Going Down Another Lane

John Young

Ashwood Books

First published in Australia March 2020 by Ashwood Books
PO Box 73, Franklin, Tasmania 7113
ISBN Paperback: 978-0-9874111-2-9
ISBN Kindle: 978-0-9874111-3-6
This edition © Ashwood Books
Text © J M R Young 2020

Acknowledgements

I thank my daughter, Sue Young, who reminded me of the details of some memorable occasions and helped me get my grammar and syntax right; my son Stephen Young made it possible, with great patience, for me to write this book on a computer; my son, Philip Young took me sailing in the Southern Ocean, took care of many major tasks that would otherwise have delayed me even further from completing this book, and set an example to me, by writing his own book. I hope he's forgiven me for letting my two ton boat fall on top of his fibreglass canoe. Most of all, I thank my wife, Ruth, who has overcome many difficulties, has always supported me at times when I have most needed it, and filled my life with love.

Thanks also to those who generously gave me permission to publish their work: the photographers Graeme Duckworth, Captain H M Denham, Jenny Scott, David Walker, Chris Burke, Bruce Hutchinson, Southerly Dolling, Stephen Young, Richard Forster, the late Mike Peters and the Huon Valley News. Tony Millatt of the Mersey Museum, Essex, helped me to locate the photo of the Thames Barge, *Leofleda*; the State Library of South Australia provided the photo of *Annie Watt*; Alan Cato provided the photo of Egg Island Canal and Don Ash (on behalf of photographer, Edward Ash) gave permission to reproduce it; the map of Eastern Fiji, including *Leofleda*'s track was created for me in 2014 by the School of Land and Food, UTAS. Thanks to Joel Pett for the use of his cartoon "Climate Summit;" to Steve Gadd for the use of his poem *The Lions' Den* and to Adrian Dean for his drawing of the trading schooner he has designed.

Jonathan Sturm, of Ashwood Books who undertook the task of publishing the book and postponed his own very significant deadline to do so. He has given me much food for thought and good advice.

Any profits from the sale of this book will go to a fund for the construction of Adrian Dean's trading schooner. Without the co-operation of the people listed here, this book would never have been completed.

Contents

Acknowledgements 2
Glossary 6
Chapter 1:   The Pig and the Crocodile 1
Chapter 2:   "A Most Likeable Scoundrel?" 16
Chapter 3:   "Un-gentlemanly sentimentalities" 34
Chapter 4:   Youth at Risk 62
Chapter 5:   Actor, Sailor, Boat builder, Failure? 74
Chapter 6:   The Beginning of the getting of wisdom 90
Chapter 7:   "If this be Love indeed, Tell me how much" 110
Chapter 8:   The Challenges of Reality... 124
Chapter 9:   Boats, Teaching, Dreaming spires, and Babies 139
Chapter 10: The course of true love never did run smooth 161
Chapter 11: Building a Career 176
Chapter 12: Babes in the Wood 199
Chapter 13: Adelaide History and the South Seas........................ 230
Chapter 14: Midlife Complexity 262
Chapter 15: One and All 279
Chapter 16: "Earth might be fair and all men glad and wise" 306
Chapter 17: Career Changes: From Theory to Practice 327
Chapter 18: "Whatsoever things are lovely…" 358
Chapter 19: "Men make their own History…" 393
Chapter 20: "…but they do not make it just as they please" 423

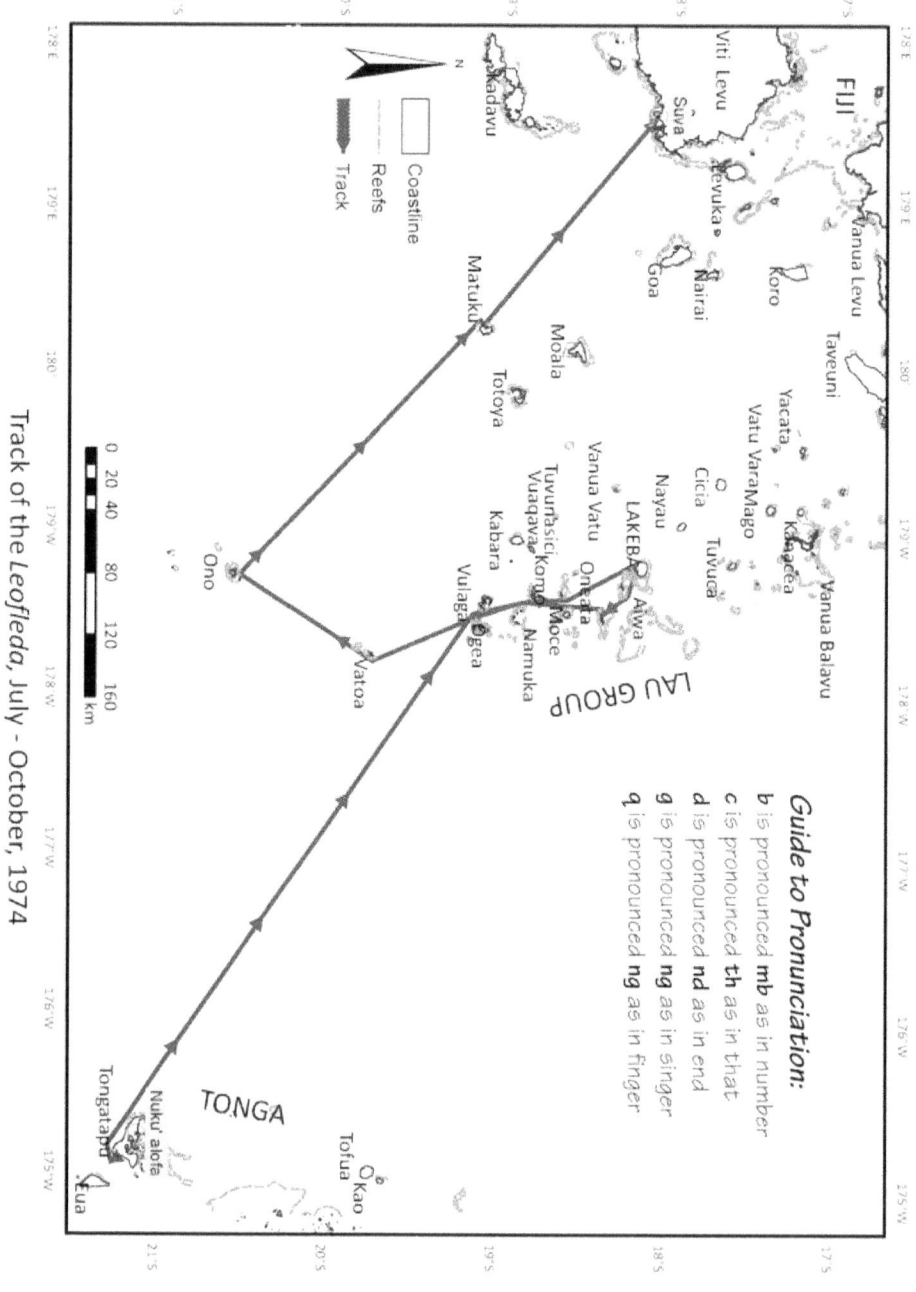

Track of the *Leofleda*, July - October, 1974

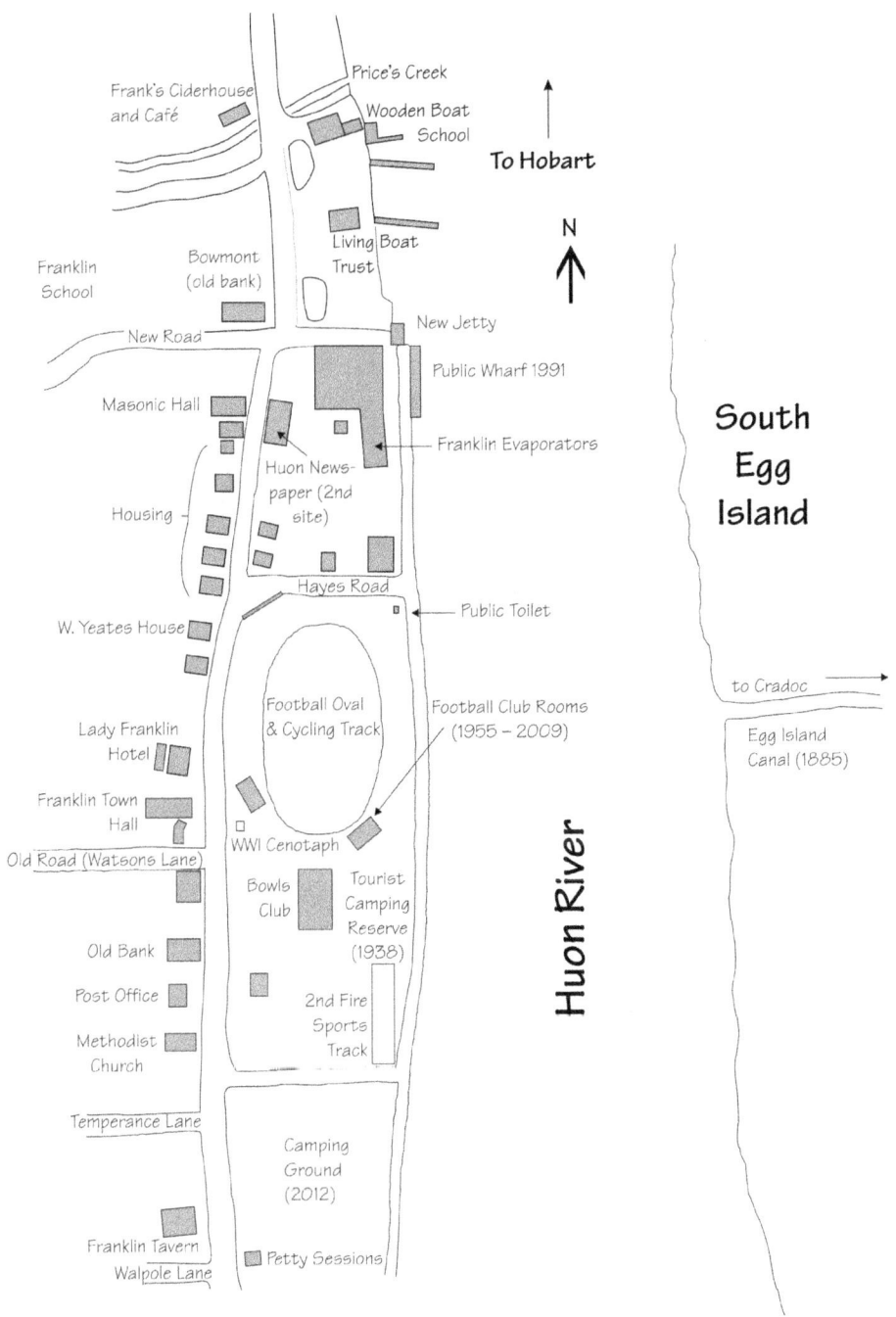

Mudmap of Franklin township.
(not to scale)

Glossary

Bure	A Fijian house built of whatever natural materials are locally available.
Caulking	Using an iron or wooden tool to fill the external gap between strakes of a wooden boat with cotton or oakum or both.
Close-hauled	Sailing as nearly into the wind as you can without allowing the sails to flap.
CMS	The Anglican Church Missionary Society
Cutter	A fore and aft rigged vessel with a mainsail and two headsails. The naval open boat, 31 feet long, however, only has one headsail, and is actually rigged as a sloop.
Dolly	A short, hand held shaft of iron or steel, held against the head of a nail while the point of the nail is peened with a hammer.
Fairmile	A motor launch designed and built by the Fairmile company during World War II for anti-submarine work. It became a general purpose vessel when the war was over.
Grappa	A home- made alcoholic drink made by the Italian community.
Grecian	Grecian—in this context, a senior student at Christ's Hospital School. Deputy Grecians were the equivalent of Year 11.
Girt	A horizontal timber along the side of a shed.
Heave-to	A manoeuvre to maintain the position of a sailing vessel by sheeting the sails on opposite sides, while holding or lashing the tiller on the leeward side of the vessel, thus pointing her into the wind. A sea anchor will help too.
Ketch	A two masted vessel with a mainsail, mizzen, and usually a foresail and a jib.
Lee	Means down-wind of a vessel or a stationary object.
Locum	A locum is a substitute for a regular employee on a break.
Mansion House	The Mansion House is the office and administration base of the City of London.
Nissen Hut	A prefabricated military building made from a half cylindrical skin of corrugated steel, conceived by American Major Norman Nissen during World War I.
Port and Starboard	Port means the left side of a vessel looking forward. Starboard, derived from Steerboard, where the Vikings placed the board they steered with. It means the right side of a vessel looking forward.
Privy	A toilet. The house on the deck of *Adi Lau*, intended for sanitary purposes.
Ribbands	The longitudinal timbers fastened to the moulds of a vessel.

	They then provide the support for the ribs as they are steamed, bent, and fastened to them. Ribbands are then replaced one at a time, by the planking.
Rode	The rope or chain attached to the anchor of a boat.
Rove	A conical washer, pushed onto the copper nails in a boat. A dolly is then held against the head of the nail while the rove is pushed onto the nail with a nail punch from the inside of the boat while another builder holds the rove punch onto the rove, cuts off the very end of the nail and then rounds the end with a peen hammer.
Scarf	A long joint between two planks, both of them identically tapered, and fastened to achieve continuous strength of a strake.
Schooner	A multi-purpose, two or more masted sailing vessel, usually fore and aft rigged. Two masted schooners have a main mast taller than the foremast.
Sea anchor	A canvas device with an open mouth tapering to a smaller tail. Put in the water over the bow, it keeps the bow pointing into the wind. Usually used to ride out a strong wind. When the wind drops the tail is pulled aboard and the vessel continues its voyage.
Seagull	A person who is a casual wharf worker and has a Seagulls Card from a wharf workers Union.
Sextant	A device used to measure the angle between the sun or moon and the horizon from the deck of the boat.
Spiling	Spiling is a technique used in building wooden boat building, in which a smaller component is used as a pattern against which the outline of a larger component can be drawn.
Stringer	A longitudinal timber lying and fastened on the inside of the ribs of a vessel
Ute	A utility vehicle, or pick-up truck.
Whaler	An open double ended boat used by European and American seamen for hunting whales between the early 17th century and the mid-20th century. Those designed by Lord Montague, of the British Navy, were also used for naval operations. They were rowed by 7 men, and were rigged with main sails, mizzens and foresails. Overall length was 27 feet.
Yaqona	Otherwise known as Kava. This is the celebration and ceremonial drink of Fiji. Originally prepared by young women who chewed the Yaqona plant until it became liquid and could be passed around to be drunk by the chiefs and guests.

Chapter 1: The Pig and the Crocodile

It was late summer in 1938 when the story of the Pig and the Crocodile came into my head. I was four and a half years old, in England, with my sister and our missionary parents on a six month "furlough" from Sierra Leone. My parents had rented a house in Broadstairs, a small seaside resort on the Isle of Thanet in Kent. It was raining and so I was bored. Normally we would have been on the beach; making sand castles, learning to swim and watching the endless procession of ships on the horizon, as they came out of the Thames estuary and turned south, beyond the Goodwin Sands, down the English Channel and across the oceans of the world.

My father, Reverend Robert Render Young, must have been equally bored, as he strove to interest me in books and games. "I'll tell you what," he said, "Let's write a story of our own." "I'm no good at writing," said I. "You make up the story then," he said, "and I'll write it down as you tell it, and then we can do the pictures together."

"What shall we call it?" I thought for a minute and said, "Let's call it *The Pig and the Crocodile*." My father got fountain pen and paper and sat down next to the big bay window that looked out onto the rainy street.

"Once upon a time," I began, "there lived a little pig, and his mother told him to go and pick some blackberries for tea. But he didn't do that," I said. "He went down another lane." (Our first stop after arriving in England from Sierra Leone was a visit to my Aunt Molly, Dad's sister and my grandfather who lived together in the village of Lockton on the North York Moors, where stone walls straggle across the heather but blackberries are used for hedges in the softer landscape of crops and grazing paddocks near the villages.)

"And at the end of the lane there was a wood," I said, "and he didn't notice that he was going further into the wood. And he saw a pool. (Here I possibly drew on a now unremembered African experience.) "And he fell into the pool, and he saw a great big mouth. And what do you suppose it was?" I asked my father, "That's up to you," said he. "It was a Great Big Crocodile!" I answered:

> *And the crocodile locked him in his house, and he got exciteder than ever.*
>
> *And some woodpeckers came and they pecked and pecked at the crocodile until they pecked his mouth off.*
>
> *Then in the afternoon some boys came; and the boys had long pockets in their trousers with swords in, and the boys stuck their swords into the crocodile, and the crocodile felt poorly and went to sleep after that.*
>
> *And then, later in the afternoon, there was A Great Big Growly Noise. And what do you suppose it was? It was a Crocodile Hound!*

(I remember a fox hunting meet in Lockton with a pack of dogs and I'd developed the theory that all species were matched by appropriate hounds, which kept things in balance).

> *It snuffed all round the crocodile, and then got the crocodile into its mouth... It had a*

great, big mouth and then it ate the crocodile all up.

And then, later in the afternoon, a farmer came and he had a very special key that could unlock any door; even if there was a key on the other side. And he unlocked the crocodile's door and then he asked the pig where he lived. And then the pig told him and he took him home and then he lived happily ever after. The End.

Then we settled down to the illustrations, with my dad interpreting my verbal descriptions to my satisfaction.

I have sometimes wondered if this story of a naive young animal has some unconscious allegorical relationship with my life that followed it, particularly the bit about the pig being diverted from his primary task of picking blackberries to go down another lane. Maybe I'll know by the time I have finished telling the real story.

Apart from that possibility, the story above has some biographical value in that it tells me a lot about my father, whom I never knew as well as I would have liked to. For most British children of my generation, growing up in wartime meant an absence of fathers. Though just too young to be a soldier in the First World War, and too old to be one in the second, Robert's family saw little of him until it was over. Later that year he was to return to his missionary post in Africa, for the next eighteen months, while our mother, knowing that war was inevitable, stayed in England to look after us children.

My parents had been travelling regularly between Sierra Leone and England since their marriage in 1926. My mother, Edith, whose maiden name was Laycock, was of Huguenot extraction, her ancestors having fled as protestant refugees, from Catholic France, in the eighteenth century. They had settled in Hull, a fishing and trading port at the mouth of the Humber River in southern Yorkshire.

Edith was the only daughter of Edward Laycock, a railway station master and his second wife. He had three older daughters by his first wife. They had left home. His second wife gave birth to Edith at the age of forty seven. I have a letter telling me how, in their retirement from the mission field, my mother and father re-visited Hull, and enjoyed the memories of Edith's childhood that came back to her. She remembered how she effectively grew up as the only child of ageing parents and her job was to "set" her father each morning before he went off to work, in return for a halfpenny every day, for her trouble.

She was sent to a large city school where she became a favourite pupil of a young teacher, my Aunt Lena, who was my father's elder sister. Sensing that Edith's domestic obligations may have restricted her opportunities to enjoy the friendship of young people her own age, Lena invited her to spend her Christmas holidays of 1915, with her own family in the North Yorkshire village of Rosedale, where her father was headmaster of the local school.

The Youngs came originally from the village of Ecclefechan, just north of the Scottish border, where the family name is still remembered. My great grandfather, Robert Young (1828–1879), is the earliest ancestor that I know anything about. He was a surveyor, who served in the British army during the Crimean War, and was married to Alice Bond (1828–1905). They had four daughters, Margaret, Emma, Lucy and Lena, and one son, William Henry Bond (known as Henry), who was my grandfather, and a significant presence during my childhood. My guess is that it was Robert and Alice who left Ecclefechan, probably at the end of the Crimean War in 1856. The populations of the towns of the north of England were increasing rapidly as the industrial revolution accelerated, and a man with a military and engineering background and a young family would have been attracted by the employment opportunities across the border.

Robert and Alice moved to Eppleton in the county of Durham, where Robert evidently worked as a surveyor. Their son, Henry, received his teacher's certificate from the Durham Training College for teachers in December 1887, at the age of twenty-two. Arthur J Bott, of the Training College staff wrote a testimonial:

Having been a student during two years, Mr Young has shown himself a pleasant and able teacher during his residence at this college, he displays a large amount of intelligence in selecting the matter for his lessons and he has the gift of placing his subject before the children in a simple and interesting manner. In addition to this he has a very quiet and pleasant manner, yet at the same time maintains excellent order.

Henry completed a required period of probation in the North Raunceby Church of England School; and had a certificate that qualified him to superintend pupil teachers. He also gained two years' practical teaching experience at North Brancepeth Colliery School, and had built on his good reputation. Thomas Vasey and M F Halliday, two of the school managers reported:

We have pleasure in certifying that Henry Young successfully completed his apprenticeship in one of the largest schools in the county. His abilities are considerably above the average. He is accustomed to large classes and his teaching power is good.

On 27 May 1890, at the age of twenty five, Henry was married, at St John's Church, Durham, to the post mistress at Brandon Colliery, Isabella Ada Render, aged twenty eight. Isabella was the daughter of Richard Render, a local draper. Since April 1888 Henry had been teaching at Eppleton school, but Isabella was soon pregnant with their first child and he decided to apply for a headmastership. He obtained a reference from Thomas Lishman, who represented the School managers, that must have helped his next move. Lishman had "not the slightest hesitation in recommending him for the position of Headmaster in any school." His next appointment took him south, on 2 June 1890, to Raunceby School in Grantham, Lincolnshire, where he taught until he got his next job, starting on 27 June 1898, at Rosedale, an ancient village ten miles west of Pickering on the southern edge of the North Yorkshire moors. The Rosedale school also provided the Headmaster with a house, and it was here that this hitherto mobile family put down roots, and brought up their children.

Until the protestant reformation, Rosedale was the seat of a Cistercian Priory, founded in 1158, and occupied by a small group of nuns. They were pioneers who made a living by running free range sheep on the adjacent moors. Other settlers followed the example of the nuns, took over the sheep farming and created a secular community. The priory was closed in 1535 because of the dissolution of the monasteries by King Henry VIII, but Rosedale survived as a moorland village until the nineteenth century, when, in 1855, small scale iron ore mining began to expand on an industrial scale, reaching a production peak in 1873. By this time, a narrow gauge railway had been built to transport ore for shipment to the convenient ports of Middlesbrough and Whitby. By the beginning of the twentieth century the industry was in decline, but still important, resulting in a busy school in which both Henry and Isabella taught until her early death from breast cancer in 1905.

Henry and Isabella had their first child, Lena, in about 1893, and there were no more children until Robert, my father, was born on 5 February 1900, soon to be followed by Molly in 1902, and Arthur in 1904. From September 1908 to July 1910, Lena replaced her mother as an assistant, presumably part time teacher, at Rosedale school, while also obtaining more practice with older children at Lady Lumley's Grammar School in the local market town of Pickering. An undated testimonial from E G Highfield, Headmaster of the Grammar school states that, "From my knowledge of her character and ability I can strongly recommend her for a post in a school and I feel sure that she will prove an exceptionally capable teacher and have a good influence over the pupils." In 1912 James Wharram, Vicar of Rosedale wrote Lena a reference for admission to the Diocesan Teacher Training College at Durham: "I have had frequent opportunities," he wrote, "in the last six and a half

My mother, Edith, 1924, aged 22.

My father, Robert Render Young, 1926, aged 26.

years, of observing her general conduct. She will prove a credit to any institution." Two years later, on 27 March 1914, Eleanor Christopher, Principal of St Hilda's Training College, Durham, had "great pleasure in recommending her as a really valuable teacher and a loyal and enthusiastic colleague." Lena's first appointment was to a large school in Hull. In 1915 she took thirteen year old Edith Laycock home for Christmas for the first time, and introduced her to her young siblings. By then the younger children had settled in well, and made friends with other children in the village, especially Joyce Moncaster, daughter of Thomas Moncaster, who was the manager of the Rosedale iron ore mine (and went on to write a history of the mine in 1936).

The Young children had always made their own fun during their school holidays. They were a creative bunch of kids, as indicated by the survival of their hand written and illustrated family magazine, *The Entertainer*. Early editions contained poems about fairies, and Art Nouveau-style illustrations. The issue of 1916 survived and was edited by Molly, aged fourteen. Other contributors were Robert Young, fifteen, Arthur Young, twelve and their friend, Joyce Moncaster, aged thirteen, who wrote an article, "The Bombardment of Scarborough," an eye witness account of the German naval attack on that harmless seaside resort on 15 December 1915. Contents of *The Entertainer* include "A Peep into Fairyland" by Molly. She still believed in fairies as an adult, and took me once when I was still young enough, to the traditional annual performance of J M Barrie's *Peter Pan* pantomime in London. The climax was an appeal to the audience to declare their belief in fairies by standing up, to save the life of Tinker Bell. We stood together. I spent a lot of time after that, trying to fit the existence of God and fairies together. Molly just said "Why shouldn't they be?"

Molly nourished a hopeful appreciation of leprechauns as well, and wrote a poem, for the *Entertainer*, about "A Summer Night," together with "Items of Interest," and an Editorial about the romantic night-life of Tom, the family cat. She also wrote "A British Chieftain's Story," a stirring tale about Celtic resistance to Roman imperialism, and a pastoral meditation called "The Coming of Spring." Arthur contributed "Dance of the Elves," a piece of piano music that plays tunefully, illustrated by a drawing with watercolours. Robert drew a pencil sketch of his father asleep in his chair, entitled "Forty Winks," and a treatise on "Six British Trees," describing their identifying features, timber qualities, habitat and useful purposes. By this time, as they had lost Isabella, their mother, Lena had become their senior, but distant, female adviser and role model.

Molly went on to write and publish poems and short stories about local characters in the distinctive dialect and idiom of the North Riding of Yorkshire. She kept a letter from her printer/publisher, Horne and Sons Ltd, offering to make a book of 32 pages, plus a cover. "You could make quite a good profit," they said, "if you sold at 2/– but you could easily earn 2/6… we shall appreciate your instructions… Candidly we **Do** like the poems." She went on writing all her life, but trained as a nurse and midwife.

The Entertainer summons up a picture of relatively well educated and energetic Edwardian family life. This was a family keen to demonstrate its literary and artistic talents in a small isolated industrial community. For my mother, Edith, meeting the Youngs was an exhilarating experience, and she took an early interest in Robert, just two years older than herself. Both of them shared a strong Christian faith and a spirit of adventure. From 1915 onwards they met regularly during school holidays. Edith found herself to be, in effect, a member of this studious and deeply Christian family. She left school when she was fourteen and trained first as a typist before she trained as a teacher in London.

Robert was a student at Pickering Grammar School when he first met Edith. After school Rob went to Durham University to train as a teacher and to read theology, in preparation for a missionary career and ordination in the Anglican Church.

My parents must have fallen gradually in love, as they looked forward repeatedly to holiday reunions. But from 1919, when they became engaged, until 1926 when they got married, theirs was a romance of constant longing. Much of their holiday time was spent at Rosedale. Rob used to ride down from Durham on his bicycle, a distance of 70 miles, while Edith travelled with Lena by busses and trains from Hull. Soon Rob and Edith developed a plan to work together as missionaries, and applied for membership of the Anglican Church Missionary Society. The *Hull Daily Mail* summarised Edith's education and new ambitions in a news item printed on 21 April 1926. There was to be a "send-off at Holy Trinity Church, in Hull, to Miss E Laycock, who is leaving Hull next week to take up work in Sierra Leone."

My parents' wedding, Freetown, Sierra Leone, 1926.

Funds had been raised by girls of the Auxiliary of the Church Missionary Society (CMS):

> ...*thus sending Miss Laycock, who was for four years a typist, to the Hull Training College, where she was very successful, and was the only student of her year to be accepted by the London County Council as a teacher. Later she attended the Kennedy Hall, London, for special training. She is taking up work in the government schools in Sierra-Leone, and is also to conduct missionary work.*

There were various speakers at the occasion. One of them was the Rev Dr D J Jordon, who sought to explain the link between mission work and education. "He looked upon Miss Laycock as a modern missionary. Modern missionaries looked at things in a new way. Education and Medical missions were quite as necessary as evangelisation." Edith was excited at the prospect. "Her work would be to superintend the native schools, and would mean constant travelling around the outlying school districts. Many of these schools had not seen other teachers for years. She would also hold missionary services, and form Girl Guides and scouts."

By this time both Rob and Edith had devoted a lot of thought to preparing themselves to work as partners, wherever God decided to send them. Edith always thought of herself, not merely as a missionary's wife, but as a missionary in her own right. Much later, in 1966 she gave a talk to an Anglican congregation in Broadstairs, about the excitement of her first assignment. After much uncertainty about their destination, she found herself on board *MV Aba* heading out alone, from Liverpool for Freetown. Robert was to join her later on another ship. She explained why:

Freetown, Sierra Leone, 1926.

I had offered to the CMS for missionary work, and as I was a teacher, there were many places where I might have been sent. In fact I was already located for Hong Kong, when there came from Sierra Leone a most unusual request for two married teachers to supervise bush schools.

I was not then married, but I was engaged, and my fiancé was also a teacher. But in those days the mission required four years unmarried service before allowing its missionaries to marry, so as we were quite young we had agreed to this condition. Then came this most unexpected request, and CMS looked round and found that they did not have two married teachers, but we were the nearest, we were engaged, and so they came to us and said "Will you get married and go and do this job?" We could only say, "this is the Lord's Doing, and it is marvellous in our eyes."

But being of a somewhat practical turn of mind, I then asked the mission doctor, "What happens if I have a baby?" You see, this was the "white man's grave," and no white children were allowed there. No one apparently had thought of that contingency, and no answer was forthcoming, but instead of going together, my fiancé was kept back to do a short medical course and I was sent on ahead to see if I could stand the climate.

She also revealed that she "was closely chaperoned by a senior woman missionary, who was returning to Lagos as head of one of the girls' schools there." Rob did come some weeks later, and they were married on 5 September 1926 at the Bishop Crowther Church in Freetown.

Edith had never enjoyed herself so much in her life. "Even seasickness has its compensations," she wrote, "when you regard it as a new experience… At least one had the great privilege of living dangerously." In July she wrote two circular letters to the friends she had left behind in Hull, and, reading them, I felt her delight

Our house at Bunumbu.

at a new and very different place, its warmth and colour, the sights of mountains and palm trees, canoes alongside the *MV Aba* in this still very underdeveloped African port. "We anchored some distance from the shore, because there is as yet no harbour at Freetown… it almost seemed that the hills were pushing the town into the sea, so close did they rise up above the houses."

There was the strangeness of black people speaking a swathe of languages, and the combination of pleasure with the company of the several expat communities, commercial, missionary, educational, government, and military, and revulsion at most of their attitudes towards native people. She played tennis, and won against her languid opponents, and enjoyed ping pong and bathing:

> *We have a lovely little beach just below the House, from which we may bathe as long as we take care to keep out of the way of the sharks. We went across to Bishop's Court, and found tennis in progress there so we joined in. Dr Lowe, (a recent female medical Graduate from St Andrew's Hospital in Edinburgh) and I played a set against Mr Humphrey, a Fourah Bay College Tutor, and a Mr Herd, one of the Government people, and we not only beat them, but I won my service with a love game. It's dreadful to crow like this isn't it? But it was lovely to achieve something on my first day in Africa, which I had never done in England.*

She also went bush walking in the hope of seeing a leopard, "but we had no such luck." At the same time, she sensed the racism of a dominant colonial culture, and hated it.

> *The average white man here regards the African as a different species of animal from himself… I think part of our job, as missionaries, is to foster a better understanding between the races, but I think we shall only do it as we mix freely with both, for you don't convince people on mere philanthropic theories.*

Parson's Piece, Hawkley, Hampshire, where I was born.

And mix she did. So did Rob. Very poorly equipped "bush schools" had been established for some time in the Protectorate that surrounded the Crown Colony of Sierra Leone. Their indigenous teachers relied for books, advice, supplies, medical help, assessment, and encouragement on regular visits from the surprisingly ecumenical cluster of Christian mission stations that had been established at Bunumbu, a village in the territory of the Mende people, a short distance from the Liberian border. Methodists, mostly American, worked with British Anglicans and the United Christian Council to establish a teachers' training college; this was eventually achieved with the founding of Union College in 1933. My parents walked along bush paths, in the absence of roads. Edith sometimes got carried in a hammock, but it made her feel uncomfortable, as she disliked the customary racial divide in principle, and this was appreciated. She kept a letter she received in 1932 from Ncole, an ordained convert who then ran the parish of Waterloo, to congratulate her on the birth of my sister, Heather Margaret Young, the previous year.

Ncole had attended the CMS grammar school in Freetown in 1879, and had then returned to his native village, where Rob had recently visited and preached. He says the baby "Margaret" (Heather's second name), should have been given an African name:

> ... *as it is the custom to give names in the language of tribal areas in which children are born. Please give our baby my kiss of peace. I always give all the children whom I baptised this kiss of peace. Kindly give your daughter this for me, and tell her it comes from a Darky.*
>
> *With warm Xtian affection and regards, I am yours ever sincerely, Ncole.*

Rob and Edith returned to England together in 1928. They had proved that it was possible to lead a healthy life in the "White Man's Grave" and they continued to commute between England and Sierra Leone for about two years each time, with six month "furloughs." Back in England, Edith trawled the length of Harley Street in search of up to date advice about contraception. She found Marie Stopes herself, and for five years my parents managed to postpone pregnancy, but not without stress. At Christmas time in 1930, they conceived for the first time, and my sister, Heather was safely delivered in a London hospital the following September. Heather went back to Sierra Leone with them as a very small infant. Two "houseboys," Ali and Bokery were employed to help with housework, gardening and child care. Furloughs were spent now at Cropton, five miles from Rosedale, where Henry taught for a short time before retirement; then at Lockton, five miles north of Pickering, just off the Whitby road.

Edith fell pregnant with me at Christmas time 1933, and as September 1934 approached, plans for my delivery had to be thought about. Molly, who was by this time a professional midwife, advised a home birth, since Edith was in good shape, and Molly was more than happy to officiate. Heather was also in good health, demonstrating the fact that white infants could survive in West Africa, so it was decided that all four of us should go to Sierra Leone this time. Passages were booked for early in October. It was then discovered that the CMS owned a most convenient property in the village of Hawkley in Hampshire; and this well maintained, capacious, thatched eighteenth century dwelling was offered to my whole family. The days of waiting for my birth were short, and by all accounts that I have heard, a wide choice of names were discussed, causing considerable mirth. Molly wanted me to be called Michael, because a senior guardian angel might be good thing to have in your corner in an emergency, and the name "Render" would acknowledge Isabella, Rob's mother. Neither name, though, could be easily shouted over a long distance. A boy was hoped for, and that would be important. So they hit on John, the name of Jesus' fondest disciple, and an easy word to shout, which was, they thought, bound to be necessary. I was born on 20 September 1934. Ten days later, my parents, Heather and I, now dubbed John Michael Render Young, were on board *MV Apapa*, and off down the Irish Sea from Liverpool, bound for Freetown.

My memories of Sierra Leone are few and flash-like. But I remember Ali and Bockery; Ali wheeling me in a push-chair and Bockery jogging down a bush path with me on his shoulders. I have spent quite a lot of my life, so far, with coloured people, and I have always felt comfortable and safe in their company, which I put down to the care and affection of those two young men. I remember the village dwellings close to our house. I used to think that our house must have been built of concrete but it was probably mud brick. It had a roof and verandah of corrugated iron anyway.

I do remember a voyage, looking down on a flat calm ocean, but which voyage that was I have no idea. There was time for two "tours" of eighteen months in Bunumbu before I would have to go to school. There is an old photograph of me dragging a black and white wooden dog called Reggie across the deck. Reggie was cleverly made so that as I pulled it along, its legs walked.

It was decided in 1938, in the shadow of war, that we children should return to Lockton for the rest of the summer and that Edith would return at the end of the

Me with "Poro" boys in background. The Poro is a male secret society in Sierra Leone, introduced by the Mende people.

Me on board MV *Apapa* with my toy dog, Reggie, 1937.

six months furlough, with Rob, to Sierra Leone. I would stay at Lockton, with Molly and our Grandfather Henry. Heather had already started school as a boarder at St Michael's, a day and boarding school which had been built at Limpsfield in Surrey, especially for the children of missionaries. It started with a kindergarten, and went on to Year 12. Heather would join us at Lockton in the holidays.

Our parents' departure for Sierra Leone is one of my worst memories. I sulked all the way in the bus from Lockton to Pickering, then to Malton where we got a train to York. We changed platforms for my parents to catch the first of a series of trains that took them to Liverpool. The train finally came in and I just said "But Africa's Too Far!" and burst into tears. I can remember now the prickly feel of my mother's fox fur as I clung to her and buried my head in her bosom as she did her best to comfort and soothe me.

Molly thought the best way to cheer us up would be to wipe away our tears and take us to have our photographs taken. And that did work — a bit. Back home in Lockton I expressed my grief and anger by climbing onto the kitchen table and pissing on the floor. Molly snatched me off the table and said that was a terrible thing to do and very wrong. I must say sorry immediately. She has mimicked me many times since then, in the North Yorkshire dialect I quickly acquired in Lockton. "A Weant say ut," said I. "Well we can't have supper 'til you do," said Molly. "Say Sorry to your Ant Molly." "A weant say ut," and so on as she took me in her arms and walked round the kitchen with me perched on her hip. In the end I got hungry, and I leant over her shoulder and whispered in her ear, "Sally Mally." "That's better," said Molly. "It'll do for now," and we sat down for the evening meal.

My "Ant" Molly was in fact, a saint. Not only as a person of deep religious faith but by her works. Like many women who reached maturity at the end of the First World War, she found it difficult to find the kind of husband she wanted and deserved. So she invented a man for herself. His name was Angus, and as children, we got to know him quite well. He was a countryman with parochial loyalties who knew a lot about North Country folklore, and liked listening to Molly's poems in Yorkshire dialect. Politically he was egalitarian, though I doubt he would vote for a labour party. He was fond of the glories of nature; good with his hands. A useful kind of man who enjoyed telling stories. A bit like Christ really.

Grandad Henry thought it might be a good idea to have a bit of home schooling in preparation for going to school. I wasn't impressed, so he said, "Alright, let's just talk about things instead." That sounded a better idea. He was a long term subscriber to the American National Geographical Magazine, which used to send out beautiful maps of countries, oceans, and continents all over the world. So we sat down with a map of the North Atlantic on the floor and talked about scale, latitude and longitude, contours, compasses, tropics and bearings. I still have that map, with a long curving row of red dots I made with a crayon as we plotted the course my parents had taken to West Africa in *Apapa*; across the Bay of Biscay, past the Spanish peninsula, around the bulge of the Sahara desert, and into Freetown harbour. "Look what a lot you've learnt," said Grandad, "without even having any lessons at all."

We did more things during successive holidays that I don't remember in the proper order. I "helped" Grandad make concrete paving tiles for a path across the back yard to the outdoor privy, and a swing off the branch of a tree in the corner of the paddock behind the vegetable garden. I enjoyed it so much that I got overenthusiastic and fell off it at its height and into a bed of nettles.

My father once brought back with him a model of a dugout canoe like the ones that came out to the ships in Freetown. I took it to bed with me. I figured that it might take a lot of time, but it was theoretically possible to make such a craft by shaping and hollowing out a log myself. Since it was built of wood I was sure it would float. There were problems, to be sure, but I read more maps and followed the moorland becks down to the River Seven in the Vale of Pickering and on past York to the Humber estuary. How could I go wrong with my unsinkable all wood canoe?

I began to eye off suitable trees and talk about Muckanoo (my canoe), the craft I would build to re-join my parents. Grandad diverted my interest in shaving and hollowing tools into making bows and arrows, with feathers from Ant Moll's chooks: Faith, Hope, Charity, and Mrs Wardle, who was named after the woman who had given her to Molly. I had a friend called Colin, who had a bicycle, and I soon became a bit of a marksman. I managed one day to shoot an arrow close to the ground to go through the spokes of the front wheel just behind the forks, which had the splendid result of causing Colin to fly over the handlebars and land, luckily, in the soft grass of the paddock.

After returning from Sierra Leone, Mother took a flat in Limpsfield, near the school, and it was hoped away from the expected bombing of London. This arrangement

On the swing my grandfather built for me in Lockton.

My "Ants," Lena (L) and Molly.

enabled her to engage vigorously in "Deputation Work," in other words, fundraising, for the CMS. It meant public speaking, which she was very good at, and a lot of travel all over Britain, both of which she enjoyed. It helped her to feel that she was doing the best she could to support her husband and fulfil her own part of the missionary vocation they shared.

In September 1939, just weeks before I turned five, it was time to start boarding school kindergarten at St Michael's, after a long train journey to London, across London in the tube, then to Limpsfield, close to the North Downs. The other kids asked me where I came from, so naturally, I told them I came from Africa. That is where I had been for most of my life. I was fairly dark skinned anyway. Someone else thought my surname must be spelt "Yung," and concluded that I was really Chinese. All these identity problems were made worse by my broad North Yorkshire dialect, so it was a while before I made friends and felt integrated. I was teased about my accent so I told a crowd of my school friends they had better shut up because I had a knife in my pocket and they had better watch out. We were in the corridor just outside the office of Mr Williams, the Headmaster, and hearing the ruckus he came out to find me with my pocket knife in my hand and the blade opened, as the crowd vanished. My parents had explained that bad behaviour at school could be punished in various ways, so I was not surprised when I was told to come into his study to be caned. I determined not to cry, and succeeded, but I have thought since then that it was a bit rough for a five year old. He took my knife too, but he gave it back at the end of term.

Not that St Michael's was a harsh school. Soon I enjoyed it because my mother had already taught me to read, and I found learning was good fun. A lot of it was rote learning, of tables, and later of conjugations. Children just enjoy the rhythm, and can learn without effort. Then they can begin to think. I must have been six or seven when I began to learn French and Latin, and anyway I was in love. The object of my affection was a beautiful young black woman called Miss Newsome, a

Grandfather Henry and Heather.

My grandfather (L) and my father.

teacher from Jamaica, who taught us nearly everything. Beginning with the classic experiment of growing the broad bean, she went on to deal in the most confident and least embarrassing way I have ever experienced, with plants, animals and humans, their anatomy and bodily functions, including reproduction. I began to read more widely. Another missionary family, Geoffrey and Dora Rogers, and their four children introduced Heather and me, to Arthur Ransome's *Swallows and Amazons*, the first of a series of children's classics that Jonathan Cape succeeded in persuading Ransome to complete, in time for every Christmas, every year. The stories were all about children my age having the time of their lives in wooden boats. They used only sails and oars, and regarded engines as positively sinful. Villains and enemies were cast as wasteful, noisy people, like the Hullabaloos of *Coot Club*, and the young, working class, petty criminals, of the *Big Six*. The books promoted high ethical standards and helped countless worried parents to keep their minds off the war. Ransome was also a countryman, who had the knack of sharing his sense of ecological appreciation and of "place" with his readers, without them even knowing it. For me, and my sister Heather, they were part of growing up.

I asked the glorious Miss Newsome if she would establish a Wolf Cub pack for us. She just said, "Yes, of course!" and got on with it. Soon we all had uniforms and were into the Mowgli stories, and learning how to track animals, and light fires with only one match.

Though Heather and I continued to see our mother at weekends at the Limpsfield flat, the school was keen to establish in us the necessary habit, for a missionary family, of writing regular letters every week, and a special time was set aside to ensure that silence was observed and the letters were obediently written. Heather, by this time was writing eloquent epistles, with no spelling mistakes or grammatical errors. My efforts were not so promising. One of them survives:

Dear Mummy and Daddy,

On Monday I played Rugger. On Tuesday I played Rugger. On Wednesday I played Rugger. On Friday I did not play Rugger. Lots of Love from John.

So not so long after the story of the pig and the crocodile came about, a bit of growing up had been done, but not much.

Chapter 2: "A Most Likeable Scoundrel?"

During the Second World War, and after the harrowing scene on the platform at York station when my parents left me with Molly and my grandfather to go to Sierra Leone, Edith decided she would stay in England until the war was over, in case of a German invasion. She took a flat in Limpsfield, not far from St Michael's, and we went home at weekends. We all were given gas masks and had to take them with us everywhere. Soon the flat below us was occupied by a family of Jewish refugees from Austria, and the reality of becoming involved in total war sank in. Limpsfield escaped bomb damage during the war, but though Rob was not in the armed forces, we shared the anxieties of the rest of the nation, because of the regular voyages he made from Liverpool to Freetown and back.

Rob travelled in ships that moved in convoy at the speed of the slowest vessel and it could take many weeks, instead of the ten days in peacetime, to complete the journey. We never knew when to expect a phone call from some British port, usually Southampton, to tell us of his arrival. The convoys sailed with the protection of destroyers, and at times, aircraft. There was one occasion, while I was at St Michael's, when the day he was expected to arrive in Liverpool came and went, without the expected telegram. My mother's face rapidly changed from that of a happy woman to a very worried and eventually desperate one, as a week, then ten days went by, and then a full month. My mother wept and I tried to comfort her, not very successfully. Like many other families at that time, a desire for news was soon displaced, as the days passed, by a fear of any news at all, in case it would be that his ship had been torpedoed, and he was dead. Then came the day when Rob told us the good news by telegram from Dundee, of all places, on the east coast of Scotland. The convoy from West Africa had been travelling at six knots, and to avoid U-boats, had taken a new and extended route far out into the Atlantic, a long way north-west of St Kilda and round Cape Wrath before landing at Dundee. The ships even survived an aerial attack. Dad brought home some shrapnel that had fallen near him on the deck from an exploding bomb. His survival was put down to the power of prayer.

My sister was doing well in 1941 at the age of ten, and could play a three quarter size violin that I envied and eventually acquired, as she grew bigger and needed a full sized instrument. I eventually gave up trying to read music, because my music teacher became tired of listening to my squeaky notes as I focussed on the music sheet and couldn't co-ordinate my eyes and brain with my fingers. He suddenly grabbed hold of the music and took it away, with the words, "Now play it again." I went on playing, with accurate notes and a degree of relaxation and enjoyment, without looking at the music. Heather went on to join the National Youth Orchestra, and has continued to play well into her old age.

In 1943, when Heather was twelve, and I was nine, things changed for us both. My parents had been married in Freetown by Cecil Horstead, Bishop of Freetown, who became their close friend, and "Uncle Cecil" to Heather and me. My mother discovered that Cecil had been schooled at Christ's Hospital, a charitable foundation originally established by the youthful King Edward VI in London in 1552, and funded largely since then by the Corporation of London. Originally a co-ed boarding school, boys and girls were physically separated in 1902. The boys were relocated some 50 miles south of London, on the railway line just past Horsham, in Sussex. It had its own railway station. The girls were taken to Hertford, well to the north, and the only contact between the two establishments from then onwards was on St Matthew's Day, 21 September, the day after my birthday and the day before Heather's, when trains from both schools took the boys and the girls to London. There they marched from their respective railway stations to the Mansion House in order to receive the traditional gift of one shilling from the Lord Mayor.

Heather was a clever girl and Cecil thought she would do well at Christ's Hospital. So she sat an exam and was successful in obtaining a subsidised place, known as a "Nomination." She did very well, ending up as Head Girl and winning a scholarship to Lady Margaret Hall at Oxford.

Further research revealed to Edith, that there were other ways in which younger children (like me) could be admitted into the school, by obtaining a "Presentation," in other words financial assistance towards the fees, to go to the prep school at the age of nine. Presentations were also the gifts of members of the charitable governing body. So she obtained a list of the Governors of Christ's Hospital, and wrote to one of them, explaining that she was in effect, a single mother with two children, and a husband who was away doing God's work in Sierra Leone most of the time, and that her daughter was going to Christ's Hospital. She would have written a good letter and her request for a Presentation for me was successful.

Above: Christ's Hospital boys and girls marching through London to meet the Lord Mayor on St. Matthew's Day.

Right: Heather and I in full Christ's Hospital uniform.

I have never been told the name of my Governor, whom, at the end of the day, I would have liked to know and thank, but I have never been able to decide whether I was fortunate or not. At one time, in adolescence, I remember telling my parents that I wished I had gone to an "ordinary school" such as Pickering Grammar School, as my father had done, and grown up in the country. Christ's Hospital turned out to be such an anal kind of school, everyone concerned about regularity of bowel habits. Many years later, I attended a reunion of former Christ's Hospital students living in Australia and met Dr. Michael Gribble, who was several years my senior. We didn't exchange much in the way of small talk. I simply said to him, "We had to take Cascara every week" and he replied, "You were lucky. In my day it was brimstone and treacle."

A positive consideration of attending Christ's Hospital was the fact that "Housey," to use the name we inherit from the Tudor orphans of Newgate, had a very good record of academic achievement, as measured by the success of its students in going to Oxford and Cambridge. Tradition was the school's key cultural ingredient, and included the school uniform: a dark blue coat with pleated skirt down to the ground, white bands at the throat, knee breeches with yellow stockings, and a leather girdle when you reached the fifth form. It was kept on the verge of falling off the loins by a silver "Broadie Buckle," which was passed down the generations from one "Old Blue" to the next. I was given mine by the Bishop of Freetown.

Christ's Hospital had a four hundred year reputation as a Religious, Royal and Charitable Foundation with the egalitarian effect, if not purpose, of levelling some, at least, of the class barriers of English society. Poor children, many of whom lost one or more of their parents during the Second World War, could expect to overcome these handicaps and leave with as good a chance of leading successful lives, as any other boy from a "public school" (as the English describe those who go to private schools).

Christ's Hospital quadrangle.
(Graeme Duckworth – Own work, CCBY-SA4.0)
https://commons.wikimedia.org/wiki/File:Christ%27s_Hospital_School_-_Quadrangle_and_Big_School.jpg

Mother took us, Heather and me, to visit the boys' school, just to look at it. For me, as an eight year old, it was an awesome experience. The school grounds covered an area of 1000 acres, allowing each of its sixteen houses its own playing field. There was a gym, an indoor swimming pool, science laboratories, acres of classrooms of different shapes and sizes, and the biggest buildings I had ever entered. These were built around the cloistered Quadrangle, the symbolic core of this culturally isolated community, in which old rituals took place, and values of loyalty and respect were commemorated and driven into our minds. To the north-northeast was the dining hall, big enough to seat eight hundred boys, fifty at each long table, underneath an amazing carved wooden ceiling. On one side there was a full size pulpit, set aside for a senior boy, a "Grecian," to recite a lengthy Grace giving thanks to our Founders and Benefactors before and after each meal. On the other side, was another pulpit for one of the masters, who was responsible for keeping order. He wielded a wooden gavel before making announcements. Opposite the dining hall was "Big School," an enormous hall seating up to a thousand people, and used as a theatre, assembly hall, examination facility, for occasional rallies to hear famous people address us, or to receive collective verbal chastisement on memorable occasions by the Headmaster, the formidable H L O Flecker.

At right angles to Big School and the dining hall was the chapel, decorated internally on each side of the aisle, by a famous series of paintings by Frank Brangwyn, of key moments in the history of Christianity; so that we could look across from the long rows of stepped pews, facing the pictures and the boys on the other side. Opposite the chapel were the laboratories, the art school and some of the classrooms. Each day at lunch time the excellent school band marched, headed up by a drum major, selected from the older boys for his physique and good looks, who tossed, twirled and caught his mace and brought the band to a halt in the middle of the Quad. In charge was the bandmaster, Sergeant Usher. His musicality was unsubtle, but sound. "Good music has two things," he said, "Toon and Rhythm." Each House with its squad of fifty boys then marched in strict time to the strains of patriotic or military music and along the avenue towards the centre of the Quad before a left or right wheel, depending on which direction they were coming from, and into the dining hall.

Behind the houses lay a continuous cover of asphalt, broken in places by fives courts, more commonly used in my time as squash courts, and a "tuck shop" where we could spend our pocket money of twelve shillings and sixpence a term, a sum that parents were counselled not to exceed, thus avoiding the seeds of class distinction. Rationing was in force, during and after the war, so most of us bought loaves of bread, hot from the oven to satisfy our hunger, which did us no harm, rather than lollies, which might have ruined our teeth. The acres of asphalt were used for backyard cricket in summer, roller skating in winter, and "double marching" punishment drills, doled out by Grecians to the smaller boys for minor misdemeanours. They were not a bad way to keep fit, as I was to discover. Orders were given by Sergeant Usher, who also assisted some of the ex-military teachers in management of the Junior Training Corps, in which enlistment and participation in uniform on Friday afternoons was compulsory.

Initially, I did not want to leave St Michael's (and Miss Newsome). However, by September 1943, the departure scene at York station in 1939 was reversed on a Victoria Station platform, where the Christ's Hospital Train, the " Housey Special" stood waiting to take me and another eight hundred boys away from their families into the Sussex countryside. By this time there were no tears from me. I longed to be into the herd and as unnoticeable as possible, anxious in fact, for my long suffering parents to be on their way and about their own business. That journey now melts into my recollection of all the others that followed. The arrival at Christ's Hospital station was followed by luggage loading onto lorries while we were introduced to the efficiency of human movement by marching in step to our destination houses, and the usual introductions and tours and rules that were to be expected.

The prep school consisted of two Houses, Prep A and Prep B (my house), in one of the eight identical H-shaped buildings. Each building contained two "houses," or groups of fifty boys. Each of them were named after distinguished pupils from the past. Charles Lamb and Samuel Taylor Coleridge were the most famous. Transition from prep school to the secondary or upper school, two years later, was automatic. Our Housemaster, Mr Willink, lived in a house with his family, attached to the side of the pupil accommodation. He also taught maths. Normally, the teaching staff of the school was entirely male, but in wartime the Housemaster's deputy was Mrs Cook, the smartly dressed, smiling wife of an army officer. She spent a lot of the time, out of lessons, trying to herd us one way or another, out of bed, into bed, onto the playing fields, down to the swimming baths, marching up to the dining hall and so on. Her instrument of authority was a clap board with a list of all our names down the left side and rows across for each day, so she could record "Black Marks" against our names. At the end of the week she would tot them up and allocate punishment drill of a length to match the number of black marks. That enabled us to start with a clean sheet for the next week. Serious crime, or a certain high number of black marks, meant we had to line up outside Mr Willink's study, where he would beat us, ritually, rather than vengefully, with his cane.

I started well in class. I think it was thanks to Miss Newsome's teaching at St Michael's, but I seem to have been a difficult child in 1943 at my new school, and felt some general resentment, probably because I was always the youngest kid doing whatever it was. My first report came at the end of Michaelmas term 1943, when I was "9.3" years old.

Housemaster (Mr Willink):

> *Has not quite learnt the meaning of discipline yet, but has started well, and but for this interruption in the infirmary,* [I think this was when I had whooping cough and was pretty ill] *would no doubt have completely settled down by now.*

Academically, things were not bad: Geography; "Quite good, progress has been steady."

English: "Very Good. Has a distinct flair for this subject. Essays imaginative and amusing."

Arithmetic [and finding this document was quite a surprise. Maths has never been my strong point]: "Is capable of good sound reasoning and his work shows promise." I suspect that promise was only hope. History was fine too: "Good. Quickly gets a clear grasp of new essential facts."

The next year was more difficult.

Lent 1944: Arithmetic: "Very good when he likes, but often naughty and inattentive — very slow to settle down to good hard work. Visible improvement since half term."

English: "Expresses his ideas well, using his imagination and sense of humour freely. But his spelling is too often just careless. He memorises easily and enjoys and appreciates good poetry and prose." Housemaster: "Good, but he is quite the most unwashed member of the house."

By the end of 1944 though, Mr Willink was losing his patience. This is his Michaelmas term report:

History: He has maintained his interest in this subject all through the term & done some very good work.

Arithmetic: I am quite convinced, by actual proof that he is very idle. When really goaded, and only then, he condescends to try.

This was because he had set me a maths test, alone, and told me that if I failed to answer every question correctly, he would give me a severe beating. He probably would not have done, but it was a useful experiment because I did answer all the questions correctly. And that helped me and raised my self confidence, possibly too much. Willink's next report as Housemaster was: "A much improved term. He is really coming on."

By this time, the war was disrupting our education considerably. In 1940, the successful defence of London by British fighter planes had brought an end to the Blitz, but in June 1944 the V1 "doodlebugs" began to fly across from the continent to resume the devastation of London. They were attacked by the newest fighter planes. I remember watching the streams of tracer bullets, through chinks in the blackout over the dormitory windows, and the noise of machine guns and engines. Some doodlebugs fell short of their targets on the way to London. One of them fell on the garage, very close to our House, where the few staff who owned cars were able to keep them. That meant that we started sleeping, not in the dormitories, but in the "Tube." This was the underground passage running from end to end of the school, and carrying all the utilities, electric cables, sewerage and steam pipes, which supplied the central heating radiators in all the buildings, and the ovens of the kitchens next to the dining hall. Some of us slept on the beds that were taken down from the dormitories; others slept beneath them on a mattress on the floor. In 1943 American Boeing B-29 Superfortresses as well as British Mosquitoes, Wellingtons and Lancasters, had begun to roar across the sky in clouds that stretched from horizon to horizon on their way to Germany. Some of us made model aeroplanes from balsa wood kits. Others made paper aeroplanes and played dogfights with them in the dayroom. Many of us hoped the war would continue until we were old enough to join the RAF as fighter pilots.

It may have been because of a sense of chaos that spread amongst us that we began to behave as if we were acting out a milder version of William Golding's *Lord of the Flies*. In Prep B, two gangs developed. We did little harm, but in retrospect the names we called ourselves are interesting. The first gang to form was known as the "KKKs," but none of my friends at the time knew, or at least none spoke, of the sinister associations that were implied. The other gang, which I think I might have started, was known as the "Bongos." This might have arisen from an association with my African background, but that is a guess. I cannot remember any kind of conflicting purpose or ideology that separated the two gangs, except that we were rivals, and used to have mock battles with mud bombs on weekend afternoons, which led to Willink's assertion that I was "unwashed."

Stephen Feaster, an historian of Cropton and brother of Adrian Feaster, my close friend during school holidays, records that "horse racing" was a custom at Cropton school: "For horse racing the older boys picked a young boy as his jockey and the race would be up and down the school yard." I claim responsibility for the introduction to Christ's Hospital of a variant of horse racing, "horse fighting," or "elephant battles," on wet days. Small boys would climb onto the shoulders of older or bigger boys and challenge opponents from the other gang to see who could wrestle the other to the ground. Sam Williams was my elephant on these occasions, and

Cropton Courthouse, where Grandfather, Ant Molly, my parents, Heather and I lived during school holidays. (Photo, Stephen Young)

we were never beaten. That was mostly because Sam was very large and strong for his age, and I was very determined. Sam left the prep school at the end of 1944 and was eventually to become the captain of the rugby team in the upper school. Then he became a South African policeman during the Apartheid era.

Mr Willink cannot have been oblivious to these developments, and my contribution to them. All my teachers complained, in my end of term reports, that I was not working hard enough. Mr Willink was disappointed, but must have detected some seed of an ability to motivate others, and sought to harness it:

> *Reported repeatedly for bad behaviour in Dining hall—and he has not been by any means an angel in sundry other ways, but he is much improved in his ways generally, and above all is never at a loose end for something to do. He has great pertinacity when he starts making anything, which in a boy of his age is unusual.*

Teaching me must have been very frustrating at this stage of my life. Apart from History, which I always enjoyed, English and Music, the constant refrain was that I was not doing as well as my teachers were convinced that I could do, and the gap between potentiality and reality was becoming wider. My woodwork teacher, whose name I don't remember said, "Lazy: could do good work if he tried." I think this was because the syllabus was all to do with making pencil boxes, while I kept working surreptitiously as much as possible building toy boats. Arithmetic: "Very Good when he likes, but often naughty and inattentive" etc.

In spite of this, Mr Willink never lost faith in me:

> *In spite of the fact that he has scored an almost record number of "black marks," that he indulged in deliberate sabotage of school property,* [I can't remember what that was about], *that he behaved very badly on one occasion in Sunday service, and has been "on the mat" far too often, I propose to make him "Head Monitor" for the start of next term and I see no reason why, if he can stand the strain of a mild reformation, that he should not make a very good one. He is a most likeable scoundrel.*

I'm sorry to have to record that I failed to live up to Mr Willink's hopes and expectations. Finding myself in a position of authority, I was too immature to relate it to an acceptance of responsibility beyond my own immediate activities and impulses. Thus when there was a crowd of boys on the brink of puberty having a naked water fight in the "Lav Ends," as the bath and shower rooms were called, I thought to organise a competition to see who could support the most wet towels on his erect penis. Unfortunately, Mr Willink heard a great deal of laughter as he came into the dormitory, and strode into the Lav End to be confronted with the competition. "Young," he said, "You will cease to be a Monitor" and strode out again.

I was of course deeply embarrassed, but my friends were kind and treated me with sympathy. Some laughed. Mr Willink clearly placed himself on my side when it came to reporting to my parents. It would have hurt them considerably if he had done otherwise, and I was in his debt for that. At the end of that term he wrote:

> *I repeat what I think I wrote last term, "A most likeable Scoundrel." I kept him on as long as I could, and after many warnings, but he has obviously been happier, (and certainly*

less trouble), as a commoner. I am going to miss him a lot next term. He has almost become an institution in Prep B, which will not seem the same without him. He has never been at a loss for something to do, and his rugger has been of great value to the house. Our best wishes go with him to the upper school where he should do well IF he behaves himself.

I settled into a kind of double life during those war years. At home in Lockton to which we had moved, I was a native of the North Riding of Yorkshire, with its heather-covered moors, deep valleys, enormous skies; its "becks" that were dammed up to make swimming pools or sheep dips according to season. And not too far away there was Whitby with its Yorkshire fishing cobles and a harbour full of small ships. At school I felt I was an outsider, even though I had many friends. My mother continued her "Deputation work" (speaking to various church groups all over the country about the work of the Church Missionary Society) with her usual energy, but Heather and I were based first, at Limpsfield, then at Lockton with Ant Molly and Grandad. The moors became a noisy place, as they were used as a training ground for tanks and Bren gun carriers destined for the African front, where Rommel was slowly driven east to Tripoli and then followed across the Mediterranean to Italy. In places like North Yorkshire, away from the bombs, people began to feel that they were on the side that would eventually win the war. I remember hearing an optimistic summer discussion in 1941, at the village store, about the arrival of Rudolf Hess, Hitler's understudy, in Scotland the previous May: "We got 'ess anyroad. It'll be 'itler next." As children, we never believed for a moment that Germany would not be defeated. My most vivid memories are of the following winter, which was very cold and snowy. We were isolated for several weeks because the snow drifts over the road often made it impossible for buses to reach the village. The postman had to walk, with snow shoes, the five miles from Pickering, over the tops of the walls and hedges to deliver the village mail.

Left: The pond (in 1978) at Cropton Mill, where Russell Clark helped me launch *Discovery* 2.

Below: Sketch of my first boat, *Discovery* 2.

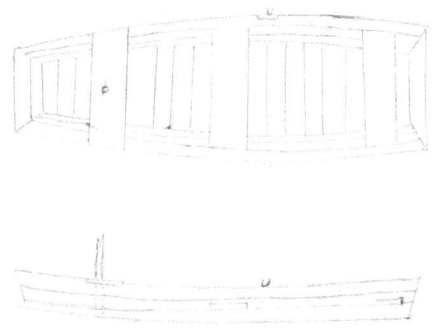

The long train journeys on the London and North Eastern Railway's "Flying Scotsman," which left King's Cross at ten in the morning every day, or back again from York, were times of cultural and linguistic transition. The telephone wires that rose and fell beside the railway reminded me each time that I must change from one form of speech, North Yorkshire dialect, to another, Soft Cockney, when I came to the end of my journey.

One day, a dispatch rider on a motor bike picked up a nearly frozen baby rabbit on the road from Whitby. He met Molly in the village. She took the rabbit home and I remember helping Grandad to make a hutch for it. We kept it as a pet, and in the next Easter holidays, took it up onto the brows in the morning sunshine and released it in the middle of a warren. It vanished down a hole, and we swore that the rabbit that came out of the hole a minute later, was *our* rabbit, and he said he was going to be OK, didn't he? Because the rabbits he'd met were going to look after him.

Later on, in 1944, my father was expected home in the summer on one of his furloughs, and my mother decided to move to Cropton, where my grandfather had concluded his teaching career as Headmaster at the village school. Part of her reason for this was that an ancient cottage, built in 1699 as the Court House, was vacant, and could be rented, probably very cheaply. Like most cottages of that age, it had exposed timber beams in the downstairs rooms, and bedrooms, at the top of steep stairs, were quaint with dormer windows, and wooden doors with wrought iron thumb latches. There was no water supply, except a small rain butt, too small to provide for the standards of cleanliness and convenience that mother's experience of an urban childhood, and as a London flat dweller in her student days had led her to expect. But the front door was about fifty yards from the village pump, fed from the pond at the top of the village. One of her first priorities was to engage a plumber to connect the water pipe that fed the pump, direct to her kitchen sink. This apparently unprecedented action caused some local comment, but she got away with it.

There was no bathroom, and so we had a galvanised tub in front of the fire in the sitting room on a Saturday night. Hot water came from copper tanks or "coppers" at the side of the fireplace, supplemented, as the water in the tub cooled, from a blackened kettle hung on a "reckon," which was a strap of iron with holes in it. They were for the hook on which the kettle was hung. Heather and I took turns in the tub so we would be clean enough for church next morning.

Sewerage was something that lay in the future for Cropton. There was a night soil service in the shape of a horse and cart and a busy man, who went round the back lane on one side of the village, took the buckets out of the little out-houses and tipped the contents into his cart. On our side of the main street there was no back lane, but each dwelling had an acre or so of land for a vegetable garden, hens, sometimes a pig, and an area big enough to bury the contents of the earth closets, sprinkled with ash from the fireplaces, deep into the ground.

The contrast between my life at boarding school and at Cropton was extreme. I felt myself to be an outsider in both places. Accent was a big problem for me because of the subtleties of the North Riding dialect. As part of the Danegeld of early medieval times, there are more Scandinavian accents and words in the North Riding, than in the language of the West or East subdivisions or "Ridings" of the county of Yorkshire. Christ's Hospital students often spoke with a mild cockney accent, more often with an understated received standard southern English accent, almost never with the accent associated with other public schools or the "upper classes."

The boys of Cropton on the other hand, seem in retrospect to have been conducting a rearguard action for the preservation of their native tongue. "Evacuees" from the industrial towns of the West Riding or Hull, who were placed in the care of North Riding families, spoke the "official" Yorkshire dialect of the comedians and sporting celebrities: "won't" becomes "woant"; "don't" becomes "doant." The Cropton variation was that "don't" became "deant," and "won't" became "weant." When my friend, Adrian Feaster (we called him "Dicky") refused to go to school, his father poked him in the back and said to him, "Tha's goin t' skeal." Adrian replied, as his father continued to poke him, "A'weant gang t'skeal," as they walked down the High street, to the village school where my grandfather had taught until he retired.

I wasn't quick enough, after my first holiday from Christ's Hospital, to put away what I now thought of as my mother tongue, and conform to the southern accent, but it took only a few minutes out of Victoria Station, to understand the need for conformity, and I developed the skill of making myself verbally indistinguishable from everyone else, wherever I was. It was just as necessary when I arrived at Cropton at the beginning of the holidays, except that I enjoyed talking North Yorkshire dialect, and resented having to conform to the unexciting norms of the received standard pronunciation, which my parents encouraged, since accent in those days was supposed to be a prime indication of class.

The short tastes of home and family life were increasingly glorious for me. My craze about boats and sailing was well under way by 1943, and having acquired an old model sailing yacht, I spent many hours learning how to sail it across the pond just at the northern end of Cropton. It was called the Dams pond, but is now filled in. The other place much frequented by me, Adrian Feaster and Peter Coupland (an evacuee from Middlesbrough) among others, was the site of "Cropton Castle," a Norman motte-and-bailey structure. It was surveyed in detail by the English Royal Commission for Historic Monuments in 1986, and is now a scheduled ancient monument of national importance. We used the site to play the war games other children played in urban streets and rural woodlands throughout the country, using mud bombs instead of hand grenades, and sticks instead of guns, but the mud bombs were more fun.

Winters were even better. There was plenty of snow, and hills that gave us frightening speed on simple sledges that our fathers made for us, or we inherited from older siblings. Sloping paddocks gave us runs with interesting obstacles to avoid, if we could. The other option was to roll off the sledge before you hit a tree. In summer and Easter holidays the family took to expeditions on bikes, including a second hand three-quarter size machine for me, when I was about ten. Mother used to have a couple of shopping bags hanging from her handlebars, with picnic food and a thermos flask to keep us going. We came to know all the local villages well: Hutton-le-hole, Lastingham, with its local saint and famous crypt, Goathland and Rosedale, with stories about our parents' courting memories and youthful escapades. On the long hot days of August we would dive and swim in the upland pools of the moorland becks, and have picnics in the heather.

Edith was anxious to bring us up with a capacity for independence. That meant being able to use a telephone, which had to wait, because the nearest telephone except the one at the pub, was five miles away in Pickering. It also meant being able to ride a horse, so she found someone with one, and persuaded us to have riding lessons. That was to come in very useful for me when I later found myself on a sheep station in New Zealand. The other skill she thought essential was to be able to row a boat, so we caught a bus to Ruswarp, near Whitby, hired a skiff on the river and learnt to row it.

My father insisted that I should have a miniature carpenter's bench for my tenth birthday, in 1944, and I took to shaping bits of wood in the vice and hollowing them out to make boats that I could sail on the village pond. When I was eleven, I suggested that a real boat would be a good idea. I think this came up when we had moved from the Court House and my father had just returned again from Africa in 1946.

It was then that a larger house, on the north side of the old Court House came on the market for six hundred pounds. Grandad Young had been unwell for some months. We were not told about the details but it was not long before he was diagnosed with a brain tumour. Resources were no doubt pooled so that the larger house could be bought. Molly and Grandad came over from Lockton to Cropton, ten miles away on the other side of Pickering, where Molly continued to look after him until his death. She brought her cat, Tom, and her chooks, Faith, Hope, Charity and Mrs Wardle with her.

Edith had been meaning to put up some shelves in the Court House for some time and had bought a few pine planks to make them with. I could see that there were plenty of shelves in this new house, and that the timber was surplus to requirements, so I nagged her quite a lot until she caved in and agreed that my father and I could build a boat with them. The boat was built without a plan, by placing a spreader between the two parallel seven foot planks, and bent amidships, where the beam was about three feet. Then we bent the planks at the bow inwards until the ends were about ten inches apart, and nailed a slightly sloped transom across to hold the planks and the transom together. Next we used a Spanish windlass to haul the two after ends together as far as we dared. Then we nailed a stern transom across the stern of what now looked something like a boat. We turned her over, bevelled the bottom edges of the planks and nailed short cross planks across for her bottom. She was just big enough for two children or one adult. We painted her with creosote.

At the end of that holiday, on the way back to school, there was just enough time between the arrival of the Flying Scotsman at King's Cross, and the departure of the Housey Special from Victoria, to fit in a visit to Captain Scott's ship, *Discovery*, moored against the Thames Embankment. My Dad took me aboard, and I managed to lie down in Captain Scott's actual bunk. So we called my boat *Discovery 2*.

The next problem, the following Easter break, was to move her to the water. The nearest river was the Seven, at the bottom of Cropton Bank, where there was a water wheel, Cropton Mill, and a farm house. My parents already knew the owners, Dr and Mrs Clark, originally from County Cork in Ireland, but instead of being Catholics, they were Quakers. In spite of that, Russell Clark, their son, had joined the Navy for the duration of the war, but at that time he was on leave and became an important supporter of Project Discovery. With his encouragement and help my parents and I managed to carry her down Cropton Bank, and along the lane leading to the mill pond. I don't remember the date of her launch, but it was not the noblest of occasions. To tell the truth, she filled with water in about one minute, but being made of wood, she didn't sink, so after she dried out Ant Molly took me with her to Pickering to seek a solution to the problem.

One of the surviving connections with the outside world in those days was the village carrier, who still used a horse and cart to cover the five miles with messages, deliveries and occasional passengers, to the shops and workshops of Pickering. I thought of various ways of caulking the vessel, but in the end took advice from the ironmonger who had a large case of pitch. Back at Cropton Mill, we melted it over a fire in an old saucepan, with a good pouring lip, and poured the molten

With my parents, Norfolk Broads.

pitch into all the seams and gaps. It immediately soaked into the wood and hardened. I clambered into her with a single paddle and set off across the millpond. To my lasting delight, she remained watertight for two minutes, before beginning to sink. However I was not at all disheartened. Russell suggested we try again with some untwisted old rope pushed into the seams. And more pitch on top of it. That helped a lot. Now I had a craft that could cover distances up to half a mile down the river before she became too wet and likely to sink. The next step was a small square-sail on a broomstick mast for fair winds on the long reach below the mill.

We came to know the Clarks well, and I became a regular visitor, not just to indulge in that most worthwhile of all activities, Mucking About In Boats, but to learn about the farm, and the animals, both tame and wild, that lived in it. Russell didn't talk about the war, but showed me where a badger lived, and took me on his daily rounds of rabbit snares, which he taught me how to set, and how to kill the rabbits caught in them as quickly and humanely as possible. With a few dairy cows, a flock of sheep, and rotated crops of barley, hay and turnips, he ran a small but successful farm, and though not a native, it was Russell who was chosen to make the speeches and accept the thanks and praise on behalf of the servicemen of Cropton when victory over Hitler was eventually celebrated in the village school.

Russell wrote to me occasionally when I was away at Christ's Hospital. On one occasion this was to tell me that there had been a great flood and *Discovery* had been washed away down the river. He said he felt responsible for her loss, but I told him I didn't mind, and I lay in my dormitory bed imagining her journey down the Seven, into the Ouse, then the Wharfe River, then the Humber and out past Hull and out to sea on a voyage that would last forever. Later in his life, Russell migrated to New Zealand, then came back to farm in Devonshire. He was a very important role model, though at the time I did not realise his importance.

Soon after the war was over, I was invited to join a Mrs Rogers and her two sons my own age for a week of camping at the mill farm. Mrs Rogers was my mother's friend from her student days at teacher training college in London. She was a Justice of the Peace, a Quaker, and an unusually well to do single mother. I soon discovered that she was unable to cook. She normally had a "woman-who-came" to do that. It became my duty to fill that gap in the holiday arrangements, which I enjoyed. The result was that, about two years later, when Mrs Rogers decided to take her sons for a sailing holiday on the Norfolk Broads, I was invited to join them as sailing master. My mother also cultivated local notables including a lady who occupied a large property known as "Keldy Castle," a relatively recently built estate house, eventually used as a military barracks in the last days of the war and then demolished in 1956. It was a kind of lesser "Brideshead" as described in Evelyn Waugh's novel. I was once asked to spend a day at Keldy Castle. Probably mother thought it would broaden my experience and improve my accent. It did that, when necessary, but I asked the lady why she hunted foxes, which ended up in a difficult situation. She claimed that they usually managed to get away, and almost enjoyed the challenge of "out-foxing their pursuers," while it also bred courage and judgement, and provided exercise for people like herself. So, for the sake of a bit of animal suffering it was worthwhile. I said it was a weak argument, looked at from the foxes' point of view. So we fell silent, and I was not invited to visit again.

One holiday was quite different. Ant Molly had promised that one day she would visit the holy island of Iona, in the inner Hebrides, where St Columba, her favourite saint, had built his monastery in 563 AD, as a base, ultimately, for the Christianisation of Scotland and Northern Britain. She asked Mother if she could borrow me as well. I loved the place because it was remote, wild and beautiful. Molly rented a shack on the western side of the island, and to begin with we went for lots of walks, and talked about Angus, her imaginary husband.

She liked walking. And so did Angus, but it was becoming more difficult for her. She seemed to have a touch of asthma, and complained when we walked up the small Iona hills, of having to breathe "in short pants." I liked her company and we laughed a lot, but I couldn't stop myself from going off on my own more than I should have. I was attracted to the little harbour on the east side of the island, in the shelter of Iona Sound, between Iona and Mull. It was there that I met Gordon, a Glasgow boy who was having a holiday on the island with his family. We discovered that the undecked 30 foot motor launch in the harbour was used for tripper cruises to other islands like Erraid, the setting of Stevenson's *Kidnapped*, and into Fingal's cave on Staffa Island, made famous by Mendelssohn. We succeeded in becoming the honorary first and second mates of the vessel by volunteering to clean her up every morning with a mop, dry her decks if there had been rain during the night, handle the warps and fenders, and help elderly people to climb on and off the boat. We persuaded Molly to come on short trips, but soon we went on our own, for free. It would have been more fun for Molly if I had still been the dependent little boy she had known before I went to school, but we were both growing older. I have often given myself a bad time over that.

I do not remember how it happened, and it must have been a co-incidence, but on the day of the European victory celebrations in 1945, the whole family was in London and we settled down to watch the troops from all the Allied forces marching through the city. Children were invited to come to the front of the crowd. We were somewhere near Piccadilly, but the crowd was many ranks thick, and was impossible to penetrate, so somewhat to the alarm of my parents I was lifted to head height and then man-handled overhead, to the front, where they found me when the long parade was over.

After the war was over in the Pacific as well, my father was asked to leave Union College in Bunumbu and return with my mother to become Principal of a new training college for CMS missionaries, in London. This called for a real family holiday. My parents came across a catalogue of Blakes Boats, which offered a large range of both sailing and motor craft for hire on the Norfolk Broads. None of us, except me, had any sailing experience. However, I had by this time read most of

Arthur Ransome's children's books, which combine story telling with detailed instructions on how to sail small boats, and also many other sailing books. From playing with sailing models, and a day or two sailing at Brightlingsea with some friends of my parents, Geoffrey and Dora Rogers, and their children, I knew enough to learn quickly if I had the chance. My parents recognised this, and my father was ready for what he expected would be a gentle and relaxing sketching holiday. In the Easter holidays of 1946, when I was 11, going on 12, we had our first family sailing holiday. Our ship was *Primrose,* twenty-four feet long with hard chines, which are unusual on the Broads, two berths, one each side of the cabin and a double cross berth up for'ard, but room on the floor of the cabin for an extra. We took an army surplus tent as well, so that Heather and I could sleep ashore whenever possible.

We left Wroxham and drifted down the River Bure in very little breeze and our sails not completely hoisted. Edith had read that if a squall came, the thing was to let out the sheets to prevent a capsize. So she concluded that heaving on the halliards so that the sails were properly hoisted was asking for trouble. Things became no better until a local man, passing in a dinghy, ventured to ask us if we would like a bit of instruction. We agreed unanimously that we did, and he came aboard.

"Well," he said, "for a start you don't want to have your sails flapping about like your washing. Pull your luff taut, then pull up your peak till the luff wrinkles, if you have any, run from your tack, here, to your peak, up there." I was expecting this, so I helped him set the sails properly, and said nothing. Soon we were actually going through the water and our Good Samaritan left us to our own devices. My father knew that sailing had become something of an obsession for me and in the most subtle way, while remaining Captain, he promoted me to the rank of Sailing Master for practical purposes. We soon mastered the art of sailing to windward without running into the reedy banks at each side of the river. My mother overcame her tendency to clutch the end of the cabin roof and look like a frightened kitten whenever the boat heeled over a little. Soon we found ourselves in the wide reaches beyond Horning and explored Ranworth, with its Norman church tower, and on to Thurne Dyke. The next day saw us at the limit of navigation on Horsey Mere, from which a dyke extends to an ancient windmill within half a mile of the North Sea. It was there that I tried to catch fish for the second time in my life. At Cropton mill I had attempted to fiddle for trout, but they were always too quick and slippery for me to succeed, and I just continued to practise unsuccessfully. Here, with a worm on a hook at the end of a line, and a float to tell me when a fish was biting, I was horrified when a small Roach became hooked. I reeled it in as fast as I could so that I could release it as soon as possible, and then burst into tears.

By the end of the week we had become a reasonable family crew. Rob had even done a few sketches and we had sailed as far as we could in the northern rivers, without going through Yarmouth. That came later because we had a similar holiday the next year in a "Summer Breeze" class, about thirty feet long, faster and more comfortable. Through my adolescent years I managed to gain a reputation as a competent sailor and so was lent to other families from time to time to enable them to have similar holidays, which suited me just fine.

But now I was in the "Upper School." I had expressed a preference for Thornton A, not because it was a house with any special reputation, like dominance of sporting or scholarly achievements, but because it was where Sam Williams, my former "horse," had gone two years before me. Of course the age gap when I was twelve and he was fifteen was now wider than when I was nine and he was twelve, so our friendship was effectively over, and it took me some time to adjust to that. In the meantime my grandfather died, and my father's appointment as Principal of the CMS training college at Blackheath in London, meant a complete domestic upheaval. Instead of the familiar rail journeys on the Flying Scotsman to Yorkshire, I was met at Victoria station and we then took a taxi because of the luggage. The CMS had acquired a large suburban dwelling called "Liskeard Lodge," on the fringe of Black Heath. It was there that the CMS Missionary Training College was established.

Objectively it was a splendid place to live. Close to London with its theatres and concert halls, churches and libraries. Edith was delighted. This meant central heating, hot water coming out of taps, and bathrooms, reminding her of her student days in London in the 1920s. For Heather it meant music, boyfriends, and young as she was, plenty of gallant interest on the part of the younger men recovering from war who had discovered their missionary vocation in its aftermath. Rob was totally absorbed in the challenges of setting up a new organisation, and adapting to the varieties of age and background of his students, mostly single men, some married couples.

For me the major attraction was the nearby Greenwich waterfront with its sailing barges, maritime museum and yacht club. And a large pond for model yachts on a corner of the heath. It also meant new friends. Christopher Rogers was a year younger than me, the son of Geoffrey and Dora Rogers, CMS missionaries who had served in what was then still known as Persia. Geoffrey had since become a leading evangelist on the "Home Front." They were based in Loughton, just to the north of London. Geoffrey had access to a holiday shack at St Osyth near Brightlingsea in Essex, and occasionally invited me to join his family for some sailing in their fifteen foot half decked sloop, *Cambridge District*, named after the railway for which Geoffrey's father had worked. His colleagues had given him the boat on his retirement. We used to sail out to the beacon on the Buxey Sands, which were exposed at low tide, giving us a desert island to play on.

Chris and I decided one day, in 1947, to ride on our bikes to Maldon, the Essex home of small boat-yards and a centre for the maintenance and repair of Thames sailing barges. It was there that I met Captain Norman Sheldrake for the first time. He was living on his barge, *Leofleda*, while she was having her chines replaced. When we started to ask questions about her, he invited us aboard. Her name consists of two Anglo-Saxon words, *Leof*, meaning "love," or "beloved" if you like, and *Leda*, which means sailor, so it's simply Anglo-Saxon for "Beloved Sailor," perhaps "Good

Sailor," or just "Nice Boat." Take your pick. But it is probably a very old name that has been given to generations of ships built on the eastern coast of England. Chris and I sat with Captain Sheldrake in his cabin while he told barging stories. His job was carrying wheat, mostly Australian, from overseas ships in the London docks, to East Mills at Colchester on the Colne River. From there he returned to a warehouse in the Pool of London with a cargo of flour. His crew consisted of one man, sometimes a boy. The barge had no engine of any kind, but she averaged one voyage each week, with a hundred tons of cargo, depending on only the knowledge, skill, and seamanship of two men. It was a great example of how to use the renewable energy of natural forces of wind and tide for serious purposes. One trick was to use the tide, which could run at nearly four knots at times, as an auxiliary engine. The crewman lowered the anchor so that the crown dragged along the bottom of the river. If the water became deeper, he let out a few links of anchor chain, to slow the barge's stern-first passage just enough to give steerage way using the rudder in reverse. If the water became shallow he hauled in the chain until the barge arrived again at a speed just a little lower than the tide. It was called drudging, and with strong tides *Leofleda* could cover fifteen miles or so in six hours of favourable tide, under perfect control.

    I was very impressed with this and Captain Sheldrake ended up by inviting us to join him for a voyage or two. I jumped at the chance, and asked my father if I could join *Leofleda* at the next opportunity. He said he would have a chat with Sheldrake and then give me an answer. Some weeks later I rode up to the Pool of London on my bike, and found the ancient, now demolished warehouse on a wharf just above Tower Bridge on the southern side of the river. *Leofleda* was unloading her cargo into a loft high above the wharf. I spoke to Captain Sheldrake and he said he'd be glad to set my father's mind at rest. So I went off on my bike to Blackheath, and returned a few hours later with Dad and left them alone. Dad came out smiling, and they had obviously impressed each other. It was agreed that I would sign on during the next school holidays. I think I must have done the same thing three times in 1947 and 1948. The second time I asked if Sam could come, which he did, but he became a bit sea-sick, and never came again. By that time he was playing for the Rugby Colts team and on the way to the Captaincy of the school First 15, so he lost interest. Later, in 1951, I wrote an article, "Corn to Colchester" for the *Boy's Own Paper* about the sailing barge experience. Eventually, on 22 February 1951, I received a letter that told me, "The Editor has read your story and likes it. He has asked me to say he will be using it, probably in the June or July BOP." I kept the letter, but never saw the article, which was my first publication.

Chapter 3: "Un-gentlemanly sentimentalities"

Back at school, I found life less interesting. Morale in Thornton A was lower than in most of the other houses. Our House Master was Fred Haselhust, who taught Latin and Greek and lived in a house built on the western side of ours, with his wife and two teenage daughters, whom we rarely saw and never formally met.

Fred was what used in those days to be called an "Old China Hand." We never knew exactly what he had done in China, but we assumed it had something to do with the opium trade. He stacked the House library with well-worn boy's adventure stories by Jack London, Marryat, Henty, Stevenson, Buchan, Kipling and harmless people like P G Wodehouse and W W Jacobs. Fred smoked a pipe continuously, and drank quite a lot. Mostly whisky. As a result he had a rather "weathered" brown and purple complexion, and at times, a bad temper. His best mate was Mr Carey, House Master of Barnes B, and an excellent rugby coach. It was due to his coaching that Christ's Hospital won the national Public Schools seven a side rugby tournament in 1950.

Both men were interested in boxing, and had created a tradition of inter house boxing matches between Barnes B and Thornton A, once a year. There was no organised boxing team or training in those days, just a tradition, and a few ancient pairs of boxing gloves, which were soaked and hardened with dried blood and old sweat. A ring was formed by placing four dayroom tables, about four metres long, as a square, and Fred and Carey took turns as referee.

Thornton A House Photo, circa 1948.
3rd Row, 2nd Left, Michael Marland, centre, Sam Williams, 2nd Right, me.
2nd Row from bottom, centre, House Master Fred Haselhust.
Bottom Row, 1st Right, Peter Ellis; 2nd Right, Michael Delves, whom I met again later in New Zealand; centre, Brian Holland.

Uniforms were expensive to make during and after World War II and all clothing was rationed. Hence younger boys wore cheaper suits, until uniforms became available again.

Thornton A had a group of "Farm Boys" (Michael Ball and David Owen were two of them), who worked on the school farm as preliminary agricultural science students. During wartime they were given an extra bread ration, so were probably in better shape than most of us.

Ball and Owen and two other boys formed the House boxing team, but it might have been a scene from the previous century. In retrospect, I realised that their skill was very basic, though their courage was considerable. No-one was seriously injured, as they might well have been with a wooden floor underneath them and hard wooden table corners to bang their heads on.

Later, the school was blessed by the arrival of a new wave of young teachers who were demobilised in 1945 and were allowed to complete their degrees in two instead of three years, in time to take teaching jobs in 1948. Among them were two men who made an enormous difference to my life, John Todd and David Jesson-Dibley.

Just as Miss Newsome had started a wolf cub group when I asked her to, Todd recognised a need for the establishment of a boxing club within the administrative framework of the National Amateur Boxing Association, which included schoolboy boxing, and an annual national competition for schools. Todd announced a preliminary meeting for boys who were interested, and I showed up. He explained the way the national organisation worked, starting with local schools and then to county championships, quarter and semi-finals and on to final national championships.

I realised immediately that this was a revolutionary concept. Public, that is private schools, normally competed in sports of all kinds against other public schools, in spite of the reality that the background of most Christ's Hospital boys was really more like that of state school boys than those of other public schools. There was an underlying apartheid of class, false class at that, in this arrangement, which was not a good thing.

Boxing first against local boys in Horsham, then perhaps in distant towns like Worthing or Brighton, then the rougher parts of London, and finally in the Albert Hall itself for the national finals, testing ourselves against boys who trained in the London Clubs, and the truly talented and fearsome contestants from the valleys of Wales, would be an exhilarating journey, and we would be able to see different parts of the country. To play rugby, representing Christ's Hospital, rather than my House, I had to wait until I was seventeen, because until then I was not big enough. Schoolboy boxing was divided up into weights, which automatically included age divisions, so you could represent your school when you were twelve, if you were good enough, against boys of the same weight and age, and go on doing it not for just one year, but every year.

So I joined the club as a road to the outside world. Todd took a few of us up to London to see the national school boxing finals at the Albert Hall later that year. We got the picture. The bouts were short, three two minute rounds in most cases. Knock downs were rare and mismatched fights were stopped before anyone became hurt, but some were close and brought out some impressive skills in the contestants. I decided to make a go of this idea.

Todd managed to raise the funds from the school coffers to purchase new gloves and training mittens, punch bags, speed balls, skipping ropes and a proper ring with bandaged ropes, virtually taking over half the gymnasium. Soon I was training for at least an hour nearly every day, often on top of a game or training session for rugby, or cross country running in preparation for the steeplechase, which made me pretty fit. Todd taught us the basic moves and punches, guards and strategies, and then put us into pairs for sparring practice. We had our first actual contests on 1 February 1947 when I was 12 years old. I lost to Timothy Dee on points, but then I began to learn. I won the next fight against Ray Arnold by what they called a technical knockout, meaning that Todd stopped us because we seemed to be mismatched. I won the next bout, the last of 1947, on 11 December, on points.

The next year the first Christ's Hospital team went in for the county championships. I won the first round of the West Sussex championships, against A Merrit, on points on 24 January 1948, and the next week, on 31 January, I had another win against Chilcot. I spent a week after that in the infirmary recovering from conjunctivitis, and on 4 February, my winning streak came to an end with a points loss in the Sussex county finals to George Moyle from Worthing. My parents and Ant Molly came down from London to see me fight. Molly was somewhat appalled, but thought Todd looked after us well. I felt encouraged.

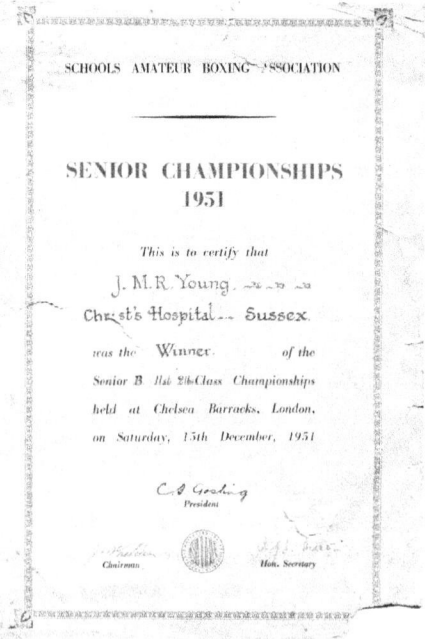

Left: Me, adopting a typical boxing photo pose, c. 1947.
Below: Schools Amateur Boxing Champion, 1951.

My year of a sudden increase of adolescent growth, strength and speed was 1950–1951. I did a lot of road and cross-country running, as part of my training and came third in the school steeple chase against a field that included a number of older boys, up to 18 years old. I was fifteen for most of that year, and won ten out of thirteen boxing contests, six of them by "Technical Knock-outs." I advanced to the national quarter finals, when I had two fights the same afternoon at the Drill Hall at Luton, North London. I won the first against D Brock on points and then lost against David Scott, who went on to win the national title. I felt, towards the end of the last round, that he was ahead on points, so I surprised him by leading with my right. It knocked him down just as the bell rang, but he won on points all the same. That was all for that season.

With the Ordinary Level or School Certificate exams coming up, I was beginning to make an effort. We were graded into "streams" according to our expected level of academic achievement, A, B, C and D. A and B streams were for students heading for University who were taught Latin and French. I was in D stream, where we were taught German, History, English, Maths, Science and Geography. I found that the system was not flexible. As I began to become interested in my work and obtained better marks, I hoped and expected to enter A or B streams. My best friend around this time was Michael Marland, who was in the same class and House as me, and was to become a champion of British comprehensive schools, headmaster of several of them, author of many good books, and a famous innovative educator. Another was Brian Holland, who went on to become a university science lecturer. We sat at the back of the classrooms and tried to speed up the pedagogical process by putting our hands up when we knew the answers to the question. Our arms ached, as others struggled; and we lowered our hands and sulked. I think the streaming process must have been a bit faulty in some way, as all three of us managed, in the end, to attend good universities and obtain good degrees.

On Sunday afternoons we were encouraged to go for unsupervised walks, and we began to explore the surrounding countryside. Nearby, close to the village of Coolham, there was a camp, or rather a group of Nissen huts, for Italian prisoners of war waiting for repatriation. They welcomed us into their accommodation, and even offered us the occasional sip of grappa. We found them to be good company and very reluctant heroes, only too glad to be living boring, but safe lives, as prisoners of war. They occupied a piece of land that was scattered with ancient clay pits that had filled with water.

One of these ponds had a kind of punt floating in it, with wooden sides and a bottom of sheet steel, a bit like my own *Discovery 2*, but larger, and a lot heavier. It was very old, and looked as if it was surplus to the requirements of some vanished industry. I had a plan for us to carry it to the nearest road, in the hope of finding some helpful person who might be willing to load it onto his truck and transport it for us to the Arun River, where we would cruise on Sunday afternoons. The Italians were keen to help, and with several Italian men and I think four of us,

Mike Marland, Brian Holland, Peter Ellis and me, we succeeded in lifting her off the ground and carrying her by hand for about two hundred yards in an afternoon. We did this at least twice, but it began to look as though it could take the rest of our lives to reach the Arun, and we started to look for other diversions. The much appreciated visits to the Italians' Nissen huts grew less frequent, while leaving in our minds a sympathetic attitude to our recent national enemies.

Another antidote to boarding school life was working on local farms to improve our finances. We used Tuesdays, set aside as a time for personal hobbies, and some weekends, to do a few hours hay making, for two shillings an hour. No school authorities ever discovered this, so I don't know whether it would have been regarded as a sign of self-reliance and initiative, or a species of truancy.

My parents thought our cross-cultural adventures with the Italian POWs might be "a bit risky," though they did not try to forbid them. My mother sought instead to "steer us in the right direction" and told us about a recently established Anglican religious commune called St Julian's near the village of Barnes Green, which was only two miles from the school and so not far to walk to. Its community included both men and women, many of whom had been in the services. They were all enthusiastic Christians, with the shared purpose of restoring an abandoned farm to productivity, and doing good works for the benefit of the local community. They also provided a venue for "Retreats" of various kinds. This was a time when similar community organisations and roving evangelists were in vogue all over Britain. Our contact, through my mother, was Florence Allshorn, who had been a missionary in Uganda. Mike and I, and Peter Ellis decided to introduce ourselves. We were welcomed warmly, and taken on a tour of the property by a very attractive young

Left: Boxing Team Coach, John Todd, 1946-7.

Below: The caravan that Heather and I lived in at Lee Abbey, while our parents were in West Africa in 1951.

woman called Ursula Watson. She had been a WREN during the war, and at this time was making a puppet theatre for a group of local children. She gave us tea and scones, and I eventually made her a grasshopper puppet. We continued to make frequent weekly visits until we left school.

St Julian's was not the kind of place we would have chosen ourselves to relieve the almost military atmosphere of Christ's Hospital, but relief is just what it provided. It initiated some creative activity, and was a refreshing contrast to the increasingly repressive atmosphere of the school at that time.

My friends and I decided to reciprocate the hospitality of St Julian's by going round singing carols and collecting money for them. This led to the idea of hiring the hall at Southbridge, close by, and putting on a play during the holidays. We sought to improve our own finances, but that inevitably led to parental intervention. We were successfully counselled to devote the proceeds to St Julian's rather than ourselves. Mick Marland was elected as our producer. Parental intervention led to the choice of a morality play, built around a story of resistance to German invasion by a group of Yugoslavian Partisans, as the main event. Mick wanted something much more sophisticated and the eventual compromise was a revue, starting with the one act morality play. We also persuaded my sister, Heather, to sing and play the violin, and an older Christ's Hospital boy that she took a shine to, Paul Roberts, put on a "20 Questions" performance, ending in a squabble with Paul's father who was in the audience. We made a profit of six pounds and six pence, which we dutifully gave to St Julian's. And that led to further theatrical ambitions.

I was finding self-esteem a bit of a struggle at this time, but winning boxing matches helped me to feel generally capable of achievement. Luckily for me, Christ's Hospital managed to recruit not only Mr Todd but also David Jesson-Dibley, an English specialist, who had gone straight from the army to Oxford, where he had joined OUDS, the famous Oxford University Dramatic Society, where he had been a successful actor and producer. The play he thought was suitable for performance by an all male cast of fifteen year olds in 1950, was Shakespeare's *Julius Caesar*. He came to our classroom and asked if any of us were interested in an audition. Michael Marland and I put our hands up, and it was arranged that we should meet him at Big School the next day. We both were given parts, Mick was to play Octavius. I was given Mark Antony, and my life was never the same again.

David soon called a first rehearsal meeting and announced a schedule of scene rehearsals at which we started reading our parts, then learning them. He also set up one-on-one rehearsals with the lead parts, to start teaching us how to act. By that time I had read the play several times and had an idea about the plot, and my character. We started with the Forum speech ("Friends, Romans, Countrymen. Lend me your ears") Act 3, Scene 2. And having had no stage experience other than as one of the shepherds in Molly's nativity pageants, I began to drone away without much understanding of what I was saying. "Use your body," said David, "and your imagination; and stop just reciting. Think about your vocal range. Get cunning, and look at the murderous gang you're trying to embarrass. Look them right in the eye. How about this?" He then gave me an electrifying demonstration of how to "Cry HAVOC," (pause) "and let *slip* the Dogs of War." He climbed off the stage and stood on the floor of Big School about fifty feet away and told me "do it again" and project my voice. I felt exhilarated and inspired.

After that, the whole process of learning some elementary stagecraft and acting in final performances in a Big School packed with 250 people was a transformatory experience. The audiences were genuinely aroused. I sensed some control of their emotions, and received as many congratulations from my peers, as well as staff, as I could handle. I had discovered there was something I was unexpectedly good at. It changed my own perception of myself.

Without that experience I might not have passed my School Certificate exams. As it was I achieved three credits and two passes, enough to surpass the earliest leaving point, and go on to sit an Advanced Level exam two years later. I began to think about my future. And how I would earn a living. I wrote about the various options in my diary: an actor, of course, at this stage or a vicar, perhaps? I might have enjoyed preaching sermons, and organising youth activities, though I had begun to lack faith. I could not make up my mind, but I wrote, in my diary, in December 1951:

I should like to be able to write well… The only time I tried before, I was successful. I sent an article up to the Boys Own Paper. It was about my trip on the barge. They gave me a pound for it, but it took them some time. I wrote that thing in March 1948. It was published in May, and I went myself to the BOP office and got my pound myself. I had written and asked for it twice before without any results. It was at the beginning of the holidays, when I desperately needed it to fit my bike out properly.

Meanwhile, my parents' lives were about to change dramatically. In June 1950, they received a letter from Max Warren, the Chairman of the Governing body of the CMS. It was written on 27 May 1950:

My Dear Rob and Dick, [Edith's nickname, her second name was "Dixon"].

Surprises should be shared, especially so when they may contain something of the shock of the unexpected. So I'm addressing you both. We want to ask you, Rob, if you could be willing to return to Sierra Leone as Principal of Bunumbu.

To cut a very long story short it looks as if that institution [Union College] *is about to founder. The Methodists cannot find a suitable person to be Principal, but faut de mieux, are considering putting in a B minus, if we cannot provide the right man. Government is really browned off with us all. I do not think I need argue that Bunumbu is a key place. Government will not consider an African yet awhile. But we know that there is **one person** whom the Government, the Africans, the Methodists and ourselves would welcome, in whom we all have complete confidence, and that is yourself.*

May we leave this to you two to think and pray over?

Warren suggested they should also consult with Bishop Horstead and himself if they wanted to. He went on:

*Let me be specific about this proposal. We do not envisage it as immediate but as following the "Lent Term" at Liskeard Lodge. That would mean sailing in April if you were satisfied that this was the right thing. We are satisfied that if they knew **You** were coming, Government will be content.*

You may well ask if we have weighed up the question of the men's training at Liskeard Lodge. We have had this in mind needless to say, and that is why the suggestion is to leave the next two terms with their program intact, and give time to think about next year.

But the important thing for us to consider at this stage is whether or not you feel that this may be a call from God to you for the job at Bunumbu.

I think we are all aware of the domestic upheaval involved, and also the personal factors which must come in. That is why we hope you will take time to think and pray about this suggestion. And you may be sure that we'll be doing the same for you both.

I do so deeply loathe being faced by big decisions of this kind myself that I am most reluctant to land one on you. But the need in Sierra Leone does seem to be more critical than most.

I would add that if you go there I can see your service there fitting into a new pattern; for Sierra Leone will have a good many changes in the near future. It will mean everything to the Church there and its future life to have one of the new team who is an old hand.

The Lord be with you both in your wrestling with this matter. Yours Affectionately,

Max.

I did not see this letter until Edith gave it to me long after Rob's death in 1961 and her migration in 1976 to live with me and my family in Australia. However she and Dad discussed the options with me and Heather, and we both supported their decision to heed God's call. Heather was then at Oxford, soon to turn twenty. Our parents sailed together in April 1951 as Max suggested. I was sixteen, supportive, but typically adolescent. Since they were doing what they wanted to do, I told myself, what was to stop me doing what I wanted to do?

It was arranged that Geoffrey Rogers (Uncle Geoff) was to take on the responsibility of becoming my legal guardian, at a time when I was keen to take advantage of the co-incidence of my parent's departure and the impending end of my schooling. I was bound to be difficult to deal with, and I must have caused Geoff and Dora a great deal of undeserved anxiety.

The first issue to arise was the question of my plans for the summer of 1951. In 1949, Rob and Edith had organised a summer locum at Ballygally, a small Episcopal parish on the coast of Antrim in Northern Ireland. Having seen the spectacle of an Orange March in Belfast, Heather and I went hitch hiking into Eire, and I became very interested in Irish history; after talking to both Protestants and Catholics on both sides of the border. I had a great ambition at the time. My career plan then was to go in for politics, and I set myself the task of finding the actual answer to the "Irish Question." Two years later, I wanted to revisit Free State Ireland, to absorb the Catholic side of the argument.

The arrangement was that after our parents departed for Africa, we would spend school and University holidays at Lee Abbey, a beautifully located Church of England property in the Valley of The Rocks on the coast of North Devon, near Lynmouth. This was the Anglican hothouse of domestic evangelism of which Geoffrey Rogers was the leader. Our parents bought a small caravan for Heather and me to live in together on the property. That was a problem for both of us. I'll leave it to your imagination. We had been before to Lee Abbey, in December 1950, probably to accustom us to the idea of living there, and to see how we would get on with Geoff and Dora. It was Christmas time, with teenagers from all over the country; a time of optimism and dreams. Years later I received a letter from a French girl, Fre'nee Gosset, which reminds me of that time of novelty, opportunity and expansion of adolescent imagination:

... and then we had a long run to Lynton don't you remember? I am quite sure this letter, written in very funny English, will please you. Anyway it is not a professor who is writing but a student of medicine. I am preparing my first exam of Physics, Chemistry and Biology. My new life of studies is wonderful. I am very open on life, I mean Arts, music, theatre, and be sure that with my studies my life is well occupied.

She went on to tell me that she wanted to meet me again:

... in order to exchange our points of view. You see, I should like to go everywhere all over the world to know, and see, and enjoy all the beauties of the world... I should like to sail by every weather and every latitude. My dream would be to obtain my grades and be a "sailing doctor." Sometimes I think it very childish to make up my mind to—But am I not young, and cannot I dream? Well dear John, after so long a silence, be sure of my real friendship. Yours, Fren'ee.

Thames Barge, *Leofleda*.
(Hervey Benham Collection, Mersey Museum)

Sadly, I received her letter after it had been forwarded from Lee Abbey, then Christ's Hospital, to a forest camp in New Zealand, then Auckland University. I wrote back, but I did not hear from her again.

Geoff gave a talk each evening on evangelical themes, sin, forgiveness and of course "Christian Sex," which seemed to encourage it. I met a nice girl called Janet, and took her for romantic walks after supper, to a spot called Jennifer's Leap, where the path comes to an end with a safety rail at a cliff face. It was a place with a sad story, and the stars sparkled in the sea below us. Janet was the first girl I ever kissed.

We did meet again, in London a year later. Both of us were just exploring, but for me the walk to Jennifer's leap was the end of an already long period of boarding school, and hence of delayed social and personal development. I determined to continue catching up with the rest of the male population of England as soon as possible. Back at school there were not many young women about, but there were some, and Horsham, with its dance halls and cinemas was only two miles away. Each pair of Houses had a Matron's office and sewing room where two girls darned socks and mended torn clothes for us. Then there were the kitchens and dining hall which employed a number of women, mostly young and single. Then there was the infirmary, which employed a number of female nurses. Bryan Magee, who was about three years older than me, and a Grecian, destined for Oxford or Cambridge, tells the story of his affair with a nurse from the Christ's Hospital infirmary, in his book, *Growing Up in a War* (Pimlico, 2007) and it is reasonable to assume that it was not an isolated event in the school's four hundred year history.

I discovered that it was possible to stand on the settle beside my bed, where I kept my clothes, and open the window, climb down the drainpipe just outside, and climb onto the asphalt safely and noiselessly. I could also climb back up the drainpipe in the early morning and return to my bed. Girls could escape their sleeping quarters much more easily. The only problem about nocturnal female companionship was making arrangements. From early 1950 to the time I left Christ's Hospital in 1952, I made several friendships with female staff members. By 1951, I was a Deputy Grecian, and was allowed to keep a bicycle at school, which enabled me to take girls away to Horsham on my cross bar for special outings. Until then we were pretty much confined to the school grounds, which increased the need for secrecy and meant loss of sleep. I have kept a note from Trudy, who worked in the kitchens and whom I have never forgotten. She was a lovely German girl who had fled to England with her family before the war. We made an arrangement, sometime in 1950, that if we were to make an assignation, I would blow my nose with my red spotted handkerchief (my talisman ever since sailing on the Thames Barge) as I walked out of the dining hall, signalling my intentions that night. Trudy confirmed the plot by passing me a surreptitious note:

Dear J.

I don't know whether you turned up last night, but if you did, don't think I didn't because I was waiting by the tuck shop from 11.45 till 12.30. Please do you think you could come out tonight or Friday, but don't come out if you think it is too bigger [sic] *risk. If you do come out, could you show your red handkerchief when you come out after Lunch, as I might not see you when I collect the cutlery boxes, because Miss Stevenson* [Dining Hall manager and dietician] *has made me do 9–16 end for smiling at the boys.*

I shouldn't come out 'til 12.30 because the night watchman does his round about 12.00 and the masters are still in their common room before then. Hoping you come tonight.

Love X Trudy.

I found her invitation irresistible, and enjoyed her company that night and on many other occasions.

The next summer holiday in 1951 was my first without either parent, and I anticipated it as an opportunity for adventure. A return to the *real* country of Ireland was high on my agenda. Colin Newbury, my geography teacher encouraged me, Brian Holland, and Michael Marland to join a Geography field trip in the Lake District, organised for boys of our age by another school. So I made a plan. After a week at Lee Abbey, I would take the ferry across the mouth of the Bristol Channel from Ilfracombe to Swansea, ride my bike to Fishguard, and take another ferry across the Irish sea to Cork, then ride over to Killarney on the west coast, up through Limerick and Galway to Donegal and across the border to Londonderry, where I would take another ferry to Glasgow. Then I would ride through Ecclefechan, the home of my ancestors, and so to Ambleside in Cumberland at the head of Lake Windermere.

I would be completely self-sufficient, taking a tent with me, and spare clothes in my pannier bags. At first Geoffrey was very alarmed by the idea, and put his foot down, but of course I appealed to my parents in Africa, and gradually wore them down. By this time, I had already explored much of southern England by bicycle, covering 100 miles in a day quite frequently, and I had camped at the Cropton mill in Yorkshire. My parents knew I could cook on a campfire, though I explained that with long distances to cover, I would use the network of "Transport Cafes" which were cheap and convenient. Since they had let me sign up for the Geography field trip, which I would have reached by bike anyway, travelling there by way of Ireland wasn't much of an ask, when it came to it, I thought. (Later, my second son Philip and my daughter, Susan and their respective girl and boy friends, wanted to catch the ferry from Melbourne to Devonport for a cycling holiday in Tasmania. Philip was a year older than I had been in 1951, and I found myself unable to think of a good reason why they shouldn't go. In fact they managed a bit better than I had done.)

The sea travel to Wales and Ireland made me feel confident, even though the Irish Sea crossing was rough and the experience of sleeping on the floor of a crowded steerage cabin, with other passengers vomiting, on the same floor, was a bit challenging. When I got on deck coming into Cork Harbour I managed to vomit over the side myself. I explored Cork that day, and found a very cheap dosshouse for bed and breakfast. The sheets were a bit grey, but I was tired and kept my clothes on.

Next day, I made an early start round the southern coast of Ireland. Soon, I overhauled two brothers, Garry and Andrew McSherry, aged eighteen and thirteen. We stopped and talked about how clean things looked, which Garry put down to the high rainfall that must keep it that way. I kept going as fast as I could and found a camping place by stopping near Bantry Bay and asking a farmer if I could pitch my tent in his paddock. Permission was followed up next morning with an offer of breakfast, my acceptance, my host's refusal to take any payment, and a strenuous day climbing the mountain roads through the McGillycuddy Reeks, and down the long winding descent to Killarney.

I may have been lucky, but the hospitality of all the people I met was astounding. I wrote later to my parents when I was back at school:

I was amazed at the kindness of everybody; not only in Ireland, though there it was much more marked. The people who were kind to me were all types including bank managers, waitresses, smugglers and sailors. My only link was that I was another human being who happened along, and there you are.

I'd read about and understood the landform history of this spectacular Ria coast line, formed by the rising seas at the end of the Ice Age, and drowning the V-shaped valleys, but I found its beauty astonishing, and I felt extremely happy. A couple of days later though, it stopped raining and I took my waterproof jacket off and strapped it to the carrier rack. Somewhere between Castleisland and Abbeyfeale, it fell off, taking my wallet with it. I made a reverse phone call to Lee Abbey and a crestfallen request for, I think it was five pounds, to see me through the rest of my journey. Geoff must have been sorely tempted to go down the "I told you so" track, but kept his powder dry for now. He was always good at resisting temptation. He sent me a telegraphic transfer that I could change at the nearest post office.

The amazing thing was that when I returned to Lee Abbey, my waterproof jacket and wallet were waiting for me. The man who found them had posted them back to my address which I had left with the local police. I wrote a thank-you letter and sent him back half of the cash that had been in the wallet, and Geoff kindly wrote off the rest.

I crossed the Shannon at Limerick, and rode up through Ennis to Galway, where I camped on the lee side of a stone wall beside Galway Bay, where a gale and heavy rain kept me sleepless and cold all night. I began to feel a bit sorry for myself as the gale howled and I shivered, but I took much comfort from a young kitten who came in from the wet in the middle of the night and crawled into my sleeping bag with me.

I was woken up in bright morning sunshine by a group of elderly women talking loudly in Gaelic on the nearby beach. They were interested in me and my tent, and the fact that I was alone except for a small cat, was enough to start a refreshing morning conversation. It ended up with taking soup and tea next to peat fires in warm kitchens, and spending most of the day with my new old lady friends. This was my first real experience of adults of another culture, and I was amazed by how much I enjoyed it. I told them I was interested in Irish history and asked them about the famous Galway Hookers, with their tumblehome black hulls and red sails, and went on to discuss the iniquity of Partition, British rule, and what should be done about it. I told them I was over for my school holidays and would be heading back to England in a few days.

I think it took me a week to wander up to Londonderry. There I met a smuggler. He smuggled horse manure from Eire to the six counties, where it attracted a government subsidy. I travelled in the night from Londonderry to Glasgow, where I stayed with Gordon, whom I had met in Iona, and his family. Then I decided to extend my journey. I cycled to Loch Lomond, and Crianlarich, then Callendar, where I stayed with Aylie, an old nursing friend of Ant Moll's, before heading back to Glasgow again. After that, I went south, through Carlisle and Ecclefechan to the head of Lake Windermere, where I joined the school geography field trip.

The base of activity was a large country house at the northern end of the Lake near the mouth of the Brathay River, which closely matches the Amazon River of Arthur Ransome's *Swallows and Amazons*. (I assumed that it must have been Ransome's inspiration for the Amazon River, but Roger Wardale's well researched study of 2010 makes a convincing case for the River Crake, which flows into Coniston Water, as the original.)

Apart from Michael Marland, Brian Holland, Peter Ellis and me, the other geography students came from another public school, I forget which, and included a New Zealander, who made New Zealand sound a very interesting place. I asked him about New Zealand and he described its egalitarian values, its rugby prowess, its Maori culture and its Kauri timber, arguably the best ship building timber in the world. I was impressed.

After a day or two we set out on an expedition to a tarn on the western side of the mountains. The plan was to climb England's highest mountain, Scar Fell, on the way to the tarn close to Wast Water. We were to camp there and make a detailed chart of the tarn, to scale. To do that we needed a canvas folding boat, which we carried with us. The trek took a whole day, and felt like quite an achievement. Mick was asthmatic, and found it hard going but made it all the same. Having just cycled round Ireland, I was as fit as I have ever been and felt really good. We had heavy packs with all our food supplies, which included pemmican and other preserved food. Our teachers included Mr Lister, a new teacher from Christ's Hospital, as well as staff from the other school who seemed very well organised. We produced a chart, and profile, using a plain table, hand bearing compass and sounding line. After a few days' work it provided an excellent illustration of glaciation, with a steep drop at the head of the tarn to a deep hollow, rising to the moraine of glacial debris where the melting glacier had dumped it, all those thousands of years ago. Thirty years later, this elementary survey experience enabled me to make accurate maps of historic Fijian fortifications in the Lau group of islands.

The expedition was a good combination, I thought, of outdoor education, serious learning, and recreation. Back at the Lake, we explored the area near the mouth of the Brathay River, and found a boat house, very much as *Swallows and Amazons* had led me to expect. Not only that, but it wasn't locked, and inside was a centreboard sailing dinghy, ready to go out on the lake. We made enquiries about its ownership, but no-one seemed to know anything about it. So we hesitated to take her for a sail in the middle of the night, but when the sun went down and the moon rose, and we were not asleep and felt a light breeze, we thought it would do no harm to go to the boathouse and at least have a look at the dinghy. In the end we decided she was too good an opportunity to miss. We borrowed her, checked all her gear, pushed her out into the river and hoisted her lug sail. The breeze was southerly, so we tacked a mile or two towards the south, probably half way towards Windermere town, and then sailed back with a fair wind. We put her carefully to bed, just as we had found her. We slept very soundly that morning.

Back at school for the Michaelmas term I was optimistic. At the end of term, in June, my academic performance was improving. I was keeping a diary at this time and it records that "Daddy Roberts [History Master] has made Marland and me full Deps." That means he made us full deputy Grecians as opposed to probationary ones. "Mick came top of Geography and I came second… Daddy R was quite pleased."

But storm clouds were gathering. As in all public schools, sex was a perpetual object of interest on the part of staff as well as students. There was no sex education at Christ's Hospital in those days, except as a side issue in the "Human Body" teaching of Mr Kirby. I was not fortunate enough to be one of his pupils, but we heard accounts of his methods. It was his custom to get straight to the point by having one of the boys take all his clothes off and come to the front of the class. Kirby would then, I have been told, take a piece of chalk and proceed to write the names of his body parts on the poor lad's skin.

Few students were shocked by this; partly because ours was to some extent a nudist culture. Swimming in the nude was normal, especially in wartime when cloth was rationed. After puberty a "Red Bather," a garment similar to the Australian "budgie smuggler," was supplied by the school, and valued as a rite of passage, but wearing them was optional. Mr Kirby was not a shy man, and used to swim amongst us naked. After all, the Greeks and Romans, our ultimate role models, were cool about the human body.

Confirmation, according to the initiation rites of the Church of England was, with hindsight, another opportunity for more specific teaching, about transition to manhood, females, reproduction, morality and contraception, but in general the opportunity was not taken. Most of us had not had the advantage in early childhood of such teachers as Miss Newsome. For most Christ's Hospital students, however, the co-incidence of Confirmation and puberty was probably not a good opportunity for sex education because for most boys it was too late. Many of our fathers were absent in those days, but there had always been older boys who provided garbled information in plenty, and did nothing to increase our understanding of women, or our respect.

Our Chaplain, an ex-military man, had his own confronting style. Some of us (not me) devised a game in chapel that took the form of a cricket match, based on the favourite phrases to be expected during the Chaplain's sermons. We agreed which side was to bat (in our imagination) with the boys sitting on the opposite side of the building, and how the score was to be kept. Every time the Chaplain said "I," a run was scored. Every time he said "God," a wicket fell. If he said, as he sometimes did, "I have seen thirteen thousand men die," there was a declaration, and the innings was over.

Confirmation class for two boys at a time (Marland and me) began with the question, "Do you fiddle with yourself?" We both confessed that, sometimes, we did. "When I was your age," the Chaplain said, "they told me, if you fiddle with yourself, YOU WILL GO MAD. I still fiddle with myself, and AM I MAD?" We laughed of course, but he failed to take the opportunity of our relaxation to move on to more important subjects.

My diary for 7 June 1950 reads:

I played squash in the afternoon and then in the evening we, [Marland and me], *went and made an image of the Chaplain out of candle wax, put it in Eastland copse and did a war dance around it as it melted, and muttered a Latin incantation round it and so on.* [Fred, our Housemaster, had started to teach us both Latin, after hours, to give us a chance of catching up with the requirements to attend a University].

Then we heard Mr Kirby and his dogs, and had to shift.

Sunday 8 July, "I heard the Chaplain's motor bike this morning, so our witchcraft has been unsuccessful."

I was becoming generally resentful of authority. My Diary, on 26 June 1951 reads: "This afternoon I went for a run as opposed to a walk; this in view of a new rule. It says that when going for walks, boys must wear white shirts and a blazer, so I got into games bags and a singlet and went for a run."

Boxing now appealed to me as a means of gaining access to the outside world. I also wanted to keep in practice for boxing the next term. It would be my last chance to win a schoolboy championship.

My friends and I also started to hitchhike down to Worthing and other coastal towns, competing at weekends to see how far we could reach and then come back in time for evening roll call and "Duty" or prayers, without being caught. I got as far as Dell Quay, beyond Chichester, where there was a Yacht Club. Soon, I took others with me and we were invited by club members to go with them for a short sail. And of course we realised that we were invited because we were students of Christ's Hospital, and could therefore be trusted. It's good to discover that Christ's Hospital now has its own sailing and cruising club.

Towards the end of November 1951 the whole atmosphere of the school changed for the worse. Daddy Roberts had our class write an essay on the subject of "School Discipline," clearly to find out what we thought about it. There were rumours of staff meetings that targeted perceived slackness and bad behaviour. People who picked up hitchhikers in uniform complained to the school. Mike Marland had been caught by our junior Housemaster, Mr Vivian, in the "Lav End" of the dormitory trying to have his essay on "School Discipline" finished by next morning. Fred took a dim view and beat him six next morning; an event followed at evening "duty" by a prayer of thanks, for "Games well played, for fun and fellowship, and for all those who have been specially kind to us today," which Fred said was most suitable. Shortly after that the gossip was, that Lamb A (named after one of our most distinguished "Old Blues," Charles Lamb) was having a crisis:

My diary on 27 November 1951 reads:

> Lamb A are victims of a purge by their Housemaster. 3 boys have been sent to the infirmary to await judgement, and probable expulsion, on the basis of information extracted from other boys. Others were to be taken to Dominics, the Horsham liquor shop, for recognition, but they, [the boys presumably] rang them up and told them [the shop keepers] to remain silent. So Mr Johnston, [their Housemaster] a puzzled man, beat them three on suspicion.

However it soon became clear that under-age drinking of alcohol was not the whole story: "The Housemaster, Mr Johnston, is not the most popular of men," I wrote. "He got all the juniors in there, and with the bribe that they would not be punished for their misdeeds, he extracted information about the three boys in question. I suppose he thinks his ends justify his means." I obviously knew, at this stage that the main issue was homosexual activity. I went on to say that Johnston's action was very wrong. "The boys in question will have a deep sense of injustice and become permanent enemies of society," I thought.

Two days later, a staff messenger came into Roberts' classroom and said Michael Marland was wanted by the Headmaster. I thought that was probably the last I'd see of him, or if he did come back it would be to send for me. He did return, and afterwards told me about his interview:

> Flecker: "You have been associating yourself with a disreputable gang." Mick denied the accusation and told me he had to stand and listen to a lot of abuse, followed by relative calm. He explained that there have been a number of masters' meetings, and that the name of Marland had come up in every unsavoury connection which had been discussed. There was no hard evidence but, "There is no smoke without a fire so write to your father and tell him that you have had a rocket from me. Then he won't be surprised if I expel you."

Fred sent for me the same day and I was not the least surprised when he told me that I had been discussed in the staff meetings, however Fred and the Chaplain had both said what a good boy I was and so "things were, for the present satisfactory."

I went on with my boxing training and I hit harder and quicker than I ever could. I broke the punch-ball. By this time the preliminary stages of the national championships were over. Very few boys old enough to be preparing for the advanced level exams were interested in boxing, so although I expected to box, about once a week, I often found myself without an opponent and went through to the next round. The semi-finals and finals were eventually scheduled for the same day, 15 December 1951, at the Chelsea Barracks in London, instead of the Albert Hall. I was annoyed about that, but it seemed I was having an easy ride.

On 9 December I wrote in my diary, "We have just been told that we are all to be in Big School in a few minutes. Presumably the headmaster will harangue us for a time on "Recent Events." I'm looking forward to it…" Then, "It has happened and I am enraged by it."

Flecker said,

"I am here because there has been, it appears, some wonder and speculation as to why certain boys have "left." They have left because they were guilty of indecent action with other boys. Such abominations will not be tolerated." He went on to say that, *"I have heard that there is an opinion that these boys were unlucky… It was bad Luck!"* Mr Flecker almost spat. *"It is unlucky that these boys ever came to Housey. It is unlucky that those boys who think they are unlucky are here now."*

I wrote on, saying that "in a single sex boarding school, some kind of homosexual action is inevitable and the system itself is at fault. He looks upon these boys as undesirable criminals which they are not, and if they are, whose fault is it?"

I blamed the stifling environment of an all male boarding school, and the difficulty we all had in socialising with girls. I was also annoyed because one of our teachers, now dead, engaged in what would now be recognised as a "grooming" process. He liked to take photographs of me, which, being vain, I didn't mind, but he eventually suggested that he take one of me in a "Red Bather" only. Perhaps I was unsophisticated, but my immediate thought was, "I know what he'll ask next." So I said no, and he dropped the idea.

Having dealt with the issue of indecent acts, Flecker went on to charge us all with what he seemed to see as a linked abomination, misbehaving as a public audience on some previous occasion. He threatened to cancel the custom of showing films in Big School from time to time and to discontinue the giving of concerts by the "big school choir," consisting of everyone who enjoyed choral singing, or the customary house plays, which were an annual event. He must have concluded, in some muddled way, we thought, that all misbehaviour of whatever kind was the consequence of insufficient repression, rather than too much of it, and our isolation from normal society.

As Bryan Magee has described in his autobiography, *Growing Up in a War*, Christ's Hospital boys went through the same stages of emotional and sexual development as everybody else:

Whenever hetero-sexual males are segregated from females and forced together for long periods there will be sexual activity among them. These men are not homosexuals, nor are they being turned into homosexuals: they are normal hetero-sexual males. Their sexual drive is so urgent, especially when they are young, that it compels an outlet.[1]

He goes on to add, "It is not possible for a normal boy [sic], to be turned into a homosexual by being sent to a boarding school." Be that as it may, my experience of Christ's Hospital leads me to the same conclusion.

---

1   Magee, B, *Growing up in a War*, Pimlico, 2007, p 220.

Privacy was not possible with large open public dormitories, and shared showers and baths. In Thornton A, the first thing we did each morning was to fill up the baths in the "Lav ends" with cold water. We took pyjamas off, formed a line, ran and plunged head first into the bath in quick succession. It put me in mind of the sheep dips on the Yorkshire moors, through which the animals were driven. I've often wondered since, how no-one cut their head open on the taps at the end of the bath. Bath water was effectively rationed. We had two bath nights a week, when we often shared a full hot bath with someone else. Inevitably in these circumstances casual explorations and sexual relationships were natural and not uncommon. Fred liked the sound of alliteration and warned us from time to time of the twin perils of growing up: "Ungentlemanly Sentimentalities" and the alternative of "Consorting with Slovenly Sluts." Avoiding both or either of these perils was to be achieved, if we found ourselves moved by our sexual fantasies, by going outside to "practise your passing" or reading some of the wholesome literature to be found in the House library. In the closing months of 1951 the school was to find itself in what seemed a confusing crisis of discipline and sexuality. The events leading up to that in my own life probably influenced my reaction, and increased my desire for independence. My diary continued with my thoughts on Christ's Hospital's good points.

This school does other things for you besides warping your attitude to sex. It solves the problems of marriages that have come unstuck, of children whose parents are dead, of families with small incomes, of families without adequate facilities for bringing up children. Housey takes boys from those situations and educates them, exercises them, develops in them their latent capabilities and corrupts them. I have thought sometimes that it should be dissolved and started again on a co-educational basis. It makes life interesting, thinking these things out, but the trouble is that I've not done much else for a considerable time. I now look forward to the national championships on Saturday, Christmas, the end of term, and a return to my mind of a sense of proportion.

Ever since I returned from the Lake District I had been trying to decide my future after I left school. I had never thought, until acting as Mark Antony successfully, that I was cut out for an academic career, or that my schoolwork could ever be of a high enough standard to contemplate it. Now I was discovering, too late perhaps, that I might have been undervaluing my abilities. My diary entry on 22 October indicates that I was having these thoughts. "My English essay turned out to be a good one. I got alpha/beta for it and Daddy R read it out to the class. I am beginning to get into gear. I am working well and enjoying it!" Back in June, Fred had offered to coach me and Michael Marland in Latin, starting from scratch, in the hope that we could pass a special O-level exam in 1952 which would open the door to entering a University. Mick persisted, passed his exam, and eventually got into Cambridge. I tagged along, but was still at this stage, more easily diverted by my other interests and dropped out after a few weeks.

On 15 December 1951 I went up to London with Mr Todd in the train for my boxing semi-final. If I won that, I would be in the final of the National Schools Boxing Championship contest on the same day. I seem to have been upset about not having the glamorous venue of the Albert Hall at my disposal and so I was a bit scornful of the Chelsea Barracks facilities, "A more depressing looking establishment," I wrote, "I hope never to see again. The hall was full of smoke. It was cold, and the changing room was even smokier." In the semi-final fight I describe a first round that I think I must have lost, against a fellow called Yates, of Berkshire. "My face felt battered and I knew I had lost the round as the bell went. My second, [MrTodd] told me it was not good enough." I had seen the other semi-final fight, and thought I could beat either of the contestants, but

> … at present it looked as if brother Yates was going to beat me… but I was better in the second round, I attacked nearly all the time, and knocked Yates down. However he got up and the opportunity for immediate victory was gone. I chased him but he was not really groggy and he could run backwards quite fast.

I won that round and thought it made us even, with me perhaps slightly ahead.

"Seconds away, Last Round." This was the best round from the spectator's point of view. It was all action. I tried most things, managed not to be knocked out myself, and as the final bell went we were standing in the middle of the ring swapping punches as hard as we could go. Mr Todd wasn't hopeful, but the referee consulted with the judges and there it was, "The winner is Young in the red corner." At this stage of the semi-finals I was the only contestant from Christ's Hospital who had won a fight.

My opponent in the final was a lanky boy called Heron. It wasn't to be a good fight though. I felt I was better than he was as soon as we started. He was clumsy and kept on swinging so as to hit me with the inside of his glove, which is not allowed. That made it easier to land some good left jabs and a few rights and hooks on him. When he came out for the second round, you could pretty well tell that his Second had told him he wasn't going to win on points so he'd better do his best to knock me out, which was good advice. He kept on throwing right hand punches, which I mainly avoided but there was a slightly groggy moment when he hit me hard on the side of my head. Then he became over excited and began to rush me, and hold and butt, with the result that, to my great disappointment, he was disqualified almost at the end of the round. I was ahead on points I think, and would have much preferred to finish the contest. But there it was, "The 11 stone 2, senior A, Schoolboy champion of Great Britain is J M R Young in the Blue corner."

I felt disappointed, because it had been relatively easy, and the quality of competition had been much better in 1950, when I only reached the quarter finals but had needed many more fights to compete against better boxers.

As well as feeling nervous about boxing and the tensions of the recent school crisis, I had spent a lot of time trying to decide what to do with my life. One reason for this was that I had become very interested in going to New Zealand, ever since

I'd talked to the New Zealander at the geography camp. I couldn't rid my mind of the thought. Geoff Rogers was coming to see Fred and Roberts about my future. If they thought I could make it to University, they might not let me go to NZ, which was a disincentive to do well academically. I had written, "I'll go. I'll be independent, and when I do return, a weary traveller, I'll perhaps think of education again. At present I can't cope with it."

Geoff's resistance to my plans for the previous summer holiday had led to correspondence, now lost, between us about the rights and wrongs of my bike ride to Ireland. It left me with no desire to spend the next four years, until I was twenty-one, in the legal custody of Geoff, and doing some boring job in austerity England. I gladly swallowed the then fashionable view, that it was better for the British Empire as a whole, if an overcrowded Britain could rid itself of surplus population by helping the development of the far distant corners. The boy from New Zealand gave his country a good rap in terms of opportunity, an egalitarian culture, and no colour bar, but it was the geography that meant most to me. Christ's Hospital was really getting me down in 1951. New Zealand was the most distant English speaking country I could find on the face of the earth. The climate was good. Huge Kauri Pines produced the best boat-building timber in the world. The coastline gave promise of excellent sailing, and it was not long before I discovered that the New Zealand Government was offering free passenger fares to intending migrants. You would only have to pay back your fare if you left in less than two years. With the higher wages and full employment in that country, that would surely not be too difficult.

But there were strong reasons for staying in England. It must have been in the Easter holiday of 1951, that I was invited by one of Heather's friends, Reverend Campbell Milford, to skipper one of a fleet of yachts, the Shearwater class, on the Norfolk Broads. Milford was in the habit of having parties of up to twenty people from different families participate in communal cruises. Four competent skippers had to be found, and word got about that, though young, I was up to the job. So I received a free skipper's berth.

The Shearwaters were four lovely wooden gaff rigged yachts, sleeping four of us each, and we couldn't help ourselves from racing. We said that whoever arrived at our agreed destination at the end of the first day didn't matter, but the boats themselves were seductive, and demanded to be sailed with concentration and efficiency. At least I thought they did, and so *Shearwater 2* always came in first. Juliet Pelly was a member of my ship's company, and though she was about a year older than me, I came to like her a lot. We went for a walk away from the boat one evening when we were moored at Potter Heigham, and we had a chance to talk. I told her a few things about Christ's Hospital, and explained about my parents going overseas and my situation at Lee Abbey. She said, "I won't let you kiss me yet," but asked me if I would like to come and spend Christmas with her family. They lived in her father's vicarage at Trowbridge in Somerset. Juliet was the third child in a family of four girls and two boys. She had an ambition to become a social worker, and said she would introduce me to her younger sister, Robina. "She's very pretty," she told me, "like a film star. You'll like her." Her mother was a doctor.

So it was agreed between parents and Geoffrey and Dora, that I would go to Trowbridge for Christmas 1951. I recorded the experience on 2 January 1952 in my diary:

> We had a wonderful party on Christmas night, and on Friday I went to an annual young people's dance at the Pump Room in Bath. Stephen Henry came to the dance and took an immediate liking for Robina. Now I did not have any intention of becoming attached to Robina, but I was her dancing partner, [Juliet had arranged this] and, well, I rather took this as a challenge, so by about 10 o'clock it began to be pretty plain that something would have to be done, so I had a glorious competition with Stephen. Robina danced with us alternately.

I had never been to any function like this before. It was like stepping back into the colourful world of Jane Austen: well played orchestral music, gracious movement and understated eye work. I loved it, especially in the "Roger de Coverley" dance at the end. It was Stephen's turn, but I did all the dancing with Robina, as I was in the next pair with Juliet. Next day was Sunday and I spent most of the day talking to Robina. I wanted to stay a bit longer with the Pellys, and they said I could if I wanted to, but Geoff told me I should come back to Lee Abbey, so I did. Robina said that she hadn't allowed Stephen to kiss her, "and" she said, "I wasn't going to let you." I made plans to return, if I could, to the Pelly household on 11 January 1952. Then I wanted to go and visit Molly at Lockton. I was very impressed by the Pelly family, and wrote a kind of tribute about them all in my diary:

> It will be lovely if I can go back to Trowbridge. The Pellys are the one and only, original happy family, a thing of which I may say, I was beginning to doubt the existence. Everybody is helpful but the great thing is that they do not talk about it. It's marvellous to live with people like that. It is not only accomplished by love and Christianity either, although that plays a large part. There is also a great deal of common sense behind everything. They are chaotic and mad and delightful. Mrs Pelly, a large, efficient woman, capable, a doctor, but feminine and motherly. Look at the things she gave me for Christmas. They were all in a large cardboard box: A box of paper and envelopes, a ping pong ball, a pair of scissors, an orange, a tooth brush, a box of chocolate, a flannel and a book of stamps. What could possibly be a more delightful combination of utility and sentiment?
>
> Then there are the children: Elizabeth aged 24, and engaged to be married to a medical student. Jane, 21, up at Oxford with Heather. Juliet of happy memory. The most perfect character I know, and I've met some pretty nice people. I am not talking about her beauty or because I like her rather a lot, but from a purely objective point of view, I think she's absolutely the cat's whiskers. She's going to be a social worker; she is one already. She stimulates one poor public schoolboy called John and gives his mind a holiday from the sordid existence he leads at school. It is most refreshing. Robina is just emerging at the age of 16, at least I should say she has emerged, from being a bit of a tomboy to becoming a most delightful young lady. She is pretty; in fact I am rather swept away by her charms,

but all the same, besides being pretty, she is good. Richard is 13. I would have guessed he was 14. He is quite big, and has a lot of common sense. Hugh is six, and funny. Through all this seeming confusion, half through it and half above it, moves Mr Pelly, an oldish man. I only heard two sermons of his. They were sane, well spoken, and downright good, without any kind of emotion. It is this beautiful chaotic, happy sanity, which makes the Pelly family so delightful and refreshing to live with.

Because my parents were away in West Africa during this rather critical time for me, I think everything that happened to me seemed both worse and better than it really was. Falling in love with Robina was a good reason for not going to New Zealand, but at seventeen I knew it would be a long time before I could even think about marrying her. We both had some growing up to do. We began to write to each other in a way that was to lead at times to an intensely emotional correspondence, as well as a useful source of biographical information.

I began cautiously. A letter, written early in 1952, reads:

"Does Stephen write to you? I suppose he must do. I have only had one letter this term from another girl, and that was Shirley. She says she would like to meet me one afternoon in Horsham. What are your views on the subject?"

I don't seem to have kept the reply. Robina probably had the sense not to give one.

Late in 1951, I answered an advertisement in the *Yachting Monthly* magazine. A man with a 32 foot yacht was looking for a crew to sail to New Zealand. I got as far as making an appointment to go and visit the yacht, but reasonably enough my parents were not willing to allow me to go, as the skipper planned to leave in August, just after their return from Sierra Leone. Meeting with Captain Sheldrake, and satisfying themselves about letting me sail with him for a week in inshore waters was one thing. This was a very different proposal. I gave up the idea, but their decision altered the way I was thinking. I explained to Robina:

"I have very nearly decided that I don't want to go to New Zealand, and certainly not if I can't sail there, so with any luck you'll have to put up with me, that is if you want to."

Just before we broke up for Christmas, I wrote again:

"I am beginning to enjoy life at school rather a lot... The trouble is that I have rather burnt my boats over the matter, and I am down as leaving in the summer. However, I want to try and work a good deal harder (I have really only been doing the minimum), so that I am in a position where I can choose."

Mr Roberts advised me not to set my hopes on getting into a university: "You would have a wonderful time, but I doubt if you would get a good degree at this stage. Later on you might do much better, but you would have wasted a lot of energy and time. If you can get a good job in New Zealand, you will be able to get started on a successful career."

Newbury had a better opinion of my academic prospects than Roberts, who quite rightly accused me of lack of factual knowledge and carelessness. Newbury advised me to attempt to gain entrance to a university in New Zealand, if that was where I was going. I had received a letter from Edith on 18 October 1951, "and she thinks it would be a good idea for me to go to New Zealand… That was the only real obstacle." So I began to make serious enquiries at New Zealand House. This resulted in an interview on 6 March 1952 at the New Zealand migration office in London. I was interviewed by Mr Rennie, and felt that I was getting on well with him. He told me that there was a possibility that I could be trained as a professional forester if I did well. That might involve going to university and obtaining a science degree at the expense of the Forestry Department, but I would spend a probationary period in a working camp. He filled in a form about me, and wrote a miniature essay in the "Remarks" space. He booked me a passage on 5 September, on a passenger ship called *Rangitoto*, after Auckland's landmark volcanic island. That night I wrote about how I felt:

I wonder if I will ever see Robina again after this year. I even wonder if I'll see England again. I might get married, settle down. A house? children? Or I may roam around the world until I'm about 40 and then come home with the best part of my life wasted. Oh well it will be fun. Six weeks on the ship, through the Panama Canal, across the Pacific. It seems like a dream, and I shall still be only seventeen when I leave England.

Geoffrey was probably a bit relieved by my decision. I received a letter from him on 28 January 1952 telling me "I was irresponsible, ungrateful and a lot more things." I recorded in my diary: "I wrote back an eight page letter, small and close, and shall be interested to read the next instalment." So we were obviously not getting on. I must have been a problem that he could well have done without. I'm grateful for his and Dora's forgiveness by the time I visited England and saw them again in 1978.

By the time I received Geoff's stiff letter I was back at school, and I was anxious to know if any of the ideas for the improvement of our behaviour that we had discussed with Mr Roberts were likely to be implemented. We had talked of forming new organisations, and extending the "dancing club," which existed for the sole purpose of an annual dance for the Grecians, who invited only the girls of the upper class Roedean school. Our idea was a dance to which we could invite our local girls.

I went and consulted Mr Roberts about the idea and he agreed, as I told Robina, "… there wasn't half enough of that kind of thing going on in the school, and he was very glad I had suggested it. He says that between us we should be able to produce about 20 'sisters,' who he thought could stay a night at various places in the

Above: Me with Chris Rogers at Appledore, 1950.
Right: Setting off for Ireland, 1951.

school." I rather fancied myself as a social reformer. I wrote: "I think I shall have to go and talk to the headmaster soon."

But I didn't need to. We did manage to obtain support for a dance at the school from the younger members of the teaching staff, especially Mr Malins, Head of the English department. Eventually, to the surprise of many, the Headmaster agreed! The date was fixed for 15 March 1952, in Big School. Mick and I went to the village of Coolham and invited eight girls. About twenty more came from the Horsham Girls High School. We wore our Tudor uniforms and collected a lot of telephone numbers, placed surreptitiously into our hands as we danced.

As the end of my schooldays drew near, Fred mellowed, and I think he must have approved of our attempts to reform the place. Hitchhiking or cycling to Birdham on the south coast became regular, and led to some very pleasant sailing lessons with a Mr Gatehouse, who invited us to sail with him and his family on his yacht, and to tea as well. Lateness back at school was inevitable, and on one occasion I didn't return to school until 8.45 pm, so Fred gated me for a month. He said he had felt it necessary to tell the Headmaster in case something serious had happened to us. "Do try to keep out of trouble," he said, "as if you get the sack I wouldn't put it beyond the Headmaster to write to New Zealand House and say he could offer no recommendation for you."

Many of our discussions of 1952 led to the conclusion that the solution to Christ's Hospital's problems would be to return to its co-educational origins of the sixteenth century. Back in 1877, as it turns out, the original decision to build a new school in Sussex for boys only was not unanimous. The Duke of Cambridge seems to have had some misgivings for purely conservative reasons. He said, "To upset an old and long lasting [ie Co-ed] institution is a very dangerous experiment to try." But as late as 1978, the idea of returning to co-education was considered impossible. I had study leave then, from my academic job in Australia and visited my old House that year and discussed the advantages that such a change would bring, with Fred's successor. I told him how me and my friends, and Mr Roberts, had considered co-education an inevitable and desirable change in 1952. He was quite horrified by my suggestion. Yet only eight years later it came to pass. What surprises me is that there is no indication in the public documents accessible from Tasmania, that motivation for the change that eventually took place in 1985 was based on anything other than the perceived financial advantages of amalgamation.

On 8 January 1952 I wrote:

> *I am anxious to find out if anything is being done about this school—I shall have to go and see Mr Roberts about it. We have only been back a week and things are becoming worse again. Nothing has been done, and very soon things will be exactly as they were before or worse. All this talk of a club house and other enlightened suggestions have come to naught, and as I wrote before, nothing has been rescued but the "Good Name of Christ's Hospital."*

The next month, some of us did manage to see Daddy Roberts:

> He says we have had a shock last term, and we hope have been sufficiently jolted to realise that something is incomplete about the education at Christ's Hospital, and in its place, there tends to be something undesirable.

So meanwhile, in 1952, we did our best to live a normal adolescent life. I continued to make nocturnal assignations with Trudy, and other girls employed by the school. My diary details a passing friendship with Josie, who endured riding on the cross-bar of my bike to a dance in Horsham, and meeting a policeman on the way back, who stopped us because of my lack of lights. He told us to return to school as quickly as possible and, "If you meet another policeman, don't say anything about meeting me." Olive was a girl who mended my trousers in the Thornton sewing room, and then, on 27 June 1952, "She suddenly flicked her arm round my shoulder and kissed me." I have a recollection of some nocturnal meetings with her, while developing what was to become a vitally important relationship by correspondence with Robina. I told myself this was quite excusable, because of my total lack of previous experience of female company, even though I had an older sister. Robina would obviously need a boyfriend, maybe, in the distant future, I told myself, a husband. But he would have to be someone who knew what girls were really like, and showed some evidence of sophistication. In 1952, we were writing to each other every week and rebuking each other when the expected letters failed to arrive. We both kept the letters we received from each other during the next four years for the rest of our lives.

Meanwhile A-Level exams loomed and I started to work hard, and to implement our ideas for a better Christ's Hospital. I told Robina that I had decided, after a meeting with Mr Newbury, my Geography teacher, that, "Really, I do the minimum of work, and that is about half as much as I could do. I am going to try an experiment, working hard, and I'll see if it makes any difference to the standard of my work and the estimate of the stuff of my intellectual capabilities." It worked to some extent, but was too late to be convincing. I think it began in late in 1951. In the Easter holidays Colin Newbury set us a holiday task of original research in the historical geography of wherever we lived. I was lucky to be living in North Devon, which had experienced a dramatic transition from cattle farming and shipbuilding in the nineteenth and early twentieth centuries to tourist dependency in the mid twentieth century. It was a story that fitted my current interests and made work a pleasure.

In 1949 Basil Greenhill, destined to become Director of the National Maritime Museum at Greenwich, wrote the first volume of his seminal work *The Merchant Schooners*, dealing with the astonishing role of the small maritime communities of Devon and Cornwall in the production of these beautiful and practical vessels. I received a copy as a present for my sixteenth birthday in 1950. Christopher Rogers and I spent some of the best days of our lives that summer, exploring the estuary of the Taw and Torridge rivers in sailing luggers we hired by the hour. We sailed over from Instow to Appledore and spoke to fishermen and shipwrights at the famous shipyard where the arts of wooden shipbuilding were being actively preserved. Lynton, also a small port in the nineteenth century, was a short bike ride away from Lee Abbey, and I used the local libraries and newspapers, and spoke to local farmers and tourist operators about the changes and relative losses and gains in their experience and attitudes. Then I took the 3 inches to the mile Ordnance Survey map of Lynton and its hinterland and made a detailed contoured relief model in plaster of Paris. Newbury gave me a straight A for that and the written discussion that went with it. The first such mark I had ever achieved. In February 1952, I began to obtain good marks most of the time, and my eventual A level results were well ahead of expectations. Colin Newbury wrote to congratulate me on my results, and advised me to "stick to the plan of getting a University course out there if it is in any way possible." Todd did not teach me, but must have received news of my sudden improvement and pointed out that if I went to the United States, there were such things as athletic scholarships and my boxing might be useful in that context. I wasn't so sure.

I still lacked consistency and determination at that age and continued to delude myself that I could afford to spend a lot of time on more immediately satisfying projects. I started a dramatic club: "Decided with Mick to do a tour of Kent with *Love's Labour Lost*." I had seen the play at the Old Vic Theatre with Michael Redgrave in the leading role the previous holiday. But the Headmaster wouldn't allow it. I optimistically record that there was going to be a Board of Studies meeting on the next Tuesday, and "We've got absolutely all the masters on our side."

This was a major preoccupation for the rest of my time at Christ's Hospital. It was the subject of intense discussion during an idyllic week on the Norfolk Broads with Michael Marland, Martin Priestly, Peter Ellis and Brian Holland in the Easter holidays. We listened to classical music as we sailed into the sunset across Hickling Broad. Then we moored at the mouth of the Hickling dyke and sang the songs we had learnt in the Madrigal choir at school. I went back to Lee Abbey after that but managed to stay the night on the way at Trowbridge to say goodbye, as it turned out, to Robina. Shortly afterwards I wrote to her about my latest idea.

> *We thought that having formed a dramatic club it would be an excellent thing if we went on tour with it. We thought about it, decided that Shakespeare would be easiest to produce, (because of the Elizabethan practice of encouraging the imagination of the audience rather than using elaborate scenery), and eventually chose Love's Labour's Lost.*

We decided, Mick and I, to do this in Kent, and as it turned out, the members of the cast, between them, knew someone in every one of the places we were going to. I told Robina:

> *We are going for a fortnight, visiting eight, perhaps nine places, giving a total of fourteen performances. We'll rehearse in the summer term, and then on August 6th we meet in London for a few days' final rehearsals, then on 9th we perform in Rochester. The other places are Faversham, Ashford, Rye, Tenderton, Battle, Lewes, Cuckfield and Westerham to finish up with.*

We called our group the Christ's Hospital Elizabethan Players, and decided to pre-book the village halls for chosen days during the summer holidays. Michael Marland was elected as producer, and the initial idea was that I should play Malvolio, but I couldn't do that if I was going to New Zealand, which gave me serious second thoughts, but by then the decision had been made. In the end, and after a lot of discussion *Twelfth Night* was chosen instead of *Love's Labour's Lost*, and was a considerable success. My Diary records, 17 June 1952: "The House is full of bits of wood as we have been making scenery for Twelfth Night. We have borrowed all the curtains we need from Colliers, [another school] and we are doing a performance at the Horsham Girls High School… thus satisfying our purpose of cultural integration with the local community." Christ's Hospital Elizabethan Players lasted longer than that single effort. It survived into the future. Mick sent me news of the successful 1952 tour much to my satisfaction.

The Christ's Hospital leaving service at the end of each term is a moving occasion, and I described it to Robina on the occasion of the funeral of George VI in February 1952 which reminded me of it, and what it meant.

It was rather like our leaving service. It leaves the sad impression that leaving school is the end of everything. "Lord thou hast brought us to our journey's end" is the last line of one of the hymns. The headmaster leads two long solemn columns, all the leavers, to the altar steps. "I charge you," he says, "never to forget the great benefits you have received in this place" and some other wise words, and presents each boy with a gilt bible. Then we all go out while the organ plays Handel's march from Scipio, an exhilarating tune that puts everyone in the right frame of mind for the end of term festivities, and reminds us that, after all, we are going home for the holidays tomorrow.

I was grateful for many good things at Christ's Hospital; and the opportunities it provided, some of which I had squandered. I was sorry that the Christ's Hospital Elizabethan Players would be having a great time without me, but I was also uplifted by the fact that I would not be coming back.

My parents returned from Sierra Leone for their first furlough on 7 July 1952, so that I spent my final weeks in England based in Blackheath with them and Heather. But there was a lot of travelling about. I went up to West Hartlepool to say goodbye to Ant Lena, who I had not seen much of as she lived so far to the north, with her partner, Gwen. I promised to write, a promise that I did not keep as well as I should have, and then caught a bus down to Lockton where I stayed for a few days with Ant Molly, who gave me her blessing and reminded me that with my Guardian Angel in my corner, I had nothing to fear. By then I was impatient to leave the country, and I remember very little about the last two weeks before I went, except that I saw the West End theatrical performance of the Rodgers and Hammerstein musical *South Pacific*, whence I was shortly to be bound. My parents and Heather came with me to the Tilbury Docks where *Rangitoto* was berthed.

She was not a spectacular liner, but a passenger and cargo ship carrying frozen lamb from New Zealand to England and back again with industrial products and migrants. I shared a cabin below the waterline with a couple and their three school children. It was a busy scene with constant movement aboard the ship and a tearful crowd on the shore. I was sad that I had not been able to say goodbye to Robina, yet again, and planned to write from our first port of call, which was to be the Dutch colony of Curaçao in the Caribbean.

Most of the passengers seemed to be migrants, like me, but there was a sprinkling of well to do New Zealanders who had spent long breaks in England, which they still referred to as "home," and young people who were returning from extended working holidays.

Soon, a band started playing the familiar military music, *The Stars and Stripes Forever* that goes with the nonsense words, "Oh be kind to my web-footed friends, for a duck may be somebody's mother." Loud hailers told non-passengers to go ashore and paper streamers were thrown from ship to shore. I left my luggage, consisting of one metal trunk and a suitcase, down below on my bunk and came on deck to say goodbye to my family. We kissed and embraced, said the usual things, like promising to write regularly, and they went ashore. Mother looked a bit teary. Mick sent me a telegram telling me to "knock them down over there just as you do here" and his parents also wished me well. The ship started to move sideways away from the shore as the band played and the streamers broke. I waved and they waved back, until I caught sight of Sybil, a New Zealand girl from Auckland who was returning with her mother after a long stay with relatives in England. She had a lovely face, white teeth and long red hair; right down to her waist.

Me at Curaçao on the way to New Zealand.

Chapter 4: Youth at Risk

Soon, *Rangitoto* was gathering speed from Tilbury towards the middle of the Thames estuary and heading east to round the North Foreland, then west down the English Channel. There was I, on one of the ships we used to watch on the horizon from the beach at Broadstairs when I was little. Sybil, her mother and I soon got to know each other over a cup of tea. There was dancing at night, for a typical migrant demographic of early middle aged parents and their families, which included about twenty boys and girls in their teens and early twenties. We soon became known as the *Rangitoto* Youth Club, and decided to put on a concert. Having led a rather sheltered social life, I knew very little about the contemporary popular songs of 1952, so, with Robina in mind, I gave a rendition of "This nearly was mine," the song that was still in my head from *South Pacific*.

Sybil and I got on well and went ashore together at the first opportunity while *Rangitoto* re-fuelled at Curaçao. It was my first tropical island. I was very impressed and bought a sombrero hat. I wrote about my impressions to my sister, Heather. By this time she was a much travelled young woman, fluent in both French and German and making the best of it. But I wanted her to know that there was another world beyond Europe that I wanted to find out about or even to be a part of:

We went with prosperous negroes in beautiful American cars through cactus covered hills where enormous goats ambled about as though they owned the place. Alongside the main street the sloops and schooners stuck their bowsprits over the harbour wall into the market place and the crews set up stalls on the ships, thus cutting out the middle man. I went on board, although I couldn't persuade Sybil to come with me. The skipper of the schooner showed me down below. They are about the same size as a Thames Barge.

Sybil wanted some earrings. I had no money, so she bought some for herself. The salesman wrapped them up and said, "Now you will dance beautifully tonight," which she did. What panache, I thought. Heather had written a letter to wait for me at Curaçao. It contained sad news, of the death in childbirth of Ursula Watson, the former WREN who had befriended me at St Julian's. The news made me regret leaving England, and I felt very depressed. It was not exactly, I told my sister, that I felt homesick. But that "I do think, Oh Purpose, Oh Future, Oh God! What next… and why?"

Balboa was even more interesting, I told Heather, "And very, very educational. A man came up to me in the street, with gold teeth, a black skin, and a 'wide-boy' suit and said, 'would you like to come to the House of Lov?' It's all right," I told my sister. I didn't go, but I stood there, regarding him for so long, taking mental notes for a novel (that I felt sure I would write), that I think he thought I was coming with him. However, when I refused he was not in the least offended and said, "I *quite understand*" as though he meant it. I'm still wondering why. A bit further on there was a Club Nocturno, where I met up with a group of passengers and some of the stewards from *Rangitoto*, who invited me to come in with them. My letter continued:

> *A lady came up to us and began to gyrate before us without any clothes on, and so the passengers went out again, much to the consternation of the proprietor who was just about to pour us out a drink. I was very inquisitive, and I still think he must have thought us very rude.*

I decided to stay at Club Nocturno with the stewards, who said they would "look after me." On reflection, I think they meant it. They knew I was an innocent abroad, and decided to keep me out of trouble. I have always been grateful. The club consisted of a large room divided into shady nooks and alcoves, and intersected at angles by wooden arches. There was a dancing place in the middle where a few couples swayed, entwined and oblivious. A little string band in a balcony produced rhythmic noise, and a mirror ball threw flakes of light into the semi-darkness where people "made lov," regardless of their surrounding audience. Eventually a huge taxi was called and we went back to the ship, past large shanties built up above the ground beneath them that teemed with life; steel bands, cooking, drinking and dancing; then to the wharf where *Rangitoto* lay "with her flood-lit superstructure rising majestically against the jungle background and the darkness of the night." Next morning, my letter gushes on, "we sailed past a line of palms standing on a low wave-washed promontory, and wooded islands of dusky green rising from the ruffled Ocean."

Nearly two weeks later, we sighted Pitcairn Island, inhabited since 1790, by the descendants of the *Bounty* mutineers and their Polynesian wives from Tahiti. Pitcairn has a "landing place" for boats, but no sheltered harbour, so we could not go ashore. Instead, we went past the island until we met two of the Pitcairn boats on the downwind side of the island. It was a dark and stormy evening when we eventually sighted the lights of the islanders' vessels, vanishing in the troughs and showing up on the crests as we came towards them. They were large open boats, about thirty-two feet long. *Rangitoto* hove to, and lines were thrown from the ship and taken aboard the boats and we towed them upwind to the other end of the island.

We lowered the boarding ladders so that the islanders could choose the right moment to step across from their boats to the bottom step of the ladder and climb up to the safety of the deck. The boats were then towed for some ten miles up to windward against a trade wind of twenty knots, in the night, so that they could return down-wind to Bounty Bay, at the northeast coast of the island. It was a spectacular demonstration of seamanship. One man stayed aboard each boat to steer. *Rangitoto* could not be steered reliably at less than seven knots, so steering the boats to keep them away from the ship in a three metre swell was hard work and very wet. The boatmen were drenched continuously. Most of the islanders came up the ladders lowered for the purpose, making nice judgements of when to step onto the lower step from the boats. They brought island craft-work with them, including a grass skirt that I bought for Sybil, but she didn't want it, so I kept it myself.

The shipboard party was mostly female, and the Pitcairn women did what they could to market their island souvenirs on the slippery deck. When we reached a point up to windward of Bounty Bay, the islanders returned to their boats down the ladders, cast off and rowed back home, singing mellifluent songs as they rowed away.

One of them stayed behind. He was sixteen-year-old Tom Christian, direct descendant of Fletcher Christian, mutineer, leader and founder of the unique Pitcairn community. Tom was leaving his island for the first time and on his way to New Zealand. He was to study to become a qualified radio operator, so that he could achieve the level of expertise and responsibility needed to maintain contact between the rest of the world and this extremely isolated community. He had a guitar and played and sang well. While our elders gambled in the ship's lounge, the Youth Club grew fond of assembling in the stern to watch the moon rise over the wake of the ship, while Tom sang the songs of Pitcairn and played his guitar. Then the rest of us would try to match his performance with the popular songs of the 1950s until midnight.

Adult passengers took an interest, as we (Sybil and I) did, in deck tennis and the swimming pool, where most of the conversation went on. Peter Wilson, aged twenty-one, was the son of a successful sheep farmer from Waipukurau, in the east of the North Island of New Zealand. I got on well with him and it turned out that I was to be posted by the Forest Department to Tikokino, not far away, so I was to see more of him.

Between the Chatham group of islands and our destination, Wellington, the capital of New Zealand, we were delayed by a bad storm that saw us hove to for twenty-four hours. It was my first real storm at sea, and I was fascinated to watch the way *Rangitoto* headed into the wind, with just enough power to make it possible to hold her position, with waves breaking over the bow and solid water flying hard against the bridge as she plunged again into the watery valleys. When the morning storm was over, we sighted the snowy summits of the 2,285 metre Kaikoura range on the eastern side of the South Island, and that evening saw us entering the harbour of Wellington. It reminded me, as we approached the wharves, of Oban in Scotland, with its surrounding hills, and their lower hillsides covered with the modest dwellings of an egalitarian society. The main difference was that in Wellington the buildings were nearly all wooden. I was told this was because of the frequency of earthquakes, which wooden houses could survive because of their ability to absorb a bit of distortion.

We arrived on 6 October 1952 and, after passing through a chain of officials, I was met by Mr Davidson from the Forestry Department, who took me away from the ship in a car for an interview. I stated my preference for working in an indigenous forest in Northland, hoping to be learning about the management of the Kauri forests, but when told about a training scheme for potential professional foresters, that involved initial training in Rotorua, and then undertaking a science degree at the University, I said that would be my priority. And as soon as possible. I was to be sent initially to Gwavas Forest in Hawke's Bay, on the eastern side of the North Island, but would be invited to return to Wellington on 28 October for another interview.

A long bus ride then took me to the little town of Waipawa, where I was met by Mr Craig, the Forester in charge of Gwavas Forest, near the small settlement of Tikokino, about twenty miles into the hinterland. I was allocated a wooden hut with a bed, a cupboard and a wood stove. It was one of a dozen or so similar buildings, clustered around the dinner shed and kitchen. I wrote to my parents later, "I was as depressed as I could be when I got here. It is mountainous country and it was raining. I was fed up with not being posted to Auckland and too depressed even to write."

Later, I went on with the letter:

I am beginning to like my surroundings quite a lot. Fifteen miles away are the Akaroas, a range of 4000 footers. Beyond them are the Ruahines, up to 5,000. There is a dramatic society about 30 miles away, which I am going to join. Most of the boys in the camp have a 303 rifle with which they shoot deer and wild pigs in the bush, and threaten upon occasions to shoot each other, but that is only for my benefit so that I can write home about it… Distances are big in this place and you are lost without transport. There are no good roads in this part, and so a bike is pretty useless too.

The main activity during working hours was "scrub cutting" which meant clearing Manuka that had been growing since the Depression of the 1930s, when many farms in the foothills were abandoned. This flowering shrub is now valued as a source of the most expensive honey in the world, but in 1952 it was seen as a weed to be removed to make way for *Pinus radiata* plantations. The cutting was done by a gang of young men using hand slashers. On 14 November, I wrote to my parents and told them I had sprained my wrist:

It's very hard work… The first day you get horrible blisters and they bleed all over… It is actually much easier when you get the knack of hitting the wood at just the right angle. Then you can slice through a stick maybe 2 inches thick with one swipe. Another time, if you don't get the angle right it bounces off and sprains your wrist.

New Zealand is a relatively new piece of land, geologically speaking, and I found the difference between New Zealand's volcanic landscape and the long smooth slopes of the Yorkshire moors or the Sussex downs disconcerting. I complained to my parents of the dozens of little valleys, all the same size and shape, and the wide chaotic strips of gravel with a trickle showing here and there that passed at that time of year, for rivers. I was also critical of my workmates:

Hawke's Bay is meant to be a snobbish region by New Zealand standards. Of course there are a lot of very wealthy farmers with big American cars, but looking around I think the weakest become workmen in the forest service. I hope I can become really interested in the service as a career, or else this part of it will not be worthwhile.

After a few visits to local towns like Waipawa and Hastings with my first friend in the camp, Bob Fortune, and a visit to Peter Wilson's farm, where I was made welcome, I considered myself to be entitled to make some social commentary in a letter written to Heather:

The Cinema in this country takes the place of the Theatre. The place is called a theatre, as opposed to a cinema, the seats are numbered, and you sit where you are told. There is "no smoking in the auditorium." The National Anthem, God Save the Queen, mind you, is played at the beginning of the film, with a portrait of the Queen projected on the screen. After the Shorts there is a short interval; all very posh.

I did nothing for the first six weeks but cut scrub, and I actually enjoyed the physical activity, and wrote on 25 November to my parents to tell them that "cutting scrub is like punching a bag. You use about the same amount of energy but the difference is that you keep it up for eight hours instead of three minutes. The result is that I am eating my meat [to please my mother], and becoming a "big tough man." The down side was boredom and worry about my future. And the fact that I had very little in common with most of my colleagues. If I was not going to work in a Kauri forest, then my interest in a forestry career was negligible. The only compensation was the possibility of going to a university.

Not that I found my colleagues uninteresting. There was Chris Welch, for example, a sailor who had jumped ship at Napier some years before, was caught, and spent nine months in gaol. I described him in a letter to my sister as "small, 29 and ugly." He had been ten years at sea and believed himself to have been the best customer at the brothels of nearly every port in the world, "but it was his fate to meet a girl called Mary in Scotland a few years ago, and he has been dogged by her ever since." When he came out of prison he obtained a contract job, earning nearly thirty pounds a week, and Mary came out from Scotland as an emigrant to join him. To begin with, he saw Mary occasionally. She came to the forest camp once and she was beautiful, well spoken, and intelligent. Chris behaved badly and would make a date with her, but forget to turn up and would leave her standing all night while he went to some other activity. On fine summer mornings he would head off to work in nothing but a pair of bright yellow swimming trunks, and a pair of boots, at the head of the gang going out to slash Manuka. He carried his slasher in his hand with a coloured handkerchief tied at the end streaming in the wind while he sang *Onward Christian Soldiers* in his raucous voice. But Mary still loved him, and one day he left us, to take her to Wellington and to marry her. We never saw them again.

Such experiences were novel and therefore interesting, but I began to feel I had made a mistake, and thought I should do my best to seek other opportunities. There was the shortage of girls. Things had been better, I began to think, at Christ's Hospital. Sybil was the only girl I knew within reach, so though I continued writing regularly to Robina, I decided to make a lightning visit to Auckland to see Sybil. It was an experience I have never forgotten, beginning with a ride in the mail car on a Friday evening to Napier. I then met a man who directed me to a cheap boarding house, and asked me if I was hitchhiking. I told him I was, so he said he was going up the Taupo road at 5.30 next morning and he would call for me. I asked the landlady for bed without breakfast, but she insisted in putting a thermos of tea and some sandwiches by my bedside so that I could eat before I went. The man who found me a bed for the night kept his word and at 5.30 I stepped out of the door of my lodgings into his lorry and away up the winding road between the mountains and the sea. New Zealand had a higher proportion of car owners than Britain, but a much smaller population. I was lucky as hitchhiking was customary to a greater degree than in Britain, so it was never difficult on the major roads. My first lift took me thirty miles, and then I procured another that took me right across the North Island to the town of Hamilton.

Sybil was living in a caravan for the time being with her mother, waiting for the time when they could return permanently to their farm at Waiuku, another sixty miles north on an inlet of Manukau Harbour. I was there at five pm. My visit, though anticipated, must have been very inconvenient. That evening we went to Auckland. "It's a lovely city," I wrote, "and much nicer than Wellington. There were big ships throwing the shadows of their superstructures on to the streets, and shops and things." Sybil and her mother stayed in a hotel that night, and there was a bus leaving for Hamilton at four o'clock next morning that would give me a good start on my journey back to the forest camp. I planned to sleep rough at the railway station, but the manager of the hotel took pity on me and told me I could sleep in the lounge, since I couldn't afford a room and was leaving early.

My first lift from Hamilton took me a long way out of my way to some small village between Bulls and Palmerston North, which I reached as it was becoming dark. There was little traffic, and I began walking. Eventually I reached a small settlement with a police station. I was very tired by now and I remembered my mother's advice when I was a child: "If ever you are lost or in trouble, John, find the nearest police station, and they will help you." So I knocked on their door, and immediately found myself in trouble. They asked me how long I had been in New Zealand, and I explained that I was a newly arrived migrant from England. I told them where I worked and where I had been. But they didn't believe me and told me I should make up something more convincing. However, I stuck to my story and asked them why they didn't believe me. The long cross examination went on for an hour or so, and I became very tired having had little sleep for the last few days. Eventually they became tired too, and told me they had suspected I was an escapee from a youth detention centre nearby. Then they let me sleep on the settee alongside the wall. I left early next morning very hungry, and soon procured a lift on my way back to the forest camp in time for the evening meal. That was the first and only experience of the dark side of the police force that I had in New Zealand. Things could have been worse, I thought.

On 24 October 1952, I had another interview in Wellington with the Forestry Department, which paid my rail fares there and back. Apparently it went reasonably well. In spite of my doubts about Forestry, I did not yet want to burn my bridges, and so I tried to forget my theatrical ambitions and concentrated on my ambition to go to university, which could only happen after a successful period at a preliminary training establishment in Rotorua. There were many probing questions. At the end of the interview, one of the interviewing panel said, "Have we undermined you at all?" I said "No, not at all." Another said, "Well we tried hard enough but you have answered well." So I left feeling confident. When I returned to Tikokino the Forest Ranger, Mr Craig, said he thought I would probably be accepted for the training scheme and science degree.

But after my visit to Auckland I began to think of other lanes, and decided to explore them as well as I could. In November, I wrote to my parents, who must have been worried about the choices I might make, without their guidance:

> *I think that whatever I do, I will want to go to Auckland University. In this country, "working your way through college" is a very practical possibility… So I am writing to Mr Newbury for the address of a geography master who left C.H. to become a tutor at Auckland.* [Mr Lister] *He knew me quite well and I think would be glad to help me. I'll write to him about what I should do.*

Then, in early December, I received a letter from the Department of Defence informing me that having turned eighteen, I was soon due to commence my National Service. I was given a choice of which service I should join. All the choices involved much shorter terms than National Service terms in England. The army would have been the shortest. But after my experience of the Junior Training Corps at Christ's Hospital, I decided on the New Zealand Navy. This meant four months of full time training and sea time, followed by three years of weekly "parades" and annual voyages at sea, as part of the Naval Reserve, which sounded far more interesting. This choice would mean that I would be called up in February 1953.

The Forestry Department went on its annual holiday shortly before Christmas, so I planned another visit to Auckland. But before I did that I had an experience which re-ignited my theatrical ambitions.

There was a Drama Club at Waipukurau. I made contact and joined up in the hope of receiving a part in a play before too long. But then I was told that a new professional theatre company had just been formed by Richard and Edith Campion. It was to be called, "The New Zealand Players." English theatre companies and even famous British actors like Lawrence Olivier and Vivian Leigh visited New Zealand regularly in those days, but this was to be the first permanent professional company of New Zealanders in New Zealand; and they would shortly be visiting Hawke's Bay on a talent seeking expedition throughout the country.

I was wildly excited and managed to make contact with the Campions, who told me they would be in Napier on their talent quest late in November. They offered me an audition. To ensure that I could reach Napier on time, I bought a small second hand 98cc, 1939 James motor cycle that was advertised in the newspaper for twenty pounds. My audition was on a Monday, so I rode the fifty miles from Tikokino on the previous day, and stayed at a cheap hotel overnight, hoping to spend the Sunday in the local library, learning my parts.

I wrote to my parents about my situation and intentions:

> *Last week I was in Napier, partly for my medical examination, as I have been accepted as a trainee by the forest service, and partly for my audition for the New Zealand*

> Players… I applied for a stage audition and was sent a form to fill in, giving my history, experience etc and it said a photograph was essential, and that I must apply immediately as auditions began in ten days' time.

The only photograph of me in the country was one I had given to Sybil, but I asked her to send it back, which she did.

I was to act two contrasting parts, one of an historical or classical character, the other modern. One of them at least, had to be of a character that was not close in age to that of the applicant. After much searching through modern scripts which I knew nothing about, I hit on a character called Denis in the play *Who is Sylvia* by Terence Rattigan (1950). For the other part, I chose my old friend Mark Antony, whose part I could still remember. The audition was at 7 pm. It was a cold day with a bit of rain. The beach was deserted and the waves made it noisy, so for three hours I learnt the dialogue for Denis and flung my Shakespearean orations at the Pacific Ocean again and again. Then I went back to my Bed and Breakfast, changed into my only suit and made my appearance. It was raining now and the studio was small, just a stage and a tiny auditorium under an iron roof. A man was asked to read the other part as I did what I could with the Denis character, and it was hard to beat the rain with drawing room chatter.

Then I brought everyone else into the auditorium and placed my characters across the stage from Caesar's corpse so that I could stand between corpse and conspirators, and walk up to challenge each in turn, as Shakespeare intended. The rain became heavy, which I thought gave the crying of "Havoc" a much more telling effect.

The Campions were very kind, and said they still had most of New Zealand to visit and couldn't "make any promises," but they liked what they saw and guaranteed me at least a place in the local reserves that were to be created in each town on their circuit. They said they thought the basic necessities of voice and technique were there, and advised me, if I wanted to be a professional actor, to gain as much experience on stage as I possibly could, and to keep in contact. I told them I had been to Auckland and was beginning to think I should move there. They advised me to contact Rex Sayers, a senior announcer on National Radio in Auckland, who was also President of the Grafton Players, the oldest and, many would say, the best amateur dramatic society in Auckland.

Thus encouraged, I visited Auckland again. This time the Navy paid the fare, as I was to have an interview because of my National Service preference. I wrote to Robina on 11 December 1952 and told her I had spent the first hour filling in forms, and then had an intelligence test. I had been led to believe at Christ's Hospital that my IQ was nothing to boast about (and apparently Mr Flecker had passed this news on to Geoff Rogers, as a reason why I should leave school at the end of year eleven). I was therefore delighted to be told that this was not the case. It was pretty high in fact, and I was regarded as potential "Officer Material." I was told that if I returned to the UK after completing the immigration requirement of two years of residence in New Zealand, I could be transferred to the Royal Navy Reserve. This interview sowed in my mind the idea that I could volunteer for extra sea time, thus gaining enough experience to secure a working passage on a ship back to England.

I then went in search of Rex Sayers, who said that his Society was always looking for male actors and that I would be welcomed as a member. He also said that he might find me a part time radio announcing job. In New Zealand in 1952, a received English accent, which I had learnt to imitate, rather than speak in my Yorkshire dialect, was a real asset.

Perhaps, I thought, I would be able to survive in Auckland, while maintaining my hard won independence, and study for an Arts degree, while gaining as much stage experience as possible. After all, university tuition in New Zealand was free. Subsistence was the only requirement, and you could study part time.

So I walked up the hill from radio station 1YA, to Auckland University, with its famous wedding cake tower, and proper cloisters round the back, just like an old university. I found the office and showed the Registrar my O-level and A-Level certificates. I was told I was eligible to apply for *ad eundem* admission to the university on the basis of my A-Level results, and was directed to Professor, and poet, Michael Joseph for guidance. I explained how I came to be in New Zealand, and my existing assumption that I would seek admission to university through the Forestry Department. Professor Joseph was encouraging, as I told him about my interests in theatre, and I came away with the idea that I now had a choice, even if it was a hypothetical one. On one hand I could have a career in plantation forestry, in which I was not interested, but it would provide financial support and enable me to earn a degree. On the other hand, since university tuition fees were free in New Zealand, I could choose to enrol part time in an Arts degree, taking subjects that I knew something about, while leaving time to earn a living independently. It would also leave me time, I thought, to do other interesting things, like acting, sailing, boxing, and developing satisfactory relationships with the opposite sex, an area in which I was still very much a beginner. I wrote to my parents just before Christmas in high spirits:

> *Believe me, I think I'm on the way now. Auckland is a really wonderful place — My Dreamland. All this manoeuvring, the audition with the NZ Players, and interviews have made me distraught. Now am having a holiday. Last night was Christmas Eve. I took Sybil to the theatre. We saw "Seagulls over Sorrento" by a British Company. Then to Midnight Mass at a "High" place,* [that is High Anglican]. *Anty Molly would have liked it. The choir were mainly Maori and sang really well. I shall return to the Forest camp for another week. I'll give you my new address as soon as I have it.*

My next address was c/o Whakatu Freezing Works, near Hastings, about forty miles away from Tikokino. The attraction was that it provided well paid seasonal work where large numbers of sheep and lambs were put to death, processed, clothed in muslin bags, frozen and then sent by rail to Napier, the nearest port, to be shipped to England. Speed was crucial, and we worked long hours, sometimes starting work at 2 am in the dark, and finishing at 5 pm. This meant a lot of overtime, and therefore high wages, but I found it a gruelling experience. For some reason I entered the building for the first time at the slaughtering end of the chain. Skilled Maori slaughtermen seized the animals as they were forced by those behind them through a gate. The slaughtermen positioned them expertly with their heads over a concrete gutter, and slit their throats. Then they lifted the back legs and pierced the fetlocks with a gimbal, and hooked the carcase onto a moving chain, while a large quantity of blood from each, still twitching, animal flowed into a concrete holding pool. There, another man in gum boots had an enormous squeegee about a metre wide which he used to push the blood into the bordering drain.

When they were on the chain, the carcasses went past a series of specialists; skins were peeled off, briskets punched, innards and heads removed by different men. At the end of that process the carcasses were re-clothed in muslin bags and hung on a series of racks on the "cooling floor," before being slid on into the freezing chamber. There they stayed until frozen solid. Beyond the chamber, I found myself working as a member of the stacking and loading gangs. We were dressed in heavy smocks and provided with woollen caps, leather gloves and sacking, in which to bind our boots to insulate us from the cold. We set up wooden chutes on trestles to slide the carcasses from the cooling floor to the storage building next to the rail siding. They were stacked there until early morning, to await loading onto the train that took them to the Napier wharves for shipment. Stacking was hard work, as we snatched each frozen carcase travelling at speed along the ice covered chutes, and threw them neatly onto a stack rising to as high as we could reach with a short and accurate throw. Sometimes the distance between cooling floor and stack was considerable, so that up to four chutes might have to be used, with a man at each corner of the run to swing the flying carcasses around the corners without dropping them onto the floor.

I have vivid memories of the early mornings, when we had to keep working hard to keep warm enough to survive in sub-zero temperatures. It was my first experience of working with Maoris, which I enjoyed. Most of them were much older than me. As soon as I spoke they knew I came from Britain and so considered it their duty to educate me on the subjects of race relations and class. Their story was that they were, indeed, cannibals, and in consequence, to be respected. "I eat Pakehas" as one of them put it. I began to ask questions about politics and religion in Maori society, so they invited me to visit the local Maori Pa, and I gained an introductory appreciation of Maori customs, and values, which I respected; and many of which I admired.

In spite of their own aristocratic and patriarchal tradition, they argued that New Zealand was a classless society when compared with England. I had to agree. Politically, they were staunch supporters of the Labour party, and were proud of New Zealand's world leadership in the early introduction of female suffrage, a National Health scheme, and victorious rugby football team. When we had intervals from work because of delayed trains, we played soccer to keep warm, and there was an atmosphere of cultural pride and mutual respect. The fact that for me, working at the Freezing Works was a temporary situation, and that I was earning good money in good company made it an experience that I have always valued.

Accommodation cost nothing. I shared a free wooden cabin, as everyone did. My mate was a young man called Rick. He was a twenty-one year old Australian on a long working holiday with a racy style about him. We went to the local pub together after work, and managed to squeeze a few drinks in before the closing time scrum in those days, at six o'clock. Alcohol was a new experience for me. Once, when Fred had taken me to London for my interview at New Zealand House, we had dinner afterwards with his family. I wrote in my diary about the amount Fred drank and remarked that, "If ever I want to get drunk, I'll have just what Fred had, and then just one more." In my early days at Tikokino, I decided on a personal experiment to discover my own limits and bought a small bottle of gin, to drink on my way home on my push bike from Waipawa. I soon succeeded in making myself vomit as my head spun, and I crashed my bike into the ditch and lay there until the cold woke me up. So my aversion to alcohol that began with my interest in keeping fit so that I could box, stayed with me for a long time, as a means of postponing death. For years after my experiment, the very thought of gin made me feel sick. I went to the pub with Ricky out of good manners, but never drank more than a single "schooner" of beer.

Smoking was another problem, because I thought it too would be bad for my health, but at "Smoko," the worker's birthright in New Zealand industrial law, it was assumed that cigarettes were always shared equally with your mates, unless you wanted to be seen as an OP, or "other People's" smoker. So I made the decision then, when I was 18, that I would be a non-smoker, and that declaration was understood, even if, in the 1950s, it was not expected.

Sex between unmarried people was also considered to be a vice as well as a sin in the religious and social context that I was used to, but my anonymous identity and the multicultural nature of my surroundings would have justified any contemporary social worker to consider me to be "at risk."

Added to that was the fact of my unusually segregated upbringing. By this time my inhibition and fear of making someone pregnant, and therefore having to marry them, was overtaken by my youthful spirit of enquiry, opportunism, and sinful lust.

Joan stood behind the bench in the cafeteria from which she served our meals as we walked past to collect them, so I saw her every day. She was the charming twenty-one year old daughter of a Maori mother and an Indian father. She had a lovely body and a cheerful and attractive countenance, full of smiles, to which I responded. After a few weeks I summoned up the courage on a Friday night to ask her if she would meet me outside after "Tea," the substantial meal that we ate at the end of the day. We met, and she asked me if I would like to take her home, which was a short distance away. She suggested that I could ride her bicycle, an old iron framed "sit up and beg" style of machine, and she would sit side saddle on the carrier behind me. And so, off we went as the sun went down and the shadows grew long across the dusty unsurfaced backroad. I was wearing an old pair of shorts with a hole in a pocket which she soon found. As dusk began to fall we rode past some trees and tall grass at the other side of a ditch. In some alarm, but more delight, I felt her hand fossick through the hole, and grasp what she was looking for. I steered into the ditch and fell off the bike and into the long grass in a high state of fear and excitement.

We lay laughing and in some discomfort on the ground as John Young the missionaries' son, and only eighteen, began, in spite of himself, and with clumsy passion, to respond to her clear invitation. But then, though a woman of few words, Joan spoke: "Let's go to my place." She explained that her own bedroom was an enclosed verandah, known in New Zealand as a sleep-out. Her parents would be out; and she told me confidently, in response to my enquiry, that her monthly cycle was at a stage at which pregnancy was impossible. Thus reassured, I pedalled at some speed the remaining mile to her house where we took our clothes off and climbed straight into her bed. Too late to repent, I let Joan take charge. I think at this point that my memory will be less useful than your imagination, where I am content to leave it.

Next morning, after an energetic night, followed by deep sleep, I woke feeling relaxed and happy. Joan's parents had come home late. Joan cooked us breakfast and we let them sleep. I expected to feel guilt, but because of my feeling that no one was hurt by our nocturnal activity, that came later. We went down to the nearby river with its sandy bottom after breakfast, and were soon joined in the clear water by a large group of Maori children. Then we played tennis with a group of teenagers and young adults. I bashfully told Robina in my next letter that "I have a girlfriend down here now, at least a Girl-Friend, if you know what I mean. She's not as nice as you."

I was grateful to Joan for her introductory tutorial on a subject which had been a mystery to me until then, and we met again on two or three occasions, but we both understood the limitations of our relationship and my inescapable obligation to go to Auckland and join the Navy. I still am grateful.

Chapter 5: Actor, Sailor, Boat builder, Failure?

Sometime between leaving Tikokino Forest, and starting work at Whakatu freezing works, I must have hitchhiked again to Auckland. One of my friends at the forest camp, whose name I remember as Barry, was planning, as I was meant to be, to enter the Forestry training establishment at Rotorua, and obtain a science degree and become a professional forester. But he was brought up in Auckland. He also had a wider knowledge than the other boys, of alternative options. I told him about my theatrical ambitions and he gave me, through his father, an important contact, Rex Sayers, who had also been recommended to me by Richard Campion.

On arriving in Auckland in the last days of 1952, I went to the radio station and sought Sayers out. I explained that I intended to be accepted as an undergraduate student of Auckland University, but only as a step towards a career as an actor, encouraged as I was by my audition with the New Zealand Players. I told him of Mr Campion's advice to gain as much experience as I possibly could; and then, perhaps, to try for a scholarship to enter the Central School of Drama in London, or the Royal Academy of Dramatic Art.

Rex was cautiously supportive. He told me that the key to success as an actor or even to join a good Drama school was to gain as much experience as possible, which would be very difficult to combine with obtaining a good degree. He gave me an informal audition as a radio announcer, and told me that my English accent and clear diction would be a satisfactory qualification, and if I intended to stay in Auckland, he thought he could offer me a part time job as a radio announcer. In the meantime he would introduce me to the Grafton Players.

I wrote a letter to my parents in January 1953 in a confident mood:

> Here I am in Auckland at last. [I was staying at a bed and breakfast, in Parnell.]
>
> There's a verandah balcony at the back, overlooking the harbour. It's nice and blue, with white sails on it. The weather is wonderful. This is what I hoped it would be like. I have arranged an audition with the Auckland broadcasting place, and I am promised a part in "The Rivals" in a month's time. I had to leave the forestry. I felt it was not what I was meant for. I could cause no delay, and I had to make my mind up... Don't grieve. I'm sure I've done the right thing. The immigration official at Hastings says there should be no objection to my coming here to Auckland University. I'm going to work my way through as a wireless announcer.

Back at the freezing works, I applied by mail to Auckland University for *ad eundem* admission to an Arts degree. The reply, dated 27 February, from the Registrar of the University was forwarded to me early in March:

> I have pleasure in informing you, that at its recent meeting, the Executive Committee of the Senate granted you Admission Ad Eundem to this University, with credit for the Entrance Qualification.

Meanwhile, I set myself the task of organizing my immediate future. Sayers told me, much to my disappointment, that I would not be able to work as a news reader after all. It was the policy of New Zealand's broadcasting association not to employ people under the age of twenty-one as announcers, so I procured a temporary job at the Auckland wool store. It was casual labour with good overtime opportunities, and so ideal for students. I was soon making friends with the young men whom I would meet again in the lecture rooms of the Wedding Cake, as the Auckland University Arts building was known.

My first address was a room in Parnell, which I did not enjoy for long. It wasn't a situation in which I could come and go as I pleased. There were meal times, and though my middle-aged landlady was a pleasant person, she expected me to have regular habits, including an English style midday meal. What with lectures, rehearsals for plays and late evenings for all sorts of reasons, it was never going to work.

I wrote to my parents from St Georges Bay Road at the end of January 1953, before I was told that the radio job was not going to happen.

> *I have a radio audition at 3 pm Monday. Things will then start moving. At five o'clock I will go to the boxing club. I've been once already, and the trainer wants me for a special session. On Tuesday night I'm going to a rehearsal for "The Rivals." Mr Sayers is going to introduce me to the gang. I've opened up four avenues to fame. I do hope I can get along one of them at least. My average day will be, 9–11 am, work at station 1YA (I hope), walk 200 yards to University Library; study, 11 am–5 pm. Lectures from 5–7 pm; 7–9 pm, either boxing or rehearsals alternate nights. I'll work* [ie. for my livelihood] *9 am–11, and study in the early mornings too. I'll be able to catch up at weekends and I'm planning a nervous breakdown about Easter.*

I hoped that, for their peace of mind, my parents didn't believe my immature rejoicings, but there was some truth in what I wrote. I moved to ideal student lodgings in the home of Mr and Mrs Dorothy Smith in 11 Kitchener Road, Takapuna in March. My room was on the first floor at the back of this pleasant dwelling, overlooking Takapuna beach. I used to wake to the noise of breaking waves and look across the water in the dawn light to the black silhouette of the volcanic cone of Rangitoto Island, whose name was also that of the ship that had brought me to where I was. Sometimes, at first, there was also an imaginary ship in my mind's eye, that I followed as she came swiftly out of Waitemata harbour and out past Great Barrier Island, to commence the passage that would take me through the Panama Canal again and back to England. That led my thoughts, on sunny mornings, to memories of Robina, and scenes of our imaginary re-union. But for now, I was increasingly happy to be in New Zealand. "Life is really speeding up now," I wrote to my parents, "and going according to plan."

> *We are about to commence the second week of "The Rivals," which is being a great success… and there is quite a feeling of importance when you see your name twice in the program, once under "street boys etc." and again under, "stage hands etc." It is a beginning… It is tremendous fun, with a fortnight of one o'clock bedtimes after a trip across the harbour, and the nights seem always to be fine.*

I went on to tell my parents that I was concentrating on an acting career and had just spent all day in a succession of auditions that had led to me being cast in the leading role in the annual University Revue, *Seize Me Caesar or There's no place like Rome*. It was due to be staged in the largest if not the most stylish theatre in Auckland, the Playhouse in Karangahape Road. My character, Sir Julius Caesar, was a spoof of the current Lord Mayor, who had a plan for a Harbour bridge for the city, as opposed to an up to date sewerage plan:

> *I am Julius — desired by two of the most beautiful girls you ever saw, Diana, who takes the part of Akarana, the one I fall for, and Marylin, who takes the part of the one who tries. I get murdered by Gasseus and Mark Antony, who are members of the Humic Drainage Brotherhood, and who think that my plans for a harbour bridge would muck up their sewerage scheme. I recover under Akarana's nursing. She is a white witch really, and brings me back to life. I smartly sing a solo, and things work up to a glorious finale. Akarana and me in duets, and there is a most stupendous chorus. It's all on a professional scale with dancing and everything. Just Lovely. There'll be such paragraphs in the newspapers — Fame at last!*

My work, before and during the Revue was at the wool store, stacking and compressing or "dumping" bales of wool, using a trolley and a wool hook to take two bales to the hydraulic press, thus doubling the weight of each load by halving the bulk of each bale, and then taking them to another stack from which they were shipped overseas. We worked until 7.30 each night, at overtime rates after 5 pm. I went on stage at 8.20, so it was a close-run existence, as exhilarating to me as it was exhausting. I told Robina that I planned to play rugby, as I had at school, when the season began.

I realised that by taking on as much stage work as I could manage, or more, I was risking failing my exams at the end of the year. But I could not stop myself. Partly it was because of my vanity and the immediate gratification I enjoyed to satisfy it, augmented by the fun of numerous parties and social acceptance of my ambitions. But there was also the background of my now long relationship with Robina. I wrote to her as soon as the Revue was over:

> *We ran for a week at a theatre that holds about 1000 people, and we had almost full houses all the time, except for the two Saturday nights, which were absolutely full. You don't get opportunities like that in England unless you are a professional.*

Acting, I told myself, was to be the speediest means of returning to England and seeing her again. And this hope was supported by the news, shortly after the revue was over, that Diana, the girl who played the part of "Akarana," would soon be leaving us, because she had won a scholarship to the Central School of Drama in London. I began to take myself even more seriously, and worry less about my studies, which were falling behind. If she could do that, why shouldn't I?

Robina seemed to have stopped writing for a while. There had been no letter from her when I boarded *Rangitoto* at Tilbury, nothing at Curaçao or Panama. Nothing at Wellington. I wrote a letter to her from the forest camp, about the middle of October 1952, not a good one, full of recriminations. But I received a jubilant letter back to tell me she must have missed me at Tilbury, but she had written me four long letters without hearing back from me, and she would go on writing once a fortnight if I would do the same. So we resumed an interchange of our personal feelings and achievements, failings, successes, and in the end, developed an affection for each other that helps me greatly now, as I write, to recall and evaluate my early life. At this point in it, I couldn't make up my mind about anything, and just let myself be swept on in whatever was the easiest or most egotistical direction.

I think I realised this, and for that reason re-started my Diary, in which my last entry was 27 June 1952, when Olive finished mending my trousers and gave me a kiss. In March 1953, I started again:

Yes, a lot has happened since Olive mended my trousers… Now, I am at Auckland University. I am a member of the New Zealand Players as one of the local reserve here up in Auckland. I am going to act like anything while I am up here, and next year I hope to get into the permanent company.

But I still wanted to have it both ways:

Someday, I'll go back to England. I'm doing History and English here, and will eventually get an MA. That will be something worthwhile, and it will just show those people at school. I think I am justified in doing it, because my A-level exam proved that I was just a little better than they thought I was.

At that stage, even being accepted to take an Honours degree, let alone achieving a good one was a long way off. My diary describes periods of depression:

I am very run down just now, but now I have money, a home, and I did have a job, at a wool store, but I finished today. I want a part time job for a short time so that I can recover my health. I have been doing without proper sleep since January and working very hard as well. It's beginning to catch up on me. This university year will be a real test. I hope I manage. One thing, boxing as an amateur is remunerative out here. You get three pounds if you win, at least a voucher to get that value from a shop.

So I went on training, but less and less frequently, with the result that later, in August, I was knocked out in the semi-finals of the Auckland championships. I began to think I should give it away, telling myself how wise I was to avoid the risk of brain damage.

Robina continued to write, and for the next two years, this became the most stabilising influence on my thinking about my future. I wrote in my diary,

I have met some nice girls in New Zealand, but it becomes more and more obvious to me that Robina is the girl I love and [when] she writes, it is the nicest idea in my head that she is interested in me. I do want her very much. I hope she loves me, but she won't say so. Perhaps she will when I go back… Perhaps.

Then, on 2 April 1953 I wrote, "She **has** said so—in her last letter; she says she is a 'little bit in love with the person who writes to her from New Zealand'. That alone should make me tremendously happy; it does." Later I wrote to my sister, "Do you ever feel the equivalent of homesick… I have to keep doing something the whole time or I do… I'm really thriving on this life, but I seldom have time to 'stand and stare' and when I do, I become browned off and 'Wanna Go Home'. So I write to Robina and tell her so."

Later, I reflected on this unsettled period in a slightly more mature fashion. I had by then met Michael Delves, who I had known quite well at Christ's Hospital. He played the clarinet in the school band, and had migrated to New Zealand with his family. He was in the orchestra of the Revue. He lived on the North Shore, a little closer to the vehicular ferry at Devonport than I was. He was doing a science degree at the University. I was working for a book distributor every morning, leaving afternoons for the library and lecture rooms of the University. My main task was making up parcels of books to be posted all over New Zealand. I accepted a lift to go to my work in Auckland City on the back of Michael's motor bike for a while. That wonderful journey across the Waitemata was a break, twice a day, from the goings on ashore; a time to settle thoughts and ponder on the mysteries of life. It was a routine I came to cherish, and Michael was a cheerful companion. So I had lifts to rehearsals and parties after the show as well.

"In some ways" I wrote, "things are going well. In other ways they're not. I have very little money, and soon I shall have no job." But I did have one minor victory;

There was a boy working there [at the book distributor] *who lives down the road. I got to know him fairly well. He had got University Entrance, and I knew he wasn't very keen on his job, so I asked him why he didn't make use of his opportunity to go to the University, which in New Zealand was virtually free. His father didn't like the idea. I knew I was not making the best of my own opportunities, but I argued with him.*

My arguments were the kind that would have helped me in my last year at school and were passed on to his father. They were all about widened choices in life, and the discovery of unsuspected abilities. Shortly after our discussion, the boy told me that his father had agreed with me. He was going to go to University next year, so I felt pleased with myself. But that did not quench my own ambition to act. I told my sister in England that I was, in both University life and acting, "up to my neck." I explained to my parents:

I am at present in three shows, The Rivals, a bit supernumerary, but my name is on the program... It was cast long before I came to Auckland. I am in "Still life"—The film was called Brief Encounter. Last Sunday, after an exhausting and nerve racking series of trials, I was given the leading part in the college revue. It isn't the biggest part, but it's all about me, "Sir Julius. The Mayor of Rome." In the meantime they are holding auditions on Sunday for St Joan, the play they have chosen for the Auckland Arts Festival.

I accepted a part in Shaw's *St Joan*, but I don't remember what it was so it can't have been very important! Soon I was successful in gaining more substantial acting experience. Alan Curnow, an English lecturer, and soon to be regarded as one of New Zealand's best poets, had written a new play, *The Axe*, about religion and acculturation in the Pacific Islands. It was to be produced by Professor Musgrove, who, like David Jesson-Dibley at Christ's Hospital, was a product of the Oxford University Dramatic Society. I auditioned successfully for a part as a Polynesian priest, and began rehearsals in July. It was quite a surprising success. A few weeks later I was in one of Auckland's pubs, when a bloke came and asked me to audition for a play. I did. It was Noel Coward's *This Happy Breed*, produced by the Grafton Players, and performed at His Majesty's Theatre, the oldest and most beautiful theatre in Auckland.

A few months before, Anthony Quinn and the British Stratford Theatre Company had performed to full houses there for a week. My role was "Billy," the young sailor, played by John Mills in the successful film version of the play. *This Happy Breed* was a fore-runner, in some ways, of the later *Family at War* television program. It was well-suited, in 1953, to the Kiwi audience. Unlike Australians, New Zealanders had retained a less critical feeling for Britain and its imperial connection. But they had not experienced the irony of Australian soldiers fighting for Britain in North Africa, while the Japanese bombed Darwin, and the consequent sense of having been let down by Britain during the Second World War. Many New Zealanders still referred to England as "Home." "The play is a bit corny," I told Heather, "and dated, but it will go over big." It did.

It was in August 1953 that the immigration department of the New Zealand Government caught up with my movements, and sent me a bill for £85, the cost of repaying my fare from England. This meant that I had to start looking for a full time job, believing that I could still handle my part time University work. I told my parents about this and they offered to pay for my fare themselves. I said I did not want them to. I wanted to be able to think of myself as independent even if I wasn't. And for several months I heard nothing more about it from them or

Left: Publicity photo for my role as "Billy" in Noel Coward's *This Happy Breed*, 1953, Grafton Players.

Below: Me (L) as a Polynesian priest in Allen Curnow's play, *The Axe*, 1953.

the New Zealand Government. But I knew that they would find raising such an amount very difficult. Our family was one in which money was never discussed. We were never allowed to be extravagant, and received the clear impression that Rob had a small salary.

Some months later I was informed that my father had paid the sum for me. I thanked him and told him I would regard it as a loan and felt bad about it. Much later, after his death in 1961, I discovered in my father's papers a letter to him from Mr Rankin, who had interviewed me in London, and booked my passage on *Rangitoto*. He must have returned to New Zealand soon afterwards. He wrote to my father to acknowledge receipt of the passage money:

> *I deeply regret that it has been necessary to require repayment in this case, and I sincerely hope that your son will do well at University and establish himself in this country.*

I still feel disappointed that I let Mr Rankin down, as well as my parents, and retrospectively very grateful to them for releasing me from what would have been such an obligation that I would not have been able to continue my student life. I had told Robina that "being a part time student is no good to me. It gives you no time to think, or write. It's just a case of hanging on." But even part time jobs had their problems. My Diary for 16 August 1953 says:

> *I have had quite a few jobs in Auckland. I made lamp shades for a while, (electric wire welding) until I got the sack. I didn't like doing the family shopping as part of my duties, or the people, so I wasn't sorry.*

What actually happened, my diary tells me, was that:

> *My boss was about to go away on a sales trip. He asked me to stay til he came back, so, being well brought up, I complied. I then went and told the Government where I was, and they sent me to a [jam] factory. That nearly drove me to distraction in three days, so I left and went to another one, — Nestlés. I made myself ill eating chocolate.*

It was company policy to allow employees to eat as much chocolate as they wanted. Beginners always gave it up after a couple of days. I did too, and then I returned to the wool store during the Easter holidays.

This Happy Breed was scheduled for the beginning of September, but it must have clashed with something else, and it was postponed until 17 October and was to run for ten days. My first exam was on the following morning. I explained to Robina:

> *We were half way through rehearsals then, [in early September] and I couldn't have dropped out then even if I had wanted to. Anyway, the last night is the night before my first exam. I'm leaving my job next week so that I'll be able to get something done.*

In a letter to Heather I tried to be optimistic:

> *If I pass it will be wonderful. I'll have done quite a lot, nearly a third of a degree, [an exaggeration] six plays and eight jobs in a year. If I fail it will look horribly as if I've fooled about to no purpose.*

My job, which I took on that August so as to be able, one day, to pay back my fare, was a full time position as a journeyman boat-builder at £10 a week at the famous shipyard of John Lidgard. He was building a beautiful fishing boat at the time, out of the very Kauri pine I had come to New Zealand to behold, and that was where I wanted to work, but it was not to be. I had done very little woodwork until then and my job was to work on a trial of the latest technology of the period, cold moulding for the construction of small dinghies. Two diagonal skins made up of strips of veneer were laid down over a softwood mould, glued and stapled together. They were then covered with a third skin of veneer strips, glued on top of them, and clamped by a fitted rubber skin, under which a vacuum was created, so as to suck the fore and aft skin evenly and tightly onto the mould. After the marine glue (resorcinol) had set, it was my job to pull all the staples out, leaving a completed shell. This then had to be followed up by fitting knees, in-wales, gunwales, risers, thwarts and breast hooks, the components that stiffened the very light vessels.

Accurate fitting was something I found very difficult. Though glues were used, they were not intended to be used as gap fillers. The standards of my workmates were still those of an industry that did not have the word "tolerance" in its vocabulary. Things fitted, or they didn't. That meant that surfaces that were meant to fit each other did so completely, curved and sometimes twisted though they were. My colleagues were astonishingly skilled, and seemed to achieve perfection without effort, so the time it took for me to manage even a fit that looked good enough but wasn't, was embarrassing. I began to improve with practice, and I think now, that if I had been given a part, however small, in building that Kauri pine fishing boat, I would never have wanted to do anything else for a living.

The skills of John Atha, who was our producer and lead actor in *This Happy Breed,* were equally impressive. He was already regarded in Auckland's theatre world as professional in all but name. He was an inspiration, with a stage presence that could extend a pause or command attention for as long as was needed; a voice that could express feeling in a totally untheatrical, but explicitly effectual style. And he had that mastery of timing, facial management, and accurate characterisation that enabled him to mesmerise a sophisticated audience and make it think, laugh, or cry as he wanted.

I was, of course, overwhelmed by the experience. I was pleased with my own performance, because I felt the support of the audience as my character wooed the object of my affections, and satisfied the ordinary expectations of a juvenile lead. I told my parents, "It was absolutely amazing the way the audience carried on." I enclosed the *Auckland Star*'s "ravishing review… We had a marvellous run after that, resulting in full houses, that is 1000 people or so every night." Then there was the last night party: "It was a staggering thing for me because I haven't had time to become well known in Auckland and everyone was asking about me." What more could an 18 year old want?

Better still, Mr Campion saw the show on the first night, and must have called around on the last night as well. I wrote to Robina to tell her he had asked me to do another audition. This time there were two things: as much of Romeo's speech, "It is the East and Juliet is the sun" that I could learn over the weekend, and my own selection of something out of *This Happy Breed*. The result was a small part in the theatrical version of the story of Ned Kelly which was put on at the same theatre by the New Zealand Players shortly after *This Happy Breed* finished. There were four performances. I proudly told my sister that "I have to appear twice, as a different character each time, in two different pubs."

J C Williams, owner/manager of the Australian Theatre Company, had offered to organise a tour to Wellington and Christchurch for us on a professional basis. That didn't happen, because as amateurs our day-jobs had to take precedence, but the expectations I had of myself as an actor at the end of the year continued to rise. I told Robina that "Mr Campion said he'd give me a job as an extra with two lines to say… They will be my first two lines in a professional capacity." But I also said, in the same letter, "I can't very well go to the University, and be in the New Zealand Players at the same time, and I think I'd better obtain a degree first."

The summer holidays lasted until late February, and this was an opportunity to earn as much money as possible. I met Emma Moore, a girl who was staying at O'Rourke Hall, the student hostel close to the University. She was a country student from the Wairarapa, on the south eastern coast of the North Island. I told her I was looking for a holiday job, and she said she would ask her parents if they could offer me one. It turned out that her parents had a huge sheep station in the Wairarapa, called "Eparaima." I told her that I had been employed to clear Manuka scrub at the forest camp, and so I ended up with a rather loose verbal "contract." I was to do whatever jobs were most urgent as they cropped up, and would have my own scrub-cutting "contract" that I could attend to whenever there was nothing else. It sounded good to me. I would keep fit and make lots of money. So I explained to my landlady, Mrs Smith, that I needed holiday work and she generously agreed to hold my room without me paying rent until I came back.

The Wairarapa property was one of 10,400 acres, right on the coast. I took a train to the nearest station at Masterton, where I was met by Emma's brother with a car and taken for a forty-mile drive to the station, about twenty miles south of Castle Point. I was given a small hut, much like those at the forest camp, a horse, called Sally, and a dog called Tip. He was just one of the station dogs, and was fed with the others, so I had no real responsibility for him, but he became my companion and we got on just fine. Soon we were rounding up sheep for shearing. Luckily, Tip knew just what he was supposed to be doing. The terrain was hilly with steep sided valleys. My job with Sally and Tip, was to come up behind the flock and keep them going downhill, often beside small dry watercourses. Tip knew where the sheep were to be found and had no difficulty in getting above them and keeping the increasing mob growing and going downhill, running every now and again along the contours, first on one side of the valley, then the other, to keep them descending with some reliability. I wrote to Robina about it in January 1954:

We set out at three one morning and rode out to the furthest paddock, about 2,000 feet up and several miles away. We'd mustered all the sheep by dinner time, and the horses were dripping and the dogs were panting so fast they could hardly keep up with themselves. It was the hottest day of the year and the sheep were lolling their tongues out and raising clouds of dust as they shambled down the bed of the river, just a trickle in a wide expanse of dust and shingle.

One of my jobs was preparation for shearing, which meant cleaning out the space between the ground and the floor of the shearing shed. The method involved using a tractor to pull a scoop through the accumulated droppings of what looked like several years, so as to make room for the muck that would soon be deposited through the grated floor of the shed. The technique was to first dig a channel through the muck at one end of the building from one side to the other, and to fasten a heavy block, that would take a half inch steel cable around it onto the timber beam on which the floor was laid. A scoop was attached to the cable so that it could be pulled by the tractor through the muck. After several scoops had been dragged out I had to shift one end of the contraption, under the shed, along the beam and the other end, to a pulley attached to an external picket outside the shed, which I moved along till it was a little more than opposite the pulley fastened to the beam, and the process was repeated.

I set to work with a hand shovel first, to make room for the tractor. As the space under the floor was only about three feet, there was a lot to be done, to begin with kneeling or lying down in the droppings, which were luckily relatively dry, but I got it done and then had to learn the more pleasant task of driving the tractor. It was pretty simple. Driving straight forward positioned the scoop so that in reverse, it would scrape along the edge of the mass of dung from the beam to the star picket, where a large pile of muck began to grow. Then I went back again to drag out another load.

When that job was finished, Emma's elder brother rode out with me to the block of land I was expected to clear of Manuka. It was a wonderful location, next to the beach. I was to be paid by the acre, which was a stimulus to industry, and I think I started well, but at the forest camp there had been an unspoken assumption of competition which made us keep going. It kept me going anyway, because I have always had a competitive streak, so I did quite well for a while, but after months as a student, I soon acquired the inevitable blisters, which slowed me down until they became calluses. And it grew hot, which made a swim at lunch time a delight. I did enjoy the gradual return of technique and strength, but I was never going to earn a lot of money, and I never did.

There were compensations for hardship. This was the closest beach to the sheep station, and at the end of the day, the workers used to come down for a swim, and to do a little cray-fishing, for tea. A small double-ended wooden clinker rowing boat was kept on the beach in summer time. It was the custom of the station staff and family members, in the evenings and at weekends, to set out drop rings in a circle, about a hundred yards in diameter. These were baited with rabbit carcasses, and kept on the bottom with half bricks in each netted drop ring, marked by a small white buoy. All we had to do was to row around the circuit, picking up each ring as we came to it, seize the crayfish from behind with a gloved hand, and drop them into a sack. It usually took only one, or at most two circular passages around the buoys to fill a large sack full of crayfish, the lobsters of the southern hemisphere. A fire of driftwood was lit on the beach and the large crays were cooked in a few minutes in an old washing copper. Small crays went back to grow bigger.

It was also a learning experience. One afternoon we hauled up a pot which contained not only a couple of crayfish, but also an octopus. Its tentacles spread from gunwale to gunwale, all eight of them! I tried not to sit on any of them, but one of the station staff, a Maori, who knew what he was doing, simply thrust his arm, which disappeared up to his elbow, into the centre of the octopus, grabbed the beak, and turned the astonished creature inside out, which ended its life. I am happy to have lived in that time of innocence, when commercial fishing was in its early infancy, and meals that would cost a lot of money in a modern restaurant could be had for nothing on the beach.

On 7 January 1954, I wrote to tell my parents what was going on:

Spent most of yesterday cutting the bad bits out of the hooves of sheep that had foot rot and dosing them with maggot juice when they were very bad. I don't think I'd make a good farmer. I suppose, after a while I'd get blunt in the imagination and it would be all right. Do you remember the fish at Horsey Mere?

Shearing time was an iconic Australasian experience. The contractors consisted of a large extended Maori family. I did have one turn at shearing sheep under very close supervision but was normally a rouseabout. Shearers prided themselves on catching their own sheep, so that they could position the animals exactly as they wanted as quickly as possible. My job was to gather each fleece together without tearing it, and take it to the table. I was taught to throw the fleeces so that they spread evenly on it. Then we removed the dags by hand and rolled the fleece and carried it to the press, where it was compressed and baled.

As shearers were contractors, paid by the number of shorn sheep, there was a competitive ethos, quite alien to me as I was accustomed to being scolded and warned of the possible perils of accident if ever I showed enthusiasm about getting a job done. Female members of the family worked as rouseabouts as hard as the men, in an instance of gender interdependence that would be regarded now as exemplary.

Shearing took about two weeks, with the contractors sleeping in a small group of huts and occupying a large and well-equipped kitchen building. When it was all over, just before Christmas, there was a big party. Emma's parents and her brothers stayed for a while and then left the shearers to celebrate as they wished, so I followed their example, only to be woken up an hour later by a sudden outburst of shouting. I looked out of my own window and saw two men running out rubbing their eyes in front of a smoking hut which soon burst into flames. Within half a minute the whole population of the station had formed a human chain from a creek next to the shearing shed and the burning hut. We filled up first one, and then many more buckets, as individuals went to fill them, and thus kept up an inefficient but constant flow of creek water onto the flames. A fire hose or even an ordinary knapsack with a hand-pump would have been much more effective, and to begin with the fire was obviously gaining the better of us. All we could do was to hold it at a fairly constant intensity, which continued to destroy the first of the huts. We kept going in the hope that we could save the next hut, which was married quarters, by stopping the radiant heat of the first hut becoming any hotter. A few people who had been asleep some distance away came to help by joining the chain and speeding up the passage of water across the gaps and reducing the spillage.

Some spillage was good because it kept us cool, and soon, there came a moment when we could see that the fire of the first hut was just beginning to diminish in intensity. That meant that if we could keep going, then only one hut would be lost and no-one would be seriously burnt. So there was a big effort with buckets moving rapidly across the space between the creek and the second, bigger hut, as the remains of the first one became a pile of ashes with plenty of steam as well as smoke.

We began to congratulate each other on our good fortune. We had been taken by surprise, but had avoided tragedy by quick thinking, energy, and the leadership of the young men of the Moore family.

Early in December, I hitchhiked to Auckland for a weekend, and promptly became ill. Mrs Smith, my landlady wrote a letter to my parents about my sheep farm experience:

He apparently loves it… Before he left us he contracted a very bad dose of flu, which he told you was mild so as not to worry you. Having had two children I insisted on his staying in bed… Young things are all the same and hate being coddled, but coddled he was, and set out to his new job rested and built up… John supplied the sunshine the home seemed to lose when both my girls were married [showing more about her warm and generous self than about me]. *Don't worry about him as he seems to be able to take on any kind of job and seems very fit and well.*

What I failed to tell Mrs Smith at the time, was news that must have made my parents worry in spite of her assurances. I discovered that I had failed my exams. I told Robina about it, and received a loving reply. She was worried about news in England of a tragic train crash in New Zealand, and happy to know I was alive. "Of course the exams make no difference. I love the boy who acts, not the one who takes exams. You'll pass next time." She described the typical winter holiday of the Pelly clan, with beagling, dances and mixed hockey matches. I was much torn.

I met my English Professor (Musgrove) in a tram. "You'll pass alright if you do some work" he told me, "Yours was one of the borderline papers. You did questions that were just beautiful empty pictures hung on the wall. Quite good reading, but I'm afraid there was nothing in them." I put the best interpretation on his words that I could, and realised he was putting me down as gently as possible, far beyond the call of duty as my teacher. I told Robina, "I suppose I will have to work a bit and not be in so many plays."

Back at Eparaima, the sheep station, I received a letter from the Navy, dated 5 December, but received on December 12. It told me to be at Admiralty Steps, Queen's Wharf, Auckland at 8.15 am on 21 January 1954, ready to travel down to HMNZS (Her Majesty's New Zealand Ship) *Tamaki*. Failure to turn up, it said, "will result in severe penalty under the Military Training Act."

This Act had been passed in 1949 after a decisive referendum which approved the introduction of National Service in New Zealand. All eighteen year old males were eligible, but were given a choice of service. The majority chose the army, because it was for a relatively short period of time. I chose the Navy, which meant an initial period of training at a base which had been established on Motuhiti Island in the Hauraki Gulf at the beginning of the Second World War in 1941. A parade ground had been built on the small hill on the eastern side, separated by a narrow isthmus from the bulk of the island, which has an interesting history. The total area of the Island is one hundred and seventy-nine hectares. It was once a quarantine station, and later an internment camp for German citizens during World War 1. Among them was the German Count Felix Von Luckner, skipper of a captured privateer vessel *SMS Seeadler*. He escaped in 1917 after capturing a local scow, which he sailed to the Kermadec Islands.

There were buildings to house a large crew of cadets, including dormitories where hammocks were slung to create the ambience of a nautical Christ's Hospital. I was a member of a "watch" or unit, honoured by the name of Drake. This shore-based Ship was composed of buildings from its former lives and additions since 1941, when the naval base chapter of its history began. They included a well equipped gymnasium, which could double as a ceremonial hall, or a ball room, and an office and dining buildings. After arriving in a naval Fairmile, we assembled in one of the larger buildings and were introduced to the petty officers who were in effect our Housemasters. I do not recollect any Wrens, and the medical staff was all male. "This

HMNZS *Tamaki* crew. I am 3rd from left, 2nd row from top.

place is just as I expected it to be," I told my parents, "The similarity to Christ's Hospital is quite hopeless." But this was a fleeting impression. I had hitchhiked from Masterton to Palmerston, where I caught the train to Auckland to make sure I would be on time. "The front of the train was full of boys from the South Island. We had a pillow fight which lasted all night with brief interludes of peace." On the first day we had what I thought was a very promising occasion: "We were all assembled this morning and those who could sail were told they'd be the crew for the naval entries in the Auckland Regatta, sailing 14 footers, Whalers and Cutters. That included me of course, and it looks as if I shall be doing quite a bit of it."

The first week was a predictable "breaking in" period, when we learnt how to march smartly. Marching had been a major part of life at Christ's Hospital, so I passed the time by falling into a trance and paying as little attention as possible. When we disturbed the peace of the night by talking loudly, singing or fighting, we were disciplined by the notion, familiar to me, of Punishment Drill. We had to climb out of our hammocks, lash them up like a sausage, and run down to the beach and back with hammocks on our shoulders, for quarter of an hour, and then rig them again, climb into them and back to sleep.

There were lectures about the responsibilities and traditional activities of the Navy in peace time, and the functions of naval vessels in war time, and soon, some lessons in seaman skills such as signalling, reading charts and tying knots. Best of all were the weekends, when we got to sail in the small fleet of fourteen foot dinghies, or in whaleboats, which belonged to *Tamaki* as they belonged to all naval ships. I soon found myself in charge of one of the 14 footers, but after a week or two, I was placed in command of a whaleboat, and given an opportunity to take part in a race around the Island. I found the boat easy to sail, and as I was used to sailing, we won. We had races, between ourselves to begin with, but then local sailing clubs were invited to compete against us, with the same results, since we had become used to the whalers and gained more confidence each week. Towards the end of the three months there was a race against the other naval ships in Auckland at the time and against the officers as well.

This time I was placed in charge of one of the two Cutters. These were larger boats than the whalers, thirty-one feet long as against twenty-seven. They were beamier too, and carried a crew of twelve instead of five. My crew consisted entirely of Maoris from the Waikato, who had no previous sailing experience, but they were very competitive, and we agreed that it was important to show the officers how it was done and that we would win. The conditions were ideal, with a strong wind for an athletic crew with good stomach muscles. They were able to sit on the gunwales and lean out with their feet hooked under the thwarts so that the boat hardly heeled over at all, and sailed fast; especially when we were tacking to windward. The boys were fairly heavy too, so we won that race and broke the record for sailing round the Island by ten minutes.

The fine weather of early autumn sometimes brought crowds of visitors at weekends, including a number of young girls. It must have been sometime in March that I met Judith Wilson on the beach, and she agreed to come for a sail with me in one of the dinghies. She was still at school, and though born and bred in Auckland, she had no experience of sailing. She learnt quickly and we got on well. Back ashore we agreed to keep in touch, and on one "long weekend" national holiday she invited me to stay with her family. She met me as we came ashore at the Admiralty steps off the naval Fairmile. I wrote a short essay about the experience that was published in a local newspaper:

It seems a long time since you saw people in such quantity, and in so many different clothes. You are dazzled by the light and noise and smiles of Queen Street on a Friday night. Smiles... It's wonderful what a uniform will do. You will always remember that weekend, because you're determined to have the time of your life, or die in the attempt.

The reality was that Judith and I went to the pictures at the Civic theatre, not a renovated stage theatre, but a modern, purpose built cinema, with lights in the blue dome of the ceiling that looked like stars. It felt romantic, but we went straight to her home in Aoraki for a late meal with her parents. It was the beginning of a long and valuable friendship.

I eventually received a cheque for my scrub-cutting efforts, and began to "walk out" with Judith at weekends to Auckland's pioneer night spots: the Peter Pan night club and the "High Diddle Griddle." And the theatre, where we saw "Private Lives," the latest production of the New Zealand Players. I was sad to be in the audience instead of on the stage, and told myself it must have been because I was in the Navy and could not have gone to rehearsals.

After two months, life in the Navy became very interesting. My air-letters to my parents included an account of the week we spent at sea in HMNZS *Tui*, an elderly Bird class minesweeper. We learnt to drop depth charges over the stern, which meant travelling at a top speed of about ten knots to get away from the explosion in the sea behind us. It lifted the after end of the ship so that the propeller raced in the aerated water, while a mushroom of foam rose in our wake, and fish, killed by the explosion rose to the surface. There was a four-inch gun for defending us against other vessels, such as surfacing submarines, and a rapid firing Bofors gun for shooting down aeroplanes with explosive shells. We learnt to load, aim and fire them to order, learnt damage control, fire fighting, how to use timber to shore up bulkheads, and counter-flooding to maintain stability. We learnt some pilotage, steered the ship in two hour "tricks" at the wheel. At any time of the day or night, we were likely to be called up on deck to man the whaleboat, and practise dropping her into the sea from the davit and sheering her away from the ship. Then we rowed her alongside and picked her up again, without anyone being hurt. I had a pretty good impression, I told my parents, of how I imagined that war would be like at sea: "violent and sudden, and if you were hit, not much time to do anything about it." We sat exams at the end of April, in seamanship, engineering, and communications. I described the questions as "superficial." But, "all the same, it's a good idea to do well, because it all helps if you want an RNVR commission."

This idea was the result of a rumour that New Zealand's flagship, *Bellona*, would be going back to the UK at the end of the year to be replaced by another ship. The authorities would be looking for willing crew. At the end of the training period, I was promoted to "leading seaman" so I let it be known that I wanted to join *Bellona* and bring her replacement back to New Zealand. Bellona was to leave just before Christmas, and the replacement would return to New Zealand in March 1955. I would be paid, and still get back to make only a slightly late start at University.

Back on Motuihe Island, things were drawing to a close. "Only 11 days 'til it's over," I wrote. "On the last Saturday there is the final sailing match, and the *Havea* cup, that is a rowing race against the rest of the navy. It's a cup that the Frigate *Havea* won when she was in the Mediterranean, that is, against the rest of the [British] Navy. I'm in the crew! It has been competed for over here ever since." I was also happy to tell my parents that I had managed to join the under twenty-one University rugby team, though that was to prove too much to continue in addition to working for a living, acting, studying and sleeping.

Judith came to the end of course dance in the Fairmile boat the Navy laid on to ship our partners from Auckland and back. The gym was decorated beyond all recognition, and a marine band was provided. I was particularly uplifted by the consequences of an unusual action of Manheena, one of the Maori "permanent" seaman boys, about fifteen years old. He asked the wife of Lieutenant Mitchell, for a dance. "She is about 23," I wrote," and really beautiful. Breath of Violets isn't in it." Then up came the Training officer, Commander somebody, RN and all that. He expected the 15 year old Maori boy to abandon his partner in favour of himself. "I'm sorry," said Mrs Mitchell, "I'm dancing with this Gentleman." How sweet it is, I thought, when power and authority are trumped by Grace.

Robina Pelly.

Chapter 6: The Beginning of the getting of wisdom

Just before leaving HMNZS *Tamaki*, I received a letter from my father letting me know that my mother was very anxious about me and was losing sleep. She had persuaded him that both of them were coming to spend their next furlough visiting me in New Zealand. They would be arriving at Wellington on *Ruahine* a week after I left the Navy.

I was appalled. I felt that their decision was a rebuke, and implied that I was not able to look after myself. In my nineteen-year-old mind, a lack of academic achievement the previous year was no reason to doubt my ability to pass my exams this time, and the presence of my parents would make it harder rather than easier to find the time for study. I was already scheming to return to England anyway, under my own steam. My enquiries to the Seaman's Union led to the conclusion that my naval service would enable me to declare HMNZS *Tui* as my "last ship." This would enable me to work my passage on a merchant vessel and make a new start, either by returning to New Zealand or by going to drama school in England. That would depend on how I got along with Robina.

I had been in contact with the New Zealand Shipping Company, and the Shaw Savill line's ship, *Rangitata*, sister ship of *Rangitoto*, as my most likely opportunity. It was sailing from Auckland to Southampton on 18 December 1954. And, who knew? I might by then have four units out of nine for a bachelor's degree. I could have them recognised and included in an Arts course that I could complete at an English University, such as Bristol, perhaps, where Robina was likely to be studying. But to do that I would need to have a foreign language. I had been learning both French and Latin at St Michael's Primary school, but I had since learnt no foreign language at all for my two years in Christ's Hospital prep school.

Then in 1945, when I moved to Thornton A, German was the language thought appropriate for the lower academic streams in the upper school, and I began to learn it, but did not take the exam as part of my School Certificate. It was with these ideas in mind, in 1954, that having missed the first term at Auckland University because of National Service, I enrolled late to repeat my first year, in History, English, Geography and Latin as well.

I was also ultimately motivated by a consequence of the fact that, in spite of my scholarly intentions and late arrival in Auckland from HMNZS *Tamaki*, I had again been offered a small part in the 1954 Revue. It was in the prevailing contemporary tradition, and entitled, *Skitsophrenia*. It opened to a full house, and received good reviews. Previous efforts had been written and produced by external semi-professionals. *Skitsophrenia* was an entirely student production, for which I was invited to audition. I told Robina that, "The script is crude but witty, topical in a strictly Auckland sense, without the heavy-handed jokes about the Prime Minister… It is all about Milk-bar Cowboys and juvenile delinquents." I was in a trio which sang a song, "Three Juvenile Delinquents, juvenile delinquents, happy as can be," sung by myself, Max Cryer and Hamish Hamilton. The newspaper review said it "was a show stopper. The audience called for more!" I was given two parts in this revue. The other was the arty and effeminate Cecil, who was allocated a pirated song, "That is the End of the News," from Noel Coward's *Sigh No More*. During the run I was offered three other parts, one of them on a professional basis. I told my parents that, "The show itself rocked the town. I had the chief comic part. We packed the playhouse every night. Once there were 300 outside in the queue when the curtain went up."

Not content with this I also auditioned for a part in the major production of the University drama club, Congreve's, *Love for Love*, to be produced by Professor Musgrove. I had the part of Ben, the other brother. I wrote to Robina about it. The letter is, like the majority of our letters, undated, but is easy to place near the end of the first term in 1954:

> *We start rehearsing Love For Love next week. I have to say some very wicked things, and make very "domestic" jokes, and it'll be the first play my parents have ever seen me in. I hate to think of the impressions they will get of the theatre in general and my life in "Art." "God be in their heads and in their understanding." The Shoemaker's Holiday* [by Thomas Dekker] *isn't a patch on it. With all my love for ever. Please, Please Write.*

Revue rehearsals ensured that I would meet Carmel Lorrigan, who was in the first year of her Arts Degree, and planned to take fourth year Honours in Latin and Greek. She had been at University for a term, and she was already famous in the student world, partly because she had come top of New Zealand in the University entrance exams, and had won a national University scholarship. She stood out too for her beauty, grace and wit. I described her to Robina, probably not the most tactful thing I could have done.

> *She has long hair and looks like Peggy Cummings, added to which, she dresses like Dorothy Dandridge* [The film" Carmen Jones" was around at the time]. *An orange skirt and black blouse are typical. She is labelled as "Brains and Sex," which is quite wrong because really she is very shy and takes cover behind the manner of a scatter-brained blond. She said, "People think I'm just acting dumb, but after a long enough time waiting for me to say something intelligent, they realise that I really am."*

It was her custom to have lunch at the student cafeteria, and then, on a sunny day, she would go outside and "hang out" on the rail at the top of the outside stairs. Soon an admiring crowd would gather, and the laughter would begin. I was interested of course, and asked her to tell me what she was *really* like. She smiled and wrinkled her nose at the same time. "Why do you do that with your nose?" I asked. "I've no idea," she said, "but I'm sure it was a friendly gesture." By then I had discovered that a classical Latin course was only available at Auckland University to students who had studied it at secondary school for four years, but Ancient Greek was taught from scratch. I asked Professor Blaiklock, Head of the Classics Department, if I could take Greek rather than Latin because I had missed a term because of Navy service, and it would be easier, and I might need a classical language if I was to decide to go to Bristol University. He eventually agreed. When I told Carmel I was going to start learning Greek, she offered to help me with it, and we started reading Xenophon together in the afternoons.

The problem of what exactly I wanted to do with my life continued to trouble me almost as much as it troubled my parents. I wrote to them on 15 June 1954:

> *I meet two kinds of people. One lot say, "Get a degree. The competition in acting is terrific." (They meant it was too hard for me to even contemplate). I see that as a negative attitude. The others say, "if you really want to be an actor you must make all other things tributary to it. The competition is so great that you must go into it with all you have got or you haven't a hope."*

Acting remained, at that time, my first choice. The other reason for wanting to return to England was because I wanted to see Robina. We were both feeling the stress of our long separation. She left school in July at the end of the English summer term, and her family moved from Trowbridge to the vicarage at Farley in Hampshire. She wrote to me about the hope we shared, that I would shortly return.

> *I can think of nothing I'd Like more, Oh Yes! If you come home with a degree. I'm stuffy, I know, to like security… Actually I don't think you'll ever be in desperate straits for money. Something will always turn up. I know you can write; after all I have a drawer full of your letters.*

I sometimes reflected on the generality of our experience in the post-war world in which we lived, a time of migration, continued war and loss of friends and family, heartache, despair or joyful reunion, all over the world, and the frustration of distance. We rationalised our plight as best we could, and assured each other of our love and hope as much as we dared.

She told me about her plans for the summer holidays, sailing on the Norfolk Broads with the Milfords, and the room in the new vicarage she had mentally booked for me when I came home at the end of the year. We also had our realistic moments: "Are we living in a fool's paradise do you think?" I asked. "If we are," she replied, "we can't do much about it, but I think and hope we are not."

I had told her about the various young women I had met:

> *Besides it doesn't make the slightest bit of difference, because I just know that you are in a different category altogether. It doesn't matter whether you know about them or not. We'd both be a bit peculiar by the time we saw each other again if we'd not enjoyed the company of the opposite sex. I take it for granted that you are having lots of beautiful enchanted evenings… so am I.*

I went on to tell her about Judith Wilson, and her graciously warm acceptance of the agreed impermanent nature of our relationship. Robina replied, "I'm glad about Judith" and went on to tell me about her new boyfriend, a medical student at Cambridge. She had spent a weekend with him there, and attempted sailing with him at St Ives in Cornwall. There was a fast car, the same age as me, and Robina thought it was very special. Her letters contained mixed indications of careful commitment, ambivalence, encouragement and love, just as mine did.

One letter came on 16 October 1954. We used air-letter forms mostly, and many of the dates are missing. This was one of the few with a date.

Two years ago I was desperately worried about you. Thank goodness that's not so now. It's funny, you now feel, if I don't write, that I've fallen in love with someone else. I used to think that, but now I never do. I think it's since you told me about Judith that I stopped worrying. If I don't get a letter now, I tell myself you are working, but worry myself that you are ill or dead. But it's less worrying that way. 12,000 [miles] of water ought to be pretty dampening one way or another, but it hasn't dampened the feeling I have for you. Coming at Christmas may be seen as a waste if things go wrong, but I don't think it ever will be. If you don't come, I will always hanker after you… But not to worry if you don't get here til later. Just come when you can. I could never be happily married to anyone, and that means you too, if I haven't seen you first. And please let it be soon. With all my love, for always, I hope. D'you remember? [Cleopatra] *"If this be love indeed, tell me how much…"* [Antony]*."There's beggary in the love that can be reckoned."*

She concluded by telling me she had been reading my old letters from when I was at school, about my desire to go away in order to grow up. Now, she thought, I had done enough of that, and it was time to come back to her. I told her about my parents' decision to come to New Zealand, and how they would be going back to England in September to board a ship back to Freetown. She invited them to visit the astonishing Pelly household while they were in England.

The winter (June–July) holiday from University was an opportunity to become organised. I stayed at the YMCA hostel in Auckland for £3 a week with all meals provided, right in the middle of Auckland within walking distance of everywhere I wanted to go, and cheaper than O'Rorke Hall, the student hostel. I arranged to rent a house at 22 Landscape Road, Mount Eden, in the Anglican Parish of St Barnabas for when my parents came. My parents had distant connections with some members of that congregation.

Unfortunately for me, the Grafton Players were looking for somewhere to hold a theatre party, and asked me if they could use my very recently acquired dwelling. I was delighted to be able to satisfy their needs. It must have looked alarming for the neighbours, the first night I took possession, to see a crowd of about forty people parking a line of cars in the road, wandering merrily in flamboyant dress, and bearing all manner of alcoholic drinks up to the normally sober suburban establishment.

As was to be expected, there was a certain amount of noise, and eventually the police paid us a visit. I was politely apologetic and we fell relatively silent, but the damage had been done, and my first call, next morning, was from my landlords, who demanded a cancellation of my tenure. I explained my predicament, that my teetotal missionary parents from Sierra Leone were arriving the next day and would have nowhere to live… it would never happen again and was just because the Grafton Players had no other venue. Luckily they believed me, and reluctantly withdrew their demand. I contacted Rex Sayers, who gallantly knocked on their door and accepted responsibility on behalf of the Grafton Players. He was not the only adult New Zealander in those years to feel responsible for me. I am still grateful.

I met my parents next day on their arrival by rail from Wellington and we began our family holiday. Restoration Comedy was not their first choice of entertainment, but they came to see *Love for Love*, and were politely appreciative. They also met Prof Musgrove, our producer, who reassured them that I had started afresh, and was making encouraging progress in both the English Language and English Literature, and that my attitude to study was much improved in comparison with the previous year. Now that my parents had arrived, I realised that they would have liked it if I had maintained my contact with the Church, so I took them to St Barnabas, the nearest Anglican Church, which did a lot to make them feel at home.

I found linguistics and learning Old English more interesting than I had expected; including *Beowulf,* the set book. Chaucer's *Canterbury Tales*, the set text for Middle English, was pure pleasure. My lecturer in New Zealand history was the great Keith Sinclair, a published poet, and son of a wharf labourer, who was working at the time on his celebrated Penguin *History of New Zealand*. It was a powerful contrast with the works of his predecessors, in that the 1840 Treaty of Waitangi, which from the English point of view, legitimised the British colonisation of Aotearoa, was not seen as the beginning of all things worth studying about the country. Sinclair was the first member of the university staff to obtain his doctorate from the University of New Zealand (on "The Origins of the Maori Wars"), instead of following the traditional path of an overseas scholarship to Oxford or Cambridge. He had the gift of inspiring us with his originality which stimulated our curiosity, and set an example of how to discover new ways of understanding the process of acculturation, and its limitations, in New Zealand society. The History Department had a collegial relationship with the department of Anthropology, in which the subject of Maori Studies provided a common means of access by Maori students to the Arts Faculty. Some of them did History as well.

Geography had been my best and favourite subject at Christ's Hospital, but then I was put off a bit by what seemed to be a problem within the discipline, of identity, or what the subject was actually about. The latest fashion in 1954 was "Regional Differentiation," as opposed to the "Environmental Determinism" of my schooldays. I was not surprised to be told ten years later that the subject consisted essentially of little else but geometric technology. The interesting part of regional differentiation has since been overtaken by "Place studies," a most interesting path indeed to important aspects of Environmental Studies and New Economics. But in 1954 I felt at home with Geography, and enjoyed its indecisive turmoil.

First Year Greek, taught by the erudite and charming Professor Blaiklock, was also a pleasure, not least because I used to sit next to Carmel in lectures, and began to understand the importance of disciplined thought, careful reading and truthful analysis, in successful scholarship. We soon developed a kind of "pidgin" Greek for personal and private conversation, which made me feel familiar with both Carmel and the language.

While I was still in the Navy, I had written hopefully to the Minister for Education Mr R M Algie, asking for a small bursary for which I was eligible because I was a student; I had been in New Zealand for a year, and was not living "at home." Eventually I received a reply:

A bursary has been awarded to you as from the beginning of this year. This bursary will provide for the payment of any tuition fees this year, and will be available for the next three years if you are successful in passing a section of your degree each year.

In retrospect I was very lucky to achieve this, after failing everything in 1953. I feel sure there must have been considerable support in the form of a reference from one of my lecturers, possibly Professor Musgrove. Whoever it was, I am eternally grateful. Mr Algie's letter made me feel a strong attachment to New Zealand, made my life much easier with an extra £40 a year to live on, and it gave me the determination to succeed.

The winter holiday that year was very busy. I moved from the YMCA to a student household with Mark Gotlieb, who was Jewish, and had leased a small house in Aoraki, quite close to where Judith lived. He was in his second year, studying architecture. He was the oldest of the student household and the most responsible. The other members of the household were Gus, a Muslim who was doing an arts degree, and John Phithian, a quiet introspective student who, I think, was doing maths. All three provided me with considerable intellectual support by sharing my growing interest in politics, young women and religion. Mark was a member of the university ski club, and two years later we spent a memorable weekend in the student built club hut, halfway up the slopes of Mt Ruapehu, the highest mountain in the North Island at 2797 metres. Accommodation consisted of a shack, built a bit at a time by repeated groups of visiting ski club members over many years. There were Primus stoves for cooking and single bunks for sleeping.

My stay on *Tamaki*, had helped my financial situation because of the lack of opportunity to spend, and the new sense of financial security, enabled me to justify to myself the purchase of an ancient (1932) Velocette motor bike for £10 from my old Christ's Hospital mate, Michael Delves. It had a 348 cc single cylinder engine, a rigid frame aft, a single, somewhat mighty, spring above the forks, a pillion seat, and it ran well. Its main problem was its inability to engage top gear, which reduced its maximum speed to 50 mph, at which velocity it would over-heat, and use a lot of petrol. It had two leather pannier bags, and I thought it a valuable asset.

I obtained a licence with great ease, since the test in those days consisted only of a brief demonstration of a capacity to kick-start the engine and drive the bike down a hill and back — a total distance of about 150 yards. Soon I worked my way through its gears, except the fourth one, and managed to steer it with some confidence through traffic. I suffered the Velocette for a very short time, and traded it in to acquire a slightly newer AJS.

I then suggested that Carmel might enjoy a weekend on the ski slopes of Ruapehu, with a mixed party of students. As I came to know her better, I realised that I was making an uninformed and unfair demand. Carmel was not focussed at all on challenging outdoor activity. Her parents, knowing their daughter better than I did, were hesitant, but eventually accepted the idea, and off we went, in a small convoy of very old cars. Importation of cars was limited at that time and New Zealand roads were distinguished by their vintage stock of them. By midday, we had reached the Chateau, the government-owned and only hostel at the foot of the mountain. We were cold as our clothing was inadequate, but excited by the romantic impulse of the journey, we soon began the ascent to the ski slopes, and the hut belonging to the student Ski club. Neither of us had skied before, and there were no lifts, but skis were stored in the hut, which we eventually reached, after abandoning the motor bike just above the snow line. We hoped that the bike would still be accessible in the morning. Carmel was pretty tired, so she became asthmatic, but we got there in the end. It rained and snowed all night and in the morning the weather was still horrible. We shouldered skis and began to walk up the beginners slopes near the hut. Our successive attempts to stay upright and mobile on skis was in the fashion of most beginners; that was by moving horizontally along the contours as far as we could, then turning, or falling over and starting again.

Domestic arrangements were primitive, with Primus stoves to cook on, and bottomless pit toilets, basins on a bench to put snow in for washing, plywood bunks against the walls for sleeping bags and separate sleeping rooms for each sex.

It rained the whole weekend. There were dry patches on the way down, but from Taupo on, it poured, and when we arrived at that very desolate and wild area in the middle of the Island, we were in clouds, and couldn't see more than about fifty yards at a time. We were warmly clad, crash helmeted and be-goggled, but it was quite gruesome all the same. Next morning we awoke to some extra snow, which had half buried the motor bike. A gallant young man offered to replace Carmel on the pillion seat for the first part of the return journey, which enabled

Left: Carmel Lorrigan, 1957.

Below: My Seagulls Card, allowing me to get a job on the Auckland Wharves. Note "Deck," written by me.

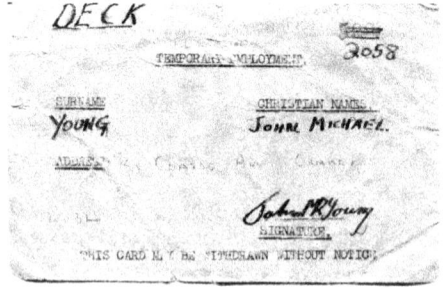

her to have a relatively warm and luxurious ride in a car for the first hour or so. The bike refused to start at first, but we set off freewheeling down the snowy slope, releasing the clutch every minute or so until the engine dried out enough to get a spark out of itself and sputtered off, largely in control of its own destiny.

Our thoughts turned to hot pools at a place called Tokaano. It turned out to be a sandy pool surrounded by native vegetation, and entirely devoid of any kind of "development." Much later, in 1986, I found it again, a small hot spring that by then had been tamed, tiled, civilised and privatised for profit after enclosing it within a fence. In 1954 we must have been part of the last Kiwi generation to experience the delight of undressing in the cold air above a steaming pool of quite hot, but not too hot water, surrounded by native vegetation. Further on, at a friend's place in Hamilton we drank cocoa in front of someone's fire. Carmel had a terrible time really, but she said she enjoyed it very much.

Work for wages was essential for survival, and the 1950s were the beginning, in both New Zealand and Australia of the "Twenty Good Years," when it was still possible for a young family to live on the wage of one parent, and save or borrow enough to own their own house by the time the children grew up and left. In New Zealand, public primary, secondary, and university education were virtually free. Full employment meant that enough could be earned by even poor students like me, to provide food and accommodation. Vacations were long, and students could earn good wages including overtime rates at weekends in wool stores and freezing works in all the big towns. The demand for quick turnarounds of ships meant that overtime was needed on the wharves most nights of the week, and often at weekends as well. This was especially so in Auckland, where coastal and trans-Tasman traffic ironed out the seasonal fluctuations of overseas shipping, based on the exports of primary agricultural products to Europe.

By the middle of 1954, I had discovered that the Waterside Workers' Union and the students union of Auckland University had recently found interests in common, because of the ideological understanding that had been reached between them during the Great Wharf Strike of 1951. Students had refused to become "scabs," and meetings of students who sympathised with the wharfies had been held in the student common room. In return, students had achieved first priority for the allocation of "Seagulls Cards" by the Waterside Workers' Union.

The cards were issued by the union for casual workers, and had to be taken down to the wharf just before work began. A union representative would come to receive vocal applications for work in the style of an auction, "Four men for *Herekino*," he might say, referring to the coastal cement carrier to and from Auckland and Whangarei. Four men would hold up their Seagulls Cards and declare their names, before leaving for the nominated wharf for their day's work. Wages were good, especially at weekends when one and a half rates per hour were paid for evening work after 5 pm on Fridays and from 8 am to noon on Saturday mornings. On Saturday afternoons or Sundays, pay was doubled.

In addition, there was "dirt money," an extra few pence an hour for some cargoes such as cement or coal, while a good meal like a roast and two vegetables and Yorkshire pudding, followed by rice pudding was served at lunchtime from the dining room, for a minimal cost.

Sometimes, in the mornings, the Union "master of ceremonies" would ask for "Deckies." These were men who were qualified to control the cargo handling machinery and signal to the gangs on the wharf and in the hold, when they were to begin or cease loading or unloading. They were paid up to 4d an hour extra. "How do you get to be a Decky?" I asked, and received the answer one morning, "You have to have a card with "Deck" written on it." There seemed to be no-one with that qualification around that morning, but no jobs left for anyone else, so, emboldened by over-confidence, I wrote "Deck" on my card and put my hand up.

I was sent to drive a winch on a typical ocean tramp ship with a cargo of sugar from Fiji, armed with nothing but the experience of watching the process in the immediate past. Two derricks were rigged, one with the pendant and hook lowered vertically into the hold and shackled to the net to be loaded with sugar bags; the other pendant, attached to the same shackle on the net, raised the load from the centre of the hold, and then carefully swung across until the net hung with the hook and pendant poised vertically above the wharf. The net was then lowered to the wharf, where the sugar bags were unloaded onto pallets and taken away by forklifts. It was a process which demanded great concentration and the ability of both winch drivers to work together. Each derrick had a steam winch which was controlled by a valve, to be unscrewed to let steam into the cylinder and set the winch in motion, hoisting the net full of sugar in bags up out of the hold. The other control was a brake used to lower the net, under control, to either the wharf or the hold.

The difficult, and potentially dangerous part of the process was a controlled swing of the cargo net from over the hold, gradually passing it across the hold and over the side of the vessel, and vice versa. Safety depended on spontaneous co-operation of the men who drove the two winches. I was asked if I had done this before, and I told the "hatchie," who was to signal to us when to hoist or lower, that I had not. My lack of any certified qualification and experience was not counted against me, and I was given a brief demonstration, and when the hatchie gave me his signal, I opened the valve and the net came up as the hold crew stepped back. When the net was raised just above the level of the top of the hatch, I closed the valve and put on the brake. My partner on the other winch, at the other side of the hold opened his valve and his cable began to haul the net across the ship, as I carefully eased my brake. The trick was to take my brake off, gradually, but not so fast as to allow the cargo net to swing out of control over the wharf.

Then both of us on the winches had to lower our cables at much the same speed, so that the net came down under control to be unloaded on the wharf. The first net was managed successfully, but the second time I hauled the empty net across the hold too fast so that it swung out over the wharf. It was still safe, since no one was on the side deck, but it scared the gang in the hold a bit, and I distinctly heard the words "take him off." However other voices came as well: "Give 'im a go"; "Let 'im learn" etc. and I was allowed to continue. The result was to increase my pay by 4d an hour on the winch, or 2d an hour, if I was relegated to the hatchie job, signalling to the "winchies" what they had to do.

Wharf work fitted very well into my schedule, as I could often earn enough to buy food and pay rent by working overtime on Friday night, all Saturday, and Sunday in term time and working full time only in vacations. On Friday nights, I found it possible to work until 5 pm, take Judith to the pictures from 6 until 7.30, put her on a bus during the interval and work a final hour and a half, missing the main feature. The next week, with luck we could alternate and see the main feature, having worked on between 6 and 7.30 and missed the "shorts."

My parents must have spent only about three weeks in New Zealand, and they realised that going to St Barnabas for church each Sunday instead of working on the wharf was not good for me from an economic point of view, but they raised my financial resources by giving me £40 to be placed in my post office savings account. St Barnabas meant a lot to Edith. It was there that my parents and I made the acquaintance of Bill and Shona Caughey, whose family were co-owners of the very successful Smith and Caughey emporium in Queen Street, Auckland. Their Christianity was a great comfort to my mother, who continued to write to Shona. And Shona responded by airmail when my parents were back in Sierra Leone, thus reducing my mother's anxiety. At the time I rather resented this parental oversight by proxy. Mother learnt from Shona, with sadness, that after they left, my attendance at St Barnabas grew occasional rather than regular. I regarded this as parental espionage, but I can understand it now.

I don't remember introducing Carmel to my parents, but she was a devout Catholic when I met her. When she was fourteen, she had felt she had a vocation to become a nun, and had attended a novitiate boarding school in Christchurch. She soon disliked the experience and came back to Auckland to complete her schooling at St Mary's, an ordinary Catholic day school staffed by the Sisters of Mercy who were renowned for their teaching ability and the achievements of their students. Carmel and I soon enjoyed some stimulating arguments about religion, especially in connexion to doctrines about sin, confession and redemption, to begin with. We moved on to papal authority, salvation by faith versus works, birth control and the history, rights and wrongs of the protestant heresies.

After my parents left New Zealand, Carmel and I began to see more of each other, and with the beginning of spring in September, and the end of a revue called *The Abominable Snow Man*, we became part of an extended group of students, including Max Cryer, Borrie Prendergast, Adrian Wilson, John Harré, and other gifted and interesting people who shared the experience of Auckland University when it was small and a mere college of the University of New Zealand. We used to have rowdy parties at which Max Cryer would play the piano with dazzling panache and without a score, relying on his memory to accompany our ribald songs, or introduce us to classical and modern music from his mysterious European background.

Living close to the Waitemata Harbour made me anxious to gain access to a boat. Each weekend hundreds of sails graced the water, and the islands and beaches make it one of the best places to sail in the world. It must have taken me a few weeks to successfully cajole my housemates into joining me in the purchase of a clinker-built half-decked vessel, belonging to the out-dated 14 foot T-class, with a sloop rig and centre case. I don't remember the sale price, but she was very cheap. We sailed her down the harbour and anchored her with the other dinghies at the Akarana Yacht club at the waterfront of the suburb of Aoraki, where we lived. Once there, we gave her a coat of paint and began to make short voyages as a breezy and sometimes boisterous spring made way for a languid summer.

I was beginning to feel that I was part of the New Zealand community now, as I had made friends from many of its branches. On 25 September 1954, I wrote to Robina about my twentieth BYO birthday party. It was held at another student share house, 768 Mt Eden Road, which I eventually moved into the following year.

This was the first time I had seen a cross-section of my friends. I thought it would be fun to ask them all… People I had met in the navy, various jobs, plays, the University. It was wonderful. It lasted til 4 in the morning. I didn't realise until then, just how I fitted into New Zealand. Everyone seemed so charming. Three girls, Helen, Wendy and Eve made me a birthday cake on the quiet without me knowing… After all, I have spent two years growing up with these people, and when I'm older I'll look back and think that they are part of the reason why I'm like I am.

After their visit to me in New Zealand, my parents spent only a short time in England, but Mother and Heather found time to accept Robina's invitation to visit her. Clearly all three agreed that my priority should be to finish my degree before going permanently back to England, and this was backed up by Ant Moll, and my maternal grandfather, who reminded me also that he was about to reach the age of 94. I evidently wrote less to my family, who up to this time had been receiving letters about once every two weeks, as had Robina.

My mother nevertheless tried to avoid restricting my choices. Knowing that I still wanted to be an actor, she wrote to Duncan Ross, Principal of the Bristol Old Vic Theatre School, and must have given him supportive details of my limited acting experience. On 6 October, mother wrote to me from Freetown, enclosing a letter from Ross.

As requested we enclose Prospectus, letter to overseas students and particulars relative to auditions. If your son is going to be in England at Christmas time we shall be very pleased to arrange an audition for him.

By that time I was really studying as hard as I could, for the first time in my life, and neglected my family. How easy it would have been if the Internet had been invented by then, to keep in touch and lower anxieties.

I began to feel the lack of the training in scholarship that I would have had if

I had stayed for a final year at Christ's Hospital, or had done some work in 1953. Slowly and painfully, I was beginning to learn the meaning of relevance and how to stick to the point in my essays. I told Robina that:

> *I shall have to keep away from Journalism, it's even creeping into my history essays. My last one I thought was jolly good... You know how you do. But I only got a B −. My tutor said the essential ideas were "too much obscured by biographical detail." It was about the Colonial reformers, Durham, Wakefield and Co, and I must have thought I was supposed to just be telling a story. I couldn't resist putting in about their respective elopements and so forth. But I don't mind, as I enjoyed writing it.*

I had chosen English as my major subject because of the mistaken notion that I would be taught to write well. But in fact, the emphasis was on the work of literary critics, whose books we had to read, in preference, when time was short, to reading and absorbing the great works themselves.

History was my other major, and just as useful an opportunity to learn how to write well. The history of New Zealand was a journey of discovery in largely uncharted waters. References to primary sources were expected from undergraduates because, in many cases, the text books and scholarly works had yet to be written. I began to be interested in parliamentary papers and old newspapers, early settlers' narratives, and political speeches, which colonial newspapers often published in full. I worked early in the mornings, when all was quiet and I could concentrate, and I often kept library books out too long, and paid the fines, as I tried to make up for lost time.

In November, my mother wrote me a sad and angry letter: "Why don't you write John? Has something gone wrong or what is it? It's five weeks since the last one arrived on 2nd Oct in England." My father was less worried, and more encouraging: "There is no doubt that you have the ability to succeed in this course... I was very glad you had the strength of character to turn down the part you coveted in the play when it conflicted with your exams. That is evidence of maturity." I don't remember what part this was but it must have been with the Grafton Players rather than the University. He went on:

> *One of my most frequent prayers for you just now is that you may "have a right judgement in all things" and that you may "know what things you ought to do" and what is even more important, that you may have "Grace and power faithfully to fulfil the same." Some of those old collects really do hit the nail on the head.*

I wrote to Robina and said, "There is just one thing, which is really not likely to happen. If I fail my exams, when I get to England, I'll stay there, and be an actor. If I pass as I think I will, I'll have to come back to New Zealand... I'll pass all the same, don't worry."

I found time, in spite of exams, to attempt a short story about "Karakaberry," one of the horses at Eparaima who was a champion jumper. It was accepted by the *New Zealand Woman's Weekly*. I was happy about that and I was feeling good about my exams, though I confessed to Robina that:

I'm not good at grammar. Heather's advice on reading the manuscript was to "go easy on the sentences without verbs." I just sat the language paper in Old English and another on Medieval History. Anyway, pass or fail, I enjoyed that paper more than any other history paper in my life… and I have been known to pass exams before.

I also made arrangements to put in voluntary sea time by joining the mine sweeper, HMNZS *Tui* again for the best part of a voyage round New Zealand. The Seaman's Union told me that my chances of "working my passage" back to England would be much enhanced if I could produce evidence of sea time, together with my leading seaman rating and Coxswain's ticket that I had been awarded in the Navy. I was told that I would be asked for the name of the "last ship" I had worked on. The naval authorities in Auckland thought doing voluntary sea time was a great idea, and booked me onto *Tui*. The week after my exams ended, *Tui* would be at the port of Bluff, at the southernmost end of the South Island. She was to cruise the spectacular Fiordland of the South Island, visit Westport, Wellington, Napier, and Tauranga before returning to Auckland on 10 December. This would work just fine for me as *Rangitata* was scheduled to leave Auckland for Southampton on 18 December. I explained to Heather that I would arrive in England on 18 January. I would then return by the beginning of March on a merchant ship, to continue my degree, or stay in England and go to Drama school.

Gael Carpenter was a girl I had met when I was living at Takapuna in 1953, and we were still good friends. For some reason we met again, and decided that, since I had finished my exams and was going away the following week, we should take a day trip to Waiheke Island and soak up the sun. So on the last Saturday morning in November 1954, that's what we did. Unfortunately, we dawdled too much and missed the ferry back to Auckland. The next one didn't leave the wharf at Matiatia until the evening of the Sunday, so we rang Gael's mother, explained our problem and told her we would have to stay in the hotel on the Island, and a very cheap and pleasant place it was. We promised Mrs Carpenter that we would "behave ourselves" and she said she knew she "could trust us." Yes, we did share a room, but not a bed. This was the fifties, remember?

All the same, there was trouble. Gael's family was living with grandparents while waiting to move into a new house. Her grandmother could distinctly remember Queen Victoria and championed the standards of sexual morality with which Her Majesty was identified. As soon as Gael walked into the house, her grandmother felt it necessary to be scandalised and walked out of the room. Gael wrote, "She implied some rather awful things about us. We're to blame alternately, depending on her mood, and Mum went in and told her it wasn't true. Real fireworks. You've no idea." Gael left as well and went to live with a girl friend in her flat. "I haven't been back," she wrote, "and I don't intend going until I get an apology. Please don't worry about it because I haven't regretted anything that happened. I only hope you don't."

The general frenzy of the occasion and my anxiety to defend my reputation led to me missing my train to Wellington, which was supposed to meet the ferry across Cook Strait and down the east coast of the South Island to Lyttleton. The ferry was timed to catch the train from Christchurch to Bluff, and my ship. I started hitch hiking at 1 pm from Auckland, in my naval uniform, which, like the sixteenth century Christ's Hospital uniform in Sussex, proved a magnet to kindly motorists and enabled me to catch the ferry across Cook Strait on Monday night. I spent the whole of the next day in the train from Christchurch to Bluff, and reached *Tui* late at night. The Officer on watch welcomed me aboard and gave me a hammock.

Next morning I really began to enjoy myself as the ship drew away from the wharf and began to follow the rugged coast to the west. It still looked much as it must have done when Cook sailed the same course. Our first anchorage was Preservation Inlet, a fiord surrounded by mountains and reaching about 40 kilometre inland. "It's the sort of beauty that you dream about," I told Robina, "and all as wild and uncivilised as it always has been... uninhabited mountains, thick bush and dark deep inlets." We anchored for the night and spent the next morning exploring in the whaleboat, and painting the ship in the afternoon. Almost as far inland as we could go, we discovered the wreck of what looked like an old sailing ship, tucked into a rocky resting place, and largely under water. On climbing aboard we looked down into the hold, almost full of water at high tide, and it was literally crawling with crayfish. It was like a magnification of a dead sheep's carcase full of huge maggots. We overcame that thought quickly, captured a few more crays than our fair share and put them in *Tui*'s freezer.

A day later and we were at the entrance to Milford Sound, probably still the most remote and staggeringly beautiful place I have ever seen, with Mitre Peak rising

Crew of HMNZ *Tui*, giving a Christmas party for children of Westport. I am 3rd left.

1692 metres straight out of the water at the entrance, and the considerably higher Mount Pembroke further inside. There was no sign whatever of humanity or its works, except for *Tui* and her crew. Due to my known experience of sailing naval boats, I was given the unexpected privilege of taking charge of a whaleboat and her crew under sail. We were launched from the davits as we were steaming past Mitre Peak, with a wind from the west behind us. I was told to raise the masts, hoist the sails and follow *Tui* to the anchorage at the head of the Sound. I wrote to Robina about it: "Just imagine it — a strong wind making exhilarating sailing. We were all wet through and going past vertical precipices dropping down from the clouds. The mountain tops were covered with snow." I told my parents, that "… you feel very small, down on the water, with 5,000 foot mountains rising up beside you, and waterfalls dropping down from the clouds into the sea. I always want to laugh when I look at mountains."

The rest of the voyage was really a public relations, or "Showing The Flag" exercise of the New Zealand Navy. Westport was our next port of call. We approached the coast in very lumpy seas, especially when *Tui* actually surfed on a huge wave to sail over the bar, then up the calm river to this wild and remote coal mining town.

One reason I remember Westport is that I received mail from a lot of my friends in Auckland to tell me that I had passed my exams (except Greek). I had expected this, but felt enormously pleased with myself as it removed my doubts about my own ability. In 1953 I had tried to discover how little work I could do and still pass. By this time, I knew that I would have to do a good bit better than ever before. I also had other letters from England. Fred, my Housemaster had died, and Mick Marland was at Cambridge, and had started a theatrical company of his own, "Michael Marland Productions Ltd." There was an article about it in the *Daily Mirror*. My father wrote to tell me he had been to Freetown to receive his MBE from the Governor of Sierra Leone, for "Services to Education," and about the festivities in Bunumbu to celebrate the twenty-first anniversary of the foundation of Union College. By this time, he was Canon of Freetown Cathedral. He clearly expected me to be in England within a short time. I reflected on the different experiences of myself and my school friends, and concluded that my choices had put me in a delicate, but promising position.

Westport. What a town! The pubs were open until one o'clock in the morning. The norm in New Zealand was the famous Six O'clock Swill, as in Australia, so I assume Westport pubs were allowed to cater for miners coming off shifts in the middle of the night. The community leaders of Westport turned on a dance for us the night we arrived. It was taken for granted that the nurses' home could be relied upon to provide us with partners. My partner was Nurse Margaret Milligan. I asked her if she had any feeling of resentment at being expected to turn out automatically for such an occasion. She of course told me she thought it was the least the nurses could do for the Navy, and that she enjoyed it. I asked her about her job, and she explained what hard work it was, and how difficult she found it when her patients died. She seemed to be valiantly depressed and we had one of those deep conversations that seem to come out of nowhere, but which you remember.

On the second day in Westport we returned hospitality by putting on a Christmas party for the children of the town. We dressed as pirates with skull and cross-bones flags and stage prop weapons, mops and scrubbers, the ships bell and anything we could scrounge from the galley to make a noise with or wear on our heads. Thus attired we marched from the ship to meet the parents and children at the middle of the town. We made presents of ice cream to the forty or so children and marched in procession back to the ship. Our band included a bugle, combs with toilet paper round them, and pots and pans. The Drum Major twirled a deck scrubber and the children followed behind. We decorated the mess deck with balloons and streamers. The wheel house was designated as the "Pirates' Lair," where one of the stokers took the part of the pirate king and stamped all of them on their innocent foreheads with the skull and cross-bones. By this time they had all completely lost their self-consciousness. One little girl got up and sang to us, and not to be out-done, the boys did too. Father Christmas turned up, gave them lollies and we marched back to restore them to their parents at the school.

We left port at 10 am the next morning, with a big crowd on the wharf, including all the children, who must have been allowed to devote school time to see us off. They sang the famous song used to farewell Maori soldiers in World War I, *Po Atarua,* otherwise known as *Now is the Hour*, thus making it a memorable occasion. Soon we were heading north again across the bar. I took up my pen to write to Robina; "It was lovely and rough today, with waves about 15 feet high and a lot of water coming aboard. Now we have just passed Cape Farewell [at the western entrance to Cook Strait], the wind is behind us and we're headed for Wellington."

We were greeted at the wharf by a group of young women, and the medical orderly issued us with condoms, but I chose not to go ashore for the evening, mainly because I couldn't come to grips with the commercial assumption that was implied, and partly because I lacked both cash and confidence. I wrote letters instead. Next day, we left early for Napier, where we enjoyed the organised hospitality of the local Returned Services Association, then to Gisborne, where I received a letter from Judith to tell me I had passed all my exams.

I wrote to my sister Heather, to explain why I was on a mine sweeper:

> *You'll be rather surprised to see this address, and will no doubt think it a peculiar way to get to England. Well, it is; but I think it will help. The trouble is that though I am a very redoubtable sailor, I have not done enough sea time to be able to join the Seaman's Union as an adult seaman. Without membership it is difficult to get a passage. The other way is to replace members of crews who have deserted. Even for that you have to fill in a form with a space for "Last Ship." Now, I will be able to say truthfully that Tui was my last ship.*

I felt a surge of confidence as we headed out again in the morning against an unusually strong easterly wind that soon became a gale. The waves came across at right angles to the course and were the largest I had experienced, making it difficult to walk on deck unless you could use your hands to prevent yourself from sliding or falling to leeward. Once round East Cape, and into darkness, with the wind behind us, I was on watch and steered the ship towards Tauranga, under instruction from the officer on watch. Keeping a steady course was a matter of learning how to counteract the tendency to oversteer, and to use as little helm as possible. It took most of the watch to learn to relax at the job.

Tauranga was crowded with summer visitors. Unlike the Wellington experience, nurses rather than prostitutes were expected to look after us. I wrote to my sister about it:

> It's a beautiful place, the equivalent of Blackpool, Scarborough, Southend and Brighton all in one. But it does it differently. There are no big dippers, just people and yachts, and lovely weather. I met a nurse, Jackie, who shared ownership of a 1926 Chevrolet called Nausea. I learnt to drive it that night.

I remember a social gathering at the Mayor's house, a dance, and an invitation to catch up with sleep, after my previous night at the wheel. I was offered an unoccupied hospital bed for what remained of the night, and was woken up by Jackie, just in time to return to *Tui* as she took in her lines and headed off for Auckland.

We arrived on schedule on 10 December, and *Rangitata*, already in port, was due to leave for England on 18 December. I packed all my belongings, and discovered that my luck was in. This was the big occasion of my life, when I would be able to work my passage back to England on *Rangitata*. I would have a choice, at last. I had about half a degree, and I planned to apply my Auckland units in History, Ancient Greek and Geography to an Arts degree at the University of Bristol. The other idea was to take up the invitation from the Bristol Old Vic to have an audition. Best of all, I would be able to renew my friendship with Robina.

As luck would have it, two men had deserted *Rangitata*, and would have to be replaced. I spoke to the Officer in charge of the ship at the time and showed him my naval credentials. He instructed me to have my passport in my hand, and to be ready at the dock on the morning of 18 December. I spent a very exciting week saying my goodbyes, having second thoughts, but sticking to my plan. The ship was to sail at noon and I was there, waiting, long before that. Passengers began to arrive, and families and friends to say goodbye. Coloured streamers were prepared and thrown from the deck to the shore, and held, waiting for them to be broken as the towering black side of the ship would move slowly away from the wharf. Music began, concluding, with the haunting *Po Atarua* in Maori as well as English.

I was at the foot of the gangway, ready to climb up it: "A quarter of an hour before twelve, I thought it was going to be all right," I wrote to Robina,

> ... two members of the crew were missing. Then they had to turn up. I'd said goodbye to everyone I knew the day before. A bit of an anti-climax. The thing is, What next? The crowd parted to allow two policemen with two hand cuffed men to march towards me, and my heart sank as I realised I would not be going up the gangplank with my black trunk and all my possessions after all.

I stayed all the same, as *Rangitata* stood clear of the wharf and began to move in a wide circle. I watched through my tears as she headed for Bean Rock and the Rangitoto Channel, then out past Great Barrier Island to Panama and England.

I returned to my share house, but told my friends there that I would still be leaving them. The house was not working as well as I had hoped. I wrote about a week later to my parents about why I had decided to move out: "It was fun at the House but it would have taken a lot of hard work to make it a really good place to live. The system when I arrived was that everyone operated as an individual. Well, if that really worked they'd adopt it in ships." I described "the time wasted, the extravagance" and put it down to religious differences, "... seeing that Mark is a Jew, Gus is a Moslem, and John had a profound disbelief in everything, it was not surprising." My own growing disbeliefs at the time were a factor, but not very profound.

I did not give up on returning to England at this stage, but described the idea as being on the back burner. Robina went to a lot of trouble to enable me to apply for a place at the University of Bristol and made successful enquiries for me about entering the Bristol Old Vic Drama School, so I was able to think I was keeping open as many options as possible. "I'm enrolling for Auckland, but also applying for Bristol, starting in September," I told my parents.

My father was anxious that I should live in a semi-supervised fashion at O'Rorke Hall, but it was going to be closed for January, and I was not enthusiastic anyway. I got on the waiting list, but said it was inconvenient as mealtimes would clash with my wharf work. In the meantime, I met an older student called Peter, who had moved out of a boarding situation with a fascinating woman, Mrs Lee, in Wakefield Street. I told my father:

She wrote and told Peter that she was alone. She doesn't like it... So I moved partly for her sake because she is a good kind woman and it was a shame. She gives me a really good hot breakfast, and tea if I'm home for it, which I'm usually not. I have a room as big as the Mt Eden [Landscape Road] *living room in which I can keep all my gear in an accessible manner instead of under the bed. I can come and go as I like. Compared with the extremely doubtful asset of living at O'Rorke, I think I am on a good wicket.*

After I had settled with Mrs Lee, I went into more detail:

Mrs Lee is a distributor of communist literature among the Chinese in NZ. She said I could pay when I liked and how much I liked. I gave her one pound for the two days I was there and she tried to give me some change! She says, "I have a great many official people to visit me, partly because I am living in a condemned house, and partly because they do not agree with my political views." She says she'd like to have me back at 2 pounds a week for bed and breakfast, a large room for myself too, as it's just that she likes someone in the house, and she lives on a pension anyway. I cook my own stuff at night. The house is about 200 yards from the University.

I came to know Mrs Lee well in the few months I stayed with her before moving into a very successful student squat. She was well read and introduced me to

Voltaire, John Stuart Mill and Karl Marx among other political thinkers, and we had many stimulating discussions.

My success in passing exams and the wide choices and possibilities open to me made me feel very optimistic at this point, but the first day of the year 1955 was to be the most disastrous of my life. Mark and Gus were away for the New Year with their families, but our boat was waiting in the shallows of the Royal Akarana Yacht Club anchorage, and the public holiday was an ideal opportunity for an expedition under sail.

Three of us set off in the middle of the morning for Matiatia Harbour on Waiheke Island. I assumed the role of skipper, and my crew consisted of John Phithian and Anne Lund, a girl we all knew who was famous as a member of the University swimming team. John was introspective and quiet. He told me he could swim, but had very little sailing experience. We had a following westerly wind and expected to complete our journey in two or three hours, camp ashore or sleep in the boat, and sail back next day. We took food, water and sleeping bags and hoped it would not rain, which it didn't.

About 10 knots of wind pushed us along nicely, gradually increasing as we headed for the gap between Motuihe and Rangitoto islands. By the time we passed the familiar island of Motuihe, the wind had reached about 16 knots. There was a slight tendency for the boat to bury her head as the waves lifted her stern, and she shot down into the troughs. We could deal with this by moving ourselves aft, but it did give me a feeling that reefing the sails would be a good idea. We didn't actually reef though, and that raised the level of tension. It wasn't far to our destination and we were soon entering the bay at top speed, with our anchor ready to drop.

The bay was full of small boats that had come in ahead of us, and there were a few moorings which made it seem crowded. We went past the outer boats and turned up into the following wind when we were about 200 yards from the beach. We dropped the anchor and paid out the rode until we were at the end of our scope, and lowered and stowed our sails. As we looked around and saw our position amongst other craft, we could see that it put us in danger of fouling other boats if the wind changed. So we hauled up towards the anchor until the crown could just trip along the bottom of the bay, as Captain Sheldrake had taught me in the Thames estuary. This slowed the drift of the boat, but allowed us to steer, as the wind blew us backwards towards the beach. About half way to the shore our anchor rope fouled the rode of another craft, and as we continued backwards towards the beach our anchor came right up to the bows of the other boat. We pulled our boat up to lie alongside of it, so that John Phithian could see what needed to be done. He stepped onto the other boat to free our anchor, but instead of hanging onto our boat or our anchor, or one of our shrouds, he let go and we dropped astern with the wind, leaving him abandoned on the other boat. I asked him again if he could swim and he said he could, so I told him he'd have to swim to us when I'd dropped our anchor again a short distance astern.

I didn't know then that he was not a confident swimmer, or that he had a serious operation on his lungs a few years previously. We anchored about 50 yards away and then watched John enter the water. I told him to leave his clothes in the boat — we could recover them later — but he kept a shirt and trousers on, and hung onto the boat for a while instead of swimming away normally. That is when I should have yelled for him to stay at all costs. We could have gone back and rescued him. I pulled up on our anchor so that we were not more than 25 yards away. Then he began to swim, but he didn't seem to make much headway at all. Anne and I decided we'd have to go and help him. We didn't really think there was any real danger at this point. I had been wearing togs all day so I dived in, and he sang out and looked panicky, and must have let go at that point, and tried to swim towards me. He wasn't hanging on to the boat when I reached it, so I looked around to see if he was hanging on somewhere else, but he must have sunk by then. The ferry, *Muritai*, was at the jetty and the skipper was on the bridge. He had seen the whole thing. He shouted and pointed downwards. I dived and swam down to look for John. I stayed down as long and as deep as I could and I could not see him. The trouble was that the surface was ruffled by the wind and by this time, there wasn't any sun any more so I couldn't see more than about three feet and didn't know in which direction to swim underwater. I just went on diving as far down as I could see, and soon Anne was out with me. Then there were more people coming from the shore. We circled and took deep breaths and dived again and again, knowing how little time there was to save his life but we couldn't find him.

The water was about fifteen feet deep with a lot of weed on the bottom. John was found about two hours later, by someone with proper diving gear, but he was dead. Anne and I spent the rest of the day at Oneroa, the Island village, making statements to the police who had by then come down in their boat from Auckland. We had no lights to sail home, so went back that night, standing in the wheelhouse of the police boat, with John's body lying on the deck. I spent the night at Anne's place. Next day was Sunday, and I went to church and prayed. John's parents had been on holiday at Tauranga and I went to the police station to find out when they were expected to be back, so that I could meet them. Someone behind me said, "Is it John Phithian you are asking about?" "Yes," I replied. "I'm his father," he said. I have lived with that moment ever since.

Mr Phithian was in more shock than I was, but showed no enmity. He wasn't going to make me feel any worse than I already did. I can't remember anything I said to him, except that I was deeply sorry and had tried to find John as well as I could. The inquest was held about a month later. I gave evidence, and the coroner concluded that the catastrophe was an accident. Judith Wilson's mother asked me to stay with her family for the next two nights and she wrote to my parents to tell them I was in recovery, was being looked after, and to give them comfort.

Chapter 7: "If this be Love indeed, Tell me how much"

After two nights with Judith's family I moved my sparse belongings to Mrs Lee's house in Wakefield Street. My mother was alarmed to begin with and tried very hard to persuade me to go to the organised student accommodation at O'Rorke Hall, but it didn't open until mid-January, and by then I was settled. I wrote to explain, as well as justify my plans, and to reassure her about my state of mind: "Everybody has been absolutely wonderful to me, especially Anne and Judith. So have their mothers." Judith's mother had given my mother Mrs Phithian's address so that they could communicate, which helped me as well as them, as I knew that the whole tragedy of John's death would now be known to everyone.

I was not blamed, even by John's parents, and this made it possible, indeed necessary, for me to blame myself. I learnt that you can't assume that everyone for whom you are responsible can be left to get themselves out of trouble. I knew that if I had not left John alone, and expected him to swim, he would not have died. I should have recognised the possibility that he wanted to test himself, and was a young man who, like most of us, thought himself immortal.

Fifty years later, I initiated and led a series of small boat expeditions in Tasmania. They included many people of all ages and dispositions and sometimes in potentially dangerous circumstances. But from 1 January 1955 onwards I had learnt the necessity of making allowances for human error and I have not since expected everyone to be invulnerable. These ten day expeditions included a number of inexperienced sailors, and when planning them, I continually told myself to think, "What will you say to the Coroner?" Our preparations included plans for every possible contingency. People did discover new personal boundaries, but we had no accidents.

By 5 January 1955 my parents must have received a telegram I sent to tell them "Staying here this year, no job for me on *Rangitata*." I had a friend come with me to Waiheke to get the boat, which still had no name, and we sailed her back to Auckland, but once I had left the House, she lay there unused for about three months. I worked for the rest of the University break on the wharves.

Looking back on the summer of 1955, it was a time when I had to make vital life choices of three kinds: where to live, who to love and what to do with myself. It was nearly too much for me.

One of the ships I worked on as a wharfie was my old ship *Rangitoto*. I was driving one of the cargo winches, which meant I was on deck, and was able to engage in conversation with members of the ship's crew as they went about their business. One of them was a children's nurse, who explained that she was having a working holiday, and the job was a lot of fun. I told Robina about this and she suggested that, since I was unable to get back to England, she could perhaps investigate the possibility of working her passage in the same way to New Zealand, so we could at least see each other, and decide on the reality and viability of our relationship. She wrote in February to say she had made enquiries, but her parents discouraged the idea: "I'm told it would only be OK," she wrote, "if I got a job of looking after children privately, because if I worked my passage as one of the ship's crew, the chances of losing my virginity would be enormous… I don't expect my parents will like the idea anyway but if you can't come… that's the plan I have in mind. I don't know why I never thought of it before. I was feeling pretty desperate. That's why it came to me."

In the end, Robina decided not to come. Unsurprisingly, my letters about my relationships with New Zealand girls were paralleled by similar accounts by Robina of her boyfriends. "I told him I wasn't in love with him and couldn't think of being until I had seen you," was balanced by my similar declarations of faithfulness until we met again:

> *The trouble is that if I do go there* [to England] *your life will be complicated enough as it is I should imagine, what with Long-Jumpers,* [one of Robina's boy-friends] *and Head Boys from Winchester,* [another one] *without any useless vagrants as well. You'll have to decide. Imagine me there and think exactly what it will be like and decide soon, because I'll have to ring you up after you get this letter.*

I didn't ring her. Probably because I didn't have enough money to do it from a phone box, and Mrs Lee despised the telephone ("if it can't wait for a letter, it's worth a visit") and did without. This was a phase of my life in which I found it very hard to make up my mind about anything, and I was beginning to unravel. For about a month, I wrote more letters than I had ever done, to a lot of people, and found it therapeutic to do so. I was probably enjoying an extended adolescence. My grip on reality was in trouble and I was not far from becoming a cynical "dropout." I wrote to my sister: "I often wonder what use a degree is in New Zealand. Most BAs are school teachers, until they become disillusioned. Then they take to truck driving and living in comfort."

Robina was a distant but very valuable friend in all sorts of practical ways as well. She had shown her love by taking a lot of trouble to make enquiries about my chances of gaining credit for the first year subjects I had passed in Auckland, as components of a Bristol degree.

"Remember," she wrote, "What you do this year will influence the whole of your life. I'm sure that degree is terribly important. Do you remember Andrew Marvell's 'To his Coy Mistress?' I *can* wait John, but I hope it isn't for too long. I WANT YOU TO COME."

In February 1955, she went through all the options she could see from my point of view.

> *I have kept out of all this. I should like you to come home as rapidly as you possibly can, but I am so afraid that thinking I am in love with you is not the same thing as being; that I cannot ask you to upset your career for me until I've seen you… I get so despondent waiting for a letter… Write to me as soon as you get this please. I can't say much on the back of an envelope, but I love you.*

In the meantime, parental anxiety was rising on all sides. Mrs Wilson wrote again to my parents in March. She had expected me to base my social life on the University but "much to our surprise, Judy and he still go out together at weekends, but I feel more just as friends and don't think either have any serious notions. And I should hope not, as Judy isn't 17 til June. I think it wise for them to mix with more at their age." Clearly she was feeling protective. I had told Judith about my now long relationship with Robina, and that I wanted to go back to England to try my luck. She saw no reason for that intention to come between us in the meantime. I told my sister that I owed Judith and her family a lot for allowing me to stay with them after John had died:

That was only one of the times since I have known her when she has stood between me and everything from homesickness to hopelessness. I will always associate her, whatever happens, with an awful lot of memorable things, passing exams, sailing in Auckland Harbour, — which is really what I came to New Zealand to do, wasn't it? She is coming to England in 1957 for a year or so. Most girls in NZ do. I will introduce you. I'm quite sure now that I will write a novel, a real landmark in New Zealand literature. Won't that be great?

My father took Mrs Wilson's hint and wrote to me to suggest that I should not make the mistake of making Judith dependent on me, and to be very careful before making any serious commitment to anyone when my own plans were unsettled. I took it as unsubtle code for urging me to put some runs on the board before I became a "professional student," that species that values university life but never finishes a degree. I might well have become one of those.

In New Zealand, even more than Australia, distance was still a tyranny in 1955. There was a lot of long distance anxiety on my account in the early months, and writing now, sixty years later, I am much more sympathetic with my family than I was then. My mother thought there must be important things going on, that I was keeping from her. I wasn't, but didn't want to tell her that my problem was not being able to make up my mind. She too was living through some kind of crisis—I have never learnt the details—but I know that ex-pat communities can be very stressful places. "Our troubles are not over yet," she wrote on 23 January, "Dear 'enemy' has now appealed to the chief minister and has asked that the termination of his engagement should be withdrawn, and he should be allowed to resign."

I don't know who "enemy" was, or anything about the troubles, but it's not hard to imagine the tension and frustration that can undermine collegiality and lead to damaging human relationships in isolated ex-pat communities. In the same letter she told me that they now planned to leave Sierra Leone in June, and find a parish somewhere in Yorkshire "… so that there will be a home for you when you do get back to England."

My aunts both felt that I must be in need of support and good advice. Lena, my "Brown Ant" (she always wore brown), Father's elder sister, wrote what I thought a rather stiff letter of consolation in February, advising me not to use John's death as an excuse for abandoning my degree in New Zealand in favour of unlikely success on the stage in England:

> *Don't run away. If you are to keep on good terms with yourself, you'll have to pull off that exam before you make tracks for home. You have chosen the hard way, haven't you John? One pays heavily for freedom and sometimes wonders if it is worth the cost. You won't know about that yet. Only time will show.*

She hoped that I was still going to church. Molly, the Black Ant (because of her thick black hair, knew me much better, and her style was a result of a much closer relationship. She wrote:

> *You know, I feel there is some work for you to do in the world. Don't delay it by doing too much acting and so on. Do work steadily and get through all your exams and get your degree. You can do it quickly if you concentrate. I have such a strong feeling about this just now, and as I am still your godmother I know you will understand… I remember how you won a star your first term at school for carrying someone who hadn't got his slippers, and you didn't want him to get a chill. Dear little Fatty, Are you still doing works of mercy? Because that is one of the things we must do, if we are to keep our vows.*

There was another letter in March, "Did you get my letter asking what colour sweater and socks you would like, and telling you to be good?"

I wish I had been a more reliable correspondent than I was. Molly was so full of love that she rarely had a severe moment, but after a long silence from me she decided on 23 April, to give me a good telling off. I took little notice of her rage at the time, but it did help me to face reality: "You know you have very good powers of concentration, so why on earth not put all you have got into your study and get a good degree and be finished with it."

She went on to make a list of difficulties if I went back to England and tried to enter Bristol University. I would no longer be eligible for a study grant, I would be called up immediately for national service (even though I still had two more years in the New Zealand Naval reserve to serve), and finding work was much more difficult and less well paid than in New Zealand. I think she thought acting would provide me with many "occasions of sin" and hoped I would put it out of my mind.

On 2 March I wrote to my parents to tell them that I had enrolled in four subjects, Second year History, Geography, English and Greek 1. I must have, by then, decided to stay in New Zealand, sub-consciously at least, because I enrolled, for the second time, in Greek 1. I wrote home "I can see now how hopeless it was to try to do it [Greek] starting in the second term last year, without even being all that familiar with grammatical terms." I reflected that if I had stayed at St Michael's instead of going to Christ's Hospital, I would have continued to learn Latin and French and would have enjoyed it. This second attempt at Greek was more encouraging.

> *It was quite exhilarating to be able to really understand everything that was going on. I've been keeping ahead of lectures in the grammar book, doing all the exercises. I'm finding it quite easy. I think I'm one of those people who doesn't develop the right attitude to study until they are about 21. When I was 11 I used to sit and dream about boats. When I was*

16 and 17 I used to be very interested and emotionally concerned, but rather contemptuous of learning any factual details. I went to see Prof Musgrove, who told me I had got good marks in 1954 for both English language and Literature... Mus says there is nothing the matter with my brain, and that I will be able to do whatever I want if I do a bit of work.

Dr Parnaby, my History tutor, told me that I could be confident about making History my main subject in the future. Carmel Lorrigan was very tactful about my failed first attempt to pass Greek 1, and said I would have no trouble the second time, so I felt encouraged. In the end, I just wanted to finish my degree as quickly as possible.

As the first term picked up momentum, my friendship with Carmel began to provide motivation as well. And so did my attitude to New Zealand, as a country, and a community with which I began to identify. I began to play rugby for the University at a relatively humble level (under 21) and I took up boxing again with a remote notion that I might join the national team for the next Empire games in London. My fare would be paid and I would be able to see Robina. That was well beyond my reach without total dedication and supreme fitness, but I did participate for Auckland in the Inter-University Tournament boxing team during the Easter break, and lost my fight on points in the semi-final. That proved to be the end of my boxing career. I feared, for the first time, that I might suffer from brain damage if I continued. However, it did give me a free ticket to the ball when the tournament was over. I took Carmel to it, and it was a lot of fun.

Robina wrote to me to tell me that she and Tym, her medical student boyfriend at Cambridge, had a car crash, and how they planned to join a group of young people for a motoring holiday in Spain, and asked what I thought of that:

He has asked me to go to Spain with him in September. I have nearly said yes, but hesitate because a) I want to see you, although I am now sure it's impossible... b) I want your consent. Somehow I won't enjoy it unless you agree.

I wrote back to say that I had no right or desire to determine who she should have holidays with, since I was doing the same, and we should not expect each other to deny ourselves the pleasures of youthful normality. She wrote back:

I am looking forward to Spain tremendously, now that you have said you don't mind. I will be going in his car with a friend of his, (a boy, and a friend of mine, a girl). Tym is determined not to be serious about me or any other girl, but four in a car in a foreign Country?... I hope you go on having a wonderful time in New Zealand. I don't mind what you do as long as you realise I only think I am in love with you. I hope with all my heart I am.

As might be expected, this threw me into a frenzy of longing to see her again before I made any commitment to Carmel. I was told that HMNZS *Bellona*'s replacement had been postponed and now she was going to leave New Zealand in September 1955. She would arrive in England in October, just as Bristol University would be admitting students. The crew would be staying in England for nine months, I was given to understand, on full pay consisting, in my case, of £9 a week plus keep! I became very keen on making the best of my weekly "parades" and working for my leading seaman's certificate, which I achieved. I told my parents that, "There is also the possibility of a commission as I am one of the ten selected for advancement, and I have part of a degree. Won't it be utterly wonderful if it comes off?" How I imagined I could fulfil my naval duties while attending Bristol University I can't remember, but it seemed a good idea at the time.

Robina had begun writing more frequently in February 1955, and her letters were an enormous comfort to my traumatised psyche. She knew about all the schemes in my mind, the alternative options I saw before me of travelling on *Bellona* and either joining the Bristol Old Vic drama school, or completing a BA at Bristol University. She wrote back with a reasoned and explicit argument that pointed out the many and varied difficulties in staying alive in austerity England, with no visible means of support. But like me, she still liked to think it was possible that we could meet again and test the reality of our relationship before we made any further decisions.

She wrote, "Let me try to say something that I don't want to say. If you can't come to England and finish your degree, you mustn't come. It's no good either of us saying "I want." You can't… I think of you so much that occasionally I see what a terrible fix we might get ourselves into." But at the end of the month she told me how she had lain in bed: "warm, sleepy and supremely happy." Then her roommate, Helen, awoke and said, "Oh what a horrid dream I had."

I replied I'd had a wonderful one. I dreamed I was sailing to America with John in a Flying Fifteen, [A famous half decked racing class designed by Uffa Fox] *in order to climb Everest. We were both quite confident that we could do it, although we'd only got as far as a seaside town in England. "Mmm," said Helen, perhaps it means you'll have a letter from him." "No, not a chance" I said, and stopped feeling happy. But I was wrong, there was a letter… It made me feel that perhaps we are wrong in trying to attempt too much, but I'm sure we can only do it if we had utter confidence. Anyhow, Let's Try.*

One of my male friends was also a competitive sailor and asked me if I would crew for him in the "Flying Twelves," the National Twelve Foot Skiff Championships that were to be held on Lake Rotorua in the Easter holidays. These boats were a development class. The only design rule was that they had to be twelve feet long overall, so they looked like small sized International 14 footers, with straight stems, deep chests, and huge rigs. They planed, even going to windward and sailing them was hard on the stomach muscles, as the sheet hand (me) spent most of the time out on a trapeze, with only his or her feet on the gunwale, while the skipper was shifting weight from the centre of the vessel to the gunwale and back, sometimes on a trapeze as well, and steering at the same time.

The skipper had a car of his own, which meant that we could tow the boat down to Rotorua on a trailer. It also meant there was room for a third person, so I asked if I could bring Carmel with us. He agreed. I had known her for about a year by then, and was gradually falling in love with her, in spite of my affection for Judith, and my hopes of love and constancy with Robina in England. Carmel and I had been members of a group of students the previous year on the slopes of Ruapehu, away from home but not alone. In Rotorua it was different. I had been chosen as crew because I could sail, not because of an established friendship with the skipper, whose name I can't remember. I do remember that he was very circumspect, and he took care to leave us alone when we were not racing. We won one race and came third in another.

Back in Auckland, Carmel invited me to take her to another ball. It involved a presentation of debutantes to the Catholic Archbishop. I told my sister that "Carmel, being an obstinate child, and sensible, was not presented, and wore green instead of white." There was a party afterwards, with Max Cryer who was to become one of New Zealand's most famous entertainers. He played the piano and we gradually felt our way from choral renderings of the revue choruses that we remembered, through the risqué *Foggy, Foggy Dew*, to the traditional drinking song of the period, sung to the tune of *Men of Harlech*:

Put an end to all frustration
Drinking may be your salvation
End it all in dissipation.
Rotten to the Core.

Such was Auckland student life in the heady days of 1955.

In spite of my best intentions to stay away from the stage, I was captivated by the social and, as I told myself, the educational advantages (if acting was to be my destiny after all), of the Revue experience. Without Carmel's influence I might well have been carried away and delayed further academic effort for another year. Carmel would have none of it. Her brains stimulated a competitive streak in me, so that I began to earn reasonably good marks, starting with a B+/A- for an English essay on Coleridge's *Rime of the Ancient Mariner* in the middle of the year. It proved itself to be the first step on a long journey.

I did take a small part in the next University Revue. There I met one of the cast who was a member of the Ponsonby Yacht Club, and proud owner of *Disgraceful*, a classic Mullet boat. The "mulletties" were, and still are, a class of small yacht about 24 feet long, designed on the lines of a shallow draft inshore fishing boat, endemic to the Hauraki Gulf. *Disgraceful* had a very large sail area, with a long bowsprit and a boom on the bottom of her gaff mainsail that extended some way past her transom. She had some inside ballast and a centreboard to give her good windward capacity, and ample beam, which made her very stiff in normal conditions. She had no bunks, just a smooth ceiling. It was possible to throw a few quilts, pillows and blankets inside her and carry quite a large number of people as human ballast below decks. I wrote to my sister about it:

It was about as cold as summer time in England and every little thing that happened seemed perfect. It was just one of those days. We didn't sleep at all. There was a crowd at the pier when we left, and we stood on the deck, and gave them one of the songs from the revue. We decided to go for a sail up to Pine Island at the top of the harbour, where we swam, then sailed out into the Waitemata harbour with a warm breeze and a clear starry

> sky. *After a misty dawn, that reminded me of the Thames estuary, came a warm sunny morning and we tacked down to the busy part, round the Bean Rock light and back again as the sun rose behind us.*

Then the weather changed. The few of us who could sail took turns sailing her, while the majority of the girls and boys, about six of them, just cuddled up in the cabin on the floor and kept warm.

> *We didn't get back to the club until 4 that afternoon after a long beat to windward with 2 reefs in, and spray and waves. Carmel turned green, and so did her sister Margaret, but they valiantly held on til we put them ashore. Back at the club we drank hot cocoa made with milk, had hot showers and managed to get some bacon and eggs to keep us alive and enable us get to the theatre only minutes before the curtain rose for the final performance. I was feeling pretty weak, but the excitement acted like a drug, and I gave the best performance I had done at all.*

Looking back, I can now see the autumn and winter months of 1955 from March to September as a time of falling in love with New Zealand, which caused turmoil in my relations with the people I loved. Having lost my semi-final bout in the boxing tournament during the Easter holidays, I was determined to make the best of the rest of the Inter University Tournament, New Zealand's own unique interuniversity occasion. Each of the University colleges, that constituted the University of New Zealand, retained independence, but valued their collective identity, which was celebrated each year by sporting and social activities. One event was an enormous picnic for all the six hundred student participants in the Tournament at Piha, a famous surf beach with black volcanic sand, on the west coast of the North Auckland Peninsula. I told my parents:

> *Perhaps I've missed something by not going to a University in Britain but not only did we enjoy ourselves as much as they do at Oxford, but we did it in our own particular way. Perhaps we had no Madrigals on the Isis, like Heather used to have, but she did not have Piha. It's got everything, sand dunes, rocks, a river, and this large stretch of sand… On the way back the bus twisted and turned higher, and gave us better views at each corner, of the spray flying up towards the rock pinnacles, and the surf yellowing in the sun. Someone nudged me and said, "Better than Brighton?" which is just what I was thinking; so I'm glad I'm having my University education here.*

I began to make friends with some of the young men I met on the sports field as well as at the library and lecture rooms, and the wharves. Barry Shorter, who was doing History with me, asked me if I would like to join him and a group of students in a house share arrangement. In addition to Barry, the other boys were Murray Francis, Scotty (alias Hamish Hamilton) and Dave Greg. Their plan was to rent a house at 768 Mt Eden Road, from a family who were planning to go to Europe for a year. Barry, Murray and Scotty were about the same age as me, but Dave was twenty-eight, and a man of the world. He was a professional seaman, at one time second mate on *Ratanui* and had lived for a year as a "beach-comber" on a South Sea Island. More recently he had played a key role in the wharf strike of

1951 in Auckland, when he had been secretary of the Seaman's Union. I think he was now the Union Treasurer. He was over six feet tall, weighed fourteen stone, and was a member of the Auckland Light Opera club. Such a man was an invaluable leader for us twenty year olds, and created an environment that we all appreciated. He was also the holder of the lease agreement with the owners.

I told Mrs Lee that I had been invited to become a member of this household, and she was sad about it, but when I told her about the others, including Dave, she said that if she had been in my position, she would have wanted to join them. I undertook to find her a replacement, and promised to visit her now and again. So we parted in a kind of warm sadness. I did visit her a few times, and she soon found another lucky student to stay with her.

All of us young students were in need of someone to organise us. Dave Greg was a natural leader without being in the least authoritarian, and he won our unqualified respect. "Wonderful things have been happening to me," I wrote to my parents, "I have moved. It's just as cheap." I explained that the shared rent was £7/10 each, every month, shared between the four of us which for me meant just a weekend plus a Tuesday on the wharf. "It's a big clean sunny house and life is brim full and wonderful." My previous experience of house sharing in Coates Avenue, Aoraki, had lacked interpersonal responsibility, and we all cooked our own food, did our own shopping, and often ate alone. Mt Eden was different.

> We have lovely neighbours who make us pies, and we have 30 fruit trees and a ¼ acre garden full of vegetables. You have no idea of the difference between this and Coates Avenue… We keep accounts and have a system for keeping the place tidy.

Domestic chores were a shared responsibility:

> Everyone devotes 4 hours a week to it. We try to give the house a thorough going over on Saturday. One of us does the washing in the washing machine, one scrubs the kitchen floor, and cleans out the cupboards. Another de-frosts the fridge and cleans out the bathroom. Another takes the vacuum around and dusts and tidies. Another digs the garden. Those who cook don't wash up. I am really learning to cook properly. I did the roast last weekend, with potatoes, pumpkin, greens and gravy; stewed apple and ice cream for pudding.

Most of the week we subsisted on "bucket stew" which began on Monday night with fresh meat and vegetables, and was then augmented next evening by more meat, and ended the week as a largely vegetable curry. Scotty said the trouble with bucket stew was that, after a while, "it pailed." Get it? For me this house-keeping regime brought back memories of Christ's Hospital, where we were all allocated "Trades" such as cleaning the baths and lavatories and sweeping the floors. Good training certainly, but at 768 Mt Eden Road, we laughed and chattered and sang as we worked, and took pride in our accomplishment.

After a while, Murray Francis, who was an excellent rugby player, was becoming tired of the relative poverty of student life. He had a successful interview with Woolworths, which led to his decision to abandon his degree and begin an early career as a store manager, enabling him to buy a second hand car. Before he left the house he found time to teach me how to drive. One weekend we went for a long drive to the Coromandel Peninsula to visit Ralph Sewell. Ralph was another influential adult I was lucky to meet. He was the "Bosun" at the Royal Akarana Yacht Club, where our T-class boat was kept. I was becoming accustomed to wheel steering instead of handlebars, when we caught up with a car travelling slowly along a straight and empty section of the road. I decided to overtake, with the result that as we returned to the left lane of the road, the inside back fender came dangerously close to the forward corner of the car I was overtaking. Thankfully, there was no collision. In May 1955 I received a summons to appear in the court at Coromandel, and so Murray and I set off once more for my first court appearance, for which I had carefully prepared. I was impressed by the style and language of the document:

Whereas information has been laid that You, the said John Michael Young... Did on 18th May 1955, at Thames, in New Zealand, drive a motor vehicle, to wit, a motor car on a public highway, to wit the Thames-Paeroa main highway, without due care and attention.

I was summoned to appear "on Thursday, 21st July, 1955, at 10 am in the forenoon, at the Magistrate's Court, Thames, to answer the said information, and to be further dealt with, according to Law."

I was quite shocked to begin with, having had no experience of the law, except the rather long interrogation by the police on the way from Auckland back to the forest camp in 1952. I had visions of unpayable fines, prison, an unfinished degree, distraught parents and an inevitable slide into crime, addiction and dismal poverty. But I was exhilarated by the prospect of having to answer "the said information," and saw it as an opportunity to defend myself in public. So I dug out a white shirt and a tie, and an old grey flannel suit that was rarely worn and only to go to church or for dances.

My accuser started by charging me with speeding to overtake her; and then cutting across dangerously in front of her. She was not a bad woman, middle aged, well dressed, and plentifully made up. I was asked, to begin with, about my name and address, my age and occupation. I still had an English accent and said I was an arts student of Auckland University. This may have helped to give a good impression of someone far from home who had been anxious to learn to drive, as indeed I was. I was then asked if I had any questions to ask my accuser, and I asked her how she knew that I was speeding. She said, as I hoped she would, that she was looking at her speedometer, which enabled me to say that she must then not have been looking at either me or the road, which may have increased the risk of collision, but for which I was not responsible. The result was that her side of the story was not accepted by the Magistrate. I was exonerated, and Murray and I drove back to Mt Eden to celebrate.

After a period of neglect, until I moved house from Mrs Lee to Mt Eden, where we had a large basement workshop, I made it my business to return the T-class boat back into shape so that she could be sold, and the proceeds distributed between the Phithian family and the other joint owners. Ralph Sewell was one of those indispensable people who have been replaced in the modern world by qualified coaches, instructors or youth workers. The 1950s were still a time when, in spite of the social changes after World War II, young people who wanted to learn about boats and seamanship had to find someone with experience and a sense of responsibility, and who regarded passing maritime knowledge onto young people as a duty. Ralph was one of that generation and background and used to see Carmel and me scraping spars, painting and varnishing, and making plans. He taught us how to do things.

Back at the basement of our house I wanted to be able to use our power drill to sand the boat in the evenings and nearly killed myself. The drill stopped, and I took it apart to fix it if I could, but ended up attaching the active lead to the Earth, with the result that when I tried to use it, I took a severe electric shock through my hand which remained as if frozen to the handle of the drill. I fell heavily to the concrete floor as I lost consciousness. Luckily the lead was short, and as I fell I pulled it out of the power plug, and awoke feeling very humble and a little bit wiser. No one else was around at the time, and if the cord had been longer, I would have died. The incident made me try to make up my mind quickly about what I wanted to do with my life.

Ralph invited Carmel and me to join him with his mother and friends on his own boat, an old 40 foot harbour launch, which he had converted himself into a ketch rigged yacht. He was impressed with my stories about sailing on the Thames barge, *Leofleda*, in England, and asked me to climb up to the cross trees and take in the topsail. He told us about the scows, coastal ketches and ocean-going schooners, on which the maritime history of Auckland was built. It was through him that Carmel and I, later on, bought our own very small mullet boat, smaller than *Disgraceful* and our first joint possession.

After our weekend at Rotorua in 1955, where we had an opportunity for privacy by ourselves, Carmel, being a good Catholic, thought she had better go to confession. Not to be outdone, and as her sin was as much mine as hers, I thought I should go as well. Confession had not been part of my middle of the road Anglican up-bringing so I sought out a "High" Anglican Priest, the Reverend Prebble, for the purpose. I explained that I had committed the sin of fornication. I expected some kind of counselling or condemnation, and was surprised by his response, "How many times?" I searched my memory and remembered my long and strenuous tutorial with Joan two years before in Hawkes Bay. My penance was some straightforward scriptural recitation, and there it was, I was forgiven. I went away feeling a bit disappointed.

Determined repentance and avoiding the occasion of sin was to prove quite a challenge as Carmel and I came to know each other more ardently. But we tried hard and sincerely in the following months, to resist temptation while arguing cheerfully with each other about the infallibility of the Pope, the existence of Hell, the Spanish Inquisition, Henry VIII, and transubstantiation. These arguments sharpened my wits but did little to improve my history essays, which still tended to lack relevance to factual and analytic questions and drifted off into theological debate. We were avoiding pregnancy by using the Catholic "rhythm method," and thus, we argued, reducing the level of sinfulness, by not using contraceptives. We began, by the end of 1955, to talk about marriage, sometime in the future, and it was discussed in the Lorrigan household. Carmel wrote to my father and told him that she had no intention of converting me to Catholicism: "He would be better off," said she, "if he could concentrate on becoming a better Anglican." But she explained that her parents would like me to undertake the twelve instructions necessary to enable her to obtain ecclesiastical permission to marry me.

Father Curran was a Dominican friar from County Mayo, in the far west of Ireland. We began the twelve instructions by agreeing that County Mayo was indeed a beautiful part of the world. I told him all about my bike ride to Ireland when I was fifteen. I also explained that I was currently discussing the implications of marriage with a Catholic girl, and that my father was a Church Missionary Society missionary in West Africa. Father Curran's response was to tell me, in his rich Irish brogue, that, "mixed marriages never work."

In spite of this, we agreed that I would go through with my intention to take instruction for the next twelve months. He told me that we should begin by understanding the proofs of the existence of God, and asked me if I believed in God. I replied that I thought that I still did, but was unsure why, and would be interested in his explanation, as I was studying the history of Europe in the sixteenth century, when the question was of universal concern to an increasingly literate European population. I wrote to my parents to tell them about the "First cause unmoved":

> *I think I told you that I was going to a priest for instructions. It's not really as helpful as I thought it would be. He began by "Proving the existence of God." The trouble is that he maintains that everything in the Christian religion can be logically proved, even the existence of God; while I don't think it can, even though it may be true… After all, no one made him, so why should anyone have made the universe? One or other could have always existed, or if one could, then the other could. But we argue for a time, and then let things pass and go on to the next stage. At present we are onto the "Authenticity of the Gospels."*

I think his County Mayo accent was something too strange for most of his parishioners. He told me it was a relief to be talking to someone who could understand what he said.

I did enjoy these sessions, which went on to the necessity of my consenting to my children, should we have any, being brought up as Catholics. Carmel told me that this would not be one of her requirements, and I said that I would have no objection. I still think that the possibility of God is one of the many foundations that is useful as a basis for a good and consistent code of ethics. Father Curran and I parted on good terms. "What a pity it is, to be sure, John. You'd make a wonderful Catholic, if only you'd turn."

For my first three years in Auckland, uncertainty was the defining condition of my life. I went on writing to Robina, and as my relationship with Auckland girls became more complicated, the more I told her about them. We both reassured each other of our emotional constancy, while endeavouring to discourage complacency. By August we had both reached the conclusion that I should stay in New Zealand and finish my degree. We both tried our best, but time and distance and other attractive people gained the better of us.

In September 1955, I had my 21st birthday party with my housemates and we invited all our girlfriends and everyone we knew and liked. Gay O'Leary, one of Carmel's school friends, was taught to sing by a famous teaching Nun who went on to train Kiri Ti Kanawa. Gay entertained us all, with songs from *Carmen*, pop songs and Mozart. "She's got such a beautiful voice," I told my parents, "that everyone suddenly stopped making a noise when she began to sing." There was also a young, and I think married couple, called Jenny and Craig, who I didn't know all that well, but they gave me a blank birthday card on which they wrote a poem that I learnt was the work of William Blake:

Thou hast a lap of good seed
And this is a fine country
Why dost thou not cast thy seed
and live in it merrily?

It must have been around this time that Robina returned from Spain and I wrote to her after a long silence:

… You asked me to write and tell you if ever I fell in love with someone else, well that is what has happened, but it's not as simple as that. I spent six weeks hoping you'd fallen in love with Tym in Spain, that is, when I was with Carmel, and the rest of the time hoping that you hadn't. I don't know how I'm going to write this letter.

And so it went. I told Robina how much she had helped me through the joy and sadness of five years of growing up, and the way I had felt that, when I was alone and happy, she was virtually with me, sharing the best of my youthful experiences. I told her that in my lowest spirits, and worst moments, she had been the person in my thoughts and the reason for my recovery. I thanked her for her time consuming efforts to find a way to return to her, and still leave my choices of career to me. Then I told her that I would not be writing *love* letters to her any more, but wished to remain her friend.

Back in England, Robina had already written and posted the letter I received the next day. She had been to Spain for her summer holiday and was now in a loving relationship with Tym, her Cambridge medical student. It seemed extraordinary that our ability to continue to love each other while realising the realities of living five years and 12,000 miles away from each other, had persisted. We had both had alternating periods of despair and hope and had continued to re-imagine our expectant futures, each time we began once more to believe in a shared life that never happened. Robina said my letter brought an end to her fears, and we congratulated each other on our fortuitous honesty.

We have written to each other again from time to time, and I asked her if, by any chance, she had kept my letters, and if she had, would she return them to me if I did the same with hers, as I wanted to write a novel one day. Her reply on 27 January 1957 was a gracious reflection on the past we had shared:

I'm glad you asked about your letters. The funny thing is that I've been keeping them for the very reason that you want them… I'm glad you are going to use them… You know your last letter was amazing, because I never realised at all that it was written before the arrival of mine. I can't tell you how glad I was to get it. It seemed so wonderful that every letter you had ever written gave me pleasure, but the last was equally happy. Thank-you John for everything you did and everything you meant to me. Wasn't it lucky that we were both honest to our feelings at the same time? It confirmed what I had always thought, that ours was, or is, a perfect friendship. Even falling in love with someone else didn't turn the love into hate.

A year later, she wrote to me from Horsham. She had a holiday job as a theatre usherette and was able to tell me that the Christ's Hospital Players were flourishing, and gaining more praise each year. "Your social revolution seems to have worked wonderfully because there is now a strong connection with the local girls' school, and the players are looked upon as an important "Thing" in the school. She ended the letter with, "Love to you and Carmel."

Chapter 8: The Challenges of Reality

I passed my exams in English, History and Geography without difficulty in 1955. By the end of the year, I was determined to make my degree my first priority. How else could I expect Carmel to have an interest in me? I majored in English and History in 1956.

My father wrote on 11 January 1956 to tell me that he and Edith were now preparing to leave Sierra Leone, but they did not know when this would happen, as a new Principal of Union College had not yet been found, and, he wrote, "The political situation is uneasy." Much of his time that year was spent in writing excellent school textbooks on the geography of the country, and on the theory and practice of Christian education. On 21 February he wrote about a new approach to African history that he was trying out on his trainee teachers:

> *Histories of Africa are all written from the European angle. How We came and what We did and saw. I'm taking it from the African angle, what the foreigners did, how they traded with us, what we learned from them etc, against a background of tribal history such as it is, and there is a fair amount of information about the old Timne Kings and the Portuguese. The students seem to like it this way and are getting on very nicely.*

This was, coincidentally, in step with the teaching of Professor Jim Davidson, the founder of the School of Pacific Island History at the Australian National University in Canberra in 1951. A decade later, I was to become one of his PhD students.

Clearly, my father was apprehensive about the future of the country to which he had devoted his life:

> *There have been a few tax riots; the people are objecting to the new taxes imposed by the native authorities, and a lot of them would like the district commissioners back in full power. They don't trust their own people to govern them in some cases. It's quieter now that taxes have been reduced, but when they are increased again, which is inevitable, there will be more trouble unless there is a careful and wise campaign to educate the people in citizenship.*

My mother's take on the values of indigenous culture were much less objective. On 13 April 1956, she wrote to tell me of a letter from the local chief about a fire, lit on top of a local sacred hill, a Home of the Spirits, by an irresponsible student of Union College. The chief said that in lighting the fire the student had, "committed a crime against the country":

> *Fire on the hill is taboo and no doubt it is believed that some disaster may come as the spirits will be offended. He said they would have to pay seven pounds, a white goat, a white fowl, and a bushel of rice. They went in a body and apologised, so I don't think the full penalty will be demanded, but I expect they will have to find the goat and the fowl— as no doubt a sacrifice will have to be offered to appease the wrath of the spirits.*

I had written to tell my parents about my religious struggles with Father Curran, and my father was typically non-judgemental about my reaction. He wrote:

> *Proofs of the existence of God are an unprofitable exercise, and would hardly convince anyone who was without faith or religious experience, and those who have those things don't need them... The only thing they can do is to show that faith is not contrary to reason... Faith is betting your life there is a God... you stake all on that assumption.*

Rob was working on the last stages of his book on the geography of Sierra Leone. My sister Heather had finished her MA after reading English at Lady Margaret Hall at Oxford, and found a job working as an editor for Heinemann, a publisher based in London. She had fallen in love with Ottó Károlyi, whom she met in the course of her support of a group of Hungarian musicians and intellectuals, who had escaped to England after the Russian invasion of Hungary in 1956.

Rob and Edith had decided to re-settle in the north of England, and find a parish, preferably in a city rather than a country village. Edith had always hankered after the conveniences of twentieth century civilisation, having been deprived of such things for much of her early life, both in Sierra Leone, and in the villages of Rosedale, Lockton and Cropton. Following Rob's appointment as Canon to the Cathedral of Freetown and his MBE for Services to Education, my parents began to anticipate my return with, perhaps, a wife, and the establishment of the extended family life in England that they had long anticipated. Rob was soon successful in gaining an appointment as Vicar of Girlington, a suburb of Bradford, but close to the Dales of the West Riding of Yorkshire, and within visiting range of Harrogate, where Molly worked as manager of a home for the blind, and Seaton-Carew, where Lena lived in retirement from her teaching life with Gwen, her female partner.

I have always regretted the fact that I never really knew my father. When I was a small child during the World War II, he was in Sierra Leone most of the time, and when I was older, and he was training missionaries at Liskeard Lodge, I was at boarding school most of the time. After that, almost until his death in 1961, I was on the other side of the world. We always got on well, but I was never able to develop the kind of relationship that I would have valued.

I do have a letter from Mrs Elizabeth Trout, a woman who was one of his parishioners, written much later, on 11 January 1975, to Dr Coggan, who was then the Archbishop of York. It shows that Rob was a master of his chosen profession and had the capacity to inspire and provide the comfort and spiritual leadership required by his congregation:

> *I feel that he was one of the finest Christians I have ever met. When I came back from college in 1958, and began teaching, Mr Young was a stranger to me. A year later I went through a period of religious upheaval and turmoil, and as I had always been a regular church goer, the doubts and fears made me quite ill. I delayed going to see him until I was quite desperate.*
>
> *I shall never forget his kindness when I did go, and also his understanding and his great intuition. The first thing he said was "Don't worry, your feelings of fear will pass." ... He piloted me through those difficult months, and I owe the formation of what I hope is a stronger and maturer faith to him. I still remember clearly his quiet manner, and his strength of faith, and his delightful smile.*

On our side of the world, Carmel continued her stellar undergraduate performance, achieving a trail of nothing but distinctions, which indicated that she would have little difficulty in winning an overseas scholarship if she wanted one. I had two plans. Plan A was that I would try to enter a British university, and gain a post-graduate degree. Carmel and I would earn our degrees and then return to academic jobs in New Zealand. Failing that (Plan B), I would follow Carmel to wherever she obtained a university job, and take a school teaching job, or have a go at working for some altruistic organisation such as UNESCO.

My father wrote to me on 9 February 1956 with some encouragement:

I think your line will be in cultural activities — in a broad sense — deepening and widening understanding of people by other people, creating community, bringing folks together and helping them to do things and enjoy things together, so it looks as if some sort of social service is your line.

He went on to say that he would contact the UNESCO representative in Sierra Leone for advice. I did not come across this letter until many decades later, when I was surprised to discover how perceptive he had been, and though I did not then see what he was hinting at, some of his expectations were eventually achieved.

I was in the habit of calling in for an evening meal at the Lorrigan household at weekends. Carmel's elder sister, Margaret, was in the final year of her law degree, and "walking out" with Robert, whom she eventually married, but he didn't join us for the evening meals. Carmel's father was a librarian and worked in Auckland's public library, where I saw him regularly later on when I started work on research for my MA thesis. He mellowed a bit, as I became seriously studious. But to begin with he was a bit cool, and referred to me as "that Pommy fellow off a boat." Both of Carmel's parents were in their sixties, and were understandably a bit alarmed at the probability that Carmel and I would go overseas and leave them alone in their old age. But by the end of the year they had accepted me, and Carmel and I used to do the washing up. Margaret would go out to meet Robert, and the parents would go to bed, leaving us to our own devices, which were never, ever, interrupted.

Carmel wrote occasionally to my parents. Several times the reason was that she wanted them to know that she had no intention of converting me to Catholicism. She wrote to Edith, "I haven't the slightest wish to see John become a Catholic. It would be quite impossible for him to do so without contradicting his principles, and it would be against mine to influence him in any way."

At the university we studied together in the library, spent as much time as we could in each other's company, and began to enjoy a reputation as, what would now be called, an "item." We were very happy. Carmel was an admired and popular member of the student world because of her style, her beauty, and wit, laced with shyness and modesty. I began to see myself as a serious student and decided to start up an "Auckland University Historical Society," since none existed at the time, though I discovered that there had been one in existence a few years previously. We drew up a constitution with the help of Owen Parnaby, one of the

history lecturers, and an announcement was made that there would be an inaugural meeting on 11 April 1956, and "Mr John Young will speak of the plans to form this society and the lines on which it is hoped the society will develop." I drew up a constitution that listed the Objects of the Society:
1. *To stimulate and maintain an interest in the study of History, by holding meetings, conferences, reading parties and social functions.*
2. *By means of the above, to maintain contact between students of history in the university and teachers of history in the schools.*
3. *To encourage the proper care of historical records, and to influence public opinion to this end.*

The staff of the History Department supported my efforts, and welcomed the beginning of an organisation that would reduce the formality of the conventional staff/student relationship. "Reading parties" took the form of camps on Waiheke Island, at which we organised discussions about things like the Suez Crisis of the time, and the implications of the South African rugby tour on race relations in New Zealand, which still involved the exclusion of Maoris from the All Blacks when they went to play in South Africa.

Another organisation, the debating society, decided to propose that "International sport does more harm than good," a sentiment that I agreed with. Carmel spoke against me in spite of her actual opinion. She was of course more rational than I was, but I had been making a habit of always attending Union meetings to practise public speaking. I told my parents that "I do enjoy union meetings very much and always make a speech. It's very good practice as the issues to be debated are not known until the delegate opens the meeting and speeches have to be completely spontaneous." As a result, I was more rhetorical; and my assertion, that "when David slew Goliath, the principle of international sport was carried to its logical conclusion" was supported by the majority.

My mother found it hard to adjust to what she saw, after her own decade long courtship with my father, as my inconsistency. On 22 October 1955, just as Carmel and I were becoming serious, she wrote to remind me that this day was the anniversary of the visit she and Heather had made to see Robina:

To me, the ironical thing is that it was in order to get to Bristol, and to Robina, that you decided to learn Greek, and in doing so, and thereby forming this attachment to Carmel, you have changed your course completely. I think you want to be very sure that this is not just the swing of the pendulum, and that, in your disappointment at not being able to get to England, you are not being thrown off your balance. To even contemplate changing your religion is a very big step to take.

I responded by doing my best to make very sure that our relationship would lead to our marriage, and so did Carmel. We both saw religious differences as being of little importance. Like many young adults of the 1950s, we both found the teachings of Christ an inspirational guide for living, but we found some of the actual doctrines we had been taught to be intellectually hard to swallow, and we concluded that they were unnecessary as a foundation for living an otherwise Christian life. I wrote back to say,

> *I suppose looking back from your point of view, there is no other advice you could give. But if you love someone, you hardly see any sense in saying, "I just want to go back and make sure that it isn't Robina I really love". Apart from that it would be expecting/presuming too much from Robina. She is in Spain now with a young man from Cambridge, and has probably forgotten about me in any case.*

In fact she had not forgotten, and neither had I. After a long interval she wrote to me to say that any doubts she had about her new boyfriend who had taken her to Spain had now gone. "I'm not certain if I knew for certain last time I wrote, that I was in love with Tym; but I am now and I'm very happy." The next news I received from her was written as she waited her turn to see her dentist, and had taken a bunch of my letters with her to pass the time, in March 1956.

> *They are a wonderful mixture* [she wrote] *of hope and despair, philosophy, narration and love. At first they made me very cheerful because the early ones are so amusing. The later ones are often amusing too, but they are also full of other things that depressed me. Please John, come and see us when you come to England. I shall find beds somehow for your wife and all your children. So please come.*

At the end of 1956 she wrote again: "It's five years since that bright frosty boxing day when we walked along the canal and talked about New Zealand; and Shakespearian sonnets."

I was offered a part, around this time, in a short evangelical film, produced by Crusade Films Ltd. My reaction to the offer reflects my state of mind about religion. The story dealt, as I told my parents, with "various people, who lead wicked lives and are then converted, and make a success of their lives." It was to be shown in Church Halls, YMCA, etc, and was to be distributed by J Arthur Rank. I wrote that it was a worthy project, and I was glad of the £6 I was paid for my acting, but, "the script is extremely corny. It presents the same sort of problem as Noel Coward's patriotism. However, I'm pleased, of course, to have a part."

New Zealand had a higher proportion of Catholic citizens than England at that time, and to my female elders, the possibility that I might marry one of them was a new and unexpected threat. Molly wrote in May: "At your age I was much attracted to Rome, but certain things are very bad." She listed (in spite of her fondness for leprechauns and fairies) Virgin Birth, Indulgences, Celibate Clergy, Immaculate Conception, and Papal Infallibility. "I do sympathise with you," she wrote, "Darling Fatty, [she still thought of me as the plump baby that she had brought into the world as mother's midwife] read your gospels, especially Mark, and do for goodness sake be honest and see whether you can square the claims and dogmas of Rome in the light of Jesus."

The owners of 768 Mt Eden Road returned at the beginning of the year, and we all had to look for somewhere else to live. The group was showing signs of breaking up anyway.

Small victories helped to sweeten my life, but my future happiness, at the start of 1956, depended on having an income I could live on, a cheap and convenient place to live, and considerable improvement in my academic achievement. I knew little about UNESCO, but with my father's encouragement, I felt it was the kind of job I would enjoy and which lay within the possible range of my ability. Carmel, I explained, had not really tried to make up my mind about the advantages of a steady job. "She just got a bit long in the face," I wrote, "at the idea of permanent pavement-bashing round Theatrical Agents with a pram." So to lay a foundation for achieving the qualifications for a steady income, I applied for a job, as many other students did, as a postman.

Post Office work was the best job I had as a student. Largely because it was the policy of the New Zealand Postal Service to make it easy for students to study and work at the same time. There was an expected demand for workers in December, because of the Christmas rush, but the Post Office was always busy and vacancies were frequent. We made a 6 am start, collected the mail addressed to the suburban area to which we were allocated, and began to sort it into the individual streets of our "run." Then we laid out the individual letters for every street, bundled in the order they were to be delivered. For the first week we were apprenticed informally to a permanent member of the staff, to learn our run. After that we were left to ourselves.

As temporary workers we were not supplied with a uniform, and I soon discovered that if I wanted to finish the job quickly, shorts, shirt and sandshoes were all the garments I needed. At first, it took me 'til 8.30 to get on the road, but I eventually cut it down to 8 am when the traffic was light, and though the leather mailbag was heavy to begin with, it grew lighter through the morning and by noon I could do a steady jog. We were paid on the assumption that we worked an eight hour day, but I could soon finish my run by 2 pm. By the middle of the year, I usually finished by noon, because I knew my run well enough to reduce the sorting time and once on the road I jogged along at a good pace.

My first run was around the end of Karangahape Road, with its heavy traffic and mixed residential, commercial, and light industrial character. There were stairs to climb to first floor offices, which slowed things up, and a modern government-funded housing estate. Later I was given a run in the Ponsonby area with its wide streets, modern houses and the sparkling sunlit water of the Waitemata Harbour at the end of many of the streets. I could get to the university or public library by about 1.30 most days, and work until nine or ten at night. I also began to play rugby on Saturday afternoons, but I explained to the coach that I couldn't attend the mid-week training sessions on account of my work and study commitments. He let me off, and still let me play the game. It was a rigorous routine, as I explained to my parents on 23 June 1956:

> Once I am out there, I only take about two hours to actually deliver the mail, but I have got the time down to a minimum now. I am playing Rugby too, just on Saturday afternoons. I can't spare the time to train during the week, but I'm probably fit enough

> through walking and running every day, so it doesn't matter. I have got on well with Greek, though somewhat at the expense of other subjects.

By the middle of 1956, I had a well established routine, and was obtaining some job-satisfaction as well:

> It has been quite fun, being a postman, and I will go back to it in the summer. I am now getting to know the people — they give me cups of tea, or drinks and beer from time to time, and tell me their troubles. I took a registered letter to a woman one day. It was from her husband, from whom she was divorced, and she told me the whole sad story. There are several families from England, and someone waits at the gate on Saturday mornings. It makes me realise how you must feel when I don't write.

I went on to explain my efforts to solve the problem of accommodation:

> The owners of 768 Mt Eden Road will soon be back, so the house will be breaking up. It doesn't matter quite so much to the other people because, apart from me, there has been a steady decline in interest taken in academic matters, and Scotty and I are really the only serious students left. Scotty and I have been very fortunate. A friend of mine, a law student, Murray Smith, lives in a flat consisting of half a house about a hundred yards from the university. His father has just been sent to New Plymouth by his firm for several years, leaving Murray with the flat, and Murray has asked us to move in. There will be four of us; Tony Courtney, who is also doing Arts and produced the last Revue, Murray Smith, and "Scotty," (Hamish Hamilton) and me… Tony and Murray Smith are extremely easy to live with, [Scotty was as well] and the atmosphere is a very happy one. Being about 50 yards from the University, we have all our meals here, and it's like being at a proper University. [I must have already begun to think of the dreaming spires of Oxford.]

This was a letter in which I tried to reassure myself, as much as my parents, that I was at last in control of my destiny. I supported Carmel's statement on religion, "She also thinks that if I become a Catholic, and am unhappy, that it would be a responsibility that she would rather do without… The point is that we both think, that, within reason, God isn't so extremely particular as people make out." It was with some implied piety, I now see, that I wrote:

> I have, for a sustained period, quite sincerely tried to see the Catholic point of view, but we both agree that it is really a matter of upbringing, which side of the fence you are dropped on. And what I can see of it, although it seems extremely reasonable, doesn't prompt me sufficiently to take the step of becoming one.

As for my career, I told them, "I thought of staying here to take an MA, then trying UNESCO." On July 24 I wrote what I thought would be a letter of reassurance of my ability to combine study, work, and romance successfully:

> I have to get in four essays in three weeks, and then I'll stop work at the PO and swot for exams… There will be three of us, 25 shillings a week for food, rent, £4 a month each. I have £38 in the bank now.

We planned a diet dominated by mince and rice and "a few greens and veg." I had no travel expenses, because we lived so close to the University. With a household of serious students, and a relatively steady job whenever it was needed, I felt confident that I was on the road to success.

But I was to learn that there was some truth in the saying that "true love never did run smooth." We decided that a house warming party would be in order. The student world was conscious of the previous story of the Mt Eden Road household as a social phenomenon, and my move to a house within easy walking distance of the library and lecture rooms, meant that a large attendance was inevitable. Invitations were informal, by word of mouth; and there was no need to remind anyone that it was a BYO event, and that included food as well as drink. Carmel was not used to the scale of imbibing that was customary, and as we proceeded past the eating and drinking stage and onto singing the favourite songs, we mingled and began to lay about on the furniture. Carmel found herself sitting on a sofa close to an ardent young man, who much to my annoyance, began a heavy petting session, that she accepted with increasing enthusiasm.

I, the host, was at a loss as to how I should behave. Until I reached Auckland, I had never had the cultural experience of the Kiwi beer party, but by this time, I was used to it and the range of behaviour that it could generate. The question was, how should I respond to it?

Should I, for instance, whisper quietly into Carmel's ear, that I'd like her to stop behaving like this, and I'd be grateful if she joined me for a private discussion outside? Should I, on the other hand, warn her ardent snogger (let's call him Jim) that he should precede me out of the house into the garden, where I would smash his face in? Or should I implement that idea right now? That would probably lead rapidly to blood on the floor, a visit by a few policemen, the departure of all our guests, a great deal of gossip, and the end of my relationship with the girl I loved, and wanted to marry.

I knew that Carmel was totally unfamiliar with alcohol. Hers was a dry household, and like me with my flask of gin on my bicycle at Tikokino, she had no previous experience by which to judge her capacity to avoid intoxication. I was her first and only boyfriend so far, and a feeling of entitlement on her part, to discover what it might feel like to be embraced by somebody else was to be expected; after all, she had lived a protected institutional life, just as I had. She had lived only in a female boarding school and with elderly parents, and was only nineteen.

My mind was frozen between the available options, and I did nothing. But the look on my face, in spite of my acting experience, could not disguise my feelings. Later on Carmel told me that I just "Looked Black," and after a short time, I left the house to express my displeasure, and went for a lonely walk to settle my thoughts. When I came back Carmel and Jim had left, much to the surprise of our guests, who had been noticing the progress of our courtship over the past three months or so. The party became quieter. I put on the best countenance I could, and resumed the role of cheerful host, but a cloud now hung over the party and it was not long before our guests began to complain of essays to be completed, and the need for early nights. I was not unhappy when people began to leave, and the four of us were left to clean up, wash the dishes and glasses and go to bed, where I was unable to sleep. Next day was spent working in the Library on *my* essay that had to be written, and feeling very sorry for myself.

When I came home that night, to an empty house, I found a letter from Carmel on the kitchen table, addressed to me. This was on 15 August 1956:

I came to explain to you what happened last night and what I have decided to do, but since you are not here I will write it instead. Please don't feel I didn't even pay you the courtesy of explaining in person though.

It is very difficult for me to put in writing what happened, but after you left, Jim and I had a conversation, and in effect he said he had not deliberately had any part in our separation, that any impressions I may have gained were the effect of my own imagination rather than any action of his and regardless of the position between you and me he did not wish to become further involved... that he had not in fact ever been involved as far as he was concerned. After that he told me to go home and I went.

All this I must add, was done very tactfully. He has behaved as well as you could wish, and you both make me feel very conscious that my own behaviour has been neither dignified nor considerate.

Poor Carmel, I thought. She must be feeling embarrassed and misunderstood. What a beautiful apology, and how courageous and honest she was, but the next part at first excited me and then depressed me.

My first impulse would be to return (abjectly) to you, but under the circumstances I cannot do so. While my feelings remain the same I cannot promise that I would be perfectly happy with you, or allow you to think so. I think it is far better for both of us not to be subjected to the sort of relationship we have been having since the Revue — one day's happiness and three of misery [This was a pattern that I had not noticed] *with you making every effort and me apparently none... I already want very much to return to you. I am sure that sooner or later I will be back quite whole-hearted if you will have me, which doesn't appear very likely, or for you, very desirable. Just now I am very far from wholehearted. If you weren't so incapable of any sort of malice you would be pleased to know I'm feeling very unhappy and very humiliated and lost.*

Next day another letter from Carmel was in our letter box. She had written it as soon as she arrived home the previous night, and then posted it. It was a long letter, written in haste, very private, and not always consistent. As I read it now, it helps me to understand Carmel's state of mind, and our subsequent relationship.

I started this as soon as I got in, to show you that I am really sorry and persuade you to realise how silly I am. I know you think I am very silly indeed, but you don't quite realise in what way. Tonight and very often I seem to be doing my best to make both of us unhappy, when the two things I want most, are for you to be happy and for me to be. It's the same thing, but I put me separately so that I could put myself after; because although I am a very selfish girl, I love you very much... in a way I am a bit bad... compounded largely by frustrated curiosity and injured pride. I never thought of the curiosity angle before, but now that I have, I think it explains most of the affair; and curiosity, you know, is not a basic passion, so it does not last. That is why I can feel confident about the future. When there is nothing to be curious about, I shan't be...

It isn't going to be much good giving you this tomorrow when I want to say these things to you, but by writing, I feel I am communicating with you tonight. Perhaps you have already shrugged and decided it's no use reasoning with me. Perhaps you can be confident that I love you. I hope so.

... I admit I get upset very easily. No-one is easy to get on with when little things go wrong. Well, we'll just have to make our married life a long succession of major crises. I'm quite good in those. Besides, I assure you, I'll be much calmer then. I won't be trying to adjust a lot of different claims, like you and my parents and my studies; you will be the only one and I promise I will devote myself to you as much as I can...

I think, in the back of my mind, that you have a very old fashioned idea of women, brainless creatures to be dallied with, but to be kept firmly in place. Well, just keep it in mind when I become difficult.

I'm not really responsible for my actions, don't know what I'm saying, aren't up to the demands of education, not to be taken too seriously. [Then she became flippant.] *What I need is a good, kind but firm husband who beats me once a week, (just you try!)*

You mustn't take me seriously about that now. But I've got exams and head-aches and I get tired, and I'm a difficult child at the best of times. If you can put up with the difficulty I will be very grateful, and will love you with all my large and loving heart, and with most of my warped, dissected, overburdened, under-equipped, distorted and otherwise peculiar mind.

If you can't, I'll chase you with unbounded energy from now til Domesday. And as you're quite a lazy boy, and can get on with anybody anyway, I'll get you in the end, whether you like it or not, so there!

Looking back some sixty years, I'm surprised that she thought she had always been so troublesome. I had thought we were getting on pretty well, which says something about my lack of sensibility. Then, I felt that I understood her much better, and I could see the kind of life we might lead in the future. Whatever happened, it would be neither uneventful nor boring, and I was attracted rather than warned about what to expect. She came to 1B Grafton Road, the next afternoon when I was the only one there, and there was only one way we could think of to celebrate our love for each other, and renew our commitment.

The effect on my studies was electric. It became essential in my mind that I raised my standards as close as possible to Carmel's. Over the next year, she would often say that if it came to a choice between marriage to me and going to Oxford or Cambridge, she would choose marriage. That made me even more determined that she should not have to make that choice.

Luckily, the support I needed at this stage arrived in the shape of a new member of staff, Bill Mandle, a young man who had attended a state grammar school in the north of England, won a state university scholarship, and had just finished his first degree at Pembroke College of Oxford University. He was twenty-one at the time of his Auckland appointment as a Junior Lecturer. I was to discover later that, much to the dismay of some of his Public School rivals, he had won the Gibbs Prize, awarded to the best performer of his year in the History School final examinations.

Bill was given the job of teaching the Medieval History of Europe, and the sixteenth century History of Britain, neither of which had attracted the very best lecturers in the past. Having drunk at the intellectual fountains inspired by Hugh Trevor-Roper, Christopher Hill, Dick Southern, A J P Taylor and their like, Bill sent shock waves through the History Department. Not all of those shock waves were welcome amongst the senior members of the university staff. Kingsley Amis, a leader of those Angry Young Men of Britain in the 1950s, had recently published *Lucky Jim*, which detailed the rebellious life of a young history lecturer in a provincial British university. Bill chose to make Lucky Jim his role model, which upset his senior colleagues rather intensely.

But for his students, including me, Bill was a breath of fresh air, introducing us to the fascinating "History Wars" between rival historians, and new ways of looking at historical evidence. Gradually, I began to understand the importance of primary sources and the most recent scholarly arguments in the history journals, rather than well-worn text books. Bill, like Lucky Jim, was enjoying his early flirtation with socialism, before his later fascination with Sir Roger Mosely, the British fascist, of whom he became the biographer. Later Bill became an expert on the history of Israel. He was only a year or two older than most of his students, and through the newly founded Historical Association, he played a significant role in student life, joining our celebrations and "Reading parties," with his wife, on Waiheke Island.

My academic record up to this point was not one to lead anyone to suppose that I could excel as a scholar of any kind, but Bill decided that some personal effort on his part might make a crucial difference. It all started with an essay I wrote for the Medieval History course, about John of Salisbury, a clerical figure of the twelfth century, whom I had always admired. Bill gave me an A-minus mark, the highest I had ever received up to that point. He didn't merely mark it but used the whole exercise as a teaching opportunity. There were not only the obligatory factual corrections and comments, but a lot of encouragement and hope. At the end of the essay he wrote: "This is good. There is a maturity about the essay that if only you'd get down in an examination, would float you to a first class degree." He then picked it apart with details of my sins of omission and of insights, and concluded, after two pages of remedial comment:

... within these limits... I think this is a fine piece of work, revealing, however, what is likely to be your greatest weakness — lack of a full body of knowledge and judgement which could only have come from your working reasonably hard in the stages 1 and 2. As it is, you lack background, and the very sharpest historical judgement, which leads, I think to the faults both Keith [Sinclair] *and I note, exaggeration, over-emphasis, and occasional shallowness. This you have the ability, most of the time to conceal, especially*

> as you are a shrewd depth analyst on occasion, which deceives people into thinking your shallower statements are therefore as deeply thought out. The trouble will arise most seriously when you try to build a case on one of your less penetrating statements. On your ability to avoid this, which I think is considerable, but not 100%, will depend, in a large part, your final result.

Not many students attain that level of intellectual discipline, critical appraisal, encouragement, and insight from their lecturers, either now, when assessment boils down too often to ticking the right box, or then, when in most universities all over the world, increasing student numbers meant, paradoxically, that many lecturers found the way to advancement was to concentrate, especially in the early stages of a career, on research rather than teaching.

I owe a lot to Bill, whatever his critics have said about him. A couple of years later, leading up to my Master's exams, he sat me down on a weekly basis and put a single question in front of me. He suggested allowing five minutes to plan an answer carefully, five minutes to write an opening paragraph which makes the examiner sit up and take notice, and within the boundaries of the evidence, goes to the root of the problem. Fifteen more minutes to explain why, and to support the conclusion with textual references, original arguments and new insights, or to perhaps refute the opinion of others. Then ten minutes to plan and deliver the confirmation of the opening sentence with a twist of irony, or humour, and then read it over to fix mistakes or cut a few words out or other stylistic improvement. It meant writing about eight hundred thoughtful and interesting words in forty minutes and avoiding mistakes. I found it hard at first, but enjoyed the idea, as I became better at it, and I still remember the day when Bill gave me back a practice exam on the foreign policy of England's Elizabeth 1. He had written on the outside of the folded paper: "This is Alpha with ease." By this time, my life had become much better in terms of my domestic arrangements and my love affair with Carmel had become intense and very happy.

The lease on 1B Grafton Road was to expire on 1 February 1957. The plan was for the four of us to move to another rental house at Mission Bay, but I was unable to afford the deposit of £50, to be paid by each of us, because I had spent all my money on a very simple and unpretentious engagement ring for Carmel. "As you know," I wrote to my parents, "we had not planned to become engaged until shortly before we get married. But we did." I told them that I had made a formal approach to Carmel's parents, who were shocked. "Next thing, you'll want to get married," said her mother. "I said that was the general idea, but we got no further." Carmel's mother said, a few days later, after talking it over with her daughter, that they didn't mind a bit. I put the little ring on her finger, next evening, down by the fishing boats in the harbour, where I had first taken her for a romantic walk nearly two years before.

My housing problem was solved because of one of my rare visits to the parish church of St Barnabas, in order for Carmel to have an Anglican experience, in return for my occasional agreement to go to Mass at her church. It was there that we again met Shona Caughey, and her husband, the couple who had impressed my mother in 1954. It was not long before Shona asked me to baby sit for her two young boys, which meant that I could rely on warmth, light and silence in which to concentrate on my studies, as the boys were heavy sleepers and never required any attention from me. They were also fascinated by my 1948 second hand AJS 500cc motor bike with which I had replaced my even more ancient 1932 Velocette. The boys used to make motor bike growling noises when they opened the imaginary throttles on their tricycles. We got on well. Shona wrote to my mother on 10 June 1957:

> *I was most amused when we asked John, rather diffidently if he could baby sit on the eve of Carmel's sister's wedding. I suggested that he might be required there to help, but he assured me there was nothing to do, and, believe it or not, Carmel came too. Mrs Lorrigan was in Hospital, and all the preparations were done by Carmel and the bride. It speaks worlds for their organising abilities.*

This was a very kind interpretation of our insatiable need for shelter and privacy in which to further our courtship, and make up for the years of same sex education that we had both experienced. Shona went on to say that we often baby sat together, and it was a great help for her and her husband to be able to rely on us to look after the boys. "Carmel is good with the children when they wake up."

As I was on good terms with the children and parents of this kind and tolerant family, it did not require much courage to approach Mr Caughey on the subject of accommodation. They had, at the back of their extensive garden, a wooden shed, which probably pre-dated their fairly modern house. It may have been a storehouse during the initial building process. It was known by the Caughey family as "Old Man's House." I wrote to tell my parents, "At last I asked Mr Caughey if I could scrub out the old man's house at the very back of the garden. Carmel has been absolutely wonderful." She was indeed delighted and tied something round her head and got stuck into it. It had one room, an old bed, an outside water tap, a power plug, a table and a primus stove. There was a toilet inside the outdoor laundry shed close by.

I offered to pay a small rent if I could have Old Man's House to live in, but Bill Caughey said that would not be necessary. I told my parents, "… so really I'm better off than we were at Cropton." I said I was going to purchase some newly fashionable straw matting for the floor, and Carmel was going to make me some curtains. Shona's mother, though, was not impressed. Her career had involved the care of unmarried mothers and their children, and she thought Bill and Shona should be aware that they might, by providing me with a place to sleep, be creating an inevitable occasion for a lot of sin. I thought it was none of her business, but she was not stupid.

Shona wrote comforting words to Edith in March 1957:

> *We are so pleased to have him here, and full of admiration for the way he has improved Old Man's House. Few people would be happy to live there with no W.C. and no hot*

water, but John sees no obstacles when he tries out a new enterprise. Carmel seems to be a very nice girl, with the rare combination of brains, beauty and common sense.

Edith was thinking further ahead when she wrote to me about what she saw as a fundamental problem of the position of the Catholic Church in relation to contraception, and made the natural assumption that Carmel would not tolerate it. There are numerous academic works, now, that deal with the social impact of reliable contraception in so-called developed societies in the 1950s and 60s. In our case, Carmel and I both rejected the idea that the use of technological contraception was sinful on the grounds that the Catholic rhythm method had exactly the same purpose as diaphragms, condoms, metallic devices, or pills; that purpose being to have children when they were wanted instead of when they were not. Until we discovered that the rhythm method was unreliable, we used it. After that Carmel mostly used a diaphragm until the blessed invention of "The Pill," which reached Britain and Australia in 1961 (for married women only).

Meanwhile, we remained focussed on the immediate problems of living and learning, as well as loving. "This is my first night here," I wrote to my parents on 4 February, 1957, "and tomorrow I start at Training College. It's as exciting as anything, playing house with Carmel. I'm sure she'll make a wonderful wife."

We had both decided to enrol at the Auckland Teachers' Training College to guarantee our solvency in the event of having children, and having therefore to stay for the foreseeable future, in New Zealand. In 1956, I passed all my exams in my major subjects, History and English, at stage three and after achieving good marks for the "Terms" examinations in Greek, I expected to complete my BA by the end of that year. But it was not to be. I hadn't passed Greek. I had been considering applying for a teaching bursary from the Education department, but I thought of this as a last resort. I told my parents:

I don't want to take a teaching bursary as it would tie me down to being a teacher. If only I can manage to get through this year, then I will be in a position to choose a job, to a certain extent. I thought of staying here to do an MA, and then trying UNESCO… and, if ever I was a successful writer, I'd like to give up whatever I was doing… I must stop now and do some Xenophon.

I went to see the history staff and they were very encouraging. Two of my lecturers, quite independently, said I should certainly do an MA, and if I worked hard, might do very well. I decided this was the best way to go and concentrated on finding a topic for my thesis. At that point I was very interested in the wharf strike of 1951, and then on the contact history of the North Auckland Peninsula, in the years before the signing of the treaty of Waitangi in 1840. Eventually I chose to accept an offer from Professor Rutherford, the Head of department, to tackle the as yet uninvestigated political history of the Auckland Province in the years before the abolition of Provincial Government in 1875.

For the whole of 1957, Keith Sinclair was my tutor/supervisor. On 1 September 1957 I told my parents that "I felt a great thing was achieved today. My tutor,

Dr Sinclair, called me John. I really feel I'm a serious student at last." I started on my thesis by reading four years of the *New Zealand Herald*, from 1871 to 1875, so as to get the feel of life in that time and place, to acquaint myself with the political characters, their beliefs and motivation, and to understand the attitudes and assumptions of that young frontier society. Auckland was described by a contemporary, W L Rees, as a transplanted suburb of Sydney, and a contrast to the transplanted British communities of the South Island:

The people of Auckland alone have no esprit de corps — no public spirit. The inhabitants of Auckland are not indeed a people. They are an aggregation of individual human atoms, each one, as a rule, thinking of his own miserable interests, and they can never work together.

It sounded interesting.

Concurrently with my first year MA, we both enrolled at the Auckland Teachers' Training College, with a generous bursary of £515 a year. My explanation of my circumstances was made in an undated letter written probably in June 1957:

The position is this: I have one unit — Greek 1 — to get to complete my B.A., and four papers, [exams] and a two year course for an History M.A. to do. It [the MA] consists of a thesis which I can do this year, to be handed in not later than two years after I complete my B.A., and four exams, which I will sit next year, and my thesis, which I will hand in at the same time.

Carmel's parents have agreed to let us get married as soon as we are able, when we will both have B.A.s. We plan to live in my shack, although we'd both be out for most of the time. Carmel says she would love it. I'm getting good marks now for my Greek prose, 18.5/20 is the best so far.

On 29 November 1957, I was able to send a telegram to my parents: "Passed Greek. Degree complete."

Chapter 9: Boats, Teaching, Dreaming spires, and Babies

Auckland Teachers' Training College was a relatively restful institution in comparison with the University. I was a student of both of them at once, but there was time, I thought, for extra-curricular activities as well. Early in the first term I was asked to address a club of city business men, the "Optimists," about University life in New Zealand, and its value to the community, which received a double column write up the next day in the *New Zealand Herald*. Soon, I found myself acting in a one act play by Shaw, *The Fascinating Foundling*, in the Orientation week celebrations. "A foolish affair," I told my parents, "but quite fun."

The College provided training for secondary school teachers throughout New Zealand, so we met graduates from Wellington, Christchurch and Dunedin as well as Auckland. The leading lecturer was Amarilda Gorrie, an Honours History and Geography graduate, who had behind her a long and illustrious career in the state schools of New Zealand. She was at the height of her career, and taught us how to plan our lessons and use a blackboard. She was also creative and set up role playing exercises to practise discussions with discontented parents about their children. She set essays for us to write on the history and changing philosophy of our chosen profession. Both Miss Gorrie and Mr Martin, the Principal of the College had a very positive approach to their task and inspired in us an enthusiastic attitude.

I liked Miss Gorrie. She asked us to write an essay on the subject of "Why should Tommy study History," "Tommy" being an average and typical 13 year old at a local state secondary school. I decided to put some effort into what I thought was a good question, so I wrote a play about it, which brought in new characters, such as Mrs Jones, Tom's mother; "about 35, who keeps a clean house, and belongs to the young mother's club at the local Anglican Church. She dresses well and has some social aspirations."

Tom Jones, the fictional father, had acquired the house after serving in World War II. But he continued to rent instead of buying it, "as he feels, quite rightly, that his country owes him something." Until the great strike of 1951, he was a member of the Waterside Workers' Union. Then, when he was de-registered, he went into partnership with an ex-serviceman friend. They bought a truck and started a carrying business. He had done very well, and bought his mate out. At the time my play was set, he owns four trucks and rents a small suburban office, where he can wear his tie and conduct his business. The fourth character was me, Tom's history teacher, and the opening scene was a classroom in the school, at 3.15 pm, where parents were able to discuss their children's problems with their teachers, when school was over for the day. Mr Jones wanted Tom to become a plumber, as they were able to earn a pound an hour.

My character asks Mrs Jones if I can come round in the evening to continue the discussion. Scene 2 is placed in the sitting room at the Jones's at 8 pm, and enables Mr Jones to put his oar in. I make a rather long speech about the educational value of historical understanding from which to endure the present and improve the future. Miss Gorrie gave me the third straight A of my student career.

Until I passed my exams in November 1957, I had been content to live one day at a time. With a guarantee of free shelter, and a salary of £515 a year as a trainee teacher, I felt some degree of financial security. For the first time in my life, I could afford to look ahead. With Carmel on the same payroll, we began to feel confidence in our future together, and early in 1957, strangely enough, I began to try and interest her in sailing. I had spotted a very small, and rather ancient sailing vessel for sale at the Akarana Yacht Club. I also convinced myself that adding a boat to my responsibilities would not compromise my chances of academic success. I began to consider the possibility that we would soon be leaving New Zealand, and I wanted to make sure that I took the opportunity to cruise the Hauraki Gulf while I was there. And I'm glad I did.

The vessel was a Mullet boat, one of a unique class of small yachts, descended from the commercial fishing craft of the Hauraki Gulf. But this one was only fifteen feet overall with a bowsprit which extended another four feet from her bow. She was gaff rigged, with no engine. Though short, she was also beamy, at six feet, and able to carry a large sail area, which included a spinnaker. Her main boom extended beyond the transom by about two feet. Like her sisters, the Cat Boats of New England, she had a large open cockpit, with stowage lockers on each side, and a small cabin with sufficient floor space on each side of the centre case, and under the side decks for one person in a sleeping bag on each side.

We named her *Grendel*, because of our Middle English studies of Beowulf, and we and our friends cruised the Hauraki Gulf in her for several memorable summer holidays and weekends. Ten years later, boats of this size and character were used as the inspiration for the plywood trailer-sailers designed by Richard Hartley and others, and enjoyed world-wide popularity. *Grendel* was much heavier, being built upside down over moulds with two sets of quarter inch Kauri diagonal planking and one fore and aft, but with no ribs. Her side decks, foredeck and the small after deck were also Kauri, coated with canvas,

Grendel in the Tamaki River.

and then painted. Mast and spars were of Oregon pine, and she had ancient canvas sails which I painted on both sides with the mixture used on Thames barges. This consisted of equal quantities of red and yellow ochre, mixed into a liquid made of kerosene, linseed oil, and hot beeswax to prevent rot, resulting in a Thames barge tan colour. I thought that would remove the necessity for sail covers. It meant I could sail off the mooring without first having to put the sails on. The spinnaker was left white.

Grendel drew about fourteen inches without her centreboard or rudder, and three feet with the centreboard down. She was moored in a shallow area of Okahu Bay, away from the deep keelers and larger vessels. After some discussion with her owner, we bought her with her mooring and a small plywood dinghy, that we used to row out to the mooring and tow behind us when we went cruising. We were given a receipt, dated 21 August 1957, for a total of £70, paid in one sum of £50, followed by another of £20 later.

It was early spring, and we began to go for day sails for an hour or two and had an early evening meal cooked on a primus stove. Usually we took another student friend with us, either Adrian Wilson, or Richard Mulgan, who was destined to become a Professor of Classics at the University of Otago at Dunedin, and was the son of John Mulgan, the author of *Man Alone* (1939), regarded to be *the* "Great New Zealand Novel." Adrian was also destined to have a successful career. She was awarded a PhD at the University of Sydney, where she went on to teach English literature.

As we grew more confident, we sailed for longer, and started to plan a summer cruise. Our agreement, to take either Adrian or Richard with us satisfied the parental protocols of the 1950s for "chaperones." Neither of them minded. I wrote about one of our expeditions to my parents:

Carmel says she told you about the last time we went out. It was rather rough, but she behaved very well indeed. [I meant the boat, not the girl, but she was alright too.] *In light weather she is fast enough. A full sail breeze and a fair wind, so you can use the spinnaker, and she does about six knots.*

… Strange to say, Carmel, who was never an outdoor girl at all, likes sailing as much as I do. She gets excited the night before we're going out and can't sleep well for fear there'll be a gale and we won't be able to go. Even when it was rough, and we ended up exhausted and soaked to the skin, she said she enjoyed it very much.

A week later, Carmel gave my parents a glimpse of her own perspective of my obsession:

I'm sorry to spend so much time on these yachting details, but yachting does seem to occupy most of our attention now. John would be perfectly happy to do nothing else, I think. He goes out to Okahu Bay at least three times a week to look at the boat, tidy it up, and give it all the loving care possible… I've never seen such devotion as John has for boats. His clothes and even his motor bike are generally falling to pieces but he hardly notices as long as Grendel is in good order… As you see, I'm beginning to share the passion. It seems to be one of the things you do with unbounded enthusiasm, or not at all. [She went on to tell them about the cuts and bruises from yesterday's expedition]... *but I find I am one of the enthusiastic ones.*

On 18 December she wrote again, probably thinking that she may have increased, rather than reduced their anxiety:

I expect John has written to you about his plans now that he has his degree. He is very keen on his history papers and thesis. I hope a completely full-time year with no worries will enable him to do as well as he can because I am sure he has set his heart on nothing but the best... I think he would have passed German a good deal more easily than Greek, but once he had decided on a classical language, nothing would change his mind... Greek has given John some experience of a subject that needs more mechanical discipline than his [other] subjects, and he needs a lot of that, if he is to do as well as he could... Anyone as ambitious as John will have to be right up with the best, but this year of training college in fairly comfortable circumstances has given him a breathing space and time to get his ideas in order. I hope it will be long enough.

Grendel continued to play a central role in our lives for two years, and records have survived of three unforgettable cruises, first, in October 1957, after which Carmel wrote to my mother:

I find, contrary to my expectation, that I like it too, though I wonder why when we get home wet through, bruised, sunburnt and exhausted. John has a fixed idea that all New Zealanders spend every moment from early childhood doing energetic things like hiking, sailing, ski-ing and mountain climbing. I have never been at all energetic, and am convinced that it's rather English girls who enjoy strenuous sports, but it's easier to become an outdoor girl myself than to convince John, and anyway I certainly enjoy sailing in spite of the rough weather we have encountered so far. We are going for a week's cruise to various islands around the Gulf after our exams, just three of us, John, and I and a friend of ours, Richard Mulgan, who has come sailing with us on most of our trips.

I wrote, in January 1958 about a cruise in the Christmas holidays when Richard was wanted at his home with his parents and we took Adrian Wilson with us to avoid any suspicion of wrong-doing, first to Waiheke Island, then to the Wade River, then Kawau Island, after sheltering from a gale in Shakespeare's Bay, then back to Auckland: "We were all encrusted to the eyes with salt, too tired to take anything ashore except ourselves. We went to Adrian's house and cooked a huge meal and drank a bottle of wine. Then we slept a little, drank coffee, had baths and little by little, made a most enjoyable recovery."

The cruise which was to be our last was in the Easter holidays in 1958. This time both Adrian and Richard came as well. The girls slept on the floor on either side of the cabin and Richard and I kept as dry as we could in the open cockpit. Carmel wrote about it in a nostalgic spirit, as she contemplated the end of a period of relative irresponsibility, and the hard work that lay ahead:

I think I enjoyed it more than the others, perhaps because it was short, and because it seemed so final; a last fling before some really hard work. Unfortunately it was so lovely that now, more than a week later, I still haven't resigned myself to work again, and this is not a usual trouble of mine. John is very single-minded and has had no difficulty in getting down to work—in fact although the holiday was his idea, I think he enjoyed it less than the rest of us because he is so keen to get on with his history... It is hard to describe the effect those four days had. The weather was rather good. There is something about fine days in Autumn that makes me feel rather sad—I get a desperate feeling that it will never be like this again, that so much of the year is too cold or too hot, and that there is something special about the quiet sunny days and grey evenings. We spent a lot of time sailing in the evening. Waiheke is very deserted at a time like Easter. Even on the island we were left quite to ourselves, and on the sea we felt almost like the Ancient Mariner, far removed from the rest of the world... All this must sound very odd to you... However, I can't write poetry. To hear me and Adrian and Richard regretting that our holiday is over you would think we were all on the brink of middle age, looking back on a sadly wasted youth, whereas all that has actually happened is that we had a wonderful time and got on very well with each other, and now find it a bit lonely, and a bit difficult to start working again at something that each of us has to do alone. The most enjoyable thing about sailing and all sharing the work at a "Bach"[1] is that no-one has to do anything alone. Although John has to take all the responsibility for our safety, and even smaller things like our course and our living, and so on, by himself; another reason why he is almost glad that the holiday is over, though he did enjoy it very much.

My take on the experience was different, but complementary:

Spent Saturday and Sunday at Waiheke, in a shack, then sailed at 10 pm on the Sunday night for the Wade [River]. *It was the most beautiful moonlit night, with hardly any wind. Got into the Wade after 20 hours of drifting, tacking, being carried backwards by the tide, anchoring and waiting for it to turn. Towing in the dinghy, sleeping and drinking coffee and singing, and then, in the morning, sailing with a good fresh breeze on our quarter, for the last 5 miles or so of our voyage.*

Just as I finished writing this paragraph, over sixty years later, I received an email from Adrian, who has written from time to time ever since:

I... was remembering those sailing trips when I was meant to be chaperone. That was a joke wasn't it? I was remembering those libations we used to make to Poseidon and goodness knows who else. It was wonderful. That love affair of you and Carmel was very special. Trying to be as naughty as we could manage we were very sweet and innocent... I was thinking of that sweet little boat of yours. We all became quite good sailors with your guidance, and it remained the only sport I ever identified with.

The next year was our last in New Zealand, and we sold *Grendel* on to a close student friend, Laurie Lambert, who was to marry Keith Sinclair's younger brother, Roy. He became a doctor in Sydney, and a lifelong friend. Living in a fifteen foot boat with Adrian and Richard was a good exercise in social compatibility. For me and Carmel, sailing had become a part of our lives. It gave us confidence in each other and optimism about our marriage and our future.

---

1   The New Zealand word for a holiday shack.

Our last years in New Zealand were crowded with ambition as well as romance. In March 1958 we were all allocated three weeks of practical teaching experience, and I found myself in front of a rowdy class of twelve and thirteen year olds, to whom I taught English and History, at Auckland Grammar School. I prepared each lesson carefully, but was easily distracted by boys who found out ways of leading me astray, and into political debate, or stories about my experience in the navy, or on the stage. Classes were large, about thirty-five boys. I soon found that it was not difficult to keep them interested in subjects I knew something about, or points of view that I was keen to defend. I gave detailed answers to questions which led to more questions. But I was lucky. Keeping order in class was never a problem. I wrote to tell my parents:

I quite enjoy teaching, but I'm sure I will be a much better lecturer. I've kept the children interested and that seems to me to be half the battle as far as discipline is concerned. You have to be more interesting than eating toffee or talking, or throwing paper or reading comics. If you can be, it's easy.

I was clearly happy to have gained confidence after weathering the kind of testing challenge that was to be expected at a big city school, but the lessons I had learnt did enable me to enjoy all the teaching at different levels, and of different subjects, that I have ever done.

My next practical teaching experience was in the totally different context of a country school at Rawene, over two hundred kilometres and several hours by train from Auckland, on the shores of Hokianga harbour, in the far north west of the North Auckland Peninsula. I was the guest of Mr Reid, one of the teachers, and his family, and he gave me an insight into this intriguing bicultural frontier community.

This was the fulfilment of one of my long standing ambitions. I wrote a letter to tell my parents that "… when I first looked at NZ on the map, and thought of coming here, I hoped there would be a forest that I would go to on the Hokianga Harbour. Well it's taken some time to get here." My failure to be posted to a Kauri forest in this part of the world was one of the main reasons why I left the Forest Service in 1952. Russell (Kororareka), in the Bay of Islands on the other (eastern) side of the peninsula was where the earliest sustained contacts had been made between Maori and Pakehas in the 1820s. It was where whalers, merchants, missionaries and escaping convicts from Sydney formed one of the most flourishing "Beach Cities" in the south Pacific.[2] Wooden ships from many countries came to the Bay of Islands because of the supplies of Kauri timber that grew in the area. Russell, with its resident shipwrights and timber supplies, became a favourite port of refreshment. It was the first Capital of New Zealand after the Treaty of Waitangi of 1840

---

2   The others were Honolulu, Papeete, and Levuka. See Ralston, Caroline, *Grass Huts and Warehouses: Pacific Beach communities in the 19th Century*, University Press of Hawaii, Honolulu, 1978. Caroline was one of the first Honours History students to choose my optional course on the Pacific Islands at the University of Adelaide. I was very fortunate to have her. This, her first book was a development of her ANU PhD thesis.

which, unlike the *Terra Nullius* assumption by the British in Australia, recognised the ownership by the Maori people of their own homeland. "Since the Capital was moved to Auckland in 1842," I told my parents, "it has been waiting for civilisation to spread in its direction, but it hasn't got here yet."

Nearly all the students of Rawene School were Maori. I found that the Pakeha staff's expectations of them were lower than their expectations of students in city schools. This struck me as a somewhat racist perception. I told my parents that "History and Geography are confused into a wishy washy thing called Social Studies. Once past the stage of learning tables, prospective mathematicians are whisked off and taught commercial practice if they are girls, and woodwork if they are boys." The Headmaster believed that clever, academically minded students should be sent away from the district as early as possible, as he had done with his own children. I attempted to assess their real abilities by setting exactly the same questions that arose from what I taught them, as I had done at Auckland Grammar, after the same amount of teaching, and found little or no difference in their ability. Not that I considered this to be a scientific proof of anything. What it did do was enable me to tell the students of Rawene School that in my opinion, they were just as able as city kids to achieve the good marks they would need to enter University, which would give them a wider choice of employment.

When it came to choices between attending school or Maori cultural priorities, culture trumped school attendance by a large margin. The maintenance of the local Maori cemetery at nearby *Omania* required the labour of the whole community, including children. This, in turn, required the preparation of a large quantity of food. The food preparation task was given to a team of women, who spent most of a day cutting up the meat of a medium sized cow and making a delicious stew with it in a 500 gallon rain tank, and simmering it on an open fire for several hours. The second week I was at Rawene school, a significant Maori Elder died, and preparations were made for a funeral, at which the presence of regional as well as local Maori aristocracy was expected. This made it necessary to repeat the culinary activity of the previous weekend, together with a traditional Hangi, in which a large pig was cooked, followed by a solemn funeral service and a wake. School children suffered considerably from lack of sleep and stayed home the following Monday. But they took pride in their cultural heritage, as I had done in the North Riding of Yorkshire.

I heard that the New Zealand Players were about to perform Shakespeare's *Merchant of Venice* in Whangarei, about 50 miles away, the largest town in Northland, so I asked to be allowed to run my class through the play in the classroom, and then take them to see it, which meant hiring a bus. The Headmaster was good enough to allow me to spend my English lessons discussing and reading the play, and the broader issues of Tudor history, the Reformation, and racial prejudice throughout the world. Then I took them to the play. For nearly all of them, it was their first experience of live theatre. They were spellbound and I was delighted with the whole thing. I began to wish I'd chosen the process of acculturation in the period before the Treaty of Waitangi as a thesis topic. It was more interesting than the politics of Auckland Province in the 1870s.

The last weekend I was there I was invited by one of my fellow training college students, Trixie McGowen to spend the weekend with her family. Her home was at Paihia, just across the Bay of Islands from Russell. Trixie and I sailed over to Russell in the family sailing dinghy, which was a big bonus for me. The Bay of Islands was the most beautiful place I had ever seen, and I looked forward to doing as much fieldwork as possible. I told my parents:

Northland is a wonderful place. I used to look at it on the map. I think it's really why I came here, [to New Zealand] *and now I'm getting really absorbed in it. I should be able to do a really good thesis on it and then come with Carmel to Oxford and do another... Something remote and obscure, lost in the dark ages. Carmel can translate the Latin manuscripts. She will do a thesis on comparative Greek and Polynesian mythology. And we will be very famous. We think we had better get married next summer.*

Carmel was thinking the same, and was feeling lonely. Her parents insisted on us waiting two years before we married. She suggested that we should marry as soon as possible and move into Old Man's House. The tapu on co-habitation would be lifted automatically if we were married. She began to write strong, intimate love letters:

Of course we simply couldn't have any children, but we could buy some Catholic books on birth control, and if that wasn't good enough we'd just have to use the other sort... I wouldn't care if I never went to Oxford anyway. It might be better if just you did. I could get a job as a school teacher and support you in comfort. I think we should insist on one year... This will have to be my last letter as it probably won't arrive til Thursday, and I wouldn't like to have one of our letters floating around un-claimed... I am delighted to be able to tell you that you are not about to become a Father... I am missing you most desperately. I feel like curling up and dying, for a week and three days. I can't think why we shouldn't just die with happiness.

Back at the Teachers' Training College, drama was considered to be a valuable opportunity to develop confidence, elocution, and stage or classroom presence, and it was customary for each annual intake of students to produce a play or musical for public performance. In spite of my decision to abandon my theatrical ambitions, this was something I could not resist. At the end of the first term, we decided to perform John Gay's *Beggar's Opera*. I auditioned, and was given the leading part of Macheath, the Highwayman hero. A week later, the student who had been chosen to be the producer withdrew for health reasons, and I was asked to fill the gap as well as perform the leading role. Laurence Olivier's film had been shown recently on New Zealand cinema screens, and it was, I thought, a timely challenge. Laurence Olivier was my role model, and his performance inspired me. We formed an orchestra, a stage crew, and everyone had a part, or helped out with costume making, scene shifting, or playing a musical instrument in the orchestra. I decided that we should include the audience in the performance as much as we could, and we built an apron stage so that the show could go on while the stage behind the proscenium was prepared for the next scene, and we could maintain the dramatic momentum. I re-wrote parts of Gay's script, and arranged for the Beggar/Town Crier, whose part was acted by Alan Ward, from Wellington, to open the show as soon as the audience was seated by walking in at the back door and along the whole length of the auditorium. He gave his prologue speech after climbing up from the stalls and onto the apron stage. He was to succeed, many years later, in becoming the Professor of History and Head of department at the University of Newcastle, New South Wales.

Like most amateur productions, ours was far from perfect. The first night was a fast-moving show. There was a tricky moment when someone forgot his lines and we had to think very quickly and *ad lib*, for the scene to make sense, but we flattered ourselves that no-one could have noticed, and we had all stayed in character and bluffed our way through it. We had full houses on each night, and we improved continuously. On the third night we really did manage to make the audience suspend their disbelief and feel part of the show. They booed the villains, really did think I was going to be hanged, and applauded when the Beggar announced my reprieve. Carmel did not want to be in the show, and told my mother that, "It occupied most of his time and all his interest in the last few weeks. It was a wonderful success." Towards the end of the year I was awarded "College Honours," a customary prize for "non-athletic achievements." I told Molly about it. "They gave me an award for general helpfulness — mainly for producing the Beggar's Opera."

Carmel must have been aware of the anxiety that this news might cause in the minds of my parents, and soon after *The Beggar's Opera* was over, she wrote them a supportive letter:

> *You would be very pleased if you could see how John is working. He has such terrific energy when he is really interested in anything, but up til now he has had such wide interests that I was afraid he wouldn't do himself justice in his exams, for wide interests are very good in themselves, but I think they have to be set aside for a while to do really well in*

Me as Macheath, behind bars in John Gay's *The Beggar's Opera*.

an honours degree. John has reached that conclusion and is working very whole-heartedly. He is enjoying it too, as he does all the things that he does wholeheartedly.

More support came from Keith Sinclair, my thesis supervisor, who told me that on my present showing, I would earn good Second Class Honours for my exam papers. My thesis, for which I had already written some short drafts, promised to be good enough, he thought, to pull me up to a First. He advised me to prioritise working like mad at the exam papers for the time being. He said that in previous years I had shown originality, but not sufficient knowledge, which was something that could be rectified. At the end of my latest essay he wrote, "Under the layers of silt I descry first class potential. But you will have to dig for it."

The annual inter-university tournament was held in September that year, and I had enough self-discipline to keep out of it, and not do any more stage work. But Carmel and I did decide to go to the ball at the end of the week, which was a big item on the social calendar. We formed a party which included our friends and classmates, Verity and Neill Maidment, who were the son and daughter of Kenneth Maidment, the Vice Chancellor of Auckland University and this led to a family conversation about Oxford.

Maidment had been a Classics Don and a Fellow of Merton College. He was also aware of our ambitions and of the contrasting levels of our past academic achievement. He offered to read *The Odyssey* with Carmel, and clearly took her success in obtaining a Commonwealth Scholarship for granted. As for me, with my less than brilliant career, he recommended an application for a Rhodes Scholarship: "There is only one applicant this year," said he, "And all they want is someone who is somewhat more than usually alive, and takes an interest in life. Put your name down!"

Maidment said that, as a University of Auckland MA graduate, I would be eligible in Oxford for either a second BA with Honours, or a PhD of some kind. He advised another BA, saying it would be a better education, and equally useful in obtaining a University lectureship. In those days, he was probably right. He thought I should try to join "a rich college like Magdalene or Merton, not a poor college like Balliol," as the meals would be better. We should go to separate colleges during term time, he thought, rather than go to St Catherine's Society,[3] and live in digs, as some married students were in the habit of doing.

We thought his advice was well meant but quaint, in view of the unlikelihood of me having a choice. Carmel would have one, and was awarded a Commonwealth Post-graduate scholarship. She applied successfully for a place at St Anne's, which was a women's college in those days, and obtained one without difficulty, with her First Class Honours in Classics in December 1957. She decided to enrol in a Bachelor of Philosophy course, which meant writing a textual analysis thesis on Greek Drama. She was able to postpone her entry until 1959 to allow time for me to enter Oxford as well. That was a more complicated process.

---

3   Now St Catherine's co-educational College.

My Auckland MA consisted of four exam papers and a thesis. The exam subjects were: The constitutional history of England 1485–1939; Seventeenth Century England; Europe in the twelfth and thirteenth centuries; and New Zealand, Australia and the Pacific. As explained earlier, I eventually settled on a History of the Province of Auckland in the 1870s as the subject of my thesis, and I had been working on it whenever opportunities arose since the middle of 1957. I started by reading newspapers in order to absorb the late nineteenth century atmosphere of the city, including the cesspools, and the limited community development, which led one contemporary writer to described the people of Auckland as:

... a very sentimental mob, always getting into a state of passionate excitement... It reads newspapers and listens to orators. Its idols are rag, bone, and bottle merchants, gentlemen who have "been in trouble on the other side" [ie. the other side of the Tasman Sea]*, and anyone who howls very loud and looks very dirty. It does not object to wealth so long as it has been earned by "the sweat of the brow," and its possessors have taken no steps to remove the proofs. These are the people who used to throw stones and mud at Sir George Grey in the streets.*[4]

Auckland Province was of special interest for me because of its differences from the planned settlements of the South, which were inspired by the ideas of Colonial reformers such as Gibbon Wakefield, who aspired to create an idealised version of pre-industrial English society in the Antipodes. Auckland, in contrast, was not planned at all. It had just grown up around the enormous natural Waitemata Harbour, which opened to the Pacific Ocean to the north, and on the isthmus that separated it from the Manukau harbour and the Tasman Sea to the south. Unlike the foundation cities of the South Island, like Christchurch and Dunedin, and Wellington in the North Island, Auckland was largely settled from Sydney rather than directly from England. Long before the crossing of the Blue Mountains in New South Wales, and the consequent development of an economy based on wool, the new colony of New South Wales had become dependent on whaling, the pork trade with Tahiti, and a sealskin trade based on the Bass Strait and Macquarie Island. Later on, I was to write my first book, *Australia's Pacific Frontier*[5] which emphasised the comparative expediency of commercial expansion, religious conquest and white settlement in the South Seas, when compared to the Australian interior, for the first thirty years of Australian settlement. By the middle of the nineteenth century, the Bay of Islands and the Waitemata had become commercial, religious and settlement outposts of New South Wales, exporting to Sydney flax for sails, Kauri timber for boat building, sealskins for the European and Chinese markets via Sydney and

---

4   From the *Timaru Herald, cit Southern Cross*, an Auckland paper, 6 October 1874. Sir George Grey had been the Governor of New Zealand from 1845 to 1853, and 1861 to 1868. In 1874, when he had become a commoner, he was elected as Superintendent of the Auckland Province, the leading opponent of abolishing Provincial Government, and a champion of an egalitarian society.

5   *Australia's Pacific Frontier: Economic and cultural expansion into the Pacific, 1795-1885*, Cassell Australia, 1967.

England, and importing hardware, nails, tools, firearms and liquor. Trade led to erratic occupation by missionaries, and small settlers. After the Treaty of Waitangi, signed on 6 February 1840 by chiefly representatives of tribal communities from both Islands, the capital was moved to the site of Auckland, on a narrow isthmus between two large natural harbours. An additional reason for making Auckland the colonial Capital was that it was located between two areas, Northland and the Waikato, in which Maoris were much more numerous than anywhere else in New Zealand. Early speculators, and shipyards were soon followed by the barracks, banks, churches, and eventually the wooden dwellings, pubs, wharves, and government offices of a colonial capital city.

I was fascinated by the challenge of culture contact history in early Northland, but soon began to realise that I lacked the background in anthropology that would be needed. I also lacked any knowledge of the Maori language. I decided that I did not have time to solve these problems in time to complete a thesis good enough to get me to Oxford within the next two years.

Instead, I accepted the task of contributing to Professor Rutherford's aim of using a team of MA students over a period of years, to research and write the history and politics of the Auckland Province from 1860 to 1875. Other students had already dealt with the earlier years, before 1870, leaving to me the last period leading up to abolition of the Provincial system of Government in 1875. I was also attracted by the impact of the return of Sir George Grey, who had been an early Governor of New Zealand, but stood for election as President of the Auckland Provincial Council, not because of support from the political class of New Zealand, but from the small settlers of remote electorates, and the working class suburbs and slums of Auckland itself.

Following Keith Sinclair's advice, I worked as hard as I could on the course leading to my examinations, and this included my reading of the then recently published *The Structure of Politics at the accession of George 111.*[6] Sir Lewis Namier, the author of this new interpretation of the nature of politics, looked beyond the theory of party ideology as the basic force behind political activity, and into the local loyalties and vested interests of members of Parliament.

Here, I thought, was an idea that could be used to discover the motivation behind the voting patterns of the Auckland Provincial Council during my chosen five years, 1870–1875. I heard at this point, that many of the primary sources had been accidently burnt in 1955, but what remained of the Provincial Council's records were now in the National Archives in Wellington. These included personal letters and papers of a series of several leading political characters, journals of the Provincial Council and "Assessment Rolls." The last consisted of the details of the ownership, location and tax value of every property occupied by those qualified to vote in Provincial Government elections. No historian had seen or used these records in the past. Here was a chance to do real primary research on a virgin subject,

---

6   By Sir Lewis Namier, McMillan, London, 1957.

using new evidence. I decided to go for it. It was, I thought, as exciting as discovering England's Domesday Book.

The trouble was that these records were stored in Wellington, not Auckland, and I would have to do a lot of travelling, find accommodation in Wellington, and take as long as I needed to do what would be have to be done. It would take away time that I would need to achieve good marks for my exams in Auckland, but I decided to do it all the same. It meant I would have to read through every debate in the provincial Council for four years, analyse every vote that was recorded, and examine the assessment rolls of every constituency, rural and urban, so that I could relate the motivation of members to the political issues of the day as they impacted on the constituencies, and the personal interests of the politicians themselves. How much easier and quicker it would have been if personal computers had been invented. They weren't, and I had to draw enormous folded charts to provide evidence to support my arguments. I set off hitchhiking to Wellington early in December 1958 on what proved to be the first of several journeys, some hitchhiking and others on my motor bike.

I arrived safely, after the first journey, and I wrote to Carmel to let her know how lucky I was:

I had a gruesome hitch-hike down here… One lift I had was with a wife and baby from Tasmania, with a husband from [Mainland] *Australia, who was dead drunk. I didn't realise he was until I got in. He chucked the bottles out of the window as we went along. This was from Taupo. I asked his wife, who kept on abusing him, if perhaps he was tired, and might he like a rest while I drove?*

In spite of the tuition I had from Murray Francis, I still had no license to drive a car, but I was confident that if she could persuade her husband to let me take the wheel, our chances of cheating death would be improved:

Luckily he agreed, instead of getting stroppy. It was quite extraordinary. Him singing "Galway Bay," and belching at the end of each line, calling his little boy a fucking bastard, and his wife other things, and changing from beer to a foul sweet wine which he spilt, and which made a sickly smell. Outside it rained so hard that I couldn't see the road, and for quite long stretches we went slowly along with the water up to the wheel caps. Then, on the Desert Road we were in the clouds, and it didn't rain so much, but I couldn't see any better… I drove them all the way to Taihape, and once I got used to the gears I went quite well and we averaged a good speed.

The people at the National Archives were very helpful, but for their own good reasons explained that they could not lend the Provincial documents of Auckland to the Auckland public library, even for me. So I soon conceived an idea of the enormous task that lay ahead of me. It was too early even for photocopying. I also visited the University of New Zealand office, to enquire about applying for scholarships to go to Oxford. The news was not good. In spite of Maidment's optimism, I was told that while I might be able to earn a place in an Oxford College on the basis of my exam marks, I would not be eligible for a Rhodes Scholarship until I had finished my MA thesis, which I had only just started working on. Other scholarships, such as Unilever and the British Council would have the same requirements. "So that is a nuisance," I told Carmel. "At least it's not really. Let's stay here another year… and in the meantime I'll do a really good thesis. There is no point in me staying here longer than a week so I'll hitch back next Saturday."

At this point, our future was uncertain. The only thing we could be certain about was that we loved each other, so we decided to marry to reduce the areas of anxiety in our lives. Then we would think about staying in New Zealand or trying to enter Oxford. Carmel's parents were also tired of uncertainty and seemed at last to be relieved at our decision. It was a small inexpensive and private ceremony. My best man was one of our best friends, Vincent O'Sullivan, who later became Poet Laureate of New Zealand and one of New Zealand's leading novelists.

Carmel's parents and her sister Margaret were the only other guests, and it was a quiet ceremony, conducted by Father McHale, at Carmel's church, the Church of the Good Shepherd, Balmoral, on 26 December 1958. McHale was insistent on my consent to having our children brought up as Catholics, should my wife so desire. I was untroubled by that because Carmel promised that she would not require such an agreement. She was probably one of the earlier brides in New Zealand to suggest that we eliminate the requirement of promising obedience to her husband, and I fully supported her.

We could not afford the expense of a honeymoon. At that time, I was working as a residential tutor at Dilworth School. When we married, I left Dilworth and we rented a small flat. Almost immediately, much to my surprise, Mr W H Cooper, the Headmaster of Auckland Grammar school knocked on our door and offered me a temporary job teaching History to his sixth form. This made it possible for the first time in our lives to save money for fares to England.

My renewed interest in research, as opposed to essays and exams, made me lean towards taking Carmel at her word about waiting until I had finished my degree before

Left: Carmel and I on our wedding day.

Below: Carmel and Stephen, 1961.

attempting to enter Oxford, but the strain of six years of student life without much to show for it proved to be a stronger force. Bill Mandle thought there was little to be lost by making an early application for a place in an Oxford College, on the grounds that if I was not successful I could apply again when I had finished my thesis, the next year, possibly with better results. He advised me to try St Catherine's Society, an organisation that was rapidly moving towards becoming a new college under the formidable leadership of Alan Bullock, who then carried the title of "Censor" of St Catherine's Society. In 1964, he became "Master" of St Catherine's, which has now become a large, co-educational, and very successful college.

Bill wrote references for me, as I applied for various scholarships, and on 26 October 1958, he asked Professor Rutherford to write another reference as well. I suspect it was a joint Mandle/Rutherford composition, which Bill copied to me, probably in hope that I would live up to it. It started with some exaggeration of my abilities, but made me feel optimistic:

Mr Young is completing his MA honours course in History. Intellectually he is good, with touches of brilliance, on a stable foundation of sound knowledge. He has a capacity for effective industry, and has applied it to good advantage. [Then came the realism.] *I cannot with certainty predict a first class degree for him, but he will at least take a high 2nd class honours.* [Then came the extras expected from applicants for a Rhodes scholarship]. *He is a young man of many attributes, good-looking; athletic; well spoken; a pleasant, cheerful personality, and an amateur actor of distinct promise. He combines a sense of responsibility with a nice sense of humour, and has enough natural self assurance to make him a natural leader.*

We thought that being married, we should not follow Maidment's advice and live in separate colleges. I delayed application for a place at St Catherine's for several months because I hoped to have some kind of financial support lined up before we booked our passages to England. Scholarships were out of the question until I completed my thesis, but I was advised by Bill to apply on the strength of my exam results, and references. "Getting a place is the first step," he told me, "without that you won't get anywhere." So I applied, and at the beginning of June 1959 I received an offer of a place at St Catherine's.

Dear Mr Young, We should be glad to offer you a place here to read History for the BA degree, your course beginning in October 1959. I believe your degree would entitle you to senior status.

This gave me two choices. I could, if I wished, enrol for a Post-graduate course, but the Dean, F C Horwood advised me that a good Oxford Honours degree would be at least as useful to me as a PhD, if I was thinking of a career as a university lecturer. He went on to say that my status entitled me "to take only two years to complete your course, but I think we would like you to take three years. Will you let me know what you think of that proposition? "

I didn't think it would be wise to reject his advice in case he changed his mind about offering me a place at all, so I agreed, still not knowing whether I would have the money to complete another three years as a student. Carmel thought I should take the three year option. My Auckland career had been relatively sketchy, as I had only started to show some promise in my third year, and I still lacked depth in my education. There would be holiday jobs for me, she thought, and the two of us could live cheaply on her scholarship if we put our minds to it. We still had time to save up some money, thanks to the job at Auckland Grammar school, followed by several summer months working as a postman again. On 10 June 1959, F C Horwood acknowledged my acceptance of a place at St Catherine's, and my agreement to spend three years over the BA. He told me that: "Your degree at Auckland exempts you from the first public examinations… Your Tutor will be Dr G A Holmes, and I am passing your letter on to him so that he can send you his advice on preliminary reading."

In the meantime my father was doing his best to find some supporting finance. He discovered that there was even a scholarship for "the sons of clergy" and also approached the Bradford County Council to find out if, as a British subject, with a place at St Catherine's, I was eligible for a "County Grant." He was told that an application form would be sent to me, to be filled in and returned, and when I arrived in England, I would have to present myself for an interview. "Take care of each other," he wrote, "and be not anxious for the morrow."

If I did obtain a County Grant, we could both concentrate on our studies. If I didn't, we told ourselves, I had completed my course at Auckland Teachers' Training College and I had a BA degree, with an Honours degree in the pipeline, so we were confident that I could find a job as a secondary school teacher, somewhere around Oxford, and Carmel could concentrate on her post-graduate degree. The next thing to do was therefore to book passages in time to reach England before the beginning of the Michaelmas term in October. The New Zealand Shipping line was not encouraging; and neither was Shaw Saville. But we discovered that there was a Dutch ship, *Johan Van Oldenbarnevelt*, built for the passage from Holland to the "Dutch East Indies" and launched in 1929. In 1959 she was on her last voyage as a migrant ship to Australia from Holland, and was to return to Holland for a major overhaul, via New Zealand, Tahiti, the Panama Canal, Miami, Bermuda and Southampton. The voyage would take four weeks.

Fortunately for us, the ship was to arrive three weeks before the start of the Oxford academic year, and would be leaving Auckland late in July. We decided that we could afford a cabin for two, instead of the dormitory accommodation typical of migrant ships, and left in high spirits, leaving Carmel's parents and sister holding the streamers on the wharf, until they broke to the familiar strains of Po Atarua, sung by a thousand voices of family members waiting on the wharf for our return.

We soon discovered that the ship was full of students, mostly from Australia, heading, like ourselves for Universities in Britain or Europe, to arrive at the beginning of the northern hemisphere academic year. We quickly made friends with many of them, and began to perform extracts from university revues of the past.

No-one had been before to our first stop, Tahiti, with its jagged mountain peaks, black sands, and its then surviving Polynesian culture. The harbour was full of ocean voyaging yachts from Europe and the United States, but as yet no airliners. Buildings were small, some built of traditional materials and in Polynesian style. We joined a group of other young people and hired a big taxi to go round the largest part of the Island, stopping at small coastal villages and beaches. It was a painfully inadequate introduction to this famous island which had raised fundamental social, moral and political questions in the minds of Rousseau, Voltaire, and many of their contemporaries and had been a stimulant of Europe's Age of Enlightenment.[7] But it was an experience that, after Pitcairn Island and New Zealand, planted a seed in my mind that put the South Pacific firmly on my intellectual agenda for the rest of my life.

The next leg was a breezy passage with *Johan* travelling at seventeen knots into the similar speed of the South East trade wind to Panama. With Carmel at my side, I felt no interest in the night life of Panama City, but it gave me a sense of victory to be on the return path through the locks and lakes of this engineering marvel, with much better prospects than I had taken with me going from the Caribbean to the Pacific in 1952. I had begun to make up for my feckless ignorance when I left school, and six years later, I had a lot more self-confidence and a chance, at least, of making up for my lack of experience and direction in what many people thought to be the best university in the world. If only I could be sure though.

Miami was a bus-ride away from the docks and little about it was unexpected, as New Zealand was already showing the effects of the global post-war cultural invasion of the United States. There were no surprises, just the road traffic, mini skyscrapers, milk bars, police, advertising and of course, the redeeming beach that we expected. It was not inspiring and did not endear me to America. It was at this point that we were told that one of the ship's famous diesel engines had broken down. For the remainder of the voyage we would be travelling at half speed, and would arrive at Southampton two weeks late.

Bermuda was off the beaten track, with a tropical colonial style of architecture. There was a yacht club, and a lot of beautiful boats. The whole place was gently relaxing, but without any historical knowledge in my head, one day was not enough to become involved. We had a good time as pure tourists, driving round the whole island in a hired car with fellow students, learning what we could. Between these stopovers, we had time to meet an unusually talented and interesting group of people, and we treasured the extra two weeks of deck tennis, sunbathing, playing water polo, and reading, completely free of stress. For the whole six weeks between Auckland and England there was nothing we could do to improve our life chances, except recover from a long period of continuous competitive study; so the rest of the time we slept or made love.

---

7   See Smith, Bernard, *European Vision and the South Pacific*, Clarendon Press, Oxford 1960.

From Southampton we took a train to London, then caught another from King's Cross to Bradford to introduce Carmel to my parents. We signed the vicarage visitor's book for 4 and 5 September 1959.

Carmel took an instant liking to my parents, especially my father, but found the approach to Bradford through a landscape of slag-heaps a bit depressing, as were the continuous terraces of cottages built long ago to accommodate the influx of the industrial revolution. But the vicarage itself was a big sunny house, with a sizeable back garden by English standards, and the civilised comforts of hot and cold water on tap, water closets, a telephone; the things which my mother had been denied for much of her life, and in which she now revelled. We saw the local sights, such as the home of the Brontë sisters, and I accompanied my father on his Parish walks, visiting the sick among his parishioners, and learning the local geography. We worked together on small carpentry jobs, and I noticed the loss of energy that had accompanied his ageing process since we had built *Discovery 2* together when I was ten.

An appointment was made for an interview with a councillor and staff of the Bradford County Council, in response to my request for a grant to enable me to accept the offer of a place at St Catherine's Society. I told them about my long journey from the New Zealand forest service to my incomplete Auckland University MA course in History, and explained my predicament as a part time student. I told them I had completed a teacher's training course, and was qualified for employment as a school teacher. But I also said that I had begun to write a Master's thesis and had become vitally interested in original historical research. I said that my ambition was to obtain a job in a University, which would naturally include research opportunities. An Oxford degree would be a passport to such a job, perhaps in the UK or, if not, in New Zealand. Either way, I would be able to contribute to historical knowledge and understanding, and to tertiary education.

After waiting alone and anxious for about half an hour, I was asked to return to the interview room and was told that I would be awarded a County Grant. This would enable me to meet living expenses as a full time student for three years. I felt thankful to the County Council of Bradford, and its rate-payers, for giving me this life-changing opportunity and to my father for his advocacy and his own high reputation, which must have had some influence. We boarded the train back to Oxford with extraordinary relief and gratitude. We had little time to find somewhere to live, and formalise our admission to St Anne's and St Catherine's before term began. We hadn't much choice, but were fortunate to be able to rent a small flat at 36 Victoria Road in Summertown, about half an hour's walk from the centre of Oxford; much quicker by bus or on bicycles, which we both bought immediately, and cheaply.

Mr Horwood had briefed George Holmes, my tutor, of our arrival. One of our first social experiences was an invitation to an evening meal with Holmes and his wife. That was a hospitable and welcoming occasion. We had an interesting conversation about the similarities and differences between England and New Zealand culture, and university life in both of them. George Holmes explained the relative intensity of the undergraduate experience at Oxford, which was going to be much more challenging than that of Auckland. Terms were short, and holidays were longer at Oxford, but instead of working on the wharves or delivering letters, I was expected to be reading intensively in preparation for the demanding routine of at least one essay each week, for each course I would be taking. For much of the time I would be engaged in two courses at once, which meant two essays a week. The core introductory course on the History of Britain from the Roman conquest to 1900, was divided into three terms' work. At the same time, I would also be taking a course on Political Thought, or a special subject based on close studies of primary sources such as "Secession and Slavery in the United States" or "The making of the Triple Entente." Lectures were neither compulsory, nor the main form of teaching, and were usually given by Dons who were writing books at the time, and offered lecture series based on recent research ahead of publication.

The unique feature of an Oxford education was the individual, one on one, or at most one Tutor with two students, Tutorial. I was given a subject or question, once a week, together with a reading list. Ideally, I was expected to have read the general works of the period in the previous vacation, but I was given a list of up to six books related to the chosen topic, and usually two or three articles in appropriate academic journals. Mr Holmes would suggest that, depending on my own interests, there were a number of lectures during the week that I might enjoy, or were being given by scholars whom he thought I would find interesting.

I had decided by this time that the best way to take notes as I read was to use 5" × 3" system cards, as I had learned to do for my Auckland thesis. I could then sort them for use in the order planned for the essay. I headed up each card with source details and subject headings, and made observations about what I read, or quotations as needed. I soon found that I could read and make notes for four days and take the last day to write the essay, usually of about 2,000 words. At Auckland I would have taken three weeks and might have written a first draft and then written it out again, after hopefully correcting and improving it. At Oxford, this was impossible. I soon developed the ability to think before I wrote and to write once, and that would be the only and final version. It took about twenty minutes to read 2,000 words intelligibly. That left another forty for my Tutor to make critical comments as we went along, and to discuss my work, verbally evaluate it, if I asked, and suggest improvements. When I was doing two courses the same week I had to work at weekends as well, which meant learning to write faster and to think more quickly. I used to read until the day before the tutorial, go to bed and wake at five in the morning. I would write until noon, eating breakfast on the hop, and go to my Tutorial, usually at two or three in the afternoon. Then I would go to the library and start on the next essay. I spent very little time in the Junior common room, but went to a trial for the college rugby team, and managed to play a match once a week.

Carmel had an easier time of it to begin with. Though a member of St Anne's, her supervisor was Mr Williams, a Fellow of Balliol. It was not yet necessary for academics to have a doctorate. In Britain a good Honours MA, was the usual requirement. Carmel had made contact before leaving New Zealand and got into it straight away. She enrolled as a Bachelor of Philosophy student (B Phil), for which the entry qualification was First Class Honours in a Bachelor degree. It was a virtually guaranteed short cut to an academic job for the very bright.

The History School at Oxford was in good shape at that time. Unlike Auckland, where in some cases, students had to sign attendance lists, lectures were not compulsory. During my three years at Oxford I went to probably more lectures than I needed, but I found some of them inspiring, especially those of Hugh Trevor-Roper, who lectured on, "The Crisis of English Society 1600–1642." Christopher Hill was in the opposite camp ideologically, and spoke on "Puritanism and Politics, 1603–1640." Politics highlights included John Plamenatz, on "Political Theory from Machiavelli to Marx." Dr Z A Pelczynski and Raghavan Iyer offered a Class, another form of teaching, which consisted of a series of group discussions on "Morals and politics from Hobbes to Marx." Isaiah Berlin drew a huge crowd to hear his views on Marx and Marxism. Later on I encountered A J P Taylor, who had the gift of either thinking aloud, and composing his lecture as he spoke, or having a memory in which his facts and judgements were stored as if in the magazine of a gun. He spoke for fifty minutes without notes, using his eyes and his hands, as well as his mouth and without stopping for breath, left us mesmerised by the extent of his knowledge and his logical and oratorical skill.

My memory of this period of my life is a series of disjointed experiences in no particular order. Partly because it was a long time ago but also because I was working as never before, and time flew. In my first year, Carmel and I valued our holidays desperately, especially in the long summer vacation of 1960. My parents expected, I think, that we would spend most of the time with them at Bradford. We did visit them for a week, but both of us wanted to see something of the rest of the country, and thought of going to France as well. In the end we settled on Devon and Cornwall. I bought a second hand Ariel motor bike with two pannier bags and we set off on a camping trip which gave us many years of happy memories. We clocked in at the Valley of the Rocks to re-visit Lynmouth, and Lee Abbey where I had spent my late adolescent holidays from school. Then on to Cornwall, which was new ground for both of us, through Barnstable and Combe Martin, and on to Penzance and Mousehole, Falmouth, and back along the south coast to Lyme Regis before heading north again to return to Oxford. We only spent a week, but it was the first holiday we ever had on land, without anything to worry about. We camped free, thanks to the hospitable landowners who allowed us to pitch our tent, and light campfires without charge.

Then we returned to our reading lists and worked hard. We joined the University sailing club, which had a fleet of Firefly sailing dinghies for us to sail on the Isis as it broadened out in the Meadows. Now and again we would walk up the towpath to the Trout Inn and have a meal. Membership of the sailing club resulted in the discovery that the club provided opportunities to crew for yacht owners in the Solent, which enabled me to obtain a berth on a Folkboat for the annual race around the Isle of Wight. Carmel wasn't keen, but encouraged me to go and enjoy the experience.

In March 1960, Carmel told me that she was pregnant. This was both joyful and terrifying news. A baby would be a challenge, but we were confident that we could rise to the occasion. There were options, and I was determined that Carmel's career should not suffer. I could withdraw from my degree course and ask for my place at St Catherine's to be deferred until Carmel had finished her B Phil. She could breast feed the child on a regular basis, but I could handle the rest of the baby's needs. Then in 1961 Carmel could take over the mother role while I returned to my degree.

Whatever happened, I was happy to do whatever was required to enable Carmel to have the time she would need. In the end we agreed that we would stand watches through the nights, and split the days and our responsibilities accordingly. After the first three months I would be able to feed the baby with a bottle. Oxford was an enlightened place to have a baby, and Carmel enrolled in the prenatal group of young women in the same condition. She was advised, as a first-time mother, to use the services of the Nuffield Hospital for the birth and we both went to the prenatal exercise sessions.

We agreed that I would be present at the birth, unusual in most British institutions, but recommended by the Nuffield authorities, and on 5 October 1960, Carmel woke up to the expected pains and we caught a taxi to the hospital. The staff took it for granted that I would stay. I held Carmel's hand as the pains came and went. She bravely shoved as hard as she could and about three hours after admission, Stephen Young was born and loudly announced his arrival. I was stoked and delighted, and we had a lot of cuddles.

Our decision to take a baby in our stride did mean notching up our daily routine. We began to go to bed with the sun, and Carmel would feed Stephen. He usually needed my attention about four hours later, when I changed his nappy and put him back to bed in his cot. As I was awake anyway, I began to work each morning, either reading, or writing my next essay until 7 am, when I woke Carmel up with a cup of tea in bed, and then made breakfast for both of us. I usually left the house at 8.30 and studied in the Radcliffe Camera or the St Catz library. I cycled home about 12.30, and if all went well I ate something. Carmel then headed off on her bike and to work at her College or the library. I took Stephen for a walk in his pram. Summertown shopping centre was a couple of hundred yards away so I could combine baby walking with shopping for necessities. Carmel's tutor, Mr Williams was a bit alarmed by Stephen's birth, but soon realised that Carmel could be extraordinarily industrious when necessary. George Holmes, and later on

Peter Dickson, my second tutor, were very supportive and fully understood what we had let ourselves in for. Carmel would return about 6 pm and cook a meal for us while I prepared the baby food for Stephen.

Stephen turned out to be a smiling, easy-going baby, who soon settled into the routine we established. At weekends we sometimes took out a punt on the river with him in a carry basket that was also part of his pram. He was always smiling a lot, seldom cried and took a great interest in his surroundings. We used the Christmas break to make a quick visit to Bradford with Stephen to introduce him to his grandparents. My mother paid us a visit when he was about six months old, and they got on well.

Chapter 10: The course of true love never did run smooth

Edith telephoned on 19 March 1961 to tell me that Rob was very ill. The aunts had gathered, and he had been diagnosed as having cancer which was inoperable. Edith told me that he was not expected to live much longer and asked me and Carmel to travel to Bradford as quickly as possible. We explained things to our tutors, packed a suitcase, put Stephen in his dual purpose carry cot and folding pram and set off for the railway station.

The next day was a grey day all the way up through the industrial heart of the country. Carmel was kind and did her best to comfort me. I accepted the fact that the father I had known only now and then would die soon, and hoped for a last talk with him. I wanted to tell him that I was glad he had followed his conscience in making his life choices and that I appreciated his support for all my endeavours and would not let him down. But as the sun began to yellow into the grey evening of slag heaps and drizzle, I felt suddenly that he was already dead.

We were met by Mr Gerald Busby, one of Rob's parishioners. He was a successful business man who was also the Church Warden. He took us to his Rolls Royce, and said he had come as quickly as he could to meet our train, and he hoped that Rob would still be alive when we reached the Vicarage. When we arrived there, Rob was in his bed, surrounded by Edith, Lena, Molly and Heather, but he had died; probably about the twilight moment when I felt that I knew it. Now, I felt emotionally numb, and was deeply shocked, but glad at least that he had lived to see his grandson.

Edith was initially in a state of anguish, but then dealt with the shattering reality of her grief by plunging into an astonishing display of energetic activity. She started spring cleaning the place, weeding the garden, and then began answering the stream of letters of condolence from all her missionary colleagues, and sending out invitations to the funeral. Heather went into Head Girl mode, and started organising the Funeral service in Rob's church, having a program printed and a public notice into the newspaper. Molly decided that there would have to be a breakfast of ham and eggs for the mourners, which she claimed was an ancient ritual, native to the north riding of Yorkshire. It was also decided that Rob would be buried in the cemetery of the Parish Church of St Mary and St Laurence at his birthplace, Rosedale Abbey.

This meant an early start from Bradford and a drive of about fifty miles to the White Horse Pub in Rosedale for the ham and eggs, and for me, Heather, Edith and Carmel, another ride with Gerald Busby in his Rolls Royce. Throughout these forty-eight hours I could not help but feel a bit of a stranger.

The next morning Carmel and I set off to continue our hectic routine at Oxford, and I soon became fascinated with the core course in the Oxford History School, which started with the Roman invasion of Britain, and ended in the nineteenth century. This course was satirised by Sellars and Yeatman in the best selling comedy novel, *1066 and All That*,[1] which I had read several times. But it was seriously interesting to me because of the things that had raised my interest in History during my childhood. I had been to the island of Iona at the impressionable age of twelve, and had knelt beside Ant Molly in the Abbey, re-built on the site of St Columba's sixth century base, from which Christianity spread throughout Scotland. Before that I had waged mock battles with my friends during World War II to defend or capture the Motte and Bailey remains of a castle of the eleventh century next to the village church of Cropton, using mud bombs as hand grenades. This was a history that depended not only on documentary evidence, but also on archaeology, anthropology, linguistics, legend, place names, and imagination based on experience. It was a history that demanded work and familiarity with past cultures and historic places as well as libraries, and could take you anywhere.

In my second year, I found myself also enjoying the course on the History of Political Thought. It involved studying the classic thinkers of the Enlightenment, such as Hobbes, Rousseau, Voltaire, J S Mill, and Marx. My Tutor for this subject was Wilfred Knapp, who was to become an expert in the history of the Middle East, but at this stage in his life, was concentrating on the history of European political thought. He provided a mixture of erudition, objectivity, encouragement and criticism that was hard to beat, and advised me to attend the lectures on the subject by Isaiah Berlin. This was a magical experience, which made essay writing a pleasure, and led me eventually to a fondness for Anarchism laced with the sentiments of Christianity.

Special Subjects were offered which were intended to provide training in historical method based on documents, and so they were exercises in the use of primary literary sources. My St Catherine's tutor in 1961 was Dr Peter Dickson, a specialist in the financial history of the eighteenth century. Peter was a little older than me, much more urbane, and destined from birth, I thought, to become an Oxford Don. Having recently finished his DPhil thesis on the foundation of the insurance industry in the eighteenth century, and its contribution to the industrial and military strength of England, he sympathised with me, with my unfinished thesis about the early days of Auckland. He confessed on his part, to moments of despair towards the end of writing his own thesis, when he had been too tired to lift a heavy book from his desk, and almost burst into tears. He treated us students as "colleagues in the pursuit of truth and a better understanding of the human condition."

The special subject choices included subjects I would have enjoyed, such as "Slavery and Secession," the only available topic in American history, and something new altogether to me, but Peter Dickson thought it would do me good to take on, "The Triple Entente" between Britain, France and Russia from 1880 until 1918. I think he thought I needed rounding out from my antipodean experience in Auckland which was much weighted towards the southern hemisphere.

---

1   *1066 and All That*. First published 1930; twenty ninth edition 1943, Methuen and Co, London.

I explained that as much of the source materials were in French, I would be at a disadvantage, since I had studied that language for only one year at the age of eight or nine at my primary school. Most of my competitors would have had at least four years of learning the language. But I rather stupidly prided myself on my tendency to rise to challenges, and took it on. Peter Dickson was delighted, and managed to persuade St Catherine's Society to supply me with a Tutor in French at no charge. I felt that this was a great honour and was very grateful, but it meant an additional class each week, and doing as much reading as I could of French documents, such as Maurice Paleologue's detailed diary at the Treaty of Versailles. It was really too much, as learning foreign languages is not one of the things I am good at, though I have learnt smatterings of German, Ancient Greek and a bit of Fijian.

The decision came at a bad time for other reasons as well. We had made friends with a Canadian student who was taking the BPhil course in Philosophy. He and his wife had local lodgings in Summertown. We got on well, but in the summer break in 1961 they went back to Canada. One afternoon when Carmel was working in the Library and I was working at home with Stephen, I was looking for a lost sock or something; and I opened a drawer and found a nest of airmail forms from Canada. They were addressed to Carmel, from the Canadian philosopher, and my first instinct was to leave them alone, but my eye caught a disturbing expression of intimate affection in ink on the blue paper, and I spent the rest of the afternoon in a state of shock and anxiety. When Carmel came home, I asked her about the letters, and she told me that she had been having an affair with the philosopher, but it was now over. This was a time to take some deep breaths.

I immediately remembered the house warming party at 1B Grafton Road, Carmel's memorable letter about her brief indiscretion with Jim, and thought that this must be one of the marital crises that she had foretold. So I was grief stricken and angry; but on reflection, not surprised. I tried to think of ways to save our marriage, because it had been all that I hoped for up to now. Having a lovely first born baby boy was a delightful source of happiness but it was unexpected. It probably did cause extra strain in the context of our two career plans. Both of us now had a responsibility to Stephen, and without each other, neither of us would find it easy to finish our degrees, let alone give a baby a good start in life. I knew that Carmel would soon be in a position from which she could realistically envisage an academic job in Oxford, and that this may have been a possible motive, conscious or not, for her infidelity. She seemed as determined for us to stay together as I was, but not apologetic. There was a lot of pride between us, but no guilt, and therefore no apology. But gradually we began to smile at each other, and even to laugh. Stephen continued to be a delight, and we both decided to get on with our lives as if nothing had happened.

There were some "frank discussions" though. This was the sixties, and women all over the prosperous countries in the world were enlarging their horizons and claiming their human rights, including the right to be the mistresses of their own bodies. We had both agreed to denial of female obedience as a condition of our marriage, and I felt that my only option was to overcome my indescribable hurt and jealousy as best I could. Life was too short for anything else. I steered clear of the notion of "forgiveness," for fear of misinterpretation, but did my best to deserve renewal of Carmel's love by a kind of second courtship, which was surprisingly successful.

The other distraction from my central concern, to obtain good exam results, was my failure to finish and submit my Auckland MA thesis before we left New Zealand. I had brought it with me, an unfinished, closely documented manuscript of 119,600 words, in my own handwriting, together with tables, notes from readings of a wide range of sources on bundles of system cards, bibliography and so on. I still had to write the final chapter and a conclusion, and managed to find time between lectures, tutorials, essays, not much sleep, and many nappy changes, to do it. Fortunately Oxford was a great place to have the manuscript professionally typed and bound. I can't remember how much it cost but it was very quickly done and I submitted it by registered airmail to Auckland University in mid 1961, my second year at Oxford, and then forgot all about it until I started writing this book in January 2016.

I found that I had been given a mark of 81%, which was safely into the first class bracket. I was confident in 1961, that I was on the right track, and decided that my chances of earning an academic job in a University would be improved if I could have an article published in a reputable academic journal. So I cut down on sleep as much as I could and wrote my first article, based on the thesis. It was immediately accepted for publication by the New Zealand academic journal *Political Science*.[2]

It was in this context of emotional recovery, necessity, renewed love and optimism about the future, that we had another surprise. Carmel finished her thesis on Greek Drama in June 1961 and became pregnant again towards the end of October. This meant, that she would be due to give birth to our second child, in June 1962, shortly before I would be sitting my exams.

We decided to move closer to the centre of Oxford to save as much time as possible, and we rented a flat on the top floor of 110 Woodstock Road, a large house a short walk from the shops, libraries and colleges, and St Catherine's Society. Another reason for the move was that we wanted to enlist the help we might need with two very young children by providing an extra bedroom for an *au pair*.

Swedish girls were usually brought up with English as a second language, and were coming to England in large numbers in the 1960s. Brigetta was one of them. She was twenty-one and an immediate success, from our point of view, because she was always happy, and very easy to get on with. We were able to share our experiences with her, and she could with us, and we had many enjoyable conversations with her. She had her own bedroom and got on extremely well with Stephen, who

---

2   Young, J M R, "The Political Conflict of 1875," *Political Science*, Vol 13, September 1961, pp 56-79.

slept in his cot in our room, and was beginning to walk and needed constant attention, especially as we lived on the top floor of a three storey building. The three of us shared the housework and cooking and we all ate together, but Brigetta did most of the cleaning. She became one of our long term friends until we lost contact several years later.

As Carmel's pregnancy progressed, she became increasingly happy. She had finished her thesis and was able to relax and concentrate on the immediate future. As her first pregnancy and Stephen's birth in hospital had been normal, she was expected to have her second baby at home, as most British mothers were at that time. She was visited regularly by her midwife, who arrived by bicycle once a week, to give her a check-up. Everything was always found to be normal.

Two weeks before my exams, Carmel's water broke and we called the midwife, who turned up in about five minutes. My job was to put a frying pan onto the cooking stove and boil some water in it to sterilise some instruments in case they were needed. I was both intrigued and horrified by a pair of scissors with a right angle bend in the end of the blades, designed to perform, if needed, an episiotomy at short notice. I was glad it wasn't needed, but the thought of it made me feel sick, and helped me to appreciate the courage Carmel needed to bear a child. Philip Young was born at about noon, on 14 June 1962, and was healthy and smiley just like his brother. Carmel rose to the task of recovery with her usual energy, and Brigetta shared our delight as if she really was one of our family.

My thoughts soon turned to the considerably increased need for a job in the near future, whatever exam results I might achieve in the next week or so. To increase my chances, I applied for several jobs. The Universities of Auckland, Townsville and Adelaide were advertising lectureships, so I sent letters of enquiry with my existing qualifications to all of them.

I also asked of the Australian National University in Canberra for details of its PhD scholarships. I had gradually developed an interest in the islands of the Pacific Ocean as a result of my Pitcairn Island experience, and my brief time spent on Tahiti on the way back to England. Auckland was always a gateway to the Pacific, and I can trace my attraction to the islands back to the island smells of the island ships I helped to unload on the wharves, the style of rugby that I played and much enjoyed against Fijian, Samoan and Tongan teams on Saturday afternoons, and the Polynesian culture that I vicariously sampled by teaching at Rawene school, and living and working for six years in New Zealand. The attraction of ANU was that it had a relatively new research School of Pacific Island History.

I wrote a letter to Professor Jim Davidson, who had been appointed in 1951, at the age of thirty-four, as the Head of the newly founded School of Pacific History at the ANU, to ask him to send me the application forms. I told him I had recently submitted my MA thesis in Auckland and was about to take my final exams for an Honours degree at Oxford. Peter Dickson and Keith Sinclair agreed to give me references. On my birthday, 20 September 1961, I received a letter from

P R Partridge of the ANU: "I think you should certainly apply for a research scholarship at the Australian National University. [He advised me to apply in the first half of 1962] Your application could then be considered, although the award of a scholarship could not be completed until the results of your finals were available, and unless they were satisfactory." Fair enough, I thought.

My first choice was a lectureship at Auckland, so I sent my application in, hoping that my MA thesis result, my published article in *Political Science* and the First Class Honours I hoped for from Oxford, would be accepted as an adequate qualification. Keith Sinclair wrote to me on 11 October:

> *I was sorry you didn't get the job, but there was strong competition, (1 Oxford doctorate, 1 ANU doctorate nearly completed) and I was not optimistic for you. But once you have an Oxford degree, especially if you get a good second or better, and with an article published, you should have no difficulty in getting a university position in NZ or Australia. There is every chance of further openings at Auckland within a year or two. Your article is published. I have read it quickly, and it is a good one. Good luck with your exams, and Carmel's.*

There was also a job going in Townsville in the far north of Queensland. I applied for that too, but received a nice letter back after a week or two to tell me that, after much consideration, the lectureship had been given to someone else.

There was one term to go before my exams, and my choices were becoming fewer. Carmel and I had discussed them at length when we weren't doing anything else important, which was hardly ever. One choice was for me to give up the idea of returning to New Zealand; write to the Auckland Teachers' Training College, ask Amarilda Gorrie for a reference and start making applications for jobs in secondary schools near Oxford. Carmel would be able to obtain a Tutorial post, publish some learned articles, or write a good book, and become a famous Don at St Anne's. I would have a less demanding career, teaching History at various secondary schools, preferably co-ed, and enjoying long holidays. We would live in Oxford most of the time, on our two salaries, but also rent a cottage and keep a boat, somewhere in Cornwall. We would travel now and again to the Mediterranean or cruise there in the yacht through the European canals to the islands of the Aegean. I even wrote to White and Austin, a boat building company of Brightlingsea, on the coast of Essex who were building wooden Folk boats. I obtained a quote for a hull only, of £756, delivery within a year, for one of those famous vessels. Once I obtained a job, I thought, we could save up for the sails and rigging. An engine would of course, not be necessary.

But we were not impressed by England in general. Too much out-dated social inequality, we thought. We did not think England's amusing fetishes about class contributed to the public good. When we became serious about our future, we remembered the best things about New Zealand. The weather, egalitarianism, racial tolerance, our friends, Carmel's family, the Waitemata and the Hauraki Gulf. Alps as good, if not quite as high, as anywhere in the world, and better beaches.

Knowing, as I did, that our future would be determined by my exam results, I went to "Collections" or informal practice exams, and tried to ignore my less stressed colleagues who laughed and joked for ten minutes or so before they started to write anything. I at least had my timing right, and an even length to my answers. In the end, as we entered the Examination schools where we would write two exam papers a day for five days, I was comforted by the traditional formality, the Commoner's gowns that we wore, and the tense atmosphere of a cohort of young, ambitious people, who shared my stress, and cheerful hope.

I found that I enjoyed the questions; and the intellectual challenge they presented. I had prepared for each paper systematically, and with the exception of the two papers on the Making of the Triple Entente, I was confident of doing well. When it came to this subject, though, I felt sick; especially when I saw the "gobbets" or extracts from diplomatic documents and some from Paleologue's diary, on which we were obliged to comment with as much knowledge, brevity and insight as we could muster.

About a week after exams were over, I joined the crowd gathered around the notice board at the examination schools, and gradually worked my way far enough through to be able to read the notices. There was a list of people who had been awarded third class honours, and that was where I looked first. My name was not there. Then I looked at a list of the names of students who were summoned to a *viva voce*, or oral examination to see whether they could rise from third to second class honours. These interviews were for a quarter of an hour, but I was not on that list either. I looked then at the list of students who had won an undisputed First. No luck there either. Then I looked at the list of students who were invited to a "Long Viva" to last, if needed, for 45 minutes, to decide whether they should be awarded first or second class honours. I was on that list, and a day or two later I stood at the door of the interview room. A door opened and I walked in to a meeting of four or five people with my exam answers and their notebooks in front of them.

They started with congratulatory remarks, and questions about my previous degree in Auckland, commenting on the fact of my unusually advanced age, for an undergraduate. So I briefly explained that I had needed time to work in order to live, and had been in effect, a part time student for six years.

Then we discussed each of the exam papers I had written. They told me they had enjoyed reading my English History and Political Thought papers. And I said that I had little confidence in my Triple Entente paper, because of my limited knowledge of French, and did not expect to have done well in that. But I confessed to thinking that I might have done well in the rest of them. I had the impression that the interview was going well and I was on the way to achieving a First. Then came my big mistake. Keith Thomas, who was to become one of the most famous historians in the country, and eventually became an expert on the fascinating subject of European Witchcraft, challenged my understanding of what was known as The Exclusion Crisis, meaning the question of excluding Catholics from becoming English monarchs.

In fact there were two such periods of public anxiety, first in the 1570s, and later from 1679 to 1681. The issue common to both was the worry that a Catholic monarch might revive the notion of the Divine Right of Kings, or Queens for that matter. Mary Queen of Scots, in the sixteenth century and James Stuart, brother of Charles II, in the seventeenth, were both seen by the Protestant majority as threats, not only to its religious freedom but to its secular liberties as well. I think Keith Thomas's challenge might have been about which crisis the question referred to. In any case his remarks threw me, and I sensed a serious challenge to my hopes of achieving a First. I looked back with enormous anxiety to the slow, prolonged, rise in knowledge and ability that I thought I had achieved. Was it all to end in failure? So I said something to the effect that whatever I had written was the truth, and whatever Thomas might think, I was unwilling to agree that I had made a mistake… Silly boy!

About a week later, when the whole thing was over, I went to see Dickson to find out how I had done. He congratulated me on earning an "Upper Second." I asked him if he knew why I had not received a First, and he told me that the committee had thought I was a bit too stubborn.

He went on to say, very kindly, that I must not have the impression that some kind of brand would now appear on my head, announcing to the world that I had not succeeded in gaining a First. The thing that mattered now was the quality of my research, writing and teaching in the future. Somewhat comforted, I went home to Carmel, who was disappointed, but just as kind.

I learnt later that Jim Davidson of the ANU took the trouble to obtain my thesis about the politics of the Auckland Province, out of the Auckland University library, and read it. He saw it as a study of race relations in a Frontier society as much as it was about colonial development and politics, and thought that I might be in a good position to tackle the same period of Fijian history, as a study of culture contact, between white settlers from Australia and New Zealand, and the Fijian people. This was the period immediately preceding the decision of the chiefs, led by Cakobau, chief of Bau, to cede Fiji to Britain in 1874. Shortly after my *viva* I received a letter from Davidson, offering me a scholarship.

I had by then decided that as a father of two, it was important for me to cover myself by applying to the University of Adelaide as well. At that point I had received no replies from anyone else, and so I accepted Jim's offer, though his conditions were challenging. He would insist that I made myself familiar with Fiji and the culture of the Fijian people, which would involve periods of absence from my young family.

His insistence reminded me of my father's report of how he was introducing the teaching of the history of Sierra Leone, by looking at it from an indigenous point of view. I read Jim's inaugural lecture of 1954, when he was appointed to the Chair of Pacific History in the new research school in Canberra, and thought it a breath of fresh air. Hugh Trevor-Roper, Oxford's Regius Professor of History, and one of my favourite lecturers, had recently given his inaugural address, in which he had expressed his scorn of attempts to write the history of non-Europeans in undeveloped countries. He declared that the study of what he called, "barbarous tribes in picturesque but irrelevant corners of the globe" were none of the historian's business. It followed that places like the South Seas were a setting for Romance, and Anthropology, but not History.

But the Oxford approach to the history of England before the Norman conquest, had led me to believe that our business is to reveal the truth of the past, and to use all the available evidence to do it; archaeology, linguistics, oral tradition, as well as documents, even if they are based on legends. Jim Davidson saw history in a new light. He acknowledged that, "It is in Imperial History that Pacific History has its more immediate origin." but went on to say:

> *This is a context of limited usefulness. Even the ablest of those who attempt the task almost inevitably impose a spurious unity on their subject matter. Events are explained without adequate consideration of factors external to the Empire, or of mainly local effect within it… Imperial history, when it insists on studying the history of European expansion by orienting all its material around the imperial factor, becomes, indeed, the negation of true scholarship… The historian normally works his way through the complex situations that confront him with the aid of his personal experience as well as his learning. He knows when he is dealing with the history of his own culture, that the way in which men thought or acted is related to a tradition to which he himself is heir. But when he is concerned with alien cultures, this advantage is denied him. The historian studying multi-cultural situations must learn to use new forms of evidence, to involve himself in other men's ways, and to avoid interpreting men's actions in terms of patterns of his own culture.³*

I found this insight very attractive, and began to think that the South Pacific should become my speciality, but there was still one more possibility of a teaching post that would provide a higher salary, and create the chance of a job for both of us at the same university.

The head of the History Department at the University of Adelaide at that time was Professor Hugh Stretton. He was a graduate of the University of Melbourne, and had served in the Australian Navy in the last years of World War II. He then won a Rhodes Scholarship and studied at Balliol College, Oxford. His undergraduate degree had culminated in a "long viva" in which, according to legend, he had, unlike me, dazzled his examiners as he talked his way into a First.

I wrote to him after I received my exam results, and asked George Holmes, Peter Dickson and Keith Sinclair for references. Stretton contacted his old friend from his student days at Balliol, Christopher Hill, who was now a Fellow of the College. I received a letter from Hill asking me to present myself for an interview at his college room. I told him that I was a trained teacher, but had turned out to be better at research and writing than I was at exams. He asked me to tell him about my

---
3   Davidson, James, "Inaugural Lecture," *Journal of Pacific History*, Vol 1. p 55, 25 November 1954.

MA thesis, which made me feel confident. Sir Lewis Namier had used information about the vested interests of the British landed gentry of the eighteenth century, to explain the political factionalism of England at that time. I told Christopher Hill that I had borrowed Namier's idea and used it in the context of nineteenth century New Zealand. I did a lot of talking, with a few words about my experience at Oxford and my domestic circumstances.

I then received a letter from Hugh Stretton to say he and his colleagues (his style was democratic and consultative) had received a letter from Hill, and were prepared to offer me a temporary lectureship, which was to be reviewed after two years. My position would then be advertised, and I would have to compete again, with any other applicants. He pointed out that, as a graduate of Auckland Teachers' Training College, I would have no difficulty in finding a job as a school teacher, if I failed to get a permanent appointment in his department. He also said that there was a good chance that Carmel would, at some stage, be able to apply for a tutorial position in the Adelaide Classics department.

Carmel was beginning to feel a bit anxious about the future from a family point of view, and in the end, we decided to accept Stretton's offer. I would have to start work at the beginning of the third term in October 1962, and Professor Stretton explained that "we can't pay fares or travelling expenses for a temporary appointment, but we stand well with Australia House, and would do our best to get you quick migrant passages." So the University of Adelaide arranged for us both, and our children, to be nominated by the University as migrants, which meant I could take advantage of my British citizenship. Ten pounds was provided by the University on my behalf. The rest of our fares were paid by the Government of Australia. My first migration to New Zealand had cost me nothing; this time, I would be a "10 pound Pom," with my wife and family nominated by my Australian employer, the University of Adelaide.

Next day I wrote to Jim Davidson telling him I had accepted Stretton's offer, and explaining my plight. I told him that I still wanted to work on Fiji, but would have to be based in Adelaide. Incredibly, he agreed to be my external supervisor, provided that I would be able to visit Canberra, and Fiji, from time to time. Hugh was also in favour of me working on a PhD. They had now become, he said, a virtual Union Ticket in the academic world, and if I was working on a doctoral thesis in a year's time, it would considerably help my prospect of retaining my job.

After a rather stormy career at the Auckland University, Bill Mandle had moved on to Adelaide University. He wrote to congratulate me on securing the job, temporary as it was, and told us he had found us a house. We started packing up. My mother had moved to York, where she was a long term guest of Dr Coggan, the Archbishop of York, and his family. Heather was working for Heinemann, an educational publisher, and had married Ottó Károlyi, her refugee musician from Hungary. There was no time for extended family farewells. We told them all that there would be study leaves now and again and we expected that we would eventually return at least for a while, to England. I knew I had to start work in Adelaide in October 1962, but there were no ships sailing at a suitable time to convey me there. We would therefore have to travel by air, at short notice.

Our tickets arrived by post soon afterwards and we headed for Heathrow. The plane was a de Havilland Comet, the first purpose-built passenger jet in the world. Our seats were as far forward as possible next to a bulkhead, with a shelf in front of us where we could place Philip's carry-cot. Stephen had a seat of his own. The flight to Australia took a total of thirty-six hours. Stephen was very excited, and I don't recall him sleeping at all. Neither did we, as we had stops along the way at Rome, Bombay, as it was still called, and Perth, arriving eventually in Sydney. The crew invited Stephen and me to enter the pilot's cabin from which we could gaze through the enormous curved window to the brown terrain of the Nullarbor Plain and inland South Australia below us. The pilot told us that it was all good cattle country.

Eventually we landed at Sydney airport, where we were met by Professor George Rudé, a very famous social historian, who was doing research in the Mitchell Library. He was his extraordinarily gracious self, and made us feel welcome and wanted. He took us to a lounge and bought us a beer each; and lemonade for Stephen. Philip was still dependent on Carmel for nourishment. Our sleep had been light and infrequent, but we did our best to stay awake. Stephen on the other hand, was hysterically active after the long confinement in the crowded cabin and began to run around the lounge and return to us to tell us about all his discoveries. In the end he decided to get up and stand on the low table between us and George, and kick over a glass of beer, as well as Carmel's handbag, which flew open and spilled much of its contents on the table. They included her contraceptive diaphragm, which rolled off the table and set off across the floor of the lounge, much to the merriment of our fellow travellers. George was equally amused, and a staff member soon mopped up the beer as I retrieved the escaping device. We had a few more laughs and went round to the gate where the much smaller Adelaide plane was to depart. An hour later Bill Mandle met us at the Adelaide airport and took all of us to the house he had found for us in Edwardstown, a southern suburb on the railway, which meant we didn't have to worry about buying a car, at least not immediately.

After I received my first pay-cheque we did buy a rather ancient Volkswagen "Beetle," which we soon used to explore the country and the beaches in the weekends. In the meantime, the railway was a blessing and quicker than a car to travel to the University and back again. Stephen liked the noise the trains made anyway, and "Dee" became his word for train. When he heard the one that arrived at Edwardstown about 5.30 pm, he would start to run about the house, because he knew that I would be on it, saying "Dee! Dee!," as a kind of alternative for Dad.

I met Hugh Stretton and the staff of the History Department. It had recently moved into the Napier building, which looked incongruous amongst the sandstone of the old University buildings, but was air-conditioned and had elevators as well as stairs. It was eight storeys high, of which two, the third and fourth, were shared between the departments of Political Science and History. A large room on the fourth floor, later to be named "the Stretton Room," was dedicated to final year Honours students, who each had their own desk.

Each member of the staff had offices of their own along the corridor running the length of the floors, with our names on the doors. Half way along the corridor, next to what is now the Stretton Room, was the Departmental office, Hugh's office and a common room, where at morning tea time, lecturers, tutors and office staff could gather with the staff of the smaller Department of Political Science, to engage in intellectual or humorous conversation, or gossip. This room was also used for formal staff meetings once a month. These were an important expression of Hugh's enlightened, democratic form of administration. Some years later he resigned from his Professorial status in order to increase his intellectual productivity, and introduced triennial elections by staff of the Chair of the Department. All our votes were of equal value, regardless of rank. It was a first move that spread throughout the universities of Australia, and brought the tradition of the "God-Professor" to an end.

In 1962, that change lay in the future, and as the junior recruit to the department, my role was to fill in the most urgent need of the moment, to relieve the teaching load borne by Dr Ian Turner, who taught Australian History to a large cohort of third year students. He also convened a class of Honours students who were to write and read short theses to the class on Australian History, which he also invited me to attend.

Australian History was a subject which I had never studied in my life, but I was now expected to teach it to third year students. I was not in a position to complain, and so I got on with it as best I could. Ian had been a member of the Communist Party of Australia for most of his life but was then in the throes of disillusionment, on account of the Russian invasion of Hungary in 1956, and its aftermath. He was ideologically aligned with historians like Brian Fitzpatrick and Russel Ward. Their interests had grown from the earlier studies of the establishment of colonial government and policy, and the feats of British explorers, to the early development of a sense of potential national identity, the social and political significance of the wool industry, and the Gold Rushes of the mid-nineteenth century. Ian's thesis was a study of the ideology and history of the Australian labour movement. He was raised in the inland town of Nhill, in Victoria, which explains his personal identification with the "Australian Outback." His unusual intelligence won him a scholarship to Geelong Grammar school, and then to the University of Melbourne. After military service in New Guinea in World War II, he went to the Australian National University in Canberra, and had recently submitted his PhD thesis, which was to be awarded in 1963. He was twelve years older than me, but both of us shared the experience of a long gap between leaving secondary school and our first permanent jobs. I found him an inspiring mentor, and we got on well, in spite of my relative ignorance of Australian History. We used to take time off in the middle of the day for a game of squash. I had some experience of this game in the Fives Courts of Christ's Hospital, but never succeeded in beating Ian at it, in spite of some limited improvement. We both enjoyed the exercise.

Ian had a nationalistic love of Australian Rules football, which he shared with Bill Mandle, who used to introduce conversation about the State Australian Rules competition into his lectures on the politics of Elizabethan and Stuart history in England. This led to a customary supporters group of students who provided Bill with his very own cheer squad every weekend in the season. For my part, I still regarded myself as a player of football of the rugby variety, rather than a spectator, and for a couple of years I played for the second University team. I also joined a local gym with a boxing ring for a short time, and did some sparring with local professionals. It was a good way of getting short bursts of strenuous activity at minimal cost of time.

Ian thought I needed some education about Australian culture, and I remember a weekend conference in Melbourne which we both attended. It included exploration of the then pioneering coffee bars of the city, which were venues for the resurgence of Australian folk music, often based on Irish songs, introduced by Irish convicts in the early nineteenth century. We also made contact with a few left wing literary and intellectual notables, including Stephen Murray-Smith and the great historian, Manning Clark. I felt that I had received a positive introduction to some very interesting people.

Soon, I was asked to contribute lectures in my new subject. Luckily, I was fortunate to have developed the habit of rising early in the morning to study for my exams. It enabled me to find time to prepare lectures to be given the same day, and to read enough of the long list of books Ian recommended, to be able to contribute intelligently to the Tutorials for the Honours students who had selected Australian History as their speciality.

This was a time of unprecedented expansion of Australian universities, following the Martin Report, instigated by Prime Minister Menzies in 1961, and published in 1964. They were attracting increasing numbers of both full time and part time students. Carmel soon had a job as a Tutor, to begin with, then, in 1966, a lectureship, in the Classics Department. Two lowly, but to us, generous salaries took some getting used to, especially for members of the continuing influx of young graduates from Britain and the USA into the departments that were included in the Arts Faculty. We soon made friends among them, particularly those with children, and spent weekends going with them and their children to the local beaches, and keeping fit by spending our lunch hours doing laps round the running track in the nearby parklands. None of us seemed to have had wealthy parents, and those of us with young children had all struggled through periods of relative poverty and hardship to become academic professionals. South Australia seemed to us to be a land flowing with milk and honey, compared with the British background of austerity that we had miraculously survived.

There was time now, I thought, to do a bit of acting, just to keep my hand in, and when the University drama club decided to present Sophocles' *Oedipus Rex*, with a professional producer, I auditioned, and received the brief, but crucially important part, of the Messenger, who brings the news to the audience, that king Oedipus has torn out his own eyes because he discovers his inadvertent patricide. That experience, thanks to Sophocles, kept up my confidence in my ability as a public performer. I still think that my acting experience made me a better lecturer than I would have been without it. I have done no acting since then. I think I found that the opportunities of lecturing about history and later about the world environmental crisis, and what to do about it, were enough to satisfy my vanity.

By the end of 1963, I was feeling optimistic that I would compete successfully for the transition from temporary to permanent employment. Ian Turner was moving on from Adelaide to Monash, the second University in Melbourne where, during the Vietnam War, he was to play an important part in the radicalisation of the student body. Australian History in Adelaide was now the responsibility of John Tregenza and Gordon Buxton, while I was asked to fill in the gap in the British Constitutional History course created by John Gilchrist's departure on study leave in 1964.

This was a course designed specifically for Law students, to provide some historical background for their legal studies, but though I had sat at the feet of celebrity Medieval historians such as George Holmes and R W Southern, I had little interest in the isolated study of Constitutional History for its own sake.

The time had come for me to apply for my job in competition with external applicants. I was asked to invite all my colleagues to attend one of my lectures. I thought my students might be interested in more social history and I had been intrigued to discover at Oxford, the latest ideas about the identity of the real Robin Hood. Fortunately, George Holmes had allowed me to write an essay about the subject, due to a recent article by RH Hilton in the journal *Past and Present*,[4] which aroused one of the many recurrent bursts of scholarly interest in the relationship between tradition and the social reality of medieval society.

Hugh Stretton gave me plenty of warning. My colleagues would be asked to vote on the issue of making my temporary status a permanent one, or not, after attending my Robin Hood lecture. They would then retire and have an open discussion, while I waited to hear their verdict.

I wrote out some notes, which I have lost, based on an old Oxford essay, which I have thrown away, but the lecture was successful. One of the staff made the unusual gesture of giving me a bit of a clap, which the students followed. Hugh came to my room to congratulate me on the lecture, and my new appointment, which most of my colleagues had voted for.

Not much later, there was another knock on my door by Dr Heinz Kent, a senior lecturer who specialised in Economic History. He told me that he wished to tell

---

4   *Past and Present*, No.14, 1958.

me to my face that he had voted against my appointment, but he added that he approved of the democratic process which had led to the decision to give me tenure, and hoped that we would continue to enjoy a collegial relationship. This, he thought, would be preferable to my being told of his opposition by somebody else. I did not ask him why he voted against my appointment, but thanked him for his openness and honesty, and told him that I appreciated his visit.

Chapter 11: Building a Career

In the next year there were some staff changes. Ian Turner left. Dr Alan Martin, an Australian History specialist from the Australian National University, joined the staff and took control of the course in Australian History, which could be taken by students at either the second or third year of their degree. I was asked to give some of the early lectures, which fitted in well with the work I was starting for my PhD. Jim Davidson agreed to be my external supervisor, which was very generous, since I had rejected his offer of a place in his department at the ANU, while Dr Ken Gillion, an Indian History specialist who had written his PhD about the Indian community in Fiji, under the supervision of Jim Davidson, was appointed as my in-house supervisor.

It was inevitable that my research work would influence my approach to my teaching. I found myself trying to combine learning about the early British colonisation of Australia in order to be able to teach it to my students, with doing scoping research for my new thesis on the cultural impact of white settlement in Fiji; starting with the motivation and background of the young people in the 1860s and 1870s who migrated to Fiji to grow cotton, taking advantage of its high price as a result of the American Civil War. Fiji, it was believed, had climatic and soil similarities with the West Indies, and various booster journalists and adventurers wrote articles in colonial newspapers encouraging young people to this new road to "making a fortune."

This movement was not an isolated one. The nineteenth century was a period of unprecedented movements of adventurous young people, in flight all over the world from the sociological consequences of the industrial revolution in Europe. I was interested in the work of the American historian, Frederick Jackson Turner, whose collected essays had been published in 1961.[1] His theory was that the nature of westward expansion of the United States in the nineteenth century had a profound cultural impact and stimulated such values as enterprise, liberty, equality and democracy in the American people. Russel Ward was the author of the then recently published book, *The Australian Legend*, in which he argued a parallel impact of Australia's outback on the Australian national character, with its climatic extremes of drought and flood, its vast distances, its apparent but deceptive emptiness.

I thought about these ideas, but I decided that the comparison did not take comparative geography into account. The *Mayflower* pilgrims standing on the Atlantic shore in 1620 had, to the east of them, an empty ocean, and beyond that, a civilised Europe. To the west lay "New England," a countryside climatically similar to its namesake, and clothed in familiar vegetation. For them, there was only one frontier, to the west, and that an inviting one. Governor Phillip, by contrast, in 1788, stood in New South Wales on the edge of a continent in which the seasons were

---

1 Billington, R A (ed), *Frontier and Section. Selected essays of Frederick Jackson Turner*, Prentice Hall Inc, 1961.

unfamiliar, the land harsh, and the animals and plants unique. He knew very little about it, and what he did know, from the log books and journals of those navigators who had tentatively skirted its coast, added up to a very unattractive picture.

But behind him, to the east lay a comparatively attractive Pacific ocean. Its main island groups had been charted by a succession of European explorers, and the most recent of them, James Cook, had taken scientists with him who had catalogued the plants, animals and people to be found there. Everything Governor Phillip knew about the Pacific added up to an extremely favourable picture.

Captain Cook himself had written of Tahiti as "These happy isles on which benevolent nature with a bountiful and lavish hand hath bestowed every blessing man could wish. The natives possessed of the same benevolent disposition, contribute willingly, cheerfully, and with a full hand to the wants of the navigator."[2] Bougainville was equally enthusiastic: "I thought," he said, "I was transported to the Garden of Eden. We found companies of men and women sitting under the shade of their fruit trees. Everywhere we found hospitality, ease, innocent joy, and every appearance of happiness among them."[3]

My instinct was to begin my PhD thesis, as I had done my MA thesis in Auckland, with an attempt to put myself into the past, in order to understand how the people of the late nineteenth century understood the world they lived in. So I started my work on Fiji by saturating myself in the contemporary literature and relevant manuscript sources of the 1860s and 70s, and with the public documents and newspapers of the time, when significant numbers of Australians and New Zealanders began to migrate to Fiji.

The gold rushes of the 1850s had brought thousands of young men, but fewer women, from Britain, the United States and Europe, to Australia, in the belief that they would soon make a fortune. Gradually, the first goldfields to be exploited by solo adventurers and male partnerships began to be taken over, at first by small companies, and then larger ones. Soon, the capital required to participate in mechanised gold mining grew to be beyond the reach of the solo diggers, and they began to look at alternatives. I followed the fortunes of individual diggers who left Australia for the new goldfields in New Zealand in the 1860s, and then went to Fiji where, at that time, journalists were describing "The Great Fiji Rush." This was not for gold, but for land, on which to grow cotton, as American supplies dwindled because of the American civil war and its aftermath.

I began to see the early British settlement of the eastern shore of Australia, and the commercial, religious, and cultural expansion into the Pacific, as something just as historically important as the early advances by squatters westward, over the Blue Mountains in search of grazing land. They, of course, assumed that the land was legally uninhabited, and according to the logic of the time, the property of the

---

2   Cit Beaglehole, J C, *The Journals of Captain Cook*, Vol II, 1961, pp 428-429.

3   Bougainville, L, Antoine de, *Voyage Round the World* (trans by J R Forster), London 1772, pp 22-9.

British Crown. I found that the first successful enterprises in Sydney were based not on sheep, but on the importation of pork from Tahiti, Kauri spars from New Zealand and sealskins and whale oil from New Zealand and the Bass Strait islands.

When Alan Martin asked me to give a few lectures in the Australian History course, I thought of it as an opportunity to learn about the Aboriginal people, who had walked onto Australia many thousands of years before the end of the last Ice Age, when climate change had led to rising seas, resulting in the separation of the Australian continent from what is now New Guinea. I believe that this was the first time a University course on Australian History had not begun with the tale of Zachary Hicks, Captain Cook's keen-eyed lookout, who was the first Englishman to see the coast of the Australian mainland in 1770. My first lecture was derived from the work of a new generation of anthropologists who had begun the task of informing the Australian public about the 60,000 year history of the most sustainable culture in the world. Moving on from a brief look at Aboriginal society, my next innovation was to look at the early history of the convict settlement of New South Wales, through the eyes of the settlers of the period. They knew that it was the government's original policy to restrict land settlement to the area between the Blue Mountain range, and the sea. It was not the promise of expansion to the west that lay behind the choice of Botany Bay by the British Government, as the initial settlement of the new colony. Rather, it was the very favourable impression of the Pacific Islands and their proximity to Botany Bay, that had been created by the early European explorers.

The claimed boundary of New South Wales encompassed islands as far east as Tahiti, close to 8,000 kilometres away — the so-called "Adjacent Islands." Early entrepreneurs of white Australia could see the advantages and attractions of the Islands included within the New South Wales borders: the Islanders' good manners and hospitality, the reports of the explorers about resources such as pigs, Kauri timber, flax, seal skins and whale oil. These all contributed to the settlers' focus on the Pacific Islands rather than the Australian hinterland, with its unusual *Acacia* and *Eucalyptus* trees, strange animals, and unreliable rainfall. They also had difficulty in their attempts either to understand anything about Aboriginal society or subdue it.

My lectures were an opportunity to introduce new research into undergraduate teaching, in the same way that the content of most of the lectures I had heard at Oxford were. Lectures there were not compulsory and not explicitly thought of as the necessary preparation for exams. That was the purpose of tutorials. Instead, lectures were often an opportunity to share the findings of the most recent research before it was actually published.

Alan Martin came to my lecture, "Australia's Pacific Frontier," and suggested that I should send a revised version of it to the academic journal, *Australian Historical Studies*. I would never have thought of doing this myself, but I was greatly encouraged, especially as it would also enable me to place the subject I had decided on for my PhD research project, within a wider perspective. Re-writing, more research, and keeping up with the task of teaching a new subject, made life just as busy as it had been at Oxford. But it was exciting.

Converting my lecture notes into a closely documented article took up a lot of time in the early mornings of several weekends. In those days, we had no computers, and I am still a slow two finger typist at the best of times. My "Junior" status meant that I had to wait my turn before I could expect the very efficient office staff to type up my final hand-written manuscript. Evaluation by the editors of *Historical Studies*, when I sent it in, was a lengthy competitive process, but my article was eventually published.[4] I sent an off-print copy to Peter Dickson, whose response was encouraging. I had started my letter with a reminder of who I was and when I had been one of his students. He regarded this as a gesture of modesty and assured me that I was not so quickly forgotten! He wrote:

> *I found your article very stimulating. I am sure that original studies of this kind, are, and about time too, going to modify profoundly the old "Nationalist" economic history, which foolishly thought the subject could be fitted within the same framework as political history.*

I had never really thought of that, but I was very happy about the compliment.

Encouragement is an important part of good teaching, and I have always tried to follow Peter's example with my own students. After my lecture on Robin Hood, I became a permanent member of the staff, and my colleagues were complimentary. I also received positive comments from several historians in other universities, and some who were teaching Australian History told me they had put the article on the reading lists for their students. A year later, I received a letter from Mr Jim Ellis, of Cassell's Australia, who wanted to discuss publication of a book on the subject of Australia's Pacific Frontier, as part of a new series entitled "Problems in Australian History." The idea was to use my article as the basis of an introduction, to be followed by chapters consisting of extracts from primary sources, introduced by short essays, to place the primary sources into their context. Soon, there were companion booklets: *Towards a Foreign Policy*; *Attitudes to non-European Migration*, *The Depression of the 1930s*, and others on the big issues of Australian History, such as *The Gold Rushes*; *Conscription in the World Wars*, and *Australia in the United Nations*.

It proved a successful venture in academic publishing, and my contribution was well reviewed by other international historians like John A Williams of the University of Washington, where it sold in a paper binding, for $US1.75:

> *This small book is part of a series called "Problems in Australian History," a series similar to American books of selected readings and an indication that Australia too is experiencing a boom in University enrolments.*
>
> *But there is an important difference between Australia's Pacific Frontier and the typical American Non-book: Mr Young's book is a work of original scholarship. The introduction is derived from a scholarly article, the documents are carefully edited and annotated, and some of the extracts are drawn from manuscript sources.*

---

4 "Australia's Pacific Frontier," *Historical Studies, Australia and New Zealand*, Vol.12, No.47, October 1966, pp 373-388.

> The book provides valuable insights into both Australian and Pacific history. The point that Australia had two frontiers, one inland and one maritime, is the overall theme of the book. Young's argument, that the maritime frontier was more important than the inland one for fifty years, and of substantial significance for fifty more, is a neglected insight that changes the perspective of much of nineteenth century Australian history. For Pacific history proper, Mr Young produces evidence modifying the extreme views of both Morehead's "Fatal Impact" and of Grenfell-Price's "Western Invasion." In addition, his bibliographical essay conveys some of the excitement of the Australian National University's work in Pacific History. If other volumes maintain this standard, Cassells' series will be a notable one.

Alan Martin wrote to me from his new job at La Trobe University: "I have just received a copy of your Cassell Booklet… It looks absolutely marvellous, so congratulations on having made something worthwhile out of a great idea." I liked to think that this and other reviews supported Peter Dickson's judgement about what was important in academic life, so it did me a lot of good and removed my remaining sorrows about my undergraduate efforts of the past.

Carmel was also getting on well in Adelaide. She had a stimulating effect on her colleagues, who were all male, and always had a smile on her face. We were accustomed to sharing domestic responsibility, and arranged our timetables so that one of us was at home with the boys most of the time. That soon became difficult, so we advertised for domestic help as well, and chose a very capable young woman called Mary, as a supplementary part time mother. The boys pronounced her name as "Way-way," but she didn't mind, and she soon became part of the family, just as Brigetta had been.

We both felt confident and happy now, and could hardly believe our good fortune, with two well paid jobs, and a house that was not expensive to rent, but more civilised and modern than anywhere either of us had ever lived before. We found ourselves to be part of a largely new cohort of young graduates, mostly from British universities, who revelled in the same sense of unexpected privilege as we did, as we walked the wide streets of what seemed an almost ideal city.

Unlike Sydney, Adelaide was planned before it was built, by Colonel William Light, at the behest of the South Australia Company, inspired by Edward Gibbon Wakefield. Wakefield's aim was not to solve the problem of rising criminality in the wake of the British industrial revolution, by transporting criminals to Australia, but to transplant an idealised version of British society, including all classes, to South Australia (and later, to Canterbury, in New Zealand). Though renowned as the "City of Churches" and advertised as a colony untarnished by the "convict stain," Adelaide was, by 1962, as socially and culturally diverse, and by then, nearly as full of people with convict ancestry as the other state capital cities. It also retained its surrounding parklands, leafy suburbs, wide streets and gracious public buildings. The River Torrens, running past the University through parklands, hosted the University rowing club, and lent a touch of grace and gentility. Cyclists thrived on the flat streets between the beaches and the Adelaide Hills, rising to 2000 feet, just ten miles from the city centre. With its museum, art gallery, theatres, symphony orchestra, and its university, the city had and still has, a cultural atmosphere not unlike that of Edinburgh.

Soon after Carmel and I arrived, Tom Playford, the leader of the State Liberal Party, and Premier for the previous fifteen years, was defeated by the leader of the Labor Party, Frank Walsh. In 1967, Don Dunstan began the first of his two stints as Labor Premier. Among his many reforms, Dunstan abolished the death penalty and created the annual Adelaide Arts Festival. Playford's social policies had, in any case, been surprisingly enlightened, including the establishment of a state owned Electricity Trust, and a State Housing Commission. He might as well have been a Socialist for all the ideological difference there was, and his genuinely liberal legacy was an ideal platform for the Dunstan revolution.

The University bought new houses from the State owned Housing Trust, and renovated old ones. These became available for the accommodation of new academic staff recruited from other parts of Australia and overseas. In 1964, we applied to rent one of them, on the Main North Road, in the suburb of Blair Athol. The rent was cheaper than our first house in Edwardstown, and we calculated that we could save quite quickly, so we could buy our own house in some desirable location, fairly soon. Like most suburban properties in Adelaide, we had a quarter acre block, with front and back gardens, a garage, and a good setback from the road. The house had been recently built, and used electricity for everything. It would have been a good asset to be improved and loved, but we were then on the make as parents, our noses deep in the works of Dr Spock, and we used the backyard as a children's playground: Australian Rules Football in winter (Stephen was keen) and cricket in summer.

Unfortunately Blair Athol was too far away from Mary's home on the other side of Adelaide. She would have had to take a bus from Norwood, where she lived with her parents, to Adelaide, then a bus to Blair Athol, and then back, so with some regret, she declined our offer to keep her on, and we parted on good terms.

The positive achievement of this period of our lives made us optimistic about our future. We had succeeded in obliterating our marital grievances, and felt full of love. We had no financial worries, which led us to consider having another child. Perhaps we would have a girl! We both came from small families and the idea of bringing up our own, slightly larger family, at home, with us, instead of in the boarding schools that we had both experienced, was an exciting one. So was the prospect of a period in which no part of our minds would be worrying about birth control. Susan Amanda Young was born on 20 January 1964. Philip was walking and talking. Stephen was maturing quickly and was deeply moved by the death of Winston Churchill, who died on the 24 January 1965. He made us watch his funeral with him on ABC television.

Carmel was offered a lectureship the following year, which led us to think, having had two previous successful experiences with additional carers, that we should employ a third. Mrs King lived locally and proved to be a competent, caring and reliable person.

Summers were the time for beaches and boats. Back in England, we had looked at maps of South Australia and noted the site of Adelaide on St Vincent's Gulf. The geography wasn't a patch on the Hauraki Gulf of New Zealand, from a sailing point of view, but both Port Adelaide, and Glenelg looked promising as places where it might be possible to keep a boat. I think it was at the end of 1964 that we joined the Port Adelaide Sailing Club, the oldest in the State, because one of its members had a small and very cheap sailing boat for sale. She was hard chined, probably amateur built, planked with Jarrah, and came with a mooring at the Club as well. She was nineteen feet long and had a large open cockpit and a small cuddy, an inboard sloop rig, and a Simplex, Australian made, single cylinder auxiliary petrol engine. It could be started only by prayer, and usually repeated manual rotation of a big flywheel. It then made a not unpleasant chugging noise. We thought she would be a good family boat to start with.

The sailing club, founded in 1887, was a venerable establishment in the industrial heart of Port Adelaide. It reminded me strongly of the Greenwich Yacht

Stephen, Susan and Philip, when we were living at Blair Athol, South Australia.

Club founded in 1908, on the Thames in London. Its members, like those of the Greenwich Club, were mainly men and women who worked on the wharves or had other boat related callings. The ancient club house, now demolished, was located just above the opening Birkenhead bridge over the Port River, surrounded by famous workshops like Bill Porter's and the Searle brothers, where wooden boats were built. We appreciated the proletarian atmosphere which went with low membership fees, and a welcoming interest in our young family. The Royal Yacht Squadron was the only alternative, but our old cheap boat would have been out of place, and membership would have been too costly for the amount of time we could afford to spend on the water.

Stephen was very impressed by the way we could sail out into the river, just above the bridge, and blow three blasts on a whistle to have it opened, then wait until the red lights on the roadway brought the traffic to a stop, and the bridge opened for us to sail through it. Then we could watch it close safely behind us. We used our boat, known as *Swallow,* no doubt named by some previous owner after Arthur Ransome's heroic vessel, to explore the shallow creeks and mangrove swamps to the north of Port Adelaide, and "out to sea" beyond the Back Pole. This usually meant tacking down a narrow well-marked channel, then around the Outer Harbour and down to one of the long beaches. We tended to ignore the engine as it was noisy and difficult to start, and I have never been much interested in them.

Our Volkswagen "beetle" was useful to take the kids to the more beautiful southern beaches. Usually our destination at weekends was Port Willunga, about forty-five kilometres south of Adelaide. It had once been a small port, where engineless wooden ketches used to load wheat. A wooden jetty had stood near the end of the mere suggestion of a peninsula, which provided some shelter in southerly winds. The beach was enormous, the water seemed always to be warm, and was often occupied by young families like ours with small children. They were content to play almost forever, while we came to know their parents, and body surfed or played beach cricket. In the cooler months we explored further afield, into the Adelaide Hills with their winding roads, nucleated villages and warm pubs, and eventually out to the vineyards of the Barossa Valley, or weekend expeditions to visit old friends from Auckland who had jobs at Broken Hill.

Our longest drive was the roughly 1000 kilometres to Canberra where we visited the Australian National University. I saw Jim Davidson and left with him a first draft of the first chapter of my PhD thesis, "Frontier Society in Fiji, 1858–1873."

I had given another copy to Ken Gillion, my Adelaide supervisor. He came to my office one day and told me, very politely, that he felt that our ideas and approaches to the subject were very different, and that he did not wish to be involved any more. Ken was really more interested in the Indians in Fiji, rather than Fiji or Fijians. I was a bit shocked at first but as we spoke I became grateful for his early decision. I waited anxiously to see if Jim would respond in the same way. But after reading my work, while Carmel and I explored the national Capital for the first time, he relieved my anxiety, and said he thought it was going to be "very interesting and well written." Soon I met other students like Peter Corris, who was to become a very successful novelist, but was then working for his PhD about the "blackbirder" labour trade, and Deryck Scarr, a graduate of Exeter University in England, who was working on his thesis about the Western Pacific High Commission, that was to be eventually published as *Fragments of Empire*.[5]

Jim told me he thought that I would find it easy to "get on" with the Fijian people, and then reminded me of the amount of primary source material there was in the Fijian National Archives, especially the records of the Land Claims Commission, appointed by Sir Arthur Gordon, Fiji's first Governor, between 1875 and 1887. The Commission's job was to examine any documents that could be found, and to hear from witnesses, sometimes in English, sometimes in Fijian, to establish the legality or otherwise of the claims by settlers to the land they said they had bought from the indigenous landowners. These papers had been stored and catalogued in the Archives in Suva, and they contained a great deal of detailed personal information about the "Adventurous Spirits,"[6] their origins, and expectations, successes and failures, beliefs and values, as well as legal documents.

It was obvious that I would need to spend some considerable time in Suva if I was to make use of such valuable evidence. I was not entitled to Study Leave until 1968, so my first opportunity was in the long summer break from late December 1965, to the middle of March 1966, and I would need to spend as much of the three months as possible in Fiji. This would mean leaving Carmel with a heavy responsibility in Adelaide and I would have to cram as much research into a short a stretch of time as possible. I needed to learn as much of the Fijian language as I could. I also needed money for travel and accommodation expenses.

Jim also told me to knock on the door of his professorial colleague, Harry Maude, who had retired from the British Colonial Service. Harry had studied Anthropology at Cambridge and then successfully applied to enter the Colonial Service in 1929. His application had included a request, as a condition of his service, that he and his wife be sent to the British Colony of the Gilbert and Ellice Islands (now Kiribati and Tuvalu). In 1949 he was appointed to the South Pacific Commission, and in 1955 was appointed as a Research Associate of the then newly established School of Pacific History at the ANU. After a career of spectacular research and publication, he was a Professor, with an encyclopaedic knowledge of the subject to which he had devoted all his working life.

Harry's "office" was also his large and roomy library. He had made it his practice throughout his working life, to obtain copies of as many publications as possible

---

5   Scarr, Deryck, *Fragments of Empire: A History of the Western Pacific High Commission 1877-1914*. ANU Press 1967.

6   *Adventurous Spirits* was the title I chose for the book based on my PhD Thesis, eventually published by Queensland University Press in 1983.

that contained information about the Islands of the Pacific Ocean. In addition, he had preserved the many and varied administrative documents produced by the governance of the Colony of the Gilbert and Ellice islands, and the South Pacific Commission. His published books alone were a valuable collection of specialist literature, including the logs and letters of explorers, trading vessels, diaries of missionaries and beachcombers, some of them the astonishingly literate ex-convicts, deserters and shipwrecked sailors of the early nineteenth century. The collection also included the work of later waves of novelists like R M Ballantyne and Robert Louis Stevenson, anthropologists like Margaret Mead, and studies of the roles of Islanders themselves in World War II.

I was inspired by Harry's love for his subject, and the fact that it promised to be one of the "new histories," along with black history, labour history, and women's history, that called for new kinds of evidence and historical thinking. I had the opportunity, I thought, to head out to still uncharted waters where no-one had been before. Much of the history I had studied so far led to learned, but sometimes stifling quarrels about the interpretation of the well-worn evidence about *why* things happened. Here was a part of the world where I would start by finding out from new evidence, *what* happened, and what difference it made. There was also the theory that the small scale, and isolated nature of islands might be an intellectual advantage. Islands were the closest the historian could come to a laboratory, in which he or she could study the process of change over time, as it were through a microscope, and that could enable him or her, to quantify the relationship between human movement, innovation, and social consequences.

I applied to the Myer Foundation for funds to cover my fares, and was successful, and I left for Fiji on 17 December, 1965. I found a room in the very cheap South Seas Private Hotel in Suva. It was a typical Colonial structure, with rooms opening to a veranda on the first floor, and the atmosphere of a Somerset Maugham novel. I was joined at the guest house by David Routledge, another post graduate student from the ANU. He was working on the formation and history of the Cakobau Government which made the decision in 1874, to cede the Fijian nation to Britain. The South Seas was within easy walking distance of the National Archives, so I got a lot done. Peter France, a recent graduate of the Pacific History School of the ANU, gave me contacts with his friends, who treated me with generous hospitality in the weekends, and gave me food for thought, and useful contacts with descendants of the ex-pat society of the nineteenth century, whose origins I was studying. They also taught me to water ski, something I had never tried before.

Suva is about 190 kilometres from Nadi, where my plane from Sydney landed, so I had to spend a night in Nadi, before heading off to Suva by bus the next morning. I was carrying an ancient, heavy suitcase, walking towards the Skylodge Hotel, a kilometre or so from the airport, when I was overtaken by Joni, a young Fijian man with the Fijian version of my own name, about my own age, who offered to carry my luggage. As I knew I had a way to go, and the case was heavy, I was torn about how to respond. How many Australians, I wondered, would offer to carry the luggage of a visitor from Fiji? I had used some old ropes to make sure of the lid staying shut, which enabled me to accept his offer by sharing my load with him, and we continued to walk together. Joni asked me why I was visiting Fiji and I explained that I was a student of Fijian history engaged in research. He became very interested and by the time we reached the Skylodge, the cheapest hotel I could find, we had talked for about ten minutes and had become friends. He then invited me to come with him the next weekend to his home village. He explained that his village happened to be accessible only by boat, as it was a long way up the Rewa River, and had no access by road. I couldn't believe my luck, and we arranged to meet in Suva the next Saturday morning.

By this time I had read some of the nineteenth century Australian newspapers, which included articles and correspondence from early Australian settlers in Fiji. In the 1860s and 70s, they were purchasing Fijian land in the *Rewa* delta, in order to establish cotton plantations. Some of them spoke of "punitive expeditions" into the interior, after local Fijian opponents of white settlement had carried out raids on individuals who made land purchases without local knowledge, or failed to obtain chiefly support from the local rulers. I was to have the opportunity to re-live the experience of both sides, in the same place and the same conditions in which the culture clashes of the past had led to compromise or bloodshed.

Joni and I met in Suva as planned. The first part of our journey was by bus to a small delta village, from which Joni's kinsfolk took us aboard a vessel described as a "punt" (very much like *Discovery 2*!), the product of the developing trans-cultural naval architecture of the twentieth century. The early Australian, would-be cotton planters, travelled usually by whaleboat, and typically, with a "beachcomber," often a shipwrecked sailor, sometimes an escaped convict, or an old resident who had spent enough time in Fiji to learn the language, conform to local customs and respect chiefly authority. As the would-be settlers made their way upstream in the 1860s, it may have been necessary to borrow a *takia*, the smallest kind of indigenous watercraft in Fiji, moved with paddles rather than sails, and used in rivers and lagoons rather than the ocean. A century later, in 1965, the *takia* had been superseded as river transport by the punt. It was a long, narrow, flat-bottomed vessel, about twelve metres in length overall, built out of sawn planks, with a beam of about one metre. With a passenger on each of her nine thwarts, she didn't have much freeboard. Her main propulsion was a vintage four horse power Seagull outboard with a big propeller. These proportions of length, and the outboard engine proved to be extremely efficient in terms of the simultaneous requirements of speed, fuel economy, and load-carrying capacity. It took about two hours of travel upstream to reach Joni's village, on the starboard bank of the Rewa River. I was introduced to family and elders, who all spoke English for my benefit, as we exchanged questions and answers about local history, including early conflicts, and social structures. We enjoyed a meal based on *dalo*, known in other parts of the world as *taro*, and eaten with our hands. I was then introduced to the drink, *yaqona,* known outside Fiji, or amongst immigrants, as *kava,* and served in a communal coconut shell.

For me this was an important initiation ceremony. And I have never felt safer. I was a mere thirty miles or so from a capital city, but I was also alone as the guest of people who succeeded in preserving their culture, and are still largely self-sufficient, living in traditional *bures,* built mainly from local and therefore renewable materials. They succeeded in retaining eighty percent of their land, as the result of the rapid acquisition of foreign political skills by their leaders, ever since the 1870s. Because of that, they have enjoyed the ability to choose which aspects of modern Western culture to include in their own culture and which to leave out.

I was intrigued by the enthusiasm of the Fijian brand of Christianity, the outstanding legacy of English missionaries of the nineteenth century. Most of them were Methodists, who rivalled their predecessors, the beachcombers, as diplomats and builders of cultural bridges. Successful beachcomber interpreters protected chiefs from British and American naval visitations, which might otherwise have harassed them. Missionaries offered education, devised an orthography for the Fijian and other island languages, and were often guarantors of safety for trading vessels and their crews. They also succeeded in bringing the practice of cannibalism to an end. By the 1850s, Fiji was a Christian country, which, from the point of view of both the white settlers and the Fijians, was a valuable achievement.

A few days later, I met another young Fijian in a Suva pub. He had been a member of the Fijian rugby team which had defeated France in a match in Paris. He told me of the extreme excitement of his experience, and how he had prayed for victory as he came onto the field. I said it must have been difficult for God to deal with the similar prayers of the French team, to which he replied that on this occasion he had prayed, not to Jesus, but to Dengei, the deified leader of the original migration to Fiji from the west some 3000 years BP. This tongue in cheek conversation was held in a pub, but began to raise not only polite laughter, but questions in my mind about how religion of all kinds develops. I believe that Fijians have succeeded in including Christianity into their cultural philosophy in a way that has re-defined the national character, but without affecting the spiritual nature of the relationship between humanity and nature; the people and the *Vanua,* or "land." *Vanua* includes human and other animal communities, forests, the ocean, reefs and mountains; the ecosystems of which they are a part, and not least, the stars by which the people navigated the Pacific Ocean, and came home again, over two thousand years before Irish monks, Vikings or anyone else in the northern hemisphere had the confidence to sail out of sight of their own home shores.

In Suva, I found the primary sources I was using more and more interesting, and had no difficulty in spending all day completely absorbed in the rise and fall of the cotton planters and the social and political consequences. Carmel and I wrote frequently to each other, and looked forward desperately to being back together again. But she was finding it difficult to manage the children on her own, and it was not hard to detect determined courage between the lines of love and support. There was also an underlying regret that I had not chosen an area of specialisation in which we could both share an interest, or for which I would not have to spend long periods away from her and the children.

I remained in Fiji until I had taken enough notes to be able to continue to write my thesis, and returned to Adelaide well before the beginning of the 1966 academic year. But it was clear that if I was ever to finish my thesis, I would have to return to Fiji, for a short period at least, as soon as possible. I began to feel tension at this stage, between my need to concentrate on my research project, and my place in Adelaide, with its responsibilities to my wife, my children and my students. My Study Leave was not available until 1968, but there was nothing to stop me spending the next holiday period in Fiji at our own expense. My feeling was that the sooner I finished my thesis, the happier we would both be.

On 22 March 1965, I received a letter from Mrs Royal Buscombe, who was the secretary of the Pan Pacific and South East Asia Women's Association. Jim Davidson had passed on to her the information that I would be returning to Fiji later in the year. He told her that I intended to bring Carmel, and my children with me. He must have suggested that Carmel might be interested in doing some research as well, while she was in the country. This would be a way of persuading someone to write a biography of a notable Fijian woman, Lolohea Solomon. She was a much admired teacher and social worker of the early twentieth century, but Jim was a bachelor, and probably under-estimated the impact such an arrangement might have on us, and our relationship. Carmel had only a spectator interest in my field of enquiry, and was about to be appointed as a lecturer in the Classics department, which would mean full commitment. Not surprisingly she was seriously underwhelmed by Mrs Buscombe's suggestion.

By then, I was beginning to feel the consequences of the very middling academic performance of my earlier days, which meant I had to work extremely hard now, during the early life of my children. I was catching up. Our visit to Canberra had been an inspirational experience, and it was followed by encouragement. In September 1965, Harry Maude wrote to me to tell me about the impending launch of a new academic journal, *The Journal of Pacific History,* to be managed and edited by Jim Davidson and himself. Harry must have heard that I had submitted my article about Australia's Pacific Frontier, to *Historical Studies*. "Please John," he said:

> ... *don't send your next article to any other Journal, but let us have it. There are so few of us doing serious work in the field... that we do need everybody's support; and especially yours as you are working on such an interesting subject... Your paper would feel so much happier in the company of all its friends and colleagues.*

I was told also, that the ANU had recently bought a house, at 30 Beach Road, Laucala Bay, a suburb of Suva, very close to the new University of the South Pacific. The house was available to visiting scholars, who would be provided with a "house girl" to assist with housework and child care. Rent would be relatively cheap. This made it possible for us to think of a family visit to Fiji as a real possibility, and we booked the house, but made it clear to Royal Buscombe that one research project would be enough. Carmel would stay at the house with the children while I made a short visit to the northern Lau group of islands. I would then return to 30 Beach Road and continue work in the National Archives of Fiji.

I was invited to contribute to a new publication, *Pacific Islands Portraits*, jointly edited by Jim Davidson and Deryck Scarr. It consisted of a series of chapters by a list of twelve students, staff, and Associates of the ANU School of Pacific History. The subject was change, through time in the South Pacific, and the individuals and groups of people, both Islanders and Europeans, who made it happen, between the beginning of the nineteenth century and the outbreak of the First World War.[7] This was also the year in which I was eventually allowed to introduce an optional course for Honours (4th year) students, on the History of the Pacific Islands. The course turned out to be very successful.

This course was focussed on primary sources, which created an atmosphere of original discovery, in the context of new opportunity. I was no more familiar with the missionary diaries, ships logs of traders and explorers, semi-literate letters from lonely settlers to their families in Australia, the speeches of beach politicians, than the students were, so we learnt together. My first two Honours students, Caroline Melville and Bronwen Douglas were very capable and motivated.[8]

Both Caroline and Bronwen achieved First Class results in History. My co-markers agreed that their exam performances were as good as I said they were. And they both went on to earn PhDs and have successful academic careers. It was a good start to a course that I believe at the time, was the only one of its kind in the world, and it kept me busy for the next ten years. Two years later, in 1970, I was allowed to teach Pacific History to between thirty and forty-five undergraduate students at third year level, but only on condition that I continued to co-ordinate, lecture, read and mark essays for about one hundred and fifty students in Australian History as well. Eventually, Pacific History at levels 2, 3 and 4 became my core teaching responsibility, supplemented by contributory work in Asian history, known as "Old Societies and New States", an excellent first year alternative, at the time, to Australian or European history, and affectionately known as "Old Socks."

I loved my job, but it took time, and I was under a lot of pressure. When my chapter of *Pacific Island Portraits* was accepted for publication, I made my first, but

---

7   Eventually published in 1970 by the ANU Press. My chapter was called "Evanescent Ascendancy: The planter community in Fiji."

8   Caroline Ralston (née Melville), wrote a chapter in *Pacific Island Portraits* about "The Beach Communities" of the early nineteenth century, and followed up with a PhD, published as *Grass Huts and Warehouses*. Later she became a lecturer at Macquarie University. Bronwen Douglas was awarded her PhD at the ANU, taught at La Trobe University for seventeen years, and became a research fellow of the Australian National University in 1997. She published many books and articles and received many honours for her work.

unsuccessful attempt, to gain promotion to the rank of Senior Lecturer. But I did receive an encouraging reply from Hugh Stretton, which clarified my priorities for me and let me down gently:

I have always thought you ought to be a workable candidate for accelerated senior lectureship, on general grounds of skill, zeal, I.Q., publications etc etc. But in a negative way, an unfinished PhD would certainly be a hindrance. Next year, with that finished, it would be reasonable to propose you be promoted.

Our stay in Suva at 30 Beach Road was short, but pleasant enough. Eta, a very capable Fijian woman with her own grown-up family was a daily visitor, and she made friends with all three of our children immediately, which enabled us to explore Suva in a leisurely way, and spend time with New Zealander friends, like Terry Donnelly, and his wife, Robina. Terry had been a member of the cast of *The Beggar's Opera*, and was then a teacher at Suva Grammar School.

I resumed my work on the Lands Claims Commission documents, but Carmel was once again landed with all the domestic responsibilities. In the end, we decided that we had made a mistake. Carmel returned to Adelaide on her own, and Eta and I took charge of the children for the next two weeks. Carmel had work to prepare for her lectures, and I needed to do some fathering. I found that at the ages of five, three and two, Stephen could climb on my back, Philip could climb on my shoulders, and I could carry Susan in my arms. We went for walks down to the beach to watch the flying boats land and take off, and to swim in the warm shallow water. Sometimes we took a bus and went into Suva to look at the Market, or the docks, or the yacht club with its diminutive café where we could order children's portions of Taveuni steak, or look at the international fleet of cruising yachts, which put ideas into my head for the future.

Back in Adelaide, there were more distractions. The major concern of the students was the introduction of conscription of 20 year olds, for the war in Vietnam, introduced as a compulsory national service in 1964. In the past, Australia had seen several schemes for compulsory military training, but only for the defence of the country in the case of invasion. Robert Menzies, the Liberal Party Prime Minister was no fool, and would have realised that Australia had a history of enthusiastic support for sending Australian soldiers overseas, provided they were volunteers. Menzies tested the water before taking the plunge. He began by introducing a National Service Act, which required 20 year old males to be conscripted for two years. The following year, in May 1965, the Act was amended to allow conscripts to be sent to Vietnam, in spite of vigorous parliamentary opposition by the Labor Party, which continued until it won the 1972 election.

There were many opposing viewpoints about conscription in Australia. Two referenda had been held in order to test public opinion about sending conscripts overseas during the World War I, in 1916 and 1917, and in both cases, voters rejected the proposal by narrow majorities. Many opponents of sending conscripts overseas in the 1960s were conscious of the referenda of the past. The results had demonstrated the opinions of most Australian voters, that while compulsory military training of young men was justified on the grounds of national defence, and for its popular ability to "turn boys into men" in peace-time, most people thought conscripts should not be involved overseas in the fulfilment of agreements with allies, however close. That was the job of the regular professional army. I decided to use my opportunity as a lecturer in Australian History, to inform the public about Australian Foreign Policy, and the historical circumstances of both World War I ("the Great War to end all wars") and the contemporary situation, in which the government had not taken the risk of public rejection by referendum and had passed a law to legalise foreign action by conscripts.

I put an advertisement in the Adelaide paper, *The Advertiser*, inviting members of the public to come to the lecture I was going to give anyway at Adelaide University, about the history of Australian Foreign Policy. Some of my colleagues criticised me, but I told them that if Universities were to think that a search for truth, and participating in public debate, should not be part of their mission, they were not worth the public expenditure they were given.

I started the lecture by comparing the reasons for Australian participation in previous offshore conflicts, including World War II, in which Australian conscripts had fought against the Japanese in New Guinea. The justification for sending conscripts "overseas" in this instance, was that the Japanese were clearly working towards an invasion of Australia, a country that had formally declared war on Japan. The Vietnam war was different, I argued. New Guinea was an Australian Mandated Territory under a Mandate of the League of Nations. Conscription of Australian twenty year olds for the war in Vietnam was not introduced because Vietnam, or anyone else was likely to invade Australia. It was because the USA needed Australian support for its own strategic and diplomatic purposes.

Our Government had defended its decision by exploiting the racist roots of the Australian psyche, the now discredited belief in the "Yellow Peril." This fear could be used to support the theory that North Vietnam was a puppet of Communist China. My research and reading about the history of China–Vietnam relations over many centuries, led me to believe that it was the focus of Vietnamese nationalism on the removal of French colonialism, that had shaped the political environment, rather than the so-called "domino theory." This held that the re-union of North and South Vietnam would be the precursor to the advance of communism down the Malaysian peninsula, and ultimately to the invasion of Australia. Someone who disagreed with me wrote to *The Advertiser* to object to my action, and signed him or herself, "Worried." I wrote back: "Dear Sir/Madam, I am glad that in opening a discussion on Vietnam at the University, I succeeded in making somebody 'worried.' That was the idea."

This incident led to other speaking invitations—not particularly illustrious ones, but interesting all the same. The debating Society of the Presbyterian Girls'

College invited me to speak to them and engage in discussion. The College secretary, Carol Dubberly, wrote me a thank you letter afterwards, which I enjoyed and kept:

The obvious enthusiasm and concern with which you spoke, and answered our questions was infectious. It was refreshing to be presented with concrete arguments, instead of a nebulous mass of rather doubtful prejudices.

Trevor Olafson, the secretary of the Bordertown Apex Club, wrote to the University Registrar to help him to find a speaker for the Club's International Goodwill annual dinner on 23 May 23 1967:

In the past our speakers have been drawn from various Embassies and Consulates. However, as International Relations Director this year, it is my hope to secure the services of a speaker with an up to the minute view of some of the international problems, and to this end, I seek your help.

This invitation was passed on to Professor Duncan, Head of the Political Science department, and to George Rudé, who was the Acting Head of the History Department while Hugh Stretton was on leave. There was a "minute" on the letterhead in the Registrar's handwriting that indicated that both men were "prepared to co-operate, and compete with the embassies." Their co-operation evidently consisted of a decision to ask me to take the job, since I had already created the extra-curricular role for myself.

Somewhat to my surprise, I found that the community of Bordertown was not in favour of conscription anyway. In spite of its support of the Liberal Party in general, the people were anxious about the impact that conscription would have on the local labour force. Young men were too valuable as a source of labour and agricultural management to be wasted, as so many other Australians' lives had been wasted in the past in defence of international and Imperial interests.

Another invitation to speak came from an Adelaide anti-war institution, which planned a large outdoor protest meeting in Light Square, a large green patch of parkland, close to the city centre, named after Colonel Light. I spent a lot of time in careful reading, including Bernard Fall's recently published book, *The Two Vietnams*.[9]

This was the first time I had spoken to a large number of people out of doors. There was a microphone and a podium, taking me back nostalgically to my Mark Antony role in 1951. Light Square was full of people, and when I stepped up to start speaking, a vehicle drew up alongside with a man and a woman with a camera. I hoped it might have been the press, but when they started filming me, as I was just about to speak, I asked them who they were. "ASIO,"[10] they answered, so I knew that I had been identified by the Government as a person of some kind of interest. I told them I was happy for them to concentrate on their job, and I would get on with mine. I never heard from them again.

---

9   Fall, Bernard, *The two Vietnams: a political and military analysis,* Frederick A Praeger, *1964.* Bernard Fall stepped on a land mine in Vietnam in 1967 and was killed.

10 Australian Security and Intelligence Organisation.

One day, I can't remember when, a law student called John Bannon, who was the President of the Student Labor Club, came to see me and asked if I would speak to a student audience about Vietnam in the Union Theatre at Adelaide University. By then I was well rehearsed and accepted the invitation. However, it was not an altogether a happy occasion. The back row of the packed theatre was filled by a mainly male line. I learnt later that the meeting had been successfully stacked by Catholic students from the Aquinas Society, and they were influenced by the strong anti-communism of the Democratic Labor Party, representing the Catholic section of the labour movement.

I congratulated them for their intelligent interest about an issue of national importance, and told them that I had been lucky in not being sent overseas as a conscript from New Zealand only a short time ago (it would have been "to deal with the Suez Crisis"). I said it was to be expected that as the Vietnam war continued, older men would be needed. The age for accepting recruits was likely to rise. I was only a few years older than them, and it was not improbable that we would meet again on the battlefield in Vietnam. We would want to know then, why the war had begun, and what kind of a war was it anyway? What was the ethical case for Australia's support? The heckling ceased and I received a fair hearing.

Soon, organisations in each Australian state were formed to oppose conscription. They began to have the effect of opposing Australia's involvement altogether. Eventually, in 1972, Gough Whitlam was elected as Prime Minister, with a Labor Party government, that withdrew Australian troops.

I was getting the hang of making political speeches, and started thinking about a career change and becoming a politician. That might have been fun, but I knew I had to return to Fiji, so I didn't think about it for long. Luckily for Australia, Neal Blewett, a new member of the Politics department, was destined to build on the early indications in South Australia, of a potentially successful campaign against conscription, and continued the good work. That led him to a very successful career, as a Labor Member of Parliament (1977) with several ministerial appointments in the 1980s, followed by a period as High Commissioner for Australia in London. I remember an occasion in the shared tea room in the Napier building, when he announced his inclination to run for Parliament, but could not decide, at that stage, to which party he should offer his talents, which were considerable.

My next visit to Fiji was a short one during the mid-year break. My main purpose was to visit the Lau group of islands, midway between Tonga and the main Fijian Island of Viti Levu. The fortunes of the early white settlers who came to Viti Levu varied very much between some successes, but more failures. On the other hand, the owners of some of the islands in Northern Lau, and the large island of Taveuni, had been strikingly successful. The owners of land in this area in 1966 were often the descendants of the original pioneers of the 1860s and 70s. I was interested to discover the reasons why these settlers had been more successful than their Viti Levu counterparts. I managed to arrange for a berth on a Government vessel, *Komaiwai*, due to visit several of the Eastern Islands on Government business. Unlike the Japanese tuna fishing boats in Suva Harbour, *Komaiwai* was small, about eighty feet long, and kept in immaculate condition. I had my own cabin and felt very privileged.

Harry Maude learnt of my good fortune and begged me to make a special effort to visit the island of Naitauba, which had been purchased in 1862 from the Tui Cakau (the "lord of the reefs"). It became a cotton and then coconut plantation as an offshoot of the main commercial establishment of the Hennings brothers at Lomaloma, on the larger island of Vanua Balavu. It was at Naitauba, however, that the business records of the largest mercantile organisation in Fiji of the period (1860–1875) had survived. Harry told me that several officials and other enthusiasts had done their best to persuade Mrs Elizabeth Hennings, who was then the owner of Naitauba, to part with the records for their value to historians. The records contained valuable historical information about the whole pre-colonial, and early colonial economy. But no-one succeeded. Harry said it was most important that the records should be given to the Fiji National Archives, and asked me to make what use I could of my powers of persuasion, to ensure that Elizabeth Hennings would allow the records to be moved.

Elizabeth (née Vogel) married Gustavus Mara Hennings, the son of William Hennings, founder of the Hennings Plantation Company, and Adi Mere Tuisalalo, who was a Fijian woman of chiefly rank. William Hennings was the first white settler at Lomaloma, Vanua Balavu, and the owner of some other islands as well, including Naitauba. He was also the German Consul to Fiji. His part German, part Fijian son, Gustavus Mara, visited Germany as a young man, probably in 1905 or 1906, and met and married Elizabeth. On his return, his father gave him the job of managing the Company's affairs on Naitauba island.

Gus' and Elizabeth's performance as custodians of Naitauba was innovative and exemplary. Instead of following the well-trodden path of a cotton monoculture and replacing the indigenous inhabitants with imported labourers from other islands or from India, which was the common practice at the time, they developed a partnership with the existing Fijian inhabitants and diversified their crops. They also encouraged and supported young islanders who sought educational opportunities; and made it their business to accept responsibility for the health and prosperity of the island community. In return, Elizabeth retained chiefly status after the death of her husband in 1955. His mother, Adi Tuisalalo, had been a chief in her own right. Elizabeth had risen to the occasion and in consequence achieved the chiefly status of her mother-in-law in the sight of the Fijian inhabitants.[11]

Komaiwai made short work of her passage, of one day and night from Suva to Lomaloma, against the steady twenty knot trade-wind so that I woke up to a vista

---

11 Scarr, Deryck, "Creditors and the House of Hennings: an elegy from the Social and Economic History of Fiji," *Journal of Pacific History*, Vol 7, 1972, pp 104 123.

that was almost a caricature of the Hollywood vision of the south seas, with a sheltering islet on one side, and on the other side, a white beach, backed by a largely Fijian style village, and a few modern buildings.

Komaiwai had Government business to attend to on the island of Kanacea, to the south-east of Lomaloma, so the plan was to send me north-east to Naitauba in the ship's tender, a fast aluminium open boat with a powerful outboard engine, and leave me there to be picked up the next day. My voyage from Lomaloma took about two hours, swooping at about twenty knots, over a calm sea with a big ocean swell. I was met on the beach on the southern corner of the island by Elizabeth Hennings herself, the owner and ruler. I thought she was probably in her seventies. We drove up from the beach to her house in an old jeep.

I had written to Elizabeth beforehand, explaining the subject of my thesis, and I stressed the historical importance, in my view, of any records that had survived of the history of her family and the commercial activities of its members. She questioned me robustly about my educational background, and teaching role at the University of Adelaide, and suggested that we should go for a drive to help me to understand the current working of the plantation. It was her custom to rise early in the morning and visit all the places where work was currently in progress, and make decisions each day about the seasonal activities that her working men and women were engaged in. I explained the tight schedule that I was working on, and I wished that I had been able to spend more time on the Island, but my dependence on the itinerary of *Komowai* made that impossible.

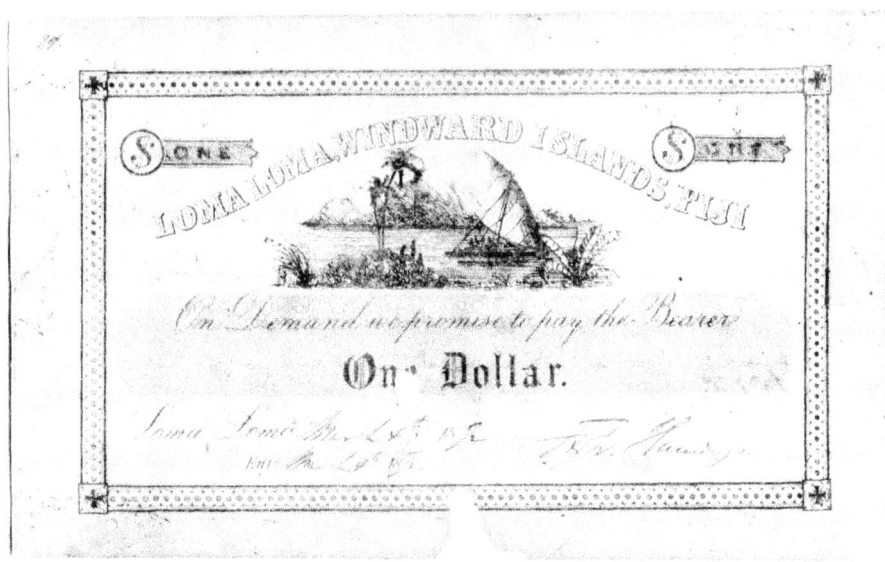

A Hennings Dollar, issued by the Hennings brothers of Lomaloma, Vanua Balavu, Fiji, in 1872.

Elizabeth was clearly ideally suited to her role as chief of the island community, responsible for the welfare of all its inhabitants, including a large number of children, as well as the management of a complicated business. We had time, as she drove, to discuss topics such as our own backgrounds and interests. She said she much preferred living on Naitauba, with its isolated beauty and purposeful community, than the alternative, of living as a member of the ex-pat community in Suva and farming out the island economy and people to some manager with a purely commercial ethos. She both valued her chiefly position and understood its deeply founded obligations to both the people and the island itself.

This fact was brought home to me very clearly as soon as we sat down in Elizabeth's house. She rang a brass bell and within seconds a young Fijian woman made a crouching entrance into the room, keeping her head below the level of Elizabeth's head as she sat in an arm chair. Tea was ordered, and the servant maid went out in the same style, returning on her knees and pushing a trolley.

I became anxious about the very short opportunity I had to build the trust I felt I needed to be able to raise the question of the commercial records I had come for. I explained that my time was limited and that I had been asked to obtain them on behalf of the Fiji National Archives. This seemed to be the right thing to say. I suspect that others had asked her to sell them to private collections. I made it clear that the Archives would be given the job of sorting the material, repairing damage and making the records available to future generations of Fijian scholars, as well as intrusive *kaivalagi* (European) academics like me.

I wrote to Carmel about my visit on 3 March 1966 when I was back on *Komowai*:

Mrs Hennings was charming. She is 81, but has the energy of a healthy 45 year old, and she is absolutely "all there." She runs the plantation, gets up at 5 am and works in the office til 7. Then she has a cup of coffee about 8.30, and goes round til eleven supervising the work. There is a staff of about 30, and she runs a store and a savings bank as well. She reads a lot—says she'd rather stay in Naitauba than go and live in Suva and talk to the people there. She is staying to run the place for Raymond Burr, who will soon be the new owner.[12] I had a splendid dinner, a comfortable bed, and Mrs Hennings said she was delighted to have someone to talk to, so we talked as long as she wanted to, about deep questions of religion and politics; not sex as such, though she would probably have been quite prepared to. In the morning she got up at five. I got up at six, and she got a man to take me all over the island in a truck.

Elizabeth pointed out a very small building, which looked to me like a chook house, and unlocked it for me. The documents were kept in four trunks and two boxes. There seemed to be a few silver fish amongst them, so I tried to impress her with both my fascination and appreciation of the significance of the documents. I could see that I should do my best to sort them into some sort of order and if possible, put them into clean containers. Soon she found a large wooden box and a few small ones, to re-pack them. I wrote to Carmel:

---

12 Burr, an American actor and television personality had recently bought the island but kept Elizabeth on as his manager.

A lot of them had been chewed by rats, and/or saturated with nasty water, but I rescued a good two thirds and packed them up in new packing cases and brought them with me, with her permission, for the Archives. I regard this as a diplomatic triumph. They consist of letter books of outward correspondence to planters, the gov't, the parent firm of Godeffroy's, and bundles of inward correspondence, letters from the same sources. Also a lot of plantation journals and account books. They go from about 1860 to 1890. I spent a whole afternoon working flat out getting them packed up as I thought the ship was coming in six hours' time. She only had one island to do before coming to get me, and the copra, from Naitauba. As it was, it poured with rain and they were delayed til next morning.

Elizabeth worked with me for a time, and in a few minutes we came across a bundle of what looked like paper dollars. Closer examinations confirmed that they were, indeed, an early form of currency, issued by the Hennings brothers of Lomaloma in 1872. Printed in a fading red ink was an announcement, signed on their behalf, by F W Hennings, that, "On demand we Promise to pay the bearer, One Dollar." Elizabeth was pleasantly surprised to find them, and took them, except two: one for the Archives, and one for me, which I photographed and included as an illustration in my thesis. I spent the rest of the day working as hard as I could to sort the documents into categories, tying ribbons around the bundles, and removing dirt and silverfish as much as I dared. I realised that it was more important to include as many documents as possible, rather than to make an amateur attempt to do the job of an archivist. The next day was fine and we took the wooden cases down to the beach landing place to wait for *Komaiwai* to arrive. I wrote again to Carmel:

I got onto the ship again at 9 for breakfast. I've got the papers safely on the ship… I meant to tell you; in one trunk, which had no lid, I found half a dozen eggs, laid God knows how long ago, by a stray fowl. It was when she was looking for eggs in an old outhouse that Mrs Hennings first found the papers herself.

That was the last I ever saw of Adi Elizabeth. I realised that I had been very lucky to be there at the right time, when the records of the island were still in her hands. Four years later I received a letter from Elizabeth's daughter, Mrs R J Miller, from Pingelly in Western Australia. She told me that her mother had been hit by a police truck "… while crossing from the Cathedral to the Defence club" in Suva, and died in hospital a few days later. Mrs Miller wanted to "read my book," which she assumed I must have written and published by then. I had to reply in sorrow and tell her that I had not yet published it, but had been very impressed by her mother. A revised version of my thesis was eventually published.[13]

Carmel wrote to me in mid-1966. We had talked a lot about our marriage and how it was going, and how to make it better:

Your second letter was very interesting, [the first one was about Mrs Hennings] *And I agree with what you say. I've been awfully intolerant and intellectually snobbish since we were at Oxford, but I suddenly feel quite different. I don't know how you have*

---

13   Young, J M R, *Adventurous Spirits: Australian Migrant Society in Pre-Cession Fiji,* QUP, 1984.

put up with it so long really. My horrible attitude must have spoiled lots of things you would otherwise have enjoyed. I was thinking yesterday about Stephen's birth and boyhood and how thrilled you were. I wish I had been more relaxed and happy. I did feel just the same about him... but there was too much work to do and too much worry.

Anyway, I am going to be quite different. I was awful about your work too, but I feel different about it now as well, and I'm really very glad I came to Fiji, as I know lots more about it now.

She was true to her word. We soon moved to a restored cottage in Barnard Street, North Adelaide, where Carmel created a joyous environment. I established a routine of working in the peace and silence of the early morning for a few hours, like Mrs Hennings, before waking Carmel up with a cup of tea. The routine enabled me to finish my thesis within the extension of time I had been granted. I submitted it in December 1968. My PhD was awarded in 1969, and I was immediately promoted to a senior lectureship.

Susan had picked up a stray female terrier dog, which she adored. We decided that as we were surrounded by parklands, and the boys wanted a proper puppy, they could have one. He was a black Labrador. We called him Sigmund. Read on to discover the reason for that.

Chapter 12: Babes in the Wood

Let me introduce Dr Clive Kneebone into this story. He was a colleague of Dr Gillen, another psychoanalyst, who began treating Carmel for depression in 1967. I became Dr Kneebone's patient towards the end of that year. He started by asking me why I wanted to see him, and I told him that I felt my marriage was in trouble. I thought it must be my fault as much as Carmel's, and I would like to be able to save it. Then he went on to describe the arrangements. I would see him for an hour twice a week, possibly for two years, depending on progress and my ability to pay his fees. Our conversations would be strictly confidential.

Clive was a classic Freudian. He cautioned me against the assumption that he could enable me to save my marriage, but said that if it was to be ended, it was likely that with the aid of my psycho-analysis, the end of it would have the psychological and family impact of a surgical operation as opposed to a road crash.

I actually lay on a couch; looking away from him in his adjacent chair, which was out of my sight. He did not ask me questions, but waited for me to open the conservation, which began with me telling him exactly what was on my mind at the time, however amusing, embarrassing or shocking it might be. If I did not speak he continued to be silent until the hour was up, and I still had to pay him. I thought this was clever, and could be interesting.

It brought to mind how, when Carmel had gone to confession after our first copulation, I felt that I should share the responsibility for her sin, and do the same. I told Clive during the early sessions, about most of the things you must have read about to get this far, and some more things that I will tell you about as we move on. Clive responded by telling me that however clever we thought we were, in terms of emotional maturity, we were both "babes in the wood."

My first meeting with Clive must have been around the end of August 1967, as I had a letter from my mother who was visiting my Ant Molly in Harrogate. Molly was very ill: "The cancer," she said, "has spread from lungs to other organs; short of a miracle, the outlook is not very hopeful… I hope Carmel is now safely back home and all is going well. I expect you find the psychiatry interesting, and I do hope that it is helping to solve some of your problems."

Some of our problems arose because of my transition, and possibly Carmel's as well, from single sex boarding school adolescence, to adulthood with three children. Carmel's return, which my mother referred to, was from a visit to New Zealand for her mother's funeral. Carmel's father had died when we were both at Oxford. Carmel was naturally depressed by her mother's death. The news about Molly filled me with a mixture of guilt and sorrow as well. Both of us were unhappy, and did our best to comfort one another.

Molly always took her responsibility as my godmother very seriously, and wrote to me more often than I wrote to her, to remind me of my vows of various sorts, as

I had not always succeeded in keeping them. My sister, Heather, also wrote later to tell me about Molly's death. She died on 3 December 1967. It was difficult to find sufficient morphine for her in her last hours, but Molly and Heather talked about the outing Molly had planned for the tenants of Tate House, the Harrogate home for the blind which Molly was in charge of. After her nursing career, Molly continued to write and publish poems and stories that were broadcast by the BBC, such as "A Christian Cantata" in which she imagined a Britain occupied by Nazi Germany, with Hitler standing in for Herod, and Mary and Joseph turning up in a village pub in a dialect-speaking Yorkshire village like Cropton or Rosedale.

Carmel's initial depression arose during my repeated absences from 1966 to 1970, and I should have realised what was happening. Given the choice of Fiji as my research area, it was to be expected that if I also spent time and energy teaching a full load and working on political issues, such as the Vietnam war, I would make her life more difficult. A letter from Carmel posted when I was in Fiji dug up some old issues:

> *I still disagree about your talks on Vietnam—I can understand you wanting to do something, but it was foolish to think talks to such odd people would really help... I just think there must be better ways of opposing the Government. Stephen has just started school in North Adelaide.*[1]

In addition to my absences at this time of our lives, she found it difficult to combine her teaching and other academic responsibilities in the Classics Department with the care of our children. And though she was lonely, no-body seemed to care. Other letters when she was in Adelaide, and I was in Fiji, told me that only one young couple could be bothered with occasional visits, "I quite like them now," she wrote:

> *Though the chief topic of conversation is never far from marital infidelity. I always espouse the Sanctity of the Home. The boys have been a lot tidier since I started hitting them more. Stephen is crazy about stories, and makes me read to him a lot. They hardly go outside unless I do.*[2]

Another letter says:

> *We have the most silent phone in Adelaide. Every so often I pick it up to see if it works, but it does! It's just that in our circle, if you have kids you might as well have Leprosy. I resent it greatly... I am on the full dose of Valium, and not finding the good doctor very understanding at all.*[3] *Stephen has been much better, rather a pet in fact, but the responsibility is very hard to take. We've spent a lot of money,* [and she gave me a list of bills] *but such a lot is coming in. It's rather splendid! Susan is yelling her little head off, so I might as well stop. Love, Carmel.*

---

1   Undated letter, but must have been February 1967, when Stephen went to North Adelaide's State Primary school.

2   She was joking. She never hit anyone, even me, but later on she did throw crockery.

3   Not Dr Gillen, her Freudian analyst, but his mainstream, chemically driven predecessor. I can't remember his name.

Philip was going to kindergarten by then, and we had moved from Blair Athol to Barnard Street, North Adelaide. The house was held in our joint names, like our boat and our car. It was an old cottage, in this, the most convenient and pleasant of the inner ring of suburbs that surround the city of Adelaide. It was ten minutes' walk across parkland to the University. The house was old, by Australian standards, and had been "done up" by a developer who had modernised the original late nineteenth century dwelling, with a new kitchen, a modern bathroom, three bedrooms, and a study. The house retained its back verandah, a garden, a garage/workshop, and its sandstone charm. With both boys out most of the day, after I arrived home, we still needed household help to look after Susan on weekdays for another year, and Mrs Upshall, whose own children were grown up, enabled us, and Susan, to have no worries.

Susan soon made friends with a stray dog, who she called Freda, to begin with, then Fred, after my housemaster at Christ's Hospital. Fred was a brown, white and black terrier of modest size, and seemed not to require oxygen to sustain life. She could often be found *in* Susan's bed, under the blankets, right at the bottom. Susan found her a great comfort. The following year Carmel and I decided to acquire a black Labrador puppy for the boys. We called him Sigmund, because of the influence that Freud was having on our lives. We felt he was black enough to represent "the sub-conscious."

Nineteen sixty-nine was a good year for me. I had my two Pacific History Honours students and was organising and delivering most of the lectures of a course at first year level on Australian History, for which I had argued a case at departmental committee meetings. I was assisted by two tutors, Decie Denholm and Peter Cahalan, and a new lecturer, Ron Norris. With their support, first year Australian History became increasingly popular. In 1969, the course attracted one hundred and twelve students. The following year, there were one hundred and fifty nine. I had two Honours students each year after that for my fourth year Honours course in Pacific History.

In 1970, I was allowed to meet demand for a second or third year course for students who wanted to major in an advanced year course in the history of the Pacific Islands. This was the first such course to be taught in Australia.[4] Between 1969 and 1978, I also supervised a total of fifteen theses by Honours students, two PhD theses, and one MA in Pacific Islands history. My two PhD students, Peter Morrison and Ian Campbell both won University prizes in successive years for their theses.

I saw the success of the first year Australian History course as an opportunity to earn some career points by presenting a paper on it at the annual ANZAAS[5] conference at the University of Queensland in 1971. My offer was accepted and that meant my air fare was provided by the University. I wanted to break the news that instead of studying Australian History in the final year of an ordinary Arts degree,

---

4   This course could be taken at either second or third year level.

5   Australian and New Zealand Association for the Advancement of Science.

perhaps as a last minute introduction to original research, Australian History in Adelaide began with a semester on local history and the use of primary sources. This enabled eighteen year-old students to find for themselves what it is like to discover the truth about the past of their own locality from primary sources. I started the lecture series on a national level by the then novel experiment of teaching the known history of Aboriginal society before the British invasion. But at the same time, I wanted the students to be introduced to the techniques of historical research and writing in their weekly tutorials.

We divided the class into tutorial groups of six to eight students, and allocated to each group, the task of contributing to the social history of the suburban expansion of Victorian Adelaide, from 1870 to 1890. Each group was given the task of dealing with one inner suburb; North Adelaide, Norwood, Unley, Prospect, Walkerville or Thebarton, all of which had developed into true suburbs between those years. I suggested that they sampled the primary sources at five year intervals — 1870, 1875, 1880, 1885 and 1890 — with pairs of students working on different kinds of historical information, such as Parliamentary debates, Assessment rolls (which evaluated every building and identified the name and occupation of individual property owners); newspapers, election results, Mayoral reports, and whatever private correspondence we could find; all for one year. Notes were to be kept uniformly on system cards, so that they could be exchanged between the pairs of students in each group and passed on to the next cohort the following year.

Tutorials became working parties, supervised by me, or one of my colleagues, in which each pair of students spoke about their discoveries and then allocated between themselves, the weekly tasks of writing up the conclusions reached by the group for the following week. Tutorials often took up to two hours instead of one. All the local Councils were very co-operative, and set aside small rooms which were used to house the documentary sources that the students worked on. At the end of the course, final summaries of each twenty-year suburban history were presented at one all-day conference. My intention was that each year, the new students would move on to the next year, 1871, 1876 and so on, and I hoped it would result in an eventual student publication of a five-year co-operative achievement. But that didn't happen.

In the long run, my Australian specialist colleagues were not keen to keep the idea of Australian History at first year level going. But the conference paper I wrote about the course, "Australian History in the first year. A report on an experiment" was well received at the ANZAAS conference that year in Brisbane. George Gregory, a journalist, attended my talk; and the substance of what I said appeared in *The Bulletin*, under the title, "Australia looks at its History."[6] Otherwise, I would have submitted my paper to an academic journal.

I kept some of the final reports that survived. But the following year there were more staff changes, and I had so many students enrolling in Pacific History that I

---

6   *The Bulletin: incorporating The Australian Financial Times*, 31 July 1971.

would not have had sufficient time to teach anything else and I was allowed to stick with my courses on Pacific History.

I used student questionnaires to find out whether the course had been a successful experiment as an introduction to the discipline of History. The consensus was that it was very demanding but also rewarding. Individual comments were also illuminating. One student said, "it made history relevant to life. A subject of personal interest." Another said, "Australian history was the best subject I have done." The question remained, did it provide a satisfactory introduction to the study of History? To quote some of the students' comments:

A good introduction to the study of history, and ways of going about things, and making me aware of the difficulties, especially the Research Project. Makes me feel unsure, having no background in European history, yet if I had the choice again I'd do Australia.

Since Australia was settled by Europeans, the ideologies, beliefs, etc of Australians in the past have been grounded on European thinking. Learning about them gives one a background in European thought.

Tutors also found the work demanding but rewarding. Peter Cahalan spent two hours with a student discussing North Adelaide in the 1870s, and finally suggested it was time for lunch. "I'm going back to the Hall," said the student, "I never stop to eat when I'm working on Assessment Books." And a second year student said: "No knowledge is irrelevant. The main effect of first year history is to develop the appropriate techniques of university level studies. Interesting courses help."

✧✧✧✧✧

By co-incidence, the same *Bulletin* issue in which George Gregory's report about my ANZAAS paper appeared, also contained an article by Peter Manning that had a bearing on the depression that Carmel and I experienced at this time. It was entitled "Permissiveness: Where will it end?" and was focussed on the changes in public morality and behaviour of the period.

The 1950s and 60s in Australia were the "Twenty Good Years," celebrated in the Harold Hopkins ABC TV series of that title. The series documented not permissiveness, but the upward mobility of a generation that came of age as the shadows of war were chased away by allied victory in World War II, in spite of new wars in Korea and then Vietnam. The period is now remembered for the positive realities of rising incomes, more educational opportunities, and more demands for the implementation of new ideas such as equal pay for women, National Health, withdrawal from the Vietnam war, University expansion, Commonwealth funded scholarships for the best students, and very low levels of unemployment.

Racism persisted, as a welded-on component of Australian culture, but slowly began to become "un-cool" in the eyes of our students. Migration from many parts of the world made Australia a more sophisticated and interesting country, and pregnancy was no longer the likely consequence of premarital sex. We really believed, in Australia, that we were on the way towards a better world.

But as Peter Manning pointed out in the *Bulletin*, there was evidence of a seismic shift of public opinion and attitude in the region of sexual morality. His article concentrated on public disapproval of censorship, the popularity of writers like Henry Miller; magazines like *Oz*, the Australian product that embarrassed London; stage shows which included nudity, like *Hair* and books like *Portnoy's Complaint*, and Sue Rhodes' *Now you'll think I'm awful*, "that outrageous book about Sex and the Australian Girl."[7] Manning wrote:

> The times are not only changing in what we are allowed to see and watch, but what we are doing and thinking. Changing attitudes to the body, to sexual relations and to marriage and family have become common fare for party talking points… In bush land settings mixed nude bathing has become commonplace. In public meetings, public speakers drop four-letter words.

I didn't think all this mattered very much. The changes in Australian society were not unique, and prudishness was something we could well do without. In retrospect, I suspect that many of our generation in the so-called Developed World were swept along in an international ideological mainstream that also meant that we lost some sense of ethical responsibility for our students, our children, and each other.

Geoffrey Badger was a new Vice-Chancellor, who wanted the Adelaide University staff to have a new lunch-time dining room, which would enable us to participate in inter-departmental or even interdisciplinary intellectual discussion, and would provide a context for positive social and intellectual development. It was a great idea, and the new staff club building was also a place to which visiting scholars could be invited.

It was not long though, before a particular table, "Table 4," became known, indeed became famous, as the place where the "Young Turks" of the university could always be found at lunch time, and where smart talk and scandal could be enjoyed. Our model was what we imagined the coffee houses of London in the time of Jonathan Swift to have been. We cultivated the art of witty conversation. Geoffrey Badger made a point of dropping in on us, now and again, no doubt to enjoy our youthful company, but I remember one day when we had scoffed a bit more wine than usual.

I think now that Geoff struggled with the problem of how to make us feel we were on the cusp of misbehaviour, without causing offence. He did well, and we agreed, one day (after he had remarked, with a carefully measured note of sarcasm, that the University of Adelaide was the only university in his experience that had what you might call a "jet set"), that we might be pushing our luck. He then left the table. I reflected that we might have been getting a bit boring for people on the other tables. Sometimes people did say funny, perhaps even witty things. Someone spilt a salt cellar across the tablecloth, and Psychology lecturer Frank Dalziel shouted, "quick, pour some red wine on it!"

---

7   Gareth Powell Associates, Gladesville NSW, 1967.

My worst memory of Table 4 was at exam time, in December 1967, when teaching had stopped, and we felt relaxed. We were looking forward to study leave, or holidays. The adjacent library was crowded with anxious students cramming as hard as they could, while Table 4 was at its loud and ugly worst. A young girl student had the considerable courage to come out of the library and ask us to moderate our volume, as everyone in the library was preparing for the exams we had set them. I'm glad to be able to say that we were suitably humbled, apologised, and went back to our studies, libraries and laboratories, to work on the preparation of the teaching, research and writing that we were supposed to be doing.

At home, Carmel and I started to discuss the state of our marriage, and the old worries about infidelity, in the light of our good luck, good jobs, and our parental responsibilities. This led to what turned out to be a calamitous discussion about the increasingly fashionable fad of so-called "open marriage." The important thing, we agreed, was that no one should suffer from the effects of one or other of us "having a fling," should we wish to. Neither of us would desert, or cease to love the other, and given that we were civilised and intelligent people, no harm could be done. Why not? we considered, was the question.[8]

Meanwhile, the semester break in the southern winter of 1972 was an opportunity for me to visit Fiji's southern Lau group. The *Komaiwai* had taken me to the island of Lakeba, the centre of power, but no further south, where none of the islands had been settled by planters. I was interested in the cultural differences between the inhabitants of the largest Fijian Island, Viti Levu, on one hand, and on the other, the widely scattered smaller islands of Lau, the upwind islands to the east. I'd finished a thesis about the European settlers of the nineteenth century. I wanted to learn about the contact history of the parts of Fiji that had not attracted many who would describe themselves as "Adventurous Spirits," but who, like Elizabeth Hennings, had successfully retained their own traditional values, while also accepting the realities of living in a traditional Fijian context.

I noticed that, though Viti Levu contained most of the Fijian population of the Nation, and was the island most exposed to the influence of the western world, and had experienced the urbanisation of Nadi and Suva, the majority of Fijian teachers and other Fijian professionals such as doctors, civil servants and politicians, were from Lau. The Prime Minister, Ratu Sir Kamisese Mara, with a Law degree from Oxford, was also the *Tui Nayau*, the senior chief of the Lau Province. He was the first Prime Minister of an independent Fiji. The paradox of Lau was that it was the least "developed" part of Fiji, but was politically and socially the most self-confident and dominant Province in the country.

The next question was how to travel there. There was an airstrip on the island of Lakeba, the political and cultural centre, but there were no regular forms of transport between Lakeba and the other islands, except in local unscheduled copra

---

8   For one answer, see: www.thephilosophersmail.com/relationships/the-stupidity-and-folly-of-adultery/

boats. As soon as I arrived, with my Tourist Visa, which allowed me to stay for a maximum of a month, I explored the Suva waterfront and enquired about local shipping. The copra boat, *Adi Lau* looked like a Bristol channel pilot cutter of the early twentieth century. I expect she had been converted to become an ocean cruising yacht and had intended to go round the world on the trade wind route from Britain, as many adventurers did in the 1950s. I guess she was delayed in Fiji. She was about to leave for Lau to collect copra for export, and according to Siveli Tavo, the skipper, *Adi Lau* would be back in Suva in about two weeks. Knowing the ropes from past enquiry, I had brought working clothes, food, a sleeping bag, a notebook, wallet, tooth brush and towel. I was ready to go the next day.

Adi Lau was about sixty feet long with a cutter rig, and a long bowsprit. She was primarily a cargo boat, but was also able to carry a few passengers. The hold may once have been a sleeping cabin for the pilots, but then it was a cargo space, empty, until we came to the islands. There was a small deck house, but we slept on deck most of the voyage. Carmel and I were writing often to each other and I received a letter from her dated 7 August 1972, just before leaving:

I don't think there is much chance of you getting this before you go on the boat. There's lots of strikes causing inconvenience in Australia. My Socialist principles are not at all undermined, but I do wish they'd improve their timing... The planes are flying again and I hope to hear from you on Monday. I am getting masses of exercise (walking to work), and my leg, kicked by our angel child, is improving... needless to say, Gillen has changed his holidays, so he'll be away from 17th to 29th, but perhaps by then some of my other worries will have lessened.

She had put on an impromptu birthday party for her own birthday on 3 August and invited a dozen or so of "the lunch people." She wrote: "I'm finding it very hard to keep really calm, but the pills, kids and dogs all help. Some of the time I'm quite happy. But I miss you more than on other occasions." When I came back to Suva, there was another letter waiting for me at the South Seas guest house:

I think Stephen was pleased with your letter, though I was not thrilled by your final comments on the Adi Lau. He has been quite good, but it's really dreadfully hard coping with all of them alone all the time. I can't really contemplate this as the pattern of our existence in the future. It is just too unpleasant. But at least this should give you enough material to keep going for a while.

Adi Lau had a large and powerful diesel engine as well as a full suite of sails, and the first part of the first journey, to Matuku Island, to the south east of Suva, was the worst, as the course was straight into the trade-wind. The boat pitched violently and a lot of spray came over the bows, keeping the deck cargo, and a few live pigs, nice and cool.

Sanitation was both practical and primitive. A privy like a bush dunny was built on the after deck to conceal a toilet bowl, and a bucket and mop. If you looked down the toilet bowl, you saw that it was fastened onto the deck on top of a gasket and a big plastic pipe, about six inches in diameter and five feet long, with no bends in it. It went through the deck and between the ribs in the bottom of the ship, through the planking, and into the ocean. I expect it was fine in calm water, but heading into twenty knots of trade wind meant that the long and graceful counter slammed down hard as the boat pitched, and the contents of the pipe could sometimes come up like a waterspout and stick to the ceiling of the privy, or fall on the floor.

I felt that a mere mop could make things worse, and that it needed a more thorough remedy. So I explored the ship until I found a scrubber on the end of a stick, and by using the scrubber and following up with the mop and many buckets of water out of the sea, I achieved great improvement, received congratulations and thanks from my fellow passengers, and stopped feeling sick.

There were about fifteen other passengers to begin with, and I made friends with two of them, Uliasi Vosabalavu, a retired public servant of chiefly status, and Pitjila Ngata, a young female schoolteacher from Lakeba. Uliasi was an invaluable tutor and willing to discuss Fijian culture and history at length. Pitjila became my virtual translator. Fijians are all taught English as a second language but in Lau especially, people preferred to speak in their own language and Pitjila's help was very valuable. Uliasi said I could call him Vosa, for short. He wrote to me back in Adelaide, concluding his letter with, "God bless you, Your Fijian Friend." He told me that I could write to Pitjila's address, in Lakeba.

The island of Matuku has a natural harbour facing west, with a narrow entrance sheltered from the prevailing wind, so we slept well. The work of shifting bags of copra from the shore, in large flat bottomed wooden barges with outboard motors, started at first light and didn't take long. We headed north west towards our next destination, Kabara, taking with us numerous new passengers, who more than replaced those that stayed on Matuku.

Uliasi Vosabalavu explained to me the cultural importance of the island for the whole district of Lau. Unlike Matuku, a basically volcanic island, and able to grow many different crops, Kabara is a limestone island, with quite low rainfall. In geomorphic terms, it is a coral reef that has been lifted up, or perhaps exposed by falling sea levels, and has relatively infertile soil, but it is soil with the qualities needed to enhance the growth of *Vesi (instia bijunga)*. A timber similar to Greenheart and Australian Jarrah, *Vesi* is a preferred material for house poles, *Yagona* (Kava) bowls, the vessels used for ceremonial occasions throughout Fiji, and as a staple of the tourist souvenir trade. The most important traditional uses of *Vesi* have been for the manufacture of war clubs, houses, hair combs, and seagoing vessels such as *Drua*. These were ocean-going sailing vessels, sometimes as long as ninety feet. The smaller *Camakau*, up to thirty feet long, were used for limited inter-island transport and fishing. Kabara has a population of about seven hundred people, living in four separate villages, and relies on the more fertile volcanic islands like Matuku, Moce and Lakeba for its food supply.

It soon became apparent that *Adi Lau* filled two distinct social and economic functions. The recorded trade was the collection of copra from the Lau islands for shipment to Suva, from which it would be shipped again to the markets of New Zealand, Australia and then, some of it, to the northern hemisphere. The unrecorded, but equally important function, was to supply the people of Lau with things like pigs and chickens, and western goods like transistor radios, which were usually gifts for both close and distant relatives. Within the islands, culturally important cargo such as Kava bowls were taken on at Kabara for delivery to Lakeba. At Moce, a volcanic island, we took on baskets of *dalo*, for delivery to Ogea, a limestone island which, like Kabara, grew *Vesi*, and built *Camakau*, but did not grow *dalo*. Much of the cargo of *Adi Lau* was ceremonial and served to consolidate the obligations of extended family life between members who lived on adjacent islands and were linked by marriage ties. This meant that ceremonial arrangements such as weddings, and lifting periods of mourning after recent deaths, or acknowledgement of visits by chiefs from other islands, had to be arranged spontaneously whenever *Adi Lau* was expected to arrive.

On arrival at Komo, I saw a new, very large *camakau*, about forty feet long, being dragged from the water by a large crowd of men and women chanting in unison like a scene from the eighteenth century. I was also invited to join a wedding ceremony followed by a splendid feast, and some excellent harmonious singing. Without the help of Uliasi and Pijila, I would have been unable to understand much of

Fijian *Drua*, painted by James Glen Wilson, 1955. Reproduced with permission of Captain HM Denham.

what was going on, or who was who, within the island communities. Nor would I have perceived the kinship-based economy that required no coinage and had survived the successive waves of exterior contacts, from castaways and missionaries, to development theorists, American Peace Corps volunteers, and economic consultants. It was an economy that depended largely on local and renewable materials, and was protected from overt ex-patriot control or influence. The copra export industry, on the other hand, was vulnerable, not only to hurricanes, but also to stock markets. I thought that the kin-based localised exchange system had lessons that, if learnt well in the West, could support the search for answers to the big questions about global sustainability.

I believe that this was because the people of Lau had not sold much of their land; and because the planters who, in some cases, bought whole islands, learnt that it was best to accept the reality of Fijian self-governance and cultural integrity, if they wished to prosper. The result is that Lau has survived the century of a temporary colonial interruption of its 3,000-year history of human occupation. And it has been able to absorb what values of the West were acceptable, including Christianity, into Fijian culture, and reject those that the people do not accept, such as Economic Rationalism.

Camakau, 1846 drawing by Louis le Breton (*Voyage au Pôle Sud et dans l'Océanie sur les corvettes L'Astrolabe et La Zélée*, Jules Dumont d'Urville, Gide Paris).

It is interesting that monetary commerce prospered in Lau in the form of co-operatives rather than companies. These were typically owned and managed by local communities. Meetings of the Provincial Councils during the colonial period were also bicultural occasions for the re-affirmation of kinship connections, sporting contests, marriages, birthdays and celebrations. *Adi Lau* found herself to be included in similar activities simply because her passengers usually included important people like Uliasi Vosabalavu, who were needed to fulfil their traditional responsibilities, and make decisions about projects of public importance.

As we completed our circuit of the islands and the lagoons around Lakeba, Moce, Ogea, Vatoa and Fulaga, I joined the crews of the local barges, to assist with loading the bags of copra and to learn as much as I could about each of the islands, and pick up historical or cultural information for future reference. In most places stacks of full bags of copra were left on the beach for us to collect. We received help from locals, passing sacks across the gunwales and stacking them on the floor of the barge. I enjoyed the work, which was about as energetic as stacking frozen sheep carcasses in the freezing works in New Zealand. But the dazzling blue water, and warmth of the lagoons made it romantic and beautiful, as the big outboards drove us rapidly back to *Adi Lau* in a cloud of cool spray. We ate fish and *dalo* on the beach.

Vatoa was the island of most interest to me. It is the only Fijian island at which Captain Cook stopped, on his second voyage of discovery on 2 July 1774. It soon became a magnet for foreign shipping because it had been reliably charted and positioned by Cook. However the ocean current that runs in a westerly direction, and is then deflected by the closely positioned reefs and islands of Central Lau to the north, led to many wrecks as a result of inaccurate navigation. I was excited by the sight of a rather nice sailing yacht, *Wei Hai*, which made me envious. Her Ship's Company consisted of Tim and Ginny Le Couter, who had sailed from England to New Zealand, then to Fiji, and were now preparing to continue their round the world voyage with the south-east trades behind them. *Wei Hai* was a bit larger than I thought I could build for myself, but she put some ideas into my head.

A vessel, perhaps big enough to go on the open ocean, but small enough to go on a ship as deck cargo from Australia, would enable a small family to explore the Lau group at their leisure with safety. A seed had been planted, and I began to think about such an idea seriously.

The most recent wreck on Vatoa was a Japanese trawler high up on a reef just to the north of the island itself. It served as a valuable land mark, and a source of recyclable building materials for local use. Walking along the shore, I happened to notice a square copper nail, about six inches long, that must have come from some sizeable wooden vessel in the early nineteenth century. It was bent around into a U-shape, and its square-pointed tip was flattened by a stone or hammer to create a useful tool like a screw driver, or, more likely, a lever to open large shell fish. This was an implement likely to have reached Vatoa as a result of some enterprising salvage work in the early decades of the nineteenth century, when American merchant ships were scouring the islands for luxury items, like sandalwood and *bêche de mer* for the Chinese market.

William Cary was the first castaway to publish an account of a wreck on the reef of Vatoa, in this case, of his whale ship, *Oeno* in 1825. Cary became a component of the tribute to be delivered in a *Drua* to the court of Malani, the sovereign chief of Lau at that time, on the island of Lakeba.[9] Cary provides a valuable account of his experience as a successful beachcomber. He served Malani as interpreter, armourer and mechanic. He provides a useful impression of the political organisation and relationship between Lau and the powerful kingdom of Bau, with its island base close to the shore of Viti Levu. *Adi Lau* proceeded on her journey in Cary's wake, calling at the smaller islands of Namuka, Moce, and Yacata on her way back to Suva.

During my trip to Lau, people on several islands mentioned the existence of the remains of very early settlements, often fortified. Their inhabitants were said to be the "first people" on these islands. It occurred to me then that an investigation of these sites might lead to an interdisciplinary study of the whole of Lau, and possibly beyond. This would include archaeologists, linguists, anthropologists and historians and could be done in collaboration with University of the South Pacific (USP), Auckland and Adelaide Universities and the Fiji Museum.

After reading Carmel's letters I was anxious to be back with her and the children as soon as I could. We settled down to another passionate re-union, and re-affirmation of love. I had plenty of material to work on, and for the rest of 1972, I resumed lectures and tutorials with renewed energy and worked in Adelaide on microfilm sources from the Fijian Archives.

And I started some new extra-mural projects. I found that indulging my interest in wooden boats could be a way of fulfilling some of my fatherly responsibilities. I bought the plans for a "Cherub" sailing dinghy, and started the building process on the sitting room floor by lofting (drawing the lines at full size) on two sheets of thin plywood, which we could remove at the end of each session and stack in the shed. The Cherub class design was the work of New Zealand designer John Spencer, in 1951. It has since become an international development class. Mine was a standard prototype, designed to be rowed as well as sailed. She was a 12 foot dinghy that could be built quickly out of plywood, and used, to begin with, for small families and later on for serious competition, if the kids or their parents developed interest in that direction. As soon as the Cherub was finished we all went down to Port Willunga, and sailed round to Aldinga, the next beach to the south. Soon the sea-breeze came in. Not a very strong wind but a good fetch of about fifty miles from the shelter of Kangaroo Island. It was the children's first experience of being in a boat among waves, which splashed water in our faces as we came out of the shelter of the point, and began a lively rising and falling across the swell. Stephen

---

9   Cary,W, *Wrecked in the Feejees*, Nantucket 1928.

started exercising his sparkling imagination. He was without fear, but when he saw a crowded beach in front of us he made the natural assumption that they were waiting, cleverly concealing their flags, banners and ticker-tape, to congratulate us for our survival of the "storm."

My father used to tell me that, when set a task, I was always apt, to "get diverted," like the pig in my early story, who "went down another lane." I think my father was right. I have always been likely to be seized by a new passion at times in my life when I could ill afford to give myself any slack. This time, it was a century old trading ketch, *Annie Watt*, which set me off on a new life-changing journey.

It all began on a rather miserable afternoon in July 1969, when one of my tutorials on Australian history became a bit off track. We were talking about the way in which Australian historians seemed to have concentrated their efforts on the themes they had been trained to look for in the histories of Britain and Europe: wars, strikes, revolutions, constitutional crises, and so on. The effect was to make Australian history a bit dull by comparison. We had only a bit-part in the drama of World War I, and Gallipoli had been, at best, an heroic defeat, not the victory that had been hoped for. There had been no civil wars, other than the quickly suppressed attack on the Eureka stockade by Her Majesty's military forces against the unfortunate gold diggers, in December 1854. Then there were the failed attempts, in both Tasmania and the mainland, to exterminate the indigenous population. The main constitutional problem, Federation of the Australian colonies in 1901, had been solved by a series of polite conferences, and a rather low-key referendum, rather than by war.

There had been strikes, the most famous of which had been the Great Maritime Strike of 1890. The text books told us that it was the key event in the formation of the Australian Labor Party. But why was the cessation of sea transport such an important aspect of life at that time as to make the government of New South Wales bring out the military with orders to shoot the strikers? It was as if strikes were the only things of any importance that wharfies and sailors did. Judging by the modern literature, shipwrecks were the only events of importance in the history of ships.

My students and I discussed the relative importance of high politics and everyday life, of the nineteenth century male dominated gender balance, of religion, sport, and nationalism. Perhaps it was in everyday life, much of which

The Pig, as drawn by my father in 1939.

had to do with ships and shipping, that the real drama of Australian history was to be found?

Some of my students, especially those who had done the first year Australian History course, where I had introduced them to research on local suburban history, thought that it would be interesting to do some research and fieldwork on the water; voyages, perhaps, during vacations, to Kangaroo Island, seventy miles south of Port Adelaide. We discussed the fact that a large part of the carrying trade had been in sailing ketches that were able to make a living by serving the small ports of the gulfs, long after the steamship had monopolised the inter-colonial trade, and even after the introduction of road haulage. *Annie Watt* and *One and All* were the only two surviving members of a large local fleet of sailing vessels that provided the same kind of service to small ports in South Australia as Thames Barges did for the small ports of Essex and Suffolk in England.

One of my students, Axel De Vries (perhaps it is significant that he was born in Holland, and not in Port Adelaide), asked me to "do something" about ensuring that at least one ketch was preserved for posterity. I said I would try. Little did I know what I was letting myself in for.

Annie Watt was built in 1870 at Port Esperance, Tasmania, for her first owner, George Watt (Annie was his daughter). The builder was John Wilson, who went on to build *One and All* at Port Cygnet for a South Australian owner in 1878.

Annie Watt at Edithburgh jetty c.1916. (State Library of South Australia, Edithburgh Collection B44828)

Annie Watt birthday party and fund raiser, Port Adelaide Sailing Club, 1970.

Both vessels were built of Tasmanian Blue Gum and built to last.[10] They had been built to carry rural cargoes like wheat, fruit and timber to the metropolitan port of Hobart from small isolated country communities. They took hardware, passengers, tools, alcohol and clothing back to the country. Lack of port development, such as wharves, in Tasmania, meant that loading often had to be achieved between tides on beaches, where horses could bring their carts and pull up alongside the ships to load or unload. So draft had to be limited to about five feet when fully loaded, and hulls had to be flat bottomed. That meant that the Tasmanian builders were quick to take up the American device of the centreboard, to enable their ships to get to windward efficiently. They were ketch rigged and ideally suited to the shallow ports and mangrove creeks of South Australia, as well as being capable of the ocean crossing from Tasmania.

In 1969 both vessels *Annie Watt* and *One and All*, were still working, carrying salt and wheat from Port Price on the western side of the top of St Vincent's Gulf to Port Adelaide under sail, with auxiliary engines. Both vessels were owned by Reg Harvey of Port Adelaide and both were up for sale. Reg had managed them successfully for his whole working life. South Australia, with its long indented coastline and very few roads, to begin with, would have been impoverished if it had not been for the ketch fleet. In the nineteenth century, funding for the purpose of building jetties became a vital target of local communities and local politics, because sailing ketches were important instruments of colonisation. But there were no studies, or even reminiscences of the maritime history of South Australia until many years later, and so no concern about restoration or preservation of old ships. This was in contrast to the local support in Adelaide, for the preservation of historic buildings, none of them very old by British standards, which struck me as good, but incongruous.

In Britain, not for profit organisations had been formed to preserve Norfolk wherries, and Thames barges, and the famous clipper, *Cutty Sark*. In the USA, coastal traders and Grand Banks schooners were being restored and re-used as charter vessels. In Melbourne, the schooner *Alma Doepel*, which had carried apples from Hobart to Melbourne on a regular basis, under sail alone, had an Association dedicated to her restoration and preservation.

Axel's request that something be done to save the ketches was only viable if they were sea-worthy. I was aware of the fact that a stationary exhibit, built out of wood, would need almost as much maintenance as a ship working at sea. *One and All* was larger than *Annie Watt*, and closer inspection revealed that she was much better preserved. After a lot of time had been spent on surveying by professionals, at no charge, we were told that *One and All* would be a much better investment. A small ship like *One and All*, the youngest vessel to combine historic value with

---

10 Graham-Evans, Alex and Wilson, Peter, *Built to Last, The story of the shipwrights of Cygnet, Tasmania and their boats 1863-1997*, Tasbook publishers, Woodstock, Tasmania, 1996. Alex was one of my Adelaide students.

sail training capacity as well, would be able to give young people the same kind of experience as the sailing barge *Leofleda* had given to me. I began to plan cargo holds slung with hammocks during the nights, but replaced by folding dining furniture during the day. I looked forward to field trips with my students, down to Kangaroo Island and across the Spencer Gulf, to Port Lincoln. These expeditions would combine seamanship with exploration and experiential education and enable the vessel to pay her own way.

I also knew that the journey, starting with an opportunity, and ending, hopefully, with public ownership of Australia's first Sail Training ship, would be extremely difficult, perhaps impossible, and would require a lot of energy. But I thought it would be worth doing. Time was precious because both vessels were for sale, so I took the first steps. The group of my students, and later my colleagues agreed to form a not for profit association, with me as Chairman, with the purpose of purchasing *One and All*. In 1970, we drew up a constitution and went through the usual rituals of registration and incorporation, as the South Australian Ketch Preservation Association Inc (SAKPA). We then approached Reg Harvey to discuss the cost of buying *One and All*.

We had a meeting with Mr Harvey and eventually agreed on a figure of $9,000 for *One and All*, less the cost of any repairs needed to enable her to satisfy the Marine and Harbours Board, for navigation between Port Lincoln and Encounter Bay. Had we been able to keep to this agreement, acquisition itself would have cost us very little.

Unfortunately, an ABC television news item about *One and All* and the plans we had for her, organised by Paula Nagel, one of my students and a reporter, became known to John Huie, an enterprising owner of a wine bar on Circular Quay in Sydney. He came over to Adelaide in a hurry, to see Reg Harvey, and offered $10,000 immediately. Reg had no hesitation in accepting his offer, and *One and All* was soon on her way with a cargo of South Australian wine, bound for Sydney. She was sold and restored in Brisbane. A crew set sail in her in 1971 to erect a navigational and radio beacon on the wreck of the freighter *Runic* but ran into bad weather and she is believed to have sprung a plank. *One and All* attempted to reach safety, but eventually foundered and sank. The crew survived some days in a life raft before being rescued.[11]

So SAKPA was left, in 1970, with the problem of re-focussing energy towards the acquisition and preservation of *Annie Watt*. She had been able to maintain her survey credentials by installing new steel bulkheads at both ends of the ship which gave her another few years of life, and surprisingly, our membership and fundraising continued to grow. We decided to celebrate her birthday on Sunday 5 July 1970, a hundred years since she was launched.

The Port Adelaide Sailing Club was chosen as the venue and we invited some potential financial supporters, but targeted ordinary people, who would be using the

---

11 Graeme-Evans, A and Wilson, P, *Built to Last*, Tasbooks, 1996, p 38.

ship themselves if we were to be successful. A lot of people provided festive food, including an enormous cake. I made a speech about what we hoped to achieve, and why, appealing equally, I hoped, to the maritime history buffs and the young adventurers. The birthday party attracted about 200 people and raised enough money to slip the vessel at Filipi's yard, so that a survey could be done to estimate the cost and practicality of restoration.

Six months later, we had 67 members: quite a few University staff and lots of students, joined by people who had nothing to do with the University, but who liked old boats and the general idea of community engagement. Membership funds began to come in after the birthday party. We started working parties at weekends, to clean *Annie Watt* out and enable us to examine her timbers closely. We also learnt that if she was to be used as a "school-ship', she needed to be self-righting in the event of a capsize and in other ways conform to the survey requirements. The Americans, who have a long tradition of school ships, enjoyed special survey requirements for their large fleet of Heritage Vessels, but at that stage, Australia did not have either the ships or the regulations.

We struggled with the legal and physical realities. Mr Filipi continued to host our restoration efforts for as long as he could, but began to lose money as we prevented his slip being used by anyone else. There were serious limits to what a group of inexperienced amateurs could achieve, but read on, and see if we arrive at a happy ending. We agreed to move her, and were given free crane service and transport by Nicholls Cranes to place her in an abandoned, but free, church yard on the outskirts of Port Adelaide. *Annie Watt* was eventually purchased by SAKPA, with the help of a loan, for $3,000 in August 1971.[12]

She then suffered the heat of a whole summer, before eventually being accepted as a component of a "Maritime Precinct," planned by the Labor State Government, as a cure for the fading prospects of Port Adelaide, resulting, largely from the technological advance of containerisation. The South Australian Maritime Museum opened at Port Adelaide in 1986 and ownership of *Annie Watt* was transferred to the Museum. While she never saw the water again, she has since served a unique purpose as a publicly visible example of nineteenth century shipbuilding techniques. As far as I know, SAKPA was never formally wound up, but its members continued to believe in the possibility of a revival of its educational purpose in a not too distant future. A few years later an opportunity arose to build on the start we had made by changing the focus of the Association's enthusiasm, from restoration of an historic vessel to building a new vessel for a broader community service.

✧✧✧✧

My son, Philip had always been the most interested of my children in boats. I bought him a very small dinghy indeed as his birthday present. It was five feet long and fitted nicely onto a box trailer that I could tow with the VW. One day we went

---

12   Bullers, Rick, "Annie Watt: the career of a coastal trading ketch," *Great Circle*,Vol. 36, No.1, p 23.

down to the mouth of the Patawalonga River at Glenelg, and started sailing lessons. Philip already understood the basic principles because of the model yachts I had made for them all. Carmel made a small lugsail for him. Philip could swim quite well by then and there was no room in the boat for anyone else, so he went off alone within the enclosed marina. That meant he would always be within earshot so that I could tell him what to do. Soon he was able to tack single handed, though without a centreboard, he wasn't gaining a lot of ground.

Among the craft in the moorings at the mouth of the Patawalonga River was one small yacht that stood out from all the rest. She was carvel built of wood and as all the other boats were made of plastic, plywood or aluminium, I couldn't keep my eyes off her. She was gaff rigged, and looked sturdy, yet graceful and ready to go somewhere. She was for sale. Sitting in her cockpit was a man whose face I recognised. It turned out to belong to David Kew, who was one of the earliest members of SAKPA from outside the University. The boat had been the *Lady Edna*, David told me, named for the wife of Leigh Anderson, a fisherman who was the previous owner and builder. David renamed her *Dauntless*, after the star wooden vessel of the *Dauntless* series of children's books, written between 1947 and 1957 by Peter Dawlish (the pseudonym of James Lennox Kerr).

Anderson had used *Lady Edna* to earn a living for most of his long life, in the Investigator Strait, between Kangaroo Island and the South Australian mainland. Only twenty-one feet long, she had been built as a single hander, with one berth in the fo'c's'le, a galley and a wet well amidships, to keep the crayfish alive till he reached port, about once a week. David bought her and converted her into a small family cruising yacht. He plugged all the drainage holes of the wet well, and made a cabin floor. Then he gave her a new deck and enlarged the cockpit to make room for two adults and two small children.

David told me that he came to South Australia from Newcastle, in the north of England, as a qualified electrician, and had worked in the busy shipyards at Whyalla. There he met Colin Burchett, who worked in the part of the shipyard that built wooden lifeboats. Together, David and Colin spent their spare time building a very

Left: Philip in his first boat. There have been many others since.

Below: The new *Leofleda*, half planked at my backyard boat yard in North Adelaide.

beautiful "Glen" class, twenty-five foot sailing yacht. David decided to abandon electricity and concentrate on woodwork and boat building. He soon became a professional woodwork teacher.

A few weeks later, we met again and I offered to buy *Dauntless*, but he told me, with some regret, that she was already sold and was in the hands of her new owner. There was a pause, until he said, "What a pity we didn't meet sooner, but if you ever want to build a boat like *Dauntless*, I'll give you a hand." I thought this was too good to be true. I explained to him that any such arrangement would be the other way round. If such a thing happened, I would be giving him a hand. "Why would you want to do this?" I asked. He said he found it frustrating to be teaching children who had no interest in what he was trying to teach them, which I realised later went far beyond the undemanding projects of the state school woodworking syllabus, and into the history of craft, tools, utility and aesthetics. David, I was to discover, had two role models, Jesus Christ and Rudolf Steiner. He went on to say that he needed time to be able to settle his mind, between escaping the frustrations of his work and the demands of his family when he arrived home, with three adolescent children and a young one. Boat building would provide an opportunity for creative concentration and would be just the thing.

My conversation with David made me think more deeply about the possibility of an inter-disciplinary study of the Lau Islands of Fiji. If I had a boat of my own and could transport it to Lau, it would be relatively easy to sail to many islands, and I could map the old village sites that the islanders had mentioned to me earlier. I would not have to rely on local copra boats to travel from one place to another. With the maps as evidence, I could obtain the support and involvement of archaeologists and anthropologists at Auckland University.

So, after some thought and discussion, I accepted David's offer, but said I would pay him for his time. We agreed on an hourly rate. I would provide all materials. With his advice, I began to collect them. He told me that the perception of the time, that wooden boats were things of the past, was to my advantage. This was the age of fibreglass and aluminium, and there was no apparent market for the high quality timber needed for boat building. But Otto and Sons, the company that had once catered for the established boat yards of Port Adelaide, was still hoarding a stack of select Western Australian Jarrah planking that had been held for seven years. They found that if they wanted to sell it as boat building grade, no one would buy it, so they were offering to sell it at a much lower price in order to get rid of it. I went to Otto's shop in Stepney, a suburb of Adelaide and bought timber for a keel, and the first few planks on each side, promising to come back for more.

A week or so later we went for a family drive to hunt for a grown "crook" which goes around a ninety degree curve between the keel and the stem. Going past a farm in the northern part of the hills, I spotted what turned out to be a Peppermint Gum, with a branch that looked exactly the shape I wanted. We drove up to the house, and I told the owner that I was building a boat, and had seen in his paddock what looked like a perfect shape for the stem. I asked him if I could buy it. He said I should make a plywood template and bring it up next weekend to see if it was the right shape. So I did that, and he was very interested in the whole project and turned out to have built his own wooden boat in the past. He encouraged me to cut the timber, and refused to let me pay for it. The branch was a fair curve, with no twist, so I was able to employ Otto's to cut it to shape on a big band saw. It has travelled through thousands of miles of coastal and ocean waters since then.

David and I went over to Corny Point, at the western end of the York Peninsula to meet Leigh Anderson himself. He was a man who had sailed the four-masted barques like *Pamir*, that carried wheat from South Australia to London on a regular basis, until the end of the World War II. He had a comprehensive knowledge of what had become erroneously known as "The Last Age of Sail"; and he agreed to draw up a set of plans to construct a slightly larger version of *Lady Edna*. He made no alteration of her beam, but set out the stations so as to add one foot to the mid length distance between them and, then set the next stations, forward and aft, at another six inches in each case, thus adding two feet to her overall length, a total of 23 feet between perpendiculars. Another hundredweight was added to her outside ballast, and she was to carry another inside her. We settled on a vessel, 23 feet long, a beam of 8 feet, drawing 3 feet 6 inches. I asked Leigh whether increasing the length but not the beam would make her more tender than *Dauntless*, but he thought not. Her initial stiffness, due to her hull shape with its reverse curves and firm bilges, would actually increase the area of the hull that would provide buoyant stability.

The keel of our new boat was laid in the backyard at North Adelaide. Once David and I had placed the moulds on their stations along the keel, we nailed battens to the moulds where the top edges of each plank would lie, to ensure that all the curves were what boat builders call "fair" curves, without bumps or irregularities, and easy on the eye.

We decided on a regular routine. We worked for four hours every Tuesday, at the end of our day jobs, and on Saturday mornings as well. As I gained confidence, I did a bit of extra work at weekends. We ended up averaging sixteen man-hours a week, working together, and another two hours of my weekend work. The whole job from start to launch took about two and a half years. And it was a profound experience. This was something I had always wanted to be able to do, and David was an excellent teacher and confidence builder. One of my proudest moments was when David couldn't make it for one week, but the next Tuesday he came into the back yard and found that I had fitted and fastened, alone, the next "strake," consisting of two planks, held together by a "butt strap" and one more seam was ready for caulking. Things went faster after that.

Carmel was not a hands-on participant, but made lovely meals for both of us and our children, every Tuesday, to begin with. David eventually decided he would arrive home by half past six, as his wife, June, preferred him to have tea with her. Fair enough, I thought. But Carmel was disappointed, as she had enjoyed the sociability, and the way, if we challenged any of his beliefs, David would hum quietly and move on to some other subject.

I mentioned earlier that we put the "open marriage" theory into action, with the naiveté of a couple of seven year olds. But as might have been predicted, our marriage became worse rather than better. Don't worry, I'm not going give you the details of our experiments. You would become bored and wouldn't read the rest of the book. I'd like to make it clear that we shared the responsibility for our troubles between us equally. There was, of course, a crisis, which put an end to the marital experiment.

Dinner was over one evening, and the children were asleep. Sigmund, the Labrador dog, was snoring, Fred was with Susan, and it was dark. Carmel and I were listening to music. There was a knock on the door, and I opened it to see a professor, who had been a beneficiary of our open marriage policy.

I turned off the music and invited him in, and for some minutes we engaged in icy, but friendly conversation. Our visitor suddenly changed his tone and announced that he intended to leave his own wife, and had come to "pick Carmel up" and take her with him, immediately, to a new house in Aldgate, a fashionable satellite suburb in the Adelaide hills. And he was serious.

My immediate reaction was to think how I could prevent this scenario from materialising. I suspected some background misunderstanding on his part, which could be sorted out later. Meanwhile I determined to prevent him from kidnapping my wife. So I just hit him, which made his nose bleed. Carmel and Sigmund fled to our bedroom. Our visitor backed away until he was beside the front door with his back to the wall beside it. I kept my own guard up in case he retaliated, but he didn't. Then I knocked him down. I dragged him up onto his feet, and told him to give me his car keys.

I was wearing sandshoes, so I decided to drive him back to his own home, about half a mile away, in his own car, and then run back. I pulled up beside his house, marched him down the path and pressed the bell. His wife came to the door and I pushed him down the passage, telling his, by now, assembled family that he had come to the wrong door and I didn't want him to come round any more. Then I gave his wife the car keys and set off on what I am sure is the fastest half mile I ever ran.

Back home I washed my face, changed my clothes and tried to look as civilised as possible. When Carmel heard two policemen arrive, she came out of the bedroom in her dressing gown. It seemed that the professor's wife suspected that I might be doing some domestic violence to Carmel by now and feared for her safety. I told the two policemen that I hit my uninvited guest, because he said he had come to take my wife away from me. So I had acted to prevent that happening, but I had stopped short of inflicting any serious injury. The policemen said that my victim seemed in bad shape all the same, and it was lucky I had not done serious damage. Carmel supported what I said and added that she had no fears that I would hurt her. It was clear to me that she had not expected the professor's visit, and was as much surprised at his suggestion as I was.

Next day I cancelled my lecture on Australian History by putting up a notice to say I was sick. I just felt that I might burst into tears at any minute, and that wouldn't be good for the students. I also had a booked session with Clive Kneebone, who was supportive as well as analytic. "This bloke," I said, "came round last night and announced he wanted to take Carmel right then. I thought it was a bit cheeky, so I hit him." We had talked about the prof in the past, so Clive knew who I was talking about:

"What did you hit him with, your fist?" he asked.

"Yes" I said.

He smiled. "He was silly to think he could win a fight with you."

"He hardly tried" I said, "to defend himself. I just wanted to put him out of action."

"You were obviously in control of yourself. You didn't lose your cool?"

"No. I wanted to make sure he wouldn't be coming around anymore, but I wanted **not** to kill him."

I never saw the professor again, and I don't have any reason to think Carmel did either. We went on with our lives, said nothing much for a day or two, then the old smiles came again. We soon got back to what seemed to be the usual loving normality. But it was not long before we began to talk about the possibility of separation. My position was that I would not leave her or the children. Ever. Carmel thought that we had damaged one another so badly that we would have happier lives separately. She had also accumulated a serious amount of study leave, which she would lose if she didn't take it, whereas I had used mine up, and would have no more until 1974.

We decided to discuss the situation with our children. Around the kitchen table, we explained that we still loved each other and them as well, but for reasons that they clearly understood, it might be better if we had a trial separation, for a while at least. I think it was this occasion that ended with a volley of crockery hurled at me by Carmel, and faithfully recorded in Philip's delightful memoir of his early life written in 2012.[13] The crockery may have had the effect of raising the possibility of more such events if we continued to live together much longer. The children agreed that separation might lead to improvement in our behaviour. It was decided, mutually, that Carmel would move out, to a flat just up the road. It belonged to Frank Dalziel, who was then on study leave.

About a month later, Carmel took her much delayed study leave, and left Australia for Oxford. The idea was that when Carmel came back in six months, the children could decide for themselves with whom they wanted to live, and if that changed from time to time as they grew older, that would be fine. I could start looking

---

13 Young, Philip, "A Pretty Ordinary Year" (in which he was in a coma for some weeks, and nearly died from an unusual tropical disease he picked up in New Guinea). December, 2013, p 7.

around for somewhere else large enough for me, the children and the dogs. In the meantime we would continue to live where we were, under the same roof, until Carmel went to England.

We agreed that we shared the responsibility for our separation, but this was all happening at a time when the divorce laws were in the process of changing. The normal procedure was that one party had to sue the other party for infidelity, or desertion, or cruelty etc. The new concept was a "No Fault" divorce, based on "irreconcilable differences."

I knew that Carmel had been, as my mother said, "carrying the heavy end of the stick," when it came to the choices we had made. In the first place, I owed my academic success, such as it was, to Carmel's inspiration and encouragement, and often her critical wisdom. She was entitled to the kind of job she had a right to expect, and have that job in Oxford, the place she would very probably have worked had it not been for me. And without me, she would probably have broken through glass ceilings galore. Now was her chance to begin the career to which she was entitled. I contacted an organisation that was campaigning for "No Fault" divorce. The alternative, providing the same result but with minimum blame, was desertion by one or other of us. We had little trouble deciding that Carmel's departure for professional reasons, could constitute desertion, and ultimately I would be able to divorce her. It took another two years for the divorce to be finalised. All Carmel and I had to do was to stay away from each other.

About a month later we took Carmel's gear up the road to Frank's flat, and the children and dogs stayed with me at Barnard Street, within easy reach. Soon after that she flew off to a little island near Padworth on the upper Thames to stay with her sister and brother-in-law, Margaret and Robert. We remained in friendly contact by writing letters to each other. Only a few have survived:

I'm not too happy here. The country really does get me down... Margaret seems less under stress than before, and there isn't much screaming or throwing things, but Robert is very worried about financial things and not his cheerful self... This isn't much of a letter I'm afraid. Margaret is talking to me, and I'm cold. I wouldn't mind being back home right now... I really need to get fixed up at Oxford and start work, dull as it may be. The newspapers are very gloomy & bomb scares and explosives are so frequent that I'm frightened to go anywhere—but I'll die of boredom if I stay here, so sooner or later I'll have to get moving... Love to all, and also Big Black Dog and Fred.

David Kew had been surprised and upset when Carmel left and offered to continue building the boat until she was finished, which, at this stage, meant another four months' work. He even offered to do it for free. I felt the offer was unfair to him, and continued to pay him a stingy wage, but he made it a condition that I would pass on in the future, what he had taught me, to at least one other person. I took this very seriously, and doing so did much to relieve my conscience.

Stephen was about to start his secondary schooling, and Carmel undertook to pay his fees as a day boy, needless to say, at Scotch College, a private school. Carmel also agreed to buy me out of my half ownership of our house in Barnard Street so I could buy another house for myself and the children.

I was naturally feeling very low most of the time. One of my students, Philippa Thomas, sensing I might need a bit of cheering up, invited me and some of my past and present students to lunch in the Adelaide Hills, where she lived with her partner, Norton Ladkin. Although I didn't feel much like partying, it was a kind gesture and I knew the kids would like to go out.

It was a lovely day. We enjoyed the drive into the hills and it was good to see my students in such a beautiful setting. Among them was Ruth. She had been a student in my third year Pacific History course in 1970. The following year, I supervised her Honours thesis — the morality tale of the short-lived 1870s land speculation in Fiji by the "Polynesia Company" — which was awarded a First. She then tutored at Flinders University in New Guinea History before going to Vietnam to help her sister, who was working in an orphanage, in what was then Saigon. At the same time, she applied successfully for a PhD scholarship and decided to work on the cultural and social impact of the tourist industry on the islanders of Fiji and Tonga, with me as her supervisor. We occasionally wrote to each other while she was in Vietnam.

Philippa suggested she saddle some horses for anyone who wanted to go for a ride. The last horse I'd ridden was Sally, my stock horse at Eparaima in New Zealand. I jumped at the chance and set off with Philippa along a narrow road. My horse was a bit keen to overtake Philippa's horse, called Robert. Robert didn't like that idea. As my horse drew alongside, Robert kicked and caught me squarely on the fibula. I felt faint and somehow dismounted. Philippa sat me down on the side of the road and rode off with both horses to obtain help. She returned with Ruth and Norton. They manhandled me into Ruth's car, picked up the kids and we went straight to a doctor, who said my leg was probably broken, and so it turned out to be.

I was in considerable pain, and Ruth stayed with me and the kids that night. This was the beginning of our, so far, forty-six year relationship. We began to spend more and more time together. Later, in the rare book collection of the Barr Smith library, I asked her to marry me. I explained to her that it might take a while for me to obtain a divorce. And she said "Yes!" she would.

Ruth was about to leave Australia to visit Tonga and Fiji to commence her PhD research, with the support of the government agencies of both countries, who arranged access to documentary materials and opportunities to interview the islander operators of tourist businesses. She remained in the Pacific for much of the last half of 1973.

My academic life was ramping up, with more teaching, writing and research. My plan was to spend my next study leave, in 1974, in the Lau Islands. I applied to the Australian Research Council for a grant to collaborate with colleagues in my first university, Auckland, to write a study of the culture-history of Fiji's Lau group of Islands. After discussions by letter, my confirmed partners at this stage were

Garth Rogers, an anthropologist and his PhD student, Simon Best, an archaeologist, both from the University of Auckland; and Bruce Knapman, an economist at Flinders University in South Australia. Ron Crocombe, the Professor of Pacific Studies at USP, was an enthusiastic supporter of the project, and put me in touch with an ideal colleague, Archie Reid, who had been Secretary for Fijian Affairs in the Colonial Government, and then British Consul to the Kingdom of Tonga. As a result, he was well known by the Fijian Community, and enjoyed virtual chiefly status. He was fluent in both Tongan and Fijian. After Archie retired, he returned to his home in Edinburgh. I wrote to him there, and he agreed to join the project as a Research Fellow for a year. He would go to Fiji and work on the sworn oral evidence of Lauan land ownership, presented to the enquiry into Fijian Land tenure in the 1930s, otherwise known as the *Tukutuka Raraba*, or "The stories of the people."

Harry Maude, on the threshold of retirement, was visiting the Barr Smith University library, to discuss his proposal that Adelaide University should become the custodian of his large and unique collection of historical works and manuscripts on Pacific History. The increasing flow of research and publication, from me and my students and the existence of other resources, led him to anticipate that the University of Adelaide might become an international centre for future inter-disciplinary studies of the Pacific Islands. There was talk of establishing a "Centre for Pacific Studies."

While Harry was in Adelaide he came to see how my boat was progressing, and offered to support my application to the Australian Research Council. The project, Harry said, was:

Essentially an interdisciplinary study, wherein lies much of its importance and at the same time, its difficulty… Culture change has been taking place from long before the beginning of documental history… The investigator must, therefore, combine in his research the techniques used by, and take advantage of the results achieved by, archaeologists, ethno-historians, anthropologists, economists and historians proper if he is to present a balanced picture of social dynamics from the settlement of the group to the present day.[14]

Harry was also my supporter when it came to the difficulty of using inter-island transport for this research, and therefore, my need to be independent of it, and to obtain funding to ship my new boat to Tonga. From there I hoped to sail her to the Lau Islands and begin mapping early village sites. Without Harry, the expedition would never have happened. He wrote:

Having spent much of my early life voyaging in the Pacific islands on small craft, I can vouch for the fact that it [my boat] *is well designed and competently built and perfectly capable of sailing in safety to and between the islands of the Lau Group.*[15]

It was imperative to have the boat finished and launched. David and I managed to do it in November 1973, but I had sold the mooring with *Swallow* at the Port

---

14 From a carbon copy of what seems to be a reference in support of my application. The first page of this document is missing so it cannot be dated.

15 *Ibid.*

Adelaide sailing Club, and had nowhere to put my new boat. I joined the recently established Small Boat Club on Garden Island, just around the corner downstream from Port Adelaide, and laid a new mooring there. Now we needed to become a bit creative with no time to lose to move her down to the Small Boat Club.

We had to make a cradle to transport the boat from North Adelaide. David managed to obtain two big truck wheels, a short wooden frame, and an axle with huge leaf springs. We attached upright posts to hold the boat steady and jacked her up carefully from the stern, and put the contraption underneath the boat. Having just two big wheels made it easy to turn her round, take a left turn to climb up a slope out of the backyard and onto the road, with the help of a four-wheel drive Land Rover I borrowed from the Geography Department. As we doubted the ability of the contraption/cradle/trailer to pass a roadworthy test, I waited til after midnight and then set off for the Small Boat Club, towing the whole outfit, weighing about two tons with no proper lights. Very slowly. Then I left her well chocked, drove back to North Adelaide and went to bed.

Next morning, I roused the children up for an early breakfast and we went back to Port Adelaide in a state of high excitement. David Kew and family and Ruth's brother, also Dave, arrived early as well. We stepped the boat's mast so that we could have something to lash ropes onto to keep her upright. Philip had a small, fairly new fibreglass canoe and he put it on the makeshift cradle. I forget how it happened, but we managed somehow to untie one of the lashings at the wrong moment, so that the boat fell onto her bilge, and would have been badly damaged had it not been for Philip's canoe acting as a fender. Luckily, it is easy to repair fibreglass canoes, but it's always been a bit of a grievance. Philip claims, "Dad never really approved of fibreglass as a boat building material. I'm not saying he crushed the canoe on purpose, but you have to wonder."[16]

On closer inspection, my boat actually came off worse than the canoe, so the boy had nothing to complain about. A plank on her bilge, underneath the starboard bunk (my bunk!), had a small split in it, and the tide was going to go out soon. David had sensibly brought a lot of tools, and he very quickly made a butt-strap to fasten on the inside of the split, with short screws, and plenty of red lead on the surfaces. It took him about ten minutes and it is still there and has never leaked. Then we were ready to launch. I slowly backed the Land Rover down the slope until the trailer was just on the edge of the flat. We attached a long rope from the cradle to a bollard, to check the boat's descent. Susan did the honours of pouring out glasses of wine for our small group of guests, and the last dribble over the boat's stem, "I name thee *Leofleda*," she said, "May God bless her and all who sail in her." Dave and I let *Leofleda* down the slope and into the water, with a few members of the Small Boat Club to cheer us, and there she was with her green topsides, varnished spars, red anti-fouling showing two inches above her waterline, and brown bulwarks, cabin sides and trim, floating right on her marks as she was designed to do. We

---

16 Young, Philip, *op cit*, p 12.

started the little air-cooled diesel engine and took her out to her mooring amongst the other boats.

Jarrah is ideal timber for the planking below the waterline. It expands powerfully when it becomes wet, and if you fit dry planks you risk the ribs cracking, or the planks warping as the timber "takes up" in the water. We had allowed for this by experiments, accurately measuring off-cuts across the grain and then measuring it again after a night spent in a bucket of water. There was a difference of 2 mm between wet and dry timber. We used some bits of old linoleum tiles to lay between each plank edge before we fastened each of them. Then we pulled the separators out and caulked the seams with caulking cotton. Until we finished caulking, you could see through the gaps. After launching, a few of the seams were squeezing out a couple of drops of water as expected, but after pumping and sponging out a miniscule amount of water, she tightened up. By the next morning she had taken up completely, and has remained dry for the last 46 years except for occasional entry of rain water. The next few weekends were taken up with sea trials. She sailed beautifully, much to my delight.

In December 1973, I decided to go to Suva, in order to organise things with the various Fijian customs and immigration authorities to prepare for study leave in mid-1974. I also wanted to visit the USP. Ron Crocombe had published an article about "Academic Imperialism." In it, he argued that archives were paid for by Fijian tax payers, but used for research by foreign, white historians, thus exploiting the Fijian tax payers. I thought he had a point, and it was good to persuade people to think about that, but it would be a kind of intellectual boycott, and could imply that history was national property. What would happen to the Archives if National boundaries were to be altered? I wanted to discuss this problem with Ron. I felt that the involvement of Fijian students from USP in my project would both help them along with their careers and ensure a culturally balanced result.

It would be better, I thought, to include Fijian students in the research projects of foreign researchers, and provide them with good supervision at Australian expense, and get more of them into Australian universities. I was delighted when Joni Madraiwiwi, a Fijian student who came to Adelaide University to read Law, attended my Honours tutorials on Fijian History. We talked about "academic imperialism" and discussed the possibility of collaboration between the USP and Adelaide University.

I booked passages for myself and the children, by air to Sydney and then by sea on the *Oronsay* to Suva. The boys had one cabin and Susan and I had the one next door. As it was the Christmas holidays, I thought a treat was in order after the stress of the last few months so that weekend in Sydney, the four of us hired a motor cruiser, of all things, from Halverson's, the famous boat-builders on the Pittwater, a marine national park just north of Sydney. The boat was much like the *Margoletta*, the motor cruiser rented by the Hullabaloos on the Norfolk Broads in Arthur Ransome's children's book, *Coot Club*. It would have been more fun in a yacht, for me anyway, but the children loved it, and it was about the safest thing I could do with them for the weekend before we boarded *Oronsay*.

Suva was the first destination, which we reached in four days of lazing about, playing deck tennis, swimming, and doing nothing. I remember a group of four women off on their holiday to "get some relief from their husbands" back on the Gold Coast. One of them was interested in us as an unusual family of three children and single father. She asked if I was expecting to meet someone special when we reached Suva. I told her that indeed I was, and as we docked at the passenger wharf in Suva Harbour I soon picked Ruth in the waiting crowd. I wept as soon as I recognised her green and white cotton dress, and saw her distant smile, but that soon changed to laughing with joy as we took each other in our arms on the wharf and then caught a taxi to a house Ruth was looking after at the USP.

We started to plan our immediate future. My next study leave began in June 1974. While I was in Suva, I talked to Ron Crocombe and John Harré, about the possibility of including Fijian students from USP in my plan for an interdisciplinary study of culture-history in the Lau group of islands. Both were supportive. John Harré had been a member of the cast in the Auckland University revue of 1954, and was Professor of Anthropology at the USP. I gave John an introductory document, to be circulated to any students who might be interested. This is most of what I wrote:

> *The Lau group, presents an ideal opportunity to break new ground in several directions. Firstly, the quantity and quality of oral traditions, and secondly, the almost entirely un-researched archaeological opportunities, will make it possible to produce a history which begins with the first human occupation, rather than the first documented records of contacts from the Northern hemisphere.*
>
> *In the context of this group of islands, the academic distinctions between Pre-history (before the arrival of people from the northern hemisphere), documented history, recorded in written languages, and contemporary society and its problems, can be forgotten.*
>
> *The task will be simply to study the process of change over time in response to both internal and external pressure, using whatever forms of evidence we can find. This presents an opportunity for collaboration between people with different cultural as well as different academic methods of inquiry. It was on this basis that the Australian Research Grants Committee agreed to provide financial support, including fares for student participants.*

Several of John Harré's own students declared an interest in joining us. They agreed to my proposal that they could choose subjects for the research component of their Honours degree courses from the evidence we hoped, with them, to discover. I met two of them, Aisea Ledua, who was a native of Lakeba, and Cema Bolabola, from the island of Koro in the Province of Lomaiviti. Aisea proposed to write a history of the early years of Provincial Government in Lau, following cession to Britain in 1874. In the spirit of Ron Crocombe's appeal for the study of Fijian History by Fijian students, I welcomed Aisea's offer of engagement, and offered to pay his fare to Lakeba from my grant. Cema was already working on a thesis about

Fijian people from Lau who were, like her, living in Suva, but retaining their links with their island communities.

Further support came from Fergus Clunie, Director of the Fijian National Museum, who wrote to the Minister of Labour on 21 January 1974:

> *I would like to state that Mr Young has the full support and co-operation of the Museum in what should prove to be a most valuable study in Fijian History. We are particularly glad to note Mr Young's policy of working though individuals and institutions who should gain valuable experience by participation in the project.*

We intended to use *Leofleda* as a means of travelling amongst the islands of southern Lau at our own pace. As luck would have it, the P & O ship *Himalaya*, built in 1948 for the Britain-Australia passage, was in Suva, and I was able to go aboard, find the Second Officer who was in charge of cargo, and with his help, and my tape measure, I checked the size of the hatch opening on the foredeck. The hatchway was twenty feet long and seventeen feet wide. *Leofleda* is twenty-three feet long on deck, with a beam, counting outside rubbing strakes, of eight feet two inches. With her mast, rudder, and bowsprit removed, the officer agreed that she and her cradle could be lifted off the wharf by the ship's cargo cranes and would pass diagonally through the hatchway. *Himalaya* was expected to arrive in Tonga from Australia in June. It would be possible to transport *Leofleda* to Tonga.

The usual Ports of Entry to Fiji for ships were Lautoka, on the western side of the Viti Levu, and Suva on the south-eastern corner. We hoped to sail downwind from Tonga to the east of Fiji. Tacking against the prevailing wind from either port to Lakeba would have taken at least a week for such a small boat as ours, and would have been slow, exhausting, no fun, and therefore dangerous for a very young crew. So I spent time in January 1974, to do the rounds of Health, Customs and Immigration for permission to use the island of Lakemba, in central Lau, as a Port of Entry. I wrote to the Prime Minister's department, for permission to do the research. I thought it prudent, to be on the safe side, to write a personal letter to Ratu Sir Kamisese Mara, who was not only the Prime Minister of modern Fiji, but the supreme chief (Tui Nayau) of the ancient kingdom of Lau, regarded as the least commercially developed part of the Fijian nation, and yet the most politically sophisticated, and "traditional":

> *Dear Sir,*
>
> *I am writing to you as Tui Nayau, to ask for your approval and support of a research project which I have planned, in conjunction with students from the USP. It also involves some of my own students from the University of Adelaide. I hope to begin working full time on this project in July, when I shall be able to return to Fiji for a period of study leave. I am in Fiji at the moment. Seven Fijian students have... responded... and it is my intention that they should become co-authors of the eventual product, and thus gain an opportunity to further their own academic careers... I would have liked to have had an opportunity to discuss the project personally with you... but I realise that it is unlikely at such short notice.*

Mr K Chandra, "for Secretary to the Cabinet" replied on 4 February 1974:

I am directed by the Right Hon, the Prime Minister, to thank you for your letter of the 29th January seeking approval and support for a research project on the Lauan Group of the Fiji Islands. Your letter has been referred to the Research Committee who considers such matters, and I shall inform you of their decision as soon as I hear from them.

Yours Faithfully.

There were no further replies to my request, sent on 31 January 1974, regarding permission to use Lakeba as a port of entry. I hoped that we would receive replies in the end, preferably before we left Australia in June.

We returned from Suva early in February 1974 to live together with the kids at North Adelaide. Carmel was still in England, but she very much wanted to stay in the North Adelaide house when she came back. Ruth and I needed to look around for somewhere else to live.

Chapter 13: Adelaide History and the South Seas

Ruth was brought up at first, in Tasmania, but the family—her mother Margaret, and seven children—had moved to South Australia, when Ruth was four. They lived in a large old house in Magill, a suburb at the foot of the Adelaide Hills. That's probably the reason we drove up the Magill Road in the first place, but we then thought it would be interesting to continue up the winding road that led to the suddenly rural landscape that she remembered exploring at weekends and holidays with her siblings and friends.

I liked the area because there were some physical similarities to the Yorkshire villages of my childhood. Once over the crest at Norton Summit, there was a sense of leaving the city altogether. We left the bitumen and bounced along a dirt road, with orchards on either side, and a creek running beside us. At the end of the road, there was a sharp turn over a small log bridge. We found ourselves in the back yard of what seemed to be an abandoned stone farm house. We later learnt that it had once been a handsome place, owned and built by the Nicholls family.

We had a very good look around both the house, which needed a lot of work, and the land. There was a large dam, pig sties and many fruit trees of different kinds, all this below a large area of bush. I wrote a note, asking if the owner was interested in selling, and taped it to the back door of the house.

About two weeks later, I received a phone call from Frank Costa and a meeting was arranged at his home in Woodville, a north-westerly suburb of Adelaide, to discuss a sale. It turned out that the Costas, a large Italian family, worked all week at the Holden car factory. Nicholls Road, Norton Summit was their place of cultural refreshment for many years: a place where they could grow their own vegetables, grow and harvest cherries, apples, plums and pears, and keep a few cows. The total area of the property was thirty-six acres. Most orchard properties in the Adelaide Hills were a bit larger, but for a big extended Italian family, it had been an ideal hobby farm and retreat, where they could speak their own language, make grappa, and maintain their kinship ties.

The Costas were what would have been called "suitcase farmers" if they had migrated to the United States. They never stayed at the farm for a night, but worked on it enough at weekends for it to provide a small income. The house had not been abandoned, but neighbours told us that it had been used as an apple store. There was also a small Caterpillar tractor, and a vintage (1940s), one ton Chevrolet truck for taking the crops to the East End market across the road from the University in Adelaide.

We could not afford the whole thirty-six acres. It was also too much land for us to look after if I intended to hold down my job. But one of the Costa cousins, a member of the Gallace family, was keen to buy some of it. We found out through a friend that another couple, Viv and Briar Ayres, were interested in buying some more. For about six weeks, and many nights spent with the Costa and Gallace families at Woodville, drinking grappa and Drambuie, Ruth and I concluded that we could afford to buy sixteen acres of the property, but we needed to organise a simultaneous three-way subdivision and sale of the other twenty acres. There would be one awful moment in time when we owned all thirty-six acres, but only a moment. This complex arrangement involved, in addition to the grappa, a lot of surveyors, lawyers, money and anxiety, but if we were prepared to fix the house ourselves we could make it possible to live in it within a short time. So we bought it.

Carmel helped a lot by agreeing on a simultaneous sale of my fifty percent of our agreed value of the Barnard Street house, to her. I would use my half as a deposit, and borrow the rest to buy the land at Nicholls Road. The Costas did not regard the house as having any value, just the land. The house was in a terrible state: the roof leaked; several walls showed clear signs of salt damp. Some of the floors were rotten and the walls and ceilings in some rooms were covered in mould, a result of being used as a place to stack apple cases. The septic tank did not comply with modern regulations. The wood-stove in the kitchen was close to being burnt out, and water came from a large rain tank which could only be filled by pumping water uphill from the creek. It was in fact a "handyman's delight." Over the next few years we relied heavily on a 1960s edition of the *Reader's Digest Home Handyman Manual* belonging to Ruth's mother, Margaret, who had behind her much experience of using it herself. The children still remember the down side of the experience. Philip remembered the house as "Damp, cold, draughty, leaky," and worse. But he went on to say:

> *The property had a fantastic dam, fringed by bull rushes, but with a perfect swimming "beach" with clay instead of sand which squished up between your toes when you walked, and down your sister's pants when you caught up with her. We had wonderful Christmases on the dam, with sailing races, swimming and generally mucking about.*[1]

My leave of 6 months was to begin in May 1974 and my grant application to the Australian Research Council was successful. So we could get ourselves and *Leofleda* to Tonga. There was almost too much to be done. We had to make our house in Norton Summit habitable within a few months, and arrange for the shipping of *Leofleda* from Adelaide, via Sydney to Tonga. I hadn't received approval of my research project from the Fijian Government. Nor had I received any word about permission to use Lakeba as a port of entry from Tonga. The reason for planning this route was that the period from May to October is the trade wind season in the South Pacific, when the wind direction, south of the equator, is reliably south-easterly. Most of the time it is steady, but not too strong, and even a boat as small as *Leofleda* can depend on safely covering up to a hundred nautical miles a day, with a fair wind behind her. [See map of Fiji, including *Leofleda*'s Lau voyage p iv].

Stephen had begun his secondary education at Scotch College. We thought it would be a bad idea for him to miss out on any of his first year of secondary teaching at his new school. He had reached an age from which he looked forward to

---
1   Young, Philip, *A Pretty Ordinary Year*, 2013, p 15.

a taste of urban life, and a bit more independence. And I think he felt a need to be with his mother. So we all agreed that he would live with Carmel in North Adelaide while Ruth, Philip, Susan and I were on *Leofleda* in Lau. Stephen, who was 13 years old, would make a short visit to Lakeba in his holidays. Philip also had his own plans and preferences, which included an international scout Jamboree in Suva. He was to fly from the island of Lakeba to Suva on his own, for the Jamboree week. Then he would fly back to join us again in Lakeba.

The P & O liner, *Himalaya* was to be taken off the work she was built for, which was carrying British passengers from Southampton to the "Far East," calling in at many ports including Bombay (Mumbai), and finishing the journey in Sydney. *Himalaya* was coming to Adelaide and then Sydney for the first *Woman's Weekly* cruise of the islands of the south-west Pacific. Some things had not changed since *Himalaya* was taken off the "Far-east run," otherwise known as POSH (Port Out, Starboard Home — that way you were always on the sunny side of the ship). We still were allotted a large allowance of hold space, as if we wanted to take a piano or two to China or India, so the cost of taking *Leofleda*, our home for the next six months, to Tonga was just $200.

Everything seemed to be going well. Checking the dimensions of *Himalaya*'s hatch in Suva, some months earlier, proved to have been a worthwhile precaution. *Himalaya* arrived at Outer Harbour of Port Adelaide, to collect the readers of the *Women's Weekly* in South Australia and us, who had booked passage on the inaugural *Women's Weekly* cruise, and it was a weekend.

Just for my own peace of mind, I went down to the ship to check that the arrangements for *Leofleda* to be loaded were in place. Much to my dismay I was told, that *Leofleda* could not be taken aboard *Himalaya,* because she would have to be loaded on the Sunday, and that would mean the additional expense of a whole gang for the weekend, at double wages. Luckily I had a booking advice from the local P & O agents. I emphasised that I had a contract with P & O, the legal implications of the refusal to load *Leofleda*, and that the tragic scale of this decision would be disastrous, in view of the numbers of people in Fiji and Australia, who would be affected and disappointed if we and *Leofleda* failed to meet our deadline. After considerable discussion, but no threats, I was told that our boat could be taken aboard on the following Friday, if I could deliver her in a cradle, not at Port Adelaide, but at a specified time, on the wharf in Sydney. She would have to be there in five days.

We received immediate help from Dieter Nass and his colleague, Sandy Van Dyke, our two friends who ran the slipway at the Small Boat Club of Port Adelaide, where *Leofleda* was moored. At this point the only conveyance we had for the boat, was the two wheeled contraption we had used to move her from North Adelaide to Port Adelaide in the middle of the night, before she was launched. We hauled *Leofleda* out of the water at the Small Boat Club and put her back onto her cradle, to see if it was strong enough for the 1,000 mile, high speed journey to Sydney.

It wasn't strong enough. The old tyres bulged out dangerously as they took up the weight of about two and a half tons. We needed to hire a large truck. Immediately. It cost $800, which made a big hole in our budget, but it made the expedition possible.

Dieter and Sandy started work on the spot, to build a cradle that could be lifted onto the back of a truck, while I scoured the phone book for a truck driver who could guarantee a fast journey to Sydney in the following three days. It took the team a whole day to gather materials for a strong cradle that would be lifted by crane onto the truck and then taken off the truck on the wharf in Sydney by a cargo derrick on *Himalaya*. Ruth and I, and Philip and Susan packed up our belongings for the drive to Sydney in our little Mazda station wagon, following the truck carrying *Leofleda*.

Luckily we had a friend, Rob Durbridge whom I had worked with in the days of student revolution of 1968 against conscription for the Vietnam war. The Vice Chancellor had refused to allow the police to arrest the students when they sought sanctuary in the administration office of the University. Rob was then in Sydney, and volunteered to look after our car for the next six months.

I remember only one stop during what remains in my mind as the most dangerous journey in my life, including all the risks we would face on the high seas in the near future. The reason for the stop was that somewhere on the Hume Highway, a large transport truck had fallen on its side and had spewed its contents across the road. Our driver was undisturbed, and assured us that he was in good shape, as he had been careful to dose himself with his customary cocktail of Coca Cola, No-Doze, and slimming pills, to keep awake, and there was a distance of only 250 miles more to go.

Exhausted and shaken, we reached the overseas passenger terminal in Sydney at the end of the next day, and slept on the boat. Loading cargo on to *Himalaya* commenced at 8 am, and we spent an hour shopping for last minute items. Our final purchase before leaving Adelaide had been a "Silva" gimballed compass, to be fitted on the after bulkhead of the cockpit, next to the tiller and away from the engine, and a small barometer hung in the cabin next to the mast.

We had swung the compass to deal with deviation with the help of a local Port Adelaide professional. But we had forgotten the need to keep dry, even in the tropics, and so we took this last opportunity to buy wet weather gear from the Crow's Nest ship chandlers. We had a lot of charts, covering Tonga and Fiji, navigation tables, and the relevant books of pilotage. I had a sextant and a stop-watch, but in spite of our navigation class (Part 1) at Port Adelaide TAFE, we had a grasp of the theory, but not the practice. We had never actually used a sextant and a stopwatch to discover our position in the open ocean.

In our rush to transport ourselves and the boat to Sydney, we did not have time to weigh *Leofleda*, with her internal ballast and anchors and chain. We knew that *Himalaya*'s derrick could safely lift three tons. So as a precaution, we removed the pigs of lead and two anchors and chain with the intention of putting them in our cabin and replacing them after *Leofleda* was safely in the water in Tonga. But we were not out of trouble yet. We arrived back at the wharf to find that the gang loading *Himalaya* had told their employers, P & O, that it would take a couple of hours more, after the lunch break, to finish loading. That would mean more overtime, and without it, *Himalaya* would not be going anywhere. At this stage, *Leofleda* was sitting in her cradle waiting to be lifted into the hold, as the last item of cargo. A conference took place over lunch (the wharfies shared their lunch with us) while we waited in a state of extreme anxiety, for the vital decision. At a bit after 2 pm, the gang leader came to the rail, and shouted triumphantly, "Another victory for the Working Class!," signalling the success of the negotiations with P & O. Perhaps the chat I'd had with the leading wharfie, in the morning, about my gratitude to the wharfies' Union in Auckland for giving me my Seagulls card helped the decision. I like to think so.

Himalaya left Sydney the evening of 23 June 1974. It was a relief to have some cruise ship luxury and less stress, despite our cabin being a minefield of lead, anchors and chain. *Himalaya* stopped briefly at Brisbane, where we were hoping to get to a supermarket, to buy provisions for the voyage from Tonga to Fiji. But the Brisbane supermarket was curiously bereft of much variety in the way of suitable non-perishable food. We bought what we could, assuming we would pick up things like flour, rice, some dehydrated food and certainly, fresh fruit and vegetables in Tonga.

When *Himalaya* stopped in Suva, we had a chance to make last minute arrangements. I had two old friends in Suva, Terry and Robina Donnelly, who had been

Leofleda in Nuku'alofa, Tonga, just after she was unloaded from *Himalaya* (in the background). The mast has just been stepped. Helping us (in white) is Derek McCabe, chippie on board *Himalaya*.

through Teacher Training College (and *The Beggar's Opera*) with me and Carmel, in Auckland in 1957. We arranged for them to meet Stephen and transport him by air to Lakeba and meet Philip at the airport for his Scout Jamboree and put him up for a week. Terry was an outstanding teacher, cricketer, and coach, at Suva Grammar School. A colleague from the University of the South Pacific, offered to receive *Leofleda*'s cradle from *Himalaya* when she called back to Suva, and look after it until we returned from Lau. It would then wait for a ship to return *Leofleda* back to Sydney. We also hoped to pick up more provisions in Suva, but the shelves of the one supermarket were completely and inexplicably empty, except for a tinned chicken, some "bullamacow" (corned beef) and some tinned ghee, all of which we bought.

We arrived at Nuku'alofa, Tonga, three days later. *Himalaya* came as close as she dared to the royal Island of Pangaimotu, where the water was deep and sheltered, heading for Nuku'alofa wharf. We prepared *Leofleda* for the re-launch with the help of the ship's "chippie," an English sailor, Derek McCabe. Six months later, he wrote to us from Hong Kong, at the end of *Himalaya*'s last voyage, to the ship breakers. Sadly he told us that when he met his girlfriend in Sydney, "My girlfriend is not my girlfriend anymore." Such is a sailor's life.

We replaced *Leofleda*'s inside ballast between the floors, laid between every three pairs of ribs. Wooden battens were screwed down on top of the lead pigs to make sure they could not move in rough seas. Then she was lifted out of the hold, still in her cradle, with me in the cockpit, and gently lowered over the side and into the transparent water. Soon the cradle was immersed enough to enable her to float free. I started the motor and drove her out of the cradle, with Derek holding a line to the ship towering above her. Once she was ahead of the cradle, it was lifted back and into the hold for my colleague to pick up in Suva, leaving *Leofleda* triumphantly afloat.

The mast was then re-stepped, with a customary coin, this time a Tongan ten *seniti*, under the foot. Spars, rigging, and sails were put aboard. The bowsprit and rudder were returned to their places. We went to our cabins and brought all our belongings on deck. Then I came alongside *Himalaya* in *Leofleda*, so that Ruth, Philip and Susan could come aboard.

We motored slowly back for about half a mile to Faua Harbour, where we were allowed to stay until we left for Lakeba. Faua was a small basin at the end of a narrow channel between two concrete moles, jutting out to the edge of the fringing coral reef. It was full of simple sailing boats from the smaller islands of Tonga: gaff rigged, with their booms extending well beyond their pointed sterns, and loading or unloading mixed cargoes of copra, timber, hardware, and "luxuries" like soap, kerosene and tobacco, animals and people.

There was mail waiting for us at the Nuku'alofa Post Office. This included the long-awaited letter, forwarded from K Chandra, Secretary to the Cabinet in Fiji, finally giving us permission to use Lakeba as a port of entry, with conditions:

Dear Dr Young,

Further to our approval of your application to do research in Fiji, you requested "permission to proceed direct to Lakeba from Tonga, without coming to Suva first." After consultation with the departments concerned, I am to inform you that approval has been granted for you to proceed direct to Lakeba, provided that:

You adhere to the Permanent Secretary for Health's letter of 31st January, 1974, [a letter I had not received] *paying particular intention to paragraph 3 of the same;* [this turned out to be about very sensible biosecurity precautions.]

You write to the Comptroller of Customs and Excise, as agreed by you earlier, informing him of the items you and your passengers would carry;

You write to the permanent Secretary for labour giving him full particulars of all persons you would be carrying, the date you leave Tonga and the expected date of arrival in Fiji, and provided that you present yourself to the Labour department as soon as you reach the first port of entry.

The delay in processing your application is very much regretted, however, you would realise, no doubt, that other departments had to be consulted before a decision could be made.

I took this message to be what I had asked for, and wrote back to confirm that I would follow instructions.

But the other letter, dated 31 January, followed a week or so later, to tell me that after arriving off the town of Tubou, on Lakeba, I was to anchor one mile off the reef entrance, fly my Australian red ensign, a yellow quarantine flag, and the Fijian Courtesy Flag, and await permission from the shore, before raising anchor and going through the passage and into the lagoon.

Will you please note that you will be required to anchor off at least a nautical mile from the mainland, and from any adjacent island until a pratique is granted by the Quarantine Officer. The vessel in this respect will have to be inspected by a Quarantine Officer.

Will you please note that a further clearance will be required from the comptroller of customs, the principle immigration officer, the Director of Agriculture, and the Manager, Coconut Pests and Diseases Board.

The ETA and other details will have to be communicated to the subdivisional Medical officer, at the Health Centre, Lakeba. Or to the Divisional Medical Officer, Eastern, Levuka, by telegraphic advice, prior to your departure from Nuku'alofa.

This letter was signed by a Mr Rao, on behalf of the Permanent Secretary for Health.

I thought that remaining a mile offshore would be difficult in view of the depth of 500 fathoms at that place. *Leofleda* would have been hardly able to float with the necessary weight of chain I would have needed! It was too late to do anything about this, except to write back and confirm that we had arrived in Tonga. We did have the yellow Quarantine flag on board. We didn't have the Fijian courtesy flag or an Australian flag, which we would somehow have to acquire in Tonga.

We had arranged in advance for Philip and Susan to sit a scholarship exam for Scotch College on 28 July. They were to do this at Tupou High School in Nuku'alofa, the Tongan capital, about a mile from Faua. We therefore knew we had to stay in Tonga for nearly a month. Most of this time was needed in any case to prepare *Leofleda*, and ourselves, for her voyage to Lakeba.

The situation in Tonga was not quite as we anticipated. For one thing, it turned out that the whole Tongatapu population was waiting, and had been for some time, for a ship to arrive from Auckland, with the very foodstuffs we needed ourselves: flour, rice, oats, tinned foods, sugar, yeast and so on, and toilet paper, which some Tongans were selling at five seniti per sheet. The absence of the ship also explained the paucity of supplies in Suva. There was plenty of taro, taro leaves, coconut, bananas and papaya at the market in Nuku'alofa, but no sign of any flags except, luckily, two small Union Jacks. It was clear we would have to make Fijian and Australian flags ourselves before we arrived at Lakeba, so we also bought some red and blue satin material.

The most important problem was navigation. Ruth and I had both enrolled for a navigation course, using the Merchant Navy method, in the hectic months before our departure, but it lasted two terms, and we were able to complete only one, before it was time to leave. We had brought our Almanacs and notes along, and the idea was to go on learning until we reached the point at which we could lose sight of land with confidence of our position. This would have meant a lot more work, but we were fortunate to meet Michael Bailes, twelve years out from England in his Folk boat, *Jellicle*.

Mike told us about his adventures. He left England and worked his way south; first to Spain, where he broke his boom, and cut down a tree to make another one. Then he crossed the Atlantic, and followed the classic route, with the North-East trade winds, and through the Panama Canal. He continued to the Galapagos, the Marquesas, Tahiti, the Cook Islands, sometimes taking adventurous islanders with him, and so to Tonga. The Tongan King asked him to establish a school of Navigation for local mariners. I told him that we were a bit green when it came to

Departing from Nuku'alofa for Nomuka.

Transporting the wedding guests from Doi to Ono Levu. Susan is in the hatchway.

ocean navigation. Michael rapidly assessed our risk of shipwreck, and thought it might be too high, though he never put it that way.

He advised us, given our shortage of time, to forget the Merchant Navy method, which we had been well and carefully taught, and to learn the air-navigation method, that he had used himself, and would take a relatively short time to learn. He even had an almost current copy of the air navigation tables to spare. This method of navigation involves using an imaginary line around the earth, and a sextant to discover how close you are to it, and at what compass bearing, first at 11 am, then at noon, and again at 2 pm. This would give us a triangle around our actual position, within five miles or so. It was much quicker than the Merchant Navy method. Mike said he would gladly exchange the air tables for a hacksaw, that he needed badly to repair his Primus stove.

It took him about an hour to teach us the process required. Once we knew the Universal Co-ordinated Time, local time, and the angle of the sun, we only had to do nineteen simple addition and subtraction sums, to find out our position within 5 sea miles.

We were committed to our first ocean passage, very soon, we hoped, but like everyone else, we had to wait for the ship from Auckland—no-one knew when this would come—and for the children to sit the exam. Faua Harbour itself was not a particularly pleasant place in which to wait. It looked polluted, so we were reluctant to fish. Our diet consisted of fresh fruit and taro. With ourselves and two young children in a boat with not much room below decks, life was quite difficult for us all. It was not long before Philip and I both succumbed to a "bug," resulting in diarrhoea and vomiting and feeling weak and poorly. I summoned up the strength to write to Stephen about this and he soon replied:

At the moment I really envy you, as I am in bed with the flu, and the thought of all of you in the sun is rather infuriating. I will see what can be done about some toily [toilet] *paper to relieve your present predicament. See if you can narrow it down to what caused Philip and Dad to be sick, and avoid it like the plague, as I can't bring more than 1,000,000 rolls of toily paper...*

Sigmund is pleased that you are not lost to him forever, Susan. And I will get him to make a paw mark on this letter.

I am not sure how large a bag I can bring, so could you sort of let me know if I'm wrong in planning to bring a Port Bag, [Stephen was a staunch member of the Port Adelaide AFL football club cheer squad] *and the toilet paper, and whatever else you ask for.*

I will now get the ALMIGHTY BLACK ONE to make a big muddy paw mark, but it might not last to Tonga.

Then there was a note from Carmel:

Sigmund's paws are too clean. All wiped off on the walls, carpets, furniture etc.
------------*Dig Dog's Paw Mark*

> Saw colour photo taken of you at Nuku'alofa. Very pretty; Very small. Good Luck.
> Love, C.

While we waited for the Auckland ship and slowly recovered from our illness, we sorted out the various practical problems presented by *Leofleda*'s small size. We had four two-gallon plastic folding water containers, and kept them under the cabin floorboards. We thought this was not quite enough in case of emergency. Our hacksaw-navigation tables transaction with Mike was symptomatic of the extreme shortage of many modern commodities in an island economy. Containers of almost any kind were always in short supply in the islands. We approached the Nuku'alofa Yacht Club, in the absence of pubs, and came away with quite a few (empty) glass spirit bottles. We washed them, filled them up with fresh water, and poked them into all the little spaces we could find under the bunks. There were five bunks altogether, one each side of the cabin, one in the fo'c's'le, for Susan, and two quarter berths. Philip slept in the port side quarter berth next to the galley. The other was for Stephen, but we used it for storage until he arrived. We filled up the fuel tank of the engine, which gave us enough diesel to motor about fifty miles in calm conditions.

Every day, we practised navigation, using the sextant and stopwatch, and Ruth's new Seiko watch, which we kept on Greenwich Mean Time, known by the short wave radio announcer in Hawaii, as Universal Co-ordinated Time, to discover where we were. We started with the comforting fact that we knew exactly where we were really; on the sea wall of Faua Harbour, as shown on our chart. To begin with, we were up to thirty miles out, but we became better at it, and as the intersecting pencil lines on the chart increased our confidence, we began to be not more than a mile from truth. Then we sailed out of the harbour to practise our newly acquired skills in the gentle slop of the wavelets beyond the Harbour wall.

I think Mike found our hacksaw as reliable as we found his tables. A few days later he set off with two island boys for Suva. A large crowd came down to Faua harbour to see him off, and as he was about to leave, Michael turned around to the crowd as if he had lost something: "I don't suppose," he said, "that anyone happens to have a spare watch?" Within half a minute, a wrist watch was passed down through the crowd. "That's awfully good of you," he said in his southern English accent. "I'm very grateful; it will make things so much easier."

Next day it was our turn to set sail, for a shake-down voyage to the island of Nomuka, in the southern Ha'apai group of islands, and back, to test our skills. We knew that underwater reefs that could not be seen from deck level in a boat as small as *Leofleda*, often show up very clearly if you could ascend even nine or ten feet up the mast. Originally, *Leofleda* was not rigged with cross-trees, as her beam of eight feet, with a 24 foot mast, gave an adequate angle of incidence between the shrouds and the mast to support the mast without cross-trees. However cross-trees are good to sit on as it is often necessary to stay aloft for long periods to con the ship through coral waters.

A local blacksmith *cum* wheelwright allowed me to use his workshop to make my cross-trees out of one inch by ⅛ inch iron strip, in return for a new ¼ inch drill bit and the loan of a small grindstone to sharpen his old ones. His greatest ambition was to save enough money to travel to Auckland in order to buy himself a good supply of tools.

There was a gentle south-easterly breeze which strengthened till noon and then fell away as it grew dark. Our little short wave transistor radio gave us regular weather forecasts which were always reassuring. We grew to love the gentle Fijian female voice every morning and evening, that told us that we would have medium strength south easterly winds, and that on the following day, conditions would be "simila," which, they were.

There are a lot of reefs to the immediate north of Nuku'alofa, but, as we expected, after 9 am, the angle of the sun made it very easy to see them if we climbed up the ratlines until our eyes were a few feet above the deck. From there, we could pick out the differences between the brownish shallows on top of the reefs, the light blue-green of the navigable shallows, maybe up to thirty feet of water, above a sandy bottom, and the deep blue of the water beyond the reefs.

We successfully made it to Nomuka island. It was a brisk sail once clear of reefs, with nothing to look out for until we sighted the island, which is low and has a large freshwater lake, and one village. Just south of the beach is Nomuka Iki island, which provides good shelter, between the two islands, from the prevailing wind. We anchored quite close to the south facing beach in two fathoms of water and pumped up our Avon rubber dinghy so that we could row ashore and have a look round. We had tried it out just once, at the Small Boat Club in Adelaide, where there was little risk of damage, but this was our first encounter with coral so we were careful to find a sandy landing. We carried the Avon up the beach, but did not like to leave it around, as it was both our tender and our life boat. We made no contact with any of the islanders, as we were keen to return to our ship in daylight, which is lost quickly in the tropics. So back we went to put up our kerosene riding light, even though we were the only vessel to be seen in the vast ocean.

Next day we had a swim and breakfast at sunrise and set off. The return passage was close hauled on the port tack, and we needed to sail through the reefs of the approach to Nuku'alofu before dark. We were lucky with the steady wind that let us stay on the same course, heading straight back to Faua Harbour, practising our sextant work and having Philip and Susan do the nineteen sums, each time we took a sight, until we were only a few miles away and could see our destination. We put in a dog-leg last tack, and slipped into our old harbour berth just before sunset, feeling pretty confident and pleased with ourselves. We had carried full working sail all day and averaged just under five knots.

In our absence, the long-awaited ship from Auckland had arrived! The shop in Nuku'alofa was reasonably stocked with the essentials. Now for the real ocean voyage. We spent the next day buying all the supplies we needed. The shop keeper gave us a large well-fitting square biscuit tin to keep our flour in. I use it still to keep old sandpaper that I might use again. Kerosene was our main source of light, inside the cabin and for navigation lights. We filled the tank up with diesel and took an extra four gallons in an army surplus can, so we could have motored for twenty-four hours if necessary. In the event we hardly used any diesel at all.

We had a pressure cooker, which we could use, with a very low flame, as an oven, on top of our methylated spirit stove. Meths proved to be a problem. It could only be obtained with great difficulty as "ships' stores." It was not sold openly in Tonga because, being an officially tee-total society, people drank it. When I eventually produced a written authority to the storekeeper to supply me with two gallons, he warned me that it was strong stuff and I should go easy on it. Meths was normally unobtainable in Lau for the same reason, so in port, when a gimballed stove was unnecessary, cooking was done on an ordinary primus stove, which we learnt to prime with kerosene to conserve what meths we could.

We tied a bunch of bananas to the lower shrouds and ate them most of the way to Fiji. But we didn't find anywhere that had any eggs. We managed to find two half bottles of Moyston Claret, produced in South Australia's Barossa Valley, which we bought for special occasions. We had some Bickford's concentrated lime juice, to stave off scurvy.

It was already August, the exams were completed and it was time to get going. We had an evening meal with Harold Gelshaw, of the trimaran, *Ariel*, from Los Angeles, with two young women from Auckland as crew and a German couple, Bernd and Elkert Fengler, who had just arrived from Europe in *Pinocchio*. *Pinocchio* was an impressive cruising yacht. She was half way through her voyage round the world. These were the first boats that we met of the continuous procession of the 1970s, when young people of many nationalities set out to do the same. Most of those we met had read, and had been inspired by, the books of Eric and Susan Hiscock, who combined storytelling with a lot of useful and encouraging advice about long distance ocean cruising. Thanks to the Hiscocks, most of this new generation of yachties succeeded. We received a letter from *Pinocchio* when they reached Singapore a year later. I envied them, but took comfort with the thought that it was even better to be able to combine cruising with a purpose, if it could be arranged.

I was considering steering a direct course to Lakeba. Our landfall would have been somewhere north of Ogea, where there were numerous islands that are hard to identify, and an enormous area of reefs, on which there had been regular wrecks in the past. There were no marked passages, nor navigation marks through the reefs. From a distance there was little means of identifying individual islands. Just before we left Tonga, we received a letter from Mike Bailes, telling us of his safe arrival in Suva. He must have been a little worried about us:

> *I still don't much like the idea of you heading straight for Lakeba, and recommend, again, making your landfall, on Ogea Levu, where the outlying reefs are not far from the 270 foot island.*

I spent some time carefully looking at the chart and understood his anxiety, and became most grateful for his concern. "… However," he concluded, "best of luck whichever way, and we hope you catch a few fish on the way across. All the best to all the family, Yours, Mike Bailes." I have often realised how fortunate we were to have met Mike. Without his experience this might have been a very different story.

We sent a telegram to Carmel and Stephen and then set sail for Fiji, with a blast from Bernd's Bavarian hunting horn, on 3 August, in the same weather as always, or so it seemed at the time. Once clear of the reefs, we set a course of 322 degrees magnetic, for the first 66 miles to avoid all hazards. Then we fixed our position and headed for the southern end of the island of Ogea, the safest entrance from the east to the ancient kingdom of Lau. Ogea, however, has no visible islands to the immediate south. Once we rounded the southern shore of Ogea, we could head north and fix our position easily by taking back bearings with a hand held compass, of the island headlands or other features that we could find on our charts. [See map on page iv]

Our first night at sea was unforgettable. At 10 pm I was at the helm for the first watch of the night, when, to my alarm a brilliant speck of light appeared on the starboard quarter. It became bigger, so I assumed it was a lit up cruise ship, like the *Himalaya*, travelling at a cruising speed of twenty-two knots. We did not have a radio transmitter to make contact with this great vessel before she ran us down. The light continued to becoming brighter and cast long shafts of light as it drew nearer. Then I suddenly realised that it was the rising moon, a thing I had never seen at sea before. It rose out of the sea as a ball and spread light everywhere. I was glad not to have woken anyone up over it, as it gave me an hour or so of feeling just a bit smug with happiness at having dealt with so many problems and crises. Soon Ruth joined me and we had the cockpit to ourselves, hugging each other, watching the bright waves, illuminated by the huge moon, and listening to the little white crests chuckling alongside as the children slept.

We had laid down a course on the chart which cleared the islands to the north of Tongatapu, to make sure that we would not be endangered as we passed any of them in the dark. We were close to where the mutiny on the *Bounty* took place on 28 April 1789. After clearing all the Tongan islands, we changed course to Ogea at the south end of the Lau group.

This brought the wind around to our port quarter, which made it possible to adjust our rig in a way that made steering without gybing much easier. In 1948, Captain Sheldrake showed me how to set the foresail of the first *Leofleda*, the Thames barge, on the port side of the mast, with the foot of the sail lashed to the pin rail and the luff hard against the mast. The clew was boomed out at right angles to the keel, and a preventer kept it that way by connecting the outboard end of the spar to the Samson post on the foredeck. With this rig, the two sails worked together like a single square sail; the wind coming across our port quarter, and no risk of an accidental gybe. Around midday, we tried some cooking on the meths stove.

This led to what might have been a disaster. As Michael Bailes had once done on

Jellicle, I allowed a bit too much meths to flow into the bowl around the flame piece, before it was hot enough to turn the liquid into gas, with the result that some of it spilt onto the shelf below the stove, where it caught alight. We had a fire in the cabin. Blue flames were soon dancing across the floor boards, into the gaps between them and into the bottom of the bilge. I successfully smothered it. In a second though, the flames burnt a hole in one of our plastic water containers, which put the fire out, but flooded the bilge between two of the floors under the table. We lost a quarter of our water supply. Things could have been worse, as we said to ourselves, and it was something that in over forty-five years of sailing has never happened since.

Around 5 pm that afternoon we saw land, and when I climbed a few steps up the ratlines I could see, not one, but two islands. We sailed on and I climbed up again to discover two more, just to the north. This was the first real test of our ability as navigators. We had been using the dead reckoning method as well as celestial navigation since we left Nuku'alofa. Dead reckoning is just a case of calculating an assumed position every hour, using the compass and patent log. Some logs are towed astern on a long revolving line attached to a propeller towed behind the ship. We had a "sum log"; a device with a small propeller attached to the hull on the outside, near the keel, with a revolving cable that leads to a readable dial fastened to a bulkhead in the cabin. It records speed through the water and a "distance run." If you know the distance you have come and the direction you have sailed, every hour, you have a fairly good idea of where you are.

But you could be wrong, especially in this part of the world, where there is a strong counter-Equatorial current, flowing from east to west. As it moves close to Fiji it has a habit of turning sharply to the south, down the subterranean barrier of the reefs and islands of the Lau group. But what is "close?" you have to ask yourself. While we still had the sun to help us we took a sight, which gave us three lines, one towards our imaginary line around the earth; the other, our course since we left Nuku'alofa, and another, a compass bearing on the southern end of what we assumed to be the island of Ogea. That gave us an assumed position, or some idea of where we were, and we continued to guess distances and take compass bearings as it began to darken. I thought we must have been about ten miles from the nearest island, with another just to the north, which is where our compass and sextant encouragingly told us we were. But what might the current do with us in the night? Or what might happen if the weather changed for the worse?

We decided to stay as close as possible to where we thought we were, and where we could see that we were safe, and wait until morning before moving close to anywhere. We hove-to, by turning *Leofleda* up into the wind so that she was on the starboard tack (with the wind blowing from the starboard side). Then we lashed the tiller to the port side of the cockpit to keep her like that, and pulled the clew of the jib over to the starboard side. That way the jib was trying to push her in a port direction, while the close-hauled mainsail was trying to push her to starboard. The rudder was trying to turn her to starboard as well, but the jib was trying to stop her, and she settled down like a duck, crabbing across the swell, and fore-reaching slowly at the same time. The balance of forces added up to a creep to windward and a sideways drift which meant that we could also use a sea anchor, a funnel shaped device with a big entry, kept open by a wooden cross-piece, and a small exit hole at the end of the funnel. When we wanted to sail again, we just pulled on the trip-line and it came in easily. Next morning the scenery looked exactly the same to me as it had when we went below the previous night. But my guess is that we must have moved about a mile closer to the nearest island during the night which, as expected, turned out to be Ogea, our Fijian landfall.

We couldn't be certain though, until we had passed south of the island and could see the shape and identify the position of Fulaga, a few miles to the west of Ogea. Then we shaped a more weatherly course between the two islands. Soon I joyfully sighted the stranded hull of a Japanese tuna boat on the reef, which I had seen beforehand from the deck of *Adi Lau*. We now knew where the unmarked entrance to the lagoon was located. It was still early in the morning and the angle of the sun, as we turned to face it, was low. We hove-to again, and waited until the sun was high enough for us to begin to see the brown coral.

We were tired from the length and stressful nature of our first ocean passage. I decided to take a chance, go through the passage, and into the lagoon for a rest. We were now heading to the northern side of the passage, into a slowly strengthening trade wind. I started the engine to offset any leeway we might make, and we continued until we could see straight into the passage between the seas breaking gently on the reefs on each side. I realised later that the sun was still too low for us to pilot through the gap safely, as there were a few coral heads scattered about. I nearly decided to turn round and go out and wait a bit longer, but there was no room to turn. Philip went up to the bow to warn of any coral heads he could see. We began to pass a few at a safe distance, but just at the end of the gauntlet we were running, we felt a definite bump as the keel under the cockpit hit something solid. By then, it was safer to continue than to turn back so we continued, past the wreck of the tuna boat, until the water turned light green and then blue, and we were safe, but we didn't know it until I had lifted the floorboards and searched for any leaks. There weren't any, so we began to feel relieved.

A *camakau* was soon heading out to see who we were. The person in charge of the vessel was Matai Waqavesi, the school Master. I explained the conditions to which I had consented, and said that I was worried about being in the lagoon, but we needed a rest. His told me that no-one outside the reef would ever hear of my arrival, as he was in charge of the Ogea radio-telephone service. He also noticed the deck-cargo we were carrying, a sack of taro (*dalo* in Fiji) that had remained on deck, lashed to the bottom of the starboard shrouds. I explained that the Department of Agriculture was expecting that I would declare any vegetables that I had carried with me from Tonga. "In that case" he said, "you will need to get rid of them before you get to Lakeba."

I have often had misgivings about the next transaction, but Matai went on to explain the shortage of nutritious items like *dalo*. They were grown on fertile islands of volcanic origin. Ogea was a limestone island, though it grew adequate quantities of *Vesi*. "Put them in the canoe," he said. "We will eat them now so that they will not be wasted. And any harmful pests will not survive our cooking. So put them in the canoe." I took his advice, and we spent the next two days on Ogea, had a fresh water bath in a creek, washed our clothes, baked bread in the pressure cooker, and made our first visit ashore on a Lauan island. Then we visited the site of the oldest fortified village. We noted its position, intending to re-visit after checking in at Tubou on the island of Lakeba. Our guide was Soku, the daughter of Macew, brother of the chief of the village. Matai Waqavesi was very hospitable and offered to send a telegram to Stephen and Carmel to say we had arrived safely in Fiji.

Next day we set off early. This time we knew where the real passage was through the reef we had entered the previous day. We sailed safely into a huge but gentle swell from the south. We passed the entrance to the Fulaga lagoon, thinking that we must not be delayed in arriving at Tubou, where we were expected to arrive.

All the way from Nuku'alofa, Ruth had been busy making our compulsory flags, an Australian red ensign and the Fijian flag, in time to fly them all when we arrived. The Australian flag was not too difficult. We had bought the Union Jack part. The Southern Cross stars were cut out of canvas sail cloth and painstakingly stitched to a red satin background. The Fijian flag was much more complex. It contains the Fijian Coat of Arms shield: a golden British lion holding a cocoa pod, as well as panels displaying a palm tree, sugar cane, bananas and dove of peace. In the end, Susan drew the shield and its contents on some sail cloth and coloured them with pencils. We then varnished the shield and stitched it to blue satin cloth.

Finding our way to Lakeba was easy as we sailed north under clear skies and obtained accurate fixes by taking bearings off the ends of the islands as we passed them. We reached the southern side of Lakeba late in the afternoon of 10 August, and took up a position a mile away from the reef, where, since we did not have 500 fathoms of chain, we hove-to, and flew our flags. Our tide tables told us that there would be a high tide at 5.30 pm, after which it would of course become dark quickly, and there would soon be a fast out-going tide through the passage, which in this case was marked. There was a visible calm water gap in the reef, about fifty yards wide, with quite large breakers falling on it at each side. We waited for an hour, but saw no sign of any shore activity that could suggest that we had been seen, or that we could expect a vessel to come out and inspect us.

After the second hour, we thought of sailing out to sea for a safe distance and heaving-to for the night, when a ship, the *Fijian Princess* appeared on the horizon, looking as if she was making for the passage. Her appearance triggered the thought that the tide was about to begin to ebb, and it might soon be too strong for us to sail in against it, so we came in close and waited to see how the *Princess* would get in. She seemed to be doing well against about two knots of tide, so we made a quick decision to follow her. At least we could depend on this reef passage being devoid of unexpected "bommies," as yachtsmen call coral heads. We turned quickly to starboard as soon as we were safely inside, sailed along the shore for a hundred yards, and dropped our anchor in two fathoms of water, just as it was becoming dark.

Next morning we arose and found that we were not close enough to the shore to make verbal contact with anyone, but it was not long before a man came past in a small canoe known as a *takia*. I asked the man for his name and he told me it was "Tui Nayau," which I took as a joke, so when he asked me my name, I said "the King of England." I knew that Ratu Mara was the Tui Nayau, and I knew what he looked like. I asked the man if it was a joke. He ended up by explaining that he was a visitor from the island of Nayau, about ten miles away. I still think he was "having a lend of me," as we say in Australia, but I explained where we had come from, and our need to obtain customs and medical inspection, and contact other officials as well. Could he ask the medical officer to come out and do his stuff, please?

In due course the medical officer, Dr Timoce Bavadra did come out in a dinghy from the shore where he lived and had his surgery. He told us that he was not a native of Lakeba, but came from Lautoka on the northwest coast of Viti Levu.

Timoce was very interested in our expedition and confirmed my expectation that none of my information about who we were and when we planned to arrive at Lakeba had come to his knowledge. He had, however, contacted the Police, and had a police corporal with him. They understood the reasons why we had decided to follow *Fijian Princess* into the lagoon. We showed him our documents, and they had a good look around the cabin and under the bunks. We yarned for a while, and Timoce said that there were no customs officials or agricultural inspectors on the island. He told us that his medical inspection was all that he could supply and all that was needed. Timoce invited us to come ashore with him, where we made the acquaintance of the "Golf Club," the elite of Tubou, who, we were told, basked in the Prime Minister's favour. Timoce asked us whether we would feel more comfortable living ashore, as he knew a couple of people, Setuata (Setu for short) and Lupe, who owned a Fijian style house in Tubou, that they would be willing to lend to us. They expected no payment but accepted a gift of two books that Ruth had finished reading, which was all we had that we didn't need. As it became obvious that we would be staying for weeks rather than days, we persuaded Setu and Lupe to let us pay a rent of $10 a week. At this point the offer of a house was something we really needed as Stephen would be arriving as soon as we could let Carmel know we were in Lakeba.

Living ashore would ease the congestion aboard, and enable Philip and Susan to find some children to play with in Tubou, which was within walking distance. The town of Tubou, consisted of Fijian style thatched houses with posts and frames of *Vesi* timber and thatched roofs, built around the multifunctional *rara*: a kind of Village Green, used for rugby matches, cricket, and public events.

At one end of the *rara*, there were some small roof-less toilet buildings, made of thatch fences, with a drain in the middle of concrete floors. The idea was to take with you a bucket of water and a towel; use the hole in the concrete floor which leads into a "bottomless pit" toilet, much like those in bush car-parks in Tasmania, but without a seat, then wash yourself all over, use your towel, put your clothes back on, and pour the remaining water in the bucket down the hole to "flush" the toilet. When the chief decides another location is needed, new enclosed toilets are built, the old concrete slabs are broken up and the land is used for something else.

Setu and Lupe's house was one huge room with sleeping mats curtained off with *masi* (tapa) cloth at one end and a cooking area at the other. Indoors, primus stoves were used; outside, with larger numbers of people, earth ovens were used. After Setu and Lupe had shown us round, we asked if we could speak to the *Matai ni Vanua,* the Orator Chief. It is his job to present and introduce visitors to the High chief, in the case of Lau, the Tui Nayau (Ratu Mara) and explain their business. It is also customary to present the chief with the traditional gift of a *Tabua,* a whale's tooth. I had managed to find one in the market just before we left Suva. We had been advised that a bottle of whisky had also become an additional traditional gift on such occasions.

The presentation of a *Tabua* is of great significance in Fiji. Its acceptance by a chief is a guarantee, on behalf of the whole community, that you are welcome, that your purposes will be supported, and that your person and property will be safe.

This was where things started to go wrong. When we met with Ratu Mara, it soon became clear that either Mara had not heard of our project, or he wanted that to be assumed. I explained that we recognised the force of the case against academic imperialism, and so had invited students from the USP to participate. Mara immediately became very agitated, and said, "I don't want any Indians poking around on my island" and added, "Are you going to teach me my own history?" "Who says you own it?" were the words in my head, but luckily they didn't come out of my mouth. Discussion became apologetic on my part, and I think, rational. Mara ended up by saying that he could not accept the *Tabua* because of our partnership with the USP.

He had a particular objection to supporting any activity in which Professor John Harré was involved. The reason for this, I discovered later, was that John Harré also worked as a marriage guidance counsellor, dealing especially with the problems of marriages between Fijians and Indians. From the Fijian perspective, such marriages carried with them the likely consequence of Indians sharing the rights of land ownership with their Fijian husbands or wives, potentially reducing the amount of land owned exclusively and permanently, by Fijians. For Mara, as a chief, responsible for the *Vanua* of his inheritance, this was an understandable objection.

Asesela Ravuvu, a Fijian anthropologist who taught Fijian culture at the University of the South Pacific (USP) clarified this concept of *Vanua,* or land, which contrasts with the generalised concept of modern "Deep Ecology" in the west. Deep ecologists assume a generalised "identification with nature" whereas *Vanua* means the specific holistic relationship between specific people and the specific land, including reefs and oceans which they live from, and are part of. Asesela explains:

> *The people are the Lewenivanua: the flesh of the land. They are the social identities of the Land, and also the means by which the land resources are protected and exploited for the sake of the Vanua, the people and their customs.*[2]

This was expressed much earlier by the Bauan chief, Cakobau, who explained his job, as the leading chief, to the first Colonial Governor, Sir Arthur Gordon: "The land and the people are one," he said, "We rule both, but we own neither."

Mara returned the *Tabua* to us (but not the bottle of whisky). The *Matai ni Vanua* said simply, and very politely, "It will be best if you go now."

This seemed a total disaster. I did not sleep very well that night, and thought we might have to just go cruising, and forget the project. We'd have to give the grant back to the Australian Research Grants Commission, but life would go on.

Then I remembered that Stephen would be joining us in a day or two, and needed to have a bit of his school holiday with his brother, sister, and new stepmother. Soon the dawn light made sleep impossible and I took the opportunity to start out on a solitary walk.

I was on the Golf course, at sunrise, when in the distance I recognised the tall figure of Ratu Mara. I wondered how well he slept as well. No one else was about and we continued to walk towards each other. It was obvious that I would have to speak to him. We met, and I wished him good morning, and asked him if he would like me to forget the project and go away. He mellowed a bit, and said he did not object to us mapping the archaeological sites I had told him about, in order to compare the record in the ground with the oral tradition. Mara repeated his declaration that the USP was not an acceptable partner. He took a plane for Suva that afternoon.

When I first thought of embarking on the inter-disciplinary history of Lau, Ron Crocombe suggested I contact a Scotsman called Archie Reid. Archie started his career in the British Colonial Service and became Commissioner and District Officer for the whole of Southern Fiji, including Lau. Ratu Mara had served under his authority as a District Officer. Archie was a fluent Fijian speaker and regarded and respected as a Chief in Lau, even though he had long since retired. I knew Archie was, at that time, working in the Archives in Suva on the *Tukutuku Raraba*. This was the source of the oral evidence, sworn in court in the 1930s, of the ownership of land established by the first Fijian ancestors and passed on to contemporary owners of the lands they lived in.

Our problem was that even though some ground had been recovered that morning, the whole of Tubou was full of gossip. People were polite to us, but wary. The co-op store politely refused to cash a cheque. And if that went on we would have to make a forced passage to Suva before we ran out of supplies. So I went to the post office, the only place on the island with a radio-telephone, and booked a call to Archie Reid in Suva. By the time I managed to make the call, a large crowd

---

2   Ravuvu, Asesela, *Vaka i Taukei—The Fijian Way of Life,* Institute of Pacific Studies, USP, 1983.

had gathered, to listen in, as was right and proper. The community was entitled to know what was going on, in order to know how they should behave towards us.

I explained our problems, and asked Archie to try and contact Mara, and do what he could to retrieve the situation. He managed to see Mara the next day. I don't know how Archie did it, but Mara agreed, conditionally, to support the project, provided that individual students from the USP were kept under close personal supervision, and would be vetted by Archie, before they came to Lau. Archie himself was the only person allowed to work on sources connected with the family history of the Tui Nayau.

Archie Reid had performed what seemed to Ruth and me to be a miracle. He set about devising a brilliant piece of diplomatic theatre to let the people of Lakeba know about Mara's change of heart. He asked me, in a letter, which was private, to ask him, by telegram or radio, which was public, to fly to Lakeba so that we could discuss the situation in detail. He arrived a few days later, coming as a guest of Tui Nayau *in absentia*. Mara had offered Archie the use of his house in Tubou, where he stayed in the style of a Chief. As soon as Archie arrived, he sent Mara's personal servant to summon me to a second audience, this time with him, as Mara's representative.

After we had talked through the situation he took me out on to the front verandah, which overlooks the *Rara*, the public space of the village, thus conferring his public blessing on the project. He then arranged to borrow a red, and therefore conspicuous, Land Rover, from Ratu Devita, Mara's brother. He invited me to join him, next day, in an anti-clockwise circuit of Lakeba island, visiting the four other island towns on the way. Archie explained our purposes and papered over the cracks, in his fluent Fijian, as we drank *yagona* with the chiefs of each village in a ritual of reconciliation. We now had Mara's consent, if not yet support. That came later, when the publication of numerous works of scholarship, confirmed the major importance of the Lau islands in the discovery, settlement and cultural development of the South Pacific.[3]

Back in Tubou, our children were welcomed by their peers, and the co-op agreed to cash our cheque. It was school holiday time in Suva and a lad called Deve, about 13 years old and a native of the island of Oneata, arrived by plane at Lakeba. Deve had been at Suva Grammar School and was keen to get home to Oneata. One of his relatives asked us if we would give him a passage to his home island on our boat. Clearly his first departure from his island home had been a harrowing experience. Stephen also arrived as expected, and we began his holiday by doing a bit of sailing in the home waters of Lakeba. Deve's need to get home and Stephen's desire to see a bit more of Fiji led us into an expedition to Oneata, a short day-sail to the south-east. Christianity had been successfully established on Oneata by the Wesleyan Church, in 1826, but only after rejection of earlier attempts. Oneata was the island on which

---

3   Young, J M R, "Lau, a Windward Perspective," *Journal of Pacific History*, 28 :2 1993, pp 159–180, "The response of Lau to foreign contact," *Journal of Pacific History*, vol 7 number 1, January 1982.

Jacaro Atai and Kei Arue, the London Missionary Society missionaries, from Tahiti landed in 1830 and succeeded, by 1835, in making converts to the Anglican variety of Christianity. This led to the much larger project of gaining chiefly support for the establishment of the new religion, known at Lakeba as the Lotu.

As we approached Oneata, Deve was greatly moved, to the extent of standing on the foredeck, and weeping, from the moment he caught sight of his island until we rowed him ashore. There was a crowd of his friends and family to give him a joyous welcome as we landed. Oneata was also the only place we had experienced since leaving Tonga, that could provide us with eggs. It was not long before we were presented with a basketful, in return for getting Deve safely home to his family. The children of Oneata were given the job of finding the nests of the numerous hens that enjoyed the free range of the island. Fences and enclosures were not to be found, but as soon as it was discovered that we needed eggs we were given as many as we wanted.

On returning to Lakeba, we met Kolinio Moce, who was a staff member of the National Archives in Suva. Ian Diamond, the Archivist, had begun his profession in Adelaide, and very kindly developed an interest in our project. Ian felt that Kolinio would be a great help to us, as an interpreter, and he thought the fieldwork would also give him some useful experience. Kolinio helped us with the mapping of three important fortifications in Lau, all of them on Lakeba, and this meant a good deal of walking and climbing as well as mapping. Young boys and women were asked, by the elders, to guide us from the coast, first, to Ulunikoro, the most ancient fortification on the island. It was eventually dated at more than 900 years old. We had to cut through some vegetation with cane knives for two hours to arrive at the remains of what must have been a formidable fortress. The ridge at the summit supported two craggy areas, joined by the remains of man-made defensive walls, and surrounded by the remains of an outer circle of stone work and ditches.

Philip, Kolinio and I used a long measuring tape, and a hand compass to take bearings, as we followed the circuit of ditches and what we presumed to have been fortifications, until we came back to where we had started. We made sketch-maps first, of Ulunikoro, and then, of the more recent fortress of Kedekede, four to five hundred years old. We were to learn later, from Simon Best, one of the project's New Zealand archaeologists, that Kedekede would have been capable of housing two thousand people, which was likely to have been the population of the whole island, in times of war.

The last archaeological site on Lakeba was called Korovusa ("old settlement"). This was where the early contacts between the local population and shipwrecked sailors from America took place. William Cary, in 1824, survived the wreck of *Oeno* on Vatoa;[4] and another seaman, John Twyning, survived the wreck of the whale-ship, *Minerva* on the Minerva reef in 1829.[5] Both men were writers later

---

4   See Cary, William, *Wrecked on the Feejees*, Nantucket, 1928.

5   Twyning, John, *Shipwreck and Adventures of John Twyning among the South Sea Islanders, giving an account of their Feasts, Massacres etc*. London, 1850, p 69. Minerva reef was previously known as "Nicholson's Shoal."

in life, and became, in effect, articles of tribute, brought to Lakemba where they could most easily become useful, as armourers, diplomats, and interpreters by the inhabitants of the small islands to the south on which they had been wrecked.

Twyning's account dates the migration to the coast as some time well before his arrival. Korovusa lies about half a mile inland from the present village of Tubou. Twyning describes a well defended fortress town, with several field guns trained to repel any attacking forces. They included "several Guns of various sizes, from a swivel to a carronade, mounted on a platform over each of the entrances to the town across the moat."

The moat is now a series of pools separated by patches of swamp, backed by a ruined wall surrounding a large enclosed area. It was closely packed with house mounds, but we did not map their location. That was left to the archaeologists, as time was running short. Cary's account describes a grand festival held at Korovusa, a precursor of the Pan Pacific Games of modern times, with an audience of two to three thousand spectators. They were seated around the large open square in the centre, with the "king" seated to one side on a stone platform. Mock club fights, using coconut timber stakes, were followed by boxing contests in which the contestants from Tonga and Samoa had their fists bound in *tapa* cloth, a refinement which was lacking in the bare-fisted boxing contests of contemporary England. A bit of unfair play excited the crowd, and a general brawl threatened, but Malani, the Tui Nayau of the time, jumped from his throne and quelled the disturbance before it got out of hand. Cary had the good fortune to become a personal friend of Malani, whom, he says "they reverence as a superior being, guarded by the spirits of his forefathers."[6]

Kolinio Moce returned to Suva at this point and unfortunately, became ill almost as soon as he arrived there, and Stephen had to go home soon. We spent several days doing the mapping of the three sites, and managed to do a bit of day-sailing before he had to go back to school in Adelaide. Having the use of Setu and Lupe's big house for all five of us was a great luxury after a long period of living at very close quarters. Stephen promised to tell Carmel that all was well, and seemed to have enjoyed himself. I think that the variety of short sails, new cultural experience, and maybe a sense of success in the face of difficulty was valuable, at his age. We met other families, living the dream, who found their older adolescent children had a different, lonelier experience. If you want to cruise far away from home with your children, take my advice and get it done early. When children are aged between seven and fourteen is your opportunity. Arthur Ransome knew what he was doing. But the greatest success on board *Leofleda,* was the development of a happy and loving relationship between Ruth, my children, and me, which has since been a joy to all of us.

By now, the mid-year break at the USP had begun, which was the opportunity for the student participants in the Lau project to begin their fieldwork. I could not have stopped Aisea Ledua from coming to Lakeba anyway, as it was his home

---

6   Cary, William, *Wrecked on the Feejees*, Nantucket, 1928, p 22.

and he had been schooled there. Archie Reid had put Aisea in the picture about Mara's objections to participation of USP students. Aisea had started work on his Honours thesis using the available sources in the Fiji Archives, but he would have come home for the holiday period in any case. Cema Bolabola was writing her thesis on urban migration by people from Lau to Suva, with no help from me.

For me, the next job was a voyage to the south to gain an understanding of the ethos of this remarkable society of some fourteen thousand people, which has managed, on one hand, to retain control of its own land and resources, and provide an exemplary model of ecologically sustainable development; and on the other hand, has succeeded in achieving relative prominence in the government and administration of the country.

From Lakeba we sailed in the wake of the tribute collecting fleets of the seventeenth, eighteenth and early nineteenth centuries, reinforcing, as they did, their links with the potentially rival power of Kabara. By then it was 10 September, and there was little chance of visiting the whole of the Lau Group before the beginning of the hurricane season. Given the choice of sailing north to Vanua Balavu, or south, nearly half way back to Tonga, it seemed better to reach those distant southern islands which were most difficult to reach by copra boat, and thus to maximise the advantage of having our own transport. So we went south.

Another factor in making this choice was a message we picked up at the post office, from our friend, Matai Waqavesi on Ogea. His people were short of baking powder, cigarettes, matches, and Coleman lantern parts. We accordingly stocked up with $25 worth, which, we were beginning to understand, would enable us to use Ogea as a base for trips to Vatoa and Fulaga, perhaps even Ono-i-Lau. Ogea is a safe anchorage in any weather, we knew that the passage was easy to find, and that reciprocal action lay at the heart of local culture.

There was advantage too, travelling as we did, subject to the same weather conditions and faced with the same problems and conditions, dependent on the same supplies of the necessities of life, as the centuries of people who built Lauan Society. It was also an attempt to develop some of the historical empathy, which hopefully enables an historian to make sensible guesses about human motivation in the past, and to understand the force of considerations which do not apply to the contemporary technological, political or geographical environment. As we made ground to the South, close hauled much of the time, to the prevailing south easterly wind, it was easy to appreciate the isolation of the communities on the limestone islands and the advantage which accrued to them from their close political and filial relationship with the powerful and relatively plentiful island of Lakeba.

Gifts and exchanges of food, labour and artefacts within a network of kinship obligations formed the basis of a self-sufficient economy that was augmented, but not replaced, by the benefits of modernity. The people of Lau, have retained a confidence in both themselves and their culture which has given them the capacity to challenge, if they choose, what their former Tui Lau, Ratu Sukuna referred to as "the omnipotence of the great octopus of the modern world."[7] At the island level, customary specialist duties to chiefs often overrode domestic commitments. When we arrived at the island of Namuka, for instance, we were told that Aca Laminaiwai, *Buli* (village chief) of Namuka, whom I had met in 1972, was away: his brother accepted *yagona* on his behalf, saying, "the trouble is, we have no king" because, as head of the Namuka branch of the *lemaki*, the carpenter clan, he was house-building on Lakeba, for Ratu Mara.

At Namuka, we experienced the expectations that were previously experienced by the beachcombers on the nineteenth century. They were expected to know all about muskets. We were expected to know all about generators. I knew nothing about them, but thankfully Philip had some kind of god-given talent with anything mechanical or electrical. The Honda generator belonging to the local church had stopped working. It had last been serviced by some earlier hapless yachtsman. Philip and I (just doing what he told me to do) fixed the starting mechanism and cleaned the carburettor and spark plug. It worked. This meant that the next day, we had to go to church.

The service was extremely impressive and the church was packed with a youthful congregation. There was a group of well-dressed young men, armed with canes, presumably to threaten children against the possibility of sacrilegious behaviour, but not surprisingly, there was none. The sermon was in Fijian, and of a violently evangelical nature. I did not need to know the language to be able to understand the message of unavoidable damnation, without very good works and impeccable faith. The singing of hymns was excellent, not only because of its sincerity, but also its musical energy. The words were Fijian, and the tunes were the uplifting, tear-jerking harmonies of Polynesia, probably developed from the original Tahitian missionaries who landed on the island of Oneata, near Lakeba in 1830.

At Komo, we came closest to shipwreck. It was 13 September 1974. Our work in Komo was interesting. Lemaki Liwai was a 14 year old who showed us the old villages. He was deaf and dumb, but clearly very intelligent. Lemaki and Kapu (his brother) were described as "the two dumbest people on the island." But Lemaki piloted us through the lagoon and found us a very safe anchorage. He used hand signals to steer us through the scattering of coral heads to a place where we put down two anchors and a long piece of rope with a short chain on one of them. The other anchor had chain all the way.

We had time to cook the usual evening meal of some kind of tinned meat and dalo, and when that was finished we told the children that it was their turn to wash up. Ruth and I went below, leaving our lovely children to impress us with their loveliness. Philip had our enamel washing bowl in his hands, when we first heard the approaching storm, as a low scream, at first, as it hit the coconut trees on the island. This was too early, I thought, for the beginning of the hurricane season.

---

7   Cit MacNaught, Timothy, *The Fijian Colonial Experience*, ANU eView, 2016, p 148.

Then we had a real gust. We were all in the cockpit when the washing up bowl was blown out of Philip's hands, over the bow and off the boat. We went inside, confident that our two anchors would keep us safe. As we sat on the bunks the wind forced the heavy rain through the louvres in the sliding hatch as if it was the rose of a watering can. I felt the jerk of the anchor ropes, as the boat reached the bitter end of their scope. In a calm moment, I went on deck and saw the anchor ropes slack and the boat turning. The wind had come from the stern and had driven the boat, bow first, into the narrowing gap between the anchor ropes. She was now firmly held with two lines; one on each side, with the stern and entrance to the cabin open to the storm. "I know what to do now," I thought, very pleased with myself, "I'll cast off one of the ropes, then she'll come round head to wind and we'll be out of the wind." I actually went up to the samson post and began to try to get the rope off it. It had pulled so tight though, and the wind was so strong that it had jammed itself round the samson post. I had no hope of getting it off without a marline spike to loosen it. Or an axe to chop it with. That realisation brought me to my senses.

I realised the danger that if I cast off the line that was holding us, we would be rapidly blown onto the reef, dragging the other anchor that was not holding. I would have to make sure that I did not let go of it. I looked across the water to see the coconut palms on the shore bending over to touch the beach. I could see that though the boat was pinned between the two ropes, she was not actually moving, and she was safe for now, even though the wind was blowing the tops of the waves over the stern. In any case, it was impossible to release either rope unless I cut it. It took only a second to work this out, and when I understood the situation, I realised that so long as the ropes held, we were safe, even though we went on getting wet, with sea water coming over the stern into the cabin.

Next day, when things had calmed down, I dived down to see what, if anything, was holding the anchors. I found that the chain of one anchor was wrapped around a coral head and that was what kept us from disaster.

We said our goodbyes on Komo, and headed for Ogea with our cargo of requested supplies. We were told that we should take the opportunity to observe the significant cultural event provided by a new enthusiasm for building *camakau*, the only reliable form of inter-island transport. Six of them were under construction in various Lau islands, and numbers of young men were given the opportunity to ensure that the skills of their forefathers were preserved for future generations. Most *camakau* were to be supplied with traditional sails made of *voivoi* (*Pandanus Caricosus*) matting. One was to have sails made from polyester bags, as an experiment.

Ogea is a limestone island, but it has close kinship ties with Moce, a volcanic island forty miles to the north, which provided a large part of Ogea's food supply. Our old friend, Matai Waqavesi told us how this reciprocal relationship with Moce gave them a measure of independence from Lakeba, "where there are too many chiefs, and everyone wants to live like the *Papalagi*." By this he meant, dependent on shipping from Suva, and eating too much canned fish, for which, he thought, they had to work too hard cutting copra, at the expense of more rewarding tasks such as building *camakau*. These boats could sail at ten knots in the right conditions. Matai thought that if they built more *camakau*, they could catch their own fish, instead of buying them back in tins, from Japan.

A festive regatta for the new vessels was being planned for Christmas of 1974 at which all six *camakau* were to compete. As in other maritime cultures, regattas are significant opportunities for strengthening social ties and creative relationships.

Vatoa, our next island lies some sixty miles to the south, but with a beam wind it was one of our fastest passages. We had full sunlight all the way, and had time to do some walking and meet people. The *Buli* Vatoa, Mosese, had plenty of stories about William Cary, and could show us where he had hidden after the wreck of his ship, before he was brought out of hiding. Cary became a friend of Mosese's ancestor, who had taken Cary to Lakeba. Joeli Vuki was the son of Mosese and anxious to meet some of his cross cousins, to do a bit of wooing, so he asked us to give him a passage to Ono-i-Lau, the next island on our schedule. Then he wanted us to invite his best friend, Tawayaco Vole, to come as well. Tawayaco said he was familiar with the reef passage into the Ono lagoon, so we agreed to take them both, partly because of the chance it gave us to return the hospitality we received, and also because of Tawayaco's anticipated nautical knowledge.

The British Admiralty pilot mentioned a length of old railway line, upright and concreted into the reef, near the entrance to the Ono lagoon, and warned of the need to go dangerously close before it could be seen. As there is only one navigable passage, the waves breaking on the south east side of the reef raise the water-level inside the lagoon so that there is always a strong current running out of it. A rising tide is a good thing if you can be so lucky, and Joeli sounded confident.

With four of us and two young men, there was not much room on *Leofleda*, especially as Joeli asked if he could bring a "suitcase" with him. I agreed, thinking it would be something very small. It turned out to be a large wooden trunk, that we called the "treasure chest." It filled the space between the two bunks in the cabin. We stowed the cabin table, which had folding legs, and put it in the port side of the fo'c's'le opposite Susan's bunk. The treasure chest had to go in its place on the cabin floor. Philip had his quarter berth. Ruth and I took the two watches, while Joeli and Tawayaco took turns in the starboard quarter berth. Ruth and I were both awake at six in the morning when the high outline of the main island in the group became visible against the background of a starry sky. The timing was good. I waited until we had a good sunrise, before calling Tawayaco up on deck to show us where to go. He seemed confident to begin with, but confessed after a few minutes, that he was not quite sure where the entrance was.

We sailed up to windward within fifty yards of the reef, while Philip looked out for bommies, then back with the wind behind us and a line of, thankfully, small breakers on the north west side of the outside of the reef. The sun began to rise soon enough for us to see, at about nine o'clock in the morning, a thing that looked like a very rusty piece of railway line. But between it and *Leofleda* was nothing but the reef. We sailed up and down a few more times, and were beginning to think of making a passage back to Vatoa, when I looked up to windward and saw the channel cutting like a scarf, diagonally across the reef, leading to the railway line, and very narrow. I started the engine and lowered the sails to make it easy to see everything clearly, and headed in. Soon we were in a channel about as wide as the boat is long, and as we went in, we began to look at the sides to see if we were moving against the current and the wind. We found that the current was strong, but we went on moving, just, in the right direction. We learnt later that the people of the island, who have canoes instead of motor boats, put crew men ashore with ropes so that they can haul the craft through the channel, which is about a hundred yards long. Our four horse-power diesel gave us a maximum of four knots, so against the three and a half knot current, it seemed to take forever, but we made it, and soon found ourselves sailing again through blue water over a sandy bottom.

We had been told that Ono is an incredibly wonderful place, and for us it lived up to its reputation. The sheltered anchorage lies between the volcanic islands of Ono Levu, the big island on the south side of the lagoon, and Doi to the north east of it. Like the other islands in Lau, village sites have changed as the need for defence from invasion decreased in the early nineteenth century. The people here look more Polynesian than the people of Viti Levu, and they are unique in their habit of addressing each other and strangers with the Tongan, rather than Fijian, words of greeting.

Later, I read the diaries of the successive District Commissioners who had governed the Lau Province in the early twentieth century. They debated about the merit of modernisation and commercial development, as opposed to self-sufficiency based on local custom. Like most of their contemporaries, the young, well-educated products of the English public school system shared the popular belief that indigenous people of the expanding British empire occupied steps on an evolutionary ladder. Australian Aborigines and Terra del Fuegians were at the bottom. American Indians, New Zealand Maori and other Polynesians were very near the top, which was occupied by white people generally, and by Englishmen in particular. Many years later, I wrote that:

> *Ono evidently made a virtue out of isolation. No missionary, trader, stipendiary magistrate or District Commissioner for 100 years failed to comment favourably on its well-being, and the "superiority of its inhabitants." In the 20th Century, Ono mirrored the paradox of modern Lau. Its inhabitants were the most pleasing pupils of the ex-prefects who were its governors, in spite of their inability, on account of its remoteness, to provide the supervision, combined with the commercial stimulation which they believed to be necessary. The same men were proud to point out the high marks that Lau as a whole was*

getting, in spite of its isolation, for population increase and educational progress.[8]

We spent a rather longer period at Ono, than we had intended, because I felt that this was a once in a lifetime experience. Surely the hurricane season could wait until we were safely back in Adelaide? It was also because of what Robert Louis Stevenson explained so well about the islands of the Pacific:

> *No part of the world exerts the same attractive power on the visitor... The first experience can never be repeated. The first love, the first sunrise, the first south-sea island, are memories apart, and touched a virginity of sense.*[9]

Ono was not my first Pacific island, but it was the least touched by Europeans and their trappings. It was a very invigorating place. It had no shops, just a co-op store, no telephones, and its people seemed to be very glad to have us with them. The chief of the island asked us if we would help out with a transport problem the day after we arrived. There was to be a wedding and the bride needed to get from the island of Doi, across to Ono Levu for the ceremony. *Leofleda* was very overloaded with about fifteen relatives and wedding guests, so she was rather low in the water, but it was one of the highlights of the expedition. We were taken into the confidence of the people who stirred our imagination about the social and political realities of pre-colonial life.

We were taken to the old fortification at the top of the hill on Ono Levu, and were told about the most celebrated and important historical events that were remembered, including the visit of Niumataiwalu, also called Niu for short, connected by marriage to the Tui Tonga and Tui Nayau.

About the time of the establishment of Korovusa in Lakeba, probably in the 1820s, Niu visited Bau, the powerful kingdom on Viti Levu, where he seduced the wife of the Vunivalu, the high chief of the kingdom. Some years later, he was sent on an expedition from Bau, to collect tribute from Ono; a test, perhaps, of the rising power of Lakeba, of which Ono was nominally a tributary. But with a consistent tendency to turbulence, supported by itinerant Tongan warriors, Niu's voyage south was preceded by a canoe from Bau carrying a Tabua of black stone, and instructions for Niu to be clubbed at a *yagona* ceremony as he stooped to drink. This was said to have occurred in the fortified town of Matokana, which occupies the highest point (370 feet) of Ono Levu. Niu was stunned but still conscious and very strong. He fought his way out and ran down to the shore. There he was overtaken by four warriors who overpowered and killed him. We were shown his grave on the southern shore of the lagoon we had crossed to bring the bride to her wedding.

Cary describes a voyage from Lakeba to Ono to collect tribute, rather than accepting a similar invitation to go to Tonga and gain protection in exchange for royal service to the Tongan monarchy. He records that "The natives were expecting us, it being the time for their annual visit to collect tribute, and had large quantities

---

[8] For a detailed discussion about subsistence versus commercial development in Lau, see my article, "Lau, A windward Perspective," *Journal of Pacific History*, 28:2 (1993), pp 59-180.

[9] Stevenson, Robert Louis, *In the South Seas*, Routledge, 2005. Introduction, p 2.

of provisions cooked and all things prepared for their annual feast."[10] It became clear, as we moved from island to island, that festivities, like political relationships were reciprocal. Annual visits were then as now, anticipated with pleasure as the social and cultural highlight of the year rather than an imposition.

Though we came to collect no tribute, and brought few gifts, we were treated with the same hospitality. We also shared the experience of self sufficiency. Ruth had a pain in her leg, which was to become a developing problem later in life, but Joeli's personal agenda had the effect of getting us an introduction to a young woman who was the traditional *vuniwai*, or doctor. Joeli had been telling us from time to time, that "the *vuniwai* is very pretty" and indeed she was. She offered to massage Ruth's leg, and though it was never going to be a permanent solution, it was a very effective remedy for some time.

Social problems also had traditional solutions. Ono has two outlying islands, Tuvana i Colo (downwind) and Tuvana i Ra (upwind). When boys reach the age of about fifteen, an annual cohort undergoes a rite of passage. They are marooned for a month on one of these islands, by their parents, who provide them with implements, like a cane knife and fishing gear. This helps them to grow up, as each of the group takes responsibility for different things, building shelters, hunting, fishing, cooking and so on. They do not read *Lord of the Flies* beforehand, but work things out and agree about who does what before they start, and evidently discover how to survive. One of these groups was brought back from Tuvana i Ra while we were on Ono, and they were all full of themselves, very proud of their achievement, and appreciative of the family support when they returned. I remembered my own effort to achieve independence by riding my bike around Ireland, and thought that I had been nearly, but not quite as lucky as they were.

The next vessel to reach Ono was our old friend the *Fijian Princess*. Joeli said he would like to take the opportunity to get a berth on her to Suva. I sought the best advice I could from his relatives, who said that his parents would be happy for him to go, so I agreed. I gave him his fare for a deck berth on the *Fijian Princess* to Suva, the next time she came to Ono. His friend asked his kin to get him back to Vatoa, and they agreed, so we decided to head straight back to Suva. Joeli felt a bit worried about his dress code in the big city, where he wanted to get a job, so I gave him my "good" pair of trousers, which fitted him well. We parted and went our different ways, heading first for the Island of Matuku.

As a parting gift, we were presented with a large gull of some kind, rather uncomfortably bound so as to be unable to fly. I asked what we were supposed to do with the bird, and they explained that she was meant to provide emergency food if we ran short before getting to our destination. As soon as we made it through the entrance, Susan suggested that she would make a nice pet, and so we started by giving her a name, eventually settling on "Geraldine." Then we reflected on the difficulty of ensuring the welfare of the bird if we took her away from her natural habitat.

---

10 Cary, W, *op cit*, p 22.

When we were close to the Yanuia islands, next to the exit from the lagoon, we cut Geraldine's restraining bonds and happily, released her, without causing offence to our hosts. She gave herself a good shake and flew towards the nearest land. We went through the passage, with the tide, and shaped our course for Matuku, about eighty sea miles away, with a fair wind and the first good weather for two weeks.

We slept at Matuku for one night, after hauling in a large dolphin fish (*Coryphaena hippurus*), otherwise known as MahiMahi, and a Barracuda on the way, using a piece of caulking cotton on our hook. We were just about to enter the sheltered harbour, but dealing with large fish like that is awkward if you have two barefooted children to worry about in a small cockpit. Both kinds of animal leap around and you need to hold the fish as still as possible with a rag and kill it as soon as possible with a knife, or they are likely to bite the children's feet, or yours. We kept enough of the fish to provide that night's meal and gave the rest to the first boy who came out in a canoe. He asked us if we planned to go to church. I told him I was too tired and wanted to reach Suva before the hurricane season began.

Shamefully, we weighed anchor at 10.30 am instead of going to church, and headed for Suva. It was a really hot day, and we sat in turn with our feet in cold seawater in a bucket. About midday we were followed by a school of sharks, but they left us after a couple of hours. By this time we could see the distant island of Kadavu, and could find our position easily by taking back bearings from both ends of the island. After that, with confidence in our navigation, we sailed at an average speed of four knots, continuing through the night, until at 3.30 am next morning. On 14 October, we saw the loom of the lights of Suva below the horizon. At 10 am we took bearings again and were thirteen miles from Suva Point. One more fix and we were five sea miles from the harbour entrance with a log reading of 256 sea miles since leaving Ono.

We knew our way and sailed on to an anchorage at the Suva Yacht Club, where we debated the priorities of cold drinks versus showers, the first for months. We chose showers, put on our clean clothes, and rediscovered the joy of getting cool drinks for the children, cold beer for ourselves, and a splendid meal of Taveuni steak, dalo and greens in the Chinese restaurant. We also met up with some of the yachties we knew from Tonga and Lau. This was a time for recovery, relaxation and celebration with new friends.

✧✧✧✧

The "Lau Project," as it came to be called, resulted in new archaeological, historical, geographical and anthropological knowledge. Many publications resulted, written by Archie Reid and myself (Adelaide University), Garth Rogers, Simon Best and Michael Rowland (Auckland University) and Cema Bolabola and Aisea Ledua (USP).

Later, my colleague, Garth Rogers from the University of Auckland, spent much more time in northern Lau than we had spent in southern Lau. He moved from one island to another in northern Lau, speaking impeccable Fijian to local people of every rank, and exploring the series of village sites, that had been occupied successively through the 3,000 years since the first human footprints were made on the beaches.

The maps we made of old fortified sites during our voyage were passed on to Simon Best and Michael Rowland, who continued the archaeological work that we initiated. Much of their work was "ground-breaking" and eventually led to continuing research within the boundaries of Fiji, Tonga and Samoa, where the formation of what is now known as "Polynesian culture" took place. It was the people of this region whose maritime technology enabled them to achieve the discovery and eventually, the first settlement by humans, of Tahiti, Hawaii, the Marquesas, the Cook Islands and New Zealand. This happened at a time when European sailors were still sticking close to their coasts.

Since the two Fijian coups of 1986, the social, historical, ecological and geographical studies of Fiji have been of international interest, notably to the *Man and the Biosphere Program* of UNESCO, who began their work in Lau in 1974. They returned in 1983. The collective work was published in 1988.[11]

The decade of Fijian history following our voyage was destined to see the rapid growth of the USP, and accelerated urbanisation, leading to the establishment of a new multiracial, and well educated middle class, which challenged the ideology of Chieftainship as the core of national political authority, as well as Fijian identity.

It was much later, that we realised that we had made the acquaintance of a man who was to become one of the most influential people in the history of Fiji, Doctor Timoce Bavadra. In 1985, Timoce began the creation of the Labour Party of Fiji, which, though led by himself, a Fijian, came to depend largely on the support of the Indian population. They were the descendants of the labourers who had been recruited in India by the British Government to provide cheap labour to the mostly Australian cotton or sugar planters, who had bought Fijian Land before Cession in 1874. This first generation of Indians had been indentured for five years, with the proviso that they could then choose to either be returned to India or stay in Fiji, as subjects of the new Colony. Many chose to stay, and succeeded, after their five year period of indenture was over, in leasing land from the Fijian owners. Many who chose to remain in Fiji claimed Fijian citizenship, became prosperous planters, and later on, business people and professionals. By 1974, the USP had more Indian than Fijian students.

Timoce's vision was a left wing multicultural community, that recognised the citizen's rights of Fijian Indians, especially those who had been born in Fiji. He formed a coalition of the Labour Party, with a largely Fijian membership, and the

---

11 Bayliss-Smith et al, *Islands, Islanders and the World: The Colonial and Post-Post-colonial experience of Eastern Fiji*, Cambridge University Press, 1988. Other useful works include Lasaqua, Isireli, *The Fijian People, Before and After Independence, 1959-1977*, Australian National University Press, 1984; Ravuvu, Asesela, *Vaka i Taukei: The Fijian Way of Life*, Institute of Pacific Studies of the USP, 1983; Robertson, R T and Tamanisau, Akosita, *Fiji-Shattered Coups*, Pluto Press, 1988.

Indian-dominated National Federation party, which achieved a sweeping victory in the election of April 1987. The coalition parties won twenty-eight seats, to the European and Fijian supported Alliance party's twenty-four. However the new government was short-lived, and was overthrown the following month by a military coup led by Colonel Sitiveni Rabuka. It now seems possible, if not likely, that Bavadra's objection to naval visits associated with Nuclear Testing in the Pacific, had led to US support of the coup of 13 May 1987, which "Rabuka has never convincingly denied."[12]

Timoce's transition from doctor to Prime Minister in April 1987, followed by his removal by a military coup a month later, was unthinkable in 1974, but in view of that decade of social change, it is easy to understand Mara's initial suspicions of the new generation of students from the USP. Sadly, Timoce died of cancer in 1989.

---

12   https://en.wikipedia.org/wiki/Timoci_Bavadra

Chapter 14: Midlife Complexity

After six months in another world, Suva was overwhelmingly ordinary. And the transition from Fijian to British colonial culture was gradual. Immediate priorities were to find a ship to take us all home, including *Leofled*a, and meet up with bio-geographer Randy Thaman, who had been looking after the cradle she was to use to get back to Australia. The P & O cruise ship *Arcadia* was due to sail for Sydney in three weeks time. In spite of his care, Randy discovered that the instructions he gave to the shipping company had not been followed. The cradle had been damaged, and placed in an auction yard to await a public auction. Randy had the energy and reliability to make an offer and bought it (eventually refunded by me) before the auction took place.

We booked *Leofleda* as cargo on *Arcadia*. Fortunately, the damage to the cradle consisted of broken timber diagonal struts rather than any of its steel components. We lived on *Leofleda* at the Yacht Club. Philip and Susan went to school in Suva. Ruth and I bought large pieces of local timber and replaced the broken diagonals using the woodworking tools we had with us.

Amongst the waiting mail in Suva was a characteristic letter from David Kew, full of the philosophical gentility, which made him such a good teacher and boat builder. It was posted in Adelaide on 26 September 1974:

Many thanks John, for your two very interesting letters from Leofleda.

From your description, I can well picture her, at home in such surroundings. I really am happy that things are going so well… Years ago I might have envied you, as I always wished to sail a boat around the world, but now I am glad that if we cannot all be fortunate, at least some of us can—So in a way you are doing it for me, and for this also, Thanks.

Captain Anderson would be pleased that his design is proving itself on the High Seas. Indeed, I would not be surprised that he is actually well pleased, for as well as I know, the "dead" do not cease to take interest in earthly events.

Another priority was to make contact with the students of the USP who had expressed an interest in joining the Lau Project. Nearly all of them had heard the news about Ratu Mara's disapproval of their participation, and had found other research subjects. I caught up with Aisea Ledua in Lakeba. His chosen subject was the establishment of the province of Lau in the early stages of British Colonisation (1870s), and the best I could do was to suggest some preliminary reading. But then I put him in touch with Archie Reid, who was a real expert. Archie had been a leading participant in the history of Fiji as Secretary for Fijian Affairs, during the colonial era. He had also become a very good and well-connected historian, who spoke the same language as Aisea. In fact, Aisea had fallen on his feet.

I did my best to help and encourage Cema Bolabola with her work on people from Lau, who had moved to Suva. I felt confident that she would do well, but I doubt if I was able to give her much support in the two weeks we had left in Suva.

I suggested a detailed reading list about the urbanisation of the Pacific Islands in general. She went on to finish her Honours degree and became a successful staff member of the School of Social Sciences at the USP. In 1986 she published a major work, shortly before the first military Coup, on the then extremely controversial subject of the land rights of Pacific women.[1]

Ron Crocombe and John Harré had obviously heard several versions of my audience with Mara, but not much of the positive side of the story surfaced in Suva before we left. Letters from the long list of students who had been interested in participation were waiting for me. Most of them were beautifully tactful essays explaining that for a wide range of reasons, they would be unable to commit to participation in the Lau project. They wrote about their work and intentions for the future, and thanked me for trying to help them. I sent a short account of our experiences to all of them who stayed in contact with me. Eventually a sunbeam broke through the clouds in the form of a letter from Mara to Archie Reid, posted on 10 January 1975, which he passed on to me:

Dear Archie,

Thank you for your letter of 20th December. I am glad to learn that there are prospects of getting a qualified Archaeologist to work on the sites of Uluinokoro and Kede-kede in due course.

Doubtless your colleague [That's me] *will make the normal approach to the Research Committee and the Ministry of Labour, but subject to them being satisfied, you may rest assured that there will be no difficulty about an Archaeologist working at Lakeba.*

Yours Sincerely, K.K.T. Mara, Prime Minister.

This letter came too late to maintain the enthusiasm of most of the students who had expressed interest in June 1974, but it cleared the way for Dr Garth Rogers, a recently appointed lecturer in the department of Anthropology and Archaeology of Auckland University. He applied successfully for permission to spend several months during 1975, visiting nearly all the inhabited islands in Northern Lau. Two of Garth's students, Simon Best and Michael Rowland wrote PhD theses based on their work in Lau, and our work on Lakeba, under Garth's supervision.

Gradually, I came to the conclusion that it was important for each of us to publish articles on the subjects that we had worked on, as soon as possible. Email had not yet conquered the "tyranny of distance" in academic life. That lay in the future, and with members of our team working in Adelaide, Sydney, Auckland, Edinburgh and Fiji, efficient collaboration would have been difficult. Joint publication of such a work would require a vast amount of correspondence over a substantial period of time. Many scholars and funding organisations knew what we had been doing, and expected news of some results. The exceptional relevance of Island history to Island politics was, unfortunately, likely to make it very difficult

---

1   Bolabola, Cema, *et al*, *Land Rights of Pacific Women*, Institute of Pacific Studies, USP, 1986.

to work in partnership with Island students at the USP, and if publication was much delayed, it was likely that further financial assistance would not be offered.

I was by no means unfazed, either, by Ratu Mara's question, "Do you propose to teach me my own History?" I spent some time in the National Archives, going over old materials to test my understanding of Fijian affairs in the light of my recent experience. I came across a letter written by Ratu Mara in his early days as a District Officer for the Lau Province. Large quantities of guano had been discovered on the island of Vatu Vara, and the Government view was that it should be mined, for the financial benefit of the colony. But Mara succeeded in changing the government's mind:

"*It is not difficult,*" [He wrote], "*to explain to the people of Vatu Vara the benefit to the colony, of the exploitation of the phosphate on their island, and the Crown's right to all minerals in the ground. But Vatu Vara, to people who are born and bred there, is the centre of the universe. They have managed, with very little government assistance, to find equilibrium with nature on the land and sea around Vatu Vara. We must therefore expect little co-operation, if not resistance, to do what they regard as the process of their extinction.*"

Reading this helped me to understand Mara better and the responsibilities of Fijian chieftainship as a protector of the *vanua* against external forces. The phosphate was still in the ground in 1974, and the people of Vatu Vara were, thanks to their chief, still living their lives with options in relation to the blessings of modernity. It was to be another fifteen years before some citizens of most "advanced economies" began to think that sustainability and continuous economic growth in a finite planet might be difficult, or that there was anything to learn about the "environmental crisis" from indigenous societies.

Leofleda anchored in Vatoa Lagoon.

I have often thought since, how easy it would have been if we had been able to take a laptop with us on *Leofleda*, and distribute our drafts between ourselves for mutual criticism, before we sent them to the academic journals. But this was all happening eight years before the internet was born. We agreed that we should not continue the attempt to produce a single volume publication at once, including all our individual efforts, but that we should publish individually so that the growing numbers of students of Fijian, and Pacific History in the world could have access to our work as soon as possible. We continued to exchange our work with each other for criticism, but published it independently.

Over the next three years, Archie Reid published three articles in the *Journal of Pacific History* and a book. I published two articles in the same journal and one in the *South Australian Journal of Anthropology*. Simon Best and Michael Rowland published articles in New Zealand's Archaeological journals. Garth Rogers wrote an article for *New Zealand Archaeology,* and several detailed accounts of his personal research in Northern Lau, as well as his long period of residence on Ono-i-Lau in 1979.[2] Garth's letters recorded a lot of energetic field work on every island in northern Lau. I had been to some of them during my short visit in 1972, but I did not have the flexibility to be able to stay or go from places that *Leofleda* had taken us to in 1974. Garth was able to use local craft to travel about on his own, and had the immense advantage of speaking and understanding the Fijian language. He began to question the authority of the *Tukutuku Raraba*, and likened its reliability to that of other written historical records, based on oral tradition, such as the books of the Old Testament, and the Anglo-Saxon Chronicle. He was lonely at times, and we

---

2   Reid, AC, *Tovata I & II*, Oceania Printers, Fiji, 1990. This title refers to the creation of Tovata ko Natokalau Kei Viti, by Ma'afu, the Governor of the Tongans living in Fiji. The Tovata was a confederation of northern and eastern Fiji, Tui Cakau and Tui Bua. On 15 February 1869, the Lakeba chiefs united with Ma'afu to establish the Kingdom of Lau, and Ma'afu was installed as Tui Lau.
See also, Reid, AC, "The fruit of the Rewa," *Journal of Pacific History*, Vol. 12, 1977, and "The view from Vatuwaqa: The role of Lakeba's leading lineage in the introduction and establishment of Christianity," *JPH*, Vol. 14, 1979; "The Crusaders: The religion and relationship background to Lakeban expansion in the 1850s," *JPH* Vol. 16, No 2, April 1981.
Young, J M R, "The response of Lau to Foreign Contact," *JPH*, Vol. 17 No 1, January 1982. And "Lau, A windward Perspective," *JPH*, Vol.28, No 2, 1993.
Best, Simon, "Preliminary Archaeological Survey of Lakeba, Lau Group, Fiji," National Geographic Society Research Report 17:453-460, 1976; "Archaeological investigation on Lakeba, Lau Group, Fiji," *New Zealand Archaeological Association Newsletter* 20:28-38, 1977. Best, Simon and Rowland, M J, "Survey and excavation on the Kedekede hill fort, Lakeba Islands, Lau Group, Fiji," *Archaeology and Physical Anthropology in Oceania*, 15(1):29-50, 1980; "Archaeology of the Lapita Cultural Complex: a critical review," *Archaeology in Oceania*, 24(3):116, 1989. Knapman, Bruce, "Fiji's economic history, 1874-1939: studies of capitalist colonial development," *Pacific Research Monograph*, No.15, ANU, 1987.

told him that we looked forward to his arrival in Adelaide, where I managed to get him a temporary job as a research assistant in the History Department.

We had five days to relax on *Arcadia* and it was a very much needed interlude with no navigational problems to keep us awake. We landed at Circular Quay in Sydney Harbour refreshed and ready to go. Rob Durbridge met us at the wharf with our car in much better shape than when we had left it with him. Very conveniently, we came across a South Australian truck driver on the wharf. He had just delivered a load of apples from the Adelaide Hills to Sydney. His truck was empty, and after a short conversation, he agreed to have *Leofleda* loaded in her cradle and to drive her back to Port Adelaide, for much less than it had cost us for the memorably dangerous drive in the other direction. Once more we followed the truck through the night and following day; and arranged for a crane to unload the truck at the Small Boat Club. Once she was on her mooring, we filled the car with bedding, clothes, and unused supplies, and took the familiar route, along Grand Junction Road, and then following Magill Road sharply to the left, we took the steep winding road up into the hills to Norton Summit, ten miles from the middle of Adelaide. Stephen, and our black Labrador, Sigmund, soon joined us.

We reached our house, where the blackberries were doing well, weaving their way up the verandah-posts and into the gutters. One look reminded us of all the renovation work that awaited us.

There were four bedrooms, kitchen, sitting room, a bathroom, of sorts, next to the kitchen, but only one tap that brought in cold creek water from the concrete-lined tank close to the back door. Almost the first neighbour we met was Jack Zachary, who had come to South Australia from Dalmatia at the end of the World War II. He knew our house well, and turned up with a "chip heater," a device that heated a lot of water in a short space of time, using small bits of wood, off-cuts and pine cones as fuel. If we wanted to have a hot bath in those early days at the house, we had to bring in a bucket of small twigs and feed them into Jack's extraordinary contraption. Within a few minutes, it could bring the water to an unbearably hot temperature, if you were not careful. So you had to jump out of the bath and turn on the only tap, which produced cold water, until the bath was cool enough; then feed just a few small sticks of wood into the heater from the bucket, while staying in the bath as the water grew hot again. Originally, the toilet was not provided with a suitable septic tank. Providing one and re-plumbing the house had been the only real improvements we succeeded in making before we left for Fiji. Some of the floors were rotten, especially the area immediately in front of the kitchen sink.

In heavy rain there were a few leaks in the roof until we climbed onto the roof and fixed them with tingles, pop rivets and silicon. There was a wood burning, "Adelect" kitchen stove, which was on the verge of burning out, with an oven and three hotplates. It lasted about a year and then we replaced it.

It was all a bit confronting, particularly for the kids; but in my case, after growing up in Cropton in the 1940s, where we bathed in front of the living room fire in a zinc tub, and went across the yard to the earth closet, I was able to look on the bright side. And Ruth had been brought up in a house which was in a never-ending state of renovation. Both of us were up to handyman level at most things that needed to be done, and so we spent a good deal of time in the early years, sitting up in bed working through the excellent Reader's Digest "Do it Yourself" publication. I had been doing domestic carpentry ever since my father began to teach me on the carpenter's bench he gave me for my tenth birthday. So there was a lot of historical and family back-up, which gave us confidence.

Two years later we had fixed the iron roof, repaired the floors, painted the exterior woodwork, and collected sufficient furniture from second hand shops, and the Ashton tip to be warm and comfortable. A retired electrician called Norm, rewired the house. He was an old man, but familiar with the electrical characteristics of the period in which the house had been built, in the early twentieth century. Once, only, we came home to find him on the verge of tears. I tried to comfort him but that just made him more despondent: "There's just too many wires coming down!" he cried, before eventually regaining his composure over a cup of tea. Soon, all the lights worked again, as did the power plugs, and none of us were electrocuted.

The old Chevrolet one-ton truck that came with the property was very useful. We were quite close to the Ashton rubbish tip, which was open to the public, with no charges. At weekends, it was more of an exchange than a dump, as a result, I think, of culture clash. Large numbers of urban families began an exodus from the sprawling suburbs of Adelaide. Some migrated to the old inner suburbs like North Adelaide, as Carmel and I had done. Such suburbs were undergoing a process of gentrification, to cater for a new wave of upward mobility, of which we were members. Others, like me and Ruth, moved to the close countryside, where people could resist the need for conformity; and where costs were a lot lower, and where wives and mothers with rural skills could celebrate self-sufficiency.

One day, I was at the Ashton tip getting rid of rusty barbed wire, and rusted out corrugated iron from the old roof, when another man came along with a modern utility truck. Amongst his load of familiar rubbish, was an ancient kitchen dresser, with glass sliding doors intact. I thought it was a very elegant piece of furniture, with several small drawers, and commodious cupboards. It was built, I guessed, in the 1930s. The man was about to drag the dresser off the back of his ute and throw it down the cliff to be buried, when I suggested that he should help me to lift it off his ute and onto the back of my truck. I even told him that I thought it was too valuable to throw away, but he said he definitely had no use for it, and I was welcome to have it. We recently sold it for a tidy sum.

The biggest challenge was the fact that the house had salt damp in two of the interior walls. We rid the stone walls of the salt damp, one side of the wall at a time. We put in new damp courses where they were needed and placed strong timber props in the gaps we had made. Doing only one side of a small section of wall at a time with second hand bricks, and mortar, prevented collapse, and it was not long before we hired a plasterer to finish the job, which enabled us also to watch and learn so that we could do more of it ourselves. We then replaced the dining room floor and organised some ventilation below it. The bed rooms all had fire places, and we used them in winter, as there was plenty of timber up the hill above the house, and the property also came with a diesel, D2 Caterpillar tractor, which could pull a trailer or pull logs along the tracks without any trouble.

We continued our friendship with the Costa and Gallace families, who reliably turned up just before Christmas every year, when we had finished picking the bulk of our cherries. The extended families set about gleaning the residue of the crop, as was their custom. They also brought champagne with them, not to mention grappa, and a crowd of small children. By midday on Christmas Eve not a cherry could be seen.

They had shown us how to start the tractor, drive it, and look after it. Starting it was a bit of an art and it took two people to achieve it. One person pulled the rope around the fly wheel which activated the petrol starter motor. After that had been running for a while, warming the diesel engine, the same person lifted the clutch lever and grabbed the decompression lever. The other person was sitting on the tractor seat waiting to get the nod signalling the moment to open the throttle. This also enabled us to use the mouldboard plough to cultivate the two acres of flat land next to the creek that flowed in the valley below the house. We had a disc plough as the local custom was to turn all the land between the fruit trees to kill whatever grew there. We ceased this habit, believing that it would lead to soil erosion. Most growth between the fruit trees was grass, so we acquired a few sheep, who kept it down, grew wool on their backs, and reduced the fire risk, as well as providing us with meat.

I used to take Stephen down to Scotch College early each morning on my way to work at the University. It was a journey that took about half an hour, often in the Chevrolet truck, for which Stephen found himself envied. In summer, we used a 125cc motor bike, which made Stephen envied even more by some boys, but he was a bit embarrassed, as some of his mates climbed out of rather sumptuous, and always warm, parental vehicles. Susan went to the State Primary school at Norton Summit, and Philip went to the new co-ed Morialta High School in Rostrevor, where Susan soon joined him. Philip often rode his bike down and up the steep hill to school. They both seemed to like their school and made some lifelong friends there.

As things turned out, Stephen loved his school too, and was untroubled by his daily separation from his siblings. He enjoyed the teaching and rowing there, and made good friends. His school reports followed a track similar to mine at his age, but with a much happier ending. Like mine, the early ones express teacher frustration due to a perception of unused ability, followed by a gradual recognition of his considerable ability as he became more mature. He was improving steadily, and he went on to get a Bachelor of Mathematical Science, a Master of Business Administration and a Master of Commercial Law.

Philip started out towards an Arts degree, but was lucky enough to be in a tutorial class taught by my good friend and Yale graduate, Norman Etherington. Norm detected an argumentative factor in Philip's work, and a somewhat unenthusiastic interest in History, and so advised him to take an Arts/Law degree. It was true that he enjoyed arguing (I think I must have given him plenty of practice) and he was good at law; he joined a law firm after graduating and quickly became a partner. Susan graduated with a Bachelor of Arts with First Class Honours in Asian Studies and History and gained a PhD in Asian Studies, her subject being Chinese political economy.

Philip was fascinated with mechanics, engines and motor cars. Our neighbours, Bob and Tiffany Bolton gave him two old black Wolseley motor cars, just like English police cars. They were identical, except that one had an unblemished body, but no engine, while the other had a very damaged body, but a reasonable engine. Philip was absolutely determined to get himself a car out of this situation, even if, for a few years, he would not be old enough to drive it on public roads. We had met his benefactor Bob Bolton, before we went to Fiji. Bob was out of work, and lived with his wife, Tiffany. Soon, he obtained a steady job in the South Australian Civil service, but his real talent was that of a Poet, and he became a very good friend. With his help and the help of the caterpillar tractor we hauled both cars up the hill behind the house, to the old pig sties, where, with a little work, we built an elementary shelter that kept most of the rain off, and we could assemble some tools. Philip was absolutely delighted, and spent many happy hours teaching himself about engines. I soon realised that he actually knew far more about cars in general and old classic cars in particular, than I ever would.

It took him about eighteen months of his spare time, mostly on his own, up in the pig sty workshop, to make one car roadworthy. I am not much of a mechanic, but when Philip started to want to put the good engine into the good body, I tried to help him. He taught me a lot, during what was eventually a successful process. I was glad to be able to do the lifting that was needed and it was about six weeks before he asked me to come up and see if we could make the good engine, now in the good car, go. I was amazed at his confidence, and surprised when he did a final check on the fuel line and asked me to crank the engine. I'll always remember the smile on his face when it started; and he just said "Thanks Dad, I feel **so** happy."

And then of course, he wanted to have a drive in the car. The brakes were good so we drove her down to the flat area in front of the house. We started the engine, went through the gears, using the clutch. He took the wheel as I sat beside him, and he drove very slowly down the dirt road, over the creek and a few hundred yards along the side of it. Then we went on until we came to the corner with Green Valley road because it wasn't wide enough to turn until we made it that far, and came triumphantly home. So at fifteen and a half, Philip had a car and very soon could drive it competently on the dirt roads around Norton Summit. But he couldn't legally drive until he received his Learner's Permit at sixteen.

Susan had been reading little girl's horsey books for years, and loved the ponies she met in the parklands next to the North Adelaide children's playground. Ruth and I took her to a riding school for a few months before we went to Fiji, and by the time we moved to Norton Summit, she was a competent rider. Philippa Thomas, one of my History Honours students who lived down the road, gave Susan the horse, called Robert, who had broken my leg, only the year before. Susan loved Robert and enjoyed him for many years.

Back at work, I found that my Pacific Islands course was attracting more students than ever, and enrolment was limited. I was also supervising PhD theses by Peter Morrison on the origins of the Australian Labor Party and Ian Campbell, on the Pacific islands beachcombers, and their cross-cultural influence. Ian Campbell was a first class Honours student from Armidale University, who later became a Professor of Pacific History at the University of the South Pacific at Suva and then at Canterbury University at Christchurch in New Zealand. He was also the first scholar to produce a comprehensive text book on the History of the Pacific Islands from the point of view of the islanders themselves, rather than from the point of view of the Europeans.

A few years later Claudia Knapman went on from an Honours degree, majoring in Pacific History in Adelaide, to a PhD thesis at the ANU, for which she was awarded a J G Crawford medal for academic excellence, followed by the publication of *White Women in Fiji, 1835–1930; The Ruin of Empire?* in 1986.[3] Angela Woollacott, another of my Honours students, went on to become the first Manning Clark Professor of History at the Australian National University.

I was very fortunate to have outstanding students at this stage of my career, and I think Jim Davidson, my supervisor in the ANU, my teachers, Oxford Tutor,

---

3   Knapman, Claudia, UQP, 1986.

Below: Susan and Robert at Norton Summit.

Right: Off Edithburgh, headed for Kangaroo Island.

Peter Dickson, and my MA supervisor, Keith Sinclair in Auckland, had a lot to do with it. It was they who put into my mind the notion that, unlike a Public school, a University was not a fundamentally hierarchical institution, but rather an egalitarian community of scholars, some more gifted or experienced than others, but working together, in search of truth. This was an approach that I took with me into my tutorials and lectures.

Harry Maude gave me a great deal of encouragement at this stage of my career. He had recently retired. He wrote to me soon after we returned from Fiji, to congratulate me, not on my publications—they were mostly yet to be written—but on our survival at sea. Morning tea discussions in the ANU Pacific Studies School had included, he told me, a few light hearted comments that we would come to grief on the reefs, or experience other nautical disasters. Since he had supported my grant application, after inspecting *Leofleda* in my backyard, he was delighted to be able to remind them of his optimistic sagacity. He wrote on 21 December 1974;

You must be delighted at the success of your ship and, not least, at your own navigational prowess. [Actually, it was Ruth's prowess. She was much quicker and more accurate than me at actually doing the sums] *This will effectively confound the critics who maintained that you would be wrecked before you had even started.*

The same letter was equally comforting politically. Harry told me that my troubles in Lau put him in mind of an eminent Pacific History scholar, who, when he was writing his thesis:

...had to make a field trip to Tonga, and despite three letters and a telegram from me, all about it, they jailed him on arrival as an undesirable they knew nothing about, but suspected of intending to seduce the girls of Tonga from their hitherto virtuous lives. And then the money the ANU promised to send did not arrive, because the finance people could only remit to a bank, and he had to sponge on the locals he was supposed to be seducing... I expect many of his strong views date from his early experience as a student.

The Education Committee of the University had become absorbed in evaluating several proposals for new developments. The Arts Faculty was considering a new department of Slavonic Studies. There was also a feeling in the Education Committee that the University should have a Department of Anthropology. For many years, the only advocates for Anthropology were members of the Department of Medicine, who, I surmised, were influenced, to begin with, by the nineteenth century focus on Physical Anthropology. I thought this subject had a ghoulish flavour, concentrating, as it did, on head measuring and the like, which perpetuated the neo-Darwinist notions of the inherent superiority of some races over others.

Physical Anthropology was a research area which was associated with the Medical School. However, the growth of academic interest and student enrolment in Pacific History created a swing towards Social Anthropology. I aligned myself with that movement, because of the obvious benefit for my students if they could include Social Anthropology in their Arts degrees. Garth Rogers had taught me how valuable social anthropology was to historians who wanted to understand the values of island societies. Thanks to Professor Austin Gough, the new head of the History Department, I was asked to represent the Department on a committee that was formed to establish an inclusive Department of Anthropology in 1974. This made Harry Maude's library valuable for anthropologists as well as historians, and led to the idea of establishing a "Centre for Pacific Studies."

Harry Maude was a leading advocate, and had written a letter to the Vice-Chancellor in July, 1973, which was also sent to me, and, I liked to think, was an indirect compliment to my teaching ability:

Nowhere has Pacific History become so firmly established as a recognised and popular interdisciplinary study, attracting not only increasing classes of undergraduate students, whose numbers have to be restricted, but also an impressive group of keen post-graduate students. In fact, nowhere else, whether in Sydney, or Melbourne, does one find such enthusiasm for Pacific Studies, and from correspondence it is evident that more post-graduate students would be glad to come if supervisory facilities could be extended.

Pacific Studies would have been a useful concept, if only as a demonstration of the utility of inter-disciplinary thinking, in order to address the problems of the twenty-first century, such as religious difference, racial conflict, climate change, resource exhaustion, land ownership and inequality. Islands can be, for both social and scientific scholarship, and because of their isolation and small size, the intellectual equivalent of a laboratory.

In the 1970s, Australia was in a good position to take advantage of these opportunities. The creation of a department of Anthropology at the University of Adelaide was a step in the right direction. But the 1980s was a period of financial reduction, by governments, for higher education. While student numbers rose, staff numbers declined, and higher education became the servant of industry rather than a search for truth.

The next thing on my mind was getting divorced from Carmel and married to Ruth. Thankfully Carmel and I were able to hold each other blameless for our separation. Ruth's Catholic mother, and her brothers and sisters, accepted the idea that their precious youngest family member, should marry a divorced English Protestant with three children. I had thought that Catholics might appreciate the position of the "High" Anglican church with its Masses, confessions, and plenty of incense. They might, I thought, accept a wedding held in such an establishment, while I expected a "low" Anglican church wedding to be out of the question. But I was wrong. Being a partly Irish family, it was the specifically English, and Royal aspect of the Church of England that was indefensible, on account of Henry VIII's adulterous relationship with Anne Boleyn, and his claim to be the head of the Church of England. That was the difficulty. Luckily, Ruth and I were not interested in the problem, but decided that since the nicest church in Norton Summit was a Baptist Chapel, lack of involvement with the Tudor dynasty meant that a decision to be married in the place we lived in was a safe one. With a congregation of Ruth's friends, family, a wonderfully warm group of people and their spouses and children, and my colleagues, past students, and some of our new neighbours, the old stone chapel was full, and we were married there on 6 September 1975. We took a week off for a leisurely honeymoon, exploring the Clare and Barossa valleys. It was a quiet time of the year, often with no other traffic on the roads, empty beaches, and time for thought about our future.

With the coming of summer, we returned emotionally to *Leofleda* for our family holidays, and renewed our membership of the unpretentious Small Boat Club of South Australia, tucked away amongst the Mangrove swamps. It was a fascinating organisation and the largest boat club in South Australia, because the cost of membership was much lower than the others. Its necessary equipment, such as moorings, a slipway, and a large clubhouse, were all the production of a generation of volunteer labour. This was largely due to the exceptional leadership of David Cambridge, a retired soldier, and a World War II veteran.

It was not only cheap, but very spacious, occupying a long reach of the tidal Angus Inlet, between Torrens Island and Garden Island. It was full of rows of moorings. Each boat lay between two floating buoys, held by chains to old railway wheels buried deep into the mud. The shore near the club house was concreted and boasted two slipways. On Torrens Island was an unsightly power station, from which hot water was released into the creek. That was the only disadvantage, because the warmth of it encouraged the growth of many forms of life on the bottoms of the boats, which made it necessary to slip, scrub, and re-paint them with anti-fouling about twice a year instead of once. The mangroves provided good shelter though, and encouraged wild life and canoes. The exit to the sea lay just to the north, where a row of posts marking the channel began. Our adventures began under sail, often by tacking down the winding channel, with the tide if possible, which gave the children good practice at handling the boat.

Port Adelaide had two other clubs that provided shore facilities and moorings for seagoing vessels and their crews and owners: the Port Adelaide Sailing Club, and the Royal Yacht Squadron.

Unlike Sydney, Adelaide itself had a minority maritime tradition, because it is inland. The first sailing club, the South Australian Yacht Club, was founded on 5 November 1869. A generation later, on 25 October 1890, Queen Victoria granted the title, "The Royal South Australian Yacht Squadron." The context was one of imperial defence and Australia's anxiety for a clear understanding that in the event of an attack on Australia, by any of Britain's enemies, South Australia, not yet part of an Australian commonwealth, could rely on British naval defence, in which South Australian yachtsmen would participate. Patriotic yachtsmen were apt to remind the public of the value of a civilian organisation, self-trained in seamanship, should a foreign naval attack be made in the future.

In contrast to the regal, and implicitly military opportunism of the Yacht Squadron, the Port Adelaide Sailing Club was founded, according to the club historian, by "a group of local working men, who met one night in 1891, in the Birkenhead

Hotel." Their ambition was to form a sailing club "specifically for the owners of small boats, without the pomp usually associated with yacht clubs." It took six years for the club to become a reality. And it was not until 1925 that its members finally achieved their ambition of opening their own club house and mooring basin just above the Birkenhead Bridge over the Port River, in the very heart of Port Adelaide.[4] When Carmel and I joined the Port Adelaide Sailing Club with *Swallow* in 1962, we used to hoist sail and spend many minutes sailing back and forth across the river, blowing a whistle to get the busy bridge attendant to open it for us, much to the delight of the children; the manoeuvre had to be repeated on our return.

Until South Australians experienced post-war rising incomes, and universal car ownership, boating was a minority activity. Coastal suburbs like Brighton held beach-based sailing competitions in specifically designed racing craft with the ability to carry a lot of sail in the strong sea breezes of the afternoons. These craft were handled by skilled young athletes, unconcerned about getting wet. Families with young children focussed on sand castles or fishing from rowing dinghies, or small boats with outboard motors, and mostly in the early morning, before the wind got up.

By 1975, both the Royal Yacht Squadron and the Port Adelaide Sailing Club had long waiting lists for moorings, and the slack was being rapidly taken up by the relatively recent foundation of the Small Boat Club. It had about 200 moored boats and around 600 members, representing the expansion of the Port Adelaide Sailing Club fraternity, rather than the much wealthier clientele of the Yacht Squadron.

The vessels of the Small Boat Club reflected the incomes and occupations of their owners, from ancient wooden converted fishing boats, to new fibreglass cabin yachts for young families, trailer sailers, and motorboats. Next to the two slipways was a large area of sloping concrete covered with all the tenders that enabled us to row out to our boats.

There was a remarkable family of dolphins at the Small Boat Club, who were very tame. They would escort us as we sailed down the marked channel towards the sea, and come alongside *Leofleda*, so close that I could touch their backs. Amongst the moorings, pelicans cruised, and sometimes one waddled up onto the concrete launching ramp, looking out to sea. Sigmund, the Labrador, was fascinated, and decided to investigate this creature, approaching slowly from behind until he was as close to the pelican as he dared go. The pelican suddenly turned his head, revealing to a startled Sigmund, the length and potential danger of that long beak. The dog sat down, and scratched his ear with his back leg, as if he had never raised the subject.

The Small Boat Club was full of distractions and characters. Dave Cambridge, then the Club Secretary, asked me to take on the job of Mooring Master. This involved allotting moorings spaces as members came and went, and regular inspections and repair of the chains between the floating buoys and the railway wheels on the bottom of the creek. The inspection equipment consisted of a pontoon with

---

4   Couper-Stuart, John, *A Sailing Club at Port Adelaide*, Port Adelaide Sailing Club, 2008.

a small crane and windlass, and an outboard motor, and sometimes Philip, as insurance in case of mechanical troubles of any kind. There was an open slot in the middle of the pontoon, so that we could hook the chain and haul it and the railway wheel up onto the pontoon deck, where we examined each link for wear or damage to links or shackles. Worn and badly rusted shackles had to be replaced, and marine growth removed. It was perhaps the dirtiest, and sometimes the most painful volunteer job I have ever done.

Around this time, Nick Wright came into our lives as a new member of the expanding History Department. He was a recent graduate from the University of Edinburgh, a medieval historian. He secured a job in the History Department of the University of Adelaide in 1975. Jackie, who became his wife two years later, was expected to join him soon. At work in the University, Nick occupied the room opposite mine on the fourth floor of the Napier building.

We soon discovered that we were both interested in sailing, and it was not long before we took Nick for a sail in *Leofleda*. He often came to visit us at Norton Summit, where he was sometimes to be found, reading a book, leaning his back against the trunk of a tree we were about to fell. He was apt to set off on walks through the scrub, sometimes with Sigmund, sometimes alone. He would return for a cup of tea, and ask a lot of questions, leading to long conversations. We liked him, and appreciated his Scottish sense of humour. Then Jackie arrived. She was a successful physiotherapist, with experience of doing good deeds in Uganda, where she had practised her profession. Both Nick and Jackie were enamoured of the Adelaide Hills. We discovered that the Ayres family, who had joined in the mutual sub-division of our original block at Norton Summit, had put the property up the hill behind us for sale. Nick and Jackie later bought it, built a house there and added two lively little boys to the growing community at Norton Summit.

The time came when we took Nick and Jackie for a sail, and it was not long before Nicholas and I started looking for a small cruising vessel for them. The boat they settled on was *Boonewa*, an Aboriginal word meaning "fast sailor."

She was a neat Bermudian sloop, about the same length as *Leofleda*, so we began to cruise together at weekends. At first we explored the coast to the north of Port Adelaide, with its mangrove swamps and winding creeks. A bit of research in old newspapers, and nautical guides like *Sawtell's Nautical Almanac*[5] exposed the maritime history of St Vincent's Gulf, as a tempting side track. An early destination was Port Gawler, now a non-existent place, just a name on the chart. I discovered that it had once been a genuine port for the ketches that tied up at the now abandoned wharf to load grain, and it had also been a place used for annual swimming races, which crowds of people gathered to watch. *Leofleda* and *Boonewa* spent a quiet night tied up where the crowds of the past had cheered the champions, and I began to ponder about the shortage of safe ports along the lee shore of St Vincent's Gulf.

---

5   Sawtell, Alfred, *Sawtell's Nautical Almanac, Tide tables and navy list of South Australia*, Port Adelaide, 1876.

We acquired the habit of putting to sea on a Friday night and heading across the gulf to Port Vincent, Stansbury, or Edithburgh on the other side, depending on the direction of the evening breeze off the land. It was a passage of around thirty sea miles, which meant we could have a meal before setting off and plot a compass course, taking three-hour watches for the crossing. As in the Pacific, we soon found the celestial bodies that could keep us on course through the starry nights. The rising sun behind us in the morning made it easy to pick up the shore marks and find a calm spot to anchor, to the north of the long shoals that curve out a mile or two from the shore towards the head of the gulf. We went ashore in our dinghies, swam, caught fish, and slept, and then sailed back with the south-westerly sea breeze behind us the next day.

Finding myself easily distracted from the routine of two lectures a week, essays to mark and four or more tutorials with up to ten students in each of them, I told myself that my privileged situation as a university lecturer included an obligation to contribute to the education of society as a whole, and to public discussions within the boundaries of my knowledge and experience. Cruising across the gulf, and then down to Kangaroo Island, and eventually to Port Lincoln and the islands in Spencer Gulf led me to think about the impact of the sudden popularity of boating on the development of coastal communities.

The Small Boat Club had a quarterly magazine, entitled *Prop and Tiller*, which identified its impartial emphasis on both sail and power, cruising and fishing, as opposed to "yachting," the focus for the Yacht Squadron. *Prop and Tiller* was free for members, and financed, like many such publications by advertising beer and fishing tackle. It recorded the social events and occasional regattas and club cruises that were organised by the committee. An editorial resignation led to a request to me from Commodore Cambridge to fill the vacancy, which I saw as an interesting opportunity to do some incidental writing.

Choosing "Pelican" as my pen name, I postured as an observant bird who knew what was going on as she paddled effortlessly between the moorings, and reported on new members and their boats, and their ambitions. I encouraged adventure by reporting on our cruises in company with *Boonewa*, illustrated by little freehand charts of anchorages. The voyage to Kangaroo Island, 70 nautical miles away was an ideal destination for a long weekend, setting sail on a Friday night, arriving mid-morning on Saturday, spending that day getting a shower at the pub ashore and provisioning if needed, then exploring, on the Sunday, places such as Pelican Lagoon, perhaps catching a few King George whiting, before sailing around Kangaroo Head to Christmas Cove for the night.

This little natural harbour was then not much bigger than a tennis court, a circular cove sheltered completely by an additional breakwater, which left a passage just big enough to allow *Leofleda* to enter into a perfect haven, and tie up to the shore. The public holiday weekends allowed time to get up early and spend the Mondays sailing home on the sea breezes of summer. We usually hugged the eastern shore of the gulf on the way home, taking back bearings of the abandoned ports, Second Valley, Port Willunga, and Port Noarlunga, where until the 1940s, the wheat of the Fleurieu Peninsula was collected by small sailing ketches, for transport to Port Adelaide. There the wheat filled the hulls of the Cape Horn clippers, who still raced half way round the world to the London Docks, where the wheat was unloaded into Thames sailing barges, including, as I knew from personal experience, the original *Leofleda*.

England and Cornwall had introduced me to the small village harbours of the regions, places like Polperro, Mousehole and Mevagissy. They had all been established centuries ago by taking advantage of small estuaries or inlets, which had been gradually improved over the centuries by adding breakwaters, built as demand arose, from local stone. Aesthetically, they were records of the energy and persistence of many generations, the Cathedrals of the coast. South Australia, had moved much more rapidly, not by building permanent havens, but wooden jetties, wherever the smallest hint of shelter could be imagined. Some of the jetties were extremely long in order to reach water deep enough to load vessels in all tidal conditions, from the shallow drafted, virtually flat bottomed, centre-board ketches of the nineteenth century.

One of Adelaide's major problems is that it is on a lee shore, lacking natural protection from the prevailing wind. But building protective sea walls as in the harbours of Cornwall was mostly too expensive for nineteenth century communities in South Australia to contemplate. When wooden jetties began to be built it was achieved by vigorous political activity, and much "log-rolling"[6] between different constituencies.

As I used *Sawtell's Nautical Almanac*, published in 1877, I reflected that something could be done, for aesthetic and safety reasons, to build on the natural protection provided by the existing reefs in South Australia, to create more sheltered anchorages on the eastern shore of St. Vincent's Gulf. Second Valley was the first possibility, where a very small headland hooked northwards just enough to protect a vessel from the sea breezes and waves in fair weather. About ten miles further north was Port Willunga, where a reef was exposed at low tide, so that quite a large area of shallow water was sheltered from all but northerly winds. North of that was Port Noarlunga, partly sheltered by a reef, running parallel to the shore, exposed except at high tide.

With the increasing activity on the water in South Australia, as the "Twenty Good Years" after the end of World War II drew to a close, new planning problems arose. The typical South Australian boat of this period, built of fibreglass, about 18 feet long, and powered with a 30 horse power outboard was kept for most of its life on a trailer. The lack of calm water led to the building of more ramps, on which fist

---

6   Colonial politicians used to bargain with other politicians, by promising to support proposals for public works in districts other than their own in return for reciprocal behavior, regardless of Party membership.

fights were known to develop as tired and hungry families queued for a place. The trouble was that the new ways of seafaring occupied only a small strip of water close to the beaches. The new boats, designed to travel at high speed, could be safe and comfortable in the early part of the summer mornings, but the afternoon sea breezes could lead to a sudden rush for the ramps, as children began to vomit when the boats crashed uncomfortably through rising waves. Behind the ramps grew large unsightly car parks, while in the sea, water skiers contested rights with slow moving children learning to swim and small dinghies with fishing lines over the side.

My theory was, of course, that the new American style motor boat designs then popular were unsuitable for the waters of St Vincent's Gulf, which lacked sheltered havens. What was needed were small harbours, which could accommodate small sailing vessels. Boats like *Leofleda* could visit these harbours and were not noisy or dangerous to anybody, and used no fuel, or very little, and added to the value of our coastal scenery. They would aid the preservation of real seamanship, by which I mean the ability to be independent of assistance from the shore, and to use natural forces of wind and tide. I talked about these notions to my colleagues over morning tea, and someone told me that the State Department of Tourism, Recreation and Sport might be interested in my thoughts for publication. There was much discussion and criticism in Adelaide at this time, about these problems, and so in the spirit of community service (I told myself) I wrote an article, "People and Boats in South Australia" which was indeed published in *Recreation and Sport* in 1977.

I like to think that this article encouraged the gradual development of North Haven, and Wirrina Marina (1997), two busy harbours that have been followed by extensive seaside housing. My only regret is that the state government did not get in first at either location, which has meant the exclusion of people with low or medium incomes. The State Housing Commission would have been a much more appropriate developer.

Chapter 15: One and All

The female side of my family was in need of support in 1976. My mother wrote to me about her medical problems. She was losing her balance and searching for answers to her questions from a sequence of practitioners; starting with members of the Church Missionary Society, who she knew and trusted, and moving on to specialists of various kinds in London hospitals, who were equally baffled.

Heather was having a difficult marriage that was in the process of breaking up. She did not tell me much about her problems, but it was not long before she was living in a rented flat with Julian, her five year old son, working for the Open University, commuting for many miles each day in the Chiltern hills by motor scooter, and visiting our mother, who was moving around a series of establishments devoted to the care of the elderly. Heather wrote several heroic letters which made me realise that she was carrying the "heavy end of the stick." To begin with, Heather was optimistic and told me that she could manage the situation without any help from me, but I began to get letters from a very well meaning young man, a friend of my mother, who told me that the place my mother was living in was somewhat Dickensian, and suggested that I should visit her, and preferably take her back with me to Australia.

Ruth was willing to take over the considerable responsibility that this would create for her. I realised that the best thing to do would be to go and visit Edith, at least to find out what she would like to do, and have some serious discussions with Heather. The university was very quick to offer compassionate leave. The Australian Government's policy (back then) of allowing the migration of family members meant that I would be able to get a migrant air passage for my mother, should she want to come to Australia with me.

I visited Heather and Edith as soon as I arrived in England. Edith was not happy with her living arrangements and needed little persuasion to come to Australia. In fact, she was delighted at the idea of yet another adventure in her adventurous life. We flew in the Qantas jet, which made her very excited, so much so that when we landed, at Rome, Mumbai, Perth and Sydney, she insisted on dispatching post cards to all her friends to let them share her adventure.

I was glad that we had managed by then to make our house at Norton Summit a liveable place. It appealed to her, with its scenery and warm climate, but it was really too dangerous for her. She had been diagnosed with Parkinson's disease, and was prone to falling, with increased danger to her person each time. It was a positive novelty for my children to finally have a grandmother within reach.

After a few months, Edith's falls became more frequent, until she finally injured herself and had to go to hospital, where the medical staff advised all of us that we needed to find a safer berth for her. I felt she would be happiest in an Anglican Home, where her life as a CMS missionary would be understood and appreciated. St Laurence's Anglican Aged Care Home was a much better outfit than anywhere she had been in England, and mother was delighted with it. We visited her quite often. On one occasion I was taking her for a walk and she suddenly stiffened up as if she had frozen solid. I felt I couldn't leave her to get help, and we weren't far from her room, so I decided to use a fireman's lift to get her onto my shoulder. It must have been a bit embarrassing, but what could I do? She was only about nine stone. But not surprisingly, we soon attracted attention.

"Excuse me, Sir," came the voice, from an elderly gentleman behind me, "but are you related to this Lady?" "Yes, she's my Mum," I replied and carried her back to the home safely.

I asked the staff how long I should expect her to live, and they said it would be difficult to tell. "People die with Parkinson's disease, not because of it," they said. So I just continued the habit of visitation and outings, such as the Australian film, *Storm Boy*, every now and again. One day she said she dreamt that my father visited her one night, and she woke up to find that she was frightened of dying. This was beyond me to deal with, but I reminded her of our family sailing holidays on the Norfolk Broads, when the yacht had heeled over and she was sure we were going to capsize. I had just turned the boat up into the wind, and as I told her it would, the sails spilled the wind and the boat sat up again. "It'll be just like that," I said.

Mother had been at St. Laurence's for about two years when the History Department had a visit from David Lewis, the author of *We, the Navigators*, a study and trial of Polynesian methods of navigation in the open ocean. He stayed with us and delighted my students. On 19 October 1979, I offered to take David for a sail in *Leofleda*. We had a great sail, but when we returned, there was a message for me to ring home. I rang from the Small Boat Club. Susan, then about fifteen, told me that my mother had died. Ruth and I went to St Laurence's to see her. I felt a terrible guilt for not being in the right place at the right time. We thanked the staff for looking after her. She wanted to be cremated and her ashes buried with my father at Rosedale. I arranged all this with Heather and she, in Ant Molly fashion, organised a tradition Yorkshire wake, which my mother would have appreciated.

At this point in my life, I began a new project which allowed me to pursue, down yet another lane, my lifelong love of boats. My mother had taught me to read long before I went to school, so I spent my childhood reading, and then dreaming, about real boats and real adventures, as I have said. Earlier I had tried to close the gap between my job and my extra-mural interest in boats, by attempting to acquire and restore one, at least, of the two remaining commercial sailing vessels still trading out of Port Adelaide, *Annie Watt* and *One and All*. In 1972, I introduced maritime history into my Australian History course. By 1974, I had managed to get myself, in a boat, in the Pacific Ocean, doing very valuable and original research. There is an ulterior motive at the heart of all of these other lanes—I like wooden sailing boats and everything about them—their history, the detail of their construction, their relative harmlessness and the resourcefulness they engender. All of this ultimately led, through many difficulties and a few triumphs, to the building, as opposed to the restoration, of a new, community-owned, 100 foot sail training brigantine, *One and All*.

Nineteen eighty was not, superficially, any more hopeful a time than 1970 had been, from the point of view of preserving or constructing historic ships. People interested in "heritage" were interested in its material manifestations alone and in particular, buildings. People interested in boats and sailing were interested in technological advances, in fibreglass, steel, aluminium and Kevlar. There was, and still is, an enormous prejudice against wooden ships, resulting partly from several decades of experience with plywoods, often of poor quality, in small boat construction. In South Australia however, we were approaching our sesquicentenary, surely the occasion for which the people of South Australia might be expected to wake up to the commercial value of the nostalgia industry.

The South Australian government had appointed a "Jubilee 150 Board" in mid 1980 and it was calling for ideas for projects to celebrate the sesquicentenary. I and many others thought that here was an opportunity to build a new sail training ship as a birthday present for South Australians.

We called the first public meeting, by invitation, in the History Department common room in June 1980. About fifty people turned up and we decided to form an incorporated body called "The Historic Sailing Ship Association." The name was changed to "The Historic Sailing Ship Project" on the advice of a psychiatrist, who said it was important to seem positive. The general characteristics of the vessel to be built were agreed upon. Bob Sexton, who was to become an influential maritime historian, produced drawings of *Postboy,* a topsail schooner built in Port Adelaide in 1874. I found some of *Postboy*'s logs in the State Archives and discovered that she had a successful career carrying passengers and mail to many of the small ports of the State. But by this time we had confirmed the fact that a replica, even of a tested vessel like this, would not be a practical proposition. The Uniform Shipping Laws Code had been recently introduced, and discussions with the Commonwealth Department of Transport revealed, that while fire safety requirements were compatible with timber construction, a replica in the strict sense would not satisfy stability, and in particular, damaged stability requirements.

We made haste to contact the Jubilee 150 Board, seeing it as a potential source of funds and sympathetic support. The Executive Officer of the Board came to a meeting in August and, as the Minutes record, suggested that we seek incorporation, not as the "Historic Sailing Ship Project," but as the "Jubilee Sailing Ship Project."[1] He explained that our objective of using the sesquicentenary as an opportunity to provide an imaginative vehicle of community identity closely fitted the expected guidelines of the Jubilee Board, and endorsement and some assistance could in due course be, confidentially, expected.

More encouragement followed. We applied for and received a grant of $1,000 from the Board, to complete a feasibility study for presentation to the Board. It

---
1   Jubilee Sailing Ship Project, Minutes, 2 August 1980.

was presented in May 1981, a document of forty-five pages, with appendices. It contained quotations from several Adelaide shipyards, showing that an eighty foot vessel could be commercially built for a cost of around $600,000.

Things began to move. The parameters of the design were established enough to approach a designer. We managed to get magnificent sponsorship from Trans Australian Airways. The Commonwealth Government owned the air line, but the marketing manager was a graduate in philosophy from the University of Adelaide. Committee members who needed to travel interstate at short notice would now be able to get free stand-by tickets for travel within Australia. I went to Hobart, queuing for the earliest morning flights, until a vacancy and return could be guaranteed, to meet the chief organiser of what was to become in 1983, the *Lady Nelson* project; the construction of a replica of the Naval vessel built in 1799 on the Thames at Deptford, and sent to Tasmania as a survey vessel. Rebecca Round was a schoolteacher who initiated the idea. She was kind enough to put me up for the short time I was in Tasmania and was very supportive of the South Australian efforts. She also introduced me to Adrian Dean, who was then making *Lady Nelson*'s mast and spars in advance of the hoped-for replica.

Adrian was originally a professional boat-builder, apprenticed to the legendary Jock Muir in Sandy Bay, Hobart. Adrian is knowledgeable in many fields, including Tasmanian history, Tasmanian timbers and the history of hand tools. He had no degree in naval architecture, but was one of the self-taught naval architects who are respected by many professionals. He has worked as a shipwright on many timber vessels, including a coastal schooner in New South Wales, and has a brain full of successfully built designs for a range of craft from sea-kayaks to big fishing boats and cruising yachts.

Adrian had recently moved on to the teaching trade, as a staff member of the Friends' School in Hobart. I talked with him for a long time about our sail training ship project, and as we talked, I began to think that he would be an ideal designer for the ship we wanted to build.

Adrian agreed to design our vessel, an offer which several Tasmanian authorities advised us to accept. He was happy to design an 80 foot topsail schooner, at no charge.

So preliminary design work commenced. But a problem emerged when the Jubilee Board wanted assurance that our designer would be a qualified naval architect. That meant that we couldn't ask Adrian Dean to do the job after all. In spite of this bureaucratic insult, Adrian had the character and broad vision to agree to be retained, as a volunteer consultant. We advertised Australia-wide for his replacement, and appointed Kel Steinman, who was a distinguished designer of very successful ocean racing yachts. But he had become emotionally attached to the global revival of wooden ship building, which was triggered by the launch of *WoodenBoat Magazine* in 1974. Kel had also begun working on *Alma Doepel*, a notoriously lovely topsail schooner, built of wood in 1903 at Bellingen, on the east coast of New South Wales. She was already being restored in Melbourne. He began working on our Jubilee ship as well, immediately, without a guarantee of ever being paid.

Kel told us that the Ship's Bounty Act would secure the project a subsidy from the Commonwealth Government, so long as the vessel was big enough. If she was 100 feet long, or displaced 150 tons, or more, she would attract a subsidy of 27.5%[2] of the cost of building. That almost doubled the size and weight of the vessel we had been thinking about, but it would also double her earning capacity, as well as supply a large proportion of the building cost. The decision was made. Kel worked quickly, and we soon attracted the interest of a professional model maker, who built a wonderful scale model, fully rigged as a topsail schooner. This we took to an inaugural Boat Show in Adelaide's Centennial Hall, and it soon attracted enormous attention.

Towards the end of the Boat Show, Bill Porter and his wife, Faye walked in. Bill was a native of Padstow on the northern coast of Cornwall. He migrated to Australia after World War II. At this time, he was one of the busiest boat builders in Port Adelaide and his eyes shone as he saw the scale model. There was a silence as he looked her over. Then he spoke. "Tell you what," he said, "I'll build that boat. Me and my boys will build that boat."

Newspaper reports followed, illustrated by photographs of the model, and an invitation of membership of the Jubilee Sailing Ship Project Inc, at $5 a head, which started to steadily increase. Nick Wright, my Medieval specialist colleague and friend became the editor of *Tall Ship*, the quarterly journal of the organisation, and which is still produced regularly today.

I approached the Premier, Mr Tonkin, leader of the Liberal Party, to ask if the State government would purchase a quantity of Huon Pine from the old Tasmanian company, Henry Jones IXL, who were offering enough Huon Pine to plank the ship at a very low price. I pointed out to Mr Tonkin, that whether or not the ship was eventually built, the acquisition of a large amount of Huon Pine, at $2 per super foot, would be a very valuable investment. He verbally agreed. The Department of Marine and Harbours agreed to provide under-cover storage for the timber. These promises never eventuated. By 1983, when we needed to begin planking, there was a different government in South Australia and Henry Jones had sold the timber to the Tasmanian government. I did try to buy it back, but in the end, the ship was planked in Jarrah and Celery Top Pine below the waterline, with Celery Top Pine and Huon Pine topsides.

We now felt sufficiently confident to anticipate a place in the proposed sesquicentenary celebrations, and financial support from the State government. We put together a business plan and submitted it, after receiving many encouraging intimations from the Jubilee Board. We also began our own fund-raising by means of raffles, fêtes, and film shows, using equipment borrowed from the University. Before long, service clubs like the Lions, Probus, Rotary and the Kiwanis, and many schools, invited me to speak and explain the value of a sail training ship to the community: how sailing and learning about sailing as crew would cultivate confidence, teach teamwork, and deliver life-changing experience for young people of both sexes. And money began

---

2   Bounty (Ships) Act, 1980, Clause 7 (c).

to come in from the service clubs, but not yet in large quantities. Michael Smee, a teacher at St Peter's College in Adelaide volunteered to become our Treasurer. It proved to be a harrowing responsibility. Michael had things set up and running, impeccably, to be eventually succeeded by several others including Brian Baldwin, a young graduate in Business Studies, who had nerves of steel.

In June 1981, I wrote to Mr James Hardy, soon to become Sir James Hardy, a very famous yachtsman who had just been appointed as Chairman of his family firm of wine makers, James Hardy and Sons. In his teens, Jim began racing 12 foot dinghies from the beach at Seacliff. Later he skippered Australia's entry in three Admiral's Cup races. The Project Committee decided to ask Jim to be our President. I used the free air ticket supplied by TAA to visit him in Sydney, because he wanted to discuss the project in some detail. To my delight, Jim accepted the position of President that we had decided to offer him. He told me of his own youthful experience rather like my own on the Thames barge, when he had joined the crew of the trading ketch, *Reginald M,* for a voyage to Kangaroo Island, and had treasured the experience. He agreed that it was the kind of opportunity that should be available to all teenagers.

Support came from diverse sections of the community, with different kinds of motivations; from historians, boat builders, educators, businesses and sailors. They were the people who stayed with us most consistently. The prospects looked bright.

On 27 June 1981, a meeting of the Sail Training Federation of Australia was held in Melbourne. The Foundation Members were the Australian Sail Training Association of New South Wales, which was restoring *New Endeavour*; Sail and Adventure Ltd of Victoria, which was restoring *Alma Doepel*; TasSail, a new organisation in Tasmania that was hoping to build the replica of *Lady Nelson*; and the Jubilee Sailing Ship Project of South Australia. The meeting was enthusiastic and cheerful and I offered to host the Federation's June 1982 meeting, timed to coincide with a general meeting of the Jubilee Sailing Ship Project, in South Australia, where the representatives from the other states could speak to our members about their own vessels. We expected that by this time, we would have a decision in our favour from the Jubilee Board.

The first hint of trouble came on 26 November 1981, when, in response to a request for permission from the Jubilee Board to seek sponsorship, in order to fund the purchase of materials, we were told we should not do so, in view of the imminent formation of a committee, which would co-ordinate all sponsorship funds for sesquicentenary events and allocate them, as needed, to the events and activities selected for endorsement.[3] An announcement of "Those events to be endorsed" would be made, we were told, on 21 February 1982, but no such announcement was made. Meanwhile, we were asked to submit a second document demonstrating that our project conformed to the guidelines, which had now been determined. We were asked to appear before an historical sub-committee of the Jubilee Board, but were never informed of the subsequent recommendations.

---

3   Mr R Piper to Secretary, Neil Keech, 26 November 1981.

We seemed to get no further ahead. My repeated phone calls to the Secretary to the Jubilee Board, were answered by long winded explanations about the very many proposals with which the Board had been inundated. But there was always some encouragement and promises to give us a formal reply as soon as possible. We soon began to worry. We knew that it might take several years to build a ship such as we envisaged. There was also a distant possibility that Jonathan King,[4] who had been planning since 1978 for a First Fleet Re-enactment in 1987–88, would invite our ship to join, because she would be the only ship in the fleet built in Australia. That meant we had a goal to work towards.

We wrote again for specific permission to approach potential sponsors and received a letter back, dated 21 April 1982, giving consent.[5] A week later, we received a letter from the Chairman of the Board refusing both funding and endorsement.[6]

I asked for the reasons and was told that the history sub-committee of the Board had rejected our proposal, because we were not intending to build a genuine replica. I explained that a replica would not have been able to sail anywhere with students aboard, because it would not be able to comply with the modern safety regulations. Flat bottomed ketches were known to have capsized. I gave him one of my lectures about the difference between an Antiquarian and an Historian and left it at that. No point in shooting the messenger I thought.

The Board itself thought that our costs had been underestimated. But there were other arguments as well. Nobody on the Jubilee Board, it seemed, had any knowledge of the existence of the many sail training vessels and supporting organisations that existed all over the world. We learned much later that three referees were consulted, two of whom made their views known either to me or to Sir James Hardy. One member had evidently read so little of our proposal that he thought we wanted to train people for military duties, and therefore our proposal to build with timber was absurd. He believed that building an ocean going vessel out of wood was then impossible. The timber was not available, the skills were lost, and the whole idea was suspect as he doubted the value of having a sail training vessel in any case.

Another referee, we were told, was a prominent yacht builder and designer. His advice was that sail training vessels should be in the high technology class, built of steel and equipped with synthetic materials. Education in such fields was what was needed for today's youngsters. Enough timber work could be incorporated into parts of such a ship to give her a "traditional feel." The evident obsession of the Project's members with history, tradition, and timber was merely a sign of the incompetence to be expected from their academic backgrounds. Later, after a Royal

---

4   Jonathan King is descended from naval officer, Phillip Gidley King, who came out in the First Fleet, returned to England and then became the third Governor of New South Wales.

5   The original is lost. It is noted in my reply to Mr J Doyle, 23 April 1982.

6   Kym Bonython to J Young, 28 April 1982.

Yacht Squadron luncheon at which I was invited to speak, this consultant confessed that had he realised, at the time, that such of his friends as Sir James Hardy were involved in the project, his report would have been entirely different.

In many ways, the two referees reflected the conventional wisdom of Australia's age of affluence, the end of which was imminent. It is often the nature of ideology to overrun the mix of circumstances that give rise to it, in this case, the circumstances still included cheap energy, and an uninformed, almost superstitious confidence in cure-all "technology." They also reflected the contemporary anti-intellectual bias in Australian society, and the widespread claims of business acuity by those who show such bias. Having called for, and received such advice, it would have been a most unusual Board that would have rejected it.

The trouble was not that the Jubilee Board had been neglectful of its responsibilities to assess the worth of our proposal. It was that the people who were consulted knew nothing whatever about sail training or wooden ships.

When our next meeting began, on the following Saturday evening, a member of our own committee introduced a member of the Jubilee Board to me and asked me to allow him to address the meeting. I consented, and I'm glad I did because our visitor, perhaps inadvertently, explained the real reason for the change of attitude of the Board towards us. He said that the Board was about to recommend to the Premier, that the State government should purchase the Dutch-built, steel motor vessel, *Falie*, which came to South Australia in 1922 as an auxiliary sailing vessel, and was not typical of the ketch fleet she was held to represent. *Falie* had traded for many years in South Australia, until she was laid up in 1982. She was to be used to celebrate the wheat-trade of the past during the sesquicentenary. We should therefore forget our plans and join forces with this proposal. He explained that he was as ignorant of ships as he was of history. It was his insight as a businessman, however, which enabled him to assure us that the Board had made the right decision. We were the wrong audience for him though, and he left without waiting for questions.

Jim Hardy then rang me to tell me that Kym Bonython, Chair of the Jubilee Board, had sought to persuade him to resign from his Presidency of the Sailing Ship Project, and become the President of the *Falie* organisation instead: "I told him I'd rather stay with the Jubilee ship," Jim said. "I think she'll go better to windward."

The difference of opinion over materials and technologies foreshadowed alternative relationships between ships and society. Building in steel might well have meant Jubilee Board endorsement, and early support from the business community. But steel is produced by large organisations that require initial heavy investment. We would have to have been in a position to make a contractual arrangement with an existing commercial shipyard.[7] Life would have been easier, but the history

---

7   Western Australia was planning a much larger Sail Training Ship, *Leeuwin II*. She was twice as big as *One and All* and cost millions more, and was built by an established shipyard, but Western Australia was having an enormous mining boom, while South Australia was in recession.

of building *One and All* would have been a less revealing social document. So to windward she went.

In spite of the setback, we held a meeting on 1 June, 1982, chaired by Sir James Hardy, at which we decided to press on regardless. This was a time of high unemployment, and incipient depression, at the beginning of the decade that was to be characterised by the statement that, "Greed is Good."[8] Support for going ahead in a negative context was probably risky, but it eventually worked.

Having decided to abandon us, the Board was anxious to eliminate us as a competitor for public support and funding. On 28 June 1982, a short item appeared in *The Advertiser*, headed "Sailing Ship Project Ends." I received a copy, though, of a "joint press release," issued by the Jubilee Board, which did not say that at all. It said that the Board did not endorse our project, and that media comparisons between the two vessels were unfair, as they would be used for different purposes.[9] We were able to get a retraction of the statement next day, and a headline, "Sailing Ship Project to Continue."[10]

Bill Porter (W G Porter and Sons) was appointed as Master builder of the project. David Nash, aged 16 years old, was taken on as his apprentice. David Nash and Jock Geddes, who was a retired shipwright from the Clyde in Scotland, lofted Kel Steinman's plans[11] in Bill Porter's workshop at Port Adelaide, and they then started building the moulds for a 100 foot sailing ship, using plantation grown Radiata Pine, donated by the Department of Woods and Forests.

TAA airlines flew Bill Porter, our builder, Kel Steinman, our designer, and me, as participant historian, to Kyogle, in Northern New South Wales where Kel had located a sawmill, owned by sawmiller Norm Mackintosh, that specialised in Australian Grey Ironwood (*Eucalyptus Paniculata*). Norm's career had been largely based on supplying timber for ship and boat builders. He wrote to me to say that he had found the perfect tree for our keel. We told Channel 7 TV that we would be going to find and fell the tree in Kyogle. Australian National Rail had already offered to provide free transport for the keel to Port Adelaide.

Norm's mill was an amazing place with beautiful forest surroundings, and the first thing we did was to take a walk of about two miles into the forest, where we came across an immense Ironbark trunk about 80 feet tall, with no branches until

---

8   From the speech by the Character Gordon Gecko in the film *Wall Street*, 1987: "Greed clarifies, cuts through, and captures the essence of the evolutionary spirit. Greed, in all its forms, greed for life, for money, for love, knowledge, has marked the upward surge of mankind… The point is, Ladies and Gentlemen, that greed, for lack of a better word, is Good."

9   Joint communiqué from the South Australian Jubilee 150 Board and Sir James Hardy, 28 July 1982.

10   *The Advertiser*, 30 July 1982.

11   Drawing lines or parts of the construction plans full size on the floor to determine the shapes of timber components of the ship.

the top was almost reached. The diameter was five feet at chest height. Bill Porter put on a great performance for the cameras, knocking on the trunk with the back of his axe to make sure it was solid all through, and declaring it to be just the job for the keel of a ship that would "last a hundred years, or more! No trouble at all."

Television Channel 7 roguishly screened a news item featuring the model of the ship and footage taken in Kyogle. This was followed by two "State Affair" programmes. There was more publicity when the Sunday Mail agreed to help us to run a "Name the Ship" competition. Sir James Hardy, as he had then become, agreed to judge the very long list of suggestions that we received from all over the state, and to choose the winner, who was to be one of the first to go on the ship's maiden voyage.

Many people wanted to celebrate the memory of their sea going ancestors, and the several hundred suggestions with their accompanying stories is a wonderful source for maritime historians. The most popular name was "One and All," the name of the vessel we had wanted to buy for use as a sail training vessel in 1970. The original was fondly remembered in South Australia until she was lost near Middleton Reef. Bill Porter also reminded us, that "One and All" was the motto of the County of Cornwall. Bill told us, it was the slogan of a successful campaign to raise a ransom for the return of the King of Cornwall to his people, after he had been captured by Vikings. True or not, the story resonated in the state of South Australia, to which many Cornish people had migrated when the collapse of tin mining in Cornwall coincided with the discovery of copper in South Australia in the 1850s.

Thousands of people warmed to the message of the name itself, which we emphasised with much help from the media. This ship would not be given to the people of South Australia by some great benefactor, or an enlightened government. She was to become the gift of thousands of people who donated their time, their money, their skills, their labour, and their influence to their own community.

Then the developers of a new marina on waterfront swamp land that was to become the suburb, "North Haven," led by Malcolm Kinnaird, decided to donate a building site, free of charge for the time it took to build the ship and a free mooring on completion. It was at this point that we began to feel confident of ultimate success.

Readymix donated a concrete slab on which to lay the keel at the North Haven site. Bill Porter started to work voluntarily on the backbone of the vessel, squaring the two pieces of Ironbark from Kyogle which made up the keel. They were scarfed together at a "Laying the Keel" ceremony, conducted by Sir James Hardy on 31 October 1982. Then the after section was held down by u-shaped steel staples, bedded into the concrete. The long process of bending the sap-filled forward part of the keel began. A jack was placed towards the forward end of the keel. It was David Nash's job, for the next three months, to come down to the site at seven o'clock every morning to give the jack a turn or two, and the green timber was then soaked with linseed oil, donated by Taubmans Pty Ltd, and applied by volunteers from Thebarton Youth Centre. The timber soon began to achieve a gradual curve to create a rocker to lift the bow, making it easier for the vessel to go about when tacking into the wind. It took about three months to achieve the required amount of curve. The moulds, made in Bill's workshop, were then brought to North Haven. Once they began to be fastened so that anyone could see that a ship was being built, crowds began to be interested.

We started a full time fund raising unit by offering two unemployed people, John Ford and his partner Marguerite, the task of enrolling members and selling goods on a commission basis, from a mobile stall that could be towed to supermarkets and other public venues. By the beginning of 1983, our membership expanded to four hundred.

Thus invigorated by public support, we were among the first South Australian community organisations to apply for funding under the Community Employment Program. This was a Federal Government scheme of the Hawke Government, designed to provide work opportunities and wages for long-term unemployed people, who were to work on socially beneficial projects. I found out about it by going to the office of the Industrial Relations Department in Rundle Street, where I met Mr Wally Bean. He was the most intelligent and helpful public servant that I have ever met. He had read the news about the laying of the keel, and immediately understood the whole range of ideas behind the project, from public education, to the merit of using renewable building materials and the use of natural sources of energy. He helped me through the application process for a hefty "seeding grant," to get us going. In May 1983, we were told that our application for $151,000 over 12 months, including $28,000 for materials, had been successful. The grant became available to us on 1 June 1983.

We thought it wise to found a Trustee Company to own the vessel and operate her in the public interest, on behalf of our existing incorporated body. What we badly needed was a shed. Dick Fidock, who was Chairman of the Co-operative Building Society of South Australia, and of our internal sponsorship sub-committee, secured a grant of $2500 from the Co-Op, and a further grant of the same amount from the Hindmarsh Building Society, in return for public acknowledgment on the site. Boral Cyclone provided the framework of a 120 foot long building shed, at cost. Lysaght donated the corrugated iron cladding. Brambles, a haulage company, provided free transport of materials. We then registered the Incorporated body as a "shipyard," in order to be eligible for the 27.5% Ship's Bounty towards the cost of building.

We sought to distance ourselves publicly from the Jubilee Board, but the media continued to refer to us as "The Jubilee ship." This tendency was accelerated, rather than decreased, by a circular, sent to all media chiefs of staff in Adelaide. It was, ironically, signed by the same official of the Board who had suggested, in 1980, that we include the word "Jubilee" in our title. It said that: "The One and All was not endorsed by the Board, and it is entirely misleading to refer to her as 'the Jubilee ship.' This title properly belongs to *Falie*."[12] This secured for us the enviable position in Australia of "the under-dog."

On the side of the new shed, John Ford painted a very large schooner under sail, that could be easily seen from the windows of the never ending stream of cars driving north on the coastal road to Outer Harbour. The shed was built around the existing keel of the ship. A month later we felt confident enough to invite all comers to a Shed Opening ceremony. It was a chance to congratulate the now hundreds of people, businesses and institutions who had supported us through a major struggle, and to re-assure them of our determination to see the project to the end. This is part of what I, as Chairman of the Sailing Ship Project, said on that occasion:

There have been people who have been sceptical about the One and All. They confused the concepts of cost and value. They could not envisage any way in which a project could be started without a large amount of money in the bank, and the backing of a few important bodies and individuals. You have shown them that there are indeed "more things in Heaven and Earth than were dreamt of in their limited philosophy"... You have shown the critics "how to give, and not to count the cost, to fight, and not to heed the wounds, to toil, and not to seek for rest, to labor, and not to ask for any reward." Perhaps the time has come for the critics and the cynics to follow your example... To give and not to count the cost.

We began to discover that news about us had reached distant shores and had established our credibility. Captain Mark Kemmis-Betty, RN, skipper of *Sir Winston Churchill*, Britain's sail training ship, paid us a visit in January 1983. He was favourably impressed: "Given that you are blessed with superb materials like Ironbark, Jarrah, and Huon Pine, you'd be crazy to use anything else." He told us that his own ship, built of steel in 1966, was then running into serious and very expensive maintenance problems: "You can slip your ship anywhere, and you can maintain her with ordinary hand tools anywhere in the world. Take my advice and keep her simple."

Building in timber attracted a huge amount of volunteer labour. We had relatively low overheads, and in the early stages, used traditional hand tools. Individual timber orders were placed as money was raised. Work experience was provided for unemployed people, and secondary school students. Thebarton Youth Services was a Council initiative by Graham Baker, a History graduate of 1981. It provided work experience, using donated equipment, in an area of extremely high unemployment. We provided an instructor, Tom Vosmer[13], from our committee, to follow up the Thebarton Council activity, by taking gangs of young people with chainsaws, on timber getting expeditions into the Adelaide Hills in a Council truck, looking for grown red gum crooks and sweeps donated by landowners.

---

12 Director, Promotions and Community Liaison, Jubilee Board to all Chiefs of Staff and News Editors, 26 December, 1983.

13 Tom Vosmer came to Adelaide from Canada and had personal experience of the Maine-based revival of wooden boat building. He became a PhD student in marine archaeology and was to become the director of the National Maritime Museum of Oman.

One morning I went down to the yard to find two men digging a trench in the sandy soil from the road towards the shed we used as an office. They told me they were working for Telecom, Australia's Government owned telephone company. I said that I didn't know whether anyone had asked Telecom to connect us, and asked them how had we obtained a place in the phone directory? How should we pay for all this? One of the men said, "Don't you worry about it John. We think it's a good idea!" A month later the new issue of the telephone directory was delivered. We never received a bill until *One and All* was launched.

Our Community Employment Grant alone was not expected to be nearly enough to finish the ship, and we continued our fund-raising activities. The gift from ATCO industries of two small buildings provided an office and a small shop. The supply of material from the Grant enabled us to employ an initial team of five men, who began to set up the workshop, and then put up the little office and shop. The idea of the shop was to sell T-shirts and post cards depicting the building of the ship to visitors. Wally Bean allowed us to use some of the funding to employ John Ford and Ally Fricker as shopkeepers and tour guides. Ally Fricker was a member of one of Port Adelaide's old ketch owning families, and was also a radical student politician of the nineteen seventies, who I had known as a colleague during the student movement against conscription for the Vietnam war. She was very beautiful, good at public speaking, and at dealing with crowds. With one side of the shed left open so that visitors could see inside from a safe distance, they began to come in large numbers. John Ford was technically unemployed, but already a self-taught marine artist. He has since made a very successful career of it. He had been a member of the Project since it began and started taking visitors for walks around the vessel as she grew, in return for a dollar each. This soon began to draw in a useful amount of money.

Around the same time, owners of old, as well as prospective "tall ships" such as ours, met together in Melbourne to discuss Jonathan King's plan for a First Fleet Re-enactment, to celebrate the bicentenary of the arrival of the original fleet in New South Wales in 1788.

We were very keen that *One and All* participate in the re-enactment voyage as it would ensure a share of funding. Jonathan was devoted to the purpose of raising public consciousness of national history, which I thought was a good idea, rather than celebrate a conquest. His view was that the re-enactment was an opportunity for a new start, a chance to acknowledge that Aboriginal land had been stolen. He was also keen on a

David Nash in foreground and Bill Porter forcing a rocker into the keel timber of *One and All*.

treaty. Jon is no fool, and knew that the re-enactment would provoke inevitable questions. He invited the famous aboriginal actor, author and advocate, Burnum Burnum, to come to our meeting. Burnum Burnum arrived a bit late into a crowded room, apologising, and explaining that, as he had no vehicle, he had walked and it had taken longer than he had expected. Then he told us that, as he walked, "No one looked me in the eye. Do you know why nobody looked me in the eye? Let me tell you why. They would not look me in the eye because we are at war. And we have been at war for two hundred years."

Jon gave a personal apology for the massacres of women and children, the seizure of land, the destruction of ecosystems, the spread of introduced disease and the loss of culture. And in particular, the failure of two centuries of occupation to repair the damage that has been inflicted by the original denial of Aboriginal ownership of land.[14] I supported him by pointing out the absence of a treaty between the eighteenth century aboriginal population and the invaders. I attempted a defence of the First Fleet re-enactment, on the grounds that the new fleet would inevitably arouse public discussion, and lead to some understanding, at least, of the historical reality of attempted genocide, and its failure, and the necessity of both recognition and legislative repair. On 26 January, 1988, Burnum Burnum stood on the white cliffs of Dover, and planted the Aboriginal flag, thereby claiming England as Aboriginal land, just as Arthur Phillip had done with the Union Jack on the beach

---

14 For Jonathan King's views about the Re-enactment and the need for reconciliation see, King, J, *Tall Ships and Tall Tales*, Scribe Publications, Victoria, 2013, pp 84–5.

December 1983: moulds in place, showing the shape of the ship to come.

on Sydney Harbour. This set me on a course of using our ship, if possible, to bring Australia to its senses about this archaic assumption of land rights for invaders.

About this time, the young men and women who were building *One and All*, decided to challenge the people working on the restoration of *Falie* to a cricket match. The landlord of the British Hotel in Port Adelaide donated a silver "Shipwright's plate" for us to compete for. It was a one day match, held at the Semaphore Oval and it turned out to be a gripping contest, with fortunes alternating throughout the day. The point was reached when the *One and All* team had one wicket in hand and one run to get for victory. Luckily, the man facing the ball was our Treasurer, Brian Baldwin, who had the steely nerves of a financial tightrope walker. He won the match and the "Shipwright's Plate" with a magnificent boundary at about tea time in the afternoon.

Sail Training, as such, was a new idea in South Australia in the 1980s, though it was well understood in Britain and New Zealand. Some journalists however, took it upon themselves to enlighten their readers, and analyse its educational value. On 21 April 1984, Paul Lloyd of *The Advertiser* wrote:

> *There are in One and All, also hidden messages for young people, in the ship's emphasis on using renewable resources instead of churning up metals and plastics and petrochemicals. The boat is built in timber, Real Wood, that you can smell and touch and hear. Wood from trees, not factories… "Also," says Dr Young, "timber is in the long run cheaper than steel. For a boat it is quieter, and easier to maintain. Most important is that the ship's majority source of power is the wind."*[15]

Building in timber began to prove the financial advantage we had anticipated. Volunteers helped with the early work, and even dull, cold weekends drew as many as four hundred visitors, bringing $150–$250 per day in donations and purchases. By this time, people not only saw the ship, soon they began to smell the timber. Then they wanted to touch it. Once they touched it, they wanted to help.

---

15   *The Advertiser*, 21 April 1984.

Above: Ribs in place, bottom planking on, replacing ribbands, which are visible above the planking.

Right: Launch of *One and All*, North Haven, 1 December 1985. Note the water level on the bulldozer on the right. (Photo by Jenny Scott, with permission, SLSA B73778)

In 1984 we broke new ground by employing Donna Axelsen, who was looking for a job, and was reputedly, Australia's first female shipwright. She was soon approached by a female sculptor, who eventually obtained Donna's consent to use her as a model for the Huon Pine figurehead of the ship, a role for which she had a perfect figure. She was soon part of the building team, and joined by two other young women, Alison Parkin and Lucinda Castanelli. Together with the five young men, they soon began to gain proficiency, and worked well together, absorbed into the atmosphere of energy and dedication created by Bill Porter. Later they were joined by Tom Vosmer and other young people from interstate as well as South Australia.[16]

Once the keel of *One and All* was laid, the rest of the backbone was completed. The stern post, of Jarrah from West Australia, was fastened to the aft end of the keel with long copper bolts through deadwoods and a stern knee, cut from a large Red Gum grown in the Adelaide hills. Similar pieces of Blue Gum came over from Tasmania for the chock piece, following the curved joint between keel and stem. This was straight-grained Blue Gum three feet wide and eighteen inches thick. Finally two and a half inch rebates were cut, one on each side, the whole length of the ship, ready to accept the planking. The Premier and Treasurer, John Bannon, came down to the site to place the final fastening in the garboard strake. He took the opportunity to announce, to a large crowd of sponsors and supporters, shipwrights and friends that he would provide a guarantee to enable *One and All* to receive the Ship's Bounty payments in advance.

The tools used in the construction included adzes, large chisels and power planes. Construction and scantlings conformed to local twentieth century practice for the construction of large timber fishing vessels rather than nineteenth century practice for the construction of cargo vessels. Kel aimed to save weight without sacrificing strength, so instead of massive timber floors, which are equivalent to joists in a house, we used bronze floors, cast for free in the workshops of Australian National Rail in Adelaide.

Karri, another Western Australian timber, was used for the ribs, for the stringers, the horizontal timbers which would lie inside the ribs, and for the girts of the workshop structure. These timbers were purchased at cost from the Forest Department of Western Australia, which also waived the royalty on the tons of two and a half inch thick Jarrah planking. The laminated Karri ribs were placed eleven inches apart. Each rib consisted of four, one inch by four inch planks, up to twenty feet long. They were steamed for three quarters of an hour, in a steel steamer box manufactured on site. Each one inch thick plank was independently steamed and then hurriedly passed and carried to the crew inside the growing skeleton of the

---

16   The workforce, 1982-1986 was as follows: Bill Porter (Master Shipwright), Jock Geddes, David Nash, John Ford, John Hayter, Keith Brimson, Debbie Kschammer, Craig Haynes, Phil Jackaman, Donna Akselsen, Faith Mason, Bruce Porter, Nigel Campbell, Alison Parkin, Trevor Copeland, Lucinda Casttanelli, Graham Hodges, Alexandra Fricker, Greg Baldwin, Daryl Henley, Vince Jones, Darren Whelan and Scott Parker.

vessel, where they were temporarily laminated with clamps to begin with, and then nailed with steel nails to ensure that the rib retained its curved shape as it dried out. Finally, steel nails were removed, one at a time, to be replaced by copper bolts.

Jarrah planking for the rounded bottom of the ship was kiln dried in Western Australia. Bunnings delivered the timber at cost, which over a distance of 2,693.3 km, was a valuable saving for *One And All*. A flying visit to Tasmania by Bill Porter secured a few flitches of Huon Pine for the transom, and part of the topsides, but the rest was Celery Top Pine, much cheaper, stronger, and more plentiful than Huon Pine, almost as rot resistant, and it shrinks very little across the grain. It was delivered for free by the Holyman shipping company of Tasmania as deck cargo.

The shape of each plank had to be spiled, using a thin batten, and copying the shape of the sister plank on the other side of the ship. The edge of each plank was planed so as to allow the inside edge to fit the adjacent plank perfectly. A bevel was cut on each plank edge to leave a caulking gap, of an eighth of an inch on the outside of the ship, and inside the plank with a perfect watertight fit.

We bought copper rod, $^3/_8$ inch in diameter, and made bolts and threaded them by hand. Much of the early metal work was done by Donna Axelsen. She cut the copper rod with a hacksaw, heated one end of it with an acetylene torch and then put it in a huge and powerful metal vice, and used a heavy ball peen hammer to shape the rounded head. Then she turned the six inch piece of rod end for end, and cut the thread to take the nut, with a washer underneath it. The crew would eventually attach each plank to a four by four inch laminated rib. Such work is monotonous, as well as skilful, and was shared, so the crew changed jobs so that they learnt a range of skills by the time the work was completed.

At this stage, in August 1984, our financial situation was complex, reasonably healthy, but unpredictable. We received over $100,000 worth of donations of goods and services in kind. The Marketing Unit had raised about $50,000. The State Government gave us a small grant to enable us to continue to pay people who had worked for a year on the Community Employment Program, thus ending their entitlement. We received a new grant from the Community Employment program to cover wages of twenty-three people for another year. Brian Baldwin estimated that the total cost of construction would be $1,000,079. Of that, the Commonwealth Government would have supplied about half, including Wage Pause, Community Employment Programs, and Ships' Bounty payments. According to our calculations the shortfall when she was completed would be $205,512, and that was our fund-raising target for the next two years.

In 1984, I wrote a small book, which turned out to be a mid-project report on how things were going, with a promise that all the proceeds of the book would go to the wages fund to keep the CEP crew employed so we could continue the work until the ship was launched and ready for sea. I called it, *A Touch of Magic, The Building of the One and All*. The title was borrowed from Bill Porter's pitch during his televised interview with Ross Bray of Channel 7 in the program *State Affair* in May 1984.

> Ross Bray: *Can you tell me why you want to build a ship like this?*
> Bill Porter: *Oh it's a magic job, building a wooden boat.*
> Ross Bray: *But can you tell me why?*
> Bill Porter: *Well there's all the feeling that goes into it, the actual planking for instance, when you're planking a timber boat… you can actually feel her going through the water. That's the magic of it.*

All the copies printed sold out quickly, and it may be that the message Sir Francis Drake to his ship's company as they prepared to sack Cadiz on 19 April 1587, which I put on the last page, pushed the project on a bit:

> … it is not the beginning of any great enterprise, but the continuing of the same until it be thoroughly finished, that yieldeth the true glory.

By this time global forces of many kinds were beginning to make life difficult for local activities all over the world. Our discussions with the Commonwealth Department of Transport had led us to believe that *One and All*, being the first purpose-built sail training vessel in the country, would become the prototype of the species, and that her construction would set the precedents. Kel would in effect become a consultant to the Department, in drawing up the rules. This would have been a really good idea.

That plan had been overtaken in 1983, when Australia incorporated regulations for Sail *Training* vessels into the Universal Shipping Laws Code, which was, I thought, an early manifestation of what globalism could do to stifle local initiatives. The Commonwealth decided that Trainees were not crew, but technically, passengers; and passenger vessels must be made of steel. But since the construction of the wooden *One and All* was already under way, and had been funded to a large extent by the Commonwealth Employment Program, it was eventually agreed that exceptions could be made. In fact many exceptions were made. It was a time-consuming process, as each exception had to be justified on its own merits, after hours of discussion. It meant visits to the site by the designer and local surveyors, and sometimes me, to discuss the practicalities of making changes on the run. It required great ingenuity, a spirit of co-operation on the part of our surveyors, and determination of everyone involved not to allow twentieth century bureaucracy to override the product of a millennium of experience.

But it did mean that an ultimate cost blow-out was inevitable. The basic philosophy of the design had to change. The decision to enlarge the ship to an overall length of 100 feet had seemed a good idea at the time, because of the Ship's Bounty. But it put us in the category of "passenger" vessels, that must have five steel, fireproof, and watertight bulkheads, which in a copper-fastened wooden ship, makes for a lot of potential electrolytic problems and extra expense. It meant, too, that instead of the natural ventilation of some of the European ships that joined the First Fleet Re-enactment in 1988, with wind chutes down the hatches, and a cool breeze blowing through the ship in the tropics, *One and All* had to have a forty horsepower diesel generator, which would be going a lot of the time, as well as a four hundred horsepower auxiliary engine. The matchless sensation of the silent power of a large sailing vessel would be a rare experience.

✧✧✧✧✧

Somehow, I managed to hold down my job while *One and All* was being managed and built. The early 1980s was a period of unprecedented re-organisation and new thinking about the role of Universities in Australian society. Hugh Stretton had become frustrated by the amount of time he had to spend, as Head of the History Department, on administration, when he wanted to complete several books. In 1969, he decided to take the then unusual step of resigning from his role as Chair of the History Department, in order to fulfil his destiny as a scholar, when he produced some of his best books. This triggered the eventual establishment all over the University of what became known as "Departmental Government": the transfer of power and responsibility from "God Professors" to elected Chairs of departmental committees, which were made up of the whole of the teaching staff of each department. Most members of the History Department came to expect temporary election as Head of their department, sooner or later.

My straw was drawn in 1983, right in the middle of *One and All*'s joys and sorrows. I became the Chairman of the History Department for the next two years. I welcomed the opportunity to have a voice on inter-departmental matters in the University's Education Committee, and thought it was the duty of the department to attract good students. So I did some research to discover what kinds of employment History graduates could expect, and encouraged employers of many different kinds to consider the intellectual qualities that historians could provide for them. I collected statistics of the current employment of historians, and published a small pamphlet *What has History got for business; What's business got for history?*[17] I argued that historians were good at critical thought, research, discovering causation in human affairs, judgement and writing; and could therefore be useful planners, critics, and leaders in business, as well as in their traditional roles as teachers or civil servants.

I always took seriously Peter Dickson's vision of the university as an egalitarian society of seekers of truth. And so I welcomed the expansion of departmental democracy. The student union was running a campaign to have student representatives included in the departmental staff committees that were then the governing bodies of the departments. The History Department staff were divided, largely on the basis of age, I thought. And when it came to a motion in favour of the inclusion of two undergraduates into the committee, the debate lasted for a long time. The department was divided equally and the resolution to include two student representatives in the Committee of the department passed, but only with my casting vote.[18]

But during my time as departmental Chairman, I was unable to show as much leadership as I should have, because of the other lanes in my life diverting me. Without

---

17 Young, J M R, History Department, University of Adelaide 1983.

18 Committee Minutes, 20/6/1983, *cit* Dare, R, "Power," in Prest, Wilfred, (Ed) *Pasts Present: History at Australia's Third University*, Wakefield Press, Adelaide, 2014, p 53.

the excellent work of the office staff, the History Department could have suffered considerably. I admit that academic administration and even university politics was not my forte. My colleagues nevertheless supported my extra-mural activity. Firstly they supported the initial aim of ketch restoration, in the 1970s, and then the eventual tasks in the 1980s of getting the *One and All* into the water, and later my work teaching environmental studies. They deserved, and received, my gratitude.

At home in the hills, Ruth and I made many friends and began to feel that we were members of an interesting community. We had very happy and co-operative relationships with our neighbours and we found Norton Summit an enjoyable place to live. We became members of the local co-operative organisation, the Ashton Co-op, where we could get advice about shearing our sheep, or pruning our fruit trees; and where we could buy essential equipment for fencing.

Another institution of even greater importance was the Norton Summit Country Fire Service (CFS). Training sessions were attended at weekends and we practised lighting fires in the spring, to learn about how to put them out before the dangerous period of very hot weather began in December. Voluntary membership of this organisation was, of course, automatically expected of the able-bodied. It was also a way of building, preserving and protecting a rural community. Many of us, including me, spent most of our daily lives in the city, but being members of the CFS made us feel like countrymen, and protectors of our neighbours as well as ourselves.

Practice fire drill left much to the imagination, but one year we were provided with a natural fire on a fairly cool day around the end of January. It wasn't much more than a grass fire, but we felt rather clever when we used a combination of back pack pumps and "flatos" to tackle it. Our neighbour and benefactor, Bob Bolton explained to me how, as a beginner, he had been confused when ordered to "Get the flatos!," and had looked vainly for a flat hose, which he imagined to be a flat canvas thing that would be rolled up and unwound when needed. This time, he told me with some pride, as a man who knew what was what, that the "flato" was a flat hoe, which we used to pull soil over burning grass, and so deprive the little fires of oxygen.

Ash Wednesday, 16 February 1983, was not so easy to deal with. I went to work as usual, in the Chevrolet truck, with half cases of cherries to take to the East End Market, across the road from the University. The sky was grey and the air still, but by the time I arrived at my University office it had become humid and threatening. I had no lectures to give that day, just a continuous day of tutorial groups and appointments with individual students. By the end of the first tutorial, about 10.30 am, the sky was darker still, and I went to the History office for the tea break, only to see my worried colleagues listening to various radios in the common room, and discussing the weather situation. I rang the Bureau of Meteorology for a forecast, and received a report, that there was a large fire at Clare. By early afternoon it had moved south to the northern Adelaide Hills. I rang Ruth, who was busy filling the gutters with water, plugging the drainpipes, putting buckets of water in the roof cavity, pumping up water from the creek to fill the water tank next to the house and listening to the repeated and increasingly threatening scenarios on the radio. She told me what she was doing to prepare for the fire. I stuck a notice on my door to tell the students I was going home, and told Ruth that I was on my way and would be with her soon.

I was not able to drive fast though, because of the traffic density that increased the stress. At last I hit the bottom of the Old Norton Summit Road, and wound my way up the hairpin turns through clearing smoke as the wind direction strayed and the smell of burning bush became more alarming. At the summit itself, I was stopped by a man with a white garment over his uniform of some kind. He told me I could go no further ahead, and must go either left or right. I told him I had come home from the city to save my wife who was alone in my house less than half a mile away, at the end of Nicholls Road, waiting for my arrival. He let me go through, and I drove through the smoke along the rough road as fast as I safely could.

Coming into the back yard Ruth was there putting clothes, personal documents, tools, and the cat and the dog, into the back of our station wagon as fast as she could. I put the Chev straight into the shed where it belonged, took the hose off the ground where Ruth had put it and cooled what I could of the house which I quite expected to burst into flames any minute.

Then came the change that characterises the arrival of a cold front in South Australia. The wind suddenly moved from north west to south east, but there was no sign of rain. I looked up the valley to its southern end. There was an almighty roar and the fire front itself suddenly lit up the hill about four hundred yards away and then travelled down the valley towards the house. Just at the bottom of our driveway was a dam, above the place where the road crossed the creek that took water from the dam. The face of the dam, next to the driveway was covered with dried out blackberries, which I could see would erupt in a mass of flame if nothing was done. Above the burning blackberry bushes, near the house was an ancient Radiata pine tree, where generations of children had swung on old rubber tyres. The tree gave shade to most of the backyard.

The dog and cat were already in the car and we had moments to choose between a very quick getaway, round the corner below the house and back north beside the creek. Or alternatively, we could get inside the house and use it for protection.

Just as I had thought it best to run the gauntlet by getting into the car with the animals, and driving away, the wind changed again, this time from south to east. The air was suddenly filled with twigs and branches whipped off the trees on the east side of the creek and blowing across the valley over the top of the house. With the broken twigs and branches came the fire itself, or so it seemed, as the grass and bracken up the eastern side of the valley caught alight, leaving the house itself unscathed.

Once the fire front passed, we were alive and well but the house was still in danger. It seemed as if there was a secondary fire down in the bottom of the valley, while the introductory fire storm had been content to scare the wits out of us, leaving us to ponder on the need to control the growth of blackberries in the future.

That was all very well, but we could see that the secondary fire was mopping up the remaining growth on both sides of the driveway to the back door, and would soon reach the big pine tree. It would then burn, and possibly explode, inevitably falling on the house.

We took buckets down to the dam. Ruth filled them and poured the water into the fire-fighting knapsack on my back. My job was to prevent the fire reaching the growth on each side of the road, by drenching the roots of the fire with a device that looked like a bicycle pump, and stopping it reaching the unburnt grass, bracken and blackberries, underneath the big Pine tree. I aimed at the base of the fire to put it out, with plenty of water, moving from the growth closest to the big tree, and then following up with the next bucket full.

Each full knapsack took about one minute to empty, which gave Ruth time to climb up the dam, fill the bucket, come down the slope and fill the knapsack again. It was hard work, but the realisation that just then, only we could save our lives, was equally powerful. After about half an hour, we could see that vegetation that had been drenched was no longer catching fire again. The time eventually came, when we felt half dead, but we could follow up with the hose from the tank that Ruth had pumped water into. We gave the whole area a good drenching. Our young dog, Darwin, seemed a bit disappointed that we hadn't gone for a drive, but waited until we lay down, to lie across the foot of the bed, and waited until the children came home from the university.

The follow-up of the fire by the Government and local authorities was quick and efficient, as were the insurance companies. Real danger has the power to bring out the best in people, and organisations. I was asked, as Chairman of the History Department to recommend that staff who had been affected by the fire, be given paid leave in the next few days, to enable them to attend to their properties and their personal affairs.[19]

The worst part of the fire for us was the sight of our normally human-shy sheep, black rather than white, attempting to walk towards us on their burnt hooves, in great pain. We lost all our sheep, and most of our fences and fruit trees in the Ash Wednesday fire, but we were so much better off than so many other people in South Australia and Victoria, who lost their lives, houses or livelihoods.

✧✧✧✧✧

As if *One and All*, the Chair of the History Department and repairing the damage caused by fire on our property were not enough, at this time, I discovered another lane. I blame Hugh Stretton for this. Hugh wanted to go on his long-delayed study leave to UK. He asked me to take over his job of giving a series of introductory lectures, entitled "Environmental Synthesis," the core subject of the Master of Environmental Studies course. The course had been established largely as a result of the contribution Hugh had made, as a member of the founding committee of

---

19   Mc Neill, Registrar, to Young, Chairman, History Department, 23 February 1983.

the Centre for Environmental Studies in 1970. Its aim was to provide an opportunity for Bachelor Degree Honours graduates, to bridge the gap between the Arts and Sciences. This had become manifestly necessary, if the wide range of the earth's environmental problems, and their infinite ramifications, were to be understood, let alone solved.

At that time, the Masters course was open only to students with Honours degrees in a science subject. It also included a short thesis, to be supervised by a lecturer in the "appropriate" Science department. All the departments in the University thought they were appropriate, except Dentistry and Music.

The Environmental Studies students themselves, however, in 1975, had written a series of essays. They called them "The Green Papers," and presented them to the Inter-Faculty Committee in Environmental Studies. The students argued that while individual subjects, and specialised research, could solve many individual problems, students would find it difficult to determine the many and various **causes** of the current "State of the Earth," without an understanding of several Arts subjects, like geography, economics, law, politics, sociology, philosophy, anthropology and history. In retrospect I think a study of literature, art and drama would also have revealed some important truths, and relevant considerations.

By this time I was developing an interest in environmental problems; both local and global; and I had begun to read the current surge of environmental literature. I spent a lot of time when riding my bike, or sailing *Leofleda,* reflecting on the experiences in Fiji that had made me think about the growing environmental crisis.

I admired the Fijian notion of *Vanua*, the habitat of land, sea, reefs and oceans, of which Fijians feel themselves to be part, rather than owners; and for whose welfare and social sustainability, humans were responsible. Many other indigenous societies have similar ideas. While recognising the legitimisation of autocracy that chieftainship implies, and which even some of my Fijian students themselves rejected, I appreciated the implication of humility as members rather than masters of the earth. I began to warm to the ideas and argument of James Lovelock in his book, *Gaia: a new look at life on Earth*, and of new environmental specialists, such as Barry Commoner, Rachel Carson, Alan Schnaiberg, Fritz Schumacher, David Suzuki and Hugh Stretton.[20]

The annual conference of the Australian and New Zealand Association for the Advancement of Science, was due to be held at the University of Queensland in Brisbane in May 1981, so I submitted an Abstract of the paper I wanted to give. I called it; "History, Science, and the Environment." It was accepted; which meant I had to write the paper, and that scared me a bit. Science had never been my strong point.

---

20 Lovelock, J, *The Closing Circle: Confronting the Environmental Crisis*, London, 1972; Carson, Rachel, *The Silent Spring*, Boston, 1962; Schumacher, E F, *Small is Beautiful: A study of Economics as if People Mattered*, Blond & Briggs, London, 1973; Schnaiberg, Alan, *The Environment: From surplus to scarcity*, Oxford University Press, 1980; Hugh Stretton, *Capitalism, Socialism and the Environment*, Cambridge University Press, 1976.

I enjoyed science, and did reasonably well at it at school, but it was taught first to me by a Christ's Hospital teacher, who photographed me in my Tudor school uniform, holding an outsize puffball as big as my head. This was the man who later wanted to photograph me in my red bathers, and nothing else. I was relieved to be able to drop science after getting my O level certificate, when I was sixteen.

All over the country, and probably the world, the problems of how Environmental Science, as it was usually called, should be taught, and by whom, were being considered. Governments and universities were influenced by the works of scientific writers who drew attention to the need for scientific education so that the threats of large scale pollution, population growth and global warming could be understood.

Existing schools and departments of indisputably scientific disciplines saw the onset of an environmental crisis, in the 1970s, as an opportunity for departmental expansion, and it was a natural gift to chemistry, physics, mathematics, and earth sciences. Geographers had always regarded ecology as a sister discipline, together with climatology and geology. But it was not long before courses in environmental law and environmental engineering became popular, together with architecture. Funding applications that contained the word "environmental" had a good chance of success in the allocation of staff and funding.

Anthropology, archaeology and economics could all claim to have relevance to the subject of the environment, if you thought about it, together with botany, but history was excluded, often by historians themselves. I thought this was strange, since historians are concerned with change over time, and what has caused it. Historians had not generally contested the sovereignty of science, but it had become evident, since the flurry of concern about the environment in the early 1970s, that the inability of reductionist science, alone, to do anything more than apply band-aids to individual problems (such as holes in the ozone layer, or protecting threatened wildlife habitats) had been demonstrated. There were no technological fixes that could overcome the recurrent famines in Africa, almost continuous warfare somewhere on earth, massive refugee movements, or worst of all, the phenomenal increase of inequality throughout the world. These, I thought, were the historical, political and ethical issues, at the core of the environmental crisis.

I gave the paper at the ANZAAS conference, in May 1981, at the University of Queensland to a full house, and it made an unexpected impact. Discussion was short, because I had spoken for too long, but I was told in the tea room that my paper should have been classified as a "keynote address," and should have been given more oxygen. Several scientists from the University of Adelaide asked for copies of the paper, and it was widely read and discussed within the University, which gave me a lot of confidence.

The question of where the Adelaide University's Centre for Environmental Studies was to be placed for purposes of administration was a top agenda item for many meetings of the Education Committee during the next few months. It was decided, eventually, that Environmental Studies should be placed in the Faculty of

Arts, at least as a temporary arrangement. Dr John Hailes was appointed as the first Director of the Centre in 1975. By 1981, Ken Dyer became Director. I was seconded from the History Department to the Centre for Environmental Studies for one year in 1984, largely on the strength of my conference paper and my lectures in Environmental Synthesis.

I think that there was some kind of psychological and emotional connection between my new concern for the environment and my continuing interest in wooden boats. It was a passion that probably originated in my distant childhood, and had been periodically encouraged by two sea voyages between 1934 and 1939, to Africa and back, and then making, and sailing, toy boats with my father, and moving on to playing with real ones. Dugout canoes in both my bath, and then in Freetown harbour were, to me, unsinkable miracles, because they were made of wood. My three voyages as crew of *Leofleda*, the Thames sailing barge, gave me enormous food for thought, as we carried around 100 tons of wheat or flour between London and Colchester without using any kind of fuel. Instead we studied the tides and watched the weather, relying on the wisdom of Captain Sheldrake, who never thought of his environment as a force to be feared, or mastered, just to be understood and put to good use; through experience and knowledge.

On the *One and All* front, I knew that John Bannon, the Premier of South Australia would be anxious about the chances of *One and All* ever being completed, but he was equally anxious about his chances of victory in the coming election, which was to be held on 7 December 1985, a week after *One and All* was to be launched. I thought he might feel that his presence, by the sea at North Haven, at six o'clock in the morning, with an enormous crowd of people, would be a political advantage. By the beginning of December, *One and All* had her hull completed, and her big diesel engine and fuel tanks installed. There was still an enormous amount of work to be done, but she could travel on her own bottom. National Rail, which had carried her keel from Kyogle, had also prepared a railway underneath her, and a cradle around her. The plan was to launch her and take her up the Port River to the McLaren Wharf where she would be seen by thousands of commuters every day. So I asked John Bannon if he would like to attend and speak at the launch, and he agreed. I was glad, because I thought his patronage would be decisive for both the ship and the Labor Party. And so it turned out to be.

In summer, the tides at Port Adelaide are low around the middle of the day and high around sunrise and dusk. On 1 December 1985, high tide was at 6 am. Dawn brought a bit of thunder and a bit of rain. Ruth and I had slept in the back of our truck under cover, with our Labrador dog Darwin, for warmth, that Saturday night, to make sure we were there for the top of the tide on the Sunday morning. A sense of occasion, and much urging over the previous few days, by media people like Keith Conlon and Carol Whitelock brought a crowd, later estimated by the Police Force at 10,000, to North Haven that morning. Premier Bannon was surprised to find himself immobilised at the back of an endless queue of cars on Lady

Gowrie Drive. He was a successful marathon runner in his spare time, and ran the last half mile to get to the ship in time to catch his breath.

The Premier had made a commitment to provide a loan to complete the build. The launch was his chance to remind the crowd of his determination before the election. My job was to provide a thankful introduction. This is some of what I said:

My task is to give thanks, but the tide commands me to be brief, so I won't recite a list of all the many hundreds of people, the builders, the volunteers, the sponsors and government departments, and the South Australians they represent… Such a list could never be complete. Instead, I'll explain how it comes about that so many of us are sufficiently demented to be standing here in the early morning on the sea shore when we could be still in bed. The reason is that everyone here is either a builder or a sponsor or a volunteer… or a taxpayer, whose taxes made the community employment program a reality.

I have a memory of quoting St Ignatius about the importance of fighting but not heeding the wounds, and that kind of thing, when covering our history of political struggle with the Jubilee Board. I thanked the Board:

Because they have compelled you to maintain your enthusiasm and a touch of that productive rage that is needed to ensure the sacrifice of time and thought and work this ship has needed, and will continue to demand… The building of a wooden-hulled sail training ship is a means of addressing the problems of an ailing society on several levels. She will commemorate an under-valued maritime heritage, and at the same time provide a public education in aesthetics, craftsmanship and the intelligent use of renewable resources. The post-industrial society of the future will not need, nor will it be able to afford, increased mindless "productivity," in order to finance the social welfare, prisons and asylums required in a fractured society. Among its needs will be work that is interesting and creative, in order to reduce the need for social welfare, asylums and prisons. This was a community achievement that we should all be proud of and that is why it will ultimately succeed.

When John Bannon had come to the ship the previous year, to drive a ceremonial bolt into the garboard strake, he had also announced that he would guarantee to enable us to receive Bounty payments in advance of completing the ship. At the launch, he was more cautious, but made an optimistic and very competent speech, and won the election.

John Ford's partner, Marguerite, smashed a bottle of champagne on the bow and *One and All* began her journey down the railway. Once in the water, but not yet afloat, she stopped.

Luckily there was a couple of bulldozers standing by, chartered by National Rail especially for the occasion. One driver sprang onto the driving seat and placed the giant blade firmly against the base of the cradle and began to push *One and All* further into the water. Soon the water came up to the tracks and covered them but the ship still failed to move any more. Two bulldozers were then used. The exhaust of one was, happily, a vertical chimney, so the crowd began to cheer the driver on, while the owner of the machine began to yell at the driver to stop. But the driver was being cheered on by 10,000 people with hundreds of cameras in their hands, and so to the cheers of the massive crowd, he persisted until the water covered the tracks of the bulldozer completely. And at that moment, *One and All* began to move, and the crowd roared with joy as her engine in reverse pulled her gently out of the cradle. The builders stayed on board for the delivery passage to the Mclaren Wharf, where she was to be rigged and fitted out.

The Advertiser had by this time taken a leading role as the teller of an increasingly interesting story, very much in the Australian tradition of the eventual victory of the underdog. Shortly after the launch, the reporter, Christabel Hirst visited the ship lying alongside the wharf in Port Adelaide, and wrote a slightly premature, but very powerful article.[21]

The heading, was "He read the wind, set sail and brought the One and All home safely," with a photograph of me with a big smile on my face in the foreground. I was very grateful, but the truth was that the worst part of the adventure was still to come. The ship had debts to pay. Without the continued support of the South Australian community and government, the dedication and resourcefulness of a mixture of both old and new volunteers and committee members, without the work of my successors Dick Fidock and Malcolm Kinnaird, post-launch manager David Addison, and John Ford, who founded and managed the Supporters' Club, *One and All* would not have survived, and thousands of young people would have missed the adventures of their lives.

I had hoped that the moment of launching would be the end of my personal contribution to what then looked like success. I originally and optimistically made a commitment to lead the Jubilee Sailing Ship Project for two years, but it had already stretched to five. I'd been holding down a day job running the History Department, as well as lecturing on a new subject, in the Centre for Environmental Studies. I was also on call round the clock, and the calendar, for the building of a ship. But there were others willing to take over. I was likely to lose my entitlement to my accruing research leave if I neglected to take it. So at the end of 1985, when my secondment to Environmental Studies ended, I resigned as Chair of the History Department, and of the Jubilee Sailing Ship Project, and applied for study leave in which to get back into my research, this time to write a book about Environmentalism. I soon discovered that my background in history and wooden ship building was relevant to many aspects of environmental politics and management.

---

21 *The Advertiser*, 4 December 1985.

Chapter 16: "Earth might be fair and all men glad and wise"[1]

I continued to fill in for Hugh Stretton, teaching the introductory Environmental Synthesis course, while he took Study Leave with Patsy, his wife, and then returned to the History Department. We corresponded while he was away. He paid a visit to Cropton, the Yorkshire village I still regard as the place to which I belong. Hugh evidently loved it, and sent me a post card:

Except perhaps for the weather, we can't think why you left. The country around about is beautiful! The Postman, regrettably, doesn't remember you, (he's a mere lad). Thank you for the map, Love to Ruth.

Then he asked me if I had kept any notes of the lectures I had been giving in Environmental Synthesis while he'd been away. Of course I had notes. Unlike Hugh, who was celebrated for his ability to walk into his lecture room with his hands in his pockets and just start talking, while making eye contact with all the students he was talking to, I always needed at least a list of prompts to consult now and again. Hugh suggested that I must have enough material to be able to work on a book. Sensing, perhaps, that I might need a bit of pushing, to convert my very rough notes into a publishable form, he offered to read each chapter as I wrote it. And he would send them back with comments.

What an offer! I thought, from a man of such eminence and intellectual stature. I started immediately in case he changed his mind. The University had an internal mail system. This was before email came into regular use, and Hugh and I fell into the ostentatious habit of always using the same paper envelope, delivered by the internal mail system, to send the drafts back and forth between us, as if to demonstrate our ecological righteousness. We did no damage to the earth this way. The envelope lasted out till we reached Chapter Five, "Small is beautiful, but can we afford it?" Hugh sent it back in a clean, new envelope, complaining that there were limits to virtue. If we kept on with the original envelope much longer, we might lose the next chapter. Hugh's comments were, I'm glad to say, mostly complimentary, and his suggestions were very useful.

One day, Iain Stevenson, a visitor from Belhaven Press in Britain, walked in unexpectedly, searching for people with manuscripts of new books. With Hugh's encouragement behind me I promised, having decided on the general structure of the book, that I would send him a draft manuscript of the first chapter as soon as possible. That was not going to be very soon. Ruth and I had already made plans, including research for the book, for long overdue study leave combined with recreational leave.

It was hard to get away from administrative duties. In May 1986, I was asked to visit the Institute of Advanced Studies at the Australian National University in Canberra, which wanted me to assist in a review of the Department of South-East Asian and Pacific History. We arrived in Canberra on 18 May, and I wrote my

---

1 Hymn, by Clifford Bax, 13 July 1886, 18 November 1962.

report, based on a long list of interviews, before going on leave on 21 May. I felt honoured, but very weary.

So Ruth and I began our journey by flying to Auckland, where there were some links between radical environmentalism and Maori culture and where Garth Rogers was living, close to Auckland University. Garth was by then, married to a Fijian woman, Alanieta Waqaniu. She was the niece of Asesela Ravuvu, the Fijian anthropologist who had worked with Garth in Fiji. We were also delighted to meet Myra Rogers, their two-year old daughter. Myra was expert at hitting on various ways of maddening Garth when he was trying to bath her or feed her, such as climbing about on furniture, or laughing while rolling on the floor, until Garth was at his wits' end. When she was certain that she could make him really enraged if she wanted to, she would suddenly smile very beautifully, and say, "'K Garth" and climb onto his knee.

Garth had settled somewhat, and had an enviable reputation as a lecturer and a prolific writer of articles and reports of his research on Fijian and Tongan cultures. All three of the family came to meet us at the airport. On the way back to their home, Garth, who was driving, got into a joyful mood, and started to sing, and then began to clap his hands, in time with his song. Alanieta seemed to be used to this dangerous behaviour, but in the end just said, "I'll clap Garth, and you sing."

Next day they took us up to a wonderfully beautiful piece of land, well into the North Auckland Peninsula, beyond Kaukapakapa, where at last, I could have a look at the giant Kauri trees that had drawn me to New Zealand in the first place. This was where they planned to build a house, amongst the trees and in sight of the ocean. They had already planted an orchard there. Later on, when we were in Fiji, we paid a visit to Asesela, who said that Garth would often talk about his plans to go north and build a house on "The Land," a place where he might retire in his old age and live a country-based, self-sufficient life, with his family. "But," Asesela said, with emphasis, "He won't do it!!"

Garth was an extraordinary man, both a scholar and an adventurer. He lived a very useful life, infecting his many students and all his friends, with enthusiasm about everything he did. But I think he must have known, in 1986, when we saw him last, that he was slowly dying of cancer. He had a lot in common with "Saint" David (Kew), as we called him, with his practicality, generosity and unselfishness. Garth died in 1989. I knew then that my dream of a collaborative inter-disciplinary history of Lau was beyond my reach. I continued to write more articles about Fiji from my own perspective, and my colleagues did the same, but from then on, as I learnt more about the environmental crisis, I used my study of Fijian society as an example of intelligent relations between ecosystems and humanity.[2] My father would probably have told me that I was going down another lane, which is one of my weaknesses.

---

2   Young, J M R, "Lau, A windward perspective," *JPH*, 28, 2,1993, and "The response of Lau to Foreign Contact," *Journal of Pacific History*, 28, 2,1993. *Sustaining the Earth*, Harvard University Press, 1990, Chapter 2, "The real garden of Eden."

Another factor at this time was our daughter, Susan. While doing a Bachelor of Arts in Asian Studies, she had taken a year off to teach English at the Chengdu College of Geology in Sichuan, China, to improve her Chinese before returning to complete her degree. After graduating with first-class honours in History and Asian Studies, Susan returned to teach in Chengdu again, as during her first year there she had fallen in love with Shaohua Zhou, one of her Chinese students, in his final year of a Masters degree in Geology. They wanted to get married almost immediately, and wanted us to come to their wedding.

Shaohua had been sent to work in the countryside after high school like others of his generation, but was among the first cohort to sit the national university entrance exams when they were reinstated after the Cultural Revolution. His academic performance was broad and exceptionally good, but this did not mean that he had a wide choice of career. In China, that was something to be decided by the perceived needs of the State, rather than his own. Shaohua was allocated a place at the Chengdu College of Geology, in the south west of the country, and trained as a geophysicist specialising in oil exploration.

We booked various means of travel to enable us to get to Chengdu for the wedding. We flew from Auckland to Hong Kong and then caught a river ferry, inland to Guangzhou, where we stayed in a very modern and gracious hotel called the White Swan. It was the most luxurious experience of my life, not so much because of the modernity and architectural splendour of the building, but because of the intense hospitality of the staff. It took some getting used to.

Stephen decided to come to China from Melbourne where he lived. Next morning we probably caught a taxi (I'm not going to pretend I have remembered everything) to a large, mostly grass covered airport. The airport building was made of corrugated iron and it was very crowded. It seemed to take a long time to get to the side of the building with fenced exits onto the bitumen. Some hundreds of people stood waiting in a large paddock with a roof on some of it, and a guarded exit where travel documents were inspected, until an official (we called him a Red Guard) walked and climbed over luggage, and people, to the exit gate.

We walked past him on to the open field before us, and soon found ourselves herded on to an open vehicle, with standing room only, which took us, it seemed, about half a mile, to where our plane was waiting to take off. All the planes faced in the same direction and took off in quick succession. We were then quickly served with small cakes in a cardboard box, to keep us going.

Susan arranged for us to stay in guest accommodation at Chengdu College. Before we left Australia, she told us that their student wedding was going to be a very modest affair. She explained that at that time in China the official marriage registration process was about as ceremonial as registering a bicycle. Couples then had a small party to announce to the world that they were married. Once we arrived in China, however, it turned out that Susan did want to have quite a Western-style ceremony, with vows, and after we had asked her enough questions about what kind of wedding she wanted, we realised that what she was getting at was something very like the Anglican Marriage Service.

So Stephen and Ruth and I sat down and tried to remember all the words that Susan wanted, leaving out the obedience bit. None of my children had been to more than a few church weddings, and I was only an occasional church goer. Carmel was a Catholic, and had told my parents that she had no intention of attempting my conversion. But I was happy about Susan's instinctive respect for Christian ethics, and the principles of Christian marriage.

Susan had made her own dress of Chinese silk, with a pattern I had picked out in Adelaide with her friend, Clare. Since Susan's feet were too big to fit into the white shoes available in China, we also took a pair of those (which miraculously, fitted perfectly), plus a Western-style wedding cake made by Ruth's mother. After a very pleasant dinner with Shaohua, his parents and members of the Geology College staff, the wedding itself was celebrated the next day in Susan's living room and included some traditional Chinese activity, like holding the bride up in the air so that she could pluck a bouquet of flowers from the ceiling with her teeth. They seemed to have a lot of good friends, some of them have stayed in touch with both of them, in spite of a lot of movement around the world. We managed to remember most of the Anglican ceremony, and in spite of my lack of either ecclesiastical, or secular qualifications, I had the honour of presiding as "priest" as they took their vows to each other, and declaring them to be man and wife. My words were translated into Classical Chinese by Shaohua's friend, Yu Jiashun.

I assumed my role as priest was to be a one-off, but some years later, I did it again. An American student and his girl-friend asked me to officiate for their informal wedding, before the real thing happened when they returned home. The ceremony took place in 2004 on Roaring Beach, near Dover, just outside the entrance to the estuary of the Huon River. Then the bride and groom and all the guests went swimming with a pack of local dogs and the seals and dolphins.

Susan and Shaohua returned to Australia, where they both won PhD scholarships at the University of Adelaide, she to research the development of private enterprise as China's official communist economy opened up, and Shaohua to continue in geophysics. Susan soon obtained a lectureship in the Adelaide Asian Studies Department. Their first and second children, Lindsay and Helen were born in Adelaide. Then Shaohua obtained a job as Assistant Professor in Geophysics at the University of Copenhagen, and there Karen was born. Ruth and I visited them in 1995.

In 1986, Chengdu was a rapidly growing city, close to a large river and an ancient monastery. We saw a track cut into the cliffs on the side of a gorge. It had been made centuries ago to enable large numbers of people to act as tugs, pulling barges upstream with long ropes against a powerful current. Human energy was still the power that facilitated a lot of industrial development. In Chengdu itself, coal was transported along the streets by often quite elderly, but very fit women.

They rode low geared tricycles, attached to carts, each carrying what looked to me like half a ton of coal.

Ruth and I travelled on to London, after arriving at Heathrow in June. We caught trains to Horsham and stayed with Heather, her husband, Ken Goodare and my nephew, Julian. Heather and Ken met each other at a camp, where they soon discovered a shared passion for Classical music. Heather was a leading fiddle player since her school girl days in the English National Youth Orchestra, and Ken was an equally competent player of the clarinet. We arranged to later hire a cottage together for a week at a little town called Gweek, at the head of navigation of the Helford River in Cornwall. Heather was interested in the plan to send *One and All* to sail to England to join the First Fleet Re-enactment back to Australia, and was helping with British contacts and publicity. We had a restful few days with them in Horsham before setting off for Ludham in Norfolk for a holiday on the Norfolk Broads.

The Broads are the old peat quarries of medieval England, that rain, tides and time, have turned into shallow, but navigable lakes. This time, instead of repeating an earlier trip up the Ant River to Barton Broad, where the youthful Lord Nelson learnt to sail, we sailed south, in the wake of Arthur Ransome's Coots,[3] to the southern broads, linked to each other by the Yare and Waveney rivers.

The Broads are renowned as just about the safest place on earth to learn how to sail. The flat landscape provides steady winds. The river banks are mostly soft, and the worst that can happen to an inexperienced sailor is to run into the reedy bank. Getting off it is simple; just drop sail and push the boat back into the river with a "quant," a long pole carried on the side deck, used also in calms as a punting pole to shift the vessel along until the wind comes back. The more difficult parts of the Broads are the lower reaches of the three main rivers, Bure, Yare and Waveney, which are tidal. So to get to the big rivers from the north, you have to navigate through Yarmouth, with its bridges, tides, and hard edges of man-made obstacles.

Most Broads hire craft now have auxiliary engines, and as they approach the bridges, sails are lowered and engines started. The only problem then is the lowering of the mast to get under the bridges. It's much more satisfying, though, to do without the engine altogether. Fortunately, the boat we hired was a *Hustler*, built in the 1930s, with no engine. We followed the example of the Norfolk wherries of the past which, for lack of good roads, carried cargoes of rural produce to the towns of Norwich, Yarmouth, Potter Heigham and Wroxham, and took back urban products and luxuries to the small villages until well into the 20th century. If you have your timing right you will go across the meeting place of the Bure and Yare, the inner harbour of Yarmouth in effect, at low tide. Then you can hoist the mast, raise the sails and jill about until the railway bridge opens to let you into Breydon Water.

The thing is to work the tides; and rely on renewable energy, mostly the tidal kind, as you get near Yarmouth. If the tide is still running fast you must tie up to the bank when you still have some distance to go before you come to the first

---

3   As described in Arthur Ransome's *Coot Club* and *The Big Six*.

bridge. You get your mast down, which is easy because it is stepped on a tabernacle—a couple of strong posts joined together, and rising about two feet through the deck in front of the cabin. The mast pivots on the tabernacle between the two posts coming up through the deck. Lowering the mast is easy because of a heavy leaden weight on the bottom end the mast. When the mast is lowered the lead ballast comes up through a hatchway on the foredeck; to balance the weight of the long mast, as the top end is lowered onto a pair of crutches, which look like a big wooden pair of scissors, on the stern deck.

As soon as the tide slows a bit, you get going before it starts to flow in the opposite direction. Shove off the bank and put the mud anchor (a ten kilogram deadweight) on to the bottom of the river over the bow, but hold onto your chain so that it drags slowly along the soft and muddy bottom of the river. Then use the tiller to steer backwards, stern first. You can control the direction you go in, by letting the anchor just slow you up a bit, but have the water still running past the boat. If she goes too fast, put out more chain, and she will slow up. If she gets into deeper water and speeds up too much, let out more chain and you can stop, if you want to. It's a trick Norman Sheldrake taught me, on a bigger scale in *Leofleda*, the Thames barge, in 1948, and it helps to combat global warming, as well as being much more fun than starting a noisy engine.

We went on to explore as far as Lowestoft, where the International School of Wooden Boatbuilding was established. I was most impressed with the atmosphere of commitment and excitement, as young people worked on several boats at different stages of construction. Some of them, at least, expected to work at Hunter's Yard when they graduated. The spark of wooden boat revival that began in Maine in 1974 had, it seemed, jumped the Atlantic. Apprenticeships in wooden boat building

Cruising on the Norfolk Broads in *Hustler II*, 1986.

were becoming few and far between, but it seemed that dedicated schools like this were filling the gap. As Jon Wilson remarked in his first editorial for *WoodenBoat* magazine, "wood is, after all, the only renewable building material on the planet."[4] I began to think about wood as material for the future.

When we returned, I had work to do in London for my new book. We stayed in what was then known as "London House,"[5] in Mecklenburgh Square, right in the centre of London. It was established in the 1930s as a residence for research students and roaming academics from distant parts of the British Empire. It was set up on the lines of a University College, with twin sleeping rooms and communal meals at regular times. It was cheap, and placed in a leafy square, close to places like Australia House, and the British Library. Australia House was useful because it received copies of all the major Australian newspapers, and this included *The Advertiser* from Adelaide. One day, I dropped in to read the paper and found that *One and All* was running into financial trouble.

We learnt later that new international laws relating to the safety of passenger ships had been introduced. Sail training ships were counted as passenger ships, and wooden ships were at a disadvantage because it was necessary for those that were the size of *One and All*, to have five steel bulkheads, not only to prevent flooding in the event of collision, resulting in a hole in the vessel, but also to prevent fire spreading through her. My *One and All* colleagues in Adelaide at first thought that construction would have to cease, to save money, while negotiations could take place, on the grounds that the new laws should not apply to vessels that were under construction before new laws were introduced. The young men and women who were very close to completing their job were dismissed. But there was a photograph in the newspaper of their march through the streets of Port Adelaide, and a story of their decision to continue to work as volunteers until their task was completed. Bill Porter also worked for free, and I received a letter from David Addison, a retired school teacher and old friend who had taken on the job of managing the administration side of the organisation. He told me that there was a proposal that, because of the inability to pay off the debt now owed to the State Government, *One and All* would have to be sold, just as her completion was within reach. This was what the street march was all about.

David Addison was managing the attempt to complete the ship in time to sail to Portsmouth to join the First Fleet. He wrote to us: "Don't worry. They'll have to drag me away in chains before I'll quit." I hated the fact that there was nothing I could do to make much difference to the Port Adelaide situation, except to tell David that if he could hold on until I arrived home, I would pull out all stops when I got there.

London House was a useful place, with its own library. As we walked everywhere we had to go, we were able to clearly see the downside of Mrs Thatcher's economic philosophy. London was full of beggars. Rubbish collectors were on strike and bins and skips were overflowing onto the footpaths. People were living with

---

4   *WoodenBoat*, Vol 1, No 1, 1974.

5   Now Goodenough College.

extreme poverty, in cardboard boxes and sleeping on park benches. We felt we were extremely fortunate to have an Australian job that included travel allowances, gave us access to wonderful libraries and other research opportunities, and enabled me to have a go at suggesting how some of the problems of the world might be solved, and get paid for it.

There was also the vibrant atmosphere of a big city full of cultural experiences. One highlight was the contribution of a group of residential American students, who put on a performance of Mozart's *Marriage of Figaro* at the height of summer, not in a theatre but in Mecklenburgh Square and under a starry sky.

When our work in London was finished, we wanted to travel cheaply to distant parts of England, Wales and Scotland, to visit a number of environmental, alternative energy and organic agriculture establishments (also wooden boat building schools). So we answered an advertisement for a tandem bicycle, in kit form. The reason for getting the tandem instead of two bikes was that Ruth had problems with circulation in her legs. With the tandem, I would be able to do most of the hard pedalling. At the same time her exercise would be useful to her, whenever she could manage it. If she had to pedal too hard she was prone to painful cramps, but she could free-wheel until her legs were better. Before leaving Australia, we bought a British Rail Pass, which enabled us to cover some of the distances, particularly through busy industrial areas or big cities, by rail, with the bike in the Guard's van. All the local explorations could be done by bike. We could carry everything we needed in pannier bags, with a tent and bedding rolled up and lashed on. The only place we could assemble the bike and keep it, was in the corridor, outside our bedroom in London House. Nobody seemed to mind.

We were happy to leave London. We took the bike on a train to Penzance and from there rode to Gweek, which is near to Falmouth, to join Heather, Ken and Julian. With them we explored the south Cornwall coast from Gweek to Land's End. I had already been in touch with Pete Greenfield, who lived in Gweek. He was the founder and editor of a new periodical, *Classic Boat*, which in many ways, was an English equivalent to America's *WoodenBoat*. In anticipation of *One and All*'s eventual arrival in Portsmouth in 1987 as part of the First Fleet re-enactment, I had written an article about the political problems of building her. I hoped for publication in England if possible, to enable her, perhaps, to attract some English participants for the voyage back to Australia.[6] I visited Pete at Gweek. He liked the article and it was published in *Classic Boat*.[7]

Heather and Ken had a car, so we went on several day trips from Gweek to a few of Cornwall's magical coastal villages. One of them was Padstow, because we wanted

---

6   *One and All* couldn't make it to Portsmouth in time. We decided to take the Suez route, through the Mediterranean and across the Atlantic Ocean to join the fleet at Rio de Janeiro. She arrived in Sydney with the rest of the fleet on 26 January 1988.

7   "One and All: The practicalities and politics of building a wooden sailing ship in South Australia." *Classic Boat,* No 4, September 1987, pp 25-32.

to see where Bill Porter came from. It was also a place with a good surf beach nearby. We learnt that the beach was under threat from a new sewerage scheme. Heather told us that a group of local people planned to stage a typical "demo," as we would have called it in Australia, and as the would-be author of a new book about the environment, I felt it was a good opportunity for some fieldwork in the area of eco-political activity.

The protest took the form of a mass swim by protesters of all genders and ages. There were some body-surfers, and a few good board riders, though the surf was small by most Australian standards. There was a police presence, but of the most democratic kind, which was good for the media coverage and brought political power to the occasion. The story did get into the local newspaper, so we all felt that we had done something useful with ourselves though I failed to follow up the story and I never found out whether the developers or the local protesters were victorious. We had left our clothes on the beach and joined the demonstration dressed for swimming, and when we were dressed again I rummaged in my pocket for my wallet and found it wasn't there. We went back to where we had last opened the car door before we went swimming. It wasn't there either, and I began to worry about my credit card and all the implications of losing it so far away from Australia. We drove in silence to the Padstow police station, and there, of course, it was. Some honest English person had handed it in.

My youthful experience of prolonged cross-examination in the police station in New Zealand, in 1952, had given me a bad impression of constabulary behaviour. That had reversed my Irish experience in 1951, of having my windcheater recovered, with my wallet in its pocket, thanks to the good Irishman who picked my stuff up off the road between Castlisland and Abbeyfeale and gave it to the local police station. I was delighted with my good fortune, and although I still had some resentments of England from my schooldays, I felt that it was time to get over them. If I could lose my wallet, not once but twice (so far) in my lifetime, from my pocket, and get it back again because of somebody's personal honesty, there was still hope, I thought, for the planet.

We left Heather and her family in Cornwall, and, with a large leek sticking out of our pannier bag, we caught trains to a station in the south of Wales and then found our way by bike to Machynlleth. This is the home of the famous Centre for Alternate Technology, set up in an abandoned slate quarry and founded in 1973 by Mr Morgan-Grenville of the Society for Environmental Improvement. Like the ethos of Fijian chiefs, its central doctrine was the identification of mankind as part of nature, rather than its master. The Society also promoted grass roots democracy, that was not specifically socialist. It had become rapidly famous as a tourist attraction, for people who wanted to learn about consistent ideas of different kinds, such as using renewable energy. Dwellings were built out of renewable materials, especially straw bales and rammed earth, as opposed to mud. Public toilets contributed to compost, and energy was supplied by windmills, water-mills and early solar panels, feeding a site-wide energy grid. There was a vegetarian and vegan restaurant, and a green bookshop. Soon, it was to become a tertiary educational institution, running practical courses, and issuing nationally accredited qualifications. Some of the public literature told me that "The Centre doesn't set itself up as some kind of Utopia... Just to point out some sustainable ways of living gently on our planet. Despite our weaknesses, people seem to like that."

The Centre also ran short residential courses, and a volunteer training program for people who wanted to work there. A volunteer guide told us that they were getting fifty thousand visitors a year. The community at this time, consisted of around thirty people, all on the same wage, with extra for families. Ten acres of small holdings were farmed organically using human waste composted with bracken and returned to the soil, "much to the disgust of fastidious visitors." We were told that:

...people who come expecting some sort of technopark can get quite cross about the peace badges and socio-political "nonsense" displayed alongside the heat pumps and windmills. They feel that technology is somehow politically neutral; it isn't!

Much stimulated, we kept going north, after cutting across the industrial heartland of England with the marvellous British Rail timetable to guide us. Ruth soon found that the truth of it could be relied upon, and began to plan days ahead accordingly. Our friends, Nick and Jackie Wright, had other friends, Simon and Sally Barham, who lent us their holiday house at Brancaster Staithe. This is an ancient medieval port on The Wash, very much exposed, geographically, to Viking raiders in the past. We settled down to enjoy a bit of English country life, and local exploration on the bike. It was a part of England that I had grown up knowing about without going there.

I have two unforgettable memories from our stay in that part of England, both of them about animals and their relationships with humans. Our neighbours, two elderly women, were custodians of the Barhams' house. They had a grudge against the local moles, who were living under the front lawn of the house we were living in. The ladies explained that they were accustomed to poisoning our moles. There probably was a reason for this, but we didn't know it. Not wanting to create some kind of stoush with the ladies, I felt it wise to simply cover up any evidence of mole nocturnal activity early each morning and say nothing about it. The ladies were very kind to us. They showed us how to catch shrimp with a push net at low tide and we had shrimp on toast for lunch. They also taught us about the dietary value of samphire grass.

On our return trip to London, we spent a night with Simon and Sally and met their ageing black Labrador, Titus. I volunteered to take him for a walk next morning and he couldn't have been more excited about the idea. After the walk (not a very energetic one for either of us), Titus immediately limped into the next room, and returned, dragging his bed, a huge bean bag. He dumped the bean bag at my feet, which I consider about the highest honour a Labrador can pay a white man, and some kind of award for good ethical behaviour. I think this is the wonderful part of travel; the people, and sometimes dogs, if you are lucky, that you meet, and all the things they can teach you.

By this time, our British Rail Pass had well and truly paid for itself. It meant that all our onward travel was free. We set off for a visit to the Scottish island of Iona. When I had been to Iona with my Aunt Molly as a twelve-year-old boy, it was mainly a religious experience for her — a search for the spirit of St Columba, who had brought Christianity from Ireland to Scotland, and started building his Cathedral on Iona before St Augustine brought Christianity from Rome to Canterbury. This time, I wanted to go to Iona again partly for sentimental reasons, but mostly for research for my book. Iona was an isolated place and imported large amounts of fossil fuel to meet its heating and transport needs. Being a cold place, at the very extremity of the national electricity grid, the island suffered from frequent power cuts. The Iona Community is primarily a Christian institution. In conjunction with the Iona Renewables Group, it has focussed its vision on providing, among other things, renewable community-owned energy from a range of sources.

We rail-cycled, and camped our way into Scotland, heading for Oban on the west coast, where we departed by steamer to the island of Mull. The ship was fully loaded with young families and couples. We cycled from Tobermory down the Ross of Mull, a peninsula pointing to the south-west of the Island. At the end there is a ferry to the holy island of Iona. It was one of our best rides, with mountain and water views all the way. We had a puncture, and had difficulty mending it, as we had no patches left. We took the wheel off and used a piece of a plastic rubbish bag, recycled from the roadside, to repair it. This was still working when we sold the bike in London, several weeks later.

I loved remembering Molly, to whom I had not written often enough from New Zealand, which made me tearful. We pitched our tent on Iona's holy beach where we could fall asleep to the sound of the Atlantic surf.

After returning to Oban again in early September, we went south by train and explored the bits of England where I had grown up but had almost forgotten. So we went to York in various trains and then cycled to Cropton, and went down to the mill where I had launched my first boat, *Discovery* 2, in 1943, just before I started prep school at Christ's Hospital. I told the householder who had recently bought the mill house and farm, that I had spent a lot of my early child life with Russell Clark, the man who filled the gap left by my father's absence in Sierra Leone. Russell had helped us to carry *Discovery*, from the main road to the mill pond. The new owner was extraordinarily hospitable, and happy to know more about Russell, who came from Ireland, but joined the British Royal Navy at the start of World War II, and was regarded as a war hero by all the young people of Cropton, who had come back from the war themselves, in 1945.

I went to the Post Office and shop in the main street, and a middle aged woman who I didn't recognise said, "Are you back then, John?" She turned out to be the sister of my friend Adrian Feaster. I wept again. Then I went up to the Court House, built in 1699, that my parents had bought at the end of the war. My mother had begun to modernise it without getting the process very far. It was well equipped with electricity instead of Aladdin kerosene lamps. There was a bathroom upstairs with running water, hot and cold, instead of a zinc tub on the sitting room floor with a kettle on the hook over the fireplace for hot water in the bath. We also met Adrian "Dicky" Feaster himself in the street and we had a good talk about old times during the war. I went in search of the pond where I had sailed my model boats, but it had been filled up when it was no longer needed as a reservoir for the village. That made me sad.

From Cropton we rode to Whitby, as I had done several times with my family in the war years, and found it virtually unchanged, with its off-shore fishing fleet, and the smaller, beach-based fleet of wooden cobles of traditional design; light enough to be launched from a beach, and hauled up above the high water mark at night. They could be sailed with a dipping lugsail as well as rowed. Then to Malton, and the Organic Farmers and Growers Co-op at Needham Market, to learn about the growing popularity of organic horticulture in both Britain and Europe.

We returned to London from York on the Flying Scotsman. I remembered my experience as a schoolboy, rehearsing my received English pronunciation, for fear of being mocked, after speaking only the North Riding dialect during school holidays. After spending a few days with our old friends, George and Judy Knapp, in Wimbledon, we rested our tired legs by going to a musical performance at the Barbican, staged by Neville Mariner, and including Vivaldi's "Gloria," a Beethoven Chorale, and an American collegiate wind band performance.

We resumed our search for environmental source material by getting onto a plane with our round the world tickets, and flying to the United States. The plane was very late, and we spent many hours reading and walking about. Finally the imminent departure was announced, to the cheers of an angry crowd at the end of its rope. At the boarding ramp we had an amazing, uniquely American experience. A man stood at the entrance to the air bridge, handing out $US100 notes to each passenger entering. Fury immediately gave way to appreciation and smiles of delight, as we found our seats, discussed how we would spend our "compo" money and just relaxed. I excused myself for participation in the dumping of carbon dioxide into the atmosphere, by concluding that the planes would go across vast distances, whether I was aboard or not. How much better for Gaia it would have been to travel by sailing vessel. I hoped that readers of my new book would understand.

We landed in La Guardia airport, New York, on 24 September 1986. My list of American friends was growing with Angela Woolacott in Santa Barbara, Marshall Sahlins, in Chicago, and Mary Emily Miller in New England. Our next stop was Boston, where we met Mary Emily Miller, of Salem, Massachusetts, who taught history at Salem State College. She had booked a bed for us at the Boston Yacht Club at Marblehead, and arranged a sail for us with a colleague in the afternoon. We spent our $200 compo from the delayed flight, to hire a car, and drove to Boston to meet Chuck and Alice Carlston. We had met their daughter-in-law, Mary Crowley, from Sausalito, California, when she visited the nearly finished *One and All* in 1985. I was keen to use her talents as an organiser of sailing cruises. Mary spent the night with us, when she visited Adelaide, and we kept in touch. When I told her we were planning to visit Maine, she told Chuck and Alice, who happened to have a "cabin" near the little village of Freedom, and we were invited to make that our base in New England. From there, I could write my book in relative peace, and learn a lot about the wooden boat revival in America.

We found our way to Chuck and Alice in Boston, collected a key and instructions and set off to drive two hundred miles to Freedom, Maine. It lies amongst a group of engaging small communities. All of them have a strong recognition of their historic importance and original colonial identity, reflected in place-names such as Liberty, Hope, Knox, and Albion. Driving was taxing, as neither of us had ever driven before on the right side of the road, or on such mighty highways. Eventually, we found a wayside restaurant and as we had not eaten for a long time, we welcomed the rather large meal. At first, that is. There was a lot of meat and vegetables and a bucket of potatoes. Less than half way through we began to flounder, and asked the waitress for a "doggie bag." We could see that we would get at least two more meals out of the leftovers.

The Carlstons' cabin was a long way into the woods, reached by my careful attention to written instructions. We were already staggered by the warmth and hospitality of everyone in America that we had met, and the cabin was as wonderful as we had come by then to expect. I thought something like "country house" would be a more appropriate description, but it was a genuine log cabin with traditional interlocking corners. There were several rooms and a very efficient wood stove that was perfect for the onset of Fall, with its carpet of leaves and astonishing range of colours.

Two minutes walk brought us to the "pond," which in Maine usually means a body of water left by melting ice at the end of the last Ice Age. These vary in size between that of a tennis court and what would be called a lake anywhere else. There was a canoe, of typical North American Indian style, with paddles kept in the house. We went for a paddle the next morning and had the privilege of meeting a beaver in a corner of the pond. Then we met Laura Pines, a young woman, who was living in a tepee, beside the pond, with her baby. Laura lent us a heap of musical tapes, which included the best of Haydn's symphonies. We invited Laura to come and have a meal with us. She soon introduced us to her local friends and her fiancé, who was a doctor. We also met a self-taught wooden boat-builder who was building an ocean cruising yacht that he had designed himself, in the corner of a paddock where he had assembled the ingredients of a temporary boat yard. He planned to sail around the world. I admired the spirit of adventure, and evidence of competence, as he worked and talked to us at the same time. It recalled my reading of Joshua Slocum and his solo voyage around the world in the 1890s.

Each of the local villages had shops that sold traditional wood working and boat building tools such as the drawknife and adze. The other items of interest were the local museums and libraries with closed reading rooms in which I could read the logs of locally built ships, describing voyages and landfalls in the south seas. We visited some coastal villages as well, including Rockport. I had read about Lance Lee and his Apprenticeshop in *WoodenBoat* Magazine and I wanted to meet him. I had an idea at the back of my mind, that should I retire early, I might investigate the notion of becoming a professional boat builder. I learnt a lot from Dave Kew, who made me promise to pass on what he had taught me to at least one other person. But I felt that I needed a lot more experience before I could contemplate doing such a thing. This turned out later to be another lane.

I found Lance in his office next to his workshop and asked him about his courses. I told him of the building of *Leofleda*. The children were grown up after all, and we would be free to go anywhere. I explained that I was conscious of my lack of experience, and recognised the fact that building one boat doesn't make you a boat builder; only experience can do that. That was why traditional apprenticeships used to take seven years. Lance said I was welcome to enrol, but he would not advise it. "You know enough now to teach yourself," he said. "Just build some more boats. And there are plenty of books if you get stuck." Ruth was inclined to agree, so we forgot about it. For a while.

The little town of Liberty was another small community with atmosphere, and a very good museum and library in the main street. I was drawn to the famous Liberty Tool Company, in search of an adze. This is a tool that can easily be mistaken for a high class weeding tool, as many of them, all over the world have often become. But this adze was the first I had ever seen in a shop. It looked new, and was sharp. It was small, and no doubt dangerous in the wrong hands, but I would be able to get it on a plane and get home with it, and learn how to use it. It is lovely to hold too, so I bought it and I still have it. And I have learnt to use it. It's much quieter and has a much nicer sound, than a power plane. Nearby was a small two-man cross cut saw, just the thing for cutting up logs, which I couldn't resist, as they don't seem to be made any more.

Our next stop was going to be San Francisco, but we took interior planes within the USA, and this meant landing at Denver, Colorado, where the cross cut saw was challenged as cabin cargo. "You can't take that on the plane!!" said our female Afro-American customs official: "You might cut someone's head off!" The "someone" whose head I might have cut off would have to have been a very co-operative soul. Nevertheless, the saw went in the plane's belly to be collected at the other end in San Francisco. I felt quite lucky about that. We hired a car and booked a cheap hotel in San Francisco for the night. Unfortunately, we left the car unlocked as we ferried our luggage to the hotel. When we got back to the car, the saw was sadly, gone.

This was the end of our study leave and holiday. We returned to Sydney in one hop, arriving on 4 November 1986. Much to my surprise, the familiar face of Wally Franklin, founder of the First Fleet Re-enactment Company, was there to greet us, with Captain Ken Edwards, who had heard about the progress *One and All* was making towards her completion. Edwards had won a Churchill Fellowship to visit England and had conducted an investigation into the activities of the Sail Training Association, for the benefit of Australia. While there was a new generation of seamen and women studying to complete their qualifications, Ken Edwards was the only person in Australia, at that stage, who was qualified to take a square rigged sailing vessel with passengers, and/or students, to sea.

One and All had only two square topsails on her foremast, but still needed a skipper like Ken, licensed to sail square-rigged sailing ships. Thankfully, the committee I left behind me had hunted Ken Edwards down, and contracted him as captain of the vessel for the voyage from Port Adelaide to Portsmouth, round Cape Horn, up the Atlantic and then back, by way of the Cape of Good Hope, to Sydney. *One and All* had to time her journey to arrive at Sydney Heads on the evening of 26 January 1988, exactly two hundred years since the actual First Fleet had arrived, with its company of soldiers and convicts, and orders to claim British sovereignty over half the continent, and "the adjacent islands" of the South Pacific.

Wally told me that financial problems were now getting serious, but the success of Jonathan King in gathering support, and financing the re-enactment of the voyage gave *One and All* a timely opportunity to utilise the First Fleet as an exotic maiden voyage, which would greatly improve our financial situation. Jonathan King had spent much of his time during the building of *One and All*, getting financial and political support for the assembly of an international fleet of sailing ships, to re-enact the original voyage to Sydney Harbour in 1788. Like our relationship with the State Government of South Australia, Jonathan encountered similar problems with the Federal Government of Australia about the great re-enactment. Both relevant Governments refused to consider community-based efforts to pull off such feats as anything more than embarrassments, but both of the voyages succeeded in the end.

One and All was the only Australian-built vessel to join the Fleet. I felt sure, as did Jonathan, that most of the Aboriginal population of Australia would feel that the very idea of celebrating a successful invasion by a distant foreign power was inexcusable, but I also thought that the aim of finishing *One and All* in time to join the First fleet in Portsmouth and sail her back to Sydney would gather support, and ensure that she would be finished for the voyage. In the end, it was an advance of $50,000 from the First Fleet Re-enactment Company, that encouraged the South Australian Government to loan a final $250,000 which enabled the ship to be completed.

The contract to join the Re-enactment was the reason that the state Government was prepared to give us a further loan, with which to finish building the ship. There wasn't much time to talk with Wally before our plane left for Adelaide. After the seemingly victorious situation I'd left behind, I felt I should try to help. I had accumulated three months of long service leave, so I took it to enable me to concentrate on salvaging the project.

The familiar drive from the Adelaide airport always seemed welcoming as we climbed the twisting road to Norton Summit at the top of the hill. Over the crest we plunged into another older, quieter world, from which the city and expanding suburbs down below were invisible. My son Philip, now a young lawyer, and his partner, Felicity Playford, training to be a teacher, had been looking after the house while we had been away, and all was as it should be, including the black Labrador, Darwin, who was glad to see us.

Next morning was the beginning of a period of extreme anxiety. I set off to the city to see Mr Dick Fidock who had taken over my role as Chairman of the *One and All* Association. He welcomed me back and told me that he was seriously ill. And when I volunteered to attempt an exercise in crisis management, he gave me his blessing, while pointing out that the alternative was a "fire sale" to pay off the tangle of debt that had accumulated.

On the ship herself, the atmosphere was much better. Money for wages had run out, but David Addison, the then unpaid manager, had assembled a heroic team of volunteers, who were still working on board; Noni Howard, a cabinet maker and artist from Tasmania; David Nash, who had been working on the vessel since before the keel was laid in 1982; Sam Gibbs, who joined the crew during the second Community Employment Scheme; Tom Vosmer, from the United States; Noel Doepel, who came across from Melbourne after working there on the restoration of *Alma Doepel*, and Igor, a rigger from Denmark, who had also worked on *Alma*. George Herbert, who had sailed a wool clipper from Port Adelaide to London in his youth, worked on the spars and rigging for nothing. John Ford was still working, unpaid, as fund raiser, and tour guide.

For me, as agreed "temporary crisis manager," it was essential to create a situation in which it would not be politically easy for the State Government to foreclose, and thus cause the sale of the ship. This meant working full time to co-ordinate volunteer work on her, while raising support from the media, and re-gaining the confidence of the First Fleet Company. Gifts came out of the blue, including that of a benefactor, who lent us $30,000 without interest, to go into the wages fund.

On 1 December 1986, Wally Franklin sent a telex to the Premier's Department, offering an increased payment from the First Fleet Company provided that the ship could get to the start of the voyage in England. Another anonymous benefactor also offered to contribute to bridging finance, on condition that the State Government, and the city of Port Adelaide would do the same. It was essential to persuade the Premier's Department, and our sponsors and creditors that the ship would be finished and on her way in time to fulfil the Re-enactment contract, and so to place her on a reasonable financial footing.

I was told that interest on the Government loan was due to begin on 31 December 1986. If we began paying interest, we would not have enough money to finish the ship. Without the prospect of a completed ship, and her participation in the First fleet Re-enactment, we could not raise any money. Therefore, unless credit could be extended we would have to liquidate, and the ship would have to be sold.

John Harrington, of Touche Ross, an old friend of Sir James Hardy, now came into the picture. On 4 December 1986, he was asked by the Premier to call a meeting consisting of Tony Lawson of the Premier's Department, Wally Bean and Amanda Bohlman of the Community Employment Program, and me, representing *One and All*, as Dick Fidock was unwell. John Harrington provided us with office space, paper, desks and telephones.

We were asked to produce a business plan for the voyage to Portsmouth and back to demonstrate that it would be a profitable enterprise. Christmas holidays were suspended while the five of us worked literally day and night for a week. For me, with no experience of organising anything more complicated than a department of a University, it was an educational experience. We succeeded in producing a two hundred page plan, detailing the cost of completing the ship, getting her to Portsmouth, and paying back her debts. This involved looking beyond the First Fleet voyage to the sail training activity for which she had been designed and built.

John Ford, who joined the team in 1982 through the Community Employment Scheme, had been co-opted to the new committee, by the Chairman, Dick Fidock. John started up a Friends of *One and All* Association. *One and All* became the centre of its universe, and the essential leadership needed to save the vessel from a fire-sale, had grown to embrace a large proportion of the South Australian population. John Ford's efforts, by the end of the year had raised $49,000, proceeds of a ball, several raffles at the British Hotel, auctions, ships visits, and public appeals. News of this activity in the centre of a busy port drew media attention, which was a great help. It demonstrated the degree to which the fate of *One and All* had become part of political life. The media played a generous and supportive role in the building and completion of the ship. The ordinary people of South Australia gave so much time, money, labour and moral support, that the momentum was maintained. Without this support, the State Government could have snuffed us out with a stroke of a pen, or even the touch of a keyboard.

On 20 January 1987, Premier John Bannon announced that "financial arrangements would be made with the Association for completion of *One and All*, and her participation in the First Fleet Re-enactment." The Premier then appointed Malcolm Kinnaird as the manager of her completion, and her maiden voyage. Malcolm then generously asked me how I felt about it. I reminded him that I had actually resigned from the Chairman's job in December 1985, expecting that I would no longer be needed. I was most grateful to both John Bannon and Malcolm Kinnaird for seeing *One and All* through to completion. As it turned out, she was not completed in time to start the homeward voyage with the rest of the fleet from Portsmouth. She made a late start, and chose the Suez Canal route, through the Mediterranean to Gibraltar. She finally caught up with the Fleet at Rio de Janeiro and sailed back with the fleet to Australia. But it was not until the end of the century that *One and All* was debt-free. Now, 32 years after her completion, *One and All* is busy and solvent.

Wally Franklin and Jonathan King very kindly invited me to join the ship's company of *One and All* for her entrance to Sydney Harbour. They arranged for *One and All* to anchor in Botany Bay the night before and pick me off the beach. I managed to book bus trips from Norton Summit, South Australia to Botany Bay, New South Wales. The bus rides were a bit of an adventure in themselves. I was there on the beach at a specified early time in the morning as the Fleet drove up the east coast with a southerly wind. *One and All* dropped anchor not far out in the Bay and sent an inflatable to get me. Soon, I was asked if I would like to take the helm, an enormous compliment, and of course, I did. We were near the after end of the growing procession of hundreds of sails, and I enjoyed the morning immensely with the Fleet spread over a square mile of water, with more craft joining us as we neared the Harbour entrance.

Before the ship left Adelaide, I gave Noni Howard, the Tasmanian craftswoman and artist, who had spent months working on the ship without getting paid, a copy of a document I wrote, in the hope that during the Re-enactment, an occasion might arise at which it could be read aloud or passed on to some radical news reporter. I would have been delighted if the Aboriginal flag could have be hoisted to the head of the mainmast on arrival in the Harbour, as a courtesy to the Aboriginal population. Unfortunately it was lost somewhere, between Rio and Sydney and no-one had an Aboriginal flag. I kept a copy of the undelivered message at home and this is what I wrote:

Two hundred years ago today, our ancestors sailed into this harbour which they thought had no name. And they hoisted a flag. They thought that by doing this, and declaring that they owned half the continent, they had established both a legal and ethical right to its possession.

We now fly, as our courtesy flag, the flag of the original owners of Australia, as a gesture of humility. We recognise the innocent arrogance of our forebears, but we now know the enormity of the cultural destruction, and genocide, which followed from their assumptions. We understand that for Aborigines, there is no cause for celebration, rather a need for mourning and remembrance for the thousands of men, women, and children who have died defending their land and their culture during the last two centuries.

We join in their grief, and we have chosen One and All, the only Australian ship in this re-enactment, to express it, for only by sharing aboriginal grief to the limits of our understanding can we dare to hope, that the end of the next 200 years of European settlement will be celebrated with more honesty than in the last two centuries, and that the Aboriginal people will be able to celebrate as well.

✧✧✧✧

Released from the responsibility of *One and All*, I could get on with my day job at the University and my book, a product of my changing interests and circumstances between 1981 and 1989, and triggered by Hugh Stretton.

Late in 1987, I was asked to head up the Centre for Environmental Studies. In those days the Centre was located on Frome Road on the northern side of the campus.

The full time staff consisted of two lecturers, Dr Ken Dyer and Dr David Corbett. Most of the teaching was in the hands of people seconded from other departments, such as Geography, Law, Biology etc, who considered that their speciality was vital to the solution of the world's problems, and rightly so. I went to the Centre and asked Ken and David if they would be happy to have me brought in from the History Department as their Director. Both agreed, and welcomed me as their future colleague. Pam Keeler, former secretary of the History Department for many years, and my great support during my period as Chair, had earlier moved from History to Environmental Studies. The fact that Pam would be Secretary was an important part of my decision to accept the Directorship.

I received a formal letter from the Vice-Chancellor asking me if I would accept a temporary secondment from the History Department to the Centre for Environmental studies:

I am writing to confirm your secondment to the University's Centre for Environmental Studies, for the period 18 July to 31 December 1988 in the first instance, with the possibility of extension until 31 December 1990. During the period of your secondment you will be the Director of the Centre. I should be grateful if you would confirm in writing that you will proceed with the secondment and accept the appointment as Director.

I replied that I would be happy to be the Director, but on two conditions. Firstly, that a current plan to review the Centre must be postponed until I had led the Centre for at least a year. Having a review earlier was clearly a ploy, I thought, designed to lead to a conclusion that the Centre should be swallowed by the Geography department. Secondly, I asked to be assured that I should return to the History Department at the end of my period of secondment. Both requests were accepted, and so I accepted the post. The Centre soon began to attract more postgraduate students than could be accommodated, and plans were being made to move it to a much larger and more public building, on the corner of North Terrace and West Terrace.

My long study leave in 1986 had introduced me to a lot of new thinking, in England and America as well as in Australia. My book was about "environmentalism," including a history of the environmental movement and environmental ideas throughout the world. It examined the attitudes to their environment, of cultures that had clung to their pre-industrial values and heritage, enabling them to survive the onslaught of modernity.

It considered the religious factors in the development of the western assumption that the world was created for the benefit of humans. The history of the relationship between science and society from the twelfth century to the present day was summarised. I argued that science in western societies was useful in the study of many individual environmental problems, but was often, and increasingly, the source of many problems, as well. While acknowledging the benefits of scientific research in many areas, I argued that science alone was likely to create new environmental and social problems, as a result of intellectual reductionism.

I looked at the effects of capitalism. If left to itself, without democratic control, it inevitably created inequality, which in turn led to war, terrorism and poverty and environmental destruction. I recommended tactical diversity based on ecological regional differentiation, and local control of resources by ethically motivated regional democracies. The hope was that successful change could be best demonstrated at a local level, in line with favourable opportunities, that are not understood by orthodox politicians and developers, and by examples of success that demonstrated the achievement of regional sustainability. Local success driven by social capital would encourage local communities, and perhaps their politicians, to take control of their local economies, rather than handing local resources or initiatives over to the international or corporate dominion.

The book ended optimistically, examining the politics of transition from continuous growth to sustainability, starting with individuals, of various political persuasions who may be content to walk to work, for example, to use stairs instead of lifts, grow their own food, but baulk at joining Green organisations. Application of the lessons learnt from small scale local experiments would lead, I theorised, to the adoption of sustainable strategies by such governments as are able to comprehend the perpetual advantages of economies based on renewable energy, community ownership and local democracy.

I wanted to call the book "Earth might be Fair." I interpreted the words of the hymn as a proposition — "Earth Might Be Fair and all men glad and wise?" — in other words, if all men were wise, earth might indeed be fair, and if earth was fair, men could be glad. But they're not and it wasn't.

The book was published in 1990 by Belhaven Press in England, with the title *Post Environmentalism*. I'm still unsure exactly what that means. The publishers were probably unfamiliar with the Church of England Hymnal, and didn't get the idea. Harvard University Press published the same text in 1990, with the title *Sustaining the Earth: the Past, Present and Future of the Green Revolution*, which I could at least understand. In 1992, the University of New South Wales Press published it with the same title.

The reviews were quite good and there were a surprising number of them. One said that my book was "... a message of hope and common sense."[8] Another reviewer wrote that I was:

...aware of the inter-relationship of environmental issues and other issues, particularly that of inequality in the distribution of the world's goods, both within societies and between them, and seeks to find formulas that will resolve these conflicts.[9]

The World Resources Institute publication, "50 of the Best Books on Earth" was generous too, perhaps too generous:

---

8   Wilson, E O, Harvard University, dust jacket.

9   Mann, Dean E, University of California, Santa Barbara.

> *No single-author environmental book of recent years has been more ambitious than Young's. With a firm grasp of environmental politics, on three continents, (North America, Australia, and Europe,) expertise on Pacific Islands culture and a perceptive take on what separates the third world from the first, Young makes the case that Environmentalism, as we know it, is about to die and a new post-environmentalism to rise, Phoenix-like from the ashes.*

Clive Crossley, a Professor of Biology at the University of Sydney and a fellow boat builder and yachtsman, wrote, "I was very glad to see your book is out in paperback as a 'Best Seller.' I've ordered copies for our biology library. Hope you get lots of royalties to keep the Stockholm Tar jar full."

Unfortunately, one can't buy much Stockholm tar with royalties from academic books and I still hanker after my optimistic title, borrowed from an old hymn. That would have been best.

Chapter 17: Career Changes: From Theory to Practice

From 1988 until 1990, I was Director of the Mawson Graduate School of Environmental Studies, newly named in honour of the famous Australian Antarctic explorer. After a great deal of discussion, it had been decided that the Master of Environmental Studies course would be open to Honours graduates, not only in science, but from any department of the University. The Centre would be administered and supported as a member of the Faculty of Arts. The students in 1988 were mostly scientists, from mathematics, chemistry, physics or biology. Some of them came from departments such as law, political science, geography, philosophy, agricultural science and anthropology. None came from the History Department. I immediately found myself dealing with conflicted perceptions of what Environmental Studies was all about. It was like the conflict between the Physical and Social anthropologists all over again.

There were a few members of the University who remained critical of my attempt to define Environmental Studies as a field that included the insights of the majority of subjects in the University Calendar. It was not, like most of the sciences, the product of reductionism, or learning more and more about less and less. But for many scientists, the degree of specialisation was a measure of intellectual status, as it is in the case of medicine, for example.

My view was that Environmental Studies should be largely a study of relationships between different subjects, and different causes of change. Much of the literature, described by some as the "Domesday books," were about the causes of the Environmental Crisis. There was a smaller range of books and articles on what should be done about it. The review of the Centre, which was to have taken place in conjunction with a review of the Geography department in 1987, had been postponed, in response to my condition of appointment, until the second year of my secondment from the History Department in 1989. That would give me time, I thought, to change the Centre from an administrative problem to an intellectual asset. It was to be a review of the Centre alone, not a preparatory ritual for subsequent amalgamation with some other department of the University.

The Centre employed me and five other full time lecturers and tutors; Ken Dyer, David Corbett, Roslyn Taplin, Philip Tighe, and Sandra Taylor. There were ten others, who taught other subjects as well as Environmental Studies. The courses offered were at two post-graduate levels. There was a one year Diploma, which could also become the first year of the Master's course, and a two year Master of Environmental Studies course, which included a short thesis. Until 1988, students were introduced to the courses only through the University Calendar, which outlined the offerings of all the departments of the University. To many potential students, Environmental Studies was a new-fangled enigma, so I introduced a specific, detailed, departmental Prospectus as well. It was printed on re-cycled, unbleached, non de-inked paper made in Australia. The black and white cover pages were adorned with a photograph of two fur seals snuggling up to each other on a deserted beach on Kangaroo Island.

The prospectus was produced and printed on plain A4 pages, consistent with its message, rather than a commercial glossy product. Black and white photographs showed field trips in wooden canoes, exploring the Coorong and the Murray River and in my own boat, *Leofleda*, sailing through the Mangrove swamps near the Small Boat Club. There were other illustrations showing students and teachers in wild places, Australian animals, urban streetscapes, beaches and dust storms. And pictures of the University assets and buildings. This prospectus attracted students from all over the world.

My teaching responsibilities from 1988 to 1990 consisted of giving fifty minute lectures, once a week, followed by a two-hour discussion seminar, in a compulsory, full year course. This was the only regular occasion when all members of each student cohort gathered together. I also supervised a number of theses, and took an interest in others, including a very interesting assessment of the overall environmental impact of cremation versus burial.

Before I was given the Director's job in 1988, I had been teaching the existing series of lectures and seminars, called "Environmental Synthesis." I felt that this was not a clear enough indication of the course content to enable students to approach the subject holistically, or to understand the causes of the impending environmental crisis, or the kind of change in human behaviour that would be needed to counteract the effects of contemporary theory and activity. So I changed the title of the course to the more explicit "Environmental Politics, Philosophy and Ethics." This suited my own search for a logical explanation of why the environmental problems of the world were getting worse, and how the forces behind them could be counteracted.

I was much encouraged by the reviews of my book, and found myself asked to give speeches about the environmental crisis to public gatherings, and then, on ABC Radio for the "Ockham's Razor" program.[1] I was pleased to discover an alliance between my ethical notions and my political preferences. My subject was "Sustainable Economics."

I took exception to the idea that the welfare of society and the welfare of the environment were alternatives, between which we must choose. It is consistent with this view, and with the view of conventional economists, that social welfare depends on continued economic growth and that if environmental priorities like national parks are to be favoured, it must be at the expense of something else, like social welfare, unless economic growth can be rapid enough to produce a surplus big enough to pay for welfare and national parks.

Near the end of 1988, the Commission for the Future produced a report, *Casualties of Change: the predicament of Youth in Australia*. It contained some horrifying statistics: suicide rates for males 15–24 had doubled in the previous twenty

---

1   "Ockham's Razor," ABC National radio, 14 May 1989.

years. Australians in this group took their own lives at the rate of one a day. Robbery, burglary and theft by young people had risen four times in the previous ten years. Rape had risen by 150% in the same period. Family disintegration, homelessness, poverty and youthful unemployment, were all increasing. Our leaders tell us that the reason we have these problems is because our economic performance isn't good enough, because we can't attract enough foreign investment. The authors of a then recent book said:

> *Australia's unemployment and poverty legacy, and the social and economic deterioration that it implies, are direct results in the decline in economic performance experienced during the 1970s and early 1980s.... The sooner output and economic growth are revived.... The sooner the scourge of high unemployment will be removed.*[2]

But after five years of relentless growth, a reduced overseas debt, a $5.5 billion surplus, we still seemed no closer to the promised land. Prime Minister Bob Hawke told us that by 1990 there would be no child poverty in Australia, but most of us were not holding our breath.

The alternative theory, was that it is growth itself, that we should blame,

> *...for the co-existence of private affluence and public squalor, the creation of imagined wants rather than real needs, the relentless exploitation of the earth's non-renewable resources, for poisoning the air and waters, for despoliation of the environment and threats to the biosphere, for crime, violence and drug addiction.*[3]

The connection between all these symptoms of crisis was not immediately obvious, but I suggested they were all related to the problem which had become the flip side of growth: increasing inequality. The role of government in industrialised countries, for the previous three decades, whatever their political complexion, had been to maintain a "balance" between economic growth and social peace, and it was a peace which was threatened whenever a slowing down of growth drew attention to its side effects, the worst of which was increasing inequality.

Growth results in increasing inequality partly because the benefits, such as more expensive cars and luxury air travel go to the rich. The costs, such as polluted air, noise, and the high cost commuting from distant suburbs are felt by the poor, as well as the rich. These are also the effects of big government, big business, and big bureaucracy. If Governments do not favour capital intensive forms of growth, as opposed to de-centralised, diverse and labour intensive forms of growth, they are judged to be inefficient. They won't be able to justify their programs or have the "runs on the board" to impress an electorate, which is trained by big media to value such yardsticks of well-being as Gross National Product and Balance of Payments.

In spite of the numbers, average families in rich countries find they need two salaries, or wages, when one is often difficult to find, in order to maintain the level

---

2   Drake, P and Nieuwenhuysen, J, *Economic Growth for Australia: Agenda for Action*, OUP, Melbourne,1988.

3   Cit Eckersley, R, *Casualties of Change: The Predicament of Youth in Australia, Commission for the Future*, Melbourne, 1988, p 40.

of consumption that they have been insistently taught to achieve. It has only been possible to prevent the development of antagonism between the people at the bottom and top, when growth has been sufficient for the relatively small gains which do filter down to the poor to result in an absolute rise in living standards. This just about offsets the resentment caused by increasing material aspirations, fuelled by advertising, in a context of increasing social inequality.

It's a very delicate balance at the best of times and it's easily upset by the intrusion of things like racism. Treading the tightrope successfully means supporting the building of office towers and casinos and tourist developments, selling off mangrove swamps for the construction of marinas, and at the same time adopting policies that distribute just enough surplus to the poor to avoid too much disturbance, and keep radical politicians out of office. Leaders like John Bannon, Bob Hawke and Mrs Thatcher performed this balancing act very well in times of good economic fortune, based on high prices for minerals and farm produce, North Sea Oil, or full order books in the arms trade, or building submarines. Without these props they know they must expect trouble.

So avoiding trouble in countries like Australia has the joint effect of maintaining present inequalities, and accelerating the degradation of the environment. We have to put up with environmental degradation, the loss of wilderness, pollution and the rest, to make the world safe for inequality.

The second, and related problem of late industrial society is that growth has not, and will not, cure unemployment. Instead of providing a growing demand for labour, a shrinking labour force in the 1990s would be able to produce a mountain of goods for those who had jobs, and could afford to buy them. Those who could not would contribute to the growth of a permanent underclass of unemployed and poorly paid part time workers.

In Britain, America, Japan, Australia and New Zealand, the underclass was already numerous. It consisted, often, of migrant workers living in inner city areas or suburban pockets, often in single parent families, or as homeless children with a low rate of literacy and a high rate of drug addiction, suicide, violence and criminality. They were thought to be unlikely to form the vanguard of a revolution because they were marginal to the economy, and some economists said, their existence is the price that modern society must pay for its "success"!

But the cost to the society, from which this large section of its youth has been removed is enormous. "No

Exploring the Angus Inlet mangroves with Environmental Studies students under sail in *Leofleda*.

Go" areas of the once great and civilised cities of the world expand. "Normal" society closes its ranks, enacts tougher penalties, talks of "law and order," and joins the unions, the police, and the bureaucracy in maintaining as much social distance as it can; which evidently isn't enough.

The problem was how to get out of the mess? I suggested that one way in which a reforming government could start would be by using different methods of accounting. GNP makes no distinction between good growth and bad growth, or the costs of growth. Car manufacturing and crash repairing for example, are both seen as aspects of growth. So are tobacco sales and funeral expenses, whereas one should be seen as the cost of the other. Railways ostensibly lose money and road haulage makes money. Both add to GNP, but having them do that doesn't show which kind of transport brings more benefit, or does more harm. Road transport has more accidents, leading to more deaths, lawyers' fees, lost days at work and insurance claims. Road transport uses more fuel per tonne/kilometre than rail does. Motorways use more land than railways do, land that could be used for residences, recreation, or production or trees. And it causes more pollution.

These things should count as losses. Adding them to growth makes them seem like profits. This kind of accounting explains why the expected benefits of growth never seem to materialise. I suggested an index called Net Human Benefit (NHB). Sailing ships would come out well ahead. The other strategy for reforming governments would be to treat the economy like the wild uncontrolled plant that it is, by selective pruning and by training it to serve socially useful goals by putting ethics into economics.

If, for example, everyone was convinced of the need for fairly drastic action, and it was clear that if this action was to be taken, and there would be equality of sacrifice, some reforms might be possible in a parliamentary democracy. One way of anticipating what might happen in this situation is to consider the history of Britain during World War II. The war itself did a lot more to equalise British society, as it turned out, than the Labour party Government that followed it. And without that increase in equality, the necessary solidarity needed for survival in "Their Finest Hour" would not have been achieved.

The purpose was to wage war effectively, but the side effects were as valuable for the environment as they were for society. Apart from military activity, Europeans on both sides consumed fewer raw materials and polluted their atmosphere and their water less, as a corollary of greater equality. The British Royal Family took the lead by having a line drawn around their bath to insure that no-one bathed in more than five inches of hot water.

Good environmental habits became customary. People repaired things. Containers of many kinds became returnable. Newspaper was recycled. Scrap metal was ruthlessly recovered. People walked, rode bicycles and used busses and trains because petrol was rationed. Marginal urban land was used intensively as householders dug for victory and composting became a topic of over the fence conversation.

The British ration book proved to be what the revolver claimed to be in America, "the great equaliser." It ended the situation in which social class coincided largely with physical size. In Britain more than half the population was better fed during the rationing period than they had ever been fed before. War time children, were usually larger and healthier than their parents and predecessors. This shows what might be possible in the way of environmental reform if the need became widely felt to be urgent and if equality became a precondition of sacrifice.

It would of course, be necessary to eliminate unemployment. Jobs can be shared; but the most important thing is to make work more interesting so that more people will want to share it. We should encourage skilful, labour intensive work, producing goods designed to last, and to be repairable. Housekeeping too should be counted as work. It contributes more to our "standard of living" than anything else in the economy, yet we don't count it. Homes, after all are the cheapest work places of all, because we have to have them anyway. Providing the maximum number of jobs at the lowest practical cost, instead of providing very expensive workplaces for capital-intensive and boring methods of production, often producing shoddy goods, should meet opposition from nobody.

The present response to unemployment by benign governments is to spend money on a series of discontinuous job creation schemes, which have increasingly fancy titles, but are directed to providing short-term jobs within the existing industrial framework. Declining real job opportunities mean that they have to be temporary to make sure that as many people as possible get a turn at a boring job. This returns people temporarily to the ranks of the consumers and improves job creation statistics.

An alternative strategy would be to work through community organisations, local Government, and volunteer organisations to fund projects that develop the kind of skills that enable people to sustain and employ themselves. The criteria for funding should be the extent to which work places are provided at low cost and require minimal use of non-renewable sources of energy. The skilful use of renewable materials should be encouraged, together with the best and most advanced appropriate technology.

The purpose would be to remove as many people as possible from as much as possible of the consumer economy. The paradoxical effect would be to reclaim them as members of society. GNP might suffer for a while, until ways of measuring it were reformed. But welfare payments would be reduced, which could reduce taxation. Such a strategy would provide increasing scope for individuality, and because it would stress liberty, while also supporting equality, it would win support from the right as well as the left, which is the hardest trick in the political book. Unemployment, the incurable symptom of a sick society, will respond only to some such antibody. This strategy might lead to logically compatible policies in areas such as agriculture, energy, defence, aid, education and medicine.

Like most of the worthwhile reforms of the past—such as the emancipation of slaves and votes for women—the transition to a sustainable economy will be difficult and frustrating. There will be backward steps and blind alleys as well as progress. If sustainable, post-industrial societies are to be achieved, they will probably not arise from the ashes of a nuclear holocaust; or from the survivors of a revolutionary apocalypse. It's more likely that as fossil fuels are exhausted, and replaced by renewable sources of energy, when the cost of militarisation, not only of the Earth, but also of space becomes unbearable, first for one superpower, then the rest, people will discover that their ability to live better, as well as more cheaply, will depend on the extent to which they can become masters rather than servants of technology, and liberate themselves from the imperatives of industrial society.

Politicians, probably in small countries to begin with, will sense votes in the positive encouragement of alternative economies, and if present trends continue, the time will come when national leaders will be able to count on majorities to understand the consistency of programs of reform, which encompass such superficially disconnected, but ethically consistent purposes as preserving rainforest, restoring land to indigenous peoples, and subsidising urban farms, protecting national parks, and building wooden ships.[4]

I was much surprised by the extraordinary reception that the content of this radio talk provoked. I have never been a formal student of economics, but I had read recent works by Hugh Stretton, Fritz Schumacher and many others. My argument was very simple. The structure of capitalism ensured that however much economic growth was achieved, it did nothing to increase equality, either in rich nations or poor ones. In fact, it usually made it worse. It was also damaging for the environment. The "trickle down" theory, whereby wealth is assumed to filter through the rich and raise the living standards of the poor is not supported by the facts. Much to my surprise, at the time, hundreds of listeners agreed with me and were spreading the word. I received and continued to receive numerous letters like this one, from Mrs Ruth Mackinnon:

> Your Sustainable Development talk on Ockham's Razor was very much appreciated. As I should like to share it with members of a discussion group, I should be pleased indeed if you are able to supply me with a printed copy. Bibliographic details of your new publication on the same subject would also be most welcome. Thank you again for that thoughtful address.

I'm glad to be able to tell you that I replied. Many other people, for example P D Day, editor of the *Queensland Planner*[5], wanted to pass the talk on to discussion groups, and local publications:

> I should like to help publicise more widely the message of your recent "Ockham's Razor" talk, and similar talks/articles of yours which I've heard/read, and admired. If you'd be good enough to send me a copy of the text of the Ockham's Razor talk, or something similar, I'd very much like to run it in the June issue of "Queensland Planner." It's a theme I've been personally plugging.

---

4   "Ockham's Razor," ABC National radio, 14 May 1989.

5   The journal of the Queensland division of the Royal Australian Planning Institute Inc.

One letter, from Dr Maureen Smith, the Director of the University Extension of the University of Western Australia was particularly encouraging. After hearing my Ockham's Razor talk, she asked me to deliver an address at the University's sixty-second Summer School of January 1990. She even offered me return airfares and two nights' accommodation. "The theme of the 1990 summer school," she told me, is "One World, One Future: Towards sustainable living." She said she had been, "extremely impressed" by my radio efforts. So I accepted her invitation, and enjoyed both giving the talk and the "meet the speaker" question and answer session that followed.[6] I hoped that my impression, that I might be stimulating the chances of change, was realistic.

My job as a teacher made a wide range of activity and intellectual innovation come together in my head. So I published a lot of articles[7], and other products stimulated by the teaching I was doing, the activities, like building *One and All*, and causes that were occupying my mind. I produced a video, called *Spelling Ecology on Kangaroo Island*, thanks to the University Educational Technology Department, about the problems and ecological considerations of agriculture on Kangaroo Island, where I went on *Leofleda*, with some of my students, to conduct a series of interviews with farmers, about their problems, ambitions and solutions. I persuaded myself that my academic and extra-mural passions were mutually complementary. And I slept well.

When Ruth and I were in Britain and the United States in 1986, the Ecopolitics Association of Australasia was born, and held the first of a series of Ecopolitics conferences, at Griffith University in Brisbane. The conferences attracted many academic contributions from political science departments, geographers, and departments of various sciences, but no other historians, to my knowledge. The conference was distinguished by also seeking papers by politicians, and lay advocates for good causes. While I was in Hobart for the third conference, I gave two papers "Strategies for a Sustainable Society," and "The Politics of Environmental Studies," both of which were published. I also spoke with Peter Hay, who was one of the founding fathers of the eco-politics movement.

I offered to organise and host the next Ecopolitics conference at the University of Adelaide, and the offer was accepted. The dates of 21–24 September 1989 were agreed on, and I set about the task of attracting what turned out to be a stellar cast of conference delegates from all over the world. But first the Centre had to face a reviewing group of five colleagues on 19 September 1989. They finished their work on 16 October 1989.

My colleague Ken Dyer offered to help with the conference organisation, which was very demanding of time and energy. We co-edited, *Changing Directions,* a 666

---

6   Dr Maureen Smith to John Young, 23 May 1989.

7   Among them Young, J M, "From Productivity to Creativity: Technological Predestination and Political Free Will," in Fischer, F, *Sustaining Gaia: Contributions to Another World View*, Monash University, Melbourne, 1987; "Sustainable Development: Doublethink of the 1990s," Ockham's Razor, ABC, 1990.

page collection of most of the papers that were delivered at the Ecopolitics conference of 1989.

We were bold in our choice of speakers, which included people of international standing, including Dr Bob Brown, the leader of the Tasmanian Greens, formerly the United Tasmania Group, the first Green political party in the world; Petra Kelly of the German Greens, and Lorna Salzman, founder of the New York Greens. We invited several Australian parliamentarians, including Bob Catley (Australian Labor Party); John Coulter, Australian Democrats Senator representing South Australia; Jennifer Cashmore, a member of the South Australian Parliament; H C "Nugget" Coombs, Australian National University and Alexander Downer, MHR. The inter-state and overseas visitors were formally welcomed by the Vice-Chancellor of the University, Dame Roma Mitchell.

The total attendance was four hundred and sixty delegates, to whom ninety-six papers were presented. The opening coincided with a prolonged airline pilots' strike which, as we said in the published account of the conference, "prevented some people from attending, caused inconvenience to many, dampened nobody's enthusiasm for the conference, and heightened most people's awareness of the environmental benefits of train and bus travel."[8]

We also invited the Labor Party Minister for the Environment, Graham Richardson, and asked him to do us the honour of opening the conference. As luck would have it, Ally Fricker, one of my history students, and an energetic fund raiser and occasional volunteer builder of *One and All*, had decided to attend the conference. She was a notable advocate, and a member of student organisations with good causes, as well. As soon as I began to introduce Minister Richardson, Ally jumped to her feet and said that I should expel him from the proceedings, on account of his political support of environmentally destructive policies. I said that I would be happy to include a discussion of the Government's environmental policy, but we could proceed no further until we allowed the Minister to declare the conference to be open. I then took a big risk. I said that I had no authority to throw anyone out of the meeting. This was a conference, not a sermon. But since this was an important idea, I proposed a motion which we could discuss, and vote on. I moved, "that the Minister should be asked to open the conference" and we could then consider whether or not he should be heard about his policy during the conference. Luckily, Minister Richardson had the sense to support my move and there was an almost unanimous vote in favour of following my recommendations. Richardson had the experience to feel the mind of the meeting, and the sense to support my bid for free speech. Next day I received a lot of notes from people who understood what I had been up to, and I hoped that Ally would forgive me.

It was encouraging to receive some good feedback. Bob Mann wrote from the University of Auckland on 6 October 2089, "I was always confident that you would

---

8   Dyer, Ken, and Young, J M R, "Changing Directions The Proceedings of Ecopolitics IV," University of Adelaide, 21-24 September, 1989.

organise Ecopolitics IV very well, but you succeeded in surprising even me. Thanks for a superb accomplishment."

Dr Jeanette Fitzsimmons, also from Auckland University wrote on 27 September:

> Thank-you for a very enjoyable conference. It was a prodigious feat of organisation especially coping with an airstrike. I particularly admired the un-rattled and democratic way you handled a very difficult situation in the final plenary. [I think she meant the opening plenary!]

Another big event which did a lot to raise the status of the Centre for Environmental Studies was a visit by David Suzuki. He is an excellent speaker, and because of his books and his charm he filled the Bonython Hall and impressed many members of the Science Faculty, with his broad understanding of the social and ethical dimensions of Environmental scholarship.

It was at this time that I was making my first attempt to gain promotion to the rank of Reader, soon to be changed to the title of Associate Professor. I thought that since I'd been an elected Chairman of the History Department and Director of the Centre for Environmental Studies; introduced and brought the teaching and research of Pacific Island History and Social Anthropology to the University; written and published several books and a reasonable number of articles, that I might be in the running. I had never lost a student from any of my courses, and had supervised some of the most outstanding post-graduate students in the University.

However, a letter arrived one day which told me that my application had failed. "Oh well!" I thought; "I knew it was going to be hard." Then I received a letter from John Gill, who was Chair of the Philosophy Department. It was a copy of a letter to Professor Kevin Marjoribanks, Vice Chancellor, dated 19 November 1990:

> A new system for promoting Readers has been introduced. But not one Arts applicant … [from the Faculty of Arts] was successful. That is a highly improbable result on statistical grounds. And given the calibre of quite a number of those eligible to apply from the Arts Faculty … the Faculty is somewhat in shock. The obvious conclusion to me is that Arts candidates were penalised by the new system, or at least by the way it operated. As a group they can hardly have been ranked appropriately in the order of merit. What they had every right to, as a group, just failed to happen.
>
> It was known that the criteria for promotion had been updated, but the whole staff of the University were now being told that no applications for promotion to the status of Reader from the Faculty of Arts, had been successful … I urge the Vice-Chancellor to act in this matter, for inaction now means that an apparent mistake becomes apparent injustice.

At this time I was so busy, and I was enjoying myself so much, that I couldn't be bothered thinking about it. I and my colleagues got on with our work while the Centre's reviewers got on with theirs.

To begin with, I was told later, four out of the five reviewers believed the Centre should be abolished. But at the end of an exhausting process, including interviews with staff and students, the reviewers had changed their minds. They reported that:

> *There has been an attempt to satisfy the educational requirements of three identifiable groups of students:*
> *(a) those who wish to pursue scholarship within the emerging field of environmental studies;*
> *(b) those who wish to begin, or advance a career in the broad area of Environmental Management;*
> *(c) those whose interests in environmental issues arise from philosophical opposition to the dominant trends in modern society.*[9]

In October 1989, the Review of the Centre for Environmental Studies was released. It was a sensible document, and there were some bits that I liked quite a lot, like:

> *The review committee accepts the point made to it that environmental studies is "no longer a loose agglomeration of disciplines centring around compulsory units in ecology, and perhaps economics, planning and sociology ... it has a unique place, which cannot be replaced by incorporating its priorities into the specialised disciplines ... [it] is the focus of a new body of knowledge"* [a quote from me!].[10]

The Review commented on the respectable amount of academic publication achieved by the those who taught in the Centre, but said "Only a fraction of this productivity, however, has been in the field of environmental studies." This was because much of the teaching was done by people who worked predominantly in other departments. We received some acknowledgement of the papers we had given in the Ecopolitics IV conference, and they made complimentary comments about my general performance: "The Current Director, Dr John Young is widely (and deservedly) respected for the energy and intellectual leadership he has given the Centre and its programmes." The students were also congratulated:

> *The Review Committee also received written and oral submissions from a range of current and past students. We were greatly impressed by these students. They had coherent and thoughtful views, which were expressed clearly and forcefully. The students that are attracted to environmental studies are very able and dedicated; this in itself reflects credit on the programme. The students were clearly appreciative and supportive of the holistic emphasis, and the broad range of the programme. Some of the teaching innovations ... are imaginative and praiseworthy.*[11]

At first I was delighted by the review, and enjoyed the congratulations. Recommendation 2 sounded good: "That the Director of the Centre should be appointed at Professorial level." But my agreement with the University was that at the end of 1990, I would return to the History Department. Then I was not so happy, and even less so when I read recommendation 12: "That the Director should be a person whose initial training is in science, with the capacity to direct a Graduate Centre for Environmental Studies." I had the capacity to direct such a department, no doubt, but I had no way to claim any scientific qualifications.

---

9   The University of Adelaide Review of the Graduate Centre for Environmental Studies, October 1989, p 9.

10 Review, p 13.

11 Review, p 9.

I did think that in the light of the Review and the rapid growth of student numbers on my watch, and the acceptance, by the Review, of my definition of the subject, that I might just make it. I even began to think of enrolling immediately, as a Science undergraduate. But I thought the Review committee had obviously decided, in spite of its comments on my "intellectual leadership," that I deserved to be discouraged.

It would have been an exhilarating challenge to contest the ruling, but I was in two minds about it, because I was beginning to think about other lanes. In 1987, I went to Hobart, mainly to attend a conference, but also to attend to some *One and All* business. There I met Mr Crook, who owned and operated a bronze foundry called Retlas Bronze, a short walk from the University of Tasmania, where the conference was held. He was making some bronze shroud plates for *Lady Nelson* and Adrian Dean had advised us to ask him to manufacture similar products for *One and All*. I soon began an interesting conversation about the other wooden ketches, like *Annie Watt* and *One and All*, that had been built in Tasmania in the nineteenth century, but for South Australian owners.

I had flown to Hobart with a cheap ticket: half price if you stayed there for a week. It was a good opportunity for me, I thought, to find out as much as I could about Tasmanian ship building. Unlike South Australia, Tasmania has some of the best ship building timbers in the world, and in the 1870s, the supply had seemed to be inexhaustible. I mentioned to Mr Crook at the foundry that I wanted to go to the little town of Cygnet in the south of the island, to see the yard where *Annie Watt* and *One and All* had been built, and he made me the extraordinary offer to lend me his car for the day. It was a round trip of over a hundred kilometres.

So I just pointed the car up Davey Street where we were standing, and drove off. Mr Crook gave good instructions for getting to Cygnet, but when I arrived at Huonville, I could see the bridge over the Huon River. I went straight on across the river, instead of turning left and going to Cygnet. The town of Huonville was soon behind me, and I was driving beside a clean river with an island in the middle, and trees on both sides. I was absorbed by the beautiful scenery for five minutes. Then the trees fell away to give a view of what was now a broad open river to my left, about one hundred yards wide. It looked very navigable, but there was not a boat to be seen.

I was suddenly in the riverside village of Franklin, named after Jane, Lady Franklin who founded the settlement in 1838. Nearly all the houses were wooden, and many of them were of pre-Federation design, which put them into the "heritage" category. I could therefore hardly believe my eyes, when I saw two excavators like marauding sharks, taking huge bites out of a row of cottages, just within the northern boundary of the village. I went on, in shock, along a very narrow road, past the sports oval on the foreshore and a hotel, the Town Hall, bank and post office, and another pub, where I stopped, hoping to find the cause of what seemed to me to be some kind of vandalism. "What's going on here?" I asked the men at the bar. "Why are they pulling those houses down?" In other states, I thought, people would be chaining themselves to such buildings. "Gotta widen the road mate," I was told, "because of the log trucks. They gotta cut 12 seconds off the time it takes for them to drive through the town." I was told that log trucks, carrying thirty tons of logs came through Franklin, round the clock at four minute intervals, carrying eucalypt timber to be transformed into woodchips, a hundred and fifty kilometres away at Triabunna. From there, the chips would be shipped to Japan to be made into paper.

Tasmania was losing thousands of acres of pristine mixed wet forest, containing a supply of some of the best furniture and boat building material in the world, while Japan made millions of yen to supply Tasmania with the machinery to clear-fell the forest and replace it with fast growing eucalypt plantations. Japan was doing very well out of the deal, but Franklin was heading toward becoming a ghost town. When I looked closely, most of the houses had peeling paint; shops were closed, their windows boarded up.

Other than these symptoms of decline, Franklin seemed to be an almost ideal place to live. At the northern entrance to the town was a stone church, just a little inland from the road and river, and raised so that walking out of the building revealed an island dividing the river into two navigable waterways, connected by a surely man-made, I thought, navigation canal across the Island. Close to the road beyond the church, were the remains of a wharf, built four generations ago. It stood to reason, I thought, that Franklin must once have been "Great." It was situated at the top of tidal movement in a navigable river on one side, and a highway on the other. The town of Franklin and its riverside setting reminded me of some of the places I had seen on my recent visit to the United States and England. I thought of the once thriving maritime communities like Mystic Seaport, in the United States, and Falmouth in England, which had found inspiration to recover their original purpose, while developing new business opportunities. In the past, the hills above Franklin had been covered with enormous trees. Later, I discovered an article in the *Huon Times* written by an anonymous "Old Resident" in 1923, about what Franklin was like in the 1870s:

> *Fifty years ago Franklin was not the proverbial one horse village ... but really a thriving community, for shipbuilding was carried on so extensively that the clang of the hammers from the building of several vessels at the same time lent an air of importance to the place.*[12]

Jim Skinner, a later resident, wrote of his joyful recollections when Franklin was the commercial centre of the Huon Valley: "There was nothing in Huonville," said Skinner "...only one little shop." In comparison, Franklin was "glorious." A trip to the town:

> *...was the highlight of our existence. It was a big bustling town ... with branches of all the big Hobart stores... Friday night shopping was a marvellous treat. It was a blaze*

---

12 *Huon Times,* 26 January 1923. Franklin also had a Hydro-electric power station using Price's Creek as its power source. It was handed on to the state owned Hydro-electric Department in 1929. One of the dams is still there.

of light. There was a street light on every pole and all the shops were ablaze with light.[13]
A walk around the waterfront stimulated other thoughts. An old toilet block stood on the edge of the river, and I saw some graffiti in huge capital letters: "How can I laugh tomorrow when I can't even smile today?" On the southern end of the smelly building was a drawing of a revolver, its short barrel pointed south to the playground, where a forlorn couple were playing with their children. Beside the drawing of the gun were the words "Eat my lead." This experience was crucial. I began to see Franklin as a community in need, and perhaps arrogantly, as  a place I could help. I remembered the letter I received from my father and his advice, when he was in Sierra Leone and I was in New Zealand in 1956:

I think your line will be in cultural activities — in a broad sense — deepening and widening understanding of people by other people, creating community, bringing folks together and helping them to do things and enjoy things together, so it looks as if some sort of social service is your line.

I decided to head on south towards Port Huon, and just as I left Franklin I saw a real estate advertisement for a waterfront property going for sixty thousand dollars. A steep drive off the road led to a yard at the back of a two storey weatherboard dwelling. I knocked on the back door, as is the Australian custom, to find a youngish couple, Martin and Ruth Fathers, with a family of seven little girls. Their plan was to sell the house as soon as possible and get back to Melbourne in the hope of getting work. The eldest girl was ambitious, and didn't enjoy her daily bus ride to Huonville High School, where she was not getting on well. I asked Martin Fathers if he would show me the fifty acres of land behind the house. The first hundred yards was a steep slope of grass, that had once been an orchard. There were a few fruit trees around the house, plums, quinces, cherries and a mulberry, but the rest were gone. Martin explained that in 1970, Britain had joined the European Common Market which meant that Tasmania no longer enjoyed the "Imperial Preference" of the past, and the Tasmanian Government had subsidised what was known as the "Tree Pull." Orchardists were able to get a subsidy to pay for their fruit trees to be pulled out and burnt. Franklin had suffered the inevitable fate of a region dependent on an economy over which it had no control. The decisions that decided its destiny had been made in London and Tokyo, not Hobart or Canberra. Small properties like this one could no longer support a family.[14]

---

13 Watson, Catherine, *Full and Plenty, An oral history of apple growing in the Huon Valley*, Twelvetrees Publishing Company, Sandy Bay, 1987, pp 36-7.

14 See Young, J M, "Back to the Future: Choosing a Meaning from Regional History," *Tasmanian Historical Studies*, Vol 5, No 1, 1995-6, pp 114-131.

Jane Franklin, the wife of Lieutenant Governor Sir John Franklin, was the founder of the town in 1838, when she bought 1,280 acres of land in order to attract free settlers of good repute to dilute the bulk of the largely ex-convict Tasmanian population. The land was subdivided into blocks of approximately fifty acres, as in New Zealand about the same time, with the expectation that each block would be enough to provide a family with a living.

Lady Franklin envisaged a self-sufficient, free, and egalitarian society, dependent on the cultivation of strips of water front land, a mile long and a hundred and thirty yards wide. The idea was to provide each settler family with access to the river, so that supplies could be delivered, and produce shipped, in the absence of roads, in wooden ketches. Next to the road were seven acres of gently sloping land for orchards and gardens. Above that was the remainder of the mile-long strip of timber-covered land for building ships and houses and for fuel.

I was attracted to the forest on the Fathers' land. It looked as if it hadn't been logged for around ninety years. Old photographs taken at the beginning of the twentieth century, and hung in the Town Hall in Huonville, show areas of bare ground littered with logs. In 1987, much of the forest had grown back, and when I walked up the steep scarp and on to more gently sloping land, there were many large Blue Gums and stringy barks, as much as three feet in diameter at chest height, and other trees of similar size. What magnificent material, I thought, for building a schooner.

The modern highway lay next to the river, and was roaring with log trucks every four minutes, but the house was far enough back from the road to muffle the noise to a tolerable level. And on the river side of the road were the remains of a jetty. I thought of how useful it would be to have our own jetty, and a mooring just off the river bank for *Leofleda*. If we were to buy the house, we would see her from the upstairs window, and keep a dinghy tied to the jetty.

In the pub they had told me about the next place of interest, Port Huon, at the mouth of the Kermandie River as it joined the Huon. So I went on, first to Shipwright's Point, and Port Huon, then about 3 kilometres further to Geeveston. Shipwright's Point is named in honour of Inches, McLaren and Harley, who established a deep water shipyard there in the 1840s. Many ships and boats were also built in Franklin, from the 1850s to the 1870s, mostly wooden ketches. Shipwright's Point, with deeper water at hand, had specialised in larger craft, rigged as schooners, some for customers in New Zealand. Shipwright's Point still had a workshop, and a slipway, designed for small vessels, mostly small cruising yachts, about fifty yards from the Huon Yacht Club. I went to the Club, explaining my credentials as Mooring Master of the Small Boat Club of Port Adelaide. The Port Huon Yacht Club was a lively and interesting club that could boast of members now retired, who had shipped a yacht to England to compete in the Fastnet Race of 1979, notorious for its overwhelming gales, and was famous for it. I enquired about membership.

I began to get involved in mental arithmetic, and when I returned to Hobart, I rang Ruth to tell her that I had a good idea. What if we were to sell our house and farm at Norton Summit? What if I took the option of early retirement, from the University, which would give me a lump sum of superannuation? We would then have enough to pay off our Norton Summit loan and to buy the Fathers' house and land in Franklin. Perhaps we could build a larger and faster vessel and take to the ocean for a cruise round the Pacific.

Ruth was born in Tasmania, and had lived there with her single mother, Margaret, and six other children. Margaret was a qualified school teacher, and had brought her family to Adelaide, with mixed feelings. Once her children were independent and she had retired from her teaching job, all she really wanted was to get back to Tasmania. She and Ruth had discussed the idea of her living with us when Margaret could no longer fend for herself. Ruth sounded on the telephone as if she would give the idea serious consideration.

I told her about Franklin, the river, the orchard and the forest. I suggested that as soon as I arrived home, she should come to Tasmania on her own, and see for herself. When she came back she was full of joy, and her mother, Margaret, was happy as well. So we began to make plans.

In early 1990, *Sustaining the Earth* had not yet been published, so I had not yet received a heap of well-expressed reviews from some of the most respected environment scholars in the world. If the book had been published earlier, that might have led to my promotion. There were many scholars in the world who might have agreed that a modern Centre for Environmental Studies would require an interdisciplinary scholar to manage it, but the decision to appoint only a scientist as my successor, passed by the Review committee, made it impossible for me to be considered as a candidate for the new Chair. Ruth and I didn't take long to decide that Tasmania would be a great adventure, and that we should retire, not that either of us thought of really retiring any time soon. This would be a change of our two careers. From academic life and farming in South Australia, to boat building, or something like that in Tasmania. We'd find out some more.

Dr Peter Hay, a poet and Reader in the Centre for Environmental Studies at the University of Tasmania, advised me to consider applying for a position as an Honorary Research Fellow in his department, which I agreed to do, and which was successful. It meant that I could teach as little or as much as I wished. I would be able to become an honorary member of the University staff, a member of the University Library and the staff club. And I would have to create my next day job for myself.

Our children were all now self-supporting. Susan and Shaohua had their first child, Lindsay and were both living and studying in Adelaide. Stephen was married to Anne and they were both working at Melbourne University. Philip and Felicity were married and he had begun a career as a lawyer and she as a teacher in Adelaide.

Ruth had different kinds of reasons for deciding to leave Adelaide and move to Tasmania. She had grown up in Launceston in the north of Tasmania. She had two brothers and three sisters, together with lavish generations of Tasmanian relatives, and so had always felt a sense of Tasmanian identity. I had made several journeys to Tasmania to further the progress of building *One and All*, and had bought a set of the relevant Admiralty charts, in case there might be need of them when I retired and we could go cruising together.

But first Ruth and I wanted to make sure that Franklin was where we wanted to live. It didn't take long to make my decision to retire, as early retirement had considerable financial attractions. And I have to admit that my non-promotion did make me a bit grumpy. But an honorary position at the Centre for Environmental Studies at UTAS enabled me to enjoy the continuity of an academic life. The Eco-politics conferences had enabled me to meet Pete Hay, Warwick Fox, Robyn Eckersley, all in the Tasmanian Centre for Environmental Studies, and Elaine Stratford. Elaine was a graduate of the Department of Geography at Adelaide University, who I had admitted to Environmental Studies in 1990 to enrol for a PhD. Elaine came to see me about doing the PhD on the last day of my membership of the University of Adelaide. She became chair of the UTAS School of Geography and Environmental Studies in 2009.

We bought the Fathers' house in 1987. We rented it out for a couple of years to a family and later to two young men and one young woman. The house needed considerable work and we decided to visit Tasmania in 1990 to do some of it. We camped in the back of our truck, parked on Franklin foreshore. Luckily, we got on well with the tenants, and we concentrated on the exterior problems like cutting the grass and re-roofing the back verandah. We were worried by the state of the piles of stone which represented the foundations of the house, but felt that we should postpone jacking the house up and dealing with it, until we were living there. So we made lists and took measurements.

I was a bit put off by the two boys' jovial account of how they had dangled the girl out of an upstairs window. The girl was frightened to death, which made me anxious to move in before some similar lark might end in tragedy. We were also a bit worried about what else Franklin people did in their spare time.

After working on the Franklin house, we really wanted a shower, so we thought we should ask at the pub if there were any about. The woman serving was Nonie Carr, and turned out to be our next-door neighbour to the south. I asked Nonie about showers. She took one look at me and said, "You certainly look as if you need one. Of course you can shower here." At that time Nonie was the Treasurer of the Franklin Progress Association founded, in 1963, which was trying to revive itself, after a period of stagnation. She soon invited us to become members.

At the beginning of 1991, back in South Australia, we packed all our stuff, including a useful number of Jarrah planks that I had bought from *One and All* after she was finished, together with our Bristol diesel tractor, which I was sure we would need when we arrived at Franklin. There was room for all our books, my tools, just everything that we possessed, in the container. It went by sea via *Mary Holyman* to Hobart. Then by truck to Franklin.

Our closest friends, Nick and Jackie Wright, had decided that they would sail their very splendid ocean going yacht, *Amadis,* back to England. For some years Nick and Jackie had joined us in *Leofleda* for wonderful cruises around St Vincent's Gulf, and down to Kangaroo Island in their smaller boat, *Boonewa*. Nick soon grew interested in going farther away, for longer voyages. He and I spent many happy hours discussing our ideas about the ideal ocean cruising yacht, which must be one of the most delightful occupations in human experience. Gradually the list of possibilities grew shorter until I showed him an article in a yachting magazine about Maurice Griffiths, and his "Good Hope" design. David Kew was living in the former rectory of the Anglican Church at Norton Summit and was keen to build her; forty feet overall length, a long straight keel, with four tons of lead ballast, and a draught of four feet six inches. With her lovely traditional looks, comfortable fit out, shallow draft and plenty of room for Nick, Jackie and their two boys, Duncan and Ben, *Amadis* was ready for her voyage and we decided that we would depart together.

The end of term in December 1990 was a bit sad. My students were sad about our departure, but understood our reasons for moving. They put on a farewell party for us on 21 December, 1990, and presented us with a brass, kerosene-fuelled riding light, to be used when we were anchored, to stop being hit by traffic. One student couldn't make it, and sent an apology for being unable to come. It brought tears to my eyes:

I'd simply like to say a very big thank-you for the past two years, I have learnt so much in your course. I have so enjoyed the Centre. It is almost like a born again feeling, (I am quite sure that is not the analogy you'd choose). In any case it was lots of fun being part of your crew.

Early in February 1991, we and the Wrights set out from the Yacht Squadron and had a great sail with the land breeze behind us during the night, as was our habit when going to Kangaroo Island, and anchored in American River. After a few days there, we rose early and set sail for Robe, a fishing port about eighty miles away.

The north-easterly land breeze gave us a good start on a south-easterly course, but as the sun rose the wind began to turn into a sea breeze and come round to the south. This put us onto a beam reach, so we went fast with a lumpy swell which put water on the foredeck. *Amadis* began to pull ahead. She was on an easterly course, close hauled against an increasing swell and, with her longer waterline and bigger sails, she was soon out of sight. The wind continued to swing round to the south east until we had to tack straight into it. It also became stronger and we decided to put two reefs in the mainsail. In sheltered waters we might have done well, but we were now in a very vast open ocean, a thousand miles to leeward of Tasmania. The waves were now huge and when we rode to the top of them we were in about thirty knots of wind. We then went down the trough and into a calm, where the sails flapped. We took bearings of the visible lights to see if we were getting anywhere, and we soon had to realise that we were simply going up and down in the ocean. And making very little headway.

We decided to try a tack towards the land to see if we could do any better and to get a more accurate idea of our position, taking bearings of the islands called "the Pages" in the middle of the Backstairs Passage. The light on South Page Island was showing on the port beam. We were able to sail a course of 070 true, which would bring us to Victor Harbour, if the wind kept coming from the same direction. We stuck to this plan, taking bearings of the South Page every hour or so. The bearings indicated that we were making about half a knot each hour through the afternoon, which was not very encouraging. We radioed *Amadis* to report our position, and told them not to wait for us. We would see them in Robe. They were romping along on a broad reach more or less about ten miles away, parallel to the coast, already off Victor Harbour.

An hour later we were a bit closer to the Pages, and we were feeling confident, but we began to see the lights of what looked like a big fleet of fishing boats heading across our bows, and it was getting dark. We were also fighting an incoming tide which was pushing us closer to South Page as we reached the top of each wave, to be thrown into the next trough by a wind that seemed to be increasing. We gave *Amadis* another radio call which was to change our lives. *Amadis* was now well beyond us and well out of sight. We told them to forget about us and do us a favour by getting as far on their way to England as possible. It was a very sad and harrowing goodbye over the radio. This was not the goodbye we'd planned. We had at least hoped to spend a few days more in Robe with our dear friends, before we went south to Tasmania and they went north on their way to England.

The fishing fleet was evidently trawling, and they would be extremely unlikely to see the lights of a vessel as small as *Leofleda*. We tried to contact with them by radio to let them know our position but without success. They were probably absorbed in the strenuous and exacting task of putting out their nets for the night. We were getting cold and tired. With considerable hazards to leeward.

At the rate we were moving, against what looked like a strong and steady easterly wind, it might take weeks, even a month or more, to reach Tasmania. We really didn't have that much time. We couldn't leave our house in Tasmania empty for that long and our tenants had already left. We then turned back to Kangaroo Island, still hoping for the right wind to sail to Tasmania.

The wind was behind us, so we moved quickly in the right direction heading just off the beach of Antechamber Bay in two fathoms of water. Ruth fell in the water when trying to get the anchor out of the fo'c's'le, but returned to the deck uninjured, and we went ashore in the inflatable dinghy to have a look round and then made ready for a morning departure. Antechamber Bay was unlikely to attract dangerous ships in the middle of the night. But it felt good to bring out our brass kerosene riding light and haul it up the forestay on the staysail halyard.

Next day we sailed to Kingscote where we sent a message, relayed to Robe, to let Nick and Jackie know we were safe. We also phoned Philip. He was very encouraging and said he would post us his auto helm for the journey to Tasmania. So we decided to wait. When we returned to *Leofleda*, there was a small bag of fresh vegetables in the cockpit. Later, when we came back from a shopping expedition ashore, someone had left us a present of some fish. Eventually we caught up with at least one of our anonymous benefactors and had a chat. It transpired that our radio conversations with Nick and Jackie, particularly our last one, had been heard by several fishermen from Kangaroo Island. Within a short time of the broadcasts, everyone there knew about us leaving our friends, and how we felt about it. Hence the gifts, and the help and comforting conversations with the islanders that followed, while we waited for the arrival of Philip's auto helm. When it did arrive, a complete stranger came aboard and helped us fit it.

But the right wind never came. Every day the south-easterly blew. We stayed in Kangaroo Island for what seemed like a long time. In the end, after a sad discussion, we decided to go back to Port Adelaide. We still had the cradle that had taken our ship to Fiji and back, so we knew we could put *Leofleda* on a train or truck to Melbourne, and deliver her to Hobart by sea.

We set sail early the next morning, caught the sea breeze back to Adelaide and left *Leofleda* at North Haven, where we knew she could be slipped and lifted on to a truck by crane. Our neighbours, Rod and Gill Brereton, who were looking after our truck, our dog and our cat, brought the truck to us so we could make arrangements for getting *Leofleda* to Tasmania. We were promised that she would arrive, via *Mary Holyman*, at Macquarie Wharf in Hobart in three weeks' time. We intended to collect the dog, at least, and drive to Melbourne, catch the ferry and meet *Leofleda* in Hobart. The whole business of *Leofleda*'s transport was so efficiently and easily arranged that we thought everything would go smoothly from that point on.

This was not quite how it turned out. As we were making final adjustments to the cradle in Holyman's depot, Ruth started to get abdominal pains, which became worse by the minute. Holyman's staff were very kind, but there was something really wrong. We drove to the hospital and Ruth went into an operating theatre. The surgeon reminded us we were very lucky that this happened in Adelaide, rather than on Kangaroo Island, or worse still, on board *Leofleda* in the middle of Bass Strait.

While Ruth was recovering in hospital and then at her mother's house, I flew to Hobart to see *Leofleda* unloaded, unscathed, into the water of Sullivan's Cove. This was in February 1991 and, as expected, *Leofleda*'s planks had opened up a bit in the hot sun. I knew she would leak, so I took a plastic bucket aboard with me as she soon as she hit the water. I prepared the little diesel engine for starting and start she did. I arranged to take her over to Constitution Dock for the duration and asked Robin Eckersley to come around and give me a hand. We motored across to the entrance to Constitution Dock, watching the little dribbles of water coming out of the seams as we took away the floor boards. There was soon enough water in the bilge to fill the pump hose-pipe lying alongside the keel. It wasn't long before I could use the pump alone, while Robin used the bucket. Within an hour of re-launching, we were using a sponge.

I was anxious to get back to Adelaide and get Ruth and the dog. Several people I didn't know offered to check on *Leofleda*, and pump her out if necessary, while I was away.

At that time, there were two ferries operating across Bass Strait from Victoria: *Abel Tasman*, which sailed overnight from Port Melbourne to Devonport, and the high-speed catamaran *Devil Cat*, which took six hours to sail from Port Welshpool to Georgetown. Thinking of our dog, Darwin, we decided to sail on *Devil Cat*, a shorter journey, and we took our time driving in our ute from the Adelaide hills to Welshpool. Darwin sat between us on the bench seat. He slept a lot whilst we were driving, making driving itself quite perilous. Darwin seemed to think that every place we stopped was going to be home. He checked everything out at every stop and clearly approved of all of them, so it took a long time to persuade him to get back into the ute. Even *Devil Cat* looked fine to him. We had been assured that there would be a box big enough for Darwin, but when we arrived at Port Welshpool, no such box existed, so we were allowed to let him stay in the car. He wasn't too keen on being there on his own. The crossing to Georgetown in Tasmania was short but very bumpy. We went and sat in a lounge for four hours. It's hard to explain to a dog that you will see him soon, so we paid periodic visits to reassure him. Each time we checked on him, he was asleep, but I still like to think that his anxiety diminished at each visit. At least he was travelling in daylight, and he made a good recovery. We drove down to Hobart in three hours, stopping at Constitution Dock, to discover that *Leofleda* had taken up beautifully, thanks to Robin Eckersley and the strangers who looked after her.

Driving back to Franklin is always a joy in good weather, especially when you reach Vince's Saddle at four hundred and ninety-five metres above sea level, and begin the descent into the Huon Valley. Just as you get past the trees, your spirit will be lifted by the sight of Mount Picton through the front window of your car. Especially in winter when it is often covered in snow. Then the landscape gets softer with re-growth forests and very green paddocks full of livestock, and orchards, heavy in late summer with apples and pears on the right, and wooded hills on the left.

The entrance to Franklin from the north had now become almost familiar. The house had a name, *Pentarba*, the first such dwelling we had ever experienced, but we decided not to use it. Its condition was as we had expected, after months of teen-aged occupancy. The walls of a small cupboard under the stairs had not been lined for years, apart from peeling wallpaper over newspaper, over hessian stuck to horizontal wooden planks. The newspaper gave us a clue about the age of the house. The earliest dated page was 1901, so the house was probably a pre-Federation structure. Shortly after we arrived in Franklin, we had a lovely sail on *Leofleda* from Hobart, marvelling at the number of wonderful anchorages in the D'Entrecasteaux Channel and Huon River on the way. We anchored her in the river across the road from our house. No more long, hot drives to get to the water!

The early months and years of habitation at Franklin were full of the similar processes that we had experienced in 1975 at Norton Summit: replacing the burnt-out wood heater in the sitting room, converting a ground floor bedroom into a modern bath room, replacing sections of rotten flooring and so on. Our container arrived quite promptly, but the driveway was too narrow for the truck carrying it to get near the house. We unloaded it gradually, tractor and all. We bought and erected a new workshop. Like most of the dwellings in Franklin, sanitation was dependent on a septic tank which had to be pumped out once a year. Franklin was destined to wait until 1999 before it gained a modern sewerage scheme. We did most of the work on repairing the house ourselves but we received a lot of advice and help from the local tradesmen.

We met many people, old residents and very recent ones. One of them was Councillor Ruth Coughlin, who was also the secretary of the Franklin Progress Association. We went along to a meeting, became members, and met the President, Garry Barnes. Garry was a professional, contract tree-feller, and a much respected leader of the Franklin community. Unlike the majority of his colleagues, he was far from satisfied with the overall strategy of Forestry Tasmania, which was to convert large areas of native mixed forest into a Eucalyptus monoculture. The practice was based on the research of Dr Max Gilbert whose Doctoral thesis at the University of Tasmania advocated a strategy of clear felling large areas of native forest, removing the best Eucalypts, and some of the rain forest and understory, and then burning the "residue." This created a man-made situation that favoured the planting of eucalyptus from the air, which could be fertilised, also from the air, which led to rapid growth of Eucalyptus to the disadvantage of other species. The disfavoured species included some of the best boat building and carpentry timbers in the world, such as King Billy Pine, Blackwood, Myrtle and Celery Top Pine. There was also a species of pink dogwood, known to have a scent attractive to crayfish, the lobsters of the southern hemisphere and therefore the best timber to use for cray pots. I was pleased to learn that we had plenty of pink dogwood on our property. Garry had lived through the growth of an industry that consisted of small sawmills, especially in the Huon Valley, that had supported the shipbuilding industry of the past. The eventual domination of the industry by pulp production for paper had put many small specialist saw millers out of business. Garry was also the owner of a small motor boat, and like me was puzzled by the complete absence of boats of any kind on the Huon River at Franklin, with the exception of the boats of the Franklin Rowing Club, which served the training requirements of the private schools in Hobart, but had few local members. It was also the preferred training ground for Australian Olympic rowing teams.

The absence of any boats on the water except for the occasional visitor could be explained by the lack of anywhere to tie them up. The waterfront was notable for the remains of many abandoned wharves and jetties, but none of them looked safe, or likely to encourage attempts to land. Garry, Ruth Coughlin and I met one evening near the remains of what was once the New Wharf at the north end of Franklin. From there, passengers had departed and arrived on a regular basis to and from Hobart and intervening destinations for a hundred years. Apples and small fruits were shipped out; shop supplies and agricultural supplies were shipped in. We decided to consult the Progress Association about creating a volunteer work force to build a new wharf, that would attract visitors. Garry said that Ruth Coughlin wanted to resign as Secretary, as her Council work was taking most of her time. So I offered to fill the gap and was accepted.

I had taught my Pacific History students in Adelaide about the cargo cults of New Guinea, which demonstrated the spiritual powers of the indigenous "Big Men" to attract trade, and assist in the universal Melanesian mission of wealth accumulation, in the form of pigs and wives. The building of a wharf might at least contribute to the creation of social capital in this part of the fourth world. Or so I thought.

I suggested to the next meeting that we should start by announcing the date on which the new wharf would be opened. In order to make this a serious proposition, I wrote a letter to Lady Bennett, the wife of Governor Sir Phillip Bennett, asking if she would be willing to open the wharf to public use on the specific date. She was kind enough to accept the invitation. Then I asked Peter Tremlett, owner of the Huon Manor restaurant in Huonville, just above the bridge, if he would be able to use his small steamer, *SS Lady Teresa* to bring Lady Bennett from Huonville down to Franklin to meet the locals and declare the wharf open. The Franklin Progress Association would contribute the firewood for the steamer.

I also made an application to the Council, explaining that Lady Bennett had accepted our invitation. Would they also agree to provide the Vice-regal party with lunch, after the announcement, to which the councillors were invited? Garry thought this might make sure the wharf was completed in time and Council agreed to support it.

For the next four months the Progress Association organised volunteer working parties in the evenings, and members provided materials and finance. Two young women, Jayne Mackay and Pam Roberts, organised a Franklin Fair on the oval with wood chopping contests and a children's pet show, which raised $2,000. This was spent on sawn timber needed for the decking and joists. Large bed logs came from land belonging to Peter Shields and labour and special skills for handling large logs and beams were provided for free by the men who had lost their jobs, at that time, due to the closure of the sawmills in the Huon Valley. As many as twenty volunteers gave their time to complete the wharf. It was opened, as forecast, on 23 November 1991 by Lady Bennett, who made a gracious speech to a sizeable crowd. This was the stimulus for many future projects that Franklin Progress Association initiated.

In the meantime, I had been introduced to Dr Dick Geeves, who was a descendent of William Geeves, the founder of Geeveston, a town famous for its timber industry. Dick was a retired geriatrician, revered for his enthusiasm, community leadership, and historical knowledge of the Geeveston area. We started talking about shipbuilding and I told him all about the building of the new *One and All* in South Australia. Soon we were talking about *Leofleda* and this led him to tell me that Athol Walter, the owner of the slipway and workshop at Shipwright's Point, was about to retire and wanted to sell up. Athol and Dick were next-door neighbours. I remember Dick's lovely wife, Barbara, telling us that if you wanted an expert on boats, you should talk to Dick, and if you wanted a medical whizz, you should talk to Athol.

Athol was a well-known boat builder. He had begun at Wattle Grove in the late 1940s and later moved to Shipwright's Point. By 1990, he had completed his forty-ninth yacht. He showed us around the workshop and said he'd help us with the slip for a while, if we wanted to buy. This seemed like a good little business for us — not too much work — but a little bit of money coming in and the chance to be around boats and people who liked them.

Athol's slip, as it continued to be called for years after we bought it, was very important to the members of the Huon Yacht Club and to a few local fishermen. We were getting to know them and as they began to know us better, they told us of their relief that we were operating the slip. We heard several yarns about Athol's increasing deafness as he aged. They spoke of their anxiety as, in contest with the noise of the winch, they would begin to hurl bits of wood, then stones or shoes against the sliding door at the front of the shed, in their attempts to make Athol stop winding the boat up, or at least slow it down before the cradle hit the shed door. With two of us, one to drive the winch, and the other to keep a lookout on the incoming cradle and to signal when to stop, the boat owners, and ourselves were much less stressed. Athol gave us his "slip book," in which the relevant measurements of all the boats were kept. This enabled us to prepare the cradle for each incoming vessel before it arrived, and mark the cradle at the expected waterline which was all hard work, but easy to get used to. Through slipping local boats, we made many friends in the Port Huon area. Various of Athol's old mates were in the habit of visiting him around lunchtime and having a chat. This didn't look like a custom that was ever going to change, so we put a little wood heater in the workshop and joined in the conversations. We learnt a great deal from those very adaptable men, who could turn their hand to almost any task.

We knew a lot about Adrian Dean, who might have become the designer of *One and All*, and was well known as a local designer and boat builder. He had moved on from boat building to teach carpentry at the Friends' School in Hobart. He had also established a short-term wooden boat building course at Margate with four students, who built five scout patrol boats in seven months. I had the idea of establishing such a school, but I knew my limitations. With the help of Dave Kew, I had gone through the process of building *Leofleda* successfully, and I never forgot David's offer to continue working on her "until she be thoroughly finished," in spite of the fact that I was running out of money. I also remembered my promise to him in return, to make sure I handed on the skills he taught me, to somebody else.

Ruth and I wanted to do something useful with our lives. We discussed the idea of setting up a boat building school, teaching a range of short recreational courses, and hiring teachers from the pool of talented Tasmanians who had expertise in the area and wanted to pass it on. In August 1991, we registered the Business Name of "Shipwright's Point School of Wooden Boatbuilding" at Athol's shed.

We advertised our first course, a "Build your own clinker dinghy" class, early in 1992. We really aimed to test the market and see if there was a demand for such a thing. But that course, due to begin in April, began to fill up. Athol's workshop was only big enough to build two or three dinghies at once, but close by was an enormous cargo shed, once the storage place for vast quantities of apples waiting for export to Europe, in the handsome ships of the Port Line. The Port Huon wharf shed was still used to store apple bins, but there was plenty of space left. In 1991, there was nothing like the quantity of apples exported from the Huon Valley as there had been before Britain had joined the European Common Market. I went to see the shed's owners, the Hobart Port Authority and asked if we could rent a portion of the shed to hold a clinker building class for ten people and their boats. The Port Authority were delighted by the idea and charged us minimal rent.

Our first applicants were an ideal mix of gender, age and skill: Dick Geeves, who had talked us into buying Athol's shed and really should be blamed for everything that followed; Lloyd Griffith, who owned and sailed a boat of his own, and was a good carpenter; Jack Miller, keen to build a boat he could use with his sons; Ted Strudwick, a friend from the Small Boat Club in Adelaide, who had retired to Tasmania. They were soon joined by Jill Paxton and Noni Howard, who was Tasmania's first qualified female carpenter, and had worked as a volunteer on the completion of *One and All*. Noni had been part of the crew that had sailed her to England and back. The idea was that Noni was to help Jill, also a woodworker, to build Jill's boat. The other students were Steve McPhee, a younger man living at Port Huon and myself. Boat building had always appealed to me, but *Leofleda* was a carvel planked vessel and I had never built a clinker boat.

Adrian Dean agreed to become our teacher, an historic agreement as it turned out. Adrian was to build the bridge between what most people thought of as the "Dying Art" of Tasmanian wooden boat building and the expansion of the art that we hoped to re-establish.

Some students who could afford it, built their dinghies using Huon Pine. Celery Top Pine was the next best. It was heavier, but at that time, much easier to find. Most of the dinghies were built to the "Robin" class design by Iain Oughtred. Instead of using marine plywood, as in the original design, we used solid wood in the traditional manner. We started with a day of lofting, for which the upper floor of the large shed was ideal. We used a roll of brown paper and cut it into large sheets. Shoes came off so that we could walk around in socks or bare feet and nail the paper to the floor with drawing pins. We enlarged the scaled drawings to full size, so that we could use them as models for the timbers that made up the back-bone of each boat, the keel, and then the stem. We went to a specialist Huon Pine saw miller, whose business it was to follow the large scale timber harvesting operations in western Tasmania, to get the natural grown curves in the roots of trees or the joining curves from the branches. In some cases they were hundreds of years old. Upright posts were fastened at the end of each building stock to support a long plank, levelled and fastened to the uprights. This plank was strong enough to support the weight of the whole boat.

Ron Martin, a Franklin friend, and I made work benches for each pair of students with vices on opposite sides of each bench. The next job was to manufacture the moulds. We used recycled *Radiata* Pine for this, as the moulds are temporary structures, spaced at each of the three stations, with the centre of the top edge of each mould placed on the exact centre of the edge of the stock plank. Smaller scrap timbers were then used as braces between the moulds, to keep them at right angles to the stock, to create a strong, boat-shaped structure. Planks were laid starting with the garboard strake alongside the keel. The next stage was very difficult, and needed much care and concentration. To begin with battens were used to mark the places on the stem and transom where the planks would be fastened.

Before the second plank was fitted, the top edges of the garboard strakes were bevelled, to receive the second plank. The bevels had to be made on the outside of the top edge of each plank, to achieve a watertight fit when the next plank was clamped onto the structure, using up to three or four clamps at once. The difficult part is the last few inches of the plank in which the bevel changes into a rebate, creating a flat surface for the last few inches of each plank.

We used rebate, or "rabbet" planes as they are called, to remove up to half the timber on the outside top of each end of each plank and corresponding rebates on the inside bottom of the next plank. As well as fitting the planks together, each plank end has to fit into the stem rebate and the transom. With the ends fitting, the contact surfaces were adjusted with a rebate plane to make sure that the seams were tight, and to create an almost invisible twist to the plank. The whole area of each seam had to be touching the bent and slightly twisted surface of the next plank. Otherwise the seam would leak. With that done the planking process could continue, with seven strakes, on each side of the boat.

Beginners might take a whole day to fit each plank, and then to clamp it to the previous plank, often lying on the floor to look at the whole seam from the outside of the boat. Only if there is absolutely no light to be seen between the planks from the inside as well, can fitting be followed by fastening, using copper nails and conical washers, known as roves, to keep the water out. Building to this standard of accuracy, and consequent beauty, takes time and persistence, but is very rewarding. Adrian taught us to "line out" the planks starting with a garboard strake up to perhaps five inches wide. We used light battens to mark out where the aft and forward ends of the planks were going to be fastened on to the stem, and then marked the transom stern. The six remaining planks gradually narrowed by $1/8$ of an inch as the planking rose, until the sheer plank was reached, and filled up the remaining space, which could be up to one inch wider than the rest, to allow for the rubbing strake.

Before each plank was fastened, the plank below it was bevelled so that the inside of the boat is a series of stepped curves, and the overlapping, flat faces are a perfect fit with each other. To begin with, two students on one boat managed to cut out, shape and fasten, one plank on each side each day, having spent the first week lofting, setting up the stocks and making moulds.

At this stage, when there was something for people to see, we decided to hold a School Opening ceremony on 30 May 1992 and invited *The Mercury* reporter Jocelyn Fogagnolo to write about it. We found that we had gained a lot of local support, largely, because the Huon Valley had a history of boat and ship building. We were seen by many as reviving something really important locally. Historically, ship building was a significant part of Tasmania's cultural identity, and this was a time when many people were mourning its demise.

Many of our Port Huon friends helped us to organise and cater for the occasion. We invited local leaders, heroes and friends, including Evan Rolley, the Manager of Forestry Tasmania. We hoped to persuade him that while dry Eucalypt forests were now supplying large quantities of pulp that ended up as paper, higher value should be placed on the mixed wet forest, with Eucalypt canopies and a rainforest under-storey. The under-storey included very valuable and unique timbers like Myrtle and Blackwood, which in the past had supported a furniture manufacturing industry, and Celery Top Pine, that we were using to build our boats. Leatherwood was the unique tree from which world famous honey was made, and by just keeping on growing provided an export as well as an important domestic industry. In the long run, the practice of clear felling and burning of mixed wet forests was a real threat to the boat building industry in Tasmania's south. Many lengthy arguments about this method of logging lay in the future.

Geeveston, three kilometres from Shipwright's Point, with its pulp mill, and its history of dependence on timber exportation as the basis of its economy, had a strong history of hostility to the green movement. It was not a good place from which to launch a head-on challenge to clear felling, burning and aerial sowing a mono-cultural plantation regime. The best thing we could do was to demonstrate an alternative way of thinking and a different strategy.

It was clear that as the operators of the only School of Wooden Boatbuilding in Tasmania we could not escape becoming involved in forestry politics. We were seen by both sides as potential allies. One of the first Tasmanians I met was Bob Brown, founder and inspiration of the first Green political party in the world. Bob had taken part in the Ecopolitics IV conference in Adelaide, and I knew that he and I shared many ideas and hopes. In particular, I discovered that Bob was not, as generally believed, an opponent of cutting down any trees at all. We shared the view that, like other animals, humans are entitled to utilise trees for domestic and other purposes, provided that we do not take more than our fair share of what the forest has to offer to all the plants and animals who depend on it for survival. Clear-fell, burn and sow advocates expected our support because, as boat builders, we were dependent on the logging industry. They thought we should consider the Greens as our enemies.

What was important to us was that we did not destroy the options for future generations by failing to perpetuate the sustainability and resilience of the forest. Modern Humans are unique in that they have an enormous ability to destroy forests, but they also have the ability to measure things, and can discover the biomass quantity of each species in a given area that has grown during a year. This indicates the quantity of timber that can be safely taken for human use, without damaging the capacity of each species to fulfil its ecological function in its original location. Each tree has its capacity for annual growth of bio-mass, and the extraction from each species should be confined to the annual increase in the same area, so that the available volume of each species can remain constant from each year to the next.

The trouble, from our point of view, was that too much of the wet mixed forest, containing rainforest under-storey, was under attack from the paper companies, who were focussed on clear felling large areas of mixed forest in order to take the eucalypts and burn the "residue" and thus prepare an ideal basis for sowing a quick growing Eucalypt monoculture. Giving chemical encouragement to speed growth also resulted in inferior timber, mostly to make paper pulp.

Bob Brown and I agreed that with modern technology, selective logging could become much easier and less dangerous than it had been in the past. Early attempts to log selectively had sometimes led to accidents. Clear felling meant that fallers were always working in the open, on the edge of the forest, and were much safer (and faster) than the selective loggers who preceded them. The introduction of portable saws such as chain-saws and Lucas mills make it possible to remove awkward branches, fell single trees and mill the trunks on the spot where they fall. Theoretically, planks can be transported by hand to the nearest track, thus reducing damage and the amount of fuel needed for the operation. For boat builders, branches can provide timber for grown ribs, knees or any other curved component of the vessel. Selective logging of wet, mixed forest is not necessarily as difficult and dangerous, as the public is led to believe.

Our conversation went on for a while until Bob asked me if I would think about standing for Parliament as a Green candidate. I asked for time to think about it, and felt it a great honour to be asked, especially by Bob. Ruth and I discussed the proposal, but I was now committed to the School, and I am very glad that Bob found a successful candidate instead of me.

Jocelyn Fogagnolo wrote in the weekend "Lifestyle" column of *The Mercury*:

The School is best introduced by its Publicity Pamphlet, "To celebrate the value of Tasmanian Timber, to bring traditional boatbuilding knowledge and skill to a new generation of students, both amateur and professional … It has been established … on a site which has a continuous tradition of wooden boatbuilding since 1841."[15]

---

15   *The Mercury*, 10 June 1992.

She introduced the elderly group of local boat builders, Athol Walter, aged 76, Jock Muir, 77 and Adrian Dean (Adrian was a bit younger), and quoted me:

> These men represent generations of wooden boat builders who have made and developed a tradition that is second to none. Nowhere else in the world has such a small group of people produced so many good boats in the past two centuries. Literally hundreds of these vessels, built on the shores the Derwent, the Huon, and other parts of the State are famous internationally for their seaworthiness, their integrity, and their beauty.

Returning to the future, Jocelyn said that I "… sounded a veiled warning about the need for a sure and constant supply of the boat building timber for which Tasmania was famous throughout the world."

The opening was a very successful and optimistic occasion. On the day we met many new people who became friends as well as teachers, such as the designer Murray Isles and the boat builders Bill Foster and Ian Johnston.

The clinker dinghies continued at a fairly slow rate, given that Adrian was only teaching on Friday afternoons and Saturday mornings. With the planking finished, the ribs were steam bent and fastened with small copper nails tapped through the laps at each rib. The last month was spent making spars, thwarts, centreboards, oars and centreboard cases. Then they were finished, with six coats of spar varnish inside and out. The students were very pleased with themselves, and we had made ends meet financially, but the whole course had taken much longer than we had anticipated. This was quite an inconvenience to our students and we learned our lesson.

Our first course began in April. In June, we ran a short weekend "Tool Seminar," also taught by Adrian Dean, who has an amazing knowledge of traditional woodworking tools. This little course was full within days of advertising. Athol's shed was a bit cold, so we held it in the Supper Room of the Palais Theatre in Franklin. We had only just completed this course, with the dinghy building course still in progress, when we were approached by Huon Skillshare. This organisation offered a variety of learning opportunities to unemployed people. The Manager, Cheryl Nicholas, was very keen to add wooden boat building to the Skillshare curriculum. So we contracted to build two 10 foot clinker dinghies with a class of ten unemployed people in Athol's shed in mid-August to mid-September. I was teaching clinker boat building to the Skillshare students only weeks or sometimes days after I was learning the techniques from Adrian at the Port Huon Wharf shed.

I was very happy to have completed my first clinker dinghy, using natural timber, and finding that, like the others, she took up quickly when we put her in the water. Now, over thirty years later she lives in the Huon River with a cover to keep the rain off, and I row her to keep fit, and sail her for fun. We called her "Clara" after Ruth's grandmother.

Getting the timber for nine dinghies gave us an opportunity to drive across the Island to Strahan and the wild west, where we chose our Huon Pine timber from the three specialist saw millers who shared between them the total production, in the world, of sawn Huon Pine timber, and even rarer, King Billy Pine. It was an amazing journey through mountains smaller than the southern Alps in New Zealand, but just as rugged. There was something else as well, a kind of identifiable sense of foreboding. I put it down to the relative geological youth of New Zealand. Tasmania is many millions of years older, less sunny, and can be intimidating to a stranger.

Bern Bradshaw's sawmill was south of the mining town of Queenstown. Randall Morrison's was on the waterfront in Strahan and Bob Crane's was close to the town of Strahan on Ocean Beach Road. We visited all three of them, and placed orders for as much as we could afford.

We decided to camp that night at Ocean Beach where we took our black Labrador dog, Darwin, for a walk. He suddenly started to open his nostrils, and pull on his lead, so we let him off it, and he ran away as fast as he could go (not very) taking us eventually, as we rounded the beach, to the unmistakable and enormous carcase of a stranded whale. From the smell, it had been there for some time.

Darwin trotted quickly around it, lifting his back leg every few yards to make sure that we, and the whole world, understood whose whale it was. Before we could stop him, he began to roll over it. He wanted to stay with his whale. We had to put his lead on, while holding our noses, and run into the ocean with him and wash him as thoroughly as we could. We stood in the remains of every wave that broke on the beach for quarter of an hour, and rid ourselves of most of the smell of dead whale. But Darwin enjoyed both the whale and the wash very much, and after a good shake, he went to sleep in the cab.

I was invited to give a talk to the members of the Royal Yacht Squadron in Hobart, and to answer questions. I told them that I was not a professional boat builder myself, but had helped to build my own boat and had tested her for six months in the Pacific ocean. I also said that I had some experience of organising Higher Education at the University of Adelaide. I hoped our boat building School would provide a bridge between generations, and thus ensure that the skills, ideals and standards of classic wooden boat building in Tasmania, would be perpetuated.

It was about this time that we noticed a tent erected during the night on the Regatta Ground between the Port Huon Yacht Club, and Athol's shed. The inhabitant turned out to be a very tall Scotsman, late of South Australia called Peter Laidlaw. He came to the shed, stayed for a cup of tea and told us of his education at Fort Augustus, Scotland (our friend, Nick Wright, had also been a victim of this school), and his training as a teacher in Adelaide. It turned out, as it sometimes does, that Ruth had been at school with his sister. He was also a very skilled woodworker and had at one stage built his own boat. He was interested in boats in general. After a few days, Peter asked us if he could sleep in our shed. He said it was a bit cold in his tent. I pointed out that, in spite of Darwin, we had seen some rats. That did not deter him, and he brought his sleeping bag and toothbrush over to our shed. He offered to help with the teaching in return for his accommodation. He soon demonstrated his entitlement to a wage as well.

The two Skillshare dinghies were finished and named *Hartz* and *Picton*, after two local mountains. Tasmania has fewer indigenous place names than the rest of Australia, which reinforces the historical darkness of the island's identity. Skillshare and the students were delighted with the boats they had built and with the well-attended launching. One dinghy was sold to interstate visitors and the other was kept by Skillshare. We developed a happy relationship with Skillshare, its staff and students and ran several boat building and repair courses for them over the next few years. We also offered several courses for Adult Education. Through our slightly crazy, but very accomplished and entertaining friend, David Perez, we began a few dinghy building courses for children from Huon Valley Council Youth Services, where David worked. We also provided the shed and tools for Sacred Heart School students to build their own wooden dinghy, under the direction of Peter Laidlaw. An Iain Oughtred design was chosen, the *Grebe,* as it was called then. The design was detailed for glued plywood construction, 13 feet 6 inches long, 4 feet 6 inches wide, with a gaff sloop rig, a centre-board, rudder, tiller and a pair of oars. This was a request that was to send out expanding waves, as from a stone thrown into the water.

The idea was to get a team of parents and children from one school at a time to work together, with help from me or Peter Laidlaw or Ruth, sometimes our students, and other people as well, depending on availability. Sacred Heart School, Geeveston, Franklin School, Geeveston District High School, Huon Valley Council, Skillshare and the Huon Cluster of Schools eventually had a Grebe of their own. The schools usually bought the timber and fittings, and paid for our supervision and teaching, or provided it themselves, with the Boat School acting as consultant. Parents, friends, and students provided the labour. A total of six Grebes were built between 1993 and 2005, usually with building crews of five or six.

Between 1992 and 1994, about one hundred students attended courses at our shed at Shipwright's Point. They built fourteen new dinghies in the traditional manner, using Tasmanian timbers, ranging from ten to seventeen feet long, and they repaired several more.

Combined with our active life with Franklin Progress Association projects, the operation of the slipway and carrying out additional commercial boat repairs, we became much busier in retirement than we'd originally intended to be.

Chapter 18: "Whatsoever things are lovely…"

Australian Amateur Boatbuilder described the Boat School as "unashamedly traditional in its orientation."[1] We had definitely hit on something. Some of our former Skillshare students had been able to get casual jobs at boat yards as a result of the skills they learnt at the School. These students and several visitors pointed out that what was really needed in Tasmania was a professional accredited course in wooden boat building. They wanted a recognised qualification.

There were very few specialist courses in wooden boat building in Australia. But I had been to Lance Lee's Apprenticeshop in Maine, USA, in 1986, and had watched the students at work, I had seen their smiles; and sensed the delight of a collective effort, and the ultimate creative glory, and I had felt the sense of achievement, as a stack of timber was transformed into a magical and useful artefact. Ruth and I began talking about a professional course in 1992. We made notes about what the content might be, and sought information about registering as a Training Provider.

One fine morning we had a visitor who came to enquire about a lofting course we had advertised. Bill Cromer was an environmental engineer who worked at solving environmental problems in urban contexts. He had a small company based in North Hobart, a wife called Hilary, who was a physiotherapist, two teenage daughters and a younger son. Bill spent a long time with us, looking at what we were doing. His family were interested in trying sailing, and eventually, Bill showed me a plan he had drawn of his dream boat, a 30 foot yacht. "Could you build me a boat like that?" he asked. "I'm not a naval architect, but this is the kind of boat I would like to have for family holidays." I thought his design was a bit boxy, but very comfortable, and family oriented. Maybe a bit too much overall windage.

I was reminded of one of my own dream ships, a Bermuda rigged cutter, called *Maori Lass*, designed by New Zealand designer, H E Cox. I'd read about *Maori Lass* in *Yachting Monthly* magazine when I was at Christ's Hospital. She was 30 feet long, had four berths, and was intended to be fit for ocean sailing as well as weekend cruising. Athol Walter had left a collection of plans in the workshop. Amongst these, I came across the blueprint lines drawings and construction plans of *Maori Lass*. This looked to me to be just the boat for Bill and his family.

I showed the plans to Bill, and explained why I thought the design would be ideal for a family cruiser. Bill agreed that *Maori Lass* was a good choice after considering cost, time needed, and expected performance. H E Cox, I discovered, had died, so I located his family in New Zealand. His wife gave us permission to use the plans Athol had hoarded, after I explained about our intention to run a professional course. She was delighted that another boat designed by her husband would be built in Australia, and asked for no royalty payment. This piece of unexpected sponsorship was vital for the feasibility of our plan.

---

1   *Australian Amateur Boatbuilder*, Vol 1, Issue 4, 1992/3.

I did not pretend that I was, myself, a professional boat builder, but I did think that Tasmania was one of the few places in which the traditional skills of wooden boat building had been preserved, as well as having access to timbers like Huon Pine, King Billy Pine, Blue Gum and Celery Top. Was there not a duty to seize this opportunity to pass on these unique skills to future generations, and to perpetuate the wise use of such magnificent renewable resources? We might be taking a big risk, but if a new generation of wooden boat builders was not able to be taught these ancient skills, then there was no chance that this craft would survive in Tasmania, and an amazing and important component of Tasmanian culture might be lost.

What we could do, initially, was to give some retired Tasmanian wooden boat builders an opportunity to teach their subject, and thus pass on their skills and values such as honesty, accuracy, and beauty into the future. Adrian Dean had demonstrated the feasibility of this with teenagers. Lifting the bar to create careers for adults would need a structure that would ensure the survival of a way of life, and a market for the product of the "Dying Art." I discussed these problems with Adrian, who has always been glad to contribute to the teaching needed to perpetuate his skills. Much later, in 2013, I used the opportunity of an invitation from the National Maritime Museum in Sydney to expand a bit on the notion of the "dying art". I was asked to give the Phil Renouf Lecture, honouring the enormous achievement of Phil Renouf, who had inspired and managed the recovery and restoration of *James Craig*, a steel Barque, built in 1874, at Sunderland, in England. I called my lecture, "Wooden Boatbuilding — Not a Dying Art," because many of the visitors who came to the Boat School had been fascinated by what they saw, but ended the conversation with the words, "But it's a dying art though, isn't it?" I would disagree, politely, and ask them why they thought so many young people all over the world were spending years of their lives learning to do it, and paying for the privilege.

In the lecture, I talked about the global resurgence of wooden boat building and put it down partly to the lessons to be learnt from the international experience of the Vietnam war. The war proved to be the first of a series of events that have unsettled the assumption that endless industrial expansion is inevitable, and that new technology will have answers to all our questions. I drew attention to the social and ecological virtues of wooden boat building, and the association that it generates between doing well and doing good. That talk attracted a full house.[2]

But I am straying off the subject. Jill Paxton, one of our "build your own dinghy" students, introduced us to Bill Foster at the official opening of the School. Bill and Adrian had been apprentices together for several years in the late 1940s. Their Master was the famous Jock Muir, who with Percy Coverdale, and other contemporaries, built a number of craft in the 1940s and 1950s that astonished the world.

---

[2] The talk was published in full on the Museum's website and in part in the journal of the National Maritime Museum, *Signals*, No 103, June-August 2013, pp 40-41.

They were small, unpretentious yachts that finished the famous Sydney to Hobart races and sometimes won them on handicap, while much larger vessels retired.

Bill Foster had been away from boat building for some time. He had several daughters and had moved to a job with a more predictable income to support his family. I asked him if he'd like to take charge of a course, building a 17 foot Whitehall skiff with a class of four students and he agreed. Unlike Adrian, Bill didn't have much teaching experience, but his knowledge of wooden boat building was profound, and itching to get out, and he soon settled in to the task. I told Bill about the professional course we'd been devising and that we needed "industry support" (difficult to find in respect of a "dying art") to get the course accredited. He suggested several people who would support the need for such a course and introduced me to Jock Muir. I also asked if he would be willing to take the role of senior teacher of the carvel building component of our new course. Adrian was prepared to begin the course with a unit in which students designed and built their own tool boxes. This demonstrated commitment, and cultivated pride in high standards of personal workmanship.

I was very impressed with Jock Muir. He understood the difference between training and education. Training, we agreed, was a process of modifying the personality of a student to fit the needs of an industrial process. Education involved the understanding of a creative process, its context, and its history. The goal of training was "competence," and qualifications consisted of a number of "competencies," a rather mediocre ambition, I thought. Education demanded excellence and initiative, starting with accuracy, which was needed for the basic capacity to build boats that did not leak, and including creativity, fitness for purpose, and beauty. We aimed to include all these concepts in our teaching.

We searched for others whose teaching we could rely on to produce graduates who would work in existing boat yards over Australia, or create their own boat yards, one day, if not immediately after graduation. We were lucky to be able to gain approval of our ambitions by such distinguished teachers. The next thing was to apply to become a Registered Training Organisation. And once we had become one, we needed to produce a very detailed curriculum of the course we would teach and get it accredited nationally. This was essential if our students were to be eligible for *Austudy*, the government financial support for tertiary students.

When we started seriously planning an Australian Qualifications Framework, Level 5, Diploma course in wooden boat building, the people in the Department of Vocational Education and Training were a bit alarmed by our proposal to focus on a major boat building project that took up half the course, instead of a series of exercises to achieve so-called "competencies" by working on mock-ups. I said that competence would not be enough. Excellence was what we should aim for. That would be ensured by inviting external surveyors to visit the school several times during the construction of each boat the students were to build, to certify that the workmanship was of a professional standard.

The Department also needed persuading that there was a demand for a course that concentrated on traditional methods, and on using real wood. My theory was that traditional wooden boat building was the best way to start a boat building career. Other materials had their place in the modern world, but wood is the only renewable building material, and applying fundamental principles to new materials was a logical process. Just as learning Latin makes it easier to learn many European languages, building a wooden boat is a useful introduction to building boats out of other materials.

They were surprised too, by titles of units such as "The wooden boat in English literature;" and "Economics and the environment in the Huon Valley." But they were satisfied in the end, as we attracted students from England, Japan, the United States, and nearly all the states of Australia. We aimed to educate as well as train. Getting the Diploma course accredited was a lengthy and demanding process.

When we first started the School, *The Mercury* published a very helpful editorial that gave us enormous encouragement. It provided just the momentum, and understanding of context that we needed. Under the heading, "Relaunching an Item of Excellence," the Editor said, "It would be short-sighted of the Tasmanian Government not to respond to requests for support from the fledging Shipwright's Point Wooden Boatbuilding School in the Huon." At that stage we had neither expected nor requested any Government support, beyond the help we received from individual public servants, who shepherded our applications for accreditation and registration through their various hurdles.[3] The Editor went on to explain that:

> *With some imaginative support the school could form the core for a re-birth of an industry that could further enhance Tasmania's growing national and international reputation as a producer of goods of excellence, and a living embodiment of the philosophy that "small is beautiful" ... This State's wooden yachts and fishing boats have an unparalleled reputation. They married the best of function and form. Those who built them had a reputation without equal in Australia. Their names are still respected in international boating circles.*[4]

Adrian Dean and Bill Foster were to succeed in continuing a process of passing on the values that a new cohort of young boat builders could pass on again to future generations, provided that Tasmania continued to grow the trees on which its excellence was based.

I discussed with Bill Cromer the idea of using his boat, the H E Cox 30, as the major project of the two year Diploma in Wooden Boatbuilding. Bill and Hilary were very enthusiastic about the idea and a great support while we developed our curriculum. We were very lucky to meet people like Adrian Howard and Therese Taylor, who acknowledged the historic and cultural significance of wooden boat building in Tasmania, and guided us through the application process, which was successfully accomplished in November 1994. This process took more than a year.

---

3   In 1997, the Tasmanian Government gave the School a grant of $15,000 to support our teaching fund.

4   *The Mercury*, 18 June 1992.

It might have taken longer if we had not had the assistance of the public servants at the Department of Vocational Education and Training, and the Tasmanian Accreditation and Recognition Committee, who combed through draft after draft of the curriculum with great dedication and enthusiasm.

We had been running our recreational courses out of Athol's shed since 1992, but it was not really big enough to cater for the demands of both recreational courses and a Diploma course. We investigated building on to the shed, approaching Esperance Council for advice. Council was keen enough, but when Athol's Title was more deeply investigated, it turned out that he had built his shed on a mixture of his own land and Crown land (which we knew about) but also a bit of the neighbour's land. There was land around the shed, but it was part of a reserve belonging to, depending on your point of view, either Shipwright's Point Regatta Association, or Esperance Council. We pursued the option of increasing the size of the shed, but it seemed impossible to make much progress and we had no wish to alienate anyone. We knew we would need Athol's shed for parts of the Diploma course and for the opportunities its slipway presented firstly, for student repairs on larger vessels and secondly, for the income it generated. In the end, we left Esperance Council and the Regatta Association to fight it out and looked instead at Franklin, our home town, for a larger premises for the delivery of the Diploma.

At the northern end of Franklin was a large area of land on the river bank, with a creek on one side, Price's Creek, named after Franklin's first, but short-lived settler, John Price. This land was an eyesore and the first sight of the town for people entering from the north. In the nineteenth century, it had been the site of the boat building yard of William Thorp, where six or seven wooden ketches had been built, including *May Queen*. Later that century, the Peacock family set up a jam factory there. [Location Map page 364] In 1993, it was a weedy, neglected piece of land. Its most recent use was as a gravel dump during the road widening of 1989.

We discovered that it was all Crown land, or so the Crown said, and we were granted a renewable thirteen-year lease. Conveniently, at that time, the Hydro-electric workshop town of Tarraleah in Central Tasmania, was being dismantled and auctioned off. We saw an advertisement in *The Mercury* for what had been the Hydro's welding shop. Its owner said it was still standing and we should go and have a look. As soon as we saw it we knew it would suit our purposes. It was a large, vertical board shed, and it cried out to be recycled. We asked around at Tarraleah and luckily found a young local man who was looking for work. He agreed to dismantle the building, stack up the panels, trusses and the framework, and label them for re-erection. He loaded it all onto a big truck, and delivered it to Franklin a week later.

As we had spent a huge amount of time renovating old houses in the past, we were not keen to rebuild the shed in Franklin ourselves. We discussed our plans with our immediate neighbours at the northern end of town, hired a draftsman and put in the appropriate applications to Council. Then we hired two local builders and an engineer to do the work, while we got on with formulating the curriculum.

But we were immediately approached by Skillshare, which wanted to run a construction course and saw our recycled shed as the ideal opportunity for their unemployed clients to gain construction skills and experience. We were not very enthusiastic, partly because we knew the construction process would probably take longer with students involved, and partly because we didn't think the builders would agree to teaching students. But Skillshare had been good to us and it was a real opportunity for unemployed people to get valuable experience. After talking about the idea to the builders, they agreed that it would take longer, but they would do it. We paid the builders, the students had the experience they wanted, Skillshare staff supervised their students and we left them to it.

One helpful co-incidence at this time, was the foundation of the Australian Wooden Boat Festival in November 1994, in the dockland area of Sullivan's Cove, Hobart. The idea had been brewing for some years in the brains of Ian and Cathy Johnston and Andy Gamlin, who had been inspired by the festival at Brest, in France.

We were aiming to begin our first two-year Diploma course in February 1995. The timing of the Festival and the finalisation of our national accreditation, meant that we had only limited time to advertise our course and recruit students. The first Festival attracted 40,000 visitors and 180 boats. The weather was sunny and bright. After that it became a regular event every two years. What we took to the Festival, by way of a display, was an old student desk from a primary school, two chairs, photos of our recreational courses and nothing much else except one copy of the detailed accredited curriculum, signed by Adrian Howard in ink as "Accredited," and a prospectus. Nevertheless, our course attracted considerable interest at the first Festival.

Our 1995–96 Prospectus lacked gloss, and was written in plain English. For the inside cover, I drew up a map of our local waterways, the Huon Estuary and D'Entrecasteaux Channel, full of cosy anchorages. It consisted of a few pages to introduce the teaching staff, including Bill Foster, Adrian Dean, Murray Isles, Peter Laidlaw, Clive Crossley, Ian Johnston, Ian Doolan, Ruth and myself, with a brief summary of the content of fifteen compulsory "modules" or subjects. The course began with each student designing and building his or her own toolbox, working through subjects about wood, marine adhesives and chine construction, small boat and displacement boat design, clinker construction, metal components in wooden boats, engine installation and boat yard and small business management, interspersed with a cluster of subjects that covered the whole process of building a carvel cruising yacht, for the Cromer family. There was also a subject about repairing and restoring wooden boats. Its delivery, of necessity, was opportunistic and extended over the whole two year period as work became available. We included some optional subjects as well, such as the "Personal Project," selected by students themselves with staff assistance, and "The wooden boat in English literature," which I enjoyed teaching.

Our budget assumed an intake of ten students every two years, but the first time we offered the course, only eight of the twelve applicants seemed suitable and likely to finish. We thought about it for a week, did some sums, and decided to go ahead with the eight we had selected, taking into account interviews, references and written applications. The Cromer family provided a full fee-paying scholarship for one student, and Forestry Tasmania offered two part-fee paying scholarships for students in our first course. One of our students received a part-fee paying scholarship from Australian Newsprint Mills.

All of our students over the following six years were courageous, talented, and interesting people, but those who applied for this first course were extraordinary, in that they were taking a huge risk. This was a new, untested course. We were new, untested providers. Although most of our staff were expert boat builders, some of them did not have much teaching experience. The wooden boat building industry was small and competitive. Enrolling in the course meant considerable upheaval for students and their families coming from other states or countries. In the case of the first students, there was not much time for them to save money to pay fees and living expenses for two years. Tasmania suffered from high rates of unemployment. In Franklin and the Huon Valley, these rates were even higher, so there was not much in the way of work available for students to supplement their incomes in the long breaks between semesters.

We turned to our friends and neighbours in the Huon Valley for help in providing accommodation, and all of the new intake found a place to live, in a range of dwellings from empty family houses to old apple pickers' huts, left behind on many former orchards. We thought ourselves lucky to have attracted what looked like a very confident and interesting group of people.

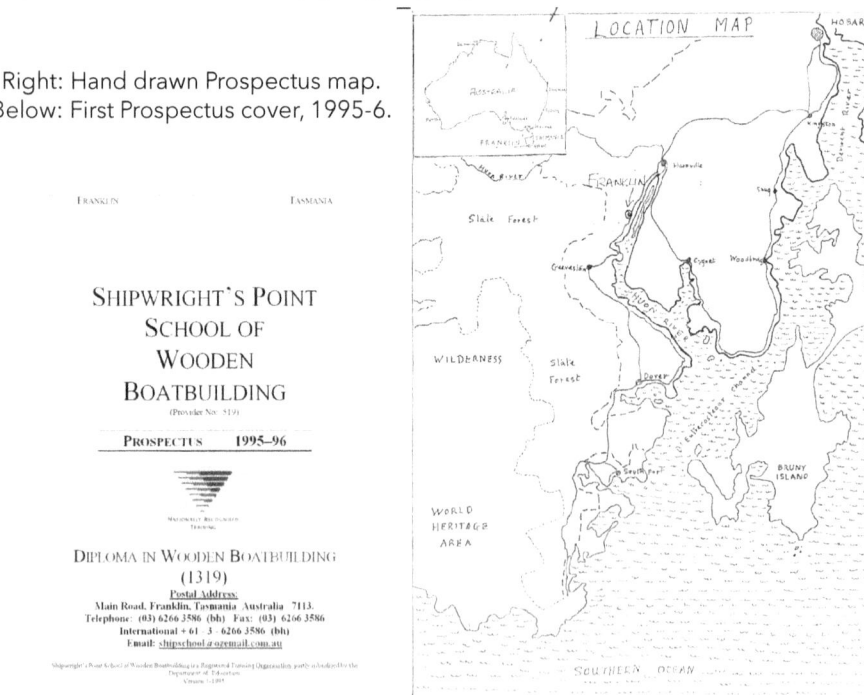

Right: Hand drawn Prospectus map.
Below: First Prospectus cover, 1995-6.

The first course as expected, attracted mostly students living in Tasmania, although all but two originated in other states. One was from England, one from New South Wales and one from the United States. The only trouble with our American was that he came under the category of an "overseas student." While the Englishman was then a British citizen, he was married to an Australian and entitled to stay in the country. The American could only stay as long as his parents were here, and they were on a temporary exchange as teachers. We had not anticipated having any overseas students in our first course, particularly as it was offered at such short notice, and to be able to accept him, we had to very quickly gain registration on the "Commonwealth Register of Institutions and Courses for Overseas Students" (CRICOS), of which we had never heard. Thankfully, we were once again helped by a public servant in Tasmania who was in charge of this aspect of education and we were accredited in time for the student to start the course.

The course began with an orientation week at the start of which I explained to the students that it was essential for the success of the School that there would be a large degree of commitment on their part. For this reason, I explained the need for continuity of effort, the value of each student to the rest of the crew, and the completion of all the tasks included in the syllabus, starting with learning how to use traditional hand tools and finishing with the launch of a completed 30 foot vessel that would be only as reliable as its builders and their judgements. Individual reliability had to be taken for granted, if everyone was to be safe and successful. We emphasised that accuracy and honesty were vital.

The Orientation week including a cruise in Adrian Dean's yacht *Claudia*, designed and built by himself; Clive Crossley's yacht, *Ananda*, also built by himself, and my own *Leofleda*. That introductory cruise was to become a custom at the start of each course, and enabled us to get to know the students very well. In addition to familiarising the students with each other and the staff, the orientation week also had a community service component, in this case, removing rubbish and a general clean-up of the Parks and Wildlife shelter on Partridge Island in the D'Entrecasteaux Channel. The local fish farm owners, Tassal, obliged by collecting the bagged rubbish in their boats and disposing of it.

The students also salvaged a sunken vessel called *Salty*, with holes in her, lying near the river bank on the bottom of the river. We wanted to make it clear that building a new vessel from scratch was often the rare high point of the boatbuilder's calling, rather than the main activity, of repair and restoration. Much of the time, repairs and restorations were exercises in imagination, originality, and determination, as the mud came off, the damage was assessed, and a quote was prepared for restoration, re-building or repair. That activity, I explained, would often support more than half of a working life.

Salty had been an early river power boat, but by 1995, her engine was just a lump of rust. Getting her to the surface from the bottom of the river was a challenge to be overcome by partially inflating two inner tubes of truck tyres on the surface of the river, and attaching them to the sunken vessel by diving down with slings to put around the ends of the hull. The tubes were then fully inflated, until *Salty* floated enough to tow her into shallow water. *Salty* provided repair and teaching opportunities for the next two years.

Adrian Dean taught the first subject of the course, a very valuable one that we called "The Boatbuilder's Tool Chest." The classroom part went through a lot of technological history, about the small tool making companies of Sheffield in England, that had amalgamated around the quality of the steel for which, during the industrial revolution, the town grew famous. Adrian dealt in categories such as measuring and marking tools, carving tools like spoke-shaves and draw knives, and fastening tools, nails, screws and bolts, percussion tools like hammers and mallets, slicks and adzes, chisels and gouges, boring tools like drills and augers. Adrian encouraged students to become connoisseurs of tools, and to be able to judge the value of any that they could find at garage sales. When they obtained old chisels for nothing, he showed them how to make and fit new handles, bound with steel or brass tubing, available from the Council's rubbish tip. They learnt how to sharpen saws, both ripping (with the grain), and cross cut, and how to sharpen planes, adzes, and chisels.

The result was growth of confidence, initiative and pride. Later on they learnt how to modify old cheap wooden planes for creating the hollows on the insides of boat planks, and the blades of calm-water oars.

In the practical part of the subject, each student designed and built their own tool chest for their own tools that they could use in the shed, in addition to the

Salty, salvaged at Huonville by Diploma students, 1995. (Photo Chris Burke)

tools we provided. These included both stationary and hand held power tools, thickness planer and band saw, which students were taught to use and were supervised until they were competent.

The first boat the students built was a flat bottomed punt designed by Murray Isles. We asked him to design a multipurpose work boat suitable for activities like collecting the logs out of the river whenever there was a bit of a flood, or as a stable platform for working on larger moored vessels. Murray designed the boat to include a number of techniques: clinker sides, and a cross planked, caulked bottom and knees, some laminated and some grown. We taught the students how to make the knees, by steaming the laminations and then bending and clamping them around a mould, the shape of which was established by making accurate patterns. When the laminations were cool and dried, they were glued together with clamps to retain their shape. Four knees were needed for the four corners of the boat, and six more for the ends of the three thwarts.

The sides of the vessel were made of seven strakes about 15 feet long, five inches wide, and one inch thick, with flat surfaces for the length of each strake. The result was similar to the construction of dories. After the sides were built, the boat was turned over and the bottom was planked with local, well-seasoned stringy bark timber. The cross-planked bottom allowed for plenty of caulking to be done by each student. They learned how hard to hit the caulking iron with the mallet; just hard enough to compress the twisted caulking cotton in the seam to keep the water out, as the seasoned timber and the caulking cotton expands, but not hard enough to split anything. Twisting the caulking cotton and hammering it into the v-shaped seams, tight on the inside and open $1/8$ of an inch on the outside, is one of those things you can only learn by practice and experience, listening for the correct "ring," given good demonstration and teaching. With eight students at work, the construction of this boat took only two weeks, and the preparing and painting another couple of days.

Just as some cultures include collecting paintings, wines, and stamps, Tasmanians collect Huon Pine, often, with the serious intention of building themselves a boat one day that they would use themselves, and then pass on to their children. The next best thing though, as they aged and children grew up, and lost interest in wooden boats or as they themselves developed a passion for cars and tents, or caravans, was to know that the timber they had cherished would, after all, be used for its intended purpose. So over time we were able to stockpile Huon Pine and other timber for our purposes. We heard news of stashes of timber by word of mouth. So, after a few telephone calls, I took our one-ton truck, with a timber rack, and asked good people all over Hobart and beyond, if they would sell their wood, that had lain in cellars, attics, and sheds, sometimes for generations. Tasmanians then knew about wood, and it had been properly stacked, with "stickers" between each level of planks, to keep it dry and unwarped. I told them that they were supporting a significant aspect of Tasmanian culture, to be nourished for future generations.

But we had not had time to acquire a stockpile of timber, when the students built their first boat. We had to get wood we could get dry "off the shelf." We bought some top quality kiln dried Radiata Pine for the planking and some hardwood for the bottom. Bill Foster was a bit ashamed that the first boat to be built by the students was planked in Radiata Pine and suggested that we use the American name for the timber, "Monterey Pine." We named her *Betsy Walton*, after a young woman who had operated a rowing ferry service between Huonville and the western side of the Huon River in the nineteenth century.

This subject prepared the students for the relatively advanced later subject, Clinker Construction, starting with the plans and a stack of timber. We divided the class into two teams. Each team built a 10 foot sailing dinghy, designed by Bill Foster, in eight weeks. I taught one group, while Peter Laidlaw taught the other. We sold the boats almost as soon as they were finished, to people who visited the workshop and met the students as they worked.

The so called "Forest Wars" of this period of Tasmanian history were an inescapable background to the whole concept of building wooden boats. An early subject in the Diploma course was called "The Wooden Boatbuilder's Medium." We thought wooden boat building was something that called for both ideological and historical knowledge, and some fieldwork in the local forests, to enable the students to understand the implications, for them, of the method of logging called "clear-felling." This involved using machines to fell swathes of old growth or old regrowth forest, regardless of age and species. The "residue" was then burnt and replaced with mono-cultural Eucalypt plantations. We invited both Forestry Tasmania managers and members of an organisation called the Southern Forests Community Group, to talk to our students. Forestry Tasmania talked to the students about their own forest management regime. The Southern Forests Group were advocates of the establishment of community forest areas in old growth forest, to be harvested one tree at a time and at a pace that would maintain the biomass of the original forest.

We also asked Roger Linnell and Andrew Skinner, two local saw millers who specialised in "Special" species like Myrtle, Blackwood and Celery Top Pine, to take us into a forest and demonstrate the technique that they used to practise selective logging. This method made it theoretically possible to limit the annual extraction of the biomass of commercial species, to what nature added to the forest each year. They demonstrated the care and judgement needed to fell single trees in thick mixed forest, and then remove the branches, and haul the logs, through the forest, using slings, pulley blocks attached to adjacent trees, and cables to steer the logs to the nearest road, while causing minimum damage to the ecosystem.

We and our students soon learnt about the ecological importance of the remaining areas of wet mixed forest, containing not only Eucalypts, but also an under storey of Special Timbers, including Celery Top Pine, Myrtle, Sassafras, Blackwood, and Leatherwood, the tree on which Tasmania's honey industry depends. Bees also need their own honey to keep well and provide pollination of many agricultural crops. Celery Top Pine is a softwood which has the strength of the best hardwoods, and reaches its most useful size for boat building in around 400 years, but because of its location in the under storey, and the protection provided to it by the tall eucalypts around it, it sheds its early branches, grows straight-grained, clear, rot resistant timber outside the knots, and extends its girth as it reaches for the light above the canopy. It also steams well when green if you want to bend it.

Ruth and I hoped for an alliance between ourselves and Forestry Tasmania, created by a compromise, establishing specialist timber areas, or "coups" that would be set aside for production of old growth timber at a slow pace. Evan Rolley, the General Manager of Forestry Tasmania agreed, but as the years went by we discovered that many of the coups supposedly dedicated to the production of "special timbers" consisted of mainly low value eucalypts, and in some cases lacked trees of any kind. We tried to establish a realistic and agreeable relationship, and invited Forestry staff to explain and defend their policy to our students. Presuming that Forestry Tasmania had nothing to hide, we obtained permission to take students into the forests before and after they were clear felled and then burnt. When the students saw the slopes of what had been forests, charred and covered with abandoned logs, some of them shed tears.

Assessment for this unit involved an essay. This was an idea based on my experience of the standards required for research projects of honours degrees in the History Department of the University of Adelaide. I set specific topics, most about forest management, but students could also choose a topic of their own, so long as the appropriate research standards were met.

Forestry Tasmania allowed us to go into the forests after they were burnt, to salvage as much as possible of the still salvageable timber. I thought it was important for the students, and the foresters to have to think about the contentious contingencies of overseas markets, local employment, risks and how to minimise them, the habitat values of healthy forest ecosystems, research opportunities, tourism and wooden boat building. Was it just a "dying art"? Or could it be the focus of a return to an economy based on renewable energy, local ownership of small businesses, and local control of regional economies?

Essay writing was something that had not been part of the educational experience of many of the students. We gave lectures about how to do the research, how to document sources, how to present a disciplined argument. The students all produced creditable essays despite their initial anxiety about the task.

The gaps between these subjects were filled with short courses on engine installation, provided by the Australian Maritime College and on naval architecture, taught by Murray Isles who had arrived in Tasmania from New South Wales. Clive Crossley had recently retired from the marine biology department of the University of Sydney and taught a two week unit on the metal components of wooden boats, dealing with the mysteries of electrolysis, and the compatibility of metals in a boat. Ruth and Murray taught a two week unit on small business and boat yard management.

The longest units covered the construction of the HE Cox design for the Cromer family. Each boat the students built was the subject of professional survey by marine surveyors. The Cox boat was surveyed at several different stages of building. The process started with lofting—using the measurements on the blueprint plans to draw the lines at full scale on the floor of the workshop. It was the natural next step after Murray's unit on naval architecture, and enabled the builders to make templates of some items, such as the keel, and taking the measurements off the loft floor to build the moulds that were to create the shape of the hull.

The first stage of constructing the yacht was to lay the keel. We were given the whole trunk of a mature Blue Gum (*Eucalyptus Globulus*) by a friend of Bill Foster who had some private forest land close to Franklin. This is a very heavy timber, immensely strong and durable, and used to build many Tasmanian coastal and ocean-going sailing ships in the nineteenth and early twentieth centuries. Wooden yachts in Tasmania are usually built with Blue Gum keels and deadwoods, and sometimes planking below the waterline, as well. Much lighter and equally durable Celery Top Pine, or Huon Pine was used for planking the topsides.

We shopped around local plumbers for scrap lead, luckily at a time when people were buying old houses, in places like Franklin, and replacing old lead piping with modern plastic. The lead keel was bolted to the wooden keel with copper bolts made by cutting 25 mm copper rod to the right lengths, using a hand-held die, to cut the threads, and a ball peen hammer to make a rounded head with the bolt held in a strong metal vice.

A small foundry made us the bronze nuts and washers we needed. Bill Foster was able to help us track down the specialist suppliers who had survived the fibreglass revolution in the industrial suburb of Derwent Park just north of North Hobart. We called it "The Centre of the Universe," because its stores and shops and workshops were seemingly the source of all things. It had not been destroyed by "progress" nor gentrified. It was the home of a working community that contained almost everything we needed. We had no machinery to lift heavy items, but we did have the experience of Bill Foster, and plenty of youthful muscle, using levers and wedges, blocks and tackles, and crowbars. A stern post was fitted to the after end of the keel, and the grown stem was taken from the large curved timber from the spreading foot of the tree that provided the keel. This use of hand tools and recycled material had an enormously encouraging effect on the students. It expanded their range of independence.

Betsy Walton with her builders.
(Photo courtesy of *Huon Valley News*)

The moulds were made by the students who had not been putting the backbone of the boat together. And they swapped jobs to give everyone a chance of working on everything. Students worked in pairs on each mould, made from second hand timber and some, of *pinus radiata*, grown fast in plantations in the north of Tasmania. After two weeks the moulds were placed on each station as marked, at right angles to the keel with two feet between stations. They were braced to each other, to ensure perfect symmetry. After the best part of a morning, with each student checking every mould with squares, measuring tapes, plumb bobs and levels; the individual pieces of wood began to come together and create the shape of the boat.

Long 40 × 40 mm "ribbands" were then fastened to edges of the moulds with steel screws to prevent any movement, They also provided a base for the ribs. The ribs were made from Celery Top Pine, in various lengths between the keel and the sheer line. They were notched into the keel, steam bent inside the ribbands, ten inches apart, and clamped until they were dry, and fastened.

Then we could see the whole skeleton of a beautiful vessel, and we could imagine how she would look when she was finished. All the energy was then applied to the same boat in the same place, and things speeded up. This size of boat had the important educational advantage of being small enough to ensure that she would be finished, including an interior fit-out, sails and rigging, on time, and big enough to make room for eight students to work together. All of them automatically held a stake in her completion, and shared pride in her quality.

Starting from the keel, ribbands were replaced by planks. Planking started with the garboard strakes, fitted along both sides of the keel; as well as the sheer strake, fitted to the level of the deck. One plank at a time was fastened on each side of the keel, with four students working together. This encouraged competition in both speed and quality, but it was never explicit. To begin with, the shape of each plank was determined by using light battens to define the upper and lower edge of each plank. Battens were fastened with small nails to each of the moulds. This process produced two templates, which were clamped onto plank timber, and marked, allowing for the tapered length of the scarf lap, usually about a 14 inches long. The outside of the scarf with the thick end went for'ard, and the thinnest end, aft. The thin end was an eighth of an inch thick to ensure a step at both ends of the scarf and a neatly fitted and fastened trailing strake, on the outside of the hull. This is perhaps the most exciting part of building a wooden boat.

Once the students had all the ribs in place and had the rhythm going, they were getting two completed strakes fastened each side of the boat each day. Planking a sizeable ocean-going vessel was a job for two pairs of builders to work together, one pair each side of the boat. The individual planks of varying length were between ten feet and eighteen feet long, and one inch thick. Each strake, was made of two planks, scarfed together, some up to just over thirty feet long, and they were measured to make sure that the scarfs were staggered, to spread the strains as the vessel leapt through the swells of the ocean. Each plank was situated at least two feet aft or forward of the adjacent scarfs alongside its neighbour strakes on both sides of the boat, and the scarfs, on both port and starboard sides, had to be exactly opposite each other.

Slight bevels had then to be put onto the lower outside edge of each new strake, with a wood to wood fit for the inward quarter of an inch, leaving the outside three quarters of an inch of the new seam, an eighth of an inch open, to take the caulking cotton. In some areas each plank had to be slightly rounded on the outside and in other places to be slightly hollowed on the inside, to create a perfect fit between the plank and the outer surface of all the ribs. Planking the area of the reverse curve between the waterline and the keel meant shaping the hollow underneath the bilge. This took great care, and to begin with, much fitting and re-fitting, but it established the standard of carpentry that was needed to build a flawless vessel, and to banish the concept of "tolerance" from the language. Things fitted, or they didn't, thanks to the wood on wood perfection insisted on, and taught to the students by Bill Foster and Adrian Dean, and to me by David Kew.

Nails were driven through the planking into the ribs by a student lying on his or her back, while the partner climbed inside the boat with a rove punch (roves are a kind of conical copper washer), a ball peen hammer, and a pair of end nippers. The outside partner had a "dolly," a home-made bit of steel shaft, weighing about a kilogram. This was held firmly against the head of each copper nail, as the student inside used a rove punch, made by drilling a hole down the middle of a piece of steel rod or hardwood, about 4 inches long, to force the rove down the nail. The

Little fleet of 10 foot clinker dinghies, designed by Bill Foster and built by Diploma class in 1999. (Photo, Chris Burke)

end of the nail was then cut off, and shaped, like a mushroom over the rove, with a ball peen hammer.

This sounds like a complicated process, and it did require good demonstration by the teacher, but it took each pair of students only a couple of trials, to be able to do it beautifully. And it then became an almost rhythmic and relatively speedy process. Having eight students at this stage was ideal. The rattle of light hammers became the background noise for the next months.

By the time the planking was begun, the School had attracted the interest of a lot of supportive organisations and individuals. Jocelyn Fogognolo wrote a regular boating page for *The Mercury* newspaper every Saturday. She often asked if we had any news for her. Her article of Tuesday 26 March 1996 was typical:

> *Next weekend the public will have a chance to see an Australian "first" in operation — The Shipwright's Point School of Wooden Boatbuilding at Franklin, on the banks of the Huon River. The school, which is offering Australia's first diploma course in wooden boatbuilding, will be open for guided tours at 11 am, and at 2 pm next Sunday.*
>
> *The tours will be a highlight of the "Taste of the Huon" festival, which this year has a strong maritime and historical theme and will be centred on the old river port of Franklin.*[5]

Anne Crawford, a journalist working for *The Australian Way* (February 1996) reported that:

> *Ruth and John Young's two year diploma is the only accredited course of its kind in Australia. The couple say it will inject a new generation of boat-builders into a field that is, if not moribund, certainly in need of revival. The school, which is housed in a former hydro-electrical commission shed, is dissected by the huge skeleton of an almost finished nine-metre carvel boat, the tangible work of the first intake of students.*[6]

Planking took about three months, and then we could dismantle the moulds and use the wood for future projects. Floors were fitted and fastened between the Celery Top ribs, and knees, in the corners of the boat and between the decking and the topsides. The stringers, the longitudinal members inside the bilge were bent to shape, placed and fastened. This was the magic moment when the whole hollow shape of the vessel could be appreciated for the first time.

The building of a yacht was the central focus of the course, and every student took part in it. There were some weeks when the boat lay in the middle of the shed, while the students were concentrating on shorter subjects.

We used the Palais Theatre as a giant sail loft, and class-room for a very short course about sail making. Ian Doolan talked about the history of his art, old and new materials, and demonstrated his rare skills, before getting the students to try them out for themselves. The floor was an ideal place to demonstrate how things were done. For example, when he wanted to show how to put the "bunt," that is the curve of the sail just above the boom, into the mainsail, he took the slack of the foot of the sail in his left hand, and used the wrist of his right hand to flick a

---

5   *The Mercury*, 26 March 1996.

6   *The Australian Way*, February, 1996, pp 76–77.

powerful curve with a measuring tape, so that it carried along the whole length of the foot of the sail, from clew to tack. Then he took a piece of charcoal and followed the crease of the curve by hand, marking it to establish the shape of the sail he wanted to cut. This was the way to create the required lift, like an aerofoil on its side, when the boat would be going to windward. Nowadays, most sail makers use a computer to do this, but Ian demonstrated the way it was traditionally done.

The students had a go as well. Not that we wanted them all to become sail makers. We wanted to demonstrate the way in which all the specialists involved in the project were contributing to the overall achievement. They were not training to be repetitive process workers, as in a factory, but to become people who understood and experienced the whole creative context in which they were working. That way, they learnt the need for continuous practice, patience and persistence on the long road to perfection. They became people who knew enough about every aspect of wooden boat building, and were able to contribute to the work of all the specialists, and each other.

My own level of experience was less than that of some of the students. This was a more complex vessel than *Leofleda*, but as I watched, I learnt more.

Our student intakes consisted of random groups of men, women and children, who had a powerful social impact on the Franklin community. They became part of the town and involved themselves in the town's activities. The reverse happened too. We had outdoor barbecues every Friday afternoon after work, and these gradually became a social occasion for the locals as well as the students. The students grew proud of their work. It was then time for the surveyor to confirm that the yacht and all the boats they built were "thoroughly finished."[7] The two year course concluded with a public launching of the yacht, *Lady Franklin*, the first of its kind launched in Franklin for many years. Bill and Hilary Cromer were pleased with their boat and we acknowledged and are indebted to them for the crucial role they played in success of the Diploma qualification. The graduation ceremony was held in the elegant Supper Room of the almost century-old Palais Theatre. After that, we and our exhausted students and teachers went out to dinner at the Franklin Tavern.

We ran three two year Diploma courses at Franklin and Port Huon between 1995 and 2000, with fascinating and often inspiring students from diverse backgrounds. They contributed to the reputation of the School and well-being of the Franklin community, both while they were enrolled and afterwards. We found that after each delivery, we altered our curriculum slightly as we learnt, largely from the students themselves, what worked and what didn't. By the end of 2000, the curriculum was in its fifth version. We started in 1995 with only one exit point, that is, Certificate IV, achieved at the end of the first year. But we found we had to create at least one other exit point, at Certificate II, in response to the request of North West TAFE

---

7   Drake's famous prayer as he and his troops stood before the siege of Cadiz, "Grant us also to know, O Lord, that it is not the beginning of any great enterprise, but the continuing of the same until it be thoroughly finished, that yieldeth the true glory." It became something of a perpetual slogan.

in Queenstown, Tasmania to offer a short boat building course to its students. We also created a course for Great Southern Regional College of TAFE in Albany, Western Australia which wanted to provide an accredited course focussed around the building of a whaleboat. These courses were licensed to the TAFEs, the licences were renewable annually.

In order to qualify our students to sail a boat, the School became an Australian Yachting Federation (now Yachting Australia) Training Institution. In addition to running the Diploma course, we also provided various levels of sail training courses for the staff and students of several local schools. We formed very good relationships with Franklin Primary School and Geeveston District High School, and we supported each other mutually.

All up, about one hundred adults and children gained a sailing qualification, ranging from beginner to instructor, from the School. We also continued to offer recreational courses in the long winter breaks between the Diploma semesters and built dinghies for, or with, Franklin Primary School and Geeveston District High School. Peter Marmion, Principal of Franklin School, asked us to build a suitable sailing vessel, eventually named *Rhonda K*, in honour of the highly valued office administrator of the school who was about to retire. I wrote to Iain Oughtred, the designer, to tell him we were building another of his designs, using King Billy Pine, since we could get it easily from the west coast of Tasmania. I received a quick reply to say that we were very lucky to have such magnificent material to work with, and to wish us well. Now, there are six clinker built Grebes, in which hundreds of children, and some of their parents have learnt to sail in safety.

Excluding the schools, 179 boat building students passed through our doors, including 23 Diploma graduates.

The competition for places in the Diploma increased as more and more was written about the School and more and more people applied for places. Our second course (1997–98) was run with nine students who built a 31 foot yacht *Atlas*, designed by Jim Brooke-Jones who had been a student in our first Diploma course; our third and last course (1999–2000) had ten students, who built the Lyle Hess "Taleisin" cutter, *Wild Honey*. Not all our graduates worked as boat builders after graduation, but several did and still are. Several also became teachers of wooden boat building, which was gratifying for us, as the whole point of the School was to pass on the skills of traditional boat building. We were fortunate to have such enterprising and interesting students and to have been able to employ the very best teachers we could ever hope for. Tradition was a Tasmanian advantage of which we were acutely aware, and the teachers were delighted with an opportunity to keep the culture going.

Sean Hogben was one of our first Diploma students. He was a Walkley Award winning journalist, working mainly for *The Australian Financial Review*, but also for other papers and journals. He wrote several articles about the School and Franklin that made an enormous contribution to our success.[8] I would like to thank him for this crucial role, at a time when it was most needed. I am especially grateful for Sean's understanding of our intention of reviving the traditional values encapsulated by Tasmania's wooden boat building tradition, and the credit he gave to Jock

---

8   "Time off on Sunday," *Sunday Tasmanian*, 24 September 1995, p 19-20; "Tasmania's Boatbuilding Tradition: Sea-kindly and Strong," *Wingspan*, July 1996, pp 10-21.

H E Cox designed, *Lady Franklin*, close hauled in a nice breeze. A credit to the first Diploma in Wooden Boat Building students 1995-6. (Photo Chris Burke)

Muir, and his apprentices, Adrian Dean and Bill Foster for their unique contribution to our efforts. Other journalists, like Rob Keeley and Jocelyn Fogagnolo also wrote about the School. And this publicity largely explains why entry to subsequent intakes became highly competitive. By the end of 2000, over a hundred men and women expressed an interest in the course beginning in 2001.

By 2000, we felt we had established something that had the potential to survive. There was a market for the Diploma, for the boats our staff and students produced and there were graduates who could maintain the standard of teaching. We were also tired and I looked forward to real retirement, since I had already changed career several times and was sixty-six years old. We decided to sell the School. An Australian mainland organisation was interested in buying it, but when the local successor of Skillshare, Southern Tasmanian Employment and Placement Solutions (STEPS) also became interested, the option to keep the School in local hands seemed attractive to us.

As part of our contract with STEPS, we agreed to recruit the next group of students for the 2001–2 Diploma Course. STEPS was to begin teaching in February 2001. We were delighted by thirty good applications from Tasmania, the United States and the Australian mainland.

We explained to the new students that we would no longer be running the school, but that the new owners would build on its established ethos. It was agreed that since Ruth and I were the people with whom the new students had made initial contact, I would introduce the STEPS staff to the students, and assure the students of the continuity of our educational philosophy and practice. I knew, from the many discussions that we had with the applicants, by email and telephone, that the established ethos was a big part of the attraction of the course from the students' point of view.

We included, as a precondition of the sale, that STEPS should pass a resolution in favour of managing the school in accordance with a "statement of ethos," which we wrote. It was in many ways a statement which reflected the ideas I had developed when I was running the Centre for Environmental Studies and writing *Sustaining The Earth*. I saw it as an opportunity to demonstrate how doing well could be used as a way of doing good. The Statement of Ethos had three principal objectives: to provide professional training in wooden boat building in the context of a wider educational experience; to demonstrate the low cost and high value of creating interesting and rewarding work by maximising added value locally and emphasising skill and quality; and to maintain an educational philosophy centred on ecological sustainability and the creation of socially useful and personally fulfilling work that is not damaging to society or the environment.

On the suggestion of Forestry Tasmania, we also asked that an Advisory Committee of the Board be established, "To assist the Manager and staff to implement the Statement of Ethos." I have a record of the first Advisory Board meeting. Others may have been held, but I was never invited to them. We left the School with ten new students, a long list of potential students and contracts for yachts for the next two courses.

I was invited to give an introductory handover lecture to staff and students of 2001. I began by congratulating the ten successful students for getting places in competition with a very capable group of applicants. I congratulated them for their success in dealing with all the obstacles that lay in their path; finding somewhere to live and the money for their fees; especially those who had to obtain overseas student visas, which meant travelling considerable distances within the USA. They were already impressing the people of Franklin with their energy, diversity and ability.

I explained the history of the School and the Diploma course and about the staff, who had established the school, and had given it a reputation of excellence. "If you can build a wooden boat," I told them, "then you can build anything else out of wood that you want."

I told them that ahead of them, lay two years of collective as well as individual achievement:

Whatever your present level of skill and experience, in two years' time you will have built at least five boats between you, to very high standards, including a 32 foot ocean-going vessel that can be sailed anywhere in the world that isn't frozen. Joining a group of complete strangers for two years is a bit like setting off in a small boat to sail across an ocean. Once you are under way you can't change the crew. There is an element of risk, but a common purpose. When you get to where you're going, there is a great sense of achievement, and in retrospect it becomes a self-defining experience. Launching the offshore vessel will be a celebration of building a group of ten qualified professional boat-builders, as well as building a boat.

It was not long before there were tensions which led to complaints by the students, often, unfortunately, to me, which put me in a difficult position. I explained that the School had a formal grievance procedure and there was little I could do except recommend that the students engage in it. Soon, some students began to leave partway through their course. This was a shock to us. Nevertheless STEPS continued with the Diploma until 2005, but by 2006 ceased to deliver accredited training in boat building, developing a non-accredited course instead.

The School, renamed the Australian Wooden Boat Centre, went on to produce many more dinghies, yachts and some boat builders. It has changed hands several times and the emphasis has changed. It now belongs to the not-for-profit organisation Franklin Working Waterfront Association Inc which raised about $60,000 from the local community and other like-minded individuals and benefitted from a huge donation from Martin and Judy Krynen. We continued to operate the slipway at Port Huon for a few years and then sold it. It too changed hands several times and is now owned by the Port Huon Sailing Club.

✧✧✧✧✧

Once I really retired, I was able to devote more time to my post as a Research Associate of the School of Geography and Environmental Studies at the University of Tasmania. I imagined immersing myself back into University life for a long time to come. This was something I really enjoyed. For me it was a valuable arrangement. I went one or two days a week to the university, where I shared an office with other research associates and was able to use the library and to help out with contributions to regular "Friday Forums." These consisted of afternoon meetings, open to the whole university, when we Associates could offer the fruits, if we had any, of our personal research. We could also participate, if our colleagues wished, in student seminars, or give lectures. Many of us supervised and/or marked student work. Our refereed publications gave Geography and Environmental Studies increased funding. We could also become members of the staff club if we wanted to. We were mostly unpaid. On one occasion my registration fees were paid for the International Small Islands Studies Association conference at the University of Hawaii College on Maui, where I delivered a paper on Tasmanian environmental problems.

I was keen to continue research and writing. Our lives in the Huon Valley provided interesting and stimulating material for these pursuits. There was the resurrection of Franklin from a potential ghost town to a real estate "hotspot." There was the conflict surrounding the management of forests in the Huon Valley and my own interest in Environmental Studies. And there was also the debate about distinctions between "education" and "training" that I first encountered operating the Wooden Boat School. I spent the next decade writing about these things and found no difficulty in getting what I wrote published.

My initial involvement in Franklin affairs came about as a consequence of joining Franklin Progress Association (FPA). In 1991, when we arrived, this was made up of a small number of people who had the energy to question the wisdom of what seemed like a series of intentional assaults on the welfare of the Franklin community. At various times between 1992 and 2003, I served as Secretary, Vice-President or President of FPA.

I remember attending a public meeting in Huonville Hall in 1991, when Huon Council, concerned by the growth of unemployment, and the closing of a pulp mill at Geeveston, was looking to find solutions to these problems that were causing high levels of anxiety throughout the Valley. The agenda was a systematic series of discussions about all the little townships, villages and settlements for which the Huon Council was responsible. Eventually the focus of the meeting came round to consideration of how Franklin could be assisted or improved. We had only recently arrived and I was alarmed when one gentleman stood up and announced that, "there's really nothing wrong with Franklin that couldn't be fixed by a couple of D9s and a good length of chain."

He drew a good laugh from his audience. D9s were the largest and most powerful class of bulldozer in daily use for the removal of native forest to be replaced by Eucalypt mono-cultural plantations. We began to wonder if coming to Tasmania had been a good idea. But in Franklin itself this incident had the effect of stiffening the blood of the community, who "disguised fair nature with hard-favour'd rage."[9] The reaction of FPA was to get started with building the wharf I have mentioned before, where visitors could tie their boats up, and where locals could fish and socialise, and perhaps have discussions about local problems. For the first time since 1970 when the apple industry began to fall apart, people like us began to buy houses and move from the Mainland.

Tasmania's economic history has consisted of a continuous chorus of "golden opportunities," none of which lasted very long. During the Australian mainland gold rushes of the 1850s, the golden opportunity was Tasmania's ability to supply construction timber for the global influx of diggers. Later, forestry became an activity focussed on the golden opportunity of woodchips with a timber by-product, instead of the other way round.

At the same time, Forestry Tasmania developed a formidable defensive rhetoric based on combating unemployment, if the systematic destruction of native forest and its replacement by plantations were to cease, or even be limited. They did not understand that the mechanisation and scale of the pulp industry was reducing employment, rather than increasing it.

Similarly, when Britain joined the European market, Tasmania destroyed many of its orchards, putting families on small holdings out of work. More recently, salmon farming has reached the point of arrogance that is leading to vigorous public disapproval as the marine environment suffers from it, and the fish insist on escaping or dying. It's much the same with live sheep, who die of heat exhaustion on the way to the Middle East, and regulation, as in the case of slavery across the north Atlantic in the 18th century, becomes a joke.

Tourism has now begun the process of self-destruction, as wild places are tamed by technology and no longer lift the spirit because of the infrastructure demanded by the "High End" requirements that re-produce the stale experience that continues to diminish the once unique delights of wild places, all over the world.

Franklin was to become one of many communities learning that by dealing locally with the big global problems, they could also have more fun, lead healthy and more interesting lives, develop their own authentic sense of place, and discover their own paths to sustainable prosperity.

After the success of the wharf building project, there was a new feeling of confidence in Franklin. The FPA enthusiastically took up its next challenge, the Palais Theatre, and it remained a challenge for at least a decade. This building, opened in 1912, had been the subject of an engineer's report in 1987. Alternative uses for the Theatre were suggested then, such as putting a big double door into the side of this basically very elegant building, and turning it into a resting place for the log trucks passing through the town, night and day, every 4 minutes. If no use could be found, the Theatre would be sold or if that didn't work, demolished. In 1987, the FPA argued that the building should be saved and restored.

---

9   Shakespeare, W, *Henry V*, Act 3, Scene 1.

Most of the structural damage to the Palais was caused by water—leaking roof, gutters, poor drainage etc—the result of neglect of normal maintenance. The main stated problem was the absence of functioning toilets and a septic tank. While the whole town did have a few septic tanks, in the period since settlement in 1836, the only sewage outlets were a series of drains, some of them buried over the years, and a few left open to run directly from domestic and public toilets into the river. The FPA gained permission from the Huon Valley Council, and began at weekends, to dig a big hole for a septic tank, a short distance from the Palais Theatre. We also replaced the old earthenware piping as a temporary solution. We managed to get a small group of people together to meet regularly and start working bees on what we hoped would develop into a full blown attempt at restoration of the whole theatre, at weekends. The building of a modern sewerage system for the whole of Franklin was eventually achieved in 1999. The Palais Theatre was nominated to the National Trust for listing in 1997. Heritage Tasmania was formed in 1998 and gazetted all the Tasmanian buildings formerly listed by the National Trust on the new Tasmanian Heritage Register in December 1998.

FPA had been the official caretaker of and fund raiser for the Palais for several years before Huon Valley Council formed the Palais Management Committee in 1998. I chaired this Committee until 2003, when David Sales took over and very ably continued the work of restoring the Theatre. It is now a successful and eclectic community venue because of the voluntary activities of hundreds of people. FPA went on to champion many successful community projects as well as providing small grants to other Franklin organisations to facilitate their work. Franklin's reputation for community development grew quickly in the first decade of the 21st century. New residents flocked to the town, many with the enthusiasm needed to continue the community-building activities of the 1990s.

Franklin became an example of the restoration of optimism and confidence that can happen when a community determines to help itself. On 30 March 1996, an article about Franklin and its symptoms of recovery, written by journalist Moya Fyfe, was published in the *Saturday Mercury*. The title was "Franklin: The town that wouldn't die." Moya reported on a town that had "dragged its way back from the brink of extinction." She chose John Caire, who had just moved into Franklin and had established the Franklin Grill Restaurant on the Main road, as her local informant. He did a good job of putting the town on the map. John was a good chef and also a good host. Until he opened the Franklin Grill, there was really nowhere in the town where you could get a sit down meal. Ruth and I became infrequent but regular customers. John used to entertain us with his detailed introductions to the menu of the day, what each dish was, and where it came from, how it was cooked and why it was good value. He introduced us to each other, and somehow created an atmosphere that invited us to move around from one table to another between courses as if we were all members of a large family. With Gail Galloway,

John Caire introduced a Sunday Food Market into the Palais, which proved very popular and contributed substantial funds towards the Palais restoration and the increasingly happy atmosphere of the town.

Moya also wrote about the boat building school and gave voice to some of my opinions about Franklin and what should be done to improve it:

> *Dr Young said the way of the future was to create a community where people wanted to live and work. That meant... not selling assets to companies which took the profits and the benefits of a variety of resources out of the region. It meant the protection of an ecological system that could provide resources on which a large number of businesses could depend indefinitely. We should stop the destruction of our old growth forests for the short term benefits of the Japanese packaging industry.*[10]

I saw the Huon Valley as a place of enormous potential for successful living, with its comfortable climate, rich soils, sheltered waterways, reliable rainfall, and beautiful beaches and landscapes. But its potential had never been reached. It had suffered from the instability of all dependent economies.[11] When we arrived in Franklin in 1991, decisions that were made for what was called "development" were not made in Huonville, or even in Hobart, but in Canberra, Tokyo and London. Such decisions served large overseas banks, corporations and industries much more than they benefitted Tasmania.

I began to research the local history of the Huon Valley and soon offered to give a paper to a meeting of the UTAS History Department. I called it "Back to the Future: Choosing a meaning from regional history," probably a rather corny title, but I had been reading Robert Putnam's book, *Making Democracy Work*, which helped to broaden the picture. Professor Michael Roe, Chair of the History Department, liked the paper enough to suggest that I offer it for publication in *Tasmanian Historical Studies*. It came out in 1995-96.[12]

It was the first of a series of publications, mostly outside the academic mainstream, such as the journal, *Friends of the Earth*[13], and *Scholastic Times*, which I don't think lasted very long, but I liked its style and thought that if it would publish my work, a lot of people might want to read it. I came across *Scholastic Times* because it contained a nice review of *Sustaining the Earth* by Ralph Robinson. I decided to offer an article derived from my analysis of the environmental problems of the Huon Valley, and the parallels it shared with many parts of what has been described as

---

10   Fyfe, Moya, "Franklin: The town that wouldn't die," The *Saturday Mercury*, 30 March 1996, p 40.

11   Simpkin, C G F, *The Instability of a Dependent Economy: Economic Fluctuations in New Zealand 1840-1914*, OUP, 1951.

12   *Tasmanian Historical Studies*, Vol 5, 1995-6, pp 114-131.

13   Culture, Democracy and Local Employment: a Strategy for Ecological Sustainable Development in Southern Tasmania", *Friends of the Earth*, Tasmania, Issue 2, pp 3-6.

the Third World. I drew attention to the policy of Forestry Tasmania, which was driven by the Japanese market for pulp. Timber was provided to pulp companies by a gullible Tasmanian Government department, depending on a process of turning the mixed wet forests of southern Tasmania into areas of Eucalyptus monoculture, designed to increase volume, and speed growth, of inferior fast grown timber. This was done at the expense of slow growing mixed forests that contain high quality hardwood, that for generations, had supported tourism, honey, woodwork, wild life, house construction, furniture making and boat building. I was asked to talk to various organisations about the unsustainability of the then current forest management practices in Tasmania over the next few years.[14]

During this time I was also able to write about my personal perception of Australian educational policy, especially in the case of the tertiary sector in which I had worked for 27 years before starting the Boat School. One of the major problems of Australian education in the past had been the assumption that economists, who were elevated to the status of prophets, could forecast the future, and in spite of the repeated failure of their predictions, we continue to believe them. So it has become the job of schools, universities, and technical colleges to prepare people for a future which turns out to be very different from what we were led to expect. We were told by the Minister for Education during the 1980s, that if we allowed industry to determine our educational priorities, then a better trained workforce would increase national productivity. This would stimulate economic growth, so that unemployment would be reduced, and we would all be better off. Australia has followed this policy, regardless of changing governments for many years, so by now, things should be pretty good!

But in fact, the "trickle-down" theory has not worked. The target for the end of the twentieth century was a reduction of unemployment to 8% of the workforce, which was then regarded as acceptable. The range of inequality of income had reached the same point as it was in the late 1890s in Australia, and just before the French Revolution, as Thomas Piketty points out.[15] As social inequality increased, so did Government cuts to education, especially to subjects like English Language, Philosophy, History, Classics or Art. The aim is to prepare people for the work force, to become servants to "the Economy," rather than to provide the opportunity for them to serve themselves, or society. The effect is to separate the concepts of education and training.

Training I claimed, was needed, but has to do with mastering particular industrial processes. It's what you do with plants that you want to grow in a particular way. Education has more to do with enabling people to discover what they are good at, and what they want to do with their lives. And what they hope to contribute to society.

---

14   "Sustainable Forests and Regional Communities," Institution of Engineers, Australia, Engineering a Sustainable Future Conference, 2-3 Sept 2002, Hobart.

15   Piketty, Thomas, (translated by Arthur Goldhammer), *Capital in the Twenty-first Century*, Harvard University Press, Massachusetts, 2014.

This kind of behaviour on my part was a legacy of my long academic life, I suppose, and I much enjoyed the opportunity the University gave me to keep my lecturing and writing in shape.

However, in spite of my so-called second retirement, 2001 turned out to be a very busy year, leading me in several different directions that I had not anticipated. The death of the mayor, Greg Norris, in May 2001 led to a by-election to fill his position as Councillor. I decided to nominate, in the hope of protecting Franklin from further neglect or indifference.

I was asked to join a group calling itself "The Community Independents," consisting of Liz Smith, a retired academic scientist; Wren Fraser, a local environmental enthusiast who lived at Lune River in the Far South of Tasmania, and me. Our chief opponent was a local entrepreneur, Mike Wilson, who had set up several local tourist, maritime and other businesses that had been very successful in the Geeveston-Port Huon area. I had no reason to attack any of these enterprises. The only differences we had of any importance were about forestry. As a citizen of Geeveston, Mike was proud of the history of industrial forestry of his native town, whatever it did. To criticise such an industry, on which the Huon Valley identity had depended for 100 years was seen as blasphemy, which was a valuable weapon for Mike Wilson.

The election period was arduous, but educational. I walked through what seemed like every street of the main towns and settlements in the Valley, knocking on doors, and having discussions with the people who let me in. Forestry was the main political subject. There were also organised meetings at which all the candidates spoke in turn to outline their policies and answer questions. My teaching experience made meetings like these relatively easy, especially in Cygnet, a little town which had attracted a wave of migrants from the eastern states in the 1970s. They included people who wrote, painted, sang and sailed, and voted Green.

Franklin people had become generally supportive, because they liked the Wooden Boat School. But the people I spoke to in the houses behind the main street in Huonville were not interested in politics at any level, and wanted me to go away. There were some surprises though. In Dover, I knocked on a door and several dogs came out to meet me, barking aggressively. I usually find that if I speak kindly to dogs they settle down, and let me pat their heads, but these ones were followed by their equally hostile owners in jeans and black T-shirts.

I told them I was a candidate in the Council election, and wanted their support. Their spokesman said he mistrusted all politicians, and he wasn't interested in voting for anyone. This was territory in which posters in favour of Green candidates were usually destroyed overnight. Politics at that time in the Huon Valley was conducted in an atmosphere of subtle, and sometimes not so subtle intimidation. A log truck with a sign saying "Say Your Prayers!" made three round trips a day through the streets of Huonville and the small towns to the south. Some people who opposed the *status quo* received threatening phone calls. Some had their animals poisoned. Opposition pamphlets sent through Australia Post did not always get delivered. Voting was secret, but it was an atmosphere that could inhibit political discussion, even within families.

I told my prospective constituents that if they didn't vote they would make politics even worse. Voting, I said, was a good way to change things. That started a stream of cusswords and barking by the dogs, and I withdrew rather politely, but one of the boys stayed with me and told me about his view of the world. He had been unemployed for most of his life since leaving school, and had spent some of his time on a "work for the dole" scheme. This was a land care project and he had been told to poison some juvenile willow trees next to a tributary of the Huon.

"And" he said, "I could see the poison was going into the river. I thought that was wrong. And I'm not even a Greenie." I congratulated him for his courage, and insight, and said that his boss must have missed out on some parts of his education. If he wanted a good book he should read *The Sea*, by Rachel Carson. He could get it from the public library in Huonville.

Voting closed a week later and counting continued into the evening. When I arrived at the Council building, counting was nearly over, and Mike Wilson and I were the only two candidates left standing for the vacant seat. On first preference votes, we were quite close. Half an hour later the announcement was made that Mike Wilson had won the seat by a respectable margin. Ruth, Liz Smith and Wren Fraser had helped me but not quite enough to win. This was my first and last dabble with a political career. In fact, I thought that the people contesting these elections should ideally have been younger than either Mike or myself. I was as surprised and pleased as I was disappointed, and thanked all the people who had voted for me for doing so.

My political ambitions ended at this point, but my concern about Tasmania's forests was heightened by my experience of standing for local government. For the next decade, Ruth and I were to become increasingly involved in the national argument about the destruction of mature, old growth forests in Tasmania to meet the requirements of the Japanese pulp industry. We felt compelled to try to halt the destruction of immature Tasmanian boat building species, caused by clear felling, because we had just spent the previous decade producing men and women skilled in wooden boat building. Not to have become involved was tantamount to setting them up for unemployment.

By 2001, the community concern about Tasmanian forest practices was more widespread than it had been before and it led to organised resistance to industrial propaganda. Front line members of the medical profession began to describe the medical impact of continuous smoke in the autumn months—a result of secondary burning of clear-felled forest coupes—especially for people with asthma. They were also concerned about dust pollution from woodchip stockpiles and possibility that the stockpiles harboured disease-carrying micro-organisms. These anxieties added to general worries about loss of native animal habitat and the use of poisons to discourage browsing native animals in young plantations and led to the rise of an organisation called "Doctors for Forests."

Some Letters to the Editor of *The Mercury* had attacked the medical profession for its agitation beyond the limits of its expertise. The Doctors asked me for a discussion paper about "Forest management and public health."[16] I suggested that although there was a legitimate assumption that foresters might know more than the rest of us about how the forest fulfilled its ecological function, the question of how its function should be manipulated for commercial purposes raised ethical problems, about which foresters were not superior or politically wiser than anybody else. In fact, doctors are probably better than the rest of us, I told them, in evaluating the risks for ourselves and for future generations of setting large forest areas on fire to create replacement forestry. Replacement forestry also threatened more seemly forest industries such as beekeeping, wooden boat building, furniture making and the craft industry.

This invitation was followed later in 2001, by an approach from a shingle-splitter, Graham Green, asking if we would attend a meeting, the intention of which was to form an incorporated association called "Timber Workers for Forests" (TWFF). This was a time of extreme polarisation, and earlier "for Forests" types of groups started out as opponents of all logging in old growth forests, a strategy that had been successful in Western Australia and had seen the undoing of the Liberal Government the previous year. They were depicted by forest industry public relations people and Government spokespersons as "front groups" for the Wilderness Society and/or The Greens.

The Forest and Forest Industry Council of Tasmania of course, knew all about Front Groups, because it had its own, in the form of the very effective, and quaintly named the "Forest Protection Society" in 1987 and renamed "Timber Communities Australia" in 1997.

Graham Green had been a member of Timber Communities Australia, and initially accepted the claims of an organisation purporting to represent the interests of all timber workers, at face value. He soon became disillusioned by the way in which the organisation he expected to protect his interests, as a shingle splitter, gave its unqualified support for a system of forest management that was systematically depriving him of the mature timber he needed for his livelihood. Timber Communities Australia acted as the champion of a single *community of interest*, the people involved in volume production of eucalypt timber, primarily for woodchip production, but in spite of its inclusive rhetoric, it did not champion those *communities of place*, the "timber towns" and villages which had once prospered through the application of hard earned local skills to add value to unique local timbers and to add meaning and pride to the lives of the people.

---

16   "Forest Management and Public Health," Doctors For Forests, Stanley Burbury Theatre, UTAS, 8 August 2001.

The inaugural meeting of TWFF was held on 15 November 2001 at the Longley International Hotel, which in spite of its impressive name and considerable elegance, is a country pub in the village of Longley. Longley has a population of about 250 souls, and lies halfway between Hobart and the Southern Forests. TWFF was to become a formal organisation that took up much of our time and energy. There, we met a remarkable group of people who worked with wood and discovered common ground across generations as well as between regions and cultures. People who worked with Tasmania's unique special timbers were, whether consciously or not, the inheritors of a continuous minority tradition of forest practice that was as much a part of Tasmania's history as the heroic vision of conquest that inspired most of our governance since 1803. Graham became the Founding President of Timber Workers For Forests and we were pleased to see some of our former Diploma students there as well.

All the people at the meeting were disgusted by the short term vision of the woodchip trade, based on maximum yield of eucalypt plantations at the expense of old growth forest, mixed forest, and pure rain forest. While endeavouring to keep our differences with the alliance of big Government and big business at a civilised level, we conducted a considerable amount of scientific and social research to demonstrate the negative consequences of the clear-fell, burn and sow regime, particularly for timber workers, including those involved in the regime itself.

The over arching aim of the Association was to "Maximise the value of Tasmania's

Aerial view of the Wooden Boat School at Franklin, 1995. (Photo by Bill Wright)

forests for the people of Tasmania in perpetuity."[17] Rather than engage in an emotive appeal to the public for change, we sought to present evidence that the clear felling of the remaining old growth forests was wasteful, costing Tasmanian jobs, causing irreversible damage to future supplies of the timbers on which we depended, and could be discontinued without loss to industrial forestry. Forestry Tasmania might then be persuaded to change methods of harvesting in old growth forest while there was still some of it left outside the World Heritage Area.

The official launch of Timber Workers For Forests took place on Saturday, 2 March 2002 on the lawns of Parliament House in Hobart. Graham Green wrote a media alert on the previous Thursday describing our membership as consisting of "saw millers, boat-builders bushmen, craftsmen, builders, cabinet makers, furniture makers, and sculptors, whose aim is to establish a new forest management structure, to be managed by a wide range of interests."[18] The ABC had done an immediate radio interview. That was followed by an interview for "The Country Hour." The launch consisted of a working display by TWFF members. It went well with attention from both the media and passersby.

In April, we called a press conference to announce the publication of the first of a series of research papers, an audit TWFF carried out of a recently clear-felled coupe, Esperance 74D, in the southern forests. It was written by Graham, who, it turned

---

17   Objects and Purposes of Timber Workers For Forests
     Advocate changes to native forest management to enable perpetual supply of special species timber and high quality eucalypts.
     Facilitate the immediate transition from clear-fell and burning of native forests to site specific management such as single stem and group selection.
     Advocate an immediate end to destruction of native forest where conversion to regrowth and plantation is the primary objective.
     Ensure the harvest of product does not compromise the ecological integrity of the forest on a Forest Management Unit level.
     Promote alternatives to the use of timbers sourced from old-growth forests and promote true labeling of timber and where it comes from.
     Promote the preservation and development of fine wood skills and crafts and of Tasmania as a centre of excellence.
     Promote the high quality work of timber workers encompassing those involved in extraction to production.
     Promote the use of solid Tasmanian timber for its highest possible value with the minimum of waste.
     Maximise opportunities for meaningful employment in the timber industry.
     Promote education of the general community in the wise management of forests, timber and production.
     Lobby authorities and developers on behalf of the community to obtain the best possible outcome in accordance with TWFF purposes.

18   The inaugural members of TWFF, described by Labor party politicians and Forestry officials as "The Usual Suspects," consisted of the following:
     G Green, I Johnston, R Davis, J Singleton, M Singleton, M Bekemma, F Whitton, N Trewartha, G Greener, R Young, J Young, J Maddock.

out, also had a PhD in science. His living was derived mainly from shingle splitting, making post and rail fences and the restoration of heritage buildings, using materials salvaged from clear-felled forests. Members of our group who had experience in identifying and using Tasmanian timbers, and some who had post graduate research and supervision experience, provided assistance with the 74D audit.

Hopes grew high, as we continued research in forest areas that had been recently cut down, by weekend examinations of wind-rows of "residue," awaiting cremation, after coups had been clear-felled. This meant identifying and recording each large remaining piece of timber in selected 10 × 10 metre quadrats. We wanted to evaluate the volume of rain forest species that were to be burnt. We marked off the quadrats of "residue" and then analysed the percentages of each of the dominant under storey and rain forest species in each square, in order to compare the consequences of continuing the dominant forest philosophy with our ideas, and their social and economic benefits and consequences.

The resulting paper quantified the amount of timber left on the ground to be burnt, and the proportion of the species that would therefore be wasted. It made recommendations for immediate waste reduction on the site in question, and both site specific and policy recommendations to avoid similar waste in the future.[19]

Before publication, comment was invited from Forestry Tasmania, but none was received. This paper was followed by another in July 2002, detailing the jobs lost in the forest industry since 1990, and also since the Regional Forest Agreement of 1998–99. It contained recommendations for alternative job creation by the selective logging of specialty timbers, using methods then being trialled in the Warra long term ecological research site by Forestry Tasmania. It also recommended the creation of training opportunities in alternative forest management and wood-skill based industries, such as furniture and wooden boat building.[20]

After the release of the Timber Industry Jobs paper, TWFF staged a stark "street theatre" illustration of the contradiction between the promises of new job opportunities, made by politicians when the Regional Forest Agreement was signed, and the devastation of lost jobs and opportunities that had followed. To represent these job losses, 1,240 cut out figures were planted on the lawns of Parliament House and then chipped.

A third paper moved from criticism of current practice to a resolution of conflict in the Tasmanian community and the creation of a policy that would allow for the satisfactory pursuit of all competing interests, based on the best interests of the forests themselves. A consultation draft was circulated to special timber saw millers for comment. Our members conducted a series of public consultation meetings in timber communities throughout Tasmania, and held draft discussion meetings

---

19 Green, Graham, *Esperance 74D(EPO74D), Logging Coupe Inventory*, Timber Workers For Forests, April 2002.

20 Green, Graham, *Tasmanian Timber Industry Jobs, Volume 1*, Timber Workers For Forests, July 2002.

with local foresters in the Huon district. No-one at Forestry Tasmania responded to our requests for feedback. So in August 2004, it was published, with the title, *Tasmania's Specialty Timber Industry: A Blueprint for Sustainability*.[21]

TWFF continued to work politically by getting its opinions into *The Mercury* letters whenever possible, building alliances with other groups like the beekeepers, documenting continued malpractice in the forests, talking to politicians and staging demonstrations.

The art and craft community had been very active about forestry issues prior to the formation of TWFF. The "One Tree" movement had managed to do a deal with the forester who ran the Forestry Tasmania base at Geeveston, where the Forest Wars had often come close to violence. Talan Atkins, the One Tree Project Co-ordinator, asked to buy one tree (literally), from Forestry Tasmania, from an area of forest that was to be clear felled. Then One Tree Inc set out to demonstrate the many valuable things it could be used for, and thus to demonstrate the waste of using it for woodchips.

Over fifty young designers, artists and crafts people used all parts of this one Stringy Bark (*Eucalyptus obliqua*) tree, from roots to leaves and sawdust to create forty-five works, including furniture, from bush styles to utility, bed frames, and sculptures, clothes pegs, tool chests, children's toys, musical instruments, textiles, puppets, paper and medicine. I was asked to write an introduction to the One Tree Exhibition programme. I thought these creative people were quite extraordinary, not just because of their talents but also because of their political acumen, determination and persistence. Between 2001 and 2007, the One Tree Exhibition toured Australia demonstrating the value-added products that had been rescued from the pulp mill.[22]

By 2003, Tasmanian artists and sculptors were as active in their opposition to clear felling as they were in their advocacy for a better future for Tasmania. One stunning example of this was an exhibition at Dick Bett's Gallery, called "Future Perfect" which expanded to many other shop fronts and restaurants in North Hobart. It was described as "a forum where artists and writers can explore our island's destiny, uncompromised and unsullied by the sponsorship of forces that sponsor the destruction of what is unique and irreplaceable on our island."[23]

Each art work was accompanied by a short essay, written by a Tasmanian writer, which complemented the art. Colin Langridge was one of the sculptors. He decided to build a large wooden fire extinguisher, to remind people of the value of timber if it was left to grow instead of getting burnt to make room for a monoculture of wood chips. I was asked to write a piece to accompany Colin's work.

---

21 All of the papers published by TWFF are available at https://www.twff.org.au/research.html

22 https://tasmaniantimes.com/2007/11/one-tree/

23 Castles, G and Bett, D, introduction to *Future Perfect: a collaboration of writers, thinkers and visual artists*, North Hobart, 2003, p 1.

After a discussion with Colin, I wrote the following:

The Future Perfect tense looks at the past through the lens of the future: I shall have asked, I shall have worked, I shall have fought, Tasmania shall have been changed!

If not, historians living in the desert of greed and mediocrity this island will have become will ask the questions we should be asking now.

How old is the wood that the artist has used?

The Celery Top Pine that became this fire extinguisher started life in about 1603. Before Tasman discovered Tasmania. Germination probably occurred as the result of a wild fire through the Arve valley in southern Tasmania, bringing down ancient Eucalypts, disturbing the ground and allowing both rain forest species and eucalypts to regenerate as the cycle was renewed.

In 2001 the whole coup it stood in was clear felled. Most of the Celery-top was immature, small, and knotty. The smaller logs, bulldozed into windrows with the rest of the understory "residue" were burnt to create a seedbed for a replacement crop of quick growing eucalypts only. Our sawlog went to a small local mill that had survived several decades of industrial transition. It had eventually produced the close grained, strong and durable layer of timber that stimulates our thoughts and senses now.

Why are old-growth forests still being clear-felled and burnt against the wishes of most Tasmanians?

Good research starts by asking the right questions, and they change with time. Half a century ago the question was "How could Tasmania's forests be best regenerated with eucalypts?" John Maxwell Gilbert gave the answer in his PhD thesis. He explained that in order to achieve successful eucalypt regeneration, the rain forest under storey must be completely removed.[24] This would produce four times the volume of pulp or timber per acre, in 80 years, as the original forest would do, but it meant huge wastage during the transition process. "The amount of slash must be sufficient" he said, "to provide a fire hot enough to kill the trees of the understory." [25]

Gilbert was aware of the long term implications of his research, and in an open society, his comments might have been expected to lead to the asking of new questions as priorities changed. He pointed out that an ecological revolution of this kind would destroy vast quantities of timber, which, if allowed to reach maturity, could provide a high value resource for future generations. But the question he was asked by the forestry industry was not how to maintain the value of Tasmania's forests for future generations. It was how to maximise the volume of pulp production and second grade timber as soon as possible. Ends justified means. Which always reveals new ethical issues. "The problem," Gilbert said, "has to be looked at in the light of demands for wood, now, in 1958."[26]

---

24   Gilbert, J M, "Eucalypt-rainforest relationships and the re-generation of Eucalypts." PhD thesis, Botany Department, University of Tasmania, 1958, p 232.

25   *Ibid*, p 235.

26   *Ibid*.

The democratic ideal of entrusting forest management to a Government department that is responsible for management of forests, in the public interest, in the future as well as the present, exists only in the minds of the naïve. The export of ever increasing volumes of woodchips through one insatiable monopoly[27] has become the dominant industrial purpose. As the pace quickens there is little left in the timber production areas of the kind of forest which produces the quality of the timber in front of you. Only if clear felling is abandoned will we be able to live off the interest of these forests, leaving their natural capital intact for the needs of future generations. Claims that single stem, selective logging is impossible, or necessarily unsafe are spurious. The Tahune forest air walk, a few kilometres from where this tree has stood for 4 centuries is a masterly demonstration of how selective logging can be done if the will is there.

This fire extinguisher is both a protest against clear felling old growth forests, and a sign of hope. In the 17th century, when our tree germinated, people were beginning to believe that the purpose of our species on earth, was the conquest of nature. This ideology has had a good innings, but now, as we begin to understand the risks of ecological ignorance, the engineering and scientific heroics of the mid 20th century come into focus as a mere episode in our intellectual history.

Tasmanians should understand that the perfect future we want is not to be achieved by vain attempts to mould our ecosystems to the fluctuating whims of the global market, but by recognising the value of our natural inheritance, and by learning to live in ways that profit from the good health of our planet.[28]

Looking back on this chapter, I have told you about a lot of things which absorbed me for more than a decade. They all hang together very consistently to me. The underlying subject is perhaps best expressed by St. Paul, in his Epistle to the Philippians:

Finally Brethren, whatsoever things are true, whatsoever things are honest, whatsoever things are just, whatsoever things are pure, whatsoever things are lovely, whatsoever things are of good report. Think on these things.[29]

---

27 This refers to Gunns Ltd.

28 Castles, G and Bett, D, *op cit*, p 8.

29 St Paul's Epistle to the Philippians, Chapter 8, Verse 3.

Chapter 19: "Men make their own History..."[1]

By the early 2000s, my children were living their own lives in different places in the world and some had families of their own. Stephen and his wife, Anne were living in Melbourne and working at Melbourne University. Philip and his wife, Felicity had three boys at this stage (with one more to come). He was working as a solicitor in Port Moresby, New Guinea. There they lived a risky and precarious life on board their boat. Susan and Shaohua had a son and two daughters. They had moved several times, first to Denmark, where we did manage to visit, then to London and finally to Saudi Arabia where Shaohua worked as an oil engineer.

It had been very difficult for us to visit them while we were running the Boat School. The students' long vacations were a frenetic time for us. During that time, we went to the West Coast of Tasmania to buy timber. We ran recreational courses to top-up the coffers for the expenses of the next semester and helped with the problems of our past, present and potential students. What this meant was that we did not see our own children very often, unless they were able to come to us in Tasmania. But when we sold the Boat School, we were able to see more of them and came to know our grand-children, and they to know their cousins. One year, the cousins got together and painted an old Sabot dinghy we'd had for years. They re-launched it at Franklin with the new name of *The Cousins*. This was a good time in our lives. We had several big family Christmases when we played about in dinghies and the *Leofleda*, pitched tents in the garden and generally relaxed and enjoyed ourselves. After the death of her husband, my first wife, Carmel also joined us for Christmas.

We had exchanged our truck for a Mitsubishi Express van, which we bought from our friends Dianne and Rob Osmond in New South Wales. They had set the van up as a campervan and it suited us very well as we intended to see some of the Australian mainland we hadn't seen before. This was about the time that Shaohua obtained a job in Saudi Arabia. This involved him having to spend a kind of probationary period of several months in Saudi alone, without Susan and their children. So instead of paying rent in London, Susan decided to just give up the lease on their house and bring everyone to Franklin for that period. This was an interesting time for us. The kids went to Franklin Primary School. Sometimes Susan or I rowed them to school from our house. They enjoyed the freedom of our land and the river, after the constraints of a London suburb. We came to know them very well and we thought they would like to see a bit of Australia.

We arranged to stay with or borrow the shacks of several friends, gutted the van's interior, replaced it with seats enough to carry the six of us and set off for the Australian East Coast. Lindsay, Helen and Karen were all mad keen on animals and we managed to spot quite a few of the wild Australian kind on our travels, and filled in the gaps by taking them to wildlife parks. In Canberra, we all went out to dinner with Cody Horgan and his wife Heather, Kat Edghill (both Cody and Kat

---

1   Marx, Karl, *The 18th Brumaire of Louis Napoleon*, 1851.

had been students in our final Diploma course) and Penny Townley, the partner of Darren McAllister, a student in 1997–98. After dinner we took the kids on what they called a "dog crawl" (named after the common Australian drinking bout, the pub crawl) to see the students' dogs at various houses in Canberra.

In the Australian Capital Territory, we stayed in a house at Tharwa, thanks to the generosity of Tony Richardson and Margaret Horn. It was a lovely property with a creek running through it and lots of lizards, kangaroos and interesting things to look at. We spent some time with our friends Diane and Rob at Woy Woy and then at their shack at Congo, further down the coast. No sooner was he out of the car than Lindsay saw a whale. Thankfully, it was alive and well and Lindsay showed no inclination to roll. It was a good trip. It made me feel more Australian and I think it might have had the same effect on Lindsay.

Back home in Tasmania, we had more sailing holidays on *Leofleda*. Randalls Bay, a sheltered anchorage south of Cygnet, was a frequent destination on our way to the D'Entrecasteaux ports. Early in 2002, we arrived at Randalls Bay just as the sun was setting. In the morning, when we went for a walk ashore, we saw that a shack directly opposite the beach was for sale. We got into conversation with the tenant, who was gardening as we were passing. She invited us inside to have a look at the house. Once inside, the first thing we saw out of the window was *Leofleda* at anchor, framed by Peppermint gums on the beach. She looked so beautiful that we didn't pay as much attention to the house itself as we should have. We decided to buy the house, thinking of the pleasant family times we could have there and the future enjoyment our grandchildren could have as they grew up.

Seeing your own boat out of the window seems a poor excuse for buying a house, but we thought "Why not?" The answer to that turned out to be that the house really needed everything done to it—new bathroom, new floors, new window frames etc. It was just the same story as all the houses we had ever bought, but as we had sold the Boat School, we were free to do what needed to be done ourselves in our own time. We soon laid a permanent mooring, in perfect shelter from both south westerly gales and the regular south-easterly sea-breezes, under the sandstone cliffs.

We were still involved with the restoration of the Palais Theatre in Franklin and our work with Timber Workers for Forests. At the same time, we became more active in a project that had been the brain-child of one of our first Diploma students, Chris Burke. Prior to enrolling in the course, Chris had a multi-faceted career which included running his own sailboard business, working on an oil rig, working as a builder and more recently as a Senior Instructor at the National Outdoor Leadership School of USA where he had gained a Diploma in Outdoor Leadership. As a student at the Boat School, Chris had watched the varied activities of the School with more intense and critical interest than we realised, until he presented a Business Plan, as part of his course in 1996, for the formation of a not-for-profit incorporated Association that he called "The Living Boat Trust" (LBT).

The aims of Chris's intended organisation were to recover and celebrate Tasmania's maritime heritage, not merely as a nostalgic sentiment, but as a practical ingredient of contemporary life. His intention was that the LBT would work with educational organisations, community groups, local government, young people at risk, families and visitors in the search for authentic cultural and practical experience, by providing opportunities for group participation in the repair of historic traditional wooden boats (like *May Queen*), replica construction, small boat adventuring with sail and oar and the preservation of plans, manuscripts, books and historic boats for study and practical use. Engaging young people in the use, as well as the restoration of historic craft would ensure the preservation of not only the artefacts themselves, but also the skills and values that they represented.

This idea probably started in Chris' mind when, as part of his Diploma course, he did a detailed study of the history and condition of *May Queen*, a 65 foot centreboard ketch, built in Franklin in 1867 by Alexander Lawson, under the auspices of William Thorp, on the river bank very close to our Franklin workshop. In 1996, Jocelyn Fogagnolo's boating column began with a paragraph about *May Queen*, "She is now," Jocelyn wrote:

> *…the last floating remnant of a once proud fleet of more than 100 similar ketches that were the lifeblood of the colony in the last century. She is the oldest trading vessel existing in Australia, the longest serving trading ketch in the country, and one of the few commercial cargo vessels of its design, and age, left in the world.*[2]

Jocelyn Fogagnolo's articles in *The Mercury* were demonstrations of her deep understanding of both the social and industrial history of Tasmanian boats. *May Queen* was an opportunity for a combination of historical research, and a feasibility study of various levels of practical restoration. In 1995–96, our course had brought in a group of students who were encouraged to look at their work in the context of Tasmania's maritime, industrial, and social history.

Since 1974, *May Queen* had been the responsibility of the Hobart Marine Board. The Board completed a full restoration in 1979 and maintained her ever since. Jocelyn reported that Chris had examined *May Queen*, and also looked at the repair and/or restoration of historic vessels in other countries, and his work contained primary as well as easily accessed secondary information. His thorough search for information, soundness of argument, and skilful interpretation, was an intellectual achievement equivalent to any university Honours level qualification. Jocelyn reported Chris's modest conclusion that, "The ideal of restoring *May Queen* to sailing condition for occasional ceremonial use or even as a floating exhibit would help revive traditional boat building skills."

Sadly, the Marine Board concluded that the cost of another complete restoration, at that time, would be too expensive, but working out the costs and technical problems, justifying choices, and writing about them, was a great educational experience for Chris Burke. Four years later, a more extensive degree of restoration

---

2   Fogagnolo, Jocelyn, "Boating," *The Saturday Mercury*, 4 May 1996.

was the first professional job undertaken by Mark Singleton, an outstanding student from the third intake of 1999–2000.

We talked with Chris and his partner, Pip about the likelihood that the Living Boat Trust could become a reality. From our point of view, such an organisation would benefit us greatly as it would enable us to concentrate solely on the delivery of professional qualifications to boat builders, while the Living Boat Trust took over our activities of teaching children to sail, building boats for schools, running recreational courses for adults and restoring old Tasmanian-built and designed boats, a task we were often presented with.

Apart from the Derwent Class yacht, the first of these historic boats we came across was the Piner's Punt. A member of the Watson family of Glen Huon asked us if we would restore a small Piner's Punt, which a family member had built himself. He'd kept a sort of diary of the building. The boat had been used, but was neglected and finally came to grief when a cow stove in part of the planking while the boat lay on the bank of the Huon River in its upper reaches. We spent a long time restoring this boat. It meant so much to the woman who inherited it. This was the kind of boat that Chris and Pip thought the Living Boat Trust ought to be preserving, together with its design details.

The Piner's Punts are reputed to have evolved from the ship's boats of the very early nineteenth century, when vessels came from the sea into the mouths of the rivers to search for fallen Huon Pine trees, if they were lucky. Otherwise, the boats had to be towed or hauled over rapids as far up stream as possible, and then the crews cut the timber. The return journey involved navigation of the rapids and towing the logs to the coast. The ship's boats were put to use for this purpose. With their sharp bows, they tended to stay on course, often driven fast by the current. They sometimes hit rocks, which caused planking near the bow to get stoved in. The thing to do then was to take a saw and cut the whole damaged part of the vessel off, at 45 degrees, at the forward end of the boat where a new, sloping forward transom, would be quickly built and fitted.

When re-launched, the slope of the new bow transom, instead of a sharp bow, allowed the boat to head to one side or the other side of any rock, in safety. When new boats began to be built for the purpose of getting Huon Pine, they were built with a small stem transom with a 45 degree slope. They were then used to collect the logs and guide them down to the nearest landing place, or take them down the river to the coastal mills.

Adrian Dean was enamoured of the Piner's Punt and used old boats as a guide to drawing a detailed design. Our friend, Tony Richardson, a keen trout fisherman, was looking for a boat for fishing in the Lakes and liked Adrian's design. When Chris graduated and was working as a boatbuilder in his own right, Tony asked him if he would build a Punt to Adrian's design. He asked for a few modifications: he wanted a sliding rowing seat, oars on outriggers for greater efficiency and a few other things. Chris and I built the boat, *Bolter*, in 1997 at Port Huon. This was followed by a request from the Tasmanian Government to build a typically Tasmanian boat as a gift to the South Korean government at the Cheju World Island Festival in 1998. Chris, Peter Laidlaw and I built the Piner's Punt, *Gus Doherty*, for this event. The boat was named after the Punt builder in Richard Flanagan's book, *Death of a River Guide*.

That year, Chris and Pip asked us if we would be members of a Committee to create the Living Boat Trust. The first Committee consisted of Pip and Chris, Ruth and me, Michele Durbin, Bill Cromer and briefly, Bill Foster. The Committee decided to incorporate and this was achieved in 1998. Chris, as Co-ordinator and Pip, as Secretary began negotiating with Crown Lands to obtain a lease of land just south of the Boat School at Franklin. This took some time and while it was happening, the LBT took over several of the Boat School's sailing instruction courses, run for the students of some of the Huon Valley Schools. Chris and Pip operated the Trust's first fund-raising venture, a rowing boat hire service, during the Tall Ships visit at Constitution Dock in 1998. The Trust also succeeded in securing a grant from the Department of Education, Community and Cultural Development to buy materials for a temporary shed on the Boat School's lease. We arranged a temporary permit with the Crown and Council and the shed was built with the physical help of volunteer members and the staff of Geeveston District High School.

In this shed, the Trust commenced construction of a replica of the Tasmanian whaleboat, *Swiftsure*, originally built in 1863. The original vessel, which was quickly purchased by a New Zealand whaling family, had been given to the Canterbury museum in Christchurch in 1915, and her lines had been taken off. Chris and I discussed the stories we were hearing about the "Atlantic Challenge" rowing race, the idea of Sir Chay Blyth. Lance Lee of Rockport, Maine, had told me all about it when I visited him. Chris, David Perez and I envisaged an antipodean equivalent such as a Tasman Sea, or Southern Ocean challenge, for New Zealand and Tasmania, based on whale boat competitions, or exploration for young people.

One of the Diploma students in our third intake, Grant Wilson (best described as an adventurer with a literary bent, but really a marine engineer), volunteered to visit the Canterbury Museum in Christchurch and get permission to copy the lines that had been taken off the original. Grant brought them back so that we could build a true replica, and use her for expeditions. He also made some very beautiful and accurate drawings of specific details from the original boat itself.

Students from Geeveston School lofted the boat on the floor of the main hall at the Palais Theatre, under the supervision of Chris, Peter Laidlaw, and Ned Trewartha, another of our first Diploma students. With the help of a donation of timber from Huon Valley Council Youth Services and the tireless fund raising efforts of the staff of Geeveston School, the keel of the new *Swiftsure* was laid in the temporary shed in August 1999. Huon Valley Council also donated all the Huon Pine planking for the whaleboat. *Swiftsure* was 32 feet long with a beam of 6 feet and is intended for six rowers. The main participants in this project were young people between the ages of 14 and 25, older people who were active volunteers and mentors, and had skills to pass on led by a paid, part time boatbuilder.

The Trust also began to seek ways of building permanent premises. We told Chris and Pip about the Carpenter's shed at Tarraleah. This was a steel-framed and clad shed which was standing next to the shed we had purchased for the Boat School in 1994. Chris and Pip went up to Tarraleah to have a look at it, and found it was still standing and available. They then approached Hydro Tasmania, explained the aims of the LBT and asked for the shed to be donated. Hydro Tasmania were clearly impressed and agreed. With the financial help of Forestry Tasmania, the shed was dismantled in panels and Hazell Brothers sponsored its transportation to Franklin.

The need to raise funds to erect the Hydro shed in Franklin had become more pressing when we decided to sell the Boat School. Once the new owners took possession, the temporary shed had to be dismantled and moved. With no "home port" for the Trust, the construction of the *Swiftsure* replica was temporarily suspended and the partly constructed whaleboat was moved, with the help of many volunteers, to a vacant shed in Geeveston. At the same time, the Trust began helping Huon Valley Council Youth Services with its "Huon Challenge Mentoring Project." This provided an opportunity for youth (13–17) who were unable to make a success of secondary school, some of whom lived in public space in Huonville in disturbing circumstances, to learn basic boat restoration and boat handling skills with a professional boatbuilder and volunteer Trust members, working with the

Chris Burke with Piner's Punt, *Bolter*, designed by Adrian Dean.
Note the sloping forward transom.

participants on a one-to-one basis. This project commenced in February 2002, and was focussed on the restoration of a "Flying 15" yacht. In the absence of permanent premises, the project was conducted at the private Tinderbox home of Ian Johnston, one of the Trust's volunteer boat builders. I provided transport for participants, often having to wake them up and chivvy them into my van, and Ian and I then worked with them.

One of the main difficulties in getting the Hydro shed erected was that Chris was working full time as the principal boatbuilder at the Boat School. Pip was also working full time. This meant that neither of them could devote the time needed to apply for grants and raise funds for building. By 2002, they were both so busy that they resigned from the LBT Committee and I was elected as the Co-ordinator. Michele Durbin stayed on as Treasurer and Ruth was Secretary. On the advice of Chris and Pip, I approached Scott Marshall from Community Foundation Tasmania (not to be confused with the Tasmanian Community Fund) and as a result of that meeting, I wrote an application for a grant which was successful. This $12,000 was a good start. I then approached some local businesses for sponsorship and this too was successful. These donations made it possible to apply for a bigger grant which would enable the shed to be erected. By early 2003, the Tasmanian Community Fund granted $20,000 to the LBT.

Ruth and I were prepared to put in a lot of work but we were not builders and we needed a builder who was really reliable. We had met a local builder, Keven McMullen when we worked together as volunteers building new toilets at the Palais Theatre. Given donations of expensive items like concrete, there was enough money to pay Keven. We felt very relieved when he said he'd do the job. The shed was constructed remarkably quickly and clad with vertical boards, in the style of local apple sheds, thanks to an employment provider in Hobart, which donated the timber. Geeveston District School staff put the roofing iron on in a day. Keven put in a toilet and kitchen and the LBT was up and ready to go.

The first thing built inside the shed was the stock to enable the completion of the *Swiftsure* replica. By this time, the partially built vessel was four years old and the Geeveston School students who had originally lofted her and set it up had left school. But the school had not left the boat. Her construction continued at a good pace with a succession of local boat builders providing supervision for students from both Geeveston and Dover and others donating glue, paint, fastenings. Anders Thiele, a boatbuilder from Lune River, took the lead supervising the planking. A grant from the Bicentenary of Tasmania Fund enabled us to employ one of our first Diploma graduates, Adrian Phillips, who worked with students and volunteers for a full day a week. Mark Singleton, another of our graduates (1999–2000) who was, by day, employed on the heavy task of restoring *May Queen*, worked on Monday evenings with other volunteers.

Monday evenings, after work, became remarkable occasions. Voluntary work started around 5 pm, and went on till 7 pm, when Ruth served up bread and soup.

Then we went back to work till about 10 pm. It wasn't long before other people like Southerly Dolling, who was a professional caterer, and Lyn Goodwin joined in. Soon soup was overtaken by sausages donated by the local butcher and cooked in a variety of ways. By this time, the LBT had about fifty members. We kept a list of our guests. There were then thirty names on it, including a person from Sweden, an American, a Norwegian, a Dane and lots of mainlander tourists, as well as old and new Tasmanians.

In the meantime, Ruth and I thought we both deserved a good holiday. We took the seats out of the van and re-equipped it as a campervan. We wanted to see Stephen and Anne in Melbourne and Philip's family and Ruth's family in Adelaide and then head mainly north. We left our house and our animals, in the hands of our neighbours, and an unusually competent house sitter. We left the Living Boat Trust and our other domestic affairs to our friend, Southerly Dolling.

The van needed servicing, so I rang a mechanic. When asked the make and model I lost my marbles and said "Mitsubishi Princess" instead of "Mitsubishi Express." This caused a lot of guffawing on the end of the phone and from my brother-in-law Dave, who came up with a new advertisement: "Mitsubishi Princess—a MAN's car". Anyway, the name stuck and we set off. I felt an obligation to become more familiar with my adopted country, accompanied by my favourite Australian.

We left Franklin to have a go at the Grey Nomad experience early in the month of May 2003, and took an annex tent with us, that we could attach to the Mitsubishi Princess, to give us an extra room. We meant to enjoy the independence of the low

Leofleda and the Russian Tall Ship *Pallada* at the Tall Ships visit to Hobart in 1998.
(Photo, courtesy Bruce Hutchison)

cost, and sometimes free, public camping sites all over Australia, mostly managed by rural local Governments.

Our first journey took us to Strathgordon, our introduction to the landscape of mountains, forests and lakes, of Tasmania's south west. Tasmania had become an electric power house by building dams after the end of World War II, when there were many thousands of migrants from Europe who came to Tasmania to rebuild their lives. And they were successful, with the encouragement of the Labor party, led by Eric Reece, a much motivated "resource developer," otherwise known as "Electric Eric."

The Hydro-electric Commission was a rare kind of industrial monopoly, both feared and loved by Tasmanians and migrants. It wielded massive political power, which allowed it to drown thousands of hectares of unique virgin rainforest, in order to store water to attract big industry to the State with the lure of cheap electricity. Some politicians spoke of the Ruhr Valley in Germany, as the model for Tasmania's future. One of Tasmania's political problems was that although hydro-electricity was a renewable source of power, it became an anathema to people who prioritised the protection of native rain forests, and other areas of infinite beauty. The Hydro, was thus the midwife, that led indirectly to the birth and increasing success of the Tasmanian Greens, the first such political party in the world.

The notorious drowning of Lake Pedder was followed by the plan to dam the Franklin River near the west coast. This was an opportunity for the Federal Labor party, led by Bob Hawke, Australia's most popular Prime Minister since Menzies, to gain the support of the emergent Australian Greens, and eventually the majority of Australian voters, to abandon the plan.

But at the local level the "Hydro" as it was known, won the support of everyone, because of the way it was woven into the Tasmanian community by its generosity. Not only did many materials necessary for rural life "fall off the back of trucks!" but it was also known that the Hydro was a reliable source of surplus building materials, engineering equipment and advice from highly qualified experts in many fields. Even some who called themselves Greens, conceded that having built a lot of dams, the Hydro had created a sustainable alternative to coal, as a source of electricity.

At the end of the twentieth century the price of Huon Pine had risen so high that it became worthwhile to re-visit the lakes that had been made by drowning big areas of forest. Special watercraft were built for harvesting ancient trees by getting brave men to dive down with compressed air chain saws, to remove branches, cut down the trunks of Huon Pine, and watch them float up to the surface, to be left to float in bays and inlets in the lakes until they were acquired by the nearest saw mill.

We visited one of the basins attached to Lake Gordon that had a large part of its surface covered by high-floating logs, chained together for later access. This was the time of the early stages of an organisation called Hydro-wood, which will be able to keep its business going for some years, but not forever, unless Huon Pine can be rationed. We discovered that this was a divisive subject that Tasmanians of all kinds could talk about for a very long time.

We took the ferry from Devonport to Melbourne and spent time with Stephen and Anne. We then drove to Ballarat, the Gold Rush town of 1851 that developed from a group of diggers into a determined community who enacted an exemplary rebellion against corrupt authority, known as the Eureka Stockade. Since then Ballarat has become a cultural, commercial and industrial society with a note of Victorian respectability.

It was a novel experience for us to have the liberty to wander as we pleased so we headed for the Glenelg National Park near the coast, and hired a canoe on the river. Not that we were short of small boat travelling, but we found this Mister Toad experience, both novel and very enjoyable. There was no challenge in it, and no noise either. No motor boats or even Hullabaloos, just an empty, winding river, with a surprise at every bend—"Nothing, absolutely nothing, half so much worth doing!" Kenneth Grahame would have loved it. Nobody was there except us, so we took the opportunity to take a bath in the clear warm water.

Next day we followed our journey through Geelong and Colac, then Port Fairy just in case we ever had a slightly larger boat than *Leofleda*, and wanted to take advantage or seek refuge from the steady south easterly winds of autumn that stopped our first attempt to sail from Port Adelaide to Tasmania. A voyage from east to northwest would, I thought, be well worth exploring along this ocean coast, but with well-staged ports of refuge.

This brought us to Warrnambool, Portland, and across the state boundary to Victor Harbour in South Australia. That was where I had once been dropped, as a History lecturer, from a helicopter, to give a short television lecture for the ABC about South Australian maritime history, and to enjoy a bit of surfing, in spite of

The Living Boat Trust's new shed from Tarraleah being unloaded.
The temporary shed on left, Wooden Boat School far left.

being frequently dumped. Ruth was a skilled surfer in her youth and taught me how to contrive a rather pedestrian version of her spectacular performance.

We headed first for the Clare valley, with its small villages, bendy roads, and rather grand houses and pubs. This was where we had spent most of our honeymoon, in 1975.

Most of Ruth's family lived in the foothill suburbs of the city of Adelaide, but her eldest brother, Stephen, had invited us to spend a few days with him in his rural hideaway farm at Jamestown, the centre of the once prosperous wheat belt for which South Australia is famous. This was where the wheat delivered to the docks in the Isle of Dogs came from, to be carried on to East Mills, Colchester and finally, as flour, to London.

Colonial agriculture, as I taught my history students, had been based on the late nineteenth century assumption, that "rain follows the plough." Planners prophesied, and railways were built on this assumption. Railway stations were constructed every ten miles or so to "open up" the country as dictated by the "Goyder Line." This was an imaginary barrier which wriggled around the upper coastline of the two gulfs, devised by George Goyder, the Surveyor-General of South Australia in 1865, to distinguish between the southern portion of South Australia, where annual rainfall usually exceeds ten centimetres, and is theoretically capable of growing wheat, and the drier land to the north, in which sheep were known to have survived.

It was supported by the Waste Lands Act of 1872. But it was soon evident that, though the boundary was theoretically a good idea, it was on average too far to the north. I used to take my Australian History students on field trips in a bus to explore the ghost towns and some towns that had survived, and to learn the determining factors of climate change and soil quality for successful large scale land use in Australia.

In Adelaide, we spent time with our families and continued our journey towards Port Augusta and then down the Eyre Peninsula to Kielpa, another once ambitious settlement, but now a ghost town with only a public notice to record the short life of a forgotten community, and on into the Darke Range Conservation Park. Ruth had memories of a young woman she had known. Her young man had been given land there after the end of World War II as a soldier settler, and had made a success of it. The stories of human endeavour, of success and failure, of death and departure seemed to be part of the landscape.

We were familiar with much of Spencer Gulf, having sailed to Port Lincoln from Port Adelaide, in *Leofleda*, but we had never been there by land. We contacted Pep Manthorpe, a famous sailor who had a long history as the skipper of several ketches, and had retired at Coffin Bay. He had been a valuable supporter and adviser for the *One and All* in her infancy, and his son, Peter, was to become one of the skippers who kept the *One and All* busy after her return from the First Fleet Re-enactment, as a sail-training vessel. This eventually enabled her to pay her debts to the South Australian Government.

Our next stop was Nadia's Landing. I thought it a wonderful place that brought questions to my mind. Who was Nadia? What can be known about her? Google tells me nothing. We spent the night there with the sounds of the sea and the clearest sky, with the biggest and brightest stars that I have ever seen.

The next day was a kind of trance, unless you were driving. We took turns. The good thing about driving on the Great Australian Bight, was that we were able to look at the sea most of the time. And the coastal views were stunningly empty, beautiful, and thought provoking. Camp sites were equally useful for stretching our legs and the protocol was to put a dollar into a tin if you wanted to stay for the night, and were honest, which we and a few other people evidently were. The best things about the Eyre Peninsula were the very vast ocean, the absence of people, and the stimulus it provided for adventurous imagination.

The drive up the Stuart Highway to Alice Springs is so unusual that you don't feel like sleep. The Wedge-tailed Eagles feed well because of the quantity of road kill on the road, which takes some getting used to, and the massive road trains in clouds of dust don't help. Coober Pedy, or originally *kupa piti*, in the local aboriginal language, is the first stop on the northern journey, and it provides a civilised experience compared with what is to come. In June, the month we arrived, the weather was just pleasantly warm, and cool at night. We stopped outside the town, and cooked on campfires under thousands of stars. In the morning we found a town of about 3,000 inhabitants, mainly from continental Europe. Buildings on the surface give the impression of a much smaller population than actually exists, especially in summer when people retire to their underground dwellings which provide cool accommodation, as well as underground shops, workshops and offices. Opal was discovered in February 1915, and mines opened quickly as the news spread. Coober Pedy is still the largest source of opal in the world.

We found a campsite well outside the town and off the road, to savour again the silence and solitude of the desert, the warmth of a small campfire and the star lit dome of the cloudless sky. You must understand that we had been living in valleys for thirty years and being able to see what seemed like the whole sky was a phenomenon. We looked forward, next day to leaving the monotony of the Stuart Highway, to visit Uluru, Australia's sacred mountain, and pay our respects to its aboriginal owners, before pressing on to the relatively metropolitan town of Alice Springs. Here we met two of our old friends from Franklin, Chris Wilson and Catherine Perez, and their half-Dingo dog Coco, who much to our delight, sang for us, with her canine soprano voice. Chris and Catherine are an adventurous couple, both of them are experienced nurses who have specialised in remote communities like Bruny Island and the Northern Territory.

The climate grew hotter as we travelled north, and places like Mataranka and Bitter Springs became magnetic. Once we reached Bitter Springs we became attached to the warm clear section of the Roper River, where we could swim and get totally clean. We were anxious to get to Darwin, partly because the Princess was due for a service, but also out of respect for the memory of the black Labrador of the same name. We delayed our arrival by going to the Litchfield National Park. It was full, to our surprise, of noisy tourists from Germany. We managed not to mention the war, and enjoyed their youthful energy as we all jumped into the water holes together.

Darwin was a bigger place than we expected, and was a welcome contrast with the desert. It was cosmopolitan, full of life, and "civilization." We moved into a cheap hotel and stayed there for two weeks. The Museum was culturally inclusive and up to date with its wonderful collection of refugee boats that had sailed from Vietnam, and arrived safely in most cases. The refugees, then, were treated with humanity as allies of the Australian soldiers who had fought with them against the Viet Cong. Which makes it hard to understand the vilification of the later maritime refugees by the political leaders of Australia.

Having come so far we headed to Kakadu, where we learnt from an Aboriginal host that his people valued the wild horses known as brumbies as part of their ecological universe. "They are our pets," he explained.

Two days later we were at the Three Ways roadhouse at the junction of the Stuart Highway and the Barkly Highway which leads to Mount Isa, and then onto what is called the Kennedy Development Road, a name that worried us a bit. It turned out to be very rough but it was a short cut to Cairns and the Queensland coast, with its offshore islands, and golden beaches, mangrove swamps and fishing villages. To begin with we were spellbound by Port Douglas, the coastal scenery, the short distances between one retirement village and the next, and the beaches we could walk on, but not swim at. But to be honest it began to get boring and repetitive as we drove south. I think it was the profusion of red brick paving in the urban areas that brought me down most and, as we drove south, the sameness of the endless marinas that had displaced so many Mangrove swamps, and thus compromised the habitat of many different kinds of fish and bird life.

We sought relief by going inland from Mackay to Rockhampton, then inland again and back to Maryborough, camping in national parks with rustic bucket showers. We went through Brisbane and on to Stradbroke island, where we caught up with Sean Hogben, the journalist/boatbuilder, and his boys, Louis and Seamus, who we had met when they were babies in Geeveston.

The next nostalgic visit was to Kyogle near the boundary between Queensland and New South Wales. This was where Bill Porter and I had gone, in 1982, to choose and fall the grey Ironbark tree that became the keel of *One and All*. The sawmill and its grey ironbark forest had continued to prosper, and to supply grey Ironbark timber to boat yards building wooden boats all over Australia.

The Byron Bay area was well on its way at this time to become a sanctuary for experimental communities and alternative lifestyles, at places like Nimbin. We made contact with Mike Foley, who really lives mainly on Huon Island in Tasmania, but was discovering the advantage, of seasonal climatic adjustment between Queensland

and Tasmania. After another week of camping in the inland forested hills we came back to the coast in time to attend the wedding of our nephew, Ben Moses and his wife Belinda at Newcastle. The wedding was a lovely family occasion where we met many old friends.

We drove round the back of Sydney to avoid the traffic, and then to Canberra, where Cody Horgan, a graduate from our 1999–2000 course, and his wife Heather lived. Kat Edghill was a student in the same course and we spent a pleasant evening together. We returned for a while to Congo, on the south-east coast of NSW, where Lindsay had sighted whales. By now, we had no feeling that we were exploring; this was coming home, and we began to think about what lay ahead when we returned to Franklin.

Once in Tasmania again, my first concern, after driving over Vince's Saddle, and looking down the Huon Valley to the melting snow on Mount Picton, was *Leofleda*, who had spent the winter on the mooring at Franklin. We would need to slip and paint her as soon as possible. We felt refreshed, and our house sitter had looked after our sheep well. *Leofleda* was unblemished after surviving a few strong winds, on her mooring, but shearing the sheep was something else to think about pretty soon.

At the Living Boat Trust, Southerly had things well under control. The construction of the *Swiftsure* replica had progressed, sailing with the schools was energetically underway and the future for the Trust looked promising.

The *Swiftsure* replica was launched on 28 November 2004. I was Co-ordinator of the LBT at the time, so I organised a celebration to mark the occasion and to thank the many volunteers, particularly the Geeveston District School staff, students and parents, politicians and the donors and supporters who had kept us going. I congratulated the founders of the Living Boat Trust, as we were combining the official opening of the workshop with the launching of the *Swiftsure II*, the first boat to be built there:

> … Chris and Pip have envisioned a place where maritime skills and arts can be preserved and shared between generations. It is to be a place through which Tasmanians can re-discover the best of their past, not as an exercise in nostalgia, but as an ingredient of contemporary life…
>
> One of the more ambitious constitutional aims of The Living Boat Trust is to "support community development." That sounds fine, and it's something we thought that building this workshop and then using it to build a whaleboat might promote, but does it work? Buzzwords like "Investing in Social capital" are useful. But at the coalface there are no magic bullets.
>
> Bonding is fine up to a point, but to build a constructive community we need networking that builds bridges. We have needed bonding networks to survive, but we need bridging networks to get ahead, and I think the Living Boat Trust and organisations that build on unifying themes such as a shared heritage and additional opportunities for the education of our children can help us to do that.

Our local MP, Harry Quick, who had been very helpful and enthusiastic about the

LBT from the start, opened the workshop. The Tasmanian Minister for Education, Paula Wriedt, launched the boat in front of about two hundred people and hopped in for a row herself. It was a very successful occasion and vindicated the trust of our sponsors, donors, members and volunteers.

Over time, people who hadn't done any work on building, but thought it was a good idea, stepped in and volunteered to cook exotic dishes for several years. The Monday night workshop meal became an institution. Soon we were using it as a continuous fund raiser, and more of a social occasion than a time for work. Tourists used to wander in at 6.45, so the committee decided to formalise the situation. *Swiftsure II* was moored in the river, making room in the workshop to replace the building stock with a set of long, narrow folding tables, creating a capacity for up to 60 guests. We became a permanent part of Franklin's night life in summer, with locals and visitors, popping in from all over the world for the sake of the conversation and the atmosphere. Cooking teams have changed, as has the fluid Franklin community. But they still continue, for a modest fee per head for varied meals on Monday evenings. Instead of rivalling the pubs and restaurants in Franklin, Monday night meals increased the local knowledge of what was going on in Franklin, to the benefit of the real estate industry and the local economy.

After the building of *Swiftsure* was over, new activities on the water absorbed the energy of the LBT. We ran a sailing school under the auspices of Yachting Australia. Some of us, including me and Pete Laidlaw, became certified coaches and others, like Southerly Dolling became instructors.

In 2004, we published our first issue of the LBT Newsletter, *Garboard Strake*, eventually producing fourteen issues, thanks to the skills of Lyn Goodwin. The *Garboard Strake* title was a metaphor; an indication that just as the Garboard strake is the first plank to be fitted and fastened onto a boat, this inaugural issue of *Garboard Strake* was the first of many that would continue to be published, I hoped, until the constitutional aims of the Living Boat Trust were achieved. The newsletters contained an editorial, articles contributed by members, news of projects in the shed and future plans.

We also established the "Swiftsure Regatta." This was held close to the end of the school year and consisted of teams from all the Huon schools racing over a short course in the Grebes. These races alternated with time trials by different crews over a set course in *Swiftsure II*. The crews were quite varied: some were older students from the High Schools, or the staff of different schools; sometimes local businesses got up a crew, and Huon Valley Council staff were regular participants. The Regattas required a huge amount of organisation by the LBT and the schools because the various crews all had to have rowing lessons for several weeks before they could compete. The same was true for the *Swiftsure* crews, but everyone seemed to enjoy the event. The results of all the races were published in the local newspaper with many photos of happy people.

By 2005, two new boats were being built in the shed. The first was sponsored by Colony 47, who organised for a group of men in difficult circumstances to build a 14 foot Piner's Punt, under the direction of Adrian Phillips. *Argo Hercules* was launched in July. The second was a Grebe built with children from several Huon Valley Schools and sponsored by the "Huon Cluster of Schools." Mark Singleton was the boatbuilder in charge and *Huon Harmony* was launched in November.

Through Adult Education, LBT offered several courses, including a "Wood Technology for Boat Owners" course run by myself, Ian Johnston and David Golding, in which different timbers, plywood grades, glues and tools and their uses were discussed, and techniques like steam-bending, laminating etc were demonstrated. We were also keen to use *Swiftsure II* to generate some income. We started with a day-long rowing trip in her, down the Huon River, with Southerly catering for lunch. We called it "A Whale of a Day." This was followed by "Small Boat Cruising the Natural Way" (ie without an engine), a course we offered for several years, and a few years later, "Messing About in Boats." The boats used for these expeditions were the Grebes that had been built by the Huon Valley Schools and Huon Council Youth Services since 1993. The LBT had become the custodian of these boats when the Boat School changed hands. In exchange for maintenance, the LBT had the use of the Grebes. This little fleet was a blessing for the LBT. The Grebes are easy to row and can carry food and shelter for up to three people in relative comfort. The most fun I remember was a delivery voyage out and back between Franklin to the Wooden Boat Festival in two days to Hobart and three back, with two grebes and our own small yacht, *Leofleda*, as mother ship.

Launch of *Swiftsure II*. Living Boat Trust's new shed in background.
(Photo, courtesy Southerly Dolling)

These courses improved the financial position of the LBT, and introduced a lot of people to open boat sailing, rowing and camping. The local geography is ideal for open boat cruising, with a many sheltered anchorages and camping places, but also broad stretches of water with plenty of wind. We organised for participants to camp in tents on the LBT site after work on a Friday afternoon. Saturday morning began with an early start about 9 am, getting to Cygnet in about three hours, or if we didn't want to bother with civilisation, we could anchor at Randalls Bay, have a swim, then sail over to Surveyor's Bay, and camp on the beach. From there it would be a quick sail with the land breeze behind us in summer, to Mickeys Bay on Bruny Island. After that we might choose our destination depending on the weather. Partridge Island has a great little harbour. Or we could cross over to Dover, in three hours, and put in to Stringer's Cove. Coming back from there to Franklin is good with a sea breeze, starting light, but perfect with a reef in the main sail and the wind on your quarter in the afternoon.

It was this type of Adult Education expedition that led to the next nautical development and another step in the recovery of Franklin as an interesting place to live. The yachting magazines of Europe began to follow the story of the "Raids," instigated in 1997 by a commercial organisation called Albacore, the brain child of Charles-Henri le Moing, a native of Brittany. The first Raid was held on the Portuguese River Douro and others soon followed in Scotland and the Baltic. In 2003, I came across an article in *The Boatman*, a British magazine. It provided an account of an organised adventure with small boats spending two weeks, stopping overnight, camping ashore, and using only oars and sails to reach their destination.

The article mentioned that Albacore was looking for waterways that would attract adventurous sailors from all over the world. Their own well-tried strategy had been to contact national governments in Portugal, Scotland and Finland, and ask for government sponsorship and assistance. Then they were looking for new and wilder or more remote places. Their collective voyages were called Raids in honour of the Scandinavian Vikings.

I wrote to Charles-Henri le Moing and told him that we, the Living Boat Trust of Tasmania, could provide not only the perfect locality for such an expedition, but also an historical background that would attract people from Europe, on account of the fact that the French explorers, Bruni d'Entrecasteaux and Huon de Kermadec had been the first Europeans to make detailed charts of what became the D'Entrecasteaux Channel and the Derwent Estuary. These waterways, I explained, were ideal for Raids as they were characterised by scattered islands, sheltered coves, mountain scenery, and, in summer, a perfect climate for camp cruising. I offered to approach the Tasmanian Government on his behalf, to get the Premier's permission to introduce what would be a great benefit to Tasmania and to Albacore. Charles-Henri replied saying he would like to come to Tasmania to check this out.

The Premier of Tasmania, Jim Bacon, was pleased to discuss the idea with me. He was an able politician with a special interest in tourism. I thought that might not be particularly useful, because of the inclination of tourism experts to concentrate on what they call the "High End" and this can lead to over-development. I argued that the Raid was a concept that could easily be shattered if it was going to be expensive and comfortable. I hoped we could make it educational, cheap and self-sufficient.

Two months later, in the summer of 2004, Charles-Henri arrived, with Johen Krauth, one of his staff, and we drove down a distance of 180 kilometres to Recherche Bay, the most southerly anchorage in Australia. Bruni d'Entrecasteaux had arrived there in January 1793 and had drawn some very deep breaths. "It will be difficult," he wrote:

... to describe my feelings at the sight of this solitary harbour, situated at the extremities of the globe, so perfectly enclosed that one feels separated from the rest of the universe. Everything is influenced by the wilderness of the rugged landscape. With each step one encounters the beauties of unspoilt nature, with signs of decrepitude. Trees reaching a very great height, and of corresponding diameter, are devoid of branches along the trunk, but crowned with an everlasting green foliage. Some of these trees seem as ancient as the world and are so tightly interlaced that they are impregnable.[3]

Thankfully, Recherche Bay is now part of a large national park and not much has changed. This is a place where the French were so overwhelmed by the safety

---

3   d'Entrecasteaux, Bruni, (Translated by Edward Duyker and Maryse Duyker), *Voyage to Australia and the Pacific 1791-1793*, MUP, 2001, p 32.

Swiftsure with her courtesy flag at the end of the 2009 Raid. She is heading for Waterman's Dock in Hobart for the Wooden Boat Festival.

and beauty of their anchorage that they made friends immediately with the local Aborigines, and it was not long before they were holding black babies, and enjoying attempts at verbal discussion, and foot races on the beach.

LBT's Treasurer, Michele Durbin had devised a Business Plan for the Raid. She and the Secretary, Southerly Dolling, dressed in their best "power suits," hired a meeting room at a posh hotel in Hobart (Hadley's), and presented Charles-Henri and Johen with the details and took questions. I didn't look half as attractive as they did, nor did I have half the business know-how they had, so I just took Charles-Henri to see Jim Bacon. They got on well. For Jim, it seemed to be a project that would become a good way of drawing international attention to Tasmania and setting high standards for the safety and management of adventure tourism. Charles-Henri went back to France with an in-principle verbal agreement of support by the Tasmanian government.

My contribution would be to ensure that an agreement would be made between The Living Boat Trust and Albacore. We would follow the example of similar events in Europe. Individuals could bring their own boats, for which we would set standards of safety, approved by Marine and Safety Tasmania. I would administer all the details and The Living Boat Trust would hire out extra boats if necessary, and safety equipment and supply a Mother ship. The Raid would start at Recherche Bay late January 2005, and conclude at Waterman's Dock on the Hobart waterfront, in the middle of the 2005 Wooden Boat Festival. Camping sites were selected in beautiful places, up to twenty sea miles apart, where we could find good shelter, set up tents, and either find public toilets, or hire portable loos.

Charles-Henri was in the habit of initiating the process in person. He believed in "going to the top," the Minister, Director or CEO as the case may be, and persuading them that it would be in their interests to support the raid because of the boost it would give to the local economy, or institution in question, because of the publicity that he could guarantee. He said that overall, only 30% of the total income of a Raid came from the customers: 70% came from "institutional support," ie sponsorship. I think he must have got it down to a fine art.

No sooner had Charles-Henri left Tasmania than we were told that Premier Jim Bacon had been diagnosed with inoperable lung cancer. We had a verbal agreement with Jim, and I had asked him if we could count on his political support. I remember him removing my doubts with the words, "I am the Premier, and I think it's a great idea." Jim died shortly after that, much to the sorrow of Tasmania. His successor was Paul Lennon, a rather different kind of person who, I felt, would be most unlikely to support us. In the end the Tasmanian government declined to provide financial support.

I thought the best way for us to go would be to ask Charles-Henri if he would mind if we took on the responsibility for running the Raid ourselves. He rang me as previously arranged. It must have cost him a packet as we talked for nearly an hour and the line kept on going off so he had to make three separate phone calls to finish the conversation. I explained that we had decided to run a small local expedition on our own, and thanked him for his inspiration and advice. He was very charming and also happy to have inspired increasing numbers of Australians to participate in what has become a regular Biennial Tasmanian event, based on his French inspiration. He was open minded about whether to work in partnership or not and was prepared to leave that decision to us.

I assume that he must have been cogitating vigorously before he phoned. He must have calculated that to manage a project like this from the other side of the world would be so expensive as to be very difficult. Meanwhile he had no objection to us borrowing his brilliant idea. This meant that a professional organisation that had successfully conducted several international, open boat expeditions, would be replaced by a group of inexperienced amateurs.

My first thought was that we should have a trial voyage from Recherche to Hobart, to find out how long it would take, and how the crew would find shelter, and deal with the difficulties that would inevitably arise. Adrian Phillips, one of our graduates and a builder of *Swiftsure II*, was keen to take charge of the trial expedition, and keep a detailed log of the voyage. The idea was to row *Swiftsure II* from Recherche Bay to Hobart with relay crews changing at different ports along the way, except for Adrian himself. He selected his own first-leg crew of six rowers. Several LBT volunteers provided support boats and acted as pilots, sources of weather forecasts and messenger boats.

Altogether, thirty-five men and women participated in the voyage. The first day was an opportunity to follow the steps of the French explorers, and row from Cockle Creek to the French vegetable garden at the northern end of Recherche Bay (this had been recently located), and then return to Cockle Creek.

Next day was so wet and windy that they stayed in Recherche, and rowed to Southport the following day, a distance of 15 miles, some of it in very open water. Southport had been a busy convict and whaling station in the nineteenth century, where ketches loaded timber for Hobart and ports on the Australian mainland. It still had a wharf and a guest house, with a big lawn area, where up to ten tents could be erected. This was followed by voyages to Dover and Randalls Bay. From Randalls Bay, *Swiftsure II* was joined by another LBT expedition: the traditional three-day sail by Franklin Primary School students in the Grebes to the Wooden Boat Festival. I was in charge of *Leofleda*, acting as Mother Ship for this voyage.

With six people rowing, *Swiftsure II* moves well. The little fleet ended up at Coningham for the night and we all then made the final passage to Waterman's Dock. By this time, the crew had become accustomed to cooking on beaches, sleeping in tents, waking at dawn and rowing well. It's important for crews of open boats to be able to live in very close quarters, and get on with each other. This was successfully accomplished with Adrian's leadership, an amazing effort for someone who had not done anything like this before.

The *Swiftsure* crews all seemed very satisfied with themselves, and rightly so. Another crew of young people rowed *Swiftsure II* back to Franklin, where we started to think about putting a rig on her. Murray Isles designed it, giving her a slightly larger version of the naval Montague Whaler rig, which works well. The choice of rig, with a small mizzen, big mainsail and jib, is perfectly balanced and in bad weather she can be sailed, with mizzen and jib alone, in some comfort.

Our first trial with rowers in *Swiftsure II* in 2005 took a lot of organising and, while it was a much smaller expedition than the international event we had discussed with Charles Henri, it turned out to be very successful. Southerly Dolling, Michele Durbin, Andy Gamlin and many other members of the LBT put many hours into making it happen.

As a result of the trial, LBT decided to go ahead with a real Raid. I took charge of two consecutive Raids, the first in 2007, the second in 2009. Each time we had more participants and made more money, which has been used to build and repair more boats, run expeditions in small sailing boats, and run elementary seamanship courses for local school children.

I found myself thinking about my responsibilities, as a kind of Admiral in charge of a fleet of twenty small open boats and a whale boat, and a total of seventy people over the whole voyage. I looked at the chart and counted the sea miles we would cover. The distance, divided into eight days work, and taking the shortest routes adds up to 92.5 sea miles but the winds would vary in speed and direction, so the distance over the ground was likely to be about 150 sea miles all told.

I thought a lot about John Phithian, and while planning the details, I asked myself, "What will you say to the Coroner?" That ensured that I left no organisational detail out. And we had no tragedies.

I spent many silent hours thinking about life jackets, weather forecasts, inter-vessel and ship to Mother ship communication and what to include in the briefings on the beach every morning. On 16 November 2006, I sent out a detailed, seven page "Participants Newsletter," detailing to all the people who had made bookings, what to bring for themselves and their boats (self-sufficiency is the essence of this expedition). Participating in a capsize drill and attendance at briefings were compulsory. I sent out the details of facilities at camping places and first aid arrangements.

In 2007, my son, Philip and my grandson, Sam sailed with me on *Leofleda* to Dover. After that, I took charge of *Swiftsure II*, while Philip and Sam sailed *Leofleda* with the fleet to Hobart. My eldest son Stephen joined me for the 2009 Raid, and I enjoyed sharing this adventure with my family.

The Raid made an educational impact in 2007 and 2009. I thought it would be valuable for the participants to experience something beyond just having a good time and making new friends. I asked my colleagues in the University of Tasmania and some post-graduate students and eminent scholars, writers, artists, Aboriginal leaders and others to give talks during the two Raids I organised. Some local musicians such as Steve and Marjorie Gadd in Franklin and the Recherche Babes at Recherche Bay organised concerts. The talks and concerts, elucidating the culture and history of the particular places where we spent the night, took place after the evening meals.

In 2007 at Recherche, local historian Greg Hogg placed the French expedition of 1792 and 1793 in the context of its revolutionary background in France, and explained its cultural significance in the contact history of Tasmania. Wren Fraser-Cameron, a local activist and historian, spoke about the communities of timber-workers, miners, fishermen, whalers, ex-convicts and shipbuilders who established a frontier society after British settlement.

On Bruny Island, setting up camp was followed by the famous Bruny Island film, *Lunawanna Kiss*, which is silent, except for the evocative music, about the romantic adventures of a lighthouse keeper's daughter, set in the 1930s. Two UTAS post-graduate students, Margie Jenkin and Rebecca Jackson, followed with a talk and Powerpoint presentation based on an oral history of Tasmanian lighthouse keeping families.

At Dover, Professor Michael Roe spoke about the impact of the 1835 wreck of the convict transport *George III,* on Imperial policy, and the details of her long voyage from Woolwich, UK to Tasmania. Cassandra Pybus who lectured at Raiwunna, the University's Centre for Aboriginal studies, spoke about the history and culture of the Aboriginal people of the Huon and Channel. For many raiders, this was the first time they had been confronted with the historical reality of the convict system, the frontier wars, and the affect the British invasion had on indigenous Tasmanian society. Speakers in 2009 included Professor Pat Quilty of the Antarctic Division, writers Peter Hay and Richard Flanagan, Aboriginal leader Jim Everett, Bruny Island activist Michael Paxton, and sculptor Wendy Edwards.

The idea of introducing history and culture into a holiday experience was based on my memories of Auckland University where I had been introduced to Chaucer's *Canterbury Tales* of the thirteenth century. Chaucer described a group of people who developed the habit of meeting at a London pub in order to commence an annual pilgrimage to Canterbury, in honour of St Thomas à Becket, and in hope of their ultimate salvation. They also came to know each other as they listened to the stories with which they entertained each other in the evenings of their 100 mile walk. I think many of our raid participants liked being thus educated, but after I stopped organising things, in later years, my successors thought it better to leave people to their own devices. The Raids still occur every two years and are a major source of income for LBT, and enjoyment for people from all over Australia.

The other side show of the expedition, in order to give people something special to think about, was the name I gave it. I was disappointed that my scheme to have a public apology for the *Terra Nullius* assumption to the First People of Australia, in 1988, had not come off. Raids were also the legacy of the Viking culture. I thought a similar gesture might be organised in honour of the much more ancient maritime adventurers of Southern Tasmania, the Melukerdee of the Huon, the Nuenonne of Bruny Island and the Lyluequonny of Recherche Bay. Tasmanian Aborigines were more inclined to peaceful journeys to honour kinship obligations, or attend to annual movements of other species than to make warlike attacks on other people as was the Viking custom.

I obtained an agreement, first from Rodney Dillon, the Melukerdee Elder of the South East Tasmanian Aboriginal Corporation, that in acknowledgement of the maritime heritage of the southern Aboriginal people of Tasmania, LBT should use an Aboriginal title for what we were doing. Rodney's translation of "raid," was two words instead of one: "Tawe" is the Melukerdee word for travel; "Nunnugah" means canoe. So with Rodney's consent on behalf of his people, we named the expedition "Tawe Nunnugah." It was intended as an implicit acknowledgement of the many thousands of years of Aboriginal maritime history since the end of the last Ice Age, when melting ice separated Tasmania from the Australian mainland. I also asked Rodney if he would lend us an Aboriginal flag to fly on the little flag-staff on the stern of *Swiftsure II*. When a foreign vessel enters the port of a country, international law requires the visiting vessel to fly the Courtesy flag of the host nation whose waters they wish to enter. This is a law commonly understood by the international maritime community.

So our approach to Sullivan's Cove on the afternoon of 9 February 2009 was an opportunity to stage a political statement. I hoisted the Courtesy flag on behalf of us foreigners, just as we reached the entrance to Constitution Dock. There was a large crowd waiting in silence as we approached them. When we were about four boat lengths away from the entrance, someone started to clap and cheer. Then the penny dropped, and they all did. I landed, thanked them for their applause, and explained that the Aboriginal flag did not mean that we were posing as Aborigines. We were reminding people that without a treaty, we were invaders, and so we were flying a courtesy flag in hope of eventual forgiveness, for the sins of our forefathers.

The LBT continued to make plenty of use of *Swiftsure II* for crews of adults and children during the Swiftsure Regattas. In 2008, the Noise and Light film company was making a gruesome film about Alexander Pearce, a convict who escaped with some of his companions from Sarah Island in Macquarie Harbour on the Tasmanian west coast in 1822. They came ashore in a whaleboat and set off to walk across Tasmania to Hobart. Lacking knowledge of bush food, they soon began to starve. Pearce turned up in Hobart as the only survivor, claiming that he had killed and eaten his mates one by one. (Sorry, but Tasmania does have a few stories of that kind.)

The film company asked us if they could hire *Swiftsure II* as a prop. Peter Lunstedt, one of the LBT members had a long trailer, so we borrowed it and Peter Laidlaw, Chris Wilson and I towed *Swiftsure* to Lake Binney in the Central Highlands, where they wanted to do a lot of filming. Pine Tiers was also used as a location. I spent some time teaching the actors how to row a whaleboat, and then, having coached one actor to steer with the 23 foot steering oar, I had to lie on the floor out of sight of the filming, to give him instructions as the boat moved along. This was all done in the depths of winter. I really admired the actors who had to swim from the beach in freezing water to get to the whaleboat, recreating the real experience of the convicts. When the actors arrived at the boat, filming stopped while we wrapped them in blankets around hot water bottles to prevent hypothermia.

We also used Swiftsure for expeditions from Franklin to Mickeys Bay on South Bruny Island, then to Dover and back to Franklin, with Year 9 students from the Friends' School in Hobart. We slept ashore, in and around an LBT member's shack at Mickeys Bay, and at the Far South Wilderness Camp behind Rabbit Island, near Dover.[4]

While we owned the Wooden Boat School, we introduced the idea of the "Clinker Clinic" where people could bring their old clinker boats for diagnoses and advice on cures. The LBT decided to run a similar afternoon course on repair and restoration of clinker boats, so that families with ancient boats that were slowly rotting under the trees could be brought back to life. The lawn beside the river next to the LBT workshop became a classroom, with Adrian Dean as the teacher and myself and Pete Laidlaw to fill gaps. We took groups of people on discussion tours to examine a range of small craft with broken ribs, split planks or rotten thwarts. Owners were asked to tell some history of the boats and having attempted a diagnosis, and the cause of their condition, we asked for suggestions on how to commence, and continue the recovery. Then we stepped in to describe and demonstrate what we thought needed to be done to repair them and how to do it. It was fun talking to lots of interested people and bringing small boats back to life.

This worked well. People dealt with their feelings of guilt at the neglect of their boats, by gaining enough confidence to start repairs. The alternative was to ask the Living Boat Trust for a quote, which turned the workshop eventually into a maritime "Men's Shed." LBT membership was cheap and open to women *and* men.

The little fleet of Grebes, built by the students of Huon Valley schools, opened up more possibilities to get children on to the water in safety when the Huon Cluster of Schools provided funding to formalise the teaching of seamanship by the LBT in 2008. This was the beginning of the very successful "On the Water" programme, which resulted in hundreds of Huon children learning first to row and then to sail. This programme was later funded by a substantial grant from the Tasmanian Labor Government in 2010. Chris Wilson became the coordinator of the programme for the duration of the grant, with supervision provided by many members of the Living Boat Trust who already had sailing or safety boat qualifications, and more who acquired those qualifications in order to help.

I had retired from the Co-ordinator's role in 2005, but continued to be involved in LBT activities. For the On the Water Programme, I specialised in capsize drill, which meant putting weight on the lee side of the boat and hauling in the sheets and forcing the boat to lean over until water came over the gunwale and she fell onto her lee side. I swam the boat round until she pointed into the wind. I requested my crew of children to hold her into the wind while I stood on the centreboard, which levered her upright again. Then I wriggled aboard over the stern and bailed with a bucket tied on to the boat with string, to shift water as quickly as possible. I helped one child at a time aboard and they bailed until more children could get

---

4   Now owned by the Friends' School, Hobart.

inside the boat. Then we sorted our rigging and sails and sailed back to the beach.

When government funding for The On the Water Programme ceased, several attempts were made to operate it on an entirely volunteer basis, with assistance from some of the school teachers, during term time. The volunteer basis has meant a reduction of teaching time. But it has been much better than nothing, and fewer drownings will happen because of greater experience and nautical knowledge.

One of the great achievements of the LBT was its support of local women who wanted to learn to row. This began with a suggestion by one of the Geeveston District High School teachers who pointed out that several mothers of her young students, particularly those with autism and other problems, would benefit from some outdoor activity away from their kids. I had already been teaching mixed crews to row *Swiftsure II* and the Grebes so they could compete in the Swiftsure Regattas. Soon there were all women crews wanting to get out on the water and making a regular thing of it. In one of the regattas, two teams of women, the "Franklin Ladies" and the "Geeveston Mums" competed very energetically, while mocking any assumption of class conscience that might be lurking around. Out of this, Lorrie Harrison in 2009, formed a group within the LBT called "Women on Water" or WOW! This group has been going strongly for ten years now. In 2012 they decided to build their own boat, a St. Ayles skiff named *Imagine*. This was followed by two more of the same design. WOW hosted the international St Ayles Skiff Regatta in Franklin in 2017 and has participated in regattas in New Zealand and Scotland.

Until very recently, I have enjoyed helping out with repairing and maintaining the LBT fleet with the "Tuesday men," a group who do these jobs every week with great dedication. I also like to row and because of this, I find that I am in a perpetual duel with David Nash for the prestigious Roger Harwood trophy.

This is a trophy for single rowers in small open boats over a distance of five kilometres. It was originally donated by the boatbuilder, Roger Harwood, for a race at the Dover Seafest. Boats started on the north of Dover harbour, and sprinted from a line on the beach to their boats, waiting with their bows in the water. The rowers dragged their boats into the water, boarded over the stern and headed off the beach for Faith and then Charity Islands, leaving them both to starboard, and then rowed back to the beach. As there were boats of many shapes and sizes, they were all handicapped on a formula based on waterline length. I enjoyed this race and found it easy to win.

But after a few years, the Dover Seafest sadly ceased.[5] Roger Harwood suggested that the race itself could continue and should be moved to Franklin, where the river could provide a visible course. Adrian Dean worked out a sophisticated handicapping formula. The race started at the pontoon at the Wooden Boat Centre, and my boat was the smallest boat so I was the first to leave, heading up towards Huonville, then turning round the northern end of the north Egg Island, down

---

5   It has since been revived.

the eastern side of the island until we reached the Egg Island canal. Going through that demanded straight rowing as the canal is not very wide and there is no room for overtaking. The race finishes with a final sprint across the river to the starting point. It takes about fifty minutes.

But David Nash, formerly the apprentice in the building of *One and All*, arrived in Franklin after sailing his boat *Yukon*, with his family, from Denmark. When David came to town and entered the race, things changed. I think I won twice by ever decreasing margins, but last year, David won. We will be at it again in a few weeks.

While the Living Boat Trust was going from strength to strength under the leadership of David Pittaway, then Chris Wilson, then Peter Laidlaw and their respective Committees, Franklin itself was facing new threats.

The delightful Franklin Football Clubhouse building at the sports oval was an extraordinary product of volunteer labour after World War II. The re-formed Franklin Lions football club members were proud of the rampant golden lion painted on the floor. By 2009, Huon Valley Council had obtained a report that recommended demolition of the building. Franklin Progress Association protested and provided an alternative costing for repairing and restoring the building. In spite of formal local protest, the building was demolished, asbestos and all, at 6 am one morning in 2009 by an excavator, hired by the Council.

This proved to be an action that did more to unite the Franklin community than anything else, and made our sense of place more powerful. Eventually, the perception by the Huon Valley community that its Council was faction ridden and dysfunctional led to its being sacked by the State Government and replaced in 2016 by an Administrator, Adriana Taylor, a wonderful woman, for two years.[6] I think this was the result of two decades of discontent created by such acts as the destruction of the Franklin Football club house, and the sentiments encapsulated by Steve Gadd in this remarkable protest poem for the Franklin Lions, "The Lions' Den":

> *On a thousand winter mornings*
> *In the fog and rain and cold*
> *The men that worked the orchards*
> *Donned The Blue, Maroon, and Gold*
> *But the Glory Days are over and*
> *The word's around Franklin Town*
> *The Huon Council ruled to tear*
> *The Den of the Lions Down.*
> *T'was in the 1940s*
> *The boys back from the War*
> *Built a clubroom at the Sports ground*
> *With a board to keep the score.*
> *Just a sturdy hardwood structure*

---

6   At the end of 2018 an election was called and a new, more youthful and energetic Council was elected.

*Built with sweat and grunt and pride,
On the South side of The oval
By the old brown Huon's side.
In the burning Summer Days
When the Cricket broke for tea
They'd go in there to find some shade
and plan their strategy.
And after each hard-fought Footy game.
When the home games ran down here.
They'd welcome the visiting team inside
And shout each man a beer.
But the Glory Days are over
and The word's around Franklin Town
The Huon Council ruled to tear
The Den of the Lions Down.
In The Sixties and the Seventies
When Football seemed like war
The Franklin boys drew strength and will
From the 'Lion on the Floor.'
Mud and Blood and Bruises
Victory and Defeat,
The Lion Heart in every breast
Matched the Lion at their feet.
But the Glory Days are over and
The word's around Franklin Town,
The Huon Council ruled to tear
The Den of the Lions Down.
After years of disappointment
When defeats seemed ne'er to stop
The Lion Roared in the 80s
And Clawed Back to the Top.
And The Clubhouse Rang with songs and drinks
Through the evening hours and more
As the Franklin folk danced Victory's Waltz
Round The Lion on the Floor.
But the Glory Days are over and
The word's around Franklin Town
The Huon Council ruled to tear
The Den of the Lions Down.
Then Back in the Nineties
When the Palais was all run down
The Clubhouse hosted the dances*

For the folk of Franklin Town.
The woman I was to marry,
I'll recall it ever more
Shared our first dance, that night
Round the lion on the floor.
Now the fellows down at Old Town hall
They Know a different Dance
Where all the steps are secret moves
And nothing's left to chance.
With clever consolations
They'll have your guard drop down
And they'll smash it in the morning
Before the Din wakes Franklin Town.
On a thousand winter mornings
In the fog and rain and cold
The men that worked the orchards
Donned
The Blue, Maroon, and Gold
But the Glory Days are over and
The words around Franklin Town
The Huon Council cruelly tore
The Den of the Lions Down.

The next challenge to Franklin's heritage came from Southern Water, formed in 2008, to take over the water and sewerage infrastructure and rights that had formerly been owned and managed by the southern councils. Knowing little about local history, Southern Water hit on a plan to obstruct the navigability of what turned out

Canal E R Ash, with permission, Don Ash, from Cato Collection.

to be the oldest working canal in Australia. The canal was built across South Egg island to connect Cradoc, on the eastern side of the river, to the more navigable water of the Franklin waterfront to the west where the water was deep enough for the Hobart-bound steamers and ketches.

Southern Water's plan in 2009 was to improve water infrastructure on both sides of the Huon River at Franklin and Cradoc, and deliver a new water system to Cygnet as part of a regional water scheme. Their engineers proposed laying down some large concrete blocks through the middle of the canal to anchor a water pipe. The Huon Valley planning process required assessments of both the European and Aboriginal heritage values of the Island and the canal. Since the heritage consultant hired to look into the European heritage values freely admitted that he did not consult primary sources, Ruth and I made a few visits to the State Archive, which revealed that the canal was first dug in the mid 1850s, funded by a local subscription. It silted up and was re-aligned, cleared, and re-dug at Government and Council expense in 1885. Although it was not the first navigation canal built in Australia, Egg Island canal turned out to be the oldest extant navigation canal in the country. Ruth decided to make an application to Heritage Tasmania for the canal to be listed.

Southern Water also wanted to place a large, noisy pump, immediately opposite the recently rescued Palais Theatre, on the ground that it would blend nicely with the adjacent change rooms and toilet block of the nineteen sixties.

It took the combined effort of a loosely formed group of individuals, calling itself informally "The Usual Suspects," to work out alternative ways of laying the pipeline and alternative locations for the pump. The Suspects consisted of several members of the newly formed Franklin History Group, the Progress Association, and the Living Boat Trust and other individuals like Alan Cato, a descendant of the Canal's builder, Henry Clark. We determined to do the research and mount an appeal. This took months of everyone's time and several appearances at the Resource Management and Planning Appeal Tribunal. In the end, the Appeal was mediated and resulted in a compromise: no pump opposite the Palais Theatre and the pipe in the canal to be buried to one side, below Lowest Astronomical Tide, so the canal remained navigable and could be cleared of debris to keep it so.

The Canal was permanently entered to the Tasmanian Heritage Register in 2013. It is used constantly by local rowers, kayakers and canoeists and has become quite a tourist attraction. But apart from its obvious historical and practical value, the most important reasons for maintaining the function of the canal were less tangible and more powerful. Charles Zuber, who had arrived recently from Queensland was an expert in art history, and he expressed it best:

> To discover the opening to the canal is a revelation for those out for their first row on the Huon River. What is it, where does it go? The answer is to be found in childhood memories of adventure. Curiosity is the impulse.
>
> Alice in Wonderland's adventures endure in our story telling for generation after generation, and for good reason, if not always entirely quantifiable… Like Alice's journey,

the canal reveals itself in ways that are not codified. There are no comparisons easily made. The experience is unique, not spectacular, or awesome, but a journey into another world. Like disappearing down a rabbit hole.

There is mystery in an excursion that takes some time to reveal the destination. From the first few dips of the oar, the banks reveal more vegetation round the bend, while reflections invite the rower to investigate further. The journey moves at a slower, more self-conscious pace, for the water is calmer, the reflections more fascinating, and without any notices, instructions or warnings.

The rower quietly slows up ... For by now, we are transported into a space of tranquillity: a childhood adventure beyond authority, angularity, regulation and rationality. Now we have lost Franklin. The stillness has slowed us. The banks shield us from society while hinting at more nature to come. And it is while negotiating the roots and branches, that we are offered a glimpse of open water ahead. The trees, all around us, frame a new landscape, and hint at new possibilities.[7]

This was a time of continuous activity to make Franklin a better place, a time of integrated action and consensus about the future and I feel privileged to have been a part of it all.

---

7   Zuber, Charles, "Introduction," in Cato, A and Young, R, *Egg Island Canal: Australia's oldest operational navigation canal*, Franklin History Group Inc, Franklin, 2013.

Chapter 20: "...but they do not make it just as they please"

When I launched the LBT's newsletter, *Garboard Strake*, I meant it to spread news about the Trust's activities, boats and members, but also as a primary source of social history. I hoped to use it as a place for discussion about local problems and solutions and new ideas for coping with global problems as they affected us locally. So in January 2008, I used my position as Editor of *Garboard Strake* to "start the conversation" with an article I called "How to really deal with the Oil Crisis."

I pointed out that Australia had ratified the Kyoto agreement. Climate change was then accepted, even by the United States Government, as a reality instead of a conspiracy. I described the content of an article I had seen in *The Mercury*. It's caption was "The first new cargo ship to harness wind power in more than 100 years."[1] In fact, the ship *The Mercury* wrote about — the 10,000 ton *Beluga Sky* — was a motor vessel, assisted by a parachute when she had a fair wind. The rig could save $1600 a day in fuel costs. "This doesn't go far enough," I said,

> ... to make much of a dent in the task of returning to a cleaner world. But now that the political balance has shifted to at least halfway action, rather than denial, there is a possibility that incentives such as carbon credits will soon be on the political agenda for commercial application, of harmless renewable energy, such as wind power.[2]

I had been deeply inspired by the notion of commercial sail ever since my holiday experiences in 1948 and 1949, as a junior volunteer on board the original *Leofleda* with Captain Norman Sheldrake. As I explained earlier, she was an engineless Thames Spritsail Barge, sailing regularly between the London docks in the Isle of Dogs, where grain was unloaded from ships from Australia, and shipped in the barge to East Mills in Colchester, Essex.

In the London docks, *Leofleda* tied up alongside big ships. Grain from Australia was poured down moveable chutes onto the smooth ceiling of the hold, while I used a big shovel to stop the tendency for the barge to lean over towards the sudden mounds of grain on the floor of the hold. Being only fifteen, I gloried in the challenge of spreading the grain to keep the barge on an even keel. Working hard to keep up with a machine made me sweat like a pig. I revelled in it as part of my boxing training.

The return cargo from Colchester was flour in bags, from East Mills, back to a warehouse at the eastern end of the southern side of the Pool of London. I count those voyages as highlights of my education. I read Hervey Benham's wonderful book, *The Last Stronghold of Sail*, which referred to the sprit-sailed Thames barges. I demanded the book (literally) from my parents for my fourteenth birthday, after browsing it in Foyles London bookshop, in September 1948. I was to read it many times. Practical experience on board the original *Leofleda* made me sad about the book's title. I have always hoped, since then, that things might change, and that I might live to experience a return to working sail.

---

1   *The Mercury*, 9 January 2008, p 36.

2   *Garboard Strake*, January 2008, p 14.

By 2050, I believe, most of us will be doing all we can to reduce climate change. Minimising marine pollution will be advanced, and the rising cost of oil based fuels will dramatically reduce their use. Vested interests may continue the use of polluting fuels, but with luck, some intelligent countries will have set an example, and demonstrated the feasibility of using renewable energy, such as hydro-electricity, hopefully without drowning any more rain forest. Tide will be a useful source of energy, and wind will probably be the easiest source of power to use for marine transport without high cost, because the human species has over 2000 years of experience with direct sail power.

There is now a global revival of commercial sail. Tom Jackson, senior Editor of *WoodenBoat* Magazine, wrote an important article, "Breeze freshening for cargo voyages,"[3] reporting a large number of organisations and single vessels using sail to move cargo from many inland and coastal regions of the United States, and many parts of Europe. Fiji has an even more radical model. It is based on abandoning diesel for inter-island shipping altogether, because of high cost, and relying on a return of the *Drua*, the traditional wooden war-ship which can carry up to 100 warriors at twenty knots. One *Drua* embarrassed Captain Cook by sailing around *Resolution* to demonstrate the superiority of the Polynesian vessel.

More recently, "Sailcargo," an organisation based in Costa Rica, has laid the keel of a 150 foot three-masted wooden schooner. She is being built to demonstrate the use of timber, our only renewable building material, with trunnels[4] instead of metal fastenings. *Sailcargo* plans to install an electrical auxiliary engine that, when needed will use the ship's propeller in neutral gear to charge her battery as she sails through the water, using renewable energy all the time. Sailcargo Inc intends not only to build a single ship, but to set an example, and stimulate the peaceful, new, global, industrial revolution, that we need to save the lives of our children and grandchildren.

How intelligent it was, I thought, back in 1948, when Captain Sheldrake took me aboard *Leofleda*, to use free, renewable energy, to carry 100 tons of wheat in one direction and 100 tons of bagged flour in the other. In those days it took five lorries, each with a crew of two men, to do the same amount of work. *Leofleda* managed with a skipper and a mate, just like the lorries did, but carried five times as much cargo and burnt no fuel at all. I was a supernumerary, but being an extra hand made me extremely happy, as Captain Sheldrake shared his weather and nautical wisdom with me, and taught me the finer points of handling *Leofleda*, our mobile floating home, while the wind and tide did the work for us.

I took my watch at the wheel, too, and felt the power of the wind, and the tide that was almost always flowing with us at up to four knots. I felt the resistance of the leeboard and rudder, as she heeled slightly, and luffed to gain distance to windward. And then bore away carefully, to keep up her speed. One particular memory has lasted for 71 years.

---

3   *WoodenBoat*, No 247, 2015.

4   Tree-nails, wooden dowels fastening timbers together, with wedges crossed at both ends.

As we sailed with the southeasterly sea breeze, around the Essex coast, we sighted some red sails of a sister ship, ahead. While I was at the helm, we slowly closed on the vessel as we swept down the Thames Estuary, towards the Buxey sands. By midday we were close enough to read the name of the barge, *Thalatta,* just ahead of us. To my delight we slowly gained on her, and eventually passed her at a polite distance, as I became better at responding to the slight changes in the wind.[5]

But I digress. Tides flow in the Thames estuary at up to four knots (nautical miles per hour). This means that it is important to know their direction and timing in order to give yourself an advantage. It also means that if the tide is against you, and you have no engine, you might as well anchor until the tide changes. You might repair things, perhaps have a cup of tea, and when the tide changed, you could make some good progress. If the gentle breeze off the land in the morning gave you four knots through the water, the ebb tide could double your speed over the seabed to eight knots, or nine miles an hour, enough to get you 54 miles on your way, from Southend, for example, to Colchester in six hours.

I was amazed by the extraordinary style of both the skipper and the one-man crew. Coming alongside wharves under sail, or getting away, was a joy to behold. Preparation took place in silence, no shouting at all, just making sure that we all knew what we should be doing and in what order. If I had not been there, they told me, no one would even be talking. Momentum was judged with great accuracy from long experience and without any noise, so that brailing up the sails, getting alongside a wharf, and setting mooring lines to check the force of 100 tons or more, moving through the water at about half a yard a second, and slowing down, could bring the vessel to a gradual halt with smiles of confidence rather than any kind of bad language. I am of course, not the first to have admired "the hard and happy men" who:

> ... *performed astonishing feats of instinctive seamanship, and never paused to consider the merits of their efforts, so natural did it all seem. And natural it was: the unnatural thing is that the slow immemorial dignity of ships on the tideways should be extinguished by the smelly, unseemly (and often uneconomical!) scurry of little lorries along the tarmac.*[6]

Not surprisingly, *Leofleda* was one of the last Thames barges to acquire an auxiliary engine, shortly afterwards, in 1952. And because of my experience on her, not surprisingly, sailing ships are integral to my version of Utopia.

Many years later, as I learned more about the ketches of Tasmania and South Australia, I was struck by the functional similarity between these Tasmanian coastal vessels, and their British contemporaries. As I became interested in problems

---

5   Four years later the name, *Thalatta*, was still lodged permanently in my memory because I was learning Ancient Greek, at the University of Auckland. The correct spelling of the Greek word for "the sea" is *thalassa*. I wondered how the misspelt Greek word, *thalatta*, had found its way to the stern of a Thames barge.

6   Benham, Hervey, *Down Tops'l: the Story of the East Coast Sailing-Barges*, Harrap & Co, London, 1951, p 16.

such as global warming in the 1970s, I enlarged my academic interests about Pacific Island and Australian history and added an interest in Environmental Studies. The idea of reviving sail power as a remedy for rising road fatalities, rising fuel costs, and climate change, began to make more sense. Sail power could be tested, and then publicised, most conveniently I thought, by small rural communities, especially in places like Franklin, with its sub-conscious memories of self-sufficient carbon neutrality in a context of ingenuity, skill, and experience, in the not too distant past.

Ruth started in 2018 to do some serious research about the trading ships built in Franklin between 1840 and 1880, and she soon discovered that many of them were snapped up by mainland owners, especially South Australians. Wooden ship building in Franklin, Hobart, Cygnet and Shipwright's Point was the successful story that changed the nature of the Huon Valley community for the better, from the 1850s to 1920, from a post-convict, violent, and dangerous society to one with libraries, schools, churches, a Mechanic's Institute, and a theatre that could seat up to 560 people. Franklin became a place where there were sometimes four ships at once being built on the land between the Evaporating Factory and the Regional Care building.

In the 1890s, refrigeration made Britain and Europe practical markets for Tasmanian apples, and civic development continued. But when Imperial Preference was withdrawn in 1970, and Britain joined the European Common Market, many orchards were "pulled" and civic development collapsed. Perhaps it was time, I thought, for

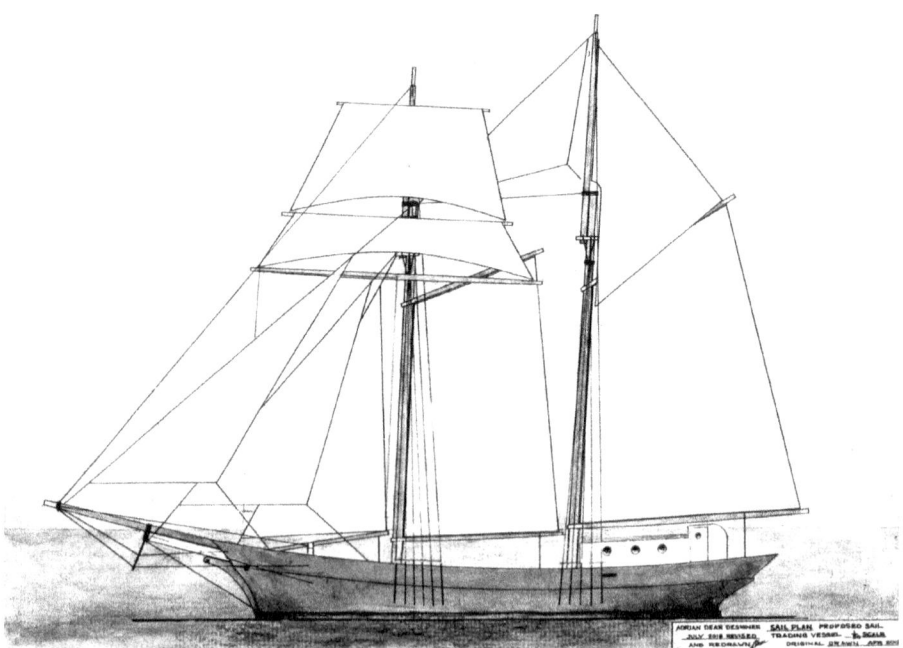

Drawing of Franklin's future trading schooner designed by Adrian Dean.
(courtesy of Adrian Dean)

a new industrial revolution based not on Imperial Preference, but on renewable shipbuilding, renewable energy and better decision-making. Franklin seems to have progressed some way towards that goal already.

In 2011, several people began meeting together to discuss the idea of building a commercial sailing vessel in Franklin. We knew she would not "save the world" on her own, but it would be a step towards that, and would provide employment, education in wooden boat building, adventure tourism, seamanship training and carry unique Tasmanian cargoes to local and mainland ports. Adrian Dean was impressed by this idea and set about designing a schooner specifically for these purposes.

Another factor, in my desire to take some tangible action to improve the prospects of the future, was that my eldest grandson, Lindsay, came from Saudi Arabia to complete his schooling at the Friends' School, and then his degree at UTAS in Hobart. Although he was boarding while at school, we saw a lot of him on weekends and during the holidays and we got to know him well. We went sailing in *Leofleda* down to the idyllic anchorages of Bruny Island and the southern Channel, discovering new safe harbours and living off the sea and vegetables from our own garden. Lindsay became an excellent free diver. We secured him a fishing licence and he kept us well fed with abalone. He and Ruth enjoyed fishing off *Leofleda*, while I slept in the cabin. Sometimes Lindsay would invite some of his friends to Randalls Bay for a weekend. We usually had our clinker dinghy, *Clara*, that I built at Port Huon in 1991, and they would row about under the sandstone cliffs, jump off *Leofleda*'s bowsprit and sunbathe on the deck.

Lindsay and I had much in common; we shared an interest in weather, public speaking, acting and a concern for the future of the natural environment. And we both wanted to "do good"—part of our missionary inheritance, I suppose. The more time I spent with Lindsay, climbing mountains, discussing the state of the world, sailing, and just mucking about, the more I became truly conscious that it would be Lindsay and Sam, Helen, Will, Karen, Nick and Henry—all my grandchildren—who would be most affected if my generation and my children's generation did nothing to stop the planet deteriorating as a feasible home for our species. Thus I badly wanted to build a merchant schooner, among other things, to demonstrate in a small way, the practicality of sailcargo.

In 2011, the Wooden Boat Centre and the Franklin Evaporating Factory both came up for sale. The factory is a huge covered space, including sheds and other buildings which had once been an apple drying factory, employing many local people. It closed in 2006. The possibility of keeping the Boat Centre in local hands and buying the Evaporators gave rise to a new organisation, the Franklin Working Waterfront Association Inc (FWWA).

Its members began talking about the planning and creation of a community managed Working Waterfront, including the building of Adrian Dean's schooner. Ruth and I had been to North America in 1986, and to Britain and Denmark in 1995, when both Susan and Shaohua had jobs at the University of Copenhagen.

We had visited Rockport in Maine, and Mystic Seaport in Connecticut, Maldon in Essex, Falmouth in Cornwall, Lowestoft in Suffolk, and Svendborg in Denmark; all of them maritime communities which had gone through economic declines, depression and war, to the cultural renaissance of the 1960s and seventies, based largely, on a return to traditional maritime activities.

Franklin Working Waterfront Association Inc envisaged Franklin as a place where there would be enough energy and expertise to become, over time, a "Port of Refreshment" for sailing ships. Shipwrights, riggers, marine engineers, naval architects, sawyers and sail-makers could set up their businesses in the Evaporators building to create employment and provide maintenance and repair services for existing wooden boats and sailing ships, and facilities for building and maintaining new ships. The ships would use the renewable energy of wind power, to reduce carbon emissions, while carrying passengers, trainees, tourists, and cargoes of local produce, to both local and Australian mainland destinations.

I had also read about Douarnenez and Brest, in France. A host of regular festivals of wooden boats had begun in Europe and the United States, and the movement had reached Tasmania. Franklin shared the same experience of decline and recovery, in the face of changing circumstances, but people also recovered an interest in local history.

I thought about the big picture of which Franklin is a part, as an example of the global and local problems arising from over-optimistic financial theory, assumed endless economic growth in a finite planet, and what could be done about it.

My first step was a paper, contributed to a departmental conference at UTAS School of Geography and Environmental Studies on 29 June 2011, entitled, "Franklin's Working Waterfront: A Template for Sustainable Prosperity."[7]

The general argument was that colonial and neo-colonial economies are dependent on decisions made in market places and parliaments in other countries. These economies are therefore vulnerable to the whims of those whose interests are not those of the colonies or neo-colonies like Tasmania. The clearest example of this reality was the mistaken faith in the doctrine of Imperial Preference which came to a sudden end when Britain joined the European Common Market in 1970. The Tasmanian government agreed to subsidise the "pulling" of many orchards to convert them into sheep or cattle farms, in response to decisions made in London, instead of Hobart or Canberra. Next came the decisions made in Tokyo rather than Hobart, to industrialise Tasmanian forest practices, that destroyed the relatively sustainable methods of traditional, small scale silviculture. These were replaced by the highly mechanised and damaging method of clear felling, and ancient mixed wet forest was replaced by rotations of quick-growing eucalypts, largely destined for making pulp. I wanted to go beyond negativity to suggest the alternative of self-sufficiency.

My narrative was a discussion of Franklin's economic history, consisting as it does, of periods of prosperity and positive cultural development (in the 1870s and the 1990s), and the periods of depression in the 1890s and 1930s. There were

---

7   Published in *Garboard Strake*, No 14, Winter, 2011.

examples of similar ups and downs in other parts of the world, and especially, Australia, but in Franklin there was a tighter connection: it was possible to relate slumps to global influences, and periods of prosperity to local initiatives and talents. A lot of positive changes were due to the shipbuilding industry, in Hobart, in Cygnet, Shipwright's Point and Franklin.

When the idea of forming a Mechanic's Institute in Franklin was first mooted in 1858, a public meeting was held at the cargo store of the steamship, *Culloden*, the only place where a meeting of its kind could be held at that time. The establishment of a Mechanic's Institute was a grand and expensive scheme for Franklin: a scheme that envisaged a better future for the town's adults and children. John Balfe, the local member of Parliament, spoke in support:

All who wish to leave an inheritance to their children and country must have their names associated with some work like the present, where-in the advantages and benefits of the public are provided for, in preference to the interests and objects of individuals.[8]

So I thought it worthwhile, following the example of the founders of the Mechanic's Institute to ask the Franklin Progress Association to call a public meeting, to consider a comprehensive plan for the northern end of Franklin, based on historical knowledge and international experience. The Evaporators could, I thought, become a home for a group of small businesses, which might provide valuable new opportunities; and create a Working Waterfront that would provide stable employment under local management.

I addressed the public meeting in the Palais Theatre about the plan for the establishment of a Working Waterfront to be managed by the local community. This is part of what I said:

Among other projects the concept of a working waterfront envisages public acquisition of the Franklin Evaporators. That could house ten maritime related shops and workshops, such as a naval architect, a maritime bookshop and chart agent, a solar, electrically-powered bronze foundry, and the rebuilding of the public wharf we built originally in 1991. An industrial museum could be included. And a collection of inter-dependent small businesses that would employ more than 30 people.

Past experience shows that such a place would rapidly become a national and international visitor attraction. But a working waterfront without ships is like a hospital without patients or a school without students. The construction of a Merchant sailing vessel would be a good way to begin, by showing how sail-power can be used for serious commercial purposes and a step in the direction of reducing Global warming.

When non-renewable sources of energy grow scarce and costly, a good thing to do will be to build a wooden sailing ship that carries both cargo and passengers. She will be built of local timber, the only renewable building material we have, and will use only renewable energy, with sails and a solar powered auxiliary. She will ply between the Huon and ports like Hobart, and in late summer, Williamstown, in Victoria, then Portland, and

---

8   Cit Martin, John, "John Donellan Balfe and the collective experience of the Huon." BA Hons thesis, History Department, UTAS, 1970, p 65.

Port Adelaide, before returning to Franklin via Port Davey, with adventure tourists and people training to become Tall Ship professional sailors.

Adrian Dean has designed the ship that will do the job. She will be a modern and more seaworthy version of the Franklin built vessels of the late 19th and early 20th centuries. Our market analysis shows that with construction funded initially through a federal program, the project could then be passed on to community ownership. Sponsorship and/or crowd funding, would be an additional activity.

Another idea would be to create a company. This was the successful strategy in Devon and Cornwall and probably in Franklin as well, in the mid-nineteenth century, which attracted people of all kinds in small villages to buy shares, with confidence that their old age would be protected from poverty.[9] The 80 foot schooner would be commercially successful by carrying 12 overnight passengers, or 36 daytime passengers, on weekly voyages between Recherche Bay and Hobart, calling at Channel and Huon River ports for large or small cargoes for delivery to the Salamanca Market in Hobart, or for collection at Waterman's Dock. The Bosun might collect a shopping list of items to be delivered at the channel ports on the way back. The use of ship's gear to handle cargo would be an added attraction for tourist or passenger photographers.

In early autumn the schooner could cross Bass Strait to Williamstown, or to Darling Harbour in Sydney as a living exhibit at the National Maritime Museum, with special Tasmanian cargoes, such as honey, wine, special timber craftwork, fruit and vegetables, and free range frozen fish. In the first few years, income will come mainly from passenger fares and catering on board. But in say, 20 years, when diesel will cost about the same as good wine, sail will be a competitive alternative.

As global warming is understood by more of us, and as politicians begin to understand that dealing with it will win votes, we may even get a subsidy for providing non-polluting forms of transport. The very large roof area of the Evaporators also makes it possible to generate solar electricity and store it in a battery. We should also be thinking of reviving the mini-hydro scheme, from the dam in Price's Creek, which provided Franklin's earliest electric street lighting in 1915.

Among other good things that will result from building the schooner will be the creation of 30 new jobs and the influx of young people of working age. Also valuable will be the children they will bring with them. Children who will increase the chances of Franklin keeping its school.[10] And with the downturn of Forestry, and the effects of Peak Oil and global warming, Tasmania will need sustainable local economies. In that context, local jobs and small local schools will be vital elements in the creation of a demographically balanced and sustainable community.[11]

---

9   Greenhill, Basil, *The Merchant Schooners*, Percival Marshall & Co, London, 1951, pp 98- 99.

10 Franklin Primary School was under threat of closure due to an apparent shortage of children. The idea was to send them in a bus each day to Huonville.

11 See Buultjens, Jeremy, *et al*, "Issues and initiatives for the future," *Australian Journal of Regional Studies*, Vol 18, No. 2, 2012.

> The history of the Huon Valley since the British invasion shows that the key to sustainability is resilience, and building on the things that are authentic and unique. That will require people with a good education, starting in primary school. But we are the generation that has the responsibility to "seize the day"[12]. To accept the challenge and encouragement of Simon Crean [Minister for Regional Development in 2012] to design our own destiny, and enable our children to inherit a better and more prosperous Tasmania.

The *Huon Valley News* reported in 2011, "overwhelming in principle support" for the establishment of a working waterfront from the forty or so people who attended the public meeting in the Palais theatre.[13]

We began to apply for grants, draw up business plans, and hold meetings. Luckily Andy Gamlin, co-founder of the Australian Wooden Boat Festival in 1994, and his partner Yvonne Buckley purchased the Wooden Boat Centre in 2011. I was the president of Franklin Working Waterfront Association at this point, and began to discuss the project of establishing a temporary wooden slipway on which to build a wooden schooner, just south of the Living Boat Trust workshop. Inside the Evaporators building, plans for a wooden boat workshop, a sail loft, student accommodation, a chart agent, a book shop, an art gallery and many other suggestions were moulded into the concept of a sustainable working waterfront. By 2012, we also had a Business Plan to retrofit the Evaporators and build a merchant schooner.[14] What we lacked was the money to buy the Evaporators and construct the schooner.

It was at about this time that a former soldier, Greg Guy arrived in Franklin. He had left the small fishing village of Kiama on the southeast coast of New South Wales, and settled in Deep Bay, just north of Randalls Bay near Cygnet in Tasmania. He was destined to have a strong influence on the Huon Valley community. He was a Vietnam veteran, and had been a Warrant Officer in the area of water transport. He had a broad experience of everything from landing craft to offshore work on HMAS *Tobruk*. He also fought as a commando on the hinterland trails from Hanoi to Saigon. He had been wounded in battle. A bullet had hit his shoulder from behind and came out of his chest. But he made a seemingly successful recovery.

In 1973 most Australian troops withdrew from Vietnam. Two years later the Tasman Bridge across the Derwent River was damaged by a bulk ore carrier and the bridge was put out of action. The Australian Army was asked to supply Hobart with a LCM-8 landing craft as part of the Military Aid to Civil Community Operations, until the bridge was repaired. Greg brought the 75 ton landing craft down the coast from Sydney. That was the reason for his first visit to Tasmania.

Greg retired from the army in 1985, and created a charter service for ocean fishing based on the very beautiful harbour of Kiama. He had gained a Master Mariner's qualification in the army so he varied his charter work with teaching at the local

---

12 "Seize the Day" is the motto of Franklin's primary school.

13 *Huon Valley News,* 23 October 2011.

14 This plan was updated several times by Ellen Witte and Michele Durbin.

New South Wales TAFE. He taught a wide range of maritime subjects for the next eighteen years, including wooden boat building.

In 2005, he arrived in Cygnet, which already had a variety of community associations, including a yacht club, a choir — the Cygnet Singers — and a Men's Shed. He bought a property at Deep Bay and built a shed there. Greg was a talented artist. He joined, and was elected Chair of the Huon Arts Exhibition Group. With them, he helped to found the Lovett Gallery in Cygnet. Later he became a Fellow of the Australian Society of Marine Artists. Greg eventually met his wonderful partner, Lynette Goodwin, the administration clerk at Franklin School, and Greg sold his Deep Bay property, bought the 50 foot ketch, *Taihoa*, sailed her to Franklin and moored her to the jetty just east of the Wooden Boat Centre. Greg worked, while living on the boat, to build himself a workshop at the top of Jackson's Road in Franklin, and devoted a lot of time volunteering at the Wooden Boat Centre and running short courses on a range of disciplines, from tying knots, to general nautical knowledge, boat building and coastal navigation.

Soon after the formation of the Franklin Working Waterfront Association in 2011, I retired from the Presidency. I nominated Greg to be President at the next AGM, and he took over, but within a year he became ill and passed that responsibility on to Vice President, David Pittaway, who was equally enthusiastic about building a schooner and creating a working waterfront.

Greg stayed in Franklin, living on his boat. That inevitably made him the voluntary Franklin Harbour Master. Many impending crises were averted over the years, especially when local children and flailing puppies decided to jump off the jetties into muddy flood water, full of invisible logs and branches. Greg's dog, Bosun, was always alert and gave warnings whenever needed. Accidents were efficiently avoided because of Greg and Bosun's presence.

By 2013, Greg was back on board as President. Franklin Working Waterfront Association continued to negotiate with the owner of Franklin Evaporators, working on various ways of raising the funds to buy it. In the meantime though, Andy Gamlin suggested to FWWA that it purchase the Wooden Boat Centre. This seemed like a very good way to kick start the Association's plans for the working waterfront and keep the Boat Centre active.

The first port of call for money to do this was the Franklin community, who pledged an initial total of about $35,000. This was soon bolstered by a generous donation of $30,000 from Helen Gasparinatos. And then in 2014, new Franklin residents, Martin and Judy Krynen donated the balance in one hit. This was a huge benefit to Franklin and gave FWWA a potential way of generating funds. A celebration of the community's ownership of the Boat Centre was held in October of that year.

Greg and I quickly contacted the Australian Maritime College (AMC) in Launceston, which is a specialist Institute of the University of Tasmania. We hoped that the Wooden Boat Centre could become a University extension, specialising in traditional wooden boat construction, and offering an associate degree course, including all the subjects and options that Ruth and I had offered from 1995 to 2000.

Negotiations commenced, and the initial exchange was optimistic, but the AMC staff members we spoke to failed to fully understand our purpose. They steered us towards a Level 3, Marine Craft Construction course in 2012. That course did not deal specifically with wood, except as an afterthought. Our course from 1995 to 2000 had been a two-year Course, at Level 5. It had successfully added qualified professional wooden boat builders to the industry and kept the tradition of Tasmanian wooden boat building alive.

The AMC offer was a one-year experience at a far less valuable level. It dealt with steel, fibreglass, aluminium, and finally wood. Shipwright's Point School of Wooden Boatbuilding had been the only Boat School in Australia devoted explicitly to traditional timbers technology, and had attracted enthusiastic national and international students because it was unique. The Allen Consulting Group revealed, in 2013, that the Victoria University ceased to deliver the Level 3 Marine Craft Construction course, because of falling student numbers and the high costs of delivery.[15]

At this time, I was much perturbed to receive an email, shortly after I turned eighty, telling me I could no longer remain an Honorary Research Associate of the University, on account of my age and the University's obligation to provide insurance. That meant that I could no longer be a member of the University library or the staff club. I complained, but was told that I had no choice, as there was too high a risk, at my age, of dying within the campus. It was a surprise to find that UTAS turned out to be a discriminator on the grounds of age. A lawyer friend did offer advice with which to sue the University for discrimination, but I never got round to it as I was too busy. Greg and I continued to talk with the frequently hard to contact AMC staff. The suggestions and the people were often changing, which meant a high risk of having to start all over again as new people came into the picture, and as the weeks, months, and years, went by. At the same time, Martin and Judy Krynen bought the Evaporators and set about making plans of their own for that space.

Not long after, Greg was diagnosed with skin cancer, which eventually spread to the lymphatic system and other organs. He prepared for the worst. The building of his coffin became a project he watched at the Wooden Boat Centre. He knew he would die soon and attended his own wake at the Centre, surrounded by his family, students and friends.

He gave a remarkable goodbye speech, about his life and family, and the capabilities of the new community that had grown up in Franklin since the end of the past century. He concluded with a request to the Working Waterfront Association to remember that one of its constitutional aims was to build a merchant schooner. He died soon afterwards, on 14 August 2017.

---

15 Allen Consulting Group, "Boat Industry Market Analysis and Conceptual Model," Victoria, 2013.

On the up-side, the recently appointed Manager of the Wooden Boat Centre, Paul D'Olier has successfully re-introduced a new accredited course that includes the construction of a seagoing wooden vessel. The Centre's volunteer staff of local people have been extraordinarily resilient, through a very anxious period, and continue to manage the day to day work with their usual energy and charm. Visitors keep the carpark area full. This is all a comfort to me and it will be good to see a new generation of students learning to build sea-going wooden boats again in Franklin.

But, looking back to that day of Greg's goodbye speech, I am ashamed of our failure, so far, as a community, to respond to his last public appeal. I am sure that if he had lived we would now be well into the construction of the lovely 80 foot merchant schooner that Adrian Dean has designed. The half model sits forlornly now, on a bench in the Boat Centre workshop. Offers have been made by community members in Franklin, to donate large trees on their properties with which to build the multi-purpose, carbon-free sailing vessel. A business plan has been devised for both construction and management, but creative action has not followed.

I took Greg's words to be a call to action, and in 2018, I thought to start some fund raising for the schooner. The six Grebe sailing dinghies built with the local schools had been lying in the boat shelter for years without being used much by anybody. The Women on Water (WOW) branch of the LBT had begun learning to row in the Grebes but had moved on to St Ayles skiffs.

Between 2011 and 2015 use of the Grebes was sporadic with different groups of people using them for different purposes. The LBT had responsibility for the boats and a "Hire and Drive" licence to hire them out. By 2015 the licence was due to expire and should have been renewed but was not. I thought it would be a sensible thing to renew it, to get the Grebes out on the water again, hire them out, and start a fund-raising effort to begin work on the schooner.

So I spent a year in 2017–2018 writing histories of all six Grebes, replacing equipment, re-writing Safe Operation Plans and recruiting volunteer "River Guides" to manage a modest boat hire business. In 2018, I secured a new licence for the Living Boat Trust to operate a Hire and Drive fleet for the next five years. I was also a member of the Men's Shed, managed by the Living Boat Trust, which has an arrangement for unemployed men to work as volunteers for two days of each week. The Tuesday Men (who come on Thursday as well) have developed high level skills which keep a fleet of wooden boats, including the six centreboard sailing dinghies, a small yacht, and three whaleboats in seaworthy condition.

Having obtained a licence to hire the boats out, I prevailed on a group of ten men and women to operate the hire fleet as volunteer River guides. The team of guides began to ask visitors if they wished to go for a row, or a sail, with, if needed, a competent guide. If we saw that the customer was competent, we rowed or sailed with them for a few minutes and then let them go on their own. If we were worried about their ability, we went with them or did the rowing ourselves. Mobile phones and life jackets were compulsory at all times. We kept *Betsy Walton*, the boat our students had built as their first project in 1995, and her outboard motor ready for use as a rescue boat. We replaced the worn leather stops on her oars.

After some initial trials, we decided to start with a full time trial of four weeks, in April 2018. It's often the best time of the year for messing about in boats; usually neither too hot nor too windy, but not this time. Sea breezes were strong, and we taught people how to reef sails, and showed them a video that we made of me and Peter Venning doing a deliberate capsize and recovery exercise, and sailing a boat back to the shore. My strategy was to ask people if they knew how to row first. Some people said "yes," but couldn't. So after a while I offered to give them a short lesson. I showed them how to reach forward, push with their feet on the footplate and swing their bodies back with their arms straight, drop their elbows vertically, to prevent digging the blades too deep into the water, and to recover by skimming the blades just above the surface as they stretched forward again.

Some visitors thought that rowing was the same as paddling. They sometimes sat down facing the bow. But most people learnt how to row reasonably well within a short time, and never looked back. Others, mothers and babies sometimes, young families, and couples, were happy for us to row them about, while we talked about the boats and the history of the river and the canal. I found it very relaxing, and enjoyed the exercise. Sailing took longer, as we had to get the mast, sails, and centreboard, ship the rudder and then show people how to step the mast, lash the shrouds and forestay, stow the anchor, hoist the sails and get going.

I usually got the centreboard down, hoisted the mainsail, then the jib, steered away from the boathouse, and then handed the tiller over as soon as I could, to one of the crew. In fine weather it was easy to explain that the crew was also the moveable ballast. There were no "passengers." Crews were taught to move, gently most of the time, to keep the boats sailing safely. As soon as the boat was clear of the shore, we explained about luffing into the wind, to avoid a chance of capsizing, and to bear away from the wind to keep the sails drawing.

Young people of both sexes learnt quickly. Older people mostly asked me to go on steering and sometimes to row for them, while having interesting conversations. Egg Island Canal was always a popular destination. We picked the weather accordingly, had no accidents, and ended up with about $400 in four weeks with an approaching winter. The dilemma was that LBT does not have a constitutional aim to build a schooner, so was not enthusiastic, but it does have a fleet of small boats that could be hired out to raise funds towards achieving that aim. Franklin Working Waterfront Association does have a constitutional aim to build a schooner, but must at present, devote all its energy to successfully delivering accredited training through the Wooden Boat Centre.

It was seven years since the meeting in the Palais Theatre had been held and reported in the *Huon Valley News* as having been "overwhelming" in its support for the establishment of the Working Waterfront, which included the building of a merchant schooner, as a goal for the community to work towards. Some of the talented boat builders in the Huon neighbourhood and young people of an adventurous disposition have told me they would love to take part in building a schooner.

I had unfortunately assumed that the community agreement of 2011 would continue to be taken for granted in view of Franklin's maritime history and reputation, accessible building materials and experienced people. This was a mistake of mine. I was surprised that the suggestion of building a schooner in 2018, exactly where many have been built before in the nineteenth century, met with an outburst of negativity. "To build a schooner," someone claimed, "would change Franklin forever." This was the first time I felt there was significant opposition to an activity that had been introduced to Franklin since 1991.

Demographic change has kept the school open, kept the Palais Theatre thriving, revived a tennis club, added to the membership of the Bowls club and Fire Brigade and increased volunteer support for the Wooden Boat Centre. At the LBT, it brought the St Ayles skiff movement into action, established the regular all-comers dinners on Monday nights, kept the On the Water program going for children, and resulted in the donation of the river launch, *Nancy*, which has become a visitor attraction.

But I should have anticipated the fluidity of the successive waves of Franklin citizens who come, stay a while, then go, just as their forebears have done. Priorities for action change with each wave; continuity of purpose can't always be assumed.

Some people may be troubled by the prospect of the effort of taking on a project that is beyond their personal knowledge or experience. And this is quite understandable. However, building a merchant schooner will, nevertheless, be worthwhile. It will create employment for young people, recruit the next generation of competent sailors and shipwrights, and develop the Huon Valley community in a positive and sustainable direction, by creating more interesting and creative jobs, attracting more visitors, and providing more options for adventure, education and experience, for both residents and visitors.

Just as important is the responsibility of this generation to remember the motto of Franklin Primary School to "seize the day." And to take opportunities. Luckily young people all over the world are now doing their very best to influence politicians to believe the science and take action to deal with the results of climate change, and they are beginning to make a difference. In 2017, Huonville High School won an international award for its contribution to environmental sustainability. But governments lag behind. The reaction of the political and corporate establishments of Tasmania to the bushfires from December 2018 to February 2019 was to fund *recovery* from bush fires, and that is a necessity, but it does not provide long term *strategies* against fires of the future caused by climate change. These are likely to be worse and more frequent all over Australia. It has taken a well-organised international school student strike to draw attention to the need to find ways of reducing the likelihood that the Tasmania of the future will cease to be inhabited by the Human species. We should follow their lead.

Some people don't believe in climate change, but that does not entitle them to prevent others, who do, from acting to protect themselves and their children. Like the Merchant schooner now being built in Costa Rica, the Fijian *Drua* and the many American and European sailing traders, sailcargo provides many good things at once; the use of renewable energy and wooden sailing ship technology, new adventure opportunities, and more school ships for educational and commercial purposes. If I am wrong, and climate change is a hoax, building a schooner would still be very worthwhile.

Franklin is part of a global industrial revolution of a new kind. I recently discovered an article by Dan Stewart with the heading "Small countries lead big on climate change."[16] Stewart quotes President Alvarado Quesada, President of Costa Rica, at the world economic forum at Davos, Switzerland in February 2019. Quesada's Government pledged to cease the use of fossil fuels entirely, in his own country by 2050, in accordance with the Paris Agreement, making Costa Rica the first nation in the world to make that commitment. Maritime use of fossil fuels accounts for 2.5% of atmospheric pollution.[17] Stewart points out that the political "heavies" in the world such as Donald Trump and Teresa May did not turn up to the Davos Economic Forum in February 2019. It is clear that as recognition of climate change becomes understood universally, change will not be inspired by the great powers or the great corporations. It will be inspired by intelligent communities and well governed nations. Probably small ones, to begin with.

President Alvarado Quesada has joined "a cohort of young idealist national leaders" in their 30s and 40s, including France's Macron, Ireland's Leo Varadka, and New Zealand's Jacinda Ardern. These leaders "make the case that developing countries can lead the world in tackling climate change; our ambition is not only to do this on our own. We want others to follow."

Given the extent of the bush fires in 2018–2019, and the news of more devastating and life threatening fires on my radio now, Tasmania would be silly not to follow Costa Rica's example. Quesada believes there is a generational shift in how governments are addressing environmental responsibility. "We are going to live longer in this world," he says, "and we [will see] the most devastating effects of climate change … and when we grow old, people are going to ask us—did you do enough about it? So we need to start answering that question today; Now!"

Lazy people say that there is little that can be done by small communities. They say that it is only the big powerful nations and corporations that can make any real difference. But historically, big philosophical changes can begin in peripheral countries, like Palestine for instance, in 31 AD.

Just as Quesada was speaking in Davos in February 2019, the wooden keel of *Ceiba*, was being laid in Costa Rica. The leader of Sailcargo Inc is a young woman

---

16   *Time*, 18 February 2019, p 24.

17   Cutcher, Nicola, "Winds of Change: the sailing ships cleaning up sea transport," *The Guardian*, 23 October 2019.

called Danielle Doggett. She offers any kind of help she can give to other people who are building sailcargo vessels.

As well-educated adults, we should not be dragging our feet. A schooner "might not be the solution to how everything is shipped in the world but we can make people think about what they're buying and how it's getting here. It's easy to feel overwhelmed and helpless. But we can all do something. We don't need one solution to everything, we need a thousand solutions that can exist simultaneously."[18] Change *for ever* of some things, is not very frightening at all. The frightening thing is the people and institutions who are doing nothing, and trying to make others do nothing as well.

Pessimists are fond of telling us that it isn't worth the effort for small places like Tasmania to do anything significant to change the world for the better. But we are now part of a global movement to introduce a return to sail as a means of carrying heavy loads, over long distances, by water. Oil and coal are likely to become very expensive and run out of steam anyway by 2050.[19]

We have been encouraged by Huon Valley Council, under new leadership, to think of plans and ideas to "raise the Huon Valley to the next level." The plan to build a wooden trading schooner is my response to this request.

We must understand the limitations of what can be achieved by ageing communities. As they age, there is a danger they may become inflexible. But we should not underestimate the power of a potentially creative community like the young people of Tasmania, especially in the Huon Valley. We will need leadership by old people with experience, confidence and skill, and young people with energy and courage, to raise funds, create jobs and set to work. Once launched, the schooner will inspire tourist adventurers, as well as full time professional sailors. We will need to be confident that stable employment will be created for both builders and sailors. We will need public investment as well as political support and public patronage.

Sailcargo.org has sent me a video of laying the keel and positioning the frames of its wooden merchant schooner. Another wooden ship will soon contribute to a cleaner world; a ship much like the schooner *Caledonia,* bound for Tonga from Sydney in the 1870s. On board was a young Victorian adventurer, Alfred St Johnston. He wrote:

I cannot think how people who have both wealth of time and money can travel by noisy, dirty, steamers, which by their very din and commotion frighten from them every wonder of the deep, when they could, if they would, Sail over the great sea, and watch it in all the

---

18 Cutcher, Nicola, quoting Alex Geldenhuys in "Winds of Change: the sailing ships cleaning up sea Transport," *The Guardian*, 23 October 2019.

19 See Young, John, *Sustaining the Earth, The story of the environmental movement–Its past efforts and future challenges,* Harvard University Press, 1990, p 201 ff.

beauty of its calm and the grandeur of its storm. Seen from the hurricane deck of a crowded steamer the sea loses all its charm.[20]

I couldn't have put it any better myself.

---

20 Alfred St Johnstone, *Camping among Cannibals*, Mc Millan, 1883, p 8.

Epilogue: For my Teachers

When I was four and a half, on a rainy morning in Broadstairs, Kent, I had no idea where my life would lead me, or what use I could be to the world. That would depend largely on my teachers of many different kinds. I have much to thank them for.

As I watched the continuous line of shipping on the horizon, turning round the North Foreland from the mouth of the Thames into the English Channel and beyond to distant destinations, I dreamt of travel and adventure. My parents took me and my sister, Heather, on bike rides during school holidays. We were carefully taught to ride bicycles, and, to observe the rule of the road, and we were encouraged to explore and read maps when we were still very young.

Our mother also believed that it was essential for us to be able to ride a horse and found friends with horses to teach us. We could swim, read a map, and use a telephone by the time we were five. Gradually I was allowed to ride on my own ¾ size bike rather than on a seat on the cross-bar on my father's bike. I fancied myself as an explorer, at first, in Kent, then, after the World War II started, around the North York Moors from Lockton and later on from Cropton. I usually returned home as expected. On the rare occasions when I was late, I rang my parents up from public telephones, and told them where I was.

I have had a fortunate life. I admired my parents, for their love, their energy and spirit of adventure, and service to others. I valued the rare, but memorable holidays with my parents, and sister Heather, exploring the countryside on our bikes, and sailing when I was eleven and fourteen on the Norfolk Broads. The people I valued most as well as my family were my teachers of many kinds.

Starting with aunts, Molly, my godmother and Aunt Lena; and Heather, my big sister, and Grandfather William Young. My father, Robert, taught me the first elements of carpentry and how to build toy wooden boats, hollow them out, and ballast them with sheet lead. My mother Edith, made sails for them.

My first school teacher was Miss Newsome, from the West Indies. She was the *Akela*, the Wolf Cub leader and teacher at St Michael's school for the children of missionaries, at Limpsfield, Surrey, UK. Next came Mr Willink, my Prep B house master at Christ's Hospital, David Jesson-Dibley who taught me to act at Christ's Hospital, and Mr Todd who taught me to box. Russell Clark at Cropton Mill helped me to build and rig *Discovery 2*, my first boat, and taught me about wild animals and farming.

Captain Norman Sheldrake, of the barge *Leofleda*, taught me seamanship; "Daddy" Roberts, as he was known, taught me history at Christ's Hospital. My girlfriends: Robina at Trowbridge, was a friend who wrote to me everywhere I lived, for 68 years and let me publish parts of her letters. Trudy at my school, and Sybil, on the *Rangitoto,* taught me about the opposite sex, as did Joan at Hawkes Bay, and Judith in Auckland, New Zealand…Thank you!

I had some good mates in Thornton A, my House at Christ's Hospital, especially Michael Marland who, after his experience of Christ's Hospital, became a famous champion of English comprehensive state schools, and Brian Holland, who became a science lecturer at Liverpool University. The three of us started at a disadvantage because of the practice of "streaming," but we all, through our friendship, helped each other to achieve our goals.

My early education was not very promising because I became interested in too many things at once, and was easily diverted. Heather did a good job of teaching me the importance of scholarly concentration, and had an exemplary career herself, as Head Girl of the girl's Christ's Hospital, and a leading violinist in the British National Youth Orchestra. She graduated with an Honours Oxford degree in English. She shook off an attack of breast cancer, writes books, continues to care for her husband Ken, and takes the lead in running the Friends of the Links in Edinburgh.

Prof Musgrove taught me English at Auckland University, from 1953 to 1957 and Keith Sinclair taught me History, and supervised my MA thesis on the history of the Auckland Province. Amarilda Gorrie of Auckland Teacher's College, taught me how to survive, and enjoy teaching secondary school students. Bill Mandle taught me how to do well enough at sitting exams to get into Oxford. Carmel Lorrigan and Prof Blaiklock taught me ancient Greek. Carmel married me, and bore my children. We went to Oxford together, and I "sat at the feet" of George Holmes, Isaiah Berlin, Peter Dickson, Hugh Trevor–Roper and Christopher Hill.

David Kew taught me the essential values and skills of wooden boat building when we built my ocean going wooden boat, *Leofleda,* in my back yard in North Adelaide. Nicholas and Jackie Wright shared our nautical self-education in off-shore sailing and are the best friends I could ever hope for. Professor Jim Davidson of the ANU was my PhD supervisor for my thesis about the "Adventurous Spirits" of Fiji. Later I was schooled by Chief Ulaiasi Vosabalavu and Fijian school teacher Pitjila Gnata, as we travelled together on the copra boat, *Adi Lau* in 1971.

Dr Clive Kneebone taught me about Freud, and much about myself. Archie Reid saved my research project about the Lau islands in Fiji from the wrath of Tui Nayau, Ratu Mara, Prime Minister of Fiji, and made a series of contributions to the interdisciplinary study of the recent history of eastern Fiji, by the group of New Zealand and Australian scholars, who worked with me. Archie Reid also published independently.

Garth Rogers was a remarkable anthropologist who made a tremendous contribution to Fijian history and anthropology, and also to my life in general. He was a brave and competent adventurer, with a voyage from New Zealand to Tonga and far beyond in a 19 foot "Sopranino" class yacht. He spoke Fijian fluently, and set an example of almost medieval humility to his colleagues. If offered anything remotely exotic he would declare that it was "too rich for anthropologists," and he was a devoted vegetarian. He had experience of farming and building, and was always a very useful person to have around to fix things, stitch up a wounded sheep, mend a fence or fight a bushfire.

My colleagues in the History Department of the University of Adelaide and especially Ian Turner and Hugh Stretton shaped my career. Hugh introduced me to a new world of ideas, and a new field of research and writing about environmental economics and politics, which led to many new publications.

Adrian Dean became involved with *One and All* and opened my eyes to the history of wooden ship building and its traditions and values. Bill Porter, originally from Padstow in Cornwall, brought with him the skills of wooden shipbuilding, and revealed to me the complexity of building *One and All*, a hundred foot brigantine. Moving from Adelaide to Tasmania took my education to the next level. Bill Foster and Adrian Dean set the standards for me and our students in the early days of our boat building workshop at Port Huon. Kevin Perkins, one of the greatest woodworkers in Australia, gave me inside knowledge of Tasmanian timbers and the importance of doing my best to save some of them for future generations.

Thanks to the School of Geography and Environmental Studies at the University of Tasmania, I had an academic context in which to blend the fruit of my experience as Director of the Mawson School of Environmental Studies at the University of Adelaide with the opportunities of running a School of Wooden Boatbuilding in Franklin.

My students—of History, Environmental Studies and Wooden Boatbuilding—have taught me that teaching is a two-way journey of mutual learning. Teaching has been an experience worth living for.

But this was only possible with the co-operation and support of my most important teacher of all, Ruth Young, the love of my life, who stimulates my brain, and teaches me about children, maths (my weak point), spelling, navigation, music, business management, gardening, leadership, tolerance, persistence and love.

As for our children, they have managed well, with good careers, and happy marriages, and have taught me a lot about everything. Each of them has had challenges to cope with that I have never had and I am proud of their courage in dealing with them and their achievements. Thanks to the ease of communication in the modern world, they are part of each other's lives as well as ours. The tyranny of distance is not what it was. I enjoy the digital proximity of South Australia, Victoria and Tasmania, where we live, and the ways in which they have all helped each other and how they all help us. And I am grateful to the Moses family for making me one of their own.

My present problem is the universal one: we don't live forever. Looking back on my 85 years, it seems as though the world is getting to be a worse and worse place: inequality is increasing; administrations are dysfunctional and secretive; rights are curtailed; the chances that the Earth can sustain life for much longer are unpredictable and there is an absence, at the governance level, of compassion, generosity and common sense. These problems can only be dealt with, at a community level, one at a time. But there are many communities and they can take action simultaneously. We in Tasmania are lucky enough to have communities and environments that are not beyond salvation. This turns potential tragedy into possibility and an opportunity to deal with the things that we know from past experience, it is possible to deal with. The revival of commercial sail is in that category. Judging from their efforts so far, I am confident that the coming generation will recognise the importance of taking local action to solve global problems.

Climate Summit, with permission, Joel Pett.

www.ingramcontent.com/pod-product-compliance
Lightning Source LLC
Chambersburg PA
CBHW052010290426
44112CB00014B/2183